Large-Scale C++

The Pearson Addison-Wesley Professional Computing Series

Brian W. Kernighan, Consulting Editor

Visit **informit.com/series/professionalcomputing** for a complete list of available publications.

The **Pearson Addison-Wesley Professional Computing Series** was created in 1990 to provide serious programmers and networking professionals with well-written and practical reference books. Pearson Addison-Wesley is renowned for publishing accurate and authoritative books on current and cutting-edge technology, and the titles in this series will help you understand the state of the art in programming languages, operating systems, and networks.

Make sure to connect with us!
informit.com/socialconnect

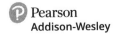

Large-Scale C++

Volume I
Process and Architecture

John Lakos

✦✦Addison-Wesley

Boston • Columbus • New York • San Francisco • Amsterdam • Cape Town
Dubai • London • Madrid • Milan • Munich • Paris • Montreal • Toronto • Delhi • Mexico City
São Paulo • Sydney • Hong Kong • Seoul • Singapore • Taipei • Tokyo

Visit us on the Web: informit.com/aw

Library of Congress Control Number: 2019948467

Cover image: MBoe/Shutterstock

ISBN-13: 978-0-201-71706-8
ISBN-10: 0-201-71706-9

1 2019

To my wife, Elyse, with whom the universe rewarded me,
and five wonderful children:
Sarah
Michele
Gabriella
Lindsey
Andrew

Contents

Chapter 2: Packaging and Design Rules   269

Chapter 3: Physical Design and Factoring   495

Preface

When I wrote my first book, *Large-Scale C++ Software Design* (**lakos96**), my publisher wanted me to consider calling it *Large-Scale C++ Software* Development. I was fairly confident that I was qualified to talk about design, but the topic of *development* incorporated far more scope than I was prepared to address at that time.

Design, as I see it, is a static property of software, most often associated with an individual application or library, and is only one of many disciplines needed to create successful software. *Development*, on the other hand, is dynamic, involving people, processes, and workflows. Because development is ongoing, it typically spans the efforts attributed to many applications and projects. In its most general sense, development includes the design, implementation, testing, deployment, and maintenance of a series of products over an extended period. In short, software development is what we *do*.

In the more than two decades following *Large-Scale C++ Software Design*, I consistently applied the same fundamental design techniques introduced there (and elucidated here), both as a consultant and trainer and in my full-time work. I have learned what it means to assemble, mentor, and manage large development teams, to interact effectively with clients and peers, and to help shape corporate software engineering culture on an enterprise scale. Only in the wake of this additional experience do I feel I am able to do justice to the much more expansive (and ambitious) topic of large-scale software *development*.

A key principle — one that helps form the foundation of this multivolume book — is the profound importance of organization in software. Real-world software is intrinsically complex; however, a great deal of software is needlessly complicated, due in large part to a lack of basic organization — both in the way in which it is developed and in the final form that it takes. This book is first and foremost about what constitutes well-organized software, and also about the processes, methods, techniques, and tools needed to realize and maintain it.

Secondly, I have come to appreciate that not all software is or should be created with the same degree of polish. The value of real-world application software is often measured by how fast code gets to market. The goals of the software engineers apportioned to application development projects will naturally have a different focus and time frame than those slated to the long-term task of developing reliable and reusable software infrastructure. Fortunately, all of the techniques discussed in this book pertain to both application and library software — the difference being the extent to and rigor with which the various design, documentation, and testing techniques are applied.

One thing that has not changed and that has been proven repeatedly is that all real-world software benefits from *physical design*. That is, the way in which our logical content is factored and partitioned within files and libraries will govern our ability to identify, develop, test, maintain, and reuse the software we create. In fact, the architecture that results from thoughtful physical design at every level of aggregation continues to demonstrate its effectiveness in industry every day. Ensuring sound physical design, therefore, remains the first pillar of our methodology, and a central organizing principle that runs throughout this three-volume book — a book that both captures and expands upon my original work on this subject.

The second pillar of our methodology, nascent in *Large-Scale C++ Software Design*, involves essential aspects of *logical design* beyond simple syntactic rendering (e.g., *value semantics*). Since C++98, there has been explosive growth in the use of templates, generic programming, and the Standard Template Library (STL). Although templates are unquestionably valuable, their aggressive use can impede interoperability in software, especially when generic programming is not the right answer. At the same time, our focus on enterprise-scale development and our desire to maximize *hierarchical* reuse (e.g., of memory allocators) compels reexamination of the proper use of more mature language constructs, such as (public) inheritance.

Maintainable software demands a well-designed interface (for the compiler), a concise yet comprehensive contract (for people), and the most effective implementation techniques available (for efficiency). Addressing these along with other important *logical design* issues, as well as providing advice on implementation, documentation, and rendering, rounds out the second part of this comprehensive work.

Verification, including testing and static analysis, is a critically important aspect of software development that was all but absent in *Large-Scale C++ Software Design* and limited to *testability* only. Since the initial publication of that book, teachable testing strategies, such as Test-Driven Development (TDD), have helped make testing more fashionable today than it was in the 1990s or even in the early 2000s. Separately, with the start of the millennium, more and more companies have been realizing that thorough unit testing *is* cost-effective (or at least less expensive than not testing). Yet what it means to test continues to be a black art, and all too often "unit testing" remains little more than a checkbox in one's prescribed SOP (Standard Operating Procedure).

As the third pillar of our complete treatment of component-based software development, we address the discipline of creating effective unit tests, which naturally double as regression tests. We begin by delineating the underlying concept of what it means to test, followed by how to (1) select test input systematically, (2) design, implement, and render thorough test cases readably, and (3) optimally organize component-level test drivers. In particular, we discuss deliberately ordering test cases so that primitive functionality, once tested, can be leveraged to test other functionality within the same component.

Much thought was given to choosing a programming language to best express the ideas corresponding to these three pillars. C++ is inherently a compiled language, admitting both preprocessing and separate translation units, which is essential to fully addressing all of the important concepts pertaining to the dimension of software engineering that we call *physical design*. Since its introduction in the 1980s, C++ has evolved into a language that supports multiple programming paradigms (e.g., functional, procedural, object-oriented, generic), which invites discussion of a wide range of important *logical design* issues (e.g., involving templates, pointers, memory management, and maximally efficient spatial and/or runtime performance), not all of which are enabled by other languages.

Since *Large-Scale C++ Software Design* was published, C++ has been standardized and extended many times and several other new and popular languages have emerged.[1] Still, for both practical and pedagogical reasons, the subset of modern C++ that is C++98 remains the language of choice for presenting the software engineering principles described here. Anyone

---

[1] In fact, much of what is presented here applies analogously to other languages (e.g., Java, C#) that support separate compilation units.

who knows a more modern dialect of C++ knows C++98 but not necessarily vice versa. All of the theory and practice upon which the advice in this book was fashioned is independent of the particular subset of the C++ language to which a given compiler conforms. Superficially retrofitting code snippets (used from the inception of this book) with the latest available C++ syntax — just because we're "supposed to" — would detract from the true purpose of this book and impede access to those not familiar with modern C++.[2] In those cases where we have determined that a later version of C++ could afford a clear win (e.g., by expressing an idea significantly better), we will point them out (typically as a footnote).

This methodology, which has been successfully practiced for decades, has been independently corroborated by many important literary references. Unfortunately, some of these references (e.g., **stroustrup00**) have since been superseded by later editions that, due to covering new language features and to space limitations, no longer provide this (sorely needed) design guidance. We unapologetically reference them anyway, often reproducing the relevant bits here for the reader's convenience.

Taken as a whole, this three-volume work is an engineering reference for software developers and is segmented into three distinct, physically separate volumes, describing in detail, from a developer's perspective, *all* essential technical[3] aspects of this proven approach to creating an organized, integrated, scalable software development environment that is capable of supporting an entire enterprise and whose effectiveness only improves with time.

Audience

This multivolume book is written explicitly for practicing C++ software professionals. The sequence of material presented in each successive volume corresponds roughly to the order in which developers will encounter the various topics during the normal design-implementation-test cycle. This material, while appropriate for even the largest software development organizations, applies also to more modest development efforts.

---

[2] Even if we had chosen to use the latest C++ constructs, we assert that the difference would not be nearly as significant as some might assume.

[3] This book does not, however, address some of the softer skills (e.g., requirements gathering) often associated with full lifecycle development but does touch on aspects of project management specific to our development methodology.

Application developers will find the organizational techniques in this book useful, especially on larger projects. It is our contention that the rigorous approach presented here will recoup its costs within the lifetime of even a single substantial real-world application.

Library developers will find the strategies in this book invaluable for organizing their software in ways that maximize reuse. In particular, packaging software as an acyclic hierarchy of fine-grained physical *components* enables a level of quality, reliability, and maintainability that to our knowledge cannot be achieved otherwise.

Engineering managers will find that throttling the degree to which this suite of techniques is applied will give them the control they need to make optimal schedule/product/cost trade-offs. In the long term, consistent use of these practices will lead to a repository of *hierarchically reusable* software that, in turn, will enable new applications to be developed faster, better, and cheaper than they could ever have been otherwise.

Roadmap

Volume I (the volume you're currently reading) begins this book with our domain-independent software process and architecture (i.e., how *all* software should be created, rendered, and organized, no matter what it is supposed to do) and culminates in what we consider the state-of-the-art in physical design strategies.

Volume II (forthcoming) continues this multivolume book to include large-scale logical design, effective component-level interfaces and contracts, and highly optimized, high-performance implementation.

Volume III (forthcoming) completes this book to include verification (especially unit testing) that maximizes quality and leads to the cost-effective, fine-grained, *hierarchical* reuse of an ever-growing repository of *Software Capital*.[4]

The entire multivolume book is intended to be read front-to-back (initially) and to serve as a permanent reference (thereafter). A lot of the material presented will be new to many readers. We have, therefore, deliberately placed much of the more difficult, detailed, or in some sense "optional" material toward the end of a given chapter (or section) to allow the reader to skim (or skip) it, thereby facilitating an easier first reading.

---

[4] See section 0.9.

We have also made every effort to cross-reference material across all three volumes and to provide an effective index to facilitate referential access to specific information. The material naturally divides into three parts: (I) Process and Architecture, (II) Design and Implementation, and (III) Verification and Testing, which (not coincidentally) correspond to the three volumes.

Volume I: Process and Architecture

Chapter 0, "Motivation," provides the initial engineering and economic incentives for implementing our scalable development process, which facilitates hierarchical reuse and thereby simultaneously achieves shorter time to market, higher quality, and lower overall cost. This chapter also discusses the essential dichotomy between infrastructure and application development and shows how an enterprise can leverage these differences to improve productivity.

Chapter 1, "Compilers, Linkers, and Components," introduces the *component* as the fundamental atomic unit of logical and physical design. This chapter also provides the basic low-level background material involving compilers and linkers needed to absorb the subtleties of the main text, building toward the definition and essential properties of components and physical dependency. Although nominally background material, the reader is advised to review it carefully because it will be assumed knowledge throughout this book and it presents important vocabulary, some of which might not *yet* be in mainstream use.

Chapter 2, "Packaging and Design Rules," presents how we organize and package our component-based software in a uniform (domain-independent) manner. This chapter also provides the fundamental design rules that govern how we develop modular software hierarchically in terms of components, packages, and package groups.

Chapter 3, "Physical Design and Factoring," introduces important physical design concepts necessary for creating sound software systems. This chapter discusses proven strategies for designing large systems in terms of smaller, more granular subsystems. We will see how to partition and aggregate logical content so as to avoid cyclic, excessive, and otherwise undesirable (or unnecessary) physical dependencies. In particular, we will observe how to avoid the heaviness of conventional *layered* architectures by employing more *lateral* ones, understand how to reduce compile-time coupling at an architectural level, and learn — by example — how to design effectively using components.

Volume II: Design and Implementation (Forthcoming)

Chapter 4, "Logical Interoperability and Testability," discusses central, logical design concepts, such as *value semantics* and *vocabulary types*, that are needed to achieve interoperability and testability, which, in turn, are key to enabling successful reuse. It is in this chapter that we first characterize the various common class categories that we will casually refer to by name, thus establishing a context in which to more efficiently communicate well-understood families of behavior. Later sections in this chapter address how judicious use of templates, proper use of inheritance, and our fiercely modular approach to resource management — e.g., local ("arena") memory allocators — further achieve interoperability and testability.

Chapter 5, "Interfaces and Contracts," addresses the details of shaping the interfaces of the components, classes, and functions that form the building blocks of all of the software we develop. In this chapter we discuss the importance of providing well-defined contracts that clearly delineate, in addition to any object invariants, both what is *essential* and what is *undefined* behavior (e.g., resulting from *narrow* contracts). Historically controversial topics such as *defensive programming* and the explicit use of exceptions within contracts are addressed along with other notions, such as the critical distinction between *contract checking* and *input validation*. After attending to backward compatibility (e.g., physical substitutability), we address various facets of good contracts, including stability, const-correctness, reusability, validity, and appropriateness.

Chapter 6, "Implementation and Rendering," covers the many details needed to manufacture high-quality components. The first part of this chapter addresses some important considerations from the perspective of a single component's implementation; the latter part provides substantial guidance on minute aspects of consistency that include function naming, parameter ordering, argument passing, and the proper placement of operators. Toward the end of this chapter we explain — at some length — our rigorous approach to embedded component-level, class-level, and especially function-level documentation, culminating in a developer's final "checklist" to help ensure that all pertinent details have been addressed.

Volume III: Verification and Testing (Forthcoming)

Chapter 7, "Component-Level Testing," introduces the fundamentals of testing: what it means to test something, and how that goal is best achieved. In this (uncharacteristically) concise chapter, we briefly present and contrast some classical approaches to testing (less-well-factored) software, and we then go on to demonstrate the overwhelming benefit of insisting that each component have a single dedicated (i.e., standalone) test driver.

Chapter 8, "Test-Data Selection Methods," presents a detailed treatment of how to choose the input data necessary to write tests that are thorough yet run in near minimal time. Both classical and novel approaches are described. Of particular interest is *depth-ordered enumeration,* an original, systematic method for enumerating, in order of importance, increasingly complex tests for value-semantic container types. Since its initial debut in 1997, the sphere of applicability for this surprisingly powerful test-data selection method has grown dramatically.

Chapter 9, "Test-Case Implementation Techniques," explores different ways in which previously identified sampling data can be delivered to the functionality under test, and the results observed, in order to implement a valid test suite. Along the way, we will introduce useful concepts and machinery (e.g., *generator functions*) that will aid in our testing efforts. Complementary test-case implementation techniques (e.g., *orthogonal perturbation*), augmenting the basic ones (e.g., the *table-driven* technique), round out this chapter.

Chapter 10, "Test-Driver Organization," illustrates the basic organization and layout of our component-level test driver programs. This chapter shows how to order test cases optimally so that the more primitive methods (e.g., *primary manipulators* and *basic accessors*) are tested first and then subsequently relied upon to test other, less basic functionality defined within the same component. The chapter concludes by addressing the various major categories of classes discussed in Chapter 4; for each category, we provide a recommended test-case ordering along with corresponding test-case implementation techniques (Chapter 9) and test-data selection methods (Chapter 8) based on fundamental principles (Chapter 7).

Register your copy of *Large-Scale C++, Volume I,* on the InformIT site for convenient access to updates and/or corrections as they become available. To start the registration process, go to informit.com/register and log in or create an account. Enter the product ISBN (9780201717068) and click Submit. Look on the Registered Products tab for an Access Bonus Content link next to this product, and follow that link to access any available bonus materials. If you would like to be notified of exclusive offers on new editions and updates, please check the box to receive email from us.

Acknowledgments

Where do I start? Chapter 7, the one first written (c. 1999), of this multivolume book was the result of many late nights spent after work at Bear Stearns collaborating with Shawn Edwards, an awesome technologist (and dear friend). In December of 2001, I joined Bloomberg, and Shawn joined me there shortly thereafter; we have worked together closely ever since. Shawn assumed the role of CTO at Bloomberg LP in 2010.

After becoming hopelessly blocked trying to explain low-level technical details in Chapter 1 (c. 2002), I turned to another awesome technologist (and dear friend), Sumit Kumar, who actively coached me through it and even rewrote parts of it himself. Sumit — who might be the best programmer I've ever met — continues to work with me, providing both constructive feedback and moral support.

When I became overwhelmed by the sheer magnitude of what I was attempting to do (c. 2005), I found myself talking over the phone for nearly six hours to yet another awesome technologist (and dear friend), Vladimir Kliatchko, who walked me through my entire table of contents — section by section — which has remained essentially unchanged ever since. In 2012, Vlad assumed the role of Global Head of Engineering at Bloomberg and, in 2018, was appointed to Bloomberg's Management Committee.

John Wait, the Addison-Wesley acquisitions editor principally responsible for enabling my first book, wisely recommended (c. 2006) that I have a structural editor, versed in both writing and computer science, review my new manuscript for macroscopic organizational improvements. After review, however, this editor fairly determined that no reliable, practicable advice with respect to restructuring my copious writing would be forthcoming.

Eventually (c. 2010), yet another awesome technologist, Jeffrey Olkin, joined Bloomberg. A few months later, I was reviewing a software specification from another group. The documentation was good but not stellar — at least not until about the tenth page, after which it was perfect! I walked over to the titular author and asked what happened. He told me that Jeffrey had taken over and finished the document. Long story short, I soon after asked Jeffrey to act as my structural editor, and he agreed. In the years since, Jeffrey reviewed and helped me to rework every last word of this first volume. I simply cannot overstate the organizational, writing, and engineering contributions Jeffrey has made to this book so far. And, yes, Jeffrey too has become a dear friend.

There are at least five other technically expert reviewers that read this entire manuscript as it was being readied for publication and provided amazing feedback: JC van Winkel, David Sankel, Josh Berne, Steven Breitstein (who meticulously reviewed each of my figures after their translation from ASCII art), and Clay Wilson (a.k.a. "The Closer," for the exceptional quality of his code reviews). Each of these five senior technologists (the first three being members of the C++ Standards Committee; the last four being current and former employees of Bloomberg) has, in his own respectively unique way, made this book substantially more valuable as a result of his extensive, thoughtful, thorough, and detailed feedback.

There are many other folks who have contributed to this book from its inception, and some even before that. Professor Chris Van Wyc (Drew University), a principal reviewer of my first book, provided valuable organizational feedback on a nascent draft of this volume. Tom Marshall (who also worked with me at Bear Stearns) and Peter Wainwright have worked with me at Bloomberg since 2002 and 2003, respectively. Tom went on to become the head of the architecture office at Bloomberg, and Peter, the head of Bloomberg's SI Build team. Each of them has amassed a tremendous amount of practical knowledge relating to metadata (and the tools that use it) and were kind enough to have co-authored an entire section on that topic (see section 2.16).

Early in my tenure at Bloomberg (c. 2004), my burgeoning BDE[5] team was suffering from its own success and I needed reinforcements. At the time, we had just hired several more-senior folks (myself included) and there was no senior headcount allotted. I went with Shawn to the then head of engineering, Ken Gartner, and literally begged him to open five "junior" positions. Somehow he agreed, and within no time, all of the positions were filled by five truly outstanding candidates — David Rubin, Rohan Bhindwale, Shezan Baig, Ujjwal Bhoota, and Guillaume Morin — four by the same recruiter, Amy Resnik, who I've known since 1991 (her boss, Steven Markmen, placed me at Mentor Graphics in 1986). Every one of these journeyman engineers went on to contribute massively to Bloomberg's software infrastructure, two of them rising to the level of team lead, and one to manager; in fact, it was Guillaume who, having only 1.5 years of work experience, implemented (as his very first assignment) the "designing with components" example that runs throughout section 3.12.

In June 2009, I recall sitting in the conference hotel for the C++ Standard Committee meeting in Frankfurt, Germany, having a "drink" (soda) with Alisdair Meredith — soon to be the library working group (LWG) chair (2010-2015) — when I got a call from a recruiter (Amy Resnik, again), who said she had found the perfect candidate to replace (another dear friend) Pablo Halpern on Bloomberg's BDE team (2003-2008) as our resident authority on the C++ Standard. You guessed it: Alisdair Meredith joined Bloomberg and (soon after) my BDE team in 2009, and ever since has been my definitive authority (and trusted friend) on what *is* in C++. Just prior to publication, Alisdair thoroughly reviewed the first three sections of Chapter 1 to make *absolutely sure* that I got it right.

Many others at Bloomberg have contributed to the knowledge captured in this book: Steve Downey was the initial architect of the **ball** logger, one of the first major subsystems developed at Bloomberg using our component-based methodology; Jeff Mendelson, in addition to providing many excellent technical reviews for this book, early on produced much of our modern date-math infrastructure; Mike Giroux (formerly of Bear Stearns) has historically been my able toolsmith and has crafted numerous custom Perl scripts that I have used throughout the years to keep my ASCII art in sync with ASCII text; Hyman Rosen, in addition to providing several

---

[5] BDE is an acronym for BDE Development Environment. This acronym is modeled after ODE (Our Development Environment) coined by Edward ("Ned") Horn at Bear Stearns in early 1997. The 'B' in BDE originally stood for "Bloomberg" (a common prefix for new subsystems and suborganizations of the day, e.g., *bpipe, bval, blaw*) and later also for "Basic," depending on the context (e.g., whether it was work or book related). Like ODE, BDE initially referred simultaneously to the lowest-level library package group (see section 2.9) in our Software-Capital repository (see section 0.5) along with the development team that maintained it. The term *BDE* has long since taken on a life of its own and is now used as a moniker to identify many different kinds of entities: *BDE* Group, *BDE* methodology, *BDE* libraries, *BDE* tools, *BDE* open-source repository, and so on; hence, the *recursive* acronym: BDE Development Environment.

unattributed passages in this book, has produced (over a five-year span) a prodigious (clang-based) static-analysis tool, **bde_verify**,[6] that is used throughout Bloomberg Engineering to ensure that conforming component-based software adheres to the design rules, coding standards, guidelines, and principles advocated throughout this book.

I would be remiss if I didn't give a shout-out to all of the *current* members of Bloomberg's BDE team, which I founded back in 2001, and, as of April 2019, is now managed by Mike Verschell along with Jeff Mendelsohn: Josh Berne, Steven Breitstein, Nathan Burgers, Bill Chapman, Attila Feher, Mike Giroux, Rostislav Khlebnikov, Alisdair Meredith, Hyman Rosen, and Oleg Subbotin. Most, if not all, of these folks have reviewed parts of the book, contributed code examples, helped me to render complex graphs or write custom tools, or otherwise in some less tangible way enhanced the value of this work.

Needless to say, without the unwavering support of Bloomberg's management team from Vlad and Shawn on down, this book would not have happened. My thanks to Andrei Basov (my current boss) and Wayne Barlow (my previous boss) — both also formerly of Bear Stearns — and especially to Adam Wolf, Head of Software Infrastructure at Bloomberg, for not just allowing but encouraging *and enabling* me (after some twenty-odd years) to finally realize this first volume.

And, of course, none of this would have been possible had Bjarne Stroustrup somehow decided to do anything other than make the unparalleled success of C++ his lifework. I have known Bjarne since he gave a talk at Mentor Graphics back in the early 1990s. (But he didn't know me then.) I had just methodically read *The Annotated C++ Reference Manual* (**ellis90**) and thoroughly annotated it (in four different highlighter colors) myself. After his talk, I asked Bjarne to sign my well-worn copy of the *ARM*. Decades later, I reminded him that it was I who had asked him to sign that disheveled, multicolored book of his; he recalled that, at least. Since becoming a regular attendee of the C++ Standards Committee meetings in 2006, Bjarne and I have worked closely together — e.g., to bring a better version of BDE's (library-based) **bsls_assert** contract-assertions facility, used at Bloomberg since 2004, into the language itself (see Volume II, section 6.8). Bjarne has spoken at Bloomberg multiple times at my behest. He reviewed and provided feedback on an early version of the preface of this book (minus these acknowledgments) and has also supplied historical data for footnotes. The sage software engineering wisdom from his special edition (third edition) of *The C++ Programming Language* (**stroustrup00**) is quoted liberally throughout this volume. Without his inspiration and encouragement, my professional life would be a far cry from what it is today.

---

[6] https://github.com/bloomberg/bde_verify

Finally, I would like to thank all of the many generations of folks at Pearson who have waited patiently for me throughout the years to get this book done. The initial draft of the manuscript was originally due in September 2001, and my final deadline for this first volume was at the end of September 2019. (It appears I'm a skosh late.) That said, I would like to recognize Debbie Lafferty, my first editor who then (in the early 2000s) passed the torch to Peter Gordon and Kim Spenceley (née Boedigheimer) with whom I worked closely for over a decade. When Peter retired in 2016, I began working with my current editor, Greg Doench.

Although Peter was a tough act to follow, Greg rose to the challenge and has been there for me throughout (and helped me more than he probably knows). Greg then introduced me to Julie Nahil, who worked directly with me on readying this book for production. In 2017, I reconnected with my lifelong friend and now wife, Elyse, who tirelessly tracked down copious references and proofread key passages (like this one). By late 2018, it became clear that the amount of work required to produce this book would exceed what anyone had anticipated, and so Pearson retained Lori Hughes to work with me, in what turned out to be a nearly full-time capacity for the better part of 2019. I cannot say enough about the professionalism, fortitude, and raw effort put forth by Lori in striving to make this book a reality in calendar year 2019. I want to thank Lori, Julie, and Greg, and also Peter, Kim, and Debbie, for all their sustained support and encouragement over so many, many years. And this is but the first of three volumes, OMG!

The list of people that have contributed directly and/or substantially to this work is dauntingly large, and I have no doubt that, despite my efforts to the contrary, many will go unrecognized here. Know that I realize this book is the result of my life's experiences, and for each of you that have in some way contributed, please accept my heartfelt thanks and appreciation for being a part of it.

0

Motivation

Large-scale, highly maintainable software systems don't just happen, nor do techniques used successfully by individual application developers necessarily scale to larger, more integrated development efforts. This is an *engineering* book about developing software on a large scale. But it's more than just that. At its heart, this book teaches a skill. A skill that applies to software of all kinds and sizes. A skill that, once learned, becomes almost second nature, requiring little if any additional time or effort. A skill that repeatedly results in organized systems that are fundamentally easy to understand, verify, and maintain.

The software development landscape has changed significantly since my first book.[1] During that time, the Standard Template Library (STL) was adopted as part of the initial C++98 Language Standard and has since been expanded significantly. All relevant compilers now fully support exceptions, namespaces, member templates, etc. The Internet has made open-source libraries far more accessible. Thread, exception, and alias safety have become common design considerations. Also, many more people now appreciate the critical importance of sound *physical design* (see Figure 0-32, section 0.6) — a dimension of software engineering I introduced in my first book. Although fundamental physical design concepts remain the same, there are important new ways to apply them.

This book was written with the practitioner in mind. The focus is closely tied to a sequential development methodology. We describe in considerable detail how to develop software in terms of the well-defined atomic physical modules that we call *components*. A rich lexicon has been assembled to characterize the process. Many existing engineering techniques have been updated and refined. In particular, we present (see Volume III) a comprehensive treatment of component-level testing. What used to be considered a black art, or at least a highly specialized craft, has emerged into a predictable, teachable engineering discipline. We also discuss (see Volume II) the motivations behind and effective use of many essential "battle-hardened" design and implementation techniques. Overall, the engineering processes described here (Volume I) complement, and are synergistic with, proven project-management processes.

Bottom line: This book is designed for professional software developers and is all about being successful at developing software that can scale to arbitrary size. We have delineated the issues that we deem integral and present them in an order that roughly corresponds to our software-development thought process. Many important new ideas are presented that reflect a sometimes harsh reality. The value of this book, however, is not just in the ideas it contains but in the cohesive regularity with which it teaches sound engineering practices. Not everything we talk about in this book is popular (yet), but initially neither was the notion of *physical design*.

---

[1] **lakos96**

0.1   The Goal: Faster, Better, Cheaper!

The criterion for successful software application development in industry is invariably the delivery of the best product at the lowest possible cost as quickly as possible. Implicit in this goal are three fundamental dimensions:

- *Schedule (faster)*: Expediency of delivery of the software
- *Product (better)*: Enhanced functionality/quality of the software
- *Budget (cheaper)*: Economy of production of the software

In practice, we may optimize the development of a particular software application or product for at most two of these parameters; the third will be dictated. Figure 0-1 illustrates the interdependence of these three dimensions.[2]

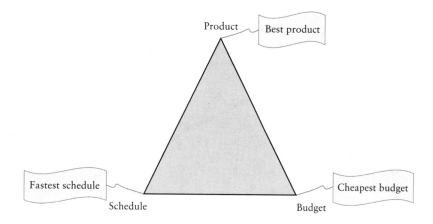

Figure 0-1: Schedule/product/budget trade-offs

At any given point, our ability to develop applications is governed by our existing infrastructure, such as developers, libraries, tools, and so on. The higher the quality goal of our product, the more calendar time and/or engineering resources it will consume. If we try to make a product of similar quality take less time and thereby improve the schedule, it will cost more — often a *lot* more, thereby negatively impacting the budget. If we have a fixed budget, the only way

---

[2] **mcconnell96**, section 6.6, "Schedule, Cost, and Product Trade-Offs," Figure 6-10, p. 126

to get the work done quicker is to do less (e.g., fewer features, less testing). This inescapable reality seems intrinsic to all software development.[3]

Still, it would be nice if there were some predictable way that, over time, we could improve all three of these parameters at once — that is, devise a methodology that, as a byproduct of its use, would continually reduce both cost and time to market while improving quality for future products. In graphical terms, this methodology would shift the faster/better/cheaper design space for applications and products further and further from the origin, as illustrated in Figure 0-2.

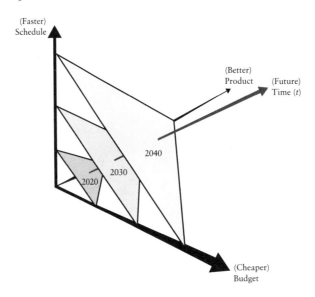

Figure 0-2: Improving the schedule/product/budget design space

---

[3] JC van Winkel has commented that these relationships are difficult to appreciate as a single graph and suggests that there are other, more intuitive ways to approach understanding these trade-offs, e.g., using *sliders*.

For a fixed schedule (calendar time to delivery), you get this slider:

(Cheaper) Budget ———█—— (Better) Product

For a fixed budget (money/resources), you get this slider:

(Better) Product —█——— (Faster) Schedule

For a fixed product (features/quality), you get this slider:

(Faster) Schedule ——█—— (Cheaper) Budget

This final slider is at the heart of the titular thesis of Fred Brooks's classic work *The Mythical Man Month* (see **brooks75**), which asserts that the idea that there is an inverse *linear* proportionality between *time* and *cost* that holds over the entire range of interest is pure fantasy. The geometric growth of interpersonal interactions (corroborated by empirical data; **boehm81**, section 5.3, pp. 61–64) suggests that — within a narrow band of relevant limits — this relationship might reasonably be modeled as an inverse *quadratic* one between time (T) and cost (C), i.e., $T \propto 1/\sqrt{C}$ (see section 0.9).

Assuming such a methodology exists, what would have to change over time? For example, the experience of our developers will presumably increase, leading to better productivity and quality. As developers become more experienced and productive, we will naturally have to pay them more, but not proportionally so. Still, there are limits to how productive any one person can be when given a fixed development environment, so the environment too must change.[4]

Over time, we might expect third-party and increasingly open-source software-development tools and libraries to improve, enhancing our development environment and thereby increasing our productivity. While this expectation is reasonable, it will be true for our competitors as well. The question is, "What can we do proactively to improve our productivity relative to the competition over time?"

Implementing a repeatable, scalable software development process has been widely acknowledged to be the single most effective way of simultaneously improving quality while reducing development time and cost. Without such a process, the cost of doing business, let alone the risk of failure, increases nonlinearly with project size. Following a sound development process is essential, yet productivity is unlikely to improve asymptotically by more than a fixed constant multiple. Along with a repeatable process, we also need some form of *positive feedback* in the methodology that will continually amplify development productivity in our environment.

Now consider that there is one essential output of all software development that continues to increase over time: the developed software itself. If it were possible to make use of a significant fraction of this software in future projects, then the prospect for improving productivity could be essentially unbounded. That is, the more software we develop, the more that would be readily available for reuse. The challenge then becomes to find a way to organize the software so that it can and will be reused effectively.

0.2 Application vs. Library Software

Application development is usually single-minded and purposeful. In large organizations, this purposefulness frequently leads both to duplicated code and to sets of interdependent applications. Each piece works, but the overall code base is messy, and each new change or addition becomes increasingly more difficult. This all too frequent "design pattern" has been coined a "Big Ball of Mud."[5]

---

[4] Upon reviewing a near-final draft of this volume, Kevlen Henney remarked, "I have recently been advocating that we ditch the term 'faster' in favour of 'sooner.' It's not the speed that matters, it's the arrival time. These are not the same concept, and the continued focus on speed is a problem rather than a desirable goal. Good design is about taking the better route to arrive sooner; whether you go faster or not is less important."

[5] **foote99**

The resulting code base has no centralized organizational structure. Any software that could in principle be useful across the enterprise either has been designed a bit too subjectively to be generally useful or is too intertwined with the application-specific code to be extricated. Besides, because the code must be responsive to the changing needs of its original master, it would be risky to rely on the stability of such software. Also, because a business typically profits from speed, there is not much of a premium on any of the traditional subdisciplines of programming such as factoring and interface design. Although this ad hoc approach often leads to useful applications in a relatively short time, it also results in a serious maintenance burden. As time goes by, not only is there no improvement in the code base, maintenance costs continue to grow inordinately faster than necessary.

To understand the problem better, we begin by observing that there are two distinct kinds of software — *application* software and *library* software — and therefore two kinds of development. An application is a program (or tightly coupled suite of programs) that satisfies a particular business need. Due to ever-changing requirements, application source code is inherently unstable and may change without notice. All source code explicitly local to an application must, in our view, be limited to use by only that application (see section 2.13).

A library, on the other hand, is not a program, but a repository. In C++, it is a collection of header and object files designed to facilitate the sharing of classes and functions. Generally speaking, libraries are stable and therefore potentially reusable. The degree to which a body of software is particular to a specific application or more generally useful to an entire domain will govern the extent and effectiveness of its reuse within an organization and, perhaps, even beyond.

These contrasting properties of specificity and stability suggest that different development strategies and policies for application and library code should apply. In particular, library developers (few in number) will be obliged to observe a relatively strict discipline to create reusable software, whereas application developers (much more numerous) are allowed more freedom with respect to organizational rules. Given the comparatively large number of application developers who will (ideally) depend on library software, it is critical that library interfaces be especially well thought through, as subsequent changes could wind up being prohibitively expensive.

Classical software design is pure top-down design. At each level of refinement, every subsystem is partitioned independently of its peers. Consideration of implementation at each level of decomposition is deliberately postponed. This process recurses until a codable solution is attained. Adhering to a pure top-down design methodology results in an inverted tree of hierarchical modules (as illustrated in Figure 0-3) having no reconvergence and, therefore, no reuse.

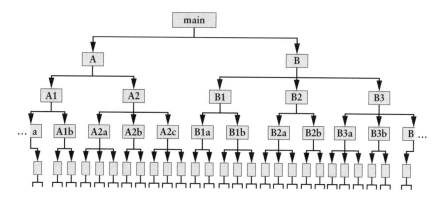

Figure 0-3: Pure top-down design (BAD IDEA)

Although the process of designing any particular application is primarily top-down, experience tells us that, within any given application domain, there are almost always recurring needs for similar functionality. Within the domain of integrated circuit computer-aided design (ICCAD), for example, we might expect there to be many separate needs for classes such as `Transistor`, `Contact`, and `Wire`. There will also be a recurring need for functionality that is common across many application domains. Examples include logging, transport, messaging, marshaling, and, of course, various high-performance data structures and algorithms, such as `std::vector` and `std::sort`, respectively. Failing to recognize common subsystems (and components; see section 0.7) would mean that each must be written anew wherever the recurring need is rediscovered. We assert that it is incumbent on any responsible enterprise to actively address such naturally recurring inefficiencies.

In an ideal application development paradigm, designers would actively seek out commonalities in required functionality across the various subsystems of their programs and, wherever practical, either employ existing solutions or design well-factored components that can serve their recurring needs. Integrating existing solutions into a top-down design makes the design process a hybrid between pure top-down and bottom-up — perhaps the most common architectural approach used in practice today. Even within the scope of a single application, there are typically ample opportunities to apply this kind of factoring for reuse to good effect.

Sadly, reusable software is not normally a byproduct of the development of applications. Because of the focused view and limited time horizon for the great majority of application development efforts, attempts to write software to exploit commonality across applications — absent a separate team of library developers (see section 0.10) — are almost never viable. This observation is not a criticism of application developers but merely reflects a common economic reality. The success of an application development team is determined by the extent to which it fulfills a business need on time and within budget. Any significant deviation from this goal in the name of reuse is likely to be penalized rather than rewarded. Given the express importance of time to market, it is a rare application developer indeed that makes decoupled, leverageable software available in a form generally consumable by others, while still meeting his or her primary responsibilities.

Library developers, on the other hand, have a quite different mission: Make the overall development process more efficient! The most common goal of library development is to increase the long-term productivity of application developers while reducing maintenance costs (e.g., those resulting from rampantly duplicative software). There are, of course, certain initial costs in setting up a library suitable for public consumption. Moreover, the incremental costs of building reusable components are higher than for similar (nonreusable) ones developed for use in a single application. But, given that the costs of developing library software can be amortized over all the applications that use it, some amount of extra cost can easily be justified.

As Figure 0-4 illustrates, there are several inherent differences between application and library software. Good application software (Figure 0-4a) is generally malleable, whereas library software (Figure 0-4b) needs to be stable (see section 0.5). Because the scope of changes to an individual application is bounded, the design of the application's pieces is often justifiably more tightly collaborative (see section 0.3) than would be appropriate in a library used across arbitrarily many applications.[6]

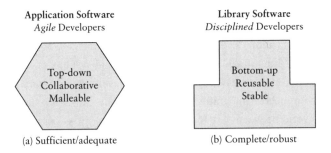

Figure 0-4: Library versus application software development

The requirements for library software are, in many ways, just the union of those of the applications that depend on it (see Volume II, section 5.7). For example, the lifetime of a separately releasable library is the union of the lifetimes of the applications that use it. Hence, libraries tend to live longer than individual applications. If an application is to be released on a particular platform, then so must any library that supports it. Therefore, libraries must be more portable than applications. Consequently, there will often be no single application team that can support a given library throughout its productive lifetime on all the platforms for which it might be needed. This observation further suggests the need for a separate, dedicated team to support shared resources (see section 0.10).

Library code must be more reliable than typical application code, and our methodology amplifies this dichotomy. For example, compared with typical application code, library code usually has more detailed descriptions of its programmatic interfaces, called *contracts* (see Volume II, section 5.2). Detailed function-level documentation (see Volume II, section 6.17) permits more accurate and thorough testing, which is how we achieve reliability (see Volume II, section 6.8, and Volume III in its entirety).

Also, library software is more stable, i.e., its essential behavior does not change (see section 0.5). More stability reduces the likelihood that bugs will be introduced or that test cases will need to be reworked due to changes in behavior; hence, stability improves reliability (See Volume II, section 5.6). Having a comparatively large number of eclectic clients will provide a richer variety of use cases that, over time, tends to prove the library software more thoroughly. Given that the cost of debugging code that you did not write (or write recently) is significantly higher than for code you are working on today, there is a strong incentive for library developers to "get it right the first time" (see Volume III, section 7.5).

When writing library software, we strive to absorb the complexity internally so as to minimize it outwardly. That is, library developers aggressively trade off ease of implementation (by them) for ease of use (by their clients). Small pockets of very complex code are far better than distributed, somewhat complicated code. For example, we assert that it is almost always better to provide two member functions than to provide a single template member function if only two parameter types (e.g., consider `const char *` and `std::string`) make sense (see Volume II, section 4.5).

More controversially, it is often better to have two copies of a `struct` — e.g., one nested/private in the `.h` file (accessible to `inline` methods and friends) and the other at file scope in the `.cpp` file (accessible to file-scope `static` functions) — and make sure to keep them in sync locally than to pollute the global space with an implementation detail. In general, library developers should plan to spend significant extra effort to save clients even a slight inconvenience. The more general the reusable component, the more developer effort can be justified (see Volume II, Chapter 6).

As with any business, the focus of ongoing library development must be to demonstrate significant value at reasonable incremental cost. Hence, any library software that is written must be *relevant* to those who would use it. Library developers need look no further than to existing applications for guidance. By working closely with application developers to solve their recurring needs, library developers stay focused on what is important: making application developers more productive!

At the same time, library developers have the important responsibility to *judiciously* and *diplomatically* resist inappropriate specific requests that would undermine the success of the development community as a whole. For example, refusing to provide a `name` attribute for a `Calendar` type might seem capricious to an application developer scrambling to make a deadline. Yet the experienced library developer knows (see Volume II, section 4.3) that providing a `name` field will destroy any useful notion of *value* for that object and render it unsuitable as the *vocabulary type* (see Volume II, section 4.4) that it was designed to be.

Even valid requests are sometimes phrased in terms of a proposed solution that is suboptimal. Instead of blindly satisfying requests exactly as they are specified (see section 3.12.1), it is the responsibility of library developers to understand the underlying needs, along with *all* of the software issues, and provide viable solutions that meet those needs (if not the wants) of all clients — both individually and collectively. Hence, the design of the client-facing interface is critically important (see Volume II, Chapter 5).

The design paradigms for application and library development are also quite different. Whereas application design is primarily top-down, libraries consisting of generally useful software are developed bottom-up. More sophisticated solutions are composed out of simpler ones. The desirable tree-like — or more accurately DAG-like — dependencies among libraries and even among the components within those libraries are not a coincidence. They are instead the result of thoughtful factoring for the express purpose of achieving fine-grained *hierarchical reuse* (see section 0.4) *across* applications.

The absolute need for clear, concise, and complete documentation also differentiates library code from its application counterpart. Since library code exists independently of any one context, far more thorough and detailed overview documentation (see Volume II, section 6.15), along with thoughtful usage examples (see Volume II, section 6.16), will be needed for clients to readily understand and use it. And, unlike applications, the performance requirements for reusable library software are not bound to any one usage and often must exceed what is provably needed today (see section 0.11).

Deployment is yet another aspect in which application and library software diverge. An application is typically released as a single executable, whereas libraries are deployed as collections of header files (see section 1.1.3) and corresponding library archives (see section 1.2.4) or, perhaps, shared libraries. While incorporating directory structure (e.g., via relative pathnames) in `#include` directives (e.g., `#include <basic/date.h>`) might be acceptable for application software, libraries should abstain from doing so, or flexibility during deployment will be compromised (see section 2.15).

Finally, application developers are invariably attempting to solve difficult, real-world problems. As Figure 0-5 illustrates, these problems are often irregular and particularly onerous to describe in all their detail. When developing a large application top-down, there is often uncertainty regarding aspects of the overall solution — perhaps some important requirements are missing or yet to be determined. Moreover, these intricate problems — and therefore the underlying application software itself — will typically grow and change over time.

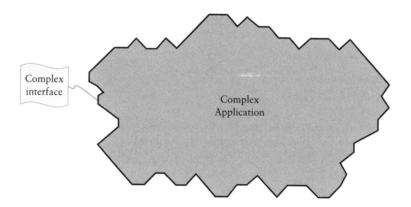

Figure 0-5: Many applications aren't regular.

Still, within such a complex application there are typically many regular, well-defined, stable subproblems whose factored solutions will find their way into the application. In such situations, we might be able to jump-start the development process by sponsoring the creation of some generally useful pieces. Working together, application and library developers might be able to identify common subsystems that help shape the requirements and/or design of the application, as illustrated in Figure 0-6. Interaction between application and library developers helps to galvanize crisply specified contracts that are relevant and generally usable, and perhaps might even be reusable (see Volume II, section 5.7).[7,8]

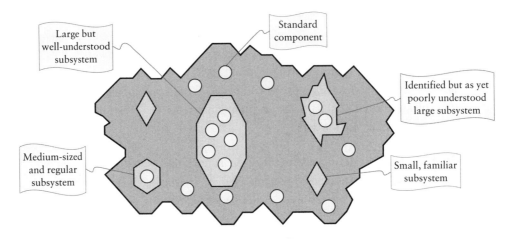

Figure 0-6: Many components and subsystems *are* regular.

By routinely solving slightly more general, more easily described subproblems that address most — but not necessarily all — aspects of a specific need, we will systematically achieve

---

[7] See also **stroustrup00**, section 23.4.1, pp. 698–700, which we summarize here.

In his book, Stroustrup makes a number of sound recommendations and observations.
- Design using existing parts.
- Hold off on creating new, eccentric, nonreusable custom parts.
- Try to make any new parts you create useful in the future.
- Only in the end create project-specific parts.

Stroustrup goes on to say that this approach can work, but it is not automatic.
- Often we cannot even identify distinct components in the final design.
- "...corporate culture often discourages people from using the model outlined here."
- "...this model of development really works well only when you consider the longer term."
- A universal/international standard for all components is not reasonable.
- A hierarchy of standards — country, industry, company, department, product — is the best we can realistically hope to achieve.
- Iteration is essential to gain experience.

[8] As noted in the preface, many of the references in this chapter in particular, such as the previous one, are to books that have had subsequent editions that "supersede" their earlier ones, but those later editions fail to carry forward the sage design advice due to length constraints. We therefore continue to reference these early (perhaps out-of-print) editions and, of course, reproduce the relevant content here for the convenience of the reader.

less *collaborative* (mutually *aware* — see section 0.3), more *stable* software, and hence more *reusable* software, even as our applications continue to evolve. Like thermal separators between concrete blocks, the gaps in functionality between assembled *reusable* components (filled in by glue logic) are what accommodate the less regular, more fickle, and ever-changing policies that large applications typically comprise (see Volume II, section 5.9).

To achieve maximal reuse, an organization must make an ongoing effort to factor out of application-specific repositories (illustrated in Figure 0-7a) as much independently comprehensible code as it can (e.g., as illustrated in Figure 0-7b). The more widely applicable that code might be, the lower in the firm-wide repository of reusable software it belongs. Only the most widely useful software would reside near the root.

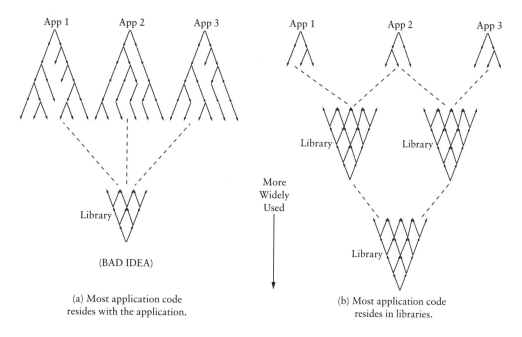

Figure 0-7: Relative application versus library sizes

Given the appropriate mandate, detail-oriented *disciplined* library developers, working closely with fast-moving *agile* application developers, have a far better chance at rendering the kind of noncollaborative, high-quality, stable pieces of software that lead to effective reuse. It is by proactively extracting an appropriate subset of the software we develop, aggressively refactoring it, and placing it into stable, accessible, and therefore potentially reusable libraries, that we might achieve substantial productivity gains in the long term.

0.3   Collaborative vs. Reusable Software

The criteria for the modularization of classically reusable software emphasize isolating manageable amounts of complexity behind interfaces that minimize collaborative idiosyncrasies. The industry recognizes that continuous refactoring — i.e., extracting, refining, and *demoting* (see section 3.5.3) widely usable functionality as it is discovered — is the only viable approach for harvesting anything more than the most basic reusable software. Even when reuse per se is not the goal, careful factoring can provide significant flexibility, leading to greater maintainability as the development effort progresses, especially as requirements change. When designing top-down, however, many developers routinely construct obscure devices that exactly meet their current needs but that are highly specific, inflexible, and clearly not useful in other contexts. The metaphors we use to characterize such poorly or inadequately factored subsystems are, respectively, the *cracked plate* and the *toaster toothbrush*.

Factoring is the art of subdividing a larger problem, illustrated schematically in Figure 0-8, into appropriate smaller ones whose independent solutions yield useful components that can be explained, implemented, tested, and recombined to solve the original problem. In a wellfactored solution, the complexity of the interface for each subsolution will be kept small relative to the complexity of the corresponding implementation that does the real work. Analogous to a sphere, the ratio of complexity across its interface (or *surface*) to that of its implementation (or *volume*) is minimized.

Figure 0-8: A large but well-defined software problem

In the worst case, the complexity of interactions across module boundaries will be no simpler than those within. To use such a module, clients will need to know essentially all details of the underlying implementation. Any change to that implementation — no matter how small — runs the substantial risk of adversely affecting the desired behavior of any of the other modules with which it interacts. Such inadequacies in logical factoring result in physical modules that can be extraordinarily difficult to maintain.

For example, imagine that we have a subsystem consisting of a suite of modules that all communicate through a common message buffer implemented as an `std::vector<char>`. Initially, the byte offsets are blocked off to correspond to a well-known structure: The first four bytes indicate the source of the transmission, the second four bytes indicate the destination, the third four bytes indicate the transmission type, and so on.

Over time (and always for valid business reasons), this structure is slowly but surely corrupted. One module adds the rule that if the most significant bit of the transmission type is set, use the "alternate enumeration" for source and destination. Some other modules, having no use for some of the fields, redefine their meaning under certain stateful conditions known only to them. Still others, not wanting to "corrupt" the message format, pre-allocate additional capacity and store "private" information beyond the logical end of the vector.[9] It remains, however, a common practice to steal the first two (or perhaps three) least significant bits (depending on the target architectures) of a pointer, based on the very practical (but not guaranteed) assumption of *natural alignment* (see Volume II, section 6.7).

What was once a relatively clean interface has become overwhelmingly complicated. The unconstrained, and now tight, logical coupling among these modules makes even minor maintenance tasks both expensive and risky. Like the pieces of a cracked plate, these modules are destined to serve exactly one useful purpose — i.e., implementing the current version of exactly one application. The resulting "partition" is illustrated schematically in Figure 0-9a.

---

[9] A previous boss of mine at Bear Stearns, Buzz Moschetti, sardonically referred to this insidious form of extreme brittleness (c. 1998) as a *zvector*.

(a) Cracked plate

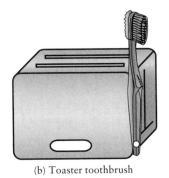
(b) Toaster toothbrush

Figure 0-9: A brittle solution

A common result of inadequate factoring is a function, object, or component that is both unfamiliar and difficult to describe. Being difficult to describe is a telling symptom of a large *surface area* (i.e., complicated interface) and a strong indication that the original problem was improperly or insufficiently factored. Disproportionate complexity in the interface results when a module is pathologically specific to the current need.

Let us now imagine that your mom is the client and you have been given a set of requirements for the morning: Brush your teeth and make toast for the family. Being the industrious type, you quickly invent a solution to both requirements as a single seamless device cast from one mold, the "toaster toothbrush" (Figure 0-9b). Although simultaneously addressing precisely the two requirements delineated by customer Mom, a `ToasterToothbrush` — much like each of the pieces of a cracked plate — is unique to the circumstances that precipitated it and is therefore entirely ineffective in the presence of change. A minor modification to any aspect of the original problem specification (e.g., Figure 0-8) could require us to revisit implementation details in every corner of the existing solution (e.g., Figure 0-9a). As it is typical for application requirements to change over time, such brittleness in the pieces of the application presents an enormous liability and a serious risk to a timely success: If your mom changes her mind — even just a little — you're toast!

Even when pathologically brittle designs are avoided, it is not unusual for application developers to create software that, while nominally independent, was clearly conceived with peer components in mind. Let's skip ahead and consider first the collaborative decomposition of the toaster-toothbrush application illustrated in Figure 0-10b. The familiar toaster object has been thoughtfully augmented with a hook that provides a handy location at which to attach the requisite toothbrush — provided, that is, the toothbrush in question has been properly customized with an appropriate hole bored through its handle. Apart from this rather specific circumstance, it is unlikely (all other things being equal) that one would opt for a toaster with an unsightly hook protruding from it to reside on their kitchen counter.

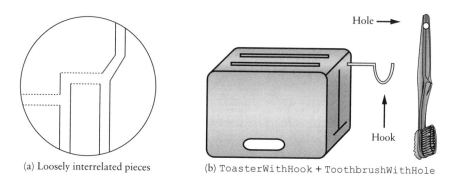

(a) Loosely interrelated pieces   (b) `ToasterWithHook` + `ToothbrushWithHole`

Figure 0-10: Collaborative solutions

Circling back to our plate analogy, it is also possible to design a software solution that has a well-defined interface and a low surface-to-volume ratio yet is nonetheless composed of highly collaborative pieces, as illustrated in Figure 0-10a. This circle, like the toaster toothbrush, is an example of a *collaborative* design — one in which, even though there might be no explicit *physical* interdependency among the submodules, the *logical* design of each piece was highly influenced by its surroundings. As you can see, fully describing any one of these pieces alone, without reference to the others, would take some doing. Like a toaster with a hook, or a toothbrush with a hole, such pieces are substantially less likely to find their way into wider use in new contexts than a less collaborative, more easily described, more *reusable* set of components.

Still, collaborative designs can be acceptable within the context of a single application, particularly if we are able to reuse the collaborative pieces across multiple versions. Compare the cracked plate of Figure 0-9a to the collaborative one of Figure 0-10a. A piece of a cracked plate is unlikely to be useful except to fit back together in the specific version of the software for which it was designed. As Figure 0-11a illustrates, brittle solutions such as this are usually limited to a single version of a single application; all of its parts must be reworked in unison with each new release. Simply put, this less-disciplined approach to software development is not effective on a large scale, which perhaps explains why so many larger projects fail (or fail to meet expectations).

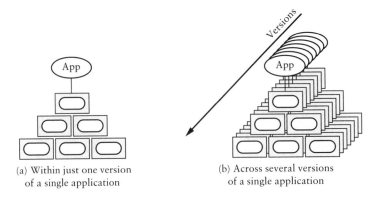

(a) Within just one version
of a single application

(b) Across several versions
of a single application

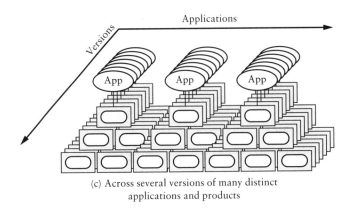

(c) Across several versions of many distinct
applications and products

Figure 0-11: Degrees of exploiting solutions to recurring problems

However, through careful factoring, we can reuse collaborative pieces *across* versions (Figure 0-11b). These pieces can reside in application-specific libraries outside of the application source code, where they can be shared *without modification* across multiple active versions of the application. By increasing the proportion of subfunctionality that remains stable across versions, we reduce not only the overall costs associated with ongoing enhancements, but also the time needed between releases.

While collaborative solutions might be reusable across versions of a single application, to achieve reuse across applications (Figure 0-11c), we must go further. Historically, *reusable* software addresses a small, well-defined problem that recurs in practice. Familiar examples include `std::vector` and `std::string` from the C++ Standard Library. In our geometric analogy, reusable software components take the form of familiar shapes, as illustrated in Figure 0-12a. Notice that each of these shapes is easy to describe in words: a *square* of side *S*, a *rectangle* of length *L* and width *W*, a (right) *triangle* of base *B* and height *H*, and a *semicircle* of radius *R*.

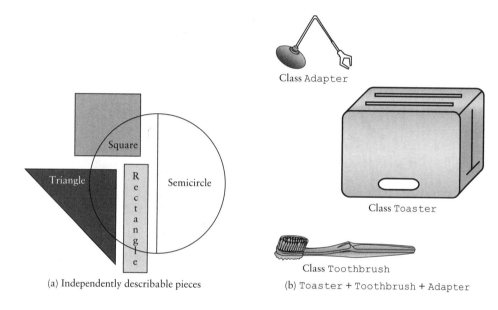

Figure 0-12: Classically reusable software

Reusable software must be easy to compose *without modification* (see section 0.5) in various ways to solve new, unforeseen problems. Having a trusted suite of prefabricated components can be a tremendous productivity aid. Assuming we had an "off-the-shelf" toothbrush (sans hole), an ordinary toaster (sans hook), and the interesting (but definitely noncollaborative) adapter of Figure 0-12b, we could readily assemble a solution very much resembling the fully custom, monolithic device of Figure 0-9b, but much more quickly *and reliably* than building it from scratch. As illustrated in Figure 0-13, such noncollaborative subsolutions will typically require some filler (Figure 0-13a); however, a bit of glue (logic) is often all that is needed (Figure 0-13b).

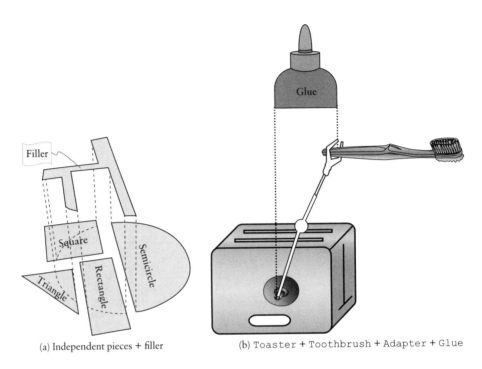

(a) Independent pieces + filler   (b) `Toaster` + `Toothbrush` + `Adapter` + `Glue`

Figure 0-13: Solving the original problem with classically reusable pieces

It is when we consider the value of a finely graduated hierarchy of truly *reusable* solutions over many versions of many distinct applications and products (Figure 0-11c) that we can begin to appreciate the vast potential benefits of component-based software in general (see section 0.7) — and *Software Capital* in particular (see section 0.9). As we will soon illustrate, it is this two-dimensional scenario that compels us to allocate the resources necessary to construct and populate a viable firm-wide repository of ultra-high-quality, *hierarchically* reusable software.

0.4   Hierarchically Reusable Software

For quite some time now, people have known that large monolithic blocks of code (illustrated in Figure 0-14) are suboptimal. As far back as 1972 — before the promise of reuse and some quarter century before physical software design concepts would come to be addressed as such — luminaries such as Parnas[10] observed that carefully separating even just the logical content of a program into its more tightly related subsystems and permitting only simple (e.g., scalar) types to pass through their interfaces alone tended to reduce overall complexity.

---

[10] D. L. Parnas is widely regarded as the father of *modular programming* (a.k.a. encapsulation and information hiding); see **parnas72**.

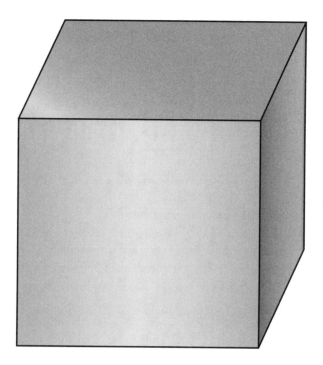

Figure 0-14: Monolithic block of software (BAD IDEA)

Some four years previous (1968), Dijkstra — known for his many important contributions to the field of mathematical computer science, such as the shortest-path algorithm that bears his name[11] — had already published the results of a body of work[12] that demonstrated the value of a hierarchical (acyclic) physical software structure for enabling the comprehension and thorough testing of complex systems. Parnas, in his seminal paper,[13] acknowledged that an (acyclic) physical hierarchy (illustrated in Figure 0-15a) along with his proposed "clean" logical decomposition (illustrated in Figure 0-15b) "are two desirable, but *independent* properties of a system structure."[14]

---

[11] **dijkstra59**

[12] **dijkstra68**

[13] **parnas72**

[14] Observing the increase in flow-of-control switches between modules in his own (then new) decomposition style, Parnas went on to correctly forecast the need for `inline` function substitution (see section 1.3.12) for modular programs to remain competitive at run time with their procedural counterparts.

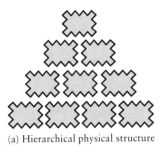
(a) Hierarchical physical structure

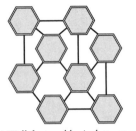
(b) Well-factored logical structure

Figure 0-15: Two desirable properties of a system structure

A few years later (1978), Myers would argue,

> ... a more powerful justification for partitioning a program is that it creates
> a number of well-defined documented boundaries within the program.
> These boundaries, or interfaces, are invaluable in the comprehension of the
> program.[15]

Although Myers happened to be referring to the maintainability of just a single program, these arguments naturally apply more generally across any physical boundaries — e.g., libraries.

Classical software design often results in a coarsely layered architecture, as illustrated in Figure 0-16. An insufficiently factored architecture such as a naive implementation of the seven layers of the OSI network architecture model[16] — or even the various layers of a compiler — is not necessarily a problem so long as the layers themselves readily admit further vertical decomposition.[17]

---

[15] **myers78**, Chapter 3, "Partitioning," pp. 21–22, specifically the last paragraph of p. 21

[16] **deitel90**, section 16.2, pp. 496–515

[17] Note that the OSI model suffers in that some "implementations" have distributed the tasks of the layers in a different way or added sublayers. An example is Ethernet II (layers 1+2) versus IEEE 802.3+802.2 where layer 2 was basically split up into 2a and 2b, adding an extra header. (This data courtesy of JC van Winkel.)

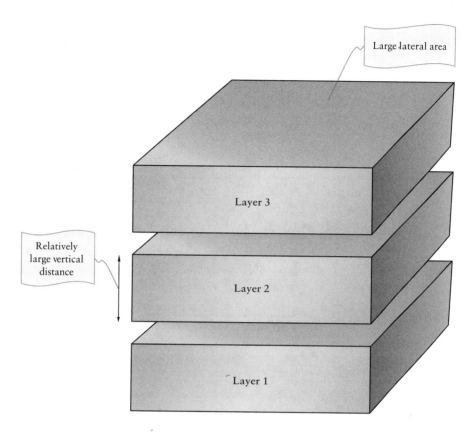

Figure 0-16: Coarse-layered software structure

A more finely graduated approach to vertical factoring is illustrated in Figure 0-17. By *finely graduated*, we mean that the amount of functionality added from one accessible level of abstraction to the next is relatively small. For example, class `Line` uses class `Point` in its interface (and therefore depends on it), but the definition of `Line` resides in a separate physical unit at a (slightly) higher level. Providing "short" logical steps from one physical level to the next dramatically improves the thoroughness with which we can understand and test our systems.

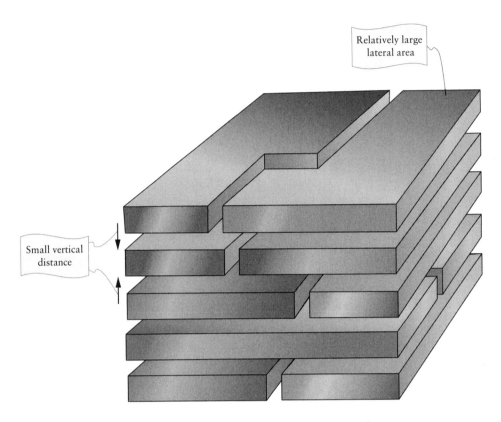

Figure 0-17: Finely graduated (but nongranular) software

Finely graduated vertical factoring alone, however, is not sufficient for efficient component-level testing (see Volume III, section 7.5) nor, due to excessive physical dependency, is it suitable for independent reuse (see section 1.8). We must also make sure to separate peer logical content — e.g., the respective definitions of `Circle`, `Triangle`, and `Rectangle` — into physically separate units (see section 3.2).

Providing broad, albeit shallow, logical content — such as a wrapper layer — will likely touch many aspects of the lower layers. If this layer resides in just one or a few large monolithic physical units, then functionality not directly needed for the current purpose will nonetheless draw in other unneeded functionality (see section 1.2.2). The result is that a disproportionately large amount of code must be compiled and linked in order to test or reuse any particular unit of logical content. The likely physical consequences are increased compilation time, link time, and executable size (see section 3.6), resulting in larger (and often slower) programs. To mitigate these problems, we must be careful to partition our logical designs laterally as well as vertically.

Classically reusable software is granular; its laterally modular structure is illustrated in Figure 0-18. By *granular*, we mean that the breadth of logical functionality implemented in any one atomic physical unit is small. The codified solution to a well-defined, recurring problem is packaged in such a way as to be readily accessible to clients yet physically independent of anything not required. We must be careful, however: If this packaging goes too far and ends up nesting (and therefore rendering inaccessible) the subfunctionality used to implement the granular functionality, the finely graduated vertical aspect is lost and with it goes *hierarchical* reuse.

Small lateral area

Figure 0-18: Granular (modular) but nongraduated (not finely layered) software

In practice, classical library reuse has tended to be bimodal: Reusable solutions are either tiny (e.g., algorithms and data structures) and devoid of policy (i.e., a specific context governing when, where, and how to use this functionality) or large and influential (e.g., databases, messaging middleware, logging systems) that more forcefully dictate their intended use.[18]

---

[18] Frameworks provide an important, but substantially different, *top-down* form of very coarse-grained, structured reuse.

Little in the way of intermediate subsolutions, however, have been broken out, documented, and made generally available.

Using the *component* (see section 0.7) as the atomic unit of logical design and physical packaging, the *finely graduated*, *granular* software structure illustrated in Figure 0-19 incorporates the benefits of fine-grained physical modularity (both horizontally and vertically) with a clean and well-documented (see Volume II, sections 6.15–6.17) logical decomposition. Like the thin layers of Figure 0-17, this organization facilitates thorough testing. And, like the independent solutions of Figure 0-18, these individual components depend on only what is needed — nothing more.

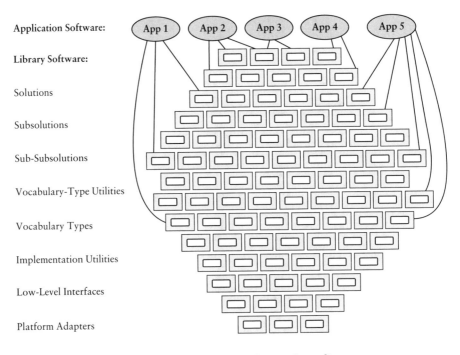

Figure 0-19: Finely graduated, granular software

If designed properly, a finely graduated, granular solution will be built from a suite of well-factored subsolutions, which in turn draws from sub-subsolutions and so on.[19] We can easily reveal, like peeling an onion, the inner levels of abstraction that, without modification (see section 0.5), provide well-factored subproblem solutions common to both the original need and often emerging new ones.

---

[19] See also **stroustrup00**, section 24.3.1, pp. 733–734.

For example, common types — especially those that flow through function boundaries, such as `Date` and `Allocator`, which we call *vocabulary types* (see Volume II, section 4.4) — are obvious candidates for reuse. These basic types might at first appear to be at one end of the reusable spectrum. Yet, virtually all concrete types are naturally layered on significantly lower-level infrastructural functionality.

Part of what makes this approach to reuse so compelling is that, unlike the software structure of classical reuse (e.g., Figure 0-12), the client is not limited to a single layer of abstraction. Recall our classically decomposed toaster, toothbrush, and adapter from Figure 0-12b. We were able to easily build the toaster toothbrush out of these parts (Figure 0-13b). However, by extending the process of factoring software across multiple finely graduated layers (as illustrated in Figure 0-20a), we are able to make available a much richer set of interoperable functionality (Figure 0-20b). This low-level functionality can be readily recombined to form new higher-level *reusable* subsolutions at substantially reduced costs — i.e., both the cost of development *and* the cost of ownership. These small, fully factored subimplementations (see Volume II, section 6.4) also lead to improved quality by enabling thorough testing (see Volume III, section 7.3).

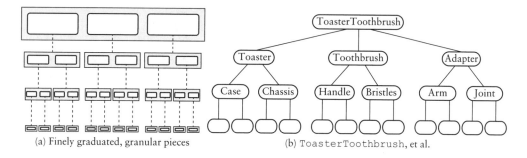

(a) Finely graduated, granular pieces   (b) `ToasterToothbrush`, et al.

Figure 0-20: Hierarchically reusable software

Consider the fully factored, fine-grained hierarchy of Figure 0-21, initially consisting of a `Toaster`, `Adapter`, and `Toothbrush`. Now suppose that we are asked to create a `ToasterFlashlight` and a `ToasterScrubbrush`. Given the classical reusable implementation of Figure 0-12b, we can easily construct a toaster flashlight by building a standard `Flashlight` type and then recombining the other two standard pieces — i.e., the toaster and the adapter — with the new flashlight to form a `ToasterFlashlight`. Proper factoring, however, will lead to additional components used to implement the flashlight — i.e., those defining `Lens` and `Stock` (Figure 0-21a).[20]

---

[20] A nice, real-world example, suggested by JC van Winkel, is that of *Phonebloks* in which a phone is built from bricks that are replaceable — e.g., don't need a camera, put in bigger battery. See www.phonebloks.com and www.youtube.com/watch?v=oDAw7vW7H0c.

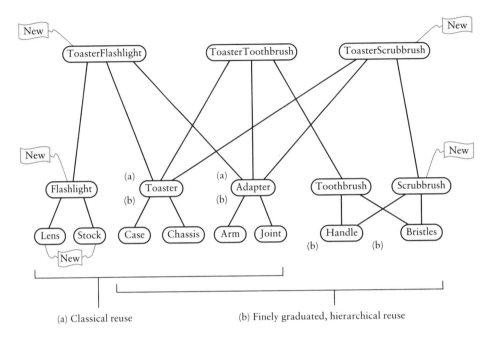

Figure 0-21: Exploiting finely factored library software

If, however, all that is needed is a toaster scrubbrush, we might be able to apply a bit more "glue" to create a new scrubbrush out of precisely the same primitive materials (i.e., `Handle` and `Bristles`) used to assemble the toothbrush! Leaving `Toothbrush` unaffected, we can then combine the new `Scrubbrush` type with the toaster via the adapter and *voilà* — a `ToasterScrubbrush` (Figure 0-21b).

Fine-grained physical modularity is essential to effective reuse. It is only by imposing fine graduations on granular solutions that we enable independent reuse at every level of abstraction as opposed to just data structures and subsystems. Moreover, it is this highly factored, hierarchically modular physical infrastructure that enables direct access (in place) to what would otherwise be inaccessible subsolutions and, therefore, have to be duplicated.

The property that distinguishes our hierarchically reusable software from conventional software is that we practically never need to *change* what we have in order to respond quickly to new situations. The more mature our repository of hierarchically reusable software solutions, the more quickly we can execute because more and more of the work has already been done for us (see section 0.9). In section 0.6, we will take a closer look at physical design aspects of our fine-grained software libraries, but first, in the next section, we explore the importance of stability to effective reuse.

0.5   Malleable vs. Stable Software

Good software generally falls into one of two broad categories: malleable or stable. *Malleable* software, by definition, is software whose behavior is easily and safely changed to reflect changing requirements. *Stable* software, on the other hand, has well-defined behavior that is deliberately *not* altered incompatibly in response to changing client needs.

The behavior of stable software can, by coincidence, also be easy to change; sound software engineering practices that facilitate malleability, such as well-documented symbolic constants (as opposed to magic numbers), of course apply to stable code as well. The important difference is that the behavior of malleable software is intended to change, whereas the behavior of stable software is not. Both kinds of software have their place, but software that is neither malleable nor stable is undesirable. Most of all, it is important never to confuse *malleable* with *reusable*. Only stable software can be reusable.

Unlike library software, the behavior of application code typically needs to be able to change quickly to respond to rapidly changing business needs. Hence, well-designed application code is malleable. Just because something is likely to change in the future does not mean that we should not expend significant up-front thought before we begin to code. Unfortunately, some well-intentioned people have treated the object-oriented paradigm as if it were a license to write code without thinking: "Let's implement some objects, and we can refine the details later." This approach might be a useful exercise in an introductory programming course, but it is far from anything we would call *engineering*.

At the far end of the "rapid" development spectrum is a general methodology known as *agile software development*[21] of which *extreme programming* (XP)[22] is an early special case. The original, stated goal of this approach[23] was to address each emerging need as quickly as possible and in whatever way maximizes current business objectives. All forms of bureaucracy are to be shunned. The extreme/agile programmer epitomizes the best of application programming by delivering the highest-quality product possible with the allotted resources on schedule. The concession is that the long term will have to be addressed later, and the software that agile programmers do write themselves will most likely soon have to change incompatibly as a result.

---

[21] **cockburn02**
[22] **beck00**
[23] **alliance01**

Most agile programmers will freely admit that they would be happy to use whatever software is available that allows them to meet their objectives. Given the opportunity to make use of a stable set of hierarchically reusable libraries, truly agile programmers most certainly would. Even the most agile of programmers cannot compete with other similarly agile programmers who, in addition to their agility, also have access to a mature library of relevant, prefabricated, stable solutions.

Without detracting from this widely practiced approach to software development, we do want to remind our readers that there is quite a bit more to this story.[24] Although agile techniques can be useful in developing modest-sized applications quickly in the short to medium term, they are generally not suitable for developing software on a large scale — especially (stable) reusable software.

Imagine, once again, that we find ourselves in need of a toaster, so we march down to our local hardware/home-improvement store and buy one. Now imagine to our surprise that one day while attempting to make toast we discover that our "dependable" toaster has morphed into, say, a toaster oven or, worse, a waffle iron. No matter how much better the mutated mechanism becomes, unless it continues to behave as originally advertised for all existing clients, whatever plans or assumptions we have made based on having a toaster are immediately called into question. It is hard to imagine this problem in real life, but sadly, this sort of thing can and often does occur in the realm of software.

Classical design techniques lead directly to software that must be modified to maintain it. By "maintain" here we sarcastically mean making a piece of code do what we want it to do *today* as opposed to what we wanted it to do *yesterday*. For example, consider the following function f designed to solve some common real-world problem:

```
f(a, b, c, x, y, z)
```

What led us to believe that six parameters were enough? What happens if, over time, we discover (or, more likely, are asked to consider) additional factors d and perhaps even e. Do we go back and change function f to require the additional arguments? Should they be optional?

In virtually all cases, the answer to these questions is no. If f is supposed to implement a documented behavior and is currently in use by several clients, we simply cannot go back and change f to do something substantially different from what it did before, or nothing that

---

[24] **boehm04**

depended on f would work anymore. By some metrics,[25] the very measure of *stability* for a given entity derives from the number of other entities that depend on it. Ideally, any change we consider would leave all of our clients' original assumptions intact (see Volume II, section 5.5).

The problem here results from a fundamentally over-optimistic approach to design: We allowed ourselves to think that there are ever enough parameters to solve any interesting real-world problem; there usually are not — not for long. The root cause of the instability can typically be traced to inadequate factoring. A more stable design would aggressively factor the implementation into a suite of simpler functions, each of which has a reasonable chance of being complete in and of themselves:

> `fa(a)    fb(b)    fc(c)    fx(x)    fy(y)    fz(z)`

As Figure 0-22 illustrates, given a more finely factored, granular design (Figure 0-22a), if we need to add new functions `fd(d)` and `fe(e)`, we might be able to leave the other functions currently in use untouched (Figure 0-22b).[26] This way, no pre-existing software applications are affected.

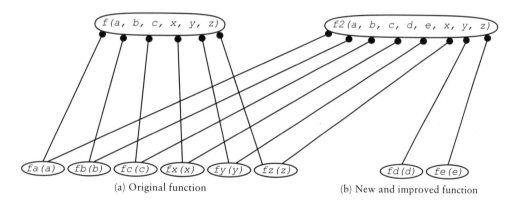

(a) Original function   (b) New and improved function

Figure 0-22: Fine-grained factoring improves stability

As a second example, suppose as part of an ultra-high-quality infrastructure we write a proprietary, high-speed parser for HTTP. Various applications begin to use this parser as part of their

---

[25] **martin95**, Chapter 3, "Metrics," pp. 246–258, specifically "(I) Instability," p. 246, and **martin03**, Chapter 20, "The Stable-Dependency Principle," pp. 261–264, specifically "(Instability I)," p. 262

[26] Throughout this book, we use the same notation (see sections 1.7.1–1.7.5) as we did in **lakos96** with a few extensions (see section 1.7.6) to support the in-structure-only nature of generic programming and concepts (which, as of C++20, are supported directly in the language).

Internet-based communication between client and server, as illustrated in Figure 0-23. The initial parser was written for HTTP version 1.0, which does not support the latest features. Over time, some clients inform us (complain) that they need the capabilities of the newer HTTP and politely request (demand) that we release a 1.1-compliant version of our HTTP parser as soon as possible (yesterday). The question now becomes, do we upgrade the original parser component (i.e., in place) or release an entirely new component that is 1.1-compliant and continue to support the original HTTP 1.0 parser component in parallel (i.e., potentially side by side in the same process)?

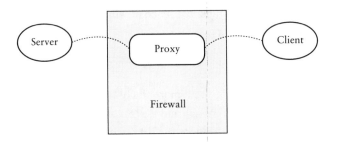

Figure 0-23: Client talking to server across firewall with proxies

The answer is that we *must* create a new component with a distinct identity and leave the original one alone! The parser is a mechanism that resides entirely within the implementation of these communication modules. For those applications that control both the client and server sides and that do not require the new features, there might never be a need to upgrade to a newer version of HTTP. Moreover, this "upgrade" is a change to existing functionality — not a bug fix and not a backward-compatible extension. As such, the decision to change properly rests entirely with each individual application owner, who cannot reasonably be required to partake in subsequent releases or otherwise be coerced according to any centralized timetable.[27]

If the proxies within the firewall require 1.1 compatibility, then exigent circumstances will oblige application developers to use the new component sooner rather than later. If, however, the proxies themselves are not yet 1.1 compatible, any such change forced upon an existing application would be catastrophic, as the newer format could not be propagated by the older

---

[27] There are times when library developers must coerce application developers to accept upgrades of libraries to a new release version to exploit new functionality. This coercion is especially necessary when continuous refactoring results in changes to types that are commonly used across interface boundaries (see Volume II, section 4.4). As long as the "upgrade" is substantially backward-compatible (Volume II, section 5.5), it is not unreasonable to expect that people will migrate in a "reasonable" timeframe (i.e., somewhat longer than the maximum length of a typical vacation). Even so, the precise timing of the upgrade *must* be orchestrated by the application developer. At least that way the application developer can avoid being in an incoherent state when the changeover occurs.

proxies across the current firewall. Among other things, this example should demonstrate the general need for occasionally supporting multiple versions of implementation-level functionality for simultaneous use even within a single program (see section 3.9).

Object-oriented or not, it is a cornerstone of our engineering philosophy that to test anything nontrivial *thoroughly*, we must be able to test it *hierarchically*. That is, at each level of physical hierarchy, we should be able to test each component in terms of only lower-level components, each of which has already been tested thoroughly (see section 2.14). Given that thorough testing (let alone correct implementation) of a component implies complete knowledge of the functionality upon which that component is built, any change — no matter how small — to the behavior of lower-level components potentially invalidates assumptions made by implementers at higher levels, leading to subtle defects and instability.

The concept of writing code whose behavior does not change is not new. Bertrand Meyer, author of the Eiffel programming language, describes this important aspect of a sound design as the *open-closed* principle[28],[29]:

> Software should be simultaneously *open* to extension yet *closed* to modification.
> That is, instead of trying to capture all potential behavior within a single
> component, we provide the hooks necessary to extend that behavior without
> necessarily having to change that component's source code.

As a concrete example, let us consider the design of a **list** component implementing std::list in the C++ Standard Template Library (STL). Being that std::list when instantiated with a value-semantic type is itself value-semantic (see Volume II, section 4.3), the component that defines std::list should (ideally) also provide a free operator that implements the standard meaning of equality comparison:

```
template <class TYPE>
bool operator==(const list<TYPE>& lhs, const list<TYPE>& rhs);
    // Return 'true' if the specified 'lhs' and 'rhs' objects have
    // the same value, and 'false' otherwise.  Two 'std::list<TYPE>'
    // objects have the same value if they have the same number of
    // elements, and elements at corresponding positions have the
    // same value.
```

---

[28] **meyer95**, section 2.3, pp. 23–25

[29] See also **meyer97**, section 3.3, pp. 57–61.

Now, suppose we find that we need to compare two lists for equality in a way other than the one provided. Perhaps all that we are interested in is, say, whether the absolute values of corresponding elements are the same. What should we do?

If it were our own class and we could modify it, we might consider adding a method `absEqual` to the class, but that "solution" is entirely inappropriate because it violates the open-closed principle. We might briefly entertain providing some sort of callback or template parameter to allow us to customize the equality operation; both are ugly, however, and none of these proposed remedies guarantees a solution to other similar problems we might face. For example, suppose we also want to print the contents of the list in some specific format. Our specialized `absEqual` method will not help us.

Changing the behavior of existing reusable functionally is wrong, and even adding new behaviors to what was previously considered a complete component is usually suboptimal. In fact, any invasive remedy addressing the needs of individual clients is highly collaborative and almost always misguided. The general solution to the stability problem is to design components in such a way that they are open to efficient, noninvasive, unilateral extension by clients; in the case of the **list** component specifically, and containers in general, that way is to provide an iterator.[30]

---

[30] Even a `Stack` type, which traditionally provides access to only its top element, would properly have an associated iterator to support similar unilateral extensions by clients. Note that there is absolutely no issue regarding encapsulation — even with a restricted interface, clients of a `Stack` class would still be able to compare two `Stack` objects for "absolute equality" (just not efficiently).

```
bool myAreAbsEqual(const Stack& lhs, const Stack& rhs)
{
    Stack u(lhs), v(rhs);  // expensive!                              (BAD IDEA)
    while (!(u.isEmpty() || v.isEmpty())) {
        if (std::abs(u.top()) != std::abs(v.top())) {
            return false;                                        // RETURN
        }
        u.pop();
        v.pop();
    }
    return u.isEmpty() && v.isEmpty();
}
```

The iterator restores that efficiency without imposing any restriction on implementation choice or additional runtime overhead.

Providing an iterator enables each client of a container to implement virtually any appropriate extension immediately. For example, both of the functions in Figure 0-24 are independent, client-side extensions of the **list** component. By designing in extensibility via iterators, we can reasonably ensure that no source-code modification of the reusable container will ever be needed for that purpose. This principle of unilateral extensibility also helps to ensure that application developers will not be held hostage waiting for enhancements that can be provided only by library developers. Note that all of the container types in the C++ Standard Library come equipped with iterators that provide efficient access to every contained element.[31]

```
bool myAreAbsEqual(const List& lhs, const List& rhs)
{
    List::const_iterator lit = lhs.begin();
    List::const_iterator rit = rhs.begin();
    const List::const_iterator lend = lhs.end();
    const List::const_iterator rend = rhs.end();

    while (lit != lend && rit != rend) {
        if (std::abs(*lit) != std::abs(*rit)) {
            return false;                                    // RETURN
        }
        ++lit, ++rit;
    }
    return lend == lit && rend == rit;
}32
```

(a) Determining whether two lists are equivalent in a particular way

---

[31] As another less general, but much more detailed, illustration of enabling the open-closed principle, see section 3.2.8.

[32] As discussed in the preface, we will sometimes note places where a more modern dialect of C++ provides features that might better express an idea. For example, given that an iterator is a well-known *concept* having well defined syntactic and semantic properties, the specific C++ type of the iterator becomes unimportant. In such cases we might prefer to use the keyword auto to let the compiler figure out that type, rather than force us to type it, or even an alias for it, each time we need it, as the code itself — e.g., lhs.begin() — makes the *concept* clear:

```
bool myAreAbsEqual(const List& lhs, const List& rhs)
{
    auto       lit  = lhs.cbegin();
    auto       rit  = rhs.cbegin();
    auto const lend = lhs.cend();
    auto const rend = rhs.cend();

    while (lit != lend && rit != rend) {
        if (abs(*lit) != abs(*rit)) {
            return false;                             // RETURN
        }
        ++lit, ++rit;
    }
    return lend == lit && rend == rit;   // We generally try to avoid placing modifiable operands
}                                        // on the left-hand side of an operator==.
```

```
std::ostream& myFancyPrint(std::ostream& stream, const List& object)
{
    stream << "TOP [";
    for (List::const_iterator it  = object.begin();
                              it != object.end();
                            ++it) {
        stream << ' ' << *it;
    }
    return stream << " ] BOTTOM" << std::flush;  //  useful for debugging
}33
```

(b) Printing the value of a list in a particular way

Figure 0-24: Unilateral client extension of operations on a `list`

Interestingly, the C++ language was originally created with a similar design goal for itself. No attempt was made to build in a complete set of useful types or mechanisms. Choosing one type or mechanism from among many competing candidates for C++ would serve to *limit* rather than *extend* its scope.

> Thus, C++ does not have built-in complex number, string, or matrix types,
> or direct support for concurrency, persistence, distributed computing, pattern
> matching, or file systems manipulation, to mention a few of the most frequently
> suggested extensions.[34]

Instead, the focus of the design (and evolution) of C++ was always to improve abstraction mechanisms (initially with inheritance and later with templates) to facilitate the efficient incorporation of arbitrary (user-defined) types and mechanisms supplied later in the form of well-organized, stable libraries. Such libraries can provide several concrete variants of any abstract type or mechanism, which could exist concurrently, even within a single program. Much of this book addresses extending this noble architectural philosophy — rooted in the language itself — toward its natural conclusion in the form of well-factored, enterprise-wide

---

[33] In this case, we might prefer a range-based `for` loop along with `auto` (introduced as part of C++11):

```
std::ostream& myFancyPrint(std::ostream& stream, const List& object)
{
    stream << "TOP [";
    for (const auto &v : object) {
        stream << ' ' << v;
    }
    return stream << " ] BOTTOM";  // '<< std::flush' is optional.
}
```

[34] **stroustrup94**, section 2.1, pp. 27–29, specifically the middle of p. 28

library-based solutions (see section 0.9). Moreover, C++ allows you to create these libraries and new types in such a way that their interfaces are the same as, and behave as if they were, first-class citizens like `int`.

Inheritance, used properly (Volume II, section 4.6), is arguably the most powerful mechanism for enabling, on a large scale, extension without modification. Consider the simple report-generator architecture of Figure 0-25. In this classical *layered* design (see section 3.7.2), the `PostscriptOutputDevice` module takes output requests and translates them into a form suitable for driving a PostScript printer. All of the detailed knowledge regarding writing accounts properly resides in the `AccountReportWriter` module (and not the `PostscriptOutputDevice` module). So far so good.

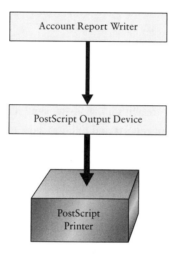

Figure 0-25: A simple `Account` report generator

We can extend the kinds of reports we can produce simply by adding new report modules, as shown in Figure 0-26. And, assuming careful fine-grained factoring, much of the code used to implement the original `AccountReportWriter` module will be common to these new report writers.

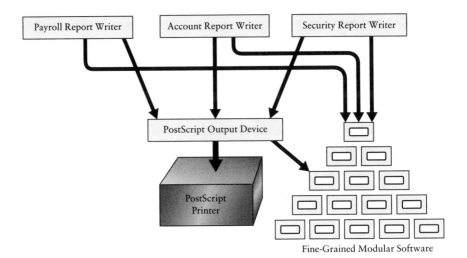

Figure 0-26: Adding new kinds of reports

But what happens when we want to add new kinds of output devices? How are we supposed to extend that architecture without modifying it? The expedient solution is to duplicate and rename the entire suite of reports and retarget them to the new output device as in Figure 0-27. Needless to say, from a maintenance perspective, this is not a good, long-term solution.

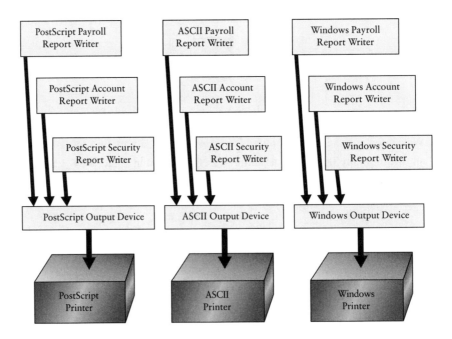

Figure 0-27: Copying code to add new kinds of output devices (BAD IDEA)

Suppose instead we decide to consolidate all of the device interfaces into one interface that can then be used to drive all appropriate devices. Given a collection of existing interfaces, we might consider making this component a wrapper that logically encapsulates the specific devices, as shown in Figure 0-28. This solution, although often employed in practice, also fails on multiple counts. Apart from having to modify the source of the output manager every time a new device comes online, we impose an outrageous physical dependency: *Every* report writer, to be used (or even tested), must link with *every* known output device. As if that were not bad enough, some devices (e.g., the Windows output device) might not exist on every supported platform! Enough said.

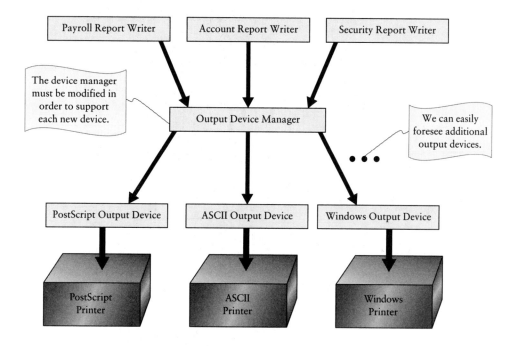

Figure 0-28: Encapsulating a readily extensible collection (BAD IDEA)

As will be a recurring theme throughout this book, we will choose to avoid encapsulating inherently extensible, nonportable, third-party, or otherwise uncontrollable or risky software that could potentially produce a destabilizing effect on our core libraries. Instead, we will capture the definition of such behavior — typically[35] as a *protocol* (pure abstract interface) class (see section 1.7.5) — along with detailed comments delineating precisely what behavior is expected. In this way, new output devices may be introduced by applications at will; the only caveat is that these new concrete implementations satisfy the *contract* (see Volume II,

---

[35] Section 3.5.7 explores protocols (see section 3.5.7.4) along with several other alternatives including concepts (see section 3.5.7.5).

section 5.2) imposed by the abstract interface. In this design, both clients and implementations co-exist as peers, each depending on only the lower-level component containing the interface. This abstract-interface approach has the further benefit of facilitating client testing through the idiomatic reuse of a ("mock") `TestOutputDevice` (see Volume II, Chapter 4, and Volume III, Chapter 9). A fully factored, bilaterally extensible, yet absolutely stable solution to our report-writing problem is provided in Figure 0-29.

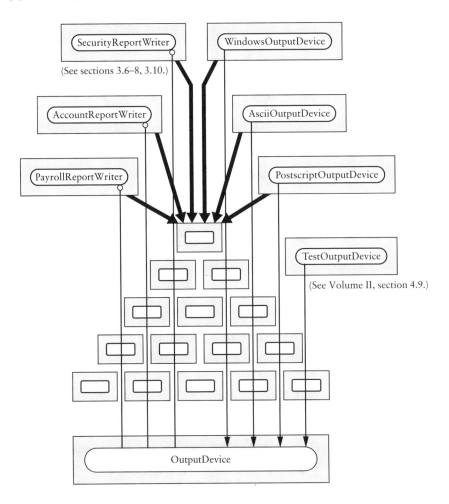

Figure 0-29: A fully factored solution

Not all software — particularly at the application level — can be stable. The behavior of each version of an application must in some way be different from the last or (apart from pure performance tuning) what would be the point? When developing high-level application code, it might be more effective to drop stability and concentrate on malleability. That is, instead of attempting to apply the open-closed principle, we accept that the code will change and focus on making such changes safe and easy. For example, it is a common practice to group code that is likely to change together in close proximity (see section 3.3.6); ideally, the amount of co-dependent code would be small enough to fit within a single component. However, when incompatible changes to existing behavior are permitted to be exposed through public interfaces, that body of software is *not* stable. Whether or not such code is considered malleable, it is definitely not reusable.

As Figure 0-30 suggests, how malleable versus stable software is used is quite different. Perhaps the most salient characteristic distinguishing malleable software from stable software is that malleable software must have exactly one master that dictates changes in its behavior (Figure 0-30a), whereas reusable software — once created — has none (Figure 0-30b). Since the number of clients that may depend on a reusable component to do what it does now is unbounded, none (i.e., no proper subset) of them may reasonably require an incompatible change.

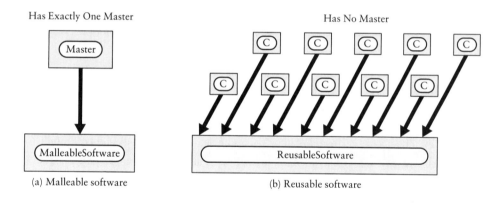

(a) Malleable software (b) Reusable software

Figure 0-30: Malleable versus reusable software

If the established behavior of software must change, then it should do so at the behest of (and affect only) a single master — i.e., a single application. The corollary is that malleable software belonging to one application must not be shared with another (see section 2.13). As Figure 0-31 illustrates, allowing more than one master the authority to unilaterally require changes to shared software leads to an over-constrained problem (Figure 0-31a), often with suboptimal results (Figure 0-31b). Even when existing logical behavior is preserved, modifications that adversely affect runtime performance or other physical properties, such as link-time dependencies, portability, and so on, can critically impact stability. To achieve effective hierarchical reuse, it is imperative that, with only rare exceptions, all aspects of a component's contract — expressed or implied — continue to be honored for the life of the component (see Volume II, section 5.5).

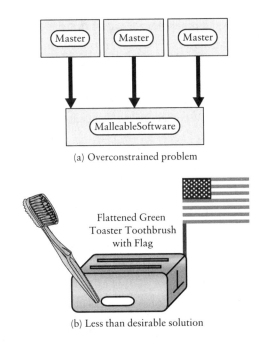

(a) Overconstrained problem

(b) Less than desirable solution

Figure 0-31: Software having multiple masters (BAD IDEA)

Infrastructure, once in use, must be maintained and enhanced. With conventional, coarse-grained factoring, the more this infrastructure software is used, the more expensive it becomes to maintain as eager users clamor for more and more enhancements. Failure to provide the enhancements leaves users feeling unsupported and unhappy, especially since there is typically no way for them to unilaterally extend that functionality themselves — a violation of the open-closed principle.

In some organizations, this increasing cost will not be sustainable, and the infrastructure group, which might not be perceived as contributing directly to the bottom line, would be the first to be sacrificed. By ensuring a fine-grained rendering of reusable infrastructure, many of the costs associated with supporting reuse are eliminated. Individual components remain stable, and any enhancements become additive instead of iterative.

To summarize, the way we achieve effective reuse is through *hierarchical* reuse. The frequency with which combinations of low, intermediate, and high-level reuse *can* occur is staggering, which we will illustrate by analogy in section 0.8. Examples of commonly reusable yet very low-level pieces include memory pools and allocators, managed/shared pointers, functors, scoped guards, and, of course, synchronization and communication primitives, just to name a few. Throughout this book, we will demonstrate the process of discovering, designing, implementing, and testing these low-level, yet highly leverageable components. Such meticulous factoring is not easy; yet, it is precisely this careful attention to fine-grained factoring that helps achieve unparalleled reuse and stability by allowing us to compose, and thereby extend, the functionality provided by our software infrastructure without always having to change it.

So far, we have characterized the software we advocate as *finely graduated* and *granular*, of having a clean decomposition, and of generally allowing only common, simple (e.g., *scalar*) types to pass through (well-documented) functional interfaces. These simple types form the basic vocabulary (see Volume II, section 4.4) by which information is transmitted across function boundaries. We have argued that interfaces having a relatively small *surface area* that are easy to describe are fundamentally more able and likely to be reused in new contexts than more complicated or *collaborative* ones.

In this section, we introduced a new dimension by which we characterize software: stability. To the extent possible, we prefer our software — particularly our library software — to be stable, and therefore potentially reusable. Designing for stability (see Volume II, section 5.6) is a staple of our daily development work. In fact, our general approach to large-scale software development fundamentally requires the construction of new software by recursively building on what we have rather than iteratively changing it.

The architectural analogy to pure functional languages (e.g., lambda calculus or pure Lisp) rather than imperative languages (such as C or Java) is also strikingly similar to the fascinating compile-time style employed by templates and metafunctions in modern generic programming using C++[36] (see Volume II, section 4.4). That is, once we "instantiate" a reusable component (i.e., write and release it), we can refer to (i.e., depend on) it, but we cannot subsequently change its "value" (i.e., change its defined or implied logical contract or substantially degrade any aspect of its essential physical characteristics). Such is how a firm-wide repository of hierarchically reusable software that is not only ultra-high quality but also ultra-stable accumulates (see section 0.9). In the next section, we will begin to take a closer look at the *physical* aspects of finely graduated, granular software.

---

[36] **alexandrescu01**, section 3.5, p. 55

0.6   The Key Role of Physical Design

Developing successful software on a large scale demands a thorough understanding of two distinct but highly interrelated aspects of design: *logical* design and *physical* design. Logical design, as we will use the term, addresses all *functional* aspects of the software we develop. A functional specification, for example, governs the overall logical design of an application, subsystem, or individual component. The decision to make a particular class concrete or instead provide an abstract interface for the needed functionality is a fairly high-level logical design choice. Whether to use blocking or nonblocking transport (i.e., interprocess communication) with or without threads would also fall under the umbrella of logical design.

Historically, most books on C++ addressed *only* logical design and often at a very low level. For example, whether a particular class should or should not have a copy constructor is a low-level yet very important logical design issue. Deliberately making a particular operator (e.g., `operator==`) a *free* (i.e., nonmember) function is also a low-level logical design choice. Even selecting the specific private data members of a class would be considered part of low-level logical design. However, logical design alone on any level fails to consider many important practical aspects of software development. As development organizations get larger, forces of a different nature come into play.

Physical design, as defined in Figure 0-32, addresses issues surrounding the placement of logical entities, such as classes and functions, into physical ones, such as files and libraries. All design has a physical aspect. That is because all of the source code that makes up a typical C++ program resides in files, which are physical. When we talk about reuse, for example, we might be thinking about a subroutine or class, but such things cannot be reused directly. What can potentially be reused is the set of files that define and implement that logical content. Hence, the way in which we aggregate our logical constructs into discrete physical modules is an essential aspect of design for reuse, in particular, and sound design, in general.

Physical Design

1. *n.* The arrangement of source code within files and
   files within libraries
2. *v.tr.* To partition source code among files and files
   among libraries

Figure 0-32: Definition of physical design

Physical design dictates *where* (physically) — e.g., in what library — codified functionality belongs relative to other functionality throughout our enterprise. Recognizing compile-time and link-time dependencies across physical boundaries will help shape both logical and physical design aspects of our software. For example, common functionality intended for firm-wide reuse belongs (physically) at a *low level* in our software repository, where application software developers working at *higher levels* can find and use it (e.g., see Figure 0-7b, section 0.2), independently of other applications.

It has become well-recognized[37,38,39] that *cyclic* dependencies among (physical) modules are to be avoided (see sections 2.2–2.4, 2.6, 2.8–2.9, 2.14, and 3.4). By employing established physical design techniques (see section 3.5), we ensure that we pay (in terms of link time and executable size) only for what we need (see section 3.6). Moreover, we want to develop reusable solutions that are *independent* of peer solutions (see section 3.7) and can co-exist with them in the same process (see section 3.9). Detailed physical design will require us to answer correctly many important questions that are simply not addressed by logical design. For example,

- Should two given classes be defined in the same header file or in two separate ones? (See section 3.3.)
- Should a given translation unit depend on some other translation unit at all? (See section 3.8.)
- Should we #include the header file containing the declaration of a given logical entity or instead simply *forward declare* it? (See Volume II, section 6.6.)
- Should a given function be declared inline? (See Volume II, section 6.7.)

These kinds of physical design questions, while closely tied to the technical aspects of development, bring with them a dimension of design with which even "expert" software developers might have little or no experience. *Physical design*, though less widely understood than *logical design*, nonetheless plays an increasingly crucial role as the number and size of the applications and libraries developed within a group, department, or company grow.

Combining thoughtful logical design with careful physical packaging will enable software developers to "mix and match" existing solutions, subsolutions, and so on, at finely graduated levels of integration (section 0.3). This combinatorial flexibility along with logical and physical

---

[37] **lakos96**, section 4.11, pp. 184–187, and section 7.3, pp. 493–503

[38] **sutter05**, item 22, pp. 40–41

[39] With respect to compile-time dependency (only), see also **meyers05**, item 31, pp. 140–148.

interoperability goes a long way toward maximizing the economies of scale made possible through *hierarchical reuse* (section 0.4).

We will return to the topic of large-scale physical design in Chapter 3, after we have presented motivation (this chapter), discussed some basic ideas involving compilers and linkers (Chapter 1), and learned how logical content can be colocated, packaged, and aggregated effectively (Chapter 2).

0.7   Physically Uniform Software: The Component

The physical form in which our software is cast plays a vital role in our ability to manage it. Apart from having a sound physical structure, requiring a *physically uniform* organization for our proprietary software greatly enhances the ability of ourselves and others to understand, use, and maintain it. Moreover, physical uniformity encourages the creation of effective development tools (e.g., rule checkers, dependency analyzers, documentation extractors) that operate on the software directly (as data). "Foolish consistency [might well be] the hobgoblin of little minds," but we're quite sure Emerson[40] was not referring to the physical form of software when he wrote that.

To motivate the importance of *physical uniformity* in software, let us take a moment to consider other forms of physical media such as video cassette tapes, compact discs, DVDs, etc. The logical content of these entities, apart from quantity, is not inherently restricted. The same physical cartridge you might rent from your local video store could contain Spielberg's last hit, a travel documentary, or even a workout video. The logical content could be anything, but the physical form is the same.

Some of us might recall that in the early days of video cassettes there were two incompatible formats, VHS and Beta. *Which was better* was not nearly as important as that *there were two*! Soon there was one! The problem resurfaced when movies became available on DVDs. Having both tapes and DVDs for video was also redundant. Renting a video requires not only finding the desired movie but also ensuring compatible equipment. The more physical forms, the more onerous the problem with interoperability.

Adopting a standard physical cartridge to represent logical content greatly simplifies the integration of supporting tools. A DVD burner, for example, enjoys economies of scale because it

---

[40] In his essay "Self-Reliance," R. W. Emerson "does not explain the difference between foolish and wise consistency" (**hirsch02**, "Proverbs," pp. 47–58, specifically p. 51).

will work on all DVDs from all manufacturers (independent of content). In contrast, imagine if each movie title came on its own physically unique medium — every title would require its own set of equipment to view and maintain it!

The same arguments for interoperability across physical devices apply to software modules. Requiring one standard physical format to hold all atomic units of software similarly facilitates the creation of a more supportive development environment. Simply knowing that tools enlisted to support one project will also be viable on the next makes their development (or procurement) more cost effective and therefore more likely. Time and time again, uniformity of this kind has invariably shown to lead to a more repeatable, predictable development process.

Consistency of physical form also brings a welcome degree of familiarity to human beings. Many people know how to view a DVD. When applied in new contexts, say, when enrolled in a video course, students would not have to learn new organizational skills to view their lectures. Analogously, a high degree of physical uniformity in software allows engineers to circulate more readily among different projects. In software, the term of art is *developer mobility*. Be it video courses or software, physical uniformity makes it easier for people to focus more of their energy on the logical content, which, after all, is the goal.

For our proprietary software to be fully interoperable across all applications, its physical form and organization must be entirely independent of the functionality that it embodies. We cannot know precisely what applications we are going to develop now — let alone in the future. However, the physical organization we are about to describe has demonstrated over time that it serves well in industries as diverse as computer-aided design and financial services. Moreover, this hierarchical *physical* structure is inherently scalable, having successfully addressed systems embodying source code with line counts ranging from less than 10,000 to more than 100,000,000. The most fundamental organizational unit in our component-based methodology is, not surprisingly, called a *component*, which we will introduce here momentarily and, in Chapter 1, explore thoroughly. Later, in Chapter 2, we will describe a global *meta*framework[41] that makes all these components play together.

The term *component* has come to mean different things in different contexts. Many system architects consider a component to be a *unit of deployment*, such as a COM component or Active X control (*plug-in*). In this sense, a `main` program (e.g., a server) could be a "component" in a distributed network of separately running executables (processes). Even an entire library could be

---

[41] A framework (a.k.a. an application framework) is typically subject (domain) specific; a *meta*framework — i.e., a framework to build frameworks — is not.

considered just a single "component" of a large development environment. Others, focusing more on individual programs, might view a component as any significant subsystem, such as an order book, a router, or a logger. Still others view a component as any discrete piece of logical content such as a class or suite of `static` methods nested within a (*utility*) `struct` (or, equivalently, free functions nested within a local namespace). Although each of these interpretations is acceptable in some appropriate context, none of them reflects what *we* mean by the term *component*.

By our definition, a *component* is the *atomic unit* of physical design. In C++, it takes the form of a `.h`/`.cpp` pair (see section 1.6).[42] Associated with each component should be a standalone test driver (see Volume III, section 7.5) capable of exercising all functionality implemented within that component. This ubiquitous physical organizational pattern, illustrated schematically in Figure 0-33, is the basic unit of packaging for *all* of our application and library software.

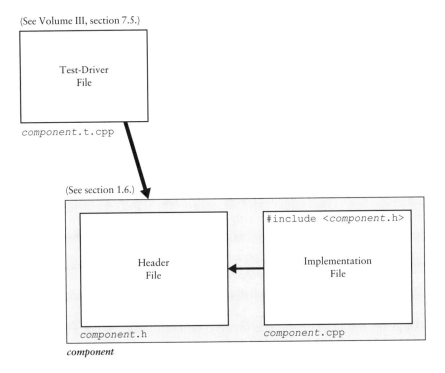

Figure 0-33: Schematic view of a component and its test driver

---

[42] We use the suffix `.cpp` to distinguish C++ source files from C source files. We will use `.h` and `.cpp` consistently throughout this book.

A component embodies a relatively *small* amount of *logical design*; its contents are cohesive in that the functionality provided naturally belongs together. We say that a component is *atomic* because (1) use of any part potentially implies use of the whole and (2) any explicit desire to use only part of a component is a strong indication that the functionality supplied by the component is insufficiently factored. Lastly, a component has a *well-defined* (and, ideally, *well-designed*) interface (e.g., it should be designed to be testable).

As a concrete example, consider the header file shown in Figure 0-34 for a "toy" stack component, **my_stack**, implementing a basic integer stack abstraction. A Stack is a kind of container. Recall from section 0.5 (and our discussion of the open-closed principle) that containers should have iterators, so it follows that our Stack class should have an iterator as well. Although access to other than the top element of a stack is not normally thought of as part of a stack abstraction, providing an iterator makes the component more generally extensible by clients and therefore more stable.

From this header file, we can see that the component contains two distinct classes, Stack and StackConstIterator. We can also see that there are two free (i.e., nonmember) operator functions implementing == and != between two objects of type StackConstIterator, as well as between two Stack objects. Finally, because a Stack represents a *value* that is meaningful outside of the current process (see Volume II, section 4.1), we have included an output operator << to render this *value* in some human-readable form.[43] Note that, for the purposes of exposition, we will defer any discussion of packaging (e.g., file prefixes and namespaces) until Chapter 2.

---

[43] In practice, we might also want to supply methods, such as streamIn and streamOut, to serialize this value to an abstract byte stream (see Volume II, section 4.1). Note that we have also provided for an optional memory allocator, supplied at construction, to be used to manage dynamically allocated memory throughout the lifetime of a stack object (see Volume II, section 4.10).

```
// my_stack.h                                      (ignoring packages for now)
#ifndef INCLUDED_MY_STACK   // internal include guard
#define INCLUDED_MY_STACK                                  (See section 1.5.)

#include <iosfwd>

// ...

namespace bslma { class Allocator; }⁴⁴          (See Volume II, section 4.10.)

// ...                    (ignoring other namespaces for now)

class StackConstIterator {   // const forward iterator
    // ...
    friend class Stack;   // single unit of encapsulation
  public:
    // ...
};

// FREE OPERATORS
bool operator==(const StackConstIterator& lhs, const StackConstIterator& rhs);
    // Return 'true' if the specified 'lhs' and 'rhs' iterators refer to the
    // same element of the same stack, and 'false' otherwise.

bool operator!=(const StackConstIterator& lhs, const StackConstIterator& rhs);
    // Return 'true' if the specified 'lhs' and 'rhs' iterators do not refer
    // to the same element of the same stack, and 'false' otherwise.

// ...

class Stack {
    // This class implements a "toy" value-semantic integer stack class...

    // DATA
    int             *d_stack_p;      // dynamically allocated array
    std::size_t      d_capacity;     // capacity of dynamic array
    vsize_t          d_length;       // length of stack (and stack pointer)
    bslma::Allocator *d_allocator_p;⁴⁵ // memory allocator; held, but not owned
                                              (See Volume II, section 4.10.)
  public:
    // TYPES
    typedef StackConstIterator const_iterator;   // typical STL-style iterator
        // Alias for a standard forward iterator.

    // CREATORS
    Stack(bslma::Allocator *basicAllocator = 0);
        // Create an empty 'Stack' object.  Optionally specify a
        // 'basicAllocator' used to supply memory.  If 'basicAlloctor' is 0,
        // the currently installed default allocator is used.
```

(continues)

---

⁴⁴ **bde14,** subdirectory `/groups/bsl/bslma/`
⁴⁵ **bde14,** subdirectory `/groups/bsl/bslma/`

(continued)

```
    Stack(const Stack& original, bslma::Allocator *basicAllocator = 0);
        // Create a 'Stack' object having the value of the specified 'original'
        // object.  Optionally specify a 'basicAllocator used to supply memory.
        // If 'basicAllocator' is 0, the currently installed default allocator
        // is used.

    ~Stack();
        // Destroy this object.

    // MANIPULATORS
    Stack& operator=(const Stack& rhs);
        // Assign to this object the value of the specified 'rhs' object, and
        // return a reference providing modifiable access to this object.

    void push(int value);
        // Append the specified 'value' to the top of this stack.

    void pop();
        // Remove the value at the top of this stack.  The behavior is
        // undefined unless 'isEmpty()' returns 'false'.

    // ...                    (ignoring "aspects" for now)

    // ACCESSORS
    const_iterator begin() const;
        // Return a standard forward iterator referring to the top element
        // of this stack, or 'end()' if this stack is empty.

    const_iterator end() const;
        // Return an iterator indicating the "one-past-the-end" position in
        // this stack.

    bool isEmpty() const;
        // Return 'true' if the number of elements in this stack is 0, and
        // 'false' otherwise.

    const int& top() const;
        // Return a 'const' reference to the top element of this stack.
        // The behavior is undefined unless 'isEmpty()' returns 'false'.

    // ...                    (ignoring "aspects" for now)
};

// FREE OPERATORS
bool operator==(const Stack& lhs, const Stack& rhs);
    // Return 'true' if the specified 'lhs' and 'rhs' objects have the same
    // value, and 'false' otherwise.  Two 'Stack' objects have the same value
    // if they have the same number of elements, and corresponding elements
    // have the same value.

bool operator!=(const Stack& lhs, const Stack& rhs);
    // Return 'true' if the specified 'lhs' and 'rhs' objects do not have the
    // same value, and 'false' otherwise.  Two 'Stack' objects do not have the
```

(continues)

(continued)

```
    // same value if they do not have the same number of elements, or any
    // corresponding elements do not have the same value.

std::ostream operator<<(std::ostream& stream, Stack& stack);
    // Write the value of the specified 'stack' to the specified output
    // 'stream' in some single-line, human-readable format...

// ...
// ... (ignoring inline [member/free-operator] function definitions for now)
// ...

#endif
```

Figure 0-34: Header file `my_stack.h` for a toy (integer) stack component

Peeking at the implementation, we would discover that both `operator==` and `operator<<` for `Stack` use class `StackConstIterator` and that `operator!=` for both classes is implemented in terms of the corresponding `operator==`. The complete set of logical entities at file scope in component **my_stack** is pictured in Figure 0-35a using the notation of section 1.7. The physical entities (`my_stack.h` and `my_stack.cpp`) along with their canonical physical relationship (see section 1.6.1) are depicted in Figure 0-35b.

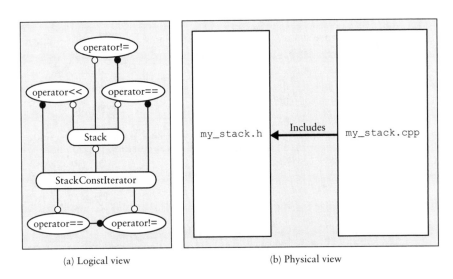

(a) Logical view   (b) Physical view

Figure 0-35: Two views of our my_stack component

More generally, a component will typically define one or more closely related classes and any free operators deemed appropriate for the abstraction it supports. As Figure 0-36 demonstrates, the component name will be reflected in every top-level logical entity it contains (see section 2.4.9). Basic types (e.g., `Point`, `Datetime`, `BigInt`, `ScopedGuard`) will each be implemented in a component containing a single class (Figure 0-36a). Generic container classes (e.g., `Set`, `Stack`, `List`) will typically be implemented in a component containing the principle class and its iterator(s) (Figure 0-36b). More complex abstractions involving multiple types (e.g., `Graph`, `Schema`, `ConcreteWidgetFactory`) can embody several classes in a single component (Figure 0-36c). Finally, classes that provide a wrapper (a.k.a. a *facade*) for an entire subsystem (e.g., `Simulator`, `XmlParser`, `MatchingEngine`) may form a thin encapsulating layer consisting of multiple principle classes and many iterators (Figure 0-36d). As a rule, however, we place each class in a separate component to avoid gratuitous physical coupling — that is, unless there is a compelling engineering reason to do otherwise. We address specific design criteria justifying colocation in section 3.3 (see Figure 3-20, section 3.3.1).[46,47]

---

[46] Note that, along these lines, if an underscore is used — e.g., `Graph_Node`, `Graph_NodeIterator` — one could keep an unambiguous correspondence between the class name and the component name. We almost fully achieve this goal (see section 2.4.6) but not quite as we have chosen to utilize the precious "underscore" identifier character (_) for something even more pressing, component-private classes (see section 2.7.3).

[47] Note that this figure differs from a similar one (**lakos96**, section 3.1, Figure 3-1, p. 102) for three reasons: (1) we now use logical package namespaces (represented here as `my::`) as opposed to prefixes such as `my_` (see section 2.4.6); (2) naming requirements are now such that the lower-cased name of every logical entity, apart from operator and aspect functions (see Volume II, section 6.14), must have the base name (see section 2.4.7) of the component as a prefix (see section 2.4.8); and (3) the iterator model (STL-style) now has the iterator used in the interface of the container (see Figure 2-54, section 2.7.4) instead of vice versa (lakos96-style), along with a renewed passion to avoid cyclic logical relationships — even within a single component!

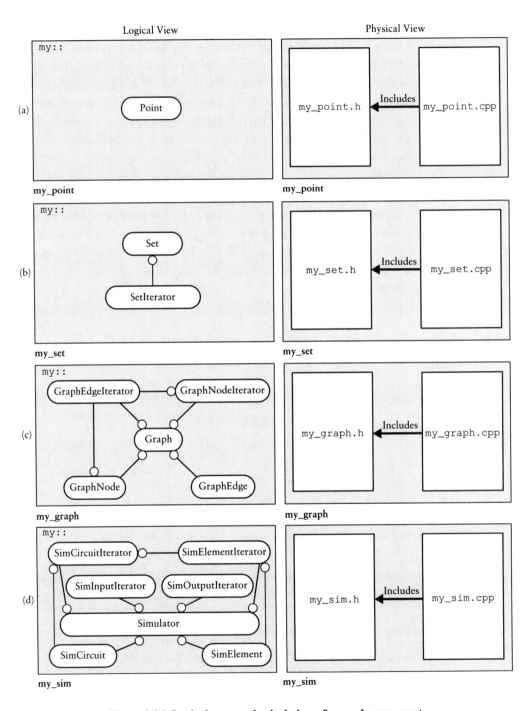

Figure 0-36: Logical versus physical view of several components

Each of the components illustrated in Figure 0-36 (like every other component) has a physical as well as a logical view. The physical view consists of the `.h` file and the `.cpp` file, with the `.h` file included (as the first substantive line) in the `.cpp` file (see section 1.6.1). Moreover, the *size* of a component, as measured by both implementation complexity and lines of source, will turn out to be relatively constant (see section 2.2.2). From a physical perspective, these components are more similar than different.

From a logical perspective, however, components such as the one shown in Figure 0-36d clearly *do* a lot more than those like the one in Figure 0-36a. Although it is plausible that much if not most[48] of the implementation of a **point** component would be embodied directly in that component's source, such is generally not the case. The implementation of a map, for example, will likely delegate part of its functionality to a few lower-level components, such as a (default) memory allocator (see Volume II, section 4.10), along with various traits and metafunctions. And, as Figure 0-37 illustrates, a more substantial piece of machinery, such as the matching engine for a trading system, will delegate to layers upon layers of subfunctionality, all of which would ideally be thoughtfully factored and placed in components of comparable size, distributed appropriately throughout our firm's repository of hierarchically reusable software (see section 0.9).

---

[48] But probably not all. Consider that a point may have associated traits such as "bitwise copyable" that it would want to include from another component. Output and serialization are two other operations that would likely depend on other components. Finally, *defensive* checks (see Volume II, section 6.8) for *narrow* contracts (see Volume II, section 5.3) would also best be imported from a separate low-level component.

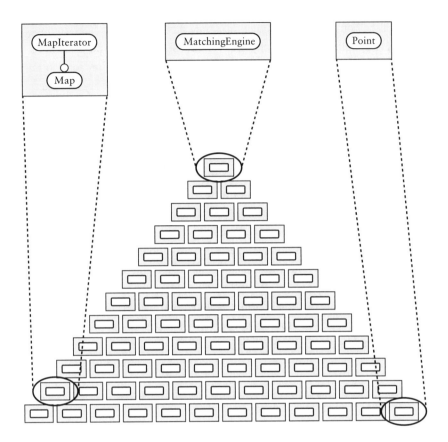

Figure 0-37: Physical location — *not* size — governs a component's scope.

It is worth noting that this view of composition — i.e., via recursive delegation to stable, reusable components — is fundamentally different from the classical nested, collaborative, and therefore private subarchitectures typical in traditional application development. In that design paradigm, systems own and isolate their subsystems, which in turn own and isolate theirs — the advantage being that the subsystems are not otherwise accessible and therefore need not be stable. The disadvantage is that there is no sharing of common subsolutions across subsystems — in other words, no reuse.

In this new compositional paradigm, the component implementing the matching engine serves as an encapsulating wrapper[49] (see Figure 3-5, section 3.1.10). Only those components that implement the (vocabulary) types (Volume II, section 4.4) that flow in and out of the wrapper

---

[49] **lakos96**, section 5.10, pp. 312–324, specifically Figure 5-95, p. 319

component itself participate in its contract (Volume II, section 5.2). Dependency on all other objects are implementation details that are not discoverable programmatically. With respect to these implementation-only components, encapsulating a component means encapsulating its *use* and not the component itself[50] (see section 3.5.10 and also Figure 3-140, section 3.11.2). This fundamentally different form of composition and encapsulation — i.e., based on dependency and not containment — is what makes hierarchical reuse (section 0.4) of stable subsolutions (section 0.5) possible.

As described here, a component serves as the appropriate fundamental unit of both logical and physical design. Components, like classes, allow for factoring, thus helping us to make small problems out of big ones, and we can solve small problems well. But components, unlike classes, enable consideration of objective physical properties (e.g., compile- and link-time dependencies) that are beyond the scope of logical design alone. Components, being physical entities, unite intimately related classes (e.g., a container and its iterators), along with closely related free operators (e.g., the output and equality operators, `operator<<` and `operator==`, respectively), in a single cohesive unit. Components, being represented in terms of files (as opposed to regions of source code), are physical modules that can be lifted individually from one *platform*[51] and deployed on another without ever having to invoke a text editor.[52] Finally, well-crafted components can be tested thoroughly because they are small and were designed with testing in mind (see Volume II, section 4.9). As we will see, the component — as *we* define it — enables us to realize the enormous synergy between good logical and physical design.

0.8   Quantifying Hierarchical Reuse: An Analogy

The business of top-down design of application software is, in effect, a series of partitioning problems that optimizes a complex global cost function. Functionality, ease of use, availability, reliability, maintainability, portability, time to market, and, of course, total development cost (to name just a few) are all potential parameters to the problem. We have also discussed the bottom-up approach of accumulating and maintaining a fine-grained hierarchy of useful and potentially reusable (stable) library solutions to expedite future application development.

---

[50] **lakos96**, section 5.10, pp. 312–324, specifically the DEFINITION on p. 318

[51] Throughout this book we will use the term *platform* loosely (but consistently) to connote a distinct combination of underlying hardware, operating system, and compiler used to build and run software such that object code compiled on any one platform is typically usable on any other.

[52] I.e., without having to physically modify source code.

So far, we have only alluded to the mathematical inclination for the scalability of our general approach, namely, the well-reasoned hierarchical reuse of component-based software. To complete the task of assessing the enormous potential benefits of hierarchical reuse in software development, we will demonstrate them quantitatively using an analogous, but far simpler, much more tractable problem.

Suppose that we want to write a program to format function documentation that avoids leaving lots of spaces at the end of a line due to a long word like `MyVeryLongType`. Figure 0-38a illustrates documentation that is formatted by placing as many words as will fit on a line before advancing to the next. Figure 0-38b illustrates a more aesthetically pleasing rendering of the same text with a less-ragged right edge. The aesthetic solution is more computationally intensive because, instead of a straightforward linear partitioning algorithm, we now have to optimize a nontrivial global cost function, much as we do in partitioning software during classical top-down design.

```
Suppose that we want to       Suppose that we want
write a program to            to write a program
format function               to format function
documentation that            documentation that
avoids leaving lots of        avoids leaving lots
spaces at the end of a        of spaces at the end
line due to a very long       of a line due to a
word like                     very long word like
'MyVeryLongType'.             'MyVeryLongType'.
```

(a) Local optimization   (b) Global optimization

Figure 0-38: Simple text-filling problem with different cost functions

More formally, we are trying to solve the following "hard" problem:

Given (1) a maximum line length L and (2) a sequence of N words $\{w_0 \dots w_{N-1}\}$, each having an independent length of from 1 to L characters, partition the words such that the sum of the results of applying some arbitrary, non-negatively valued, monotonically increasing cost function $f(x)$, say

$$f(x) = x^3$$

to the number of unused (trailing) spaces x on each line (excluding the last one) is minimized.

Notice that, as is common in reusable software, we have formulated the problem in a minimalist form to make it more widely applicable by eliminating specific details about intervening spaces. A similar minimization problem that includes an intervening space character between each word on a line can be reduced to this basic problem simply by extending, by one, the line length, L, as well as the length of each word, $|w_i|$. In fact, by choosing not to hard-code the space into the basic problem, we can also use the same solution to solve the problem for proportionally spaced fonts simply by representing the line length, the space character, and the individual characters in each word by their corresponding numbers of *points*.[53]

An instance of this basic partitioning problem is illustrated in Figure 0-39a. What makes the optimization problem "hard" is the nonlinear global cost function (Figure 0-39b). If all we needed to do was minimize the total amount of unused space at the end of all lines, we could use a *greedy algorithm* to pack in as many words as possible on each line (in linear time) in a single pass (Figure 0-39c). But, because the cost function is more general, we are instead forced to consider every viable partition to see whether it yields a best result.[54]

In this example, it turns out that by choosing not to place the third word on the first line — even though it fits — the resulting sum of the cubes of the number of trailing spaces on each line is reduced by $730 - 250 = 480$ (Figure 0-39d).

---

[53] Recall the open-closed principle proposed in section 0.5, which states that the component is open to extension (by clients) but closed to modification (by library developers).

[54] Note that this problem is inherently different from seemingly similar problems (e.g., "bin-packing" or "one-dimensional knapsack") because in this problem the words must be "packed" in the order in which they are provided.

(a) Initial sequence of words of varying lengths from 1 to L

$$totalCost = \sum_{i=0}^{M-2} trailingSpaceOnLine(i)^3$$

(b) Nonlinear global cost function to be minimized

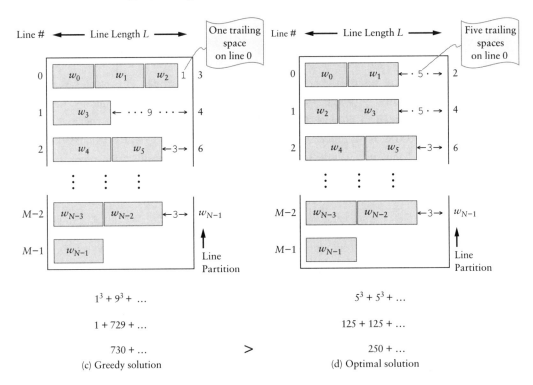

Figure 0-39: Filling text so as to minimize a nonlinear global cost function

Let us take a look at how we might go about solving this problem in software as shown in Figure 0-40. Consistent with our library-based application development methodology, the software solution to this problem — i.e., a program — is implemented as two distinct parts: (1) a single new component having a stable interface and contract that solves the basic problem (Figure 0-40a), and (2) a corresponding driver file containing `main` that adapts this well-factored, stable subsolution so that it can be invoked conveniently on arbitrary text from the command line (Figure 0-40b). All that remains now is to provide an effective implementation of `FormatUtil::calculateOptimalPartition` in the library component's `.cpp` file.

```
// xyza_formatutil.h

// ...                        (ignoring include guards for now)        (See section 1.5.)

#include <vector>

// ...                        (ignoring include guards for now)        (See section 2.4.)

struct FormatUtil {
    // Provide a namespace⁵⁵ for a suite of functions used in formatting text.

    // TYPES
    typedef double (*CostFunction)(int);⁵⁶
        // Alias for a pointer to a C-style function taking a single integer
        // argument (i.e., the number of trailing spaces) and returning a
        // (non-negative) 'double' value.

    // CLASS METHODS
    static void calculateOptimalPartition(
                                    std::vector<int>        *result,
                                    const std::vector<int>& wordLengths,
                                    int                     lineLength,
                                    CostFunction            costFunction);
        // Load, into the specified 'result', the sequence of respective
        // word indices for the specified 'wordLengths' and 'lineLength'
        // at which to insert line breaks (before the word) in order to
        // minimize the cumulative result of applying the specified
        // 'costFunction' to the number of remaining spaces at the end
        // of each line except the last one.  The behavior is undefined
        // unless, for each value of 'i', '1 <= wordLengths[i] <= lineLength'
        // and the cost function is a monotonically (at least linearly)
        // increasing, non-negative-valued function of its argument.  Note
        // that this primitive calculation packs words with no intervening
        // space; adding 1 to each element of 'wordLengths' as well as to
        // the 'lineLength' achieves the most frequently desired result.

    // ...
};

// ...
```

(a) Stable component header for core text partitioning function

---

[55] Yes, we *could* have made `FormatUtil` a `namespace` instead of a `struct`, but we deliberately chose not to do so. (See Figure 2-23, section 2.4.9.)

[56] Note that in C++11 and later, instead of a function pointer, we might consider passing either an `std::function` or making the method a function template so as to allow the use of *lambdas* (function literals).

```
// myapplication.cpp
// ...

#include <xyza_formatutil.h>

#include <vector>
#include <iostream>
#include <cctype>    // for 'isspace'
#include <cstddef>   // for 'atoi'
#include <cassert>                           (See Volume II, section 6.8.)

// ...

double calculateLineCost(int numTrailingSpaces)
    // Return the cost of a line as a pseudo piece-wise continuous
    // (non-sublinear) function of the specified 'numTrailingSpaces'.
    // The behavior is undefined unless '0 <= 'numTrailingSpaces'.
{
    assert(0 <= numTrailingSpaces);          (See Volume II, section 6.8.)
    double t = numTrailingSpaces;
    return t * t * t;
}

int loadWord(std::string *result)⁵⁷
    // Load into the specified 'result' the next word from standard input.
    // Return 0 on success, and a non-zero value otherwise.  Note that,
    // for the purposes of this example application, a word is a set of
    // contiguous printable (i.e., non-whitespace) characters.

{
    assert(result);                          (See Volume II, section 6.8.⁵⁸)

    // First, skip over whitespace.

    char c = ' ';
    while (std::cin && isspace(c)) {
        std::cin.get(c);
    }

    if (!std::cin) {
        return -1;
    }

    // Found the beginning of a word.  Load the characters from the input
    // stream to 'result'.
```

(continues)

---

[57] We could have used `<iostream>` directly from the `main` program; instead, we inserted this subroutine, in part, to introduce our coding standards. In our methodology — especially at the library level — we ensure that our code is *exception safe* in that it correctly propagates injected exceptions via RAII (Resource Acquisition Is Initialization), but generally is *exception agnostic* in that we do not `try`, `catch`, or `throw` exceptions directly (see Volume II, section 6.1), preferring instead to return error status. Note also that to signal that an argument to a function (1) is modifiable, (2) its address is retained beyond the call of the function, or (3) is optional, we pass its address; if none of these unusual conditions apply, we pass the argument by value if it is a fundamental, enumerated, or pointer type, and by `const` reference otherwise (see Volume II, section 6.12).

```
    result->clear();

    while (std::cin && !isspace(c)) {
        result->push_back(c);
        std::cin.get(c);
    }

    return 0;
}

int main(int argc, const char *argv[])
{
    // Get argument(s), specifically the line length, which defaults to 79.

    const int lineLength = argc > 1 ? std::atoi(argv[1]) : 79;

    // Read in words.  Note that we add one to each word length to include a
    // trailing space.

    std::vector<std::string> words;
    std::vector<int>         wordLengths;

    std::string word;
    while (0 == loadWord(&word)) {
        words.push_back(word);
        wordLengths.push_back(word.length() + 1);
    }

    // Process word lengths.

    std::vector<int> partition;

    FormatUtil::calculateOptimalPartition(   // ignoring namespaces for now
        &partition,
        wordLengths,
        lineLength + 1,    // Adjusted for trailing space after last word.
        calculateLineCost
    );

    // Format output, placing all words within a single partition on one line.
    // Note that, by pushing the total number of words onto the end of the
    // partition list, we are converting a list of separators into a list of
```

(continues)

---

[58] A preliminary version of a (language-based) contract-checking facility fashioned after the library-based solution advocated in section 6.8 of Volume II of this book was adopted (temporarily) into a draft of the C++20 Standard in June 2018 but was withdrawn a year later to allow time for further consideration and refinement.

(continued)

```
// terminators, where each partition indicates the word after which to
// terminate the line.

int i = 0;
int partitionIndex = 0;
partition.push_back(words.size());

while (partitionIndex < partition.size()) {
    while (i < partition[partitionIndex] - 1) {
        std::cout << words[i++] << ' ';
    }
    std::cout << words[i++] << std::endl;
    ++partitionIndex;
}
}
```

(b) Malleable top-level text-partitioning driver file containing `main`

Figure 0-40: Component-based decomposition of text-partitioning program

A first attempt at a solution to the basic problem addressed by the library component might be to iterate over all of the potential partition (i.e., newline) indices $\{1 \ldots N - 1\}$ in turn, solve each pair of subproblems recursively, and then select a solution pair having the lowest combined cost as the result. A pseudocode implementation of this algorithm is provided in Figure 0-41a; the actual C++ implementation provided in Figure 0-41b serves to make this illustration concrete.

```
If [A .. B] fits on a line

    If this is the last line (i.e., B is last word)
        Return 0.0.
    Else
        Return cost(number of trailing spaces on this line).

Else // [A .. B] doesn't fit

    For each division position [A + 1 .. B]
    {
        • Divide the text into left and right subproblems.
        • Separately solve each left/right subproblem recursively.
        • Record index and subpartitions of pair with min combined cost.
    }

Load into result: [ left-partition, index, right-partition ].

Return the combined costs of the left and right partitions.
```

(a) Pseudocode

```
// xyza_formatutil.cpp
// ...

#include <xyza_formatutil.h>
// ...

namespace {
                        // -------------
                        // LOCAL CONTEXT
                        // -------------

struct Context {
    // This structure holds "global" information used during the recursion.

    // DATA
    const std::vector<int>&  d_wordLengths;   // length of each word in text
    int                      d_lineLength;    // maximum length of each line
    FormatUtil::CostFunction d_costFunction;  // applied to trailing space

    // CREATORS
    Context(const std::vector<int>&  wordLengths,
            int                      lineLength,
            FormatUtil::CostFunction costFunction)
    : d_wordLengths(wordLengths)
    , d_lineLength(lineLength)
    , d_costFunction(costFunction)
    {
    }
};

}  // close unnamed namespace


                        // --------------------
                        // RECURSIVE SUBROUTINE
                        // --------------------

static double minCost1(std::vector<int> *result,
                       int               a,
                       int               b,
                       const Context&    context)
    // Load, into the specified 'result', an optimal subsequence of
    // respective word indices in the specified (inclusive) range '[a, b]'
    // at which to insert line breaks as dictated by the specified 'context'.
    // Return the total cost of the optimal solution.  The behavior is
    // undefined unless '0 <= a', 'a <= b', and
    // 'b < context.d_wordLengths.size()'.
{
    assert(result);                                          (See Volume II, section 6.8.)
    assert(0 <= a);                                          (See Volume II, section 6.8.)
    assert(a <= b);                                          (See Volume II, section 6.8.)
    assert(b < context.d_wordLengths.size());               (See Volume II, section 6.8.)
    double resultCost;  // value to be returned (set below)
    result->clear();    // Make sure that result is initially empty.

    // First see if current region [a, b] will fit on a line.

    int sum = 0;
```

(continues)

(continued)

```
int i;
for (i = a; i <= b && sum <= context.d_lineLength; ++i) {
    sum += context.d_wordLengths[i];
}

if (i > b && sum <= context.d_lineLength) { // if fits?
    resultCost = context.d_wordLengths.size() - 1 == b    // if last line
               ? 0.0                                       // then no charge
               : context.d_costFunction(context.d_lineLength - sum);
                                                           // else get cost
}
else if (a == b) {          // Although the behavior is unspecified if a
    resultCost = 0.0;       // single word is too long, the only reasonable
}                           // thing to do is pass it back at no charge.
else {
    assert(a < b);          Active comment

    // The current sequence is too long and must be further partitioned.
    // For each possible partition location 'k', 'a < k <= b', solve both
    // the left- and right-side problems recursively.  If the combined
    // cost of the two subpartitions is less than any so far, record 'k'
    // and the combined cost.  Finally, append 'left', 'k', and 'right' to
    // the result array and return the minimum cost.

    double lowestCost;
    int    lowestK;

    std::vector<int> lowestLeft;
    std::vector<int> lowestRight;
    std::vector<int> left;
    std::vector<int> right;

    const int first = a + 1;

    for (int k = first; k <= b; ++k) {
        double cost = minCost1(&left,  a, k - 1, context)
                    + minCost1(&right, k, b,     context);

        if (first == k || cost < lowestCost) {
            lowestCost  = cost;
            lowestK     = k;
            lowestLeft  = left;
            lowestRight = right;
        }
    }

    result->insert(result->end(),lowestLeft.begin(), lowestLeft.end());
    result->push_back(lowestK);
    result->insert(result->end(),lowestRight.begin(), lowestRight.end());
    resultCost = lowestCost;
}
```

(continues)

(continued)

```
    // '*result' holds an optimal sub-solution.

    return resultCost;
}

                    // -----------------
                    // TOP-LEVEL ROUTINE
                    // -----------------

// CLASS METHODS
void FormatUtil::calculateOptimalPartition(
                        std::vector<int>        *result,
                        const std::vector<int>& wordLengths,
                        int                     lineLength,
                        FormatUtil::CostFunction costFunction)
{
    assert(result);                          (See Volume II, section 6.8.)
    assert(0 <= lineLength);                  (See Volume II, section 6.8.)

    // Solve entire problem recursively.

    Context context(wordLengths, lineLength, costFunction);

    minCost1(result,                  // where to load partition
             0,                       // a
             wordLengths.size() - 1,  // b
             context);                // global info
}

// ...
```

(b) Actual C++ implementation

Figure 0-41: Brute-force, recursive top-down partitioning

In many important ways, a brute-force recursive solution to this relatively simple text partition-ing problem mirrors the kinds of gross inefficiencies that routinely afflict large-scale software development: An enormous amount of time and effort is squandered partitioning an initial prob-lem into subproblems and then repeatedly repartitioning those problems into sub-subproblems, and so on, until a problem of manageable size is reached. In the case of text partitioning, "manageable size" means it all fits on a single line, whereas in software our unit of manageable size is the component.

To see how this text-partitioning problem maps almost directly onto the top-down decom-position of application software, let us examine an instance of the computation in detail. The Context in Figure 0-41b (analogous to the software development environment itself) comprises all the immutable parameters (analogous to compilers, debuggers, third-party libraries, etc.) needed to perform the recursive calculation efficiently. The top-level rou-tine, FormatUtil::calculateOptimalPartition, creates an instance of the Context structure on the program stack (achieving thread safety) and then invokes the recursive subroutine `minCost1`.

The first recursion step of this brute-force text-partitioning algorithm (analogous to decomposing an application into subsystems)[59] leads to a fan-out of $N - 1$ pairs of subroutine calls. Each pair, in turn, divides the initial problem into unique left/right subproblems (analogous to potential subsystem designs). Each subproblem is solved recursively, again dividing the subproblem into all possible left/right sub-subproblem pairs (sub-subsystems), and so on, to a worst-case depth of N. In this analogy, the words (or, more precisely, word lengths) correspond to logical content (i.e., behavior/functionality) to be partitioned (i.e., designed) into physical lines (i.e., components).

Just as in top-down software design, the recursion terminates when the subregion is sufficiently small so as to fit on a line (or component) or when the subregion consists of only a single word (or the logical content of the component is atomic). It is only at this point that a cost can be assessed (i.e., the leaf component developed) and returned (i.e., released to production).

For the leaf case, the subpartition (returned via the argument list)[60] is empty. For every other case, the resulting subpartition will be determined by whichever left-right pair of subregions yields the lowest combined cost (best design). The task of determining an optimal subregion pair (implementing a subsystem) requires evaluating and comparing the results of each of the subpartitions (subsystem designs). In the end, an optimal partition (the integrated subsystem) is returned along with its total cost to the caller (the business sponsor).

Figure 0-42 illustrates the brute-force algorithm of Figure 0-41 (analogous to pure top-down design) applied to $N = 5$ words, each of which (just for computational simplicity) we'll assume here to be of length equal to the line length ($L = 1$). At every step in the recursion, each of the $2 \cdot (M - 1)$ subpartitions of the subsequence of length $M \le N$ is locally unique. For example, [bcde] decomposes into the three left-right subsequence pairs [b:cde], [bc:de], and [bcd:e], with each of the six subsequences — e.g., [bc] — indicated by a different (i, j) pair of word

---

[59] We acknowledge that the task of partitioning application software is qualitatively harder than our unidimensional text partitioning analogy. Still, the concreteness of this example serves to illustrate quantitatively what are essentially the same points.

[60] The resulting partition is represented here as a sequence of word indices that are loaded (i.e., values copied) into the modifiable `std::vector<int>` whose address was passed in as the first argument (see Volume II, section 6.12) to the recursive function. Even in modern C++ (i.e., C++11 and later), returning — by value — objects that allocate dynamic memory in what is intended to be hierarchically reusable software infrastructure remains in our view misguided — e.g., because it explicitly prevents object pooling across invocations (see Volume II, section 4.10).

indices — e.g., $(1, 2)$. Hence, every time a partitioning problem is encountered recursively, it is resolved anew leading to an exponential amount of work — in this case, 3^{N-1} subproblems.[61]

Theoretically, this simple algorithm is correct and will eventually produce an optimal solution; its exponential run time, however, makes it infeasible for problems of any substantial size N. Just as with pure top-down application development, this naive approach to partitioning does not scale.

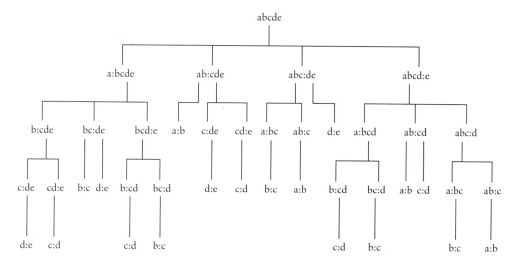

Figure 0-42: Exponential effort for naive partitioning (NO REUSE)

---

[61] This is a demonstration of recursion being 3^{N-1} for the simplified problem where `lineLength` = `wordLength`:

$$f(N) = \sum_{i=1}^{N-1} f(i) + f(N-i)$$

$$f(N) = 2\sum_{i=1}^{N-1} f(i)$$

$$f(N) = 2(\sum_{i=1}^{N-2} f(i)) + 2f(N-1)$$

$$f(N) = 3f(N-1)$$

$$f(N) = 3^{N-1}$$

This analysis, however, counts only the number of calls to f and does not address the runtime cost. For run time, we need to add overhead constants:

$$f(N) = (\sum_{i=1}^{N-2} (f(i) + f(N-i) + C_1)) + C_2$$

The key observation here is that we are doing far more work than is necessary. If there were truly an exponential number of distinct, stable subproblems, we might reasonably expect to spend an exponential amount of time solving them. Yet consider that we were able to represent each unique subproblem with just an integer pair (i, j), where $0 \le i \le j < N$, which means that the total number of unique subproblems is not exponential in N but merely quadratic.

$$\textit{Number of unique subproblems} = \frac{N(N + 1)}{2}$$

Just as in top-down application design, the number of unique partitions (like useful, well-factored software subsystems) is far smaller than the number of effective *uses* of them. If we could solve each subproblem just *once*, we'd be done in polynomial time!

To avoid the exponential costs associated with top-down design, we need to find a way to avoid solving the same subproblem over and over again. Suppose that each time we calculate an optimal subpartition we cache that solution and make it globally available. Suppose further that, instead of blindly recalculating each subproblem recursively, we first make an attempt to look up the solution in the global cache in case the very problem we are working on has already been solved.

This classic optimization technique, known as *dynamic programming*[62] (a.k.a. *memoization*), has been used successfully by many, including this author,[63] for reducing seemingly exponentially hard problems to tractable ones that can be solved in polynomial time. By simply recording and making available the optimal solution for each of the relatively few unique partitions (or subsystems) we create, the amount of time and effort expended to solve this simple text partitioning problem (or application) is reduced dramatically. What is more, unlike text partitioning where hierarchical reuse is specific to a single instance of a problem (e.g., Figure 0-11a, section 0.3), the analogous solution cache in software — i.e., enterprise-wide hierarchically reusable software libraries (see section 0.9) — can span multiple versions of multiple software applications and products (e.g., Figure 0-11c, section 0.3).

Figure 0-43 illustrates, in pseudocode, what would be necessary to achieve the proposed optimization. Notice that the previous pseudocode is unchanged (i.e., stable). Instead, two new blocks of code are added: one at the beginning to determine whether the solution to this subproblem is already known and one at the end to record each new solution for future use. The obvious analogy is that software engineers are well-advised to look for an appropriate existing solution — or at

---

[62] **bellman54**

[63] For example, see **lakos97a**.

least appropriate subparts — before creating an entirely new one from scratch. If creating a new solution is necessary, it might ultimately be appropriate to render and package it in a manner that allows it to be discovered and reused to address similar needs in the future (see section 0.10).

If [A .. B] is found in solution map
  Copy partition into result and return cost.

If [A .. B] fits on a line

  If this is the last line (i.e., B is last word)
    Return 0.0.
  Else
    Return cost(number of trailing spaces on this line).

Else // [A .. B] doesn't fit

  For each division position [A + 1 .. B]
  {
    • Divide the text into left and right subproblems.
    • Separately solve each left/right subproblem recursively.
    • Record index and subpartitions of pair with min combined cost.
  }

Load into result: [left-partition, index, right-partition].

Record cost and partition for [A .. B] in solution map.

Return the combined costs of the left and right partitions.

Figure 0-43: Pseudocode employing dynamic programming

Figure 0-44a shows how we would modify the `Context struct` of Figure 0-39b to contain a mutable cache, `d_solutionCache`, implemented as a mapping from a pair of integers, uniquely identifying the subrange of word indices, to a `Solution struct` containing (1) an optimal sequence of word indices at which to introduce line breaks, and (2) the cost associated with trailing spaces for that partition. When the `Context` object is created, `d_solutionCache` is initially empty; however, each time the modified `minCost1` subroutine (Figure 0-44b) calculates a solution for a new subrange $[i, j]$, that solution is retained so that it will be readily available the next time it is needed. Again, notice that this optimization introduced some new source code but didn't require changes to *any* existing code.

```
// xyza_formatutil.cpp
// ...

#include <xyza_formatutil.h>
// ...

namespace {                                                                    NEW
                      // --------------
                      // SOLUTION CACHE
                      // --------------

typedef std::pair<int, int> Range;
    // Alias for a pair of integers representing a range of word indices.

struct Solution {
    // This structure holds the solution/cost for a particular sub-range.

    std::vector<int> d_partition;  // word indices to receive line breaks
    double           d_cost;       // cost associated with this solution
};

typedef std::map<Range, Solution> Map;
    // Alias for a mapping of index ranges to optimal partitions/total costs.


                      // -------------
                      // LOCAL CONTEXT
                      // -------------
struct Context {
    // This structure holds "global" information used during the recursion.

    // DATA
    const std::vector<int>&  d_wordLengths;   // length of each word in text
    int                      d_lineLength;    // maximum length of each line
    FormatUtil::CostFunction d_costFunction;  // applied to trailing space
                                                                           NEW
    mutable Map              d_solutionCache; // ranges/solution association

    // CREATORS
    Context(const std::vector<int>&  wordLengths,
            int                      lineLength,
            FormatUtil::CostFunction costFunction)
    : d_wordLengths(wordLengths)
    , d_lineLength(lineLength)
    , d_costFunction(costFunction)
    { }
};

} // close unnamed namespace

// ...
```

(a) Revised Context struct with mutable solution cache

```
                        // --------------------
                        // RECURSIVE SUBROUTINE
                        // --------------------

static double minCost1(std::vector<int> *result,
                       int                 a,
                       int                 b,
                       const Context&      context)
    // Load, into the specified 'result', an optimal subsequence of
    // respective word indices in the specified (inclusive) range '[a, b]'
    // at which to insert line breaks as dictated by the specified context.
    // Return the total cost of the optimal solution.  The behavior is
    // undefined unless '0 <= a', 'a <= b', and
    // 'b < context.d_wordLengths.size()'.
{
    assert(result);                                       (See Volume II, section 6.8.)
    assert(0 <= a);                                       (See Volume II, section 6.8.)
    assert(b < context.d_wordLengths.size());             (See Volume II, section 6.8.)
    assert(a <= b);                                       (See Volume II, section 6.8.)

    double resultCost;  // value to be returned (set below)
    result->clear();    // Make sure that result is initially empty.
```
NEW
```
    // DYNAMIC PROGRAMMING: Try to look up the solution to the given range.

    Map::iterator it = context.d_solutionCache.find(Range(a,b));

    if (context.d_solutionCache.end() != it) {
        *result = (*it).second.d_partition;
        return (*it).second.d_cost;
    }

    // NOT FOUND, so proceed to calculate it recursively.
```
```
    // First see if current region [a, b] will fit on a line.

    int sum = 0;

    int i;
    for (i = a; i <= b && sum <= context.d_lineLength; ++i) {
        sum += context.d_wordLengths[i];
    }

    if (i > b && sum <= context.d_lineLength) { // if fits?
        resultCost = context.d_wordLengths.size() - 1 == b    // if last line
                   ? 0.0                                      // then no charge
                   : context.d_costFunction(context.d_lineLength - sum);
                                                             // else get cost
    }
    else if (a == b) {          // Although the behavior is unspecified if a
        resultCost = 0.0;       // single word is too long, the only reasonable
```

(continues)

(continued)

```
    }                                  // thing to do is pass it back at no charge.
    else {
        assert(a < b);

        // The current sequence is too long and must be further partitioned.
        // For each possible partition location 'k', 'a < k <= b', solve both
        // the left- and right-side problems recursively.  If the combined
        // cost of the two sub-partitions is less than any so far, record 'k'
        // and the combined cost.  Finally, append 'left', 'k', and 'right' to
        // the result array and return the minimum cost.

        double lowestCost;
        int    lowestK;

        std::vector<int> lowestLeft;
        std::vector<int> lowestRight;
        std::vector<int> left;
        std::vector<int> right;

        const int first = a + 1;

        for (int k = first; k <= b; ++k) {
            double cost = minCost1(&left,  a, k - 1, context)
                        + minCost1(&right, k, b,     context);

            if (first == k || cost < lowestCost) {
                lowestCost  = cost;
                lowestK     = k;
                lowestLeft  = left;
                lowestRight = right;
            }
        }

        result->insert(result->end(),lowestLeft.begin(), lowestLeft.end());
        result->push_back(lowestK);
        result->insert(result->end(),lowestRight.begin(), lowestRight.end());
        resultCost = lowestCost;
    }

    // '*result' holds an optimal sub-solution.
                                                                            NEW
    // DYNAMIC PROGRAMMING: Record this optimal sub-partition and its cost.

    Solution& ref = context.d_solutionCache[Range(a,b)];
    ref.d_partition = *result;
    ref.d_cost = resultCost;

    return resultCost;
}
```

(b) Revised recursive subroutine using solution cache

Figure 0-44: Actual C++ code employing dynamic programming

During the early part of execution, the optimized code of Figure 0-44 will proceed to solve each problem it encounters, much the same as our original "brute-force" implementation. However, as the computation progresses, more and more of the limited number of unique subproblems will already have been solved and made accessible in the solution cache. What started out as a laborious depth-ordered "brute-force" traversal of the tree in Figure 0-42 quickly flattens to the much more efficient, shallow traversal of Figure 0-45.

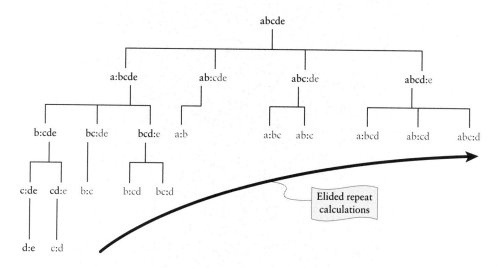

Figure 0-45: Polynomial effort achieved through hierarchical reuse

Consider how it feels the first few days after starting a new programming job. The initial projects are the most time-consuming, requiring extra effort to learn your way around, customize your development environment, set up configurations, install tools, re-create shortcut aliases, rewrite useful scripts, and so on. After the first couple of projects, additional ones become easier, as we benefit from the work done on previous ones. Without proactive planning, however, such significant gains are unlikely to continue indefinitely.

The smallness of the illustrative example discussed earlier belies the importance of not repeatedly re-solving the same problem at every level in the recursion. Recall that in our example, the brute-force solution to a text partition having N words required solving an exponential 3^{N-1} subproblems, compared with a quadratic $N \cdot (N + 1) / 2$ unique subproblems when employing a solution cache. As Figure 0-46 illustrates, we do not need N to be very large at all — just ten words — before the amount of reuse we are able to realize exceeds 99 percent! What makes this phenomenal benefit realizable, however, is not just mere reuse but full-on *hierarchical* reuse.

Problem Size	Potential Number of Subproblems	Number of Unique Subproblems	Percentage of Subproblems Presolved
1	1	1	0.0%
5	81	15	81.48%
10	19,683	55	99.7206%
15	4,782,969	120	99.997491%
20	1,162,261,467	210	99.99998193%
25	282,429,536,481	325	99.9999998849%
30	68,630,377,364,883	465	99.999999999322%
100	1.717925069106e+47	5,500	~100%
300	4.56304930195e+142	45,150	~100%
1,000	1.32207081948e+477	500,500	~100%

Figure 0-46: Quantifying the benefit of fine-grained, hierarchical reuse

Dynamic programming is a powerful metaphor for what we intend to achieve with hierarchical reuse in software development, and yet there is more to be gleaned from our analogy. Let us now consider a couple of additional refinements to our text-partitioning solution and see how they are reflected in our component-based software-development process.

First, we observe that the `Solution struct` used to implement `Map` in Figure 0-44a records an independent copy of the optimal partition for each subrange. The larger the range, the more space is needed to represent that partition. What's worse, the information contained in the partition for a larger subsolution duplicates the information stored in the solutions for the left and right subranges used to create it, resulting in a solution cache that is a full order of magnitude larger than necessary. This wasteful copying is mirrored in software development when pre-existing solutions are "copied and pasted" from one application or subsystem to the next — a malignant form of reuse that we generally discourage.[64]

The difficulty arises here because each cached partitioning `Solution` effectively *contains*, as opposed to *refers to* or *depends on* (see section 1.8), its sub-subsolutions, leading to `Solution` representations of nonuniform size. If those subsolutions were themselves subject to change, then, like application software, we would not be able to refer to (depend on) them reliably. However, once a `Solution` corresponding to a subrange is calculated (developed) and cached (released), it never changes (is stable), is potentially reusable (in place), and therefore can be referred to (depended on) safely by higher-level solutions (components). It is precisely this kind of hierarchical reuse that was illustrated in terms of software in Figure 0-19, section 0.4.

For this desirable non-copy-and-paste kind of hierarchical reuse to occur during text partitioning, we will need to restructure our solution cache to allow new solutions to refer to, rather than copy from, existing ones. By ensuring that the solutions are (1) *stable*, i.e., once instantiated do not change incompatibly (section 0.5), and (2) *ubiquitously accessible*, i.e., centrally located in a global (firm-wide) repository (see section 0.9), we can eliminate all copying and simply refer to the existing solutions *in place*, resulting in all subsolutions (like components) being of (roughly) uniform size (section 0.7).

Figure 0-47 illustrates both the current and proposed text-partitioning algorithms on a body of text containing 1,000 words. Instead of having each solution maintain an independent copy of the combined partitions of its subsolutions (Figure 0-47a), each subsolution (component) is implemented as a fixed-size `struct` retaining references to its optimal left and right sub-subsolutions (Figure 0-47b).

---

[64] Note that sometimes, however, a small amount of redundancy can go a long way toward breaking oppressive physical design cycles (see section 3.5.6).

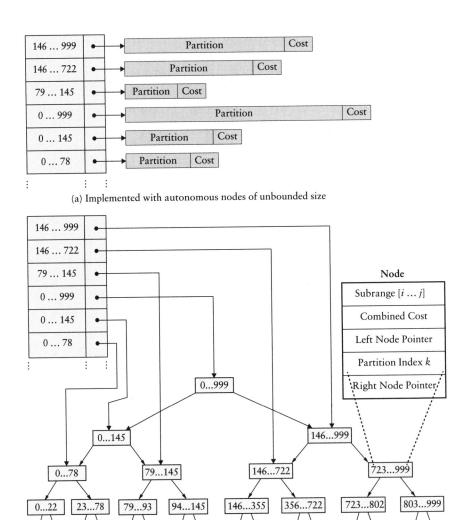

(a) Implemented with autonomous nodes of unbounded size

(b) Implemented with fixed-sized nodes referencing other nodes

Figure 0-47: Hierarchical rendering of solutions within the cache

In this latest design, each fixed-size range/solution entry in the solution cache would contain five fields.

1. Subrange $[i, j]$ of word indices corresponding to the solution

2. Total cost of the solution in terms of trailing spaces

3. Pointer to the left subsolution

4. Word index of the initial (root) partition, *k*, for this solution

5. Pointer to the right subsolution

Given a reference to a solution, a depth-ordered traversal of the subsolutions efficiently re-creates (in linear time) the full partition — i.e., the entire sequence of word indices at which to insert line breaks in the original text.

Now instead of containing the entire solution (implementation) itself, each node in the solution cache (hierarchically reusable component library) contains only a uniformly small amount of local data ("glue" logic) and pointers to (`#include` the `.h` files of) the optimal left-right subsolutions (lower-level components). Not only is the runtime (development) cost of rampant copying eliminated, but so is an order-of-magnitude excess in process size (cost of ownership).[65]

Analogies can be stretched. Still, illustrating the many compelling similarities between using dynamic programming for our nonlinear text-partitioning problem and exploiting fine-grained hierarchical reuse in software application development fairly justifies one more refinement.

Recall that our goal is to maximize productivity through hierarchical reuse of existing solutions. We would therefore expect that, as more and more subsolutions become available, a greater and greater proportion of our time will be spent attempting to locate solutions, rather than building them anew. If finding a solution is needlessly expensive, it unfairly limits the effectiveness of the overall hierarchical-reuse strategy. Hence, expediting the retrieval of relevant solutions will be the focus of our final refinement to the implementation of our dynamic-programming-based text-partitioning program.

Until now, the cost of finding a solution (or determining that it does not yet exist) has been needlessly expensive. In particular, both of the previous dynamic-programming-based optimizations used an `std::map` to associate each subproblem, described as an (*i, j*) pair, with its corresponding optimal `Solution`. As illustrated in Figure 0-48a, an `std::map` implements an ordered collection, typically as a balanced tree, guaranteeing $O[\log (N)]$ access time. However, our dynamic-programming-based optimization does not require that solutions be maintained in any particular order: The solution to a given range is either there or not. If, instead of using an `std::map`, we use an unordered (i.e., hash-based) map, such as the data structure illustrated in Figure 0-48b, we could reduce the expected cost of lookup substantially — i.e., proportional

---

[65] For concreteness, we created a complete C++ implementation (not shown) corresponding to the modified design of Figure 0-47b. The salient differences between this new dynamic-programming-based implementation and the previous one are that (1) the `Solution` type is now just a fixed-sized (POD) `struct`, (2) the recursive `minCost1` function now returns the root of a tree of `Solution` nodes representing the optimal partition, and (3) a new recursive helper function, `loadPartition`, is now used to walk the `Solution` returned to the top-level routine to populate the `std::vector<int>`, whose address was supplied by the client.

to a constant. Yet the compact nature of the [*i, j*] notation for referencing all possible solutions enables us to do even better.

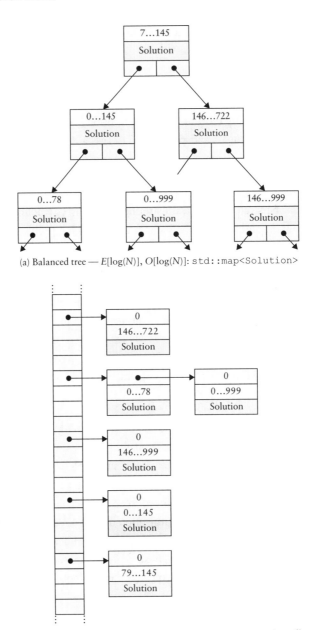

(a) Balanced tree — $E[\log(N)]$, $O[\log(N)]$: `std::map<Solution>`

(b) Hash table — $E[1]$, $O[N]$: `std::unordered_map<Solution>`[66]

---

[66] `std::unordered_map` became part of the C++ Standard Library (STL) as of C++11.

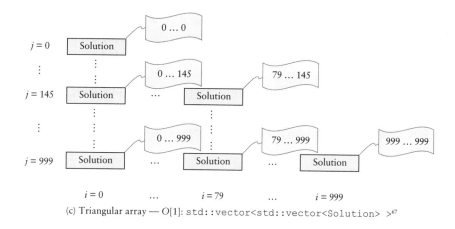

(c) Triangular array — $O[1]$: `std::vector<std::vector<Solution> >`[67]

Figure 0-48: Achieving both compact and fast access to pre-existing solutions

A general-purpose hash table must address the possibility of collisions. Suppose that instead of settling for a conventional hash function on the integer pair (i, j), we were to concoct a perfect hash function — one that would guarantee *a priori* that no conflicts could ever occur. In the case of our text-partitioning problem, a perfect hash is easy because we know all the entries ahead of time. If we replace our `std::map` with a triangular array of elements of type `Solution` — indexed first by j and then by i as illustrated in Figure 0-48c — we guarantee that we can find each solution (or not) in worst-case constant time, $O[1]$, and with a tiny constant at that! Moreover, the triangular array, unlike the other two (node-based) data structures, represents the solutions compactly — i.e., no substantial administrative storage is required.[68]

---

[67] As of C++11, the intervening space between successive right-angle-bracket (>) characters in such template instantiations is no longer required.

[68] For concreteness, we created one last complete C++ implementation (not shown) corresponding to the modified design of Figure 0-48c. The only significant difference between this and the previous implementation (corresponding to Figure 0-44) is that the new `Context` makes use of a better organized, faster, and more compact solution cache: (1) a `Solution` now has a notion of being unset (indicated by a negative partition index, k) and is constructed in an unset state by default; (2) the `std::map<Range, Solution>` is replaced by an `std::vector<std::vector<Solution>>`, which is configured to its proper triangular form by a `for` loop in the body of the `Context` constructor; and (3) instead of calling `context.d_solutionCache.find(Range(a, b))` and comparing the iterator returned with `context.d_solutionCache.end()`, we retain a reference (`result`) to the `Solution` element returned by `context.d_solutionCache[j][i]` and — as before — return `&result` immediately if available (i.e., `result.d_k >= 0`).

Just as in our text-partitioning analogy, when creating software applications that employ hierarchical reuse, as more and more components become available, the cost of development will be increasingly dominated by how quickly software engineers can locate and exploit relevant components. In this final implementation, not only is access time of the cache minimized but so is the size of the representation. Because each partial solution can be represented uniquely in a compact notation, there is no spatial overhead (e.g., like that associated with node-based containers) and no need to resort to heuristics (e.g., like those associated with hash tables).

Thoughtful packaging (see sections 2.1–2.3) facilitates a compact hierarchical naming strategy (see section 2.4) in which components can be looked up via globally unique, orthogonal identifiers — i.e., first by *package group* and then by *package*. Insisting on a compact notation with respect to organizing and locating reusable components results in similar efficiencies with respect to finding and referring to pre-existing software solutions (e.g., via fully qualified names of manageable length).[69]

Figure 0-49 recaps the four successively refined, text-partitioning solutions that we have discussed in this section and shows how the actual C++ implementations stack up in terms of run times for problems of varying size. The original top-down recursive implementation (Figure 0-41) turned out to be useless for text having more than about a dozen words. By avoiding redundant calculations via a mutable solution cache (Figure 0-44), we were able to extend the applicability of the algorithm on our example under test by more than a factor of ten.

---

[69] Effective solution-oriented documentation including usage examples (see Volume II, section 6.16) will also be crucial in realizing the full benefit of having a vast repository of fine-grain, hierarchically reusable software, yet it is our ability to find relevant solutions quickly that is most directly analogous to this final text-partitioning improvement. Having a well-organized hierarchical structure is a good start, but we will also need effective search capabilities. Having alternative indexes in the repository, such as a solution "cookbook," can help. Finally, having knowledgable in-house infrastructure developers who can also serve as librarians has, in our experience, afforded significant returns to application-developer productivity in practice.

(a) Original Solution (Brute Force): Top-down recursive solution

(b) Dynamic Programming (By Value): Used a cache to look up/record subsolutions

(c) Fixed-Size Solutions (By Ref): Avoided copying and pasting subsolutions

(d) Fast Lookup (Curated Solutions): Replaced tree-based with fast/compact *indexed* lookup

Number of Words	*Original* (a) Brute Force (Fig. 0-41)	⟵ *Dynamic Programming* ⟶		
		(b) By Value (Fig. 0-44)	(c) By Ref (Fig. 0-47b)	(d) Curated Solutions (Fig. 0-48c)
1	0.076	0.077	0.076	0.077
5	0.143	0.144	0.149	0.145
10	0.318	0.231	0.230	0.227
15	19.453	0.319	0.316	0.312
20	4,480.437	0.419	0.402	0.400
25	over a week	0.510	0.485	0.483
30		0.584	0.526	0.524
100		2.613	0.955	0.797
300		57.746	6.123	1.192
1,000		out of mem	402.550	36.712

Thrashing due to extensive memory use

All data is in "wall" seconds running on an IBM T22 ThinkPad compiled with gcc -O4.

Figure 0-49: Measuring the benefits of fine-grained, hierarchical reuse

By restructuring each `Solution` to be of a uniform fixed size (Figure 0-47b) and incorporating each of its subsolutions by reference, we were able to eliminate the overhead associated with wasteful copying and decrease the space usage by a full order of magnitude, thereby enabling problems of substantially larger size to be accommodated. Finally, we replaced the logarithmic lookup of an `std::map` with the much more efficient (and compact) constant-time *indexed* lookup of a triangular array (Figure 0-48c), allowing large problems to be solved in significantly less time.[70,71]

---

[70] Even the final implementation is by no means the best possible. For those interested in the optimal solution to this text-formatting problem, see **cormen09**, Chapter 15, Problem 15-4, pp. 406–407 (reprinted here for convenience):

15-4 Printing neatly

Consider the problem of neatly printing a paragraph with a monospaced font (all characters having the same width) on a printer. The input text is a sequence of n words of lengths $l_1, l_2, \ldots, l_n$, measured in characters. We want to print this paragraph neatly on a number of lines that hold a maximum of M characters each. Our criterion of "neatness" is as follows. If a given line contains words i through j, where $i \leq j$, and we leave exactly one space between words, the number of extra space characters at the end of the line is $M - j + i - \sum_{k=i}^{j} l_k$, which must be nonnegative so that the words fit on the line. We wish to minimize the sum, over all lines except the last, of the cubes of the numbers of extra space characters at the ends of lines. Give a dynamic-programming algorithm to print a paragraph of n words neatly on a printer. Analyze the running time and space requirements of your algorithm.

[71] Note that it was Professor Ronald Rivest at M.I.T. (c. 1980) who first introduced me to text partitioning as a homework problem, which has had a profound, positive effect on my professional career ever since.

Text partitioning is an excellent metaphor for what we want to achieve with software; the many parallels are shown in Figure 0-50. We used this relatively simple nonlinear optimization problem to demonstrate quantitatively the importance of fine-grained hierarchical reuse. Whether we are talking about text or software, there are an enormous number of ways of partitioning that can lead to essentially the same result. Rather than blindly resolving every subproblem anew each time it is encountered, if we instead strive to look up the solution and, if not found, make sure that the solution is readily available for subsequent use, the overall increase in productivity is profound. Ensuring that fine-grained subsolutions are, in fact, effectively reusable is the challenge.

Software Development	Text Partitioning
• Subjective cost function	• Objective cost function
• Application program / Suite of programs	• Entire text / Entire text (again)
• Factored design	• Partition
• Logical content	• Words
• Leaf component	• Line
• Component	• Solution
• Hierarchical reusable library	• Solution cache
• Enterprise-wide	• Globally accessible
• Source-code copy-and-paste	• Independent subsolution copies
• Software packaging strategy / Curated suite of components	• Solution-cache organization / Solution-cache organization (again)
• Uniform component size	• Uniform solution-node size
• Reusable software is stable	• Subsolutions are never modified
• Component-dependency	• Reference to subsolution
• Finding relevant components	• Finding solutions quickly

Figure 0-50: Summarizing similarities in our analogy

There are, of course, additional challenges to achieving reuse in library software that are not addressed by our dynamic-programming text-partitioning example. An important goal when crafting reusable library software is to maximize the probability that it will be reused frequently. The primary difference between partitioning text and designing modular software is that, in software, there is no reason to believe that we will necessarily come up with the same (or perhaps even similar) atomic solutions on two different branches of the top-down decomposition, let alone decompositions resulting from disparate applications.[72] The "magic" of software design is that the decomposition requires human intelligence and experience and, therefore, is not exact. Still, there is much we can do to maximize the probability of a "cache hit" in our software repository.

First, we must make each of our recursive subsolutions (components) finely graduated and granular (section 0.4); the probability of an adequate match for a hierarchical subsystem consisting of small components is much more likely than for a single large one. We must also remove arbitrary degrees of freedom that would impede effective composition. For example, insisting on minimal collaboration (section 0.3), a consistent and uniform physical form (section 0.7), a common organization (see Chapter 2), physical interoperability within a single process (see section 3.9), and use of a common set of fundamental *vocabulary* types (see Volume II, section 4.4) all serve to increase the probability of reuse.

Second, a primary goal for a reusable software developer must be to widen the applicability of each solution to encompass as many different uses as appropriate — especially for *vocabulary* types (see Volume II, section 4.4). Achieving this goal often means providing *less* functionality (see section 3.2.7) and also less policy (see Volume II, section 5.9). Recall that the text partitioning application (Figure 0-40b) adapted the basic core library component (Figure 0-40a) to accommodate intervening spaces as opposed to building that feature into the library component itself, such that the same library component — without modification — could naturally accommodate proportionally spaced fonts. Furthermore, by ensuring that component solutions in the repository are "spread out" so as to cover the intended design space, rather than overlapping each other (see Volume II, section 5.7), we increase the likelihood that there is a unique solution to meet each need, which, again, is especially important for vocabulary types.

Finally, if application development were truly analogous to our dynamic programming text partitioning example, then computers, not human beings, would determine whether some preexisting solution is a viable match and if so use it — no questions asked! Of course, the *cache*

---

[72] That is to say, there is no pair of integers (i, j) that uniquely describes every potentially useful software component.

is our software repository, and *people*, not computers, make that *subjective* determination. Therefore, there is no guarantee that even a perfectly applicable solution will be reused. We will explore this issue further in section 0.11.

To summarize, in our analogy, a vague and complex global cost function of top-down software decomposition for partitioning logical content of a program into components was replaced by a precise one for partitioning words of text into lines. In addition, a centrally located library of hierarchically reusable components is replaced by a global, mutable solution cache. Like reusable components in a library, the solutions in the cache (1) are of a fixed, uniform size, (2) are stable, and (3) comprise subsolutions (in place) by reference. Further, as with software development, the larger the solution cache becomes, the more important it is that relevant solutions be curated (organized effectively) so as to be locatable quickly.

Of course, the constraints introduced by real-world software development lead to additional complexity. To realize the enormous potential benefits that we have outlined in this section, these two statements must be true:

I. There can exist an acyclic, hierarchical, component-based rendering of all library software that we would ever care to own (see section 0.9).

II. We can identify a feasible process (see section 0.10) by which to grow a repository of such software over time having sufficient quality (see section 0.11) and in such a way that it is stable (section 0.5) from one version of the repository to the next.

It is these critical assertions to which we turn our attention in the following sections.

0.9   Software Capital

It has been said that there is never enough time to do it right, but there is always enough time to do it over. But what does it mean to *do it right*? Would we be able to *do it right* if we had enough time?

In business, *doing it right* means maximizing the firm's profits. Software is a tool — a means to an end and never an end in itself. In any business, the focus is always to *maximize profit*. The interesting question is, "In what timeframe?"

In most industries, time to market directly affects profit. The first company to provide a new or substantially improved product can often capture and retain substantial market share.

The sooner a product gets to market, the sooner it can contribute to the company's bottom line. In some industries — the financial industry in particular — the pressure to deliver quickly is especially pronounced.

Figure 0-51 illustrates the return on investment for a new financial instrument. Initially, there is no software support and, hence, no revenue. The first institution able to offer this financial product (at time t_1) will receive *all* of the business and can charge substantial premiums for the service; the revenue stream is all but unbounded!

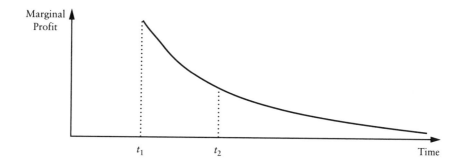

Figure 0-51: Return on investment for financial instruments

Over time, as other institutions begin to offer similar products (say, at t_2), the business will be shared by a few providers that, in an effort to attract business away from others, lower their premiums until near *perfect competition*[73] brings the instrument to its steady-state revenue profile.

Being among the first providers of a new financial product dramatically increases total profit; hence, it should not be surprising that financial software professionals are often rewarded more for getting the job done *quickly* than for "doing it right."

To better appreciate this way of thinking, consider the following analogy:

- The teenage mortality rate due to influenza among a particular segment of our population is determined to be five times the national average.
- A questionnaire has been created that each student will answer.

---

[73] **tragakes11**

- Our goal is to develop software to correlate specific answers with afflicted individuals to identify high-risk subjects.
- Each day of delay costs young lives.

How much *extra* time should we spend to *do it right*?[74]

In business, leaving money on the table is a tragedy. The sooner the product is delivered, the greater the return on the investment. To maximize that return, our primary goal must be to get the job done quickly, but how?

We could throw more people at it, as illustrated in Figure 0-52, but Fred Brooks[75] would say no. A published empirical study[76] along with our own experience suggests instead a staffing profile more like the one shown in Figure 0-53. There is simply "no silver bullet"[77] for reducing time to market for software *today*.

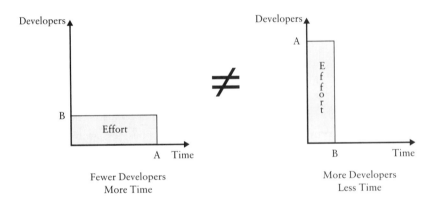

Figure 0-52: Invoking the mythical man month (BAD IDEA)

Continuing our analogy, suppose that the National Institute of Health observes that emergencies requiring the development of similar software are common. What can be done to reduce time to market for "emergency software" in the future? The answer is to *invest* in Software Capital.

---

[74] There are, of course, completely different problem domains that work differently. Examples are heart monitors, avionics (safety first!), spacecraft control software (do it wrong and your lander crashes on Mars), firmware for nonflashable hardware (do it wrong and you can have an expensive recall), etc., but we're not talking about those here.

[75] **brooks75**

[76] **boehm81**

[77] **brooks87**

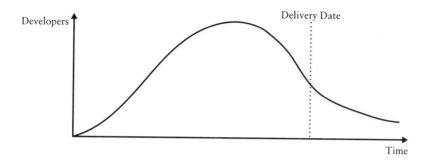

Figure 0-53: Optimal staffing profile[78]

What is Software Capital? We define the term *Software Capital*[79] to mean a proprietary suite of relevant, interoperable, reusable components.[80]

Software Capital is an asset of the firm; it does not belong to any one application or product. The secondary purpose of Software Capital is to reduce costs associated with defects and maintenance, but its primary purpose — its reason for being — is to reduce time to market for *future* applications and products (as pictured in Figure 0-54).

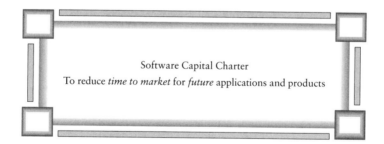

Figure 0-54: Primary motivation for developing Software Capital

---

[78] See **boehm81**, section 4.4, pp. 41–46, specifically Figure 4-4a, p. 45.

[79] The term *Software Capital* was coined by Dean Zarras, formerly a managing director in the F.A.S.T. (Financial Analytics and Structured Transactions) group at Bear Stearns. His original 1996 paper, *Software Capital — Achievement and Leverage*, however, was not published until some 20 years later (see **zarras16**).

[80] There is also a small but interesting and enlightening book on the economics of software; see **baetjer98**.

Software Capital is more than just good proprietary library software; it captures crystallized domain knowledge in a form that can be readily understood and redeployed. Unlike typical applications (and even some commercially available library software), Software Capital is approachable. Using Software Capital, a new developer — even one who is unfamiliar with the subject matter — can begin to become productive almost immediately.

With each new solution, any developer wanting to understand the relevant issues often need look no further than the library software that implements it. Each component becomes an example that has enormous potential to transmit knowledge, almost like a "runnable book." Education via concrete example is an important dimension of leverage that components offer. Properly documented (see Volume II, sections 6.15–6.17), a well-designed component is not only easy to understand and use but also instructive, both in the particular domain of the problem it solves and in the general domain of software engineering.

Software Capital also serves as the best example of good software by consistently being (1) easy to understand, (2) easy to use, (3) high performing, (4) portable, and (5) reliable. Each well-designed, well-documented component serves as a potential starting point for rendering the next, similar component — e.g., one in the same class category (see Volume II, section 4.2). This form of leverage has become critical to our daily development activity. Once again, we observe that the more Software Capital we already have, the more productive we are likely to be at writing more of it.

Collectively, these instructive examples soon permeate our quotidian workflow, providing positive feedback to the development community: educating, stimulating, motivating, and thereby *attracting* and *retaining* talented developers. The significance of these subtle business aspects of leverage are routinely underestimated.

In addition to early design reviews by senior software developers, we believe that routine peer review of rendered software is an essential part of the development process. Yet it is easy for us to understand why many might feel that peer review is generally too expensive to employ in practice. If the initial quality of the code is poor or its organization is unfamiliar, the relative cost to review the code can be unacceptably high, comparable even to that of writing the code in the first place. Polishing poorly designed code is hardly a good use of developer time. Moreover, the didactic benefit of reviewing poorly conceived code is lost.

On the other hand, high-quality software is (by our definition) easy to understand. Less *is* better: a simpler, lighter-weight solution that is easier to explain is typically *more useful* than a substantially heavier one that does more. Coming up with a tighter design that is easier to understand often requires substantial up-front thought, time, and effort. Saying exactly what you are going to do *before* you do it — both in terms of use cases and reference documentation — is neither easy nor cheap but virtually always leads to a better, more comprehensible design and less overall cost in the long run. The more effort that is spent making the software easy to understand, the less effort will be required to review it. Hence, peer reviewing high-quality software costs relatively little and achieves much for reviewer and reviewee alike.

To enjoy the economic return from creating Software Capital, we must be willing to consider diversifying our efforts along two timeframes: short and long. Creating Software Capital will unavoidably introduce a short-term opportunity cost. Much like attending college, the initial investment in such an aggressive infrastructure requires intense training and the laying of a foundation that will not immediately benefit anyone except the team developing the Software Capital itself.

After some time, a well-organized, integrated, crystal-like structure begins to emerge. Developers, realizing the unparalleled utility of the available Software Capital, begin to use it without coercion (see section 0.11). Once other library and application developers have incorporated Software Capital in their own development efforts, a few other good things begin to happen. The best practices ingrained in these well-factored highly polished components are assimilated — often subliminally — by their users. The benefit of peer review in terms of automatic developer training — although hard to measure — is by itself ample justification, and yet it is only one of many such collateral benefits.

Other developers, observing the increasingly obvious value of a regular organization for software (see Chapter 2) and the supporting metaframework and tools (see section 2.16), follow suit and begin to adopt the new way of organizing and building their own software. Soon, much of the enterprise is creating and using fine-grain components, thereby directly benefiting from this scalable, component-based approach to developing software.

Over time, the common low-level integrated infrastructure allows separately conceived libraries to interoperate with each other via a common vocabulary (see Volume II, section 4.4), facilitating almost seamless integration across product lines. The fine-grain logical factoring (section 0.4) naturally minimizes physical coupling (section 0.6). Sound physical design strategies (see Chapter 3) avoid cyclic, excessive, or otherwise inappropriate physical dependencies. The resulting application structure automatically becomes qualitatively more manageable. Because all the low-level pieces embody the five properties of Software Capital, delineated in Figure 0-55, client applications inherit this stellar quality (at absolutely no cost to them) in the form of improved reliability, portability, and performance.

---

(1) *Easy to understand*
  - Minimal surface area
  - Canonical rendering
  - Clear and complete reference documentation
  - Relevant usage examples

(2) *Easy to use*
  - Effective usage model
  - Intuitive interface
  - Appropriate level of safety
  - Minimal physical dependencies

(3) *High performing*
  - Execution (i.e., wall and CPU) run time
  - Process (i.e., in-core memory) size
  - Compile time (or the degree of compile-time coupling)
  - Link time (or the extent of link-time dependency)
  - Executable (i.e., on-disk) code size

(4) *Portable*
  - Builds on all supported platforms
  - Runs on all supported platforms
  - Produces the same results on all supported platforms
  - Achieves "reasonable" performance on all supported platforms

(5) *Reliable*
  - No core dumps
  - No memory leaks
  - No incorrect results
  - No bugs
  - No, we're not kidding!

Figure 0-55: Intrinsic properties of Software Capital

All of these benefits combine to make a compelling argument, yet none of these reasons justifies the economic investment in Software Capital as powerfully as its charter, specifically to reduce time to market for future applications and products (Figure 0-54). It is by delivering on this promise alone that we can fairly argue for the up-front investment in time and talent that will be required. The residual benefits — quality, stability, reduced maintenance cost, captured knowledge, and so on — are just happy consequences of doing business quickly *the right way*.

To realize the full benefit of this fine-grained enterprise-wide factoring effort, we must ensure that the useful software we factor out of our applications resides in a place that makes sense from both a logical and physical perspective. We assert that the questions "What should this component do?" and "Where should this component reside?" are not independent and both should be answered before development begins (see section 3.1.4). Instead of allowing existing useful functionality to be buried among application code (see sections 3.2.2–3.2.4), we carefully factor this valuable software into discrete components, which we then thoughtfully group alongside logically similar or related components (see sections 3.3.6–3.3.8) that are also characterized by the same envelope of physical dependencies. A substantial organizational and cognitive benefit results just from colocating components with cohesive logical and physical characteristics into packages and package groups (see, respectively, sections 2.7 and 2.8).

Picture the directed acyclic graph of libraries throughout our enterprise as a huge warehouse modeled after a suburban hardware/home-improvement store. This cavernous building contains prefabricated materials and parts of almost every kind and complexity. Like most hardware stores, similar parts such as nuts, bolts, screws, and nails are conveniently located on the same or adjacent shelves, as are similar kinds of materials such as lumber (e.g., pine, oak, and plywood), glass, Formica, and stone.

The shelves in this warehouse are arranged in long parallel rows, which are consecutively numbered. In this warehouse, however, the parts — from the most simple to the most complex — are all from the same manufacturer. More complex parts, such as light fixtures, doors, and window frames, are built out of less complex ones that also reside within the same warehouse. Shelves containing the more complex parts are always in rows with higher numbers than those holding the more primitive components out of which these more complex parts were assembled (see section 1.10). Shelves in still higher-numbered rows are reserved for yet more complex and involved entities: a washing machine, a bathroom vanity, and even a grand piano. In short, logical behavior and physical dependency together help to determine the physical location of items within the warehouse.

Along the same lines, we can imagine developing an application as similar to building a piece of custom furniture. Instead of starting from scratch, however, our goal is to *assemble* the desired object, selecting from an almost overwhelming abundance of prefabricated parts and materials, as illustrated in Figure 0-56. The meticulous organization (Figure 0-56a), however, makes finding what we need virtually instantaneous. Naturally, we prefer prefabricated assemblies that meet our needs over assembling raw materials ourselves. It is not coincidental that the primitives in *our* warehouse tend to coordinate aesthetically (e.g., in color and texture) and *integrate* well in the final product (see Volume II, section 4.4). The result of our effort may pull from every corner of the warehouse (Figure 0-56b), but — once instantiated (e.g., statically linked; see section 1.2) — the constituent pieces come together in similar relative order, preserving their *acyclic* physical dependencies (Figure 0-56c) just as when these components were distributed throughout the warehouse.

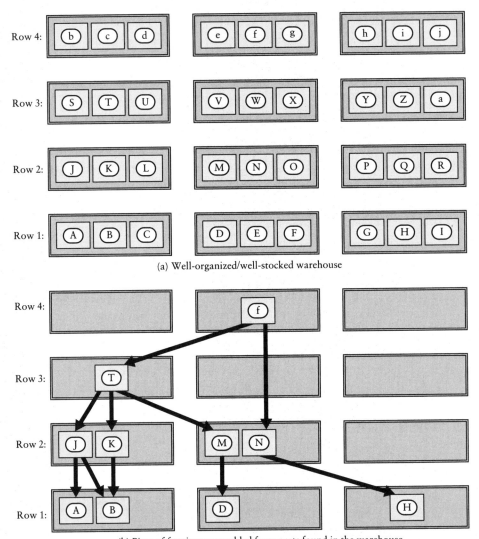

(a) Well-organized/well-stocked warehouse

(b) Piece of furniture assembled from parts found in the warehouse

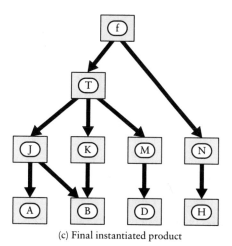

(c) Final instantiated product

Figure 0-56: Maintaining an acyclic collection of prefabricated components

On those increasingly rare occasions where the needed part is not yet available, we can immediately and reliably determine its absence. Just as in our optimized solution to the text-partitioning problem (section 0.8), we will then have to create the part ourselves on the fly. Given time, we might prepare the missing item to a sufficient level of refinement that it could, with minimal polishing by library developers, be placed in our warehouse precisely where it belongs so that we and others can readily find and use it in future projects. If, however, as is often the case, the need for some new item is urgent, we might instead concoct an ad hoc solution sufficient for us alone today, place that solution in a component local to our application (for now), and arrange (with library developers) to solve this subtask thoroughly once and for all as time permits.

For Software Capital to serve as a viable business strategy, it is important to understand that current business needs must never be held hostage by the software destined to satisfy them. Even under the best of conditions, generally useful albeit imperfect software *will* find its way into applications. As part of this *bimodal* yet evolutionary development process (see section 0.10), commonly useful software initially created for a single application (e.g., Figure 0-7a, section 0.2) will be *demoted*[81] (i.e., renamed, reworked, and placed lower in the physical

---

[81] Demotion is but one of the original nine *levelization* techniques introduced in Chapter 5, pp. 203–325, of **lakos96** (and specifically demotion in section 5.3, pp. 229–247) and are re-explained here in a more contemporary context in section 3.5 (and specifically demotion in section 3.5.3).

hierarchy) where it can be shared more widely (e.g., Figure 0-7b, section 0.2). The same process of *demotion* can also be applied profitably across different levels of library code.[82]

In this way, generally useful functionality will, over time, eventually find its appropriate place in the physical hierarchy of library software that spans our enterprise (see section 2.1). By organizing our libraries in this centralized way, each application will be able to draw from a wealth of established stable library software.

Finally, recall from section 0.1 that, for any given development organization at any point in time, there exists a design space, illustrated here in Figure 0-57a, for which schedule, product, and budget may be traded off. Our stated goal was to push that schedule/product/budget design space away from the origin, ostensibly giving development managers more of each to trade off (Figure 0-57b). By employing Software Capital, however, not only have we improved all three dimensions simultaneously, we have also moved the design space itself away from its dimensional axis (Figure 0-57c). Because applications can now be assembled largely from high-quality, highly integrated, prefabricated parts, a substantial portion of product quality — as well as the schedule (time) and budget (cost) to develop and maintain it — comes with these parts automatically and for free! That is, regardless of trade-offs, any product built substantially out of Software Capital can now reasonably take only so long, cost only so much, and be only so unreliable!

---

[82] When demoting library software, however, there might be issues of stability that need to be addressed. Unlike software confined to a single application, it might not be possible for all clients of library software to change in lockstep; hence, a rational deprecation strategy for the original library component implementation might be needed. One option is to allow the old and new implementations to co-exist for a time until all clients have had a chance to move over. It will turn out that this refactoring approach is facilitated by our methodology since nominal logical and physical name cohesion (see section 2.4) ensures that the names of all logical and physical entities contained within an architectural unit of aggregation (see section 2.2) are scoped by the name of that unit and therefore cannot conflict with logical or physical names in any other unit.

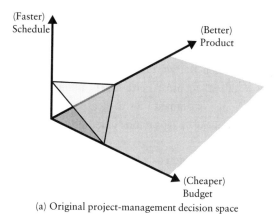

(Faster) Schedule

(Better) Product

(Cheaper) Budget

(a) Original project-management decision space

(Faster) Schedule

(Better) Product

(Cheaper) Budget

(b) Quantitatively improved decision space

(Faster) Schedule

(Better) Product

(Cheaper) Budget

(c) Qualitatively improved decision space

Figure 0-57: Improving schedule/product/budget trade-offs simultaneously

0.10   Growing the Investment

How do we create Software Capital? If reusable software is not normally a by-product of application development, then Software Capital — an ultra-high-quality, ultra-stable, enterprise-wide, reusable resource — most certainly is not either. Software Capital does not occur naturally and, without a sustained and dedicated (*tenacious*) effort, will not exist at all. To create Software Capital, we must establish an *autonomous* core development team.

> The importance of such a "standard components" group cannot be overestimated.
>
> —Bjarne Stroustrup (2000)[83]

This team must not be bound to any one project. We must grant these developers the resources and the time necessary to produce relevant prefabricated components that are easy to understand, easy to use, high performing, portable, and reliable (see Figure 0-55, section 0.9). The success of the team, however, will ultimately be measured by the (long-term) successes of its clients and the enterprise itself.

The next question is, "How big should this core team be?" That is, for a fixed staff of N developers, what fraction of them should be focused on feeding reusable software back into the development process? Given a staff of $N = 100$ developers, it is hard to imagine that 5 core developers is too many or that 50 is too few. Beyond that, almost any decision can be rationalized. Diverting m developers to the core team reduces our immediate productivity by roughly m/N (e.g., 5 to 50 percent). Remember that the more Software Capital we have, the faster, better, and cheaper it will be to write applications. And, in our methodology, the more applications we write, the more relevant Software Capital we amass.

By partitioning the teams, we hope to convert what would otherwise be the purely additive productivity of m developers:

$$P(t) = (N - m) + m + lower\text{-}order\ terms$$

into a multiplicative productivity that includes a monotonically increasing term L:

$$P'(t) = (N - m) \cdot (1 + L(m \cdot t)) + lower\text{-}order\ terms$$

---

[83] **stroustrup00**, section 23.5.1, pp. 714–715, specifically p. 714

Figure 0-58a illustrates the productivity profile associated with a typical application-only development team. Given N developers, an initial productivity rate roughly proportional to N increases with experience over time until an increasing cost of ownership begins to reduce marginal productivity.

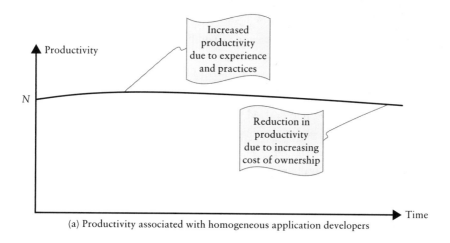

(a) Productivity associated with homogeneous application developers

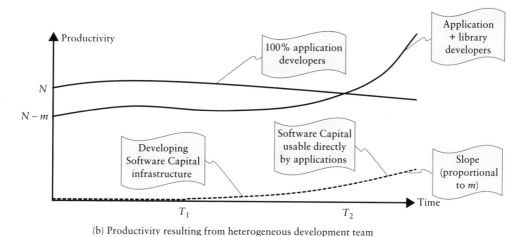

(b) Productivity resulting from heterogeneous development team

Figure 0-58: Improved productivity due to a heterogeneous development team

If instead we allocate m developers to serve as a shared resource (Figure 0-58b), the rate of productivity is initially proportionally lower.[84]

At some later time T_1, Software Capital that is directly useful to application developers becomes available and continues to grow at a rate roughly proportional to m. The productivity of the remaining developers, however, begins to increase superlinearly as more and more recurring solutions become available in near constant time.

At some yet later time T_2, the rate of productivity of the heterogeneous team exceeds that of an otherwise identical homogeneous one. This superior productivity is primarily due to the availability of pre-existing fine-grained solutions and secondarily to reduced maintenance costs resulting from the well-factored (nonduplicative) common infrastructure.[85]

Not long after T_2, the overall amount of product created by the heterogeneous team surpasses what would have been produced by the homogeneous one, and there's no looking back!

So, how exactly do we begin the process? Initially, we have no Software Capital. In anticipation, the core team establishes the development environment and implements an initial substrate of essential (hierarchically reusable) foundation components. Application developers, as always, write whatever software is needed to make their applications work. As Figure 0-59 illustrates, all program functionality implemented for Application 1 resides entirely within that application's own source code repository.[86]

---

[84] As long as the pool of developers is large enough, then we can segregate them into a large pool of application developers and a small pool of infrastructure developers and groom them appropriately.

[85] Based on a variety of empirically observable parameters, as yet unpublished formal models developed by Thomas Marshall (see section 2.16) help to quantify the expected increase in overall productivity due to this bilateral developer partitioning.

[86] Note that this proposed workflow in no way precludes use of standardized, third-party, and open-source software.

Application 1

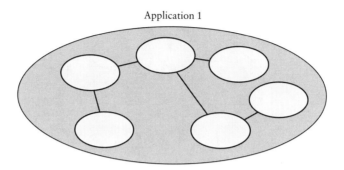

Figure 0-59: The first application gets no help.

Using this first application almost as a divining rod, the core team identifies potentially useful functionality, which the team then researches, generalizes, and reworks into a baseline reusable componentized framework, as illustrated in Figure 0-60. These new well-factored, finely graduated, granular components (section 0.4) based on real-world *bona fide* (and now documented) use cases (see Volume II, section 6.16) will then be made available for reintroduction back into the original application.

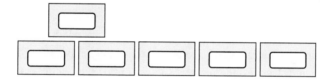

Figure 0-60: Software Capital reworked from the first application

Whether or not this new code is incorporated into a subsequent version of the original application is strictly a business decision; a revised version, v2, of Application 1 using the newly available Software Capital is illustrated in Figure 0-61. If and when the application is modified, it will exhibit increased performance, reduced maintenance cost, and inherent low-level interoperability with other similarly refactored software through the use of common *vocabulary* types (see Volume II, section 4.4). Either way, the new library software is immediately available for all future applications.

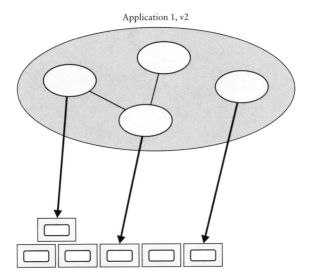

Figure 0-61: Optionally refactored first application

Figure 0-62 shows a second application that now makes limited but nontrivial use of the available Software Capital. The core team again mines this new application for generally useful functionality and builds upon the reusable framework. This core team does not merely rename and incorporate the existing source code as is but instead extracts, refactors, and rerenders the essential functionality as a hierarchy of fine-grained (hierarchically) reusable components (section 0.4), which it then distributes appropriately across our ever-growing, enterprise-wide repository.

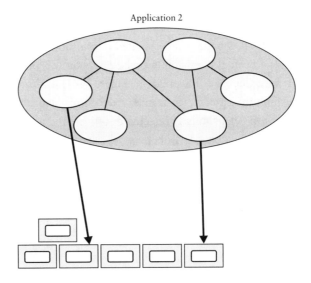

Figure 0-62: The second application gets some help.

When or even whether to fold the new Software Capital back into a revised version, v2, of Application 2 (illustrated in Figure 0-63) is, as ever, a business decision. In any event, all of the new ultra-high-quality, hierarchically reusable functionality is ready and waiting for Application 3, as illustrated in Figure 0-64. As one can plainly see, developing Software Capital is an ongoing effort.

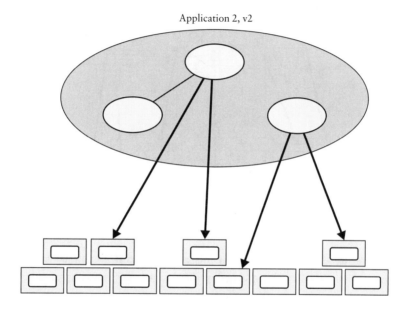

Application 2, v2

Figure 0-63: Optionally refactored second application

Immediate business needs must always be the top priority. It is therefore imperative that the creation of reusable software never stand in the way of these needs. In fact, an application developer would be as foolish to risk delay by waiting for a reusable component to be completed as a reuse engineer would be to hurry the development of a complex component. Moreover, the order in which Software Capital is developed, in addition to being guided by business needs, is highly constrained by physical laws involving dependency (see section 1.8), testability (see section 2.14), and overall correctness (see Volume II, section 6.8, and all of Volume III). To be successful in both the short and long terms, each of these two distinct development efforts must be allowed to co-exist and operate synergistically but also independently.[87]

---

[87] It is not uncommon for application groups in urgent need of specific reusable functionality to produce a pilot implementation for their own uses and then immediately turn it over to a core infrastructure team for subsequent refinement and eventual incorporation into more generally available Software Capital somewhere down the road. The hierarchical nature of the existing Software Capital along with its effective use, however, lead to prototype implementations that naturally embody largely new reusable features rather than overlapping or duplicative ones.

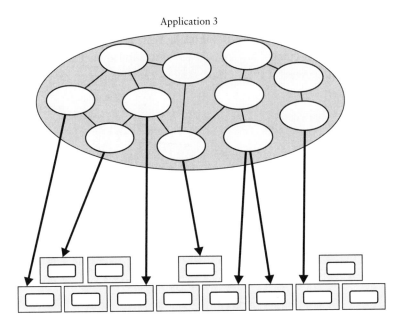

Figure 0-64: The third application is facilitated.

If we had to wait several years for this approach to demonstrate value, it would be of little practical interest. By the construction discussed here, however, such is clearly not the case. Because the units of functionality are quantized as fine-grained components, we can make new capital available as often as we care to release it (see section 2.15). And, since the defined behavior of these ultra-stable components (almost) never changes incompatibly (see Volume II, section 5.5), application developers do not risk instability by adopting such partial solutions incrementally.

To again drive home the benefit of our *recursively adaptive* approach for effective development throughout an enterprise, assume that we have the beginnings of a fairly robust repository of partial architectural solutions that we have accumulated over some time. Suppose we now find a need for a new solution similar to some existing one X, but whose realization would require an incompatible change to one of its deeply nested subsolutions *u*, as illustrated in Figure 0-65a.

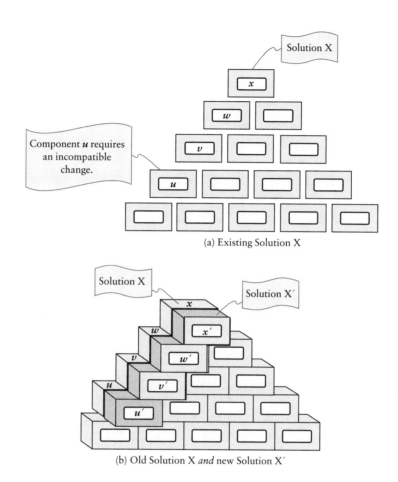

(a) Existing Solution X

(b) Old Solution X *and* new Solution X′

Figure 0-65: The incremental cost of doing business

Rather than modify **u** in place or duplicate the entire subtree rooted in **x**, we instead thought-fully re-create[88] components **u′**, **v′**, **w′**, and ultimately **x′** — each primed version having well-defined, additional *useful* behavior (and typically similar respective physical dependencies), as in Figure 0-65b. The incremental cost to create **x′** is, of course, just a tiny fraction of that needed to create **x** originally, yet there is absolutely no loss in stability nor the rampant duplication of

---

[88] This "re-creation" might sound like code duplication, but — on the contrary — it is isolating the small number of fine-grained components whose functionality needs to change; see also section 3.5.6.

code that would have resulted had we copied the entire Solution X subsystem. Both time to market and ongoing maintenance costs are reduced dramatically. In short, we can have it all!

As the process of accumulating reusable functionality continues, more and more highly leverageable, well-integrated functionality is available for use in applications from their inception. As Figure 0-66 suggests, developers will become increasingly productive, and with each success, the scope of new projects will gradually increase beyond anything that could reasonably have been considered using classical methods (Figure 0-66a). This new-found ambition is a direct consequence of both the *ease of use* and the unparalleled high performance (both space and speed) that an appropriate investment in Software Capital delivers. Over time, a mature infrastructure capable of efficiently supporting many sophisticated applications becomes a reality (Figure 0-66b).

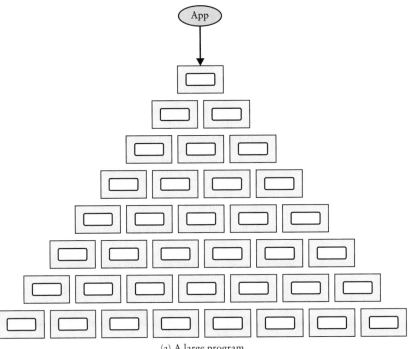

(a) A large program

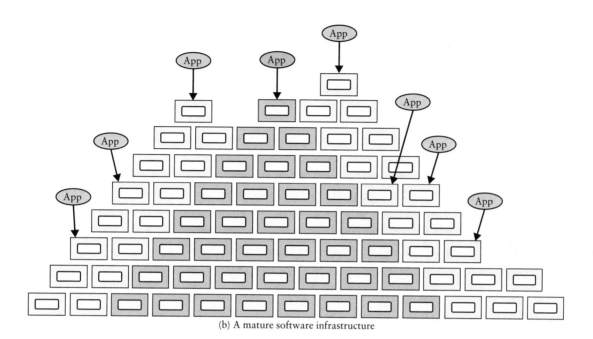

(b) A mature software infrastructure

Figure 0-66: A mature infrastructure efficiently supports many large programs.

Application developers are often domain experts who also have a good understanding of how to assemble software to produce the desired product. Without a dedicated team of library developers, however, each application developer would have to learn the details of a variety of specific software disciplines, which would interfere with their primary focus of developing useful products. Creating Software Capital serves to establish specialized in-house software expertise that application developers can exploit. For example, a high-performance multithreaded queuing system might take a single library developer several (perhaps many) months to implement properly. Yet that developer, once the software has been released, can serve as a specialized "in-house" expert resource to application and library developers alike.

Given a sizable development team, specific expertise of individuals within both the library community and the application community will serve to improve both quality and productivity. Moreover, specialists in documentation, testing, and tools will be needed to serve as reviewers, mentors, and consultants to other library developers. At least for large-scale development, the era of needing only fungible (Renaissance) programmers has passed!

Let us now try to visualize our hierarchically reusable repository of Software Capital several years hence. Figure 0-67 shows the many versions of many applications and products that led to the creation of this hierarchically organized repository and now depend on it. Because it evolved as part of building product, the history of business needs leading to our current development environment will have been well-reflected in the software repository we are postulating. The intricate and time-consuming tasks associated with partitioning many of the more complex subsolutions will have been completed long ago.[89]

---

[89] Note that this ambitious conjecture (and, in fact, even parts of this very text) date back to the late 1990s. I presented my first technical conference on Software Capital in Sydney, Australia, in the summer of 1998, and the prodigious value proposition that I then envisioned has long since been realized — e.g., at Bloomberg LP.

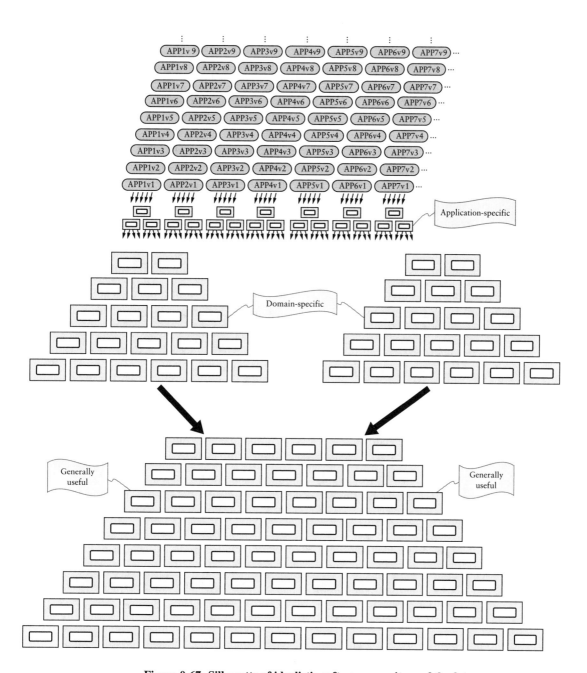

Figure 0-67: Silhouette of idealistic software repository of the future

0.11   The Need for Vigilance

The goal of reusable software is to be *reused* wherever "appropriate," and human beings — not computers — will make that determination:

> We conjecture that the barriers to reuse are not on the producer's side, but on the consumer side. If a software engineer, a potential consumer of standardized components, perceives it to be more expensive to find a component that meets his need, and so verify, than to write one anew, a new, duplicative component will be written. Notice we said *perceives* above. It does not matter what the true cost of reconstruction is.
>
> —Van Snyder (1995)[90]

To be sure, the "customers" of an enterprise-wide repository of Software Capital are application developers. It is precisely this group of individuals that we *must* satisfy if we are to justify such a substantial investment. From an engineering perspective, it is essential that we deliver the more tangible measures of quality (e.g., correctness, performance, portability). From a psychological perspective, however, the degree to which our reusable software is in fact *reused* will also be governed by criteria that is often highly subjective.

For a variety of reasons (both real and imagined), people are often unwilling to use software developed by others. Although often justified, this phenomenon — collectively referred to as the *not-invented-here* syndrome — can unfairly rob an organization of its long-term potential to reduce development time and cost while substantially improving quality. We have found — particularly when working with highly competent (and, not coincidentally, highly opinionated) developers — that legislation alone does not guarantee reuse. In practice, the benefits of reuse will be achieved only by writing software that application developers genuinely *want* to use.

Software engineering, like any other engineering practice, is a cost-benefit proposition. For any given software task, we should be able to place a value on an adequate solution and also determine the premium we are willing to pay for a "better," albeit more expensive, one. From a given application's perspective, sometimes all that is needed is an adequate solution. For example, if an application is inherently I/O-bound, there might be little added business value in coming up with an ultra-high performance in-memory data structure that further reduces the

---

[90] **brooks95**, Chapter 17, section "What About Reuse?," pp. 222–223

almost negligible CPU usage. In such cases, the premium that this application is willing to pay for "better" software is (or should be) essentially zero.

When designing Software Capital, however, there is no such thing as adequate. From a potential client's perspective, the *easier-to-understand*, *easier-to-use*, *higher-performing*, *more portable*, and *more reliable* we can make our software, the more potentially valuable it *could* be. Though there is considerable extra cost in building Software Capital, said cost would not be borne by any individual application. A single *good* solution that can be used across a variety of applications will be manifestly more cost-effective overall than a host of merely *adequate* ones created independently ad hoc (per application) if and as needed.

So, how good does Software Capital have to be? We might look to other industries for guidance. In the construction industry, for example, the goal is to build houses that are good — i.e., good enough to withstand *almost* any eventuality. No reputable construction company would admit to building anything less. Still, construction is a business. Clearly, houses could be built more sturdily with higher-quality fixtures, and more time could be spent attending to detail. In this sense, construction, like most industries, is far more akin to application development than a firm-wide repository of hierarchically reusable software.

Recall that the goal of Software Capital is not mere reusability but actual reuse.[91] Given the choice between using an unfamiliar and potentially suboptimal (let alone substandard) part or crafting their own, many software developers will automatically choose the latter. Therefore, even the *perception* that our Software Capital might be suspect can severely reduce the extent of its use.[92] Moreover, there must be some affirmative benefit that overrides our natural tendency

---

[91] According to Stroustrup, a component is not reusable unless it is usable (i.e., it works) and until someone has "reused" it (see **stroustrup00**, section 23.5.1, pp. 714–715, specifically p. 714).

[92] In his third (centennial) edition of *The C++ Programming Language* (2000), Stroustrup makes several more important observations/recommendations regarding the adoption of standard components (see **stroustrup00**, section 23.5.1, pp. 714–715):

- The "components group" must actively promote its components.
  - Traditional documentation is not sufficient.
  - Tutorials and other mechanisms that allow potential users to find a component and understand why it might be of help are required.
  - Activities associated with marketing and education must also be undertaken.
- The "components group" must work closely and directly with application developers.
  - "Components group" developers will need to allocate time for consulting with application developers.
  - Internships ("bootcamp") will allow for the transformation of information into (and out of) the "components group."

to "write it ourselves." That is, we must go beyond "good"; most successful developers (this author included) believe they too can write good software.

Returning to our nonlinear text-partitioning analogy (section 0.8), introducing a human factor is like adding a probabilistic coefficient to finding each solution in the cache. For a variety of aesthetic reasons, otherwise sound software might exhibit a coefficient considerably less than unity, precluding its otherwise valid adoption. Avoiding subjective deterrents — such as poor rendering — to otherwise appropriate reuse requires vigilance beyond what one might otherwise predict. Simply put, neatness counts!

By the same token, well-designed, well-implemented solutions (such as the containers in the STL) can and, in practice, often do achieve a coefficient of reuse that substantially exceeds unity! Application developers know that a familiar, portable, reliable, high-performance solution is compelling, even if using that solution requires nontrivial effort to adapt it to the need at hand. The more we are able to widen the attractiveness of each of our solutions and subsolutions (see Volume II, section 5.7), the fewer of them will be required to satisfy a vast majority of needs.

Clearly, the level of quality needed to ensure the unmitigated success of Software Capital does not reconcile well with conventional business models (e.g., in construction and manufacturing) primarily because the additional work that is done is ongoing and must be applied to each individual instance. The value returned by investing disproportionate amounts of time and materials on any one product in those industries (as in ours for a given application) is simply not warranted.

A better, more appropriate analogy for Software Capital would be the effort expended to develop the special paper and plates used by the Bureau of Printing and Engraving to mint the various denominations of U.S. currency. The quality of U.S. currency is, by design, irreproducible. The U.S. government makes no attempt to economize in such matters nor to hide the extent of its efforts. Like Software Capital, when it comes to the sanctity of our economic infrastructure, failure is simply not an option. Publication of such overwhelming measures further serves to discourage even the thought of inappropriate duplication (leaving reuse the only rational option). When you consider the alternative illustrated in Figure 0-68 (compared to the much more desirable scenario depicted in Figure 0-67), this stalwart, up-front effort does not seem so bad.

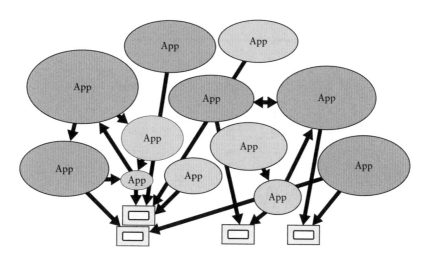

Figure 0-68: The opposite of organization is chaos!

Developing software that is actually reused is neither easy nor cheap. In addition to developing the software itself, the core team must also actively organize and promote a software development environment conducive to reuse. The core team will be responsible for providing supplementary documentation, training, tools, and consulting that minimize barriers to entry and ensure that widespread reuse becomes a reality. The good news is that the relatively high cost of successful Software Capital can be rationalized to "nonbelievers" because it will naturally be amortized over many versions of many applications (recall Figure 0-11c, section 0.3) as reprised here in Figure 0-69. The true benefits, however, are measured primarily in reduced time to market for future applications and products (see Figure 0-54, section 0.9), and secondarily in the reduced cost of ownership due to defects and maintenance (section 0.9). The challenge, however, remains to ensure that the software is, in fact, reused.

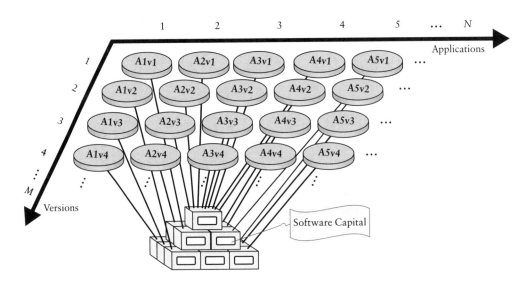

Figure 0-69: Amortized cost of Software Capital

Bottom line: For Software Capital to reach its full potential, it must be *perceived* by other developers as being far better than what they (or anyone else) could do in any practical time frame. To achieve this ambient belief throughout the development community, Software Capital often has to be *too* good! That is, the kind of reusable software we are advocating is typically of higher quality (i.e., is easier to understand and use while delivering higher performance on more platforms with fewer defects) than what could normally be rationalized for use by any one person, project, or application. It is the delineation of the organization, process, and engineering techniques we use for developing this kind of "too-good" software to which this book aspires.

0.12   Summary

Effective software development on a large scale doesn't just happen; it requires organization, planning, experience, and skill. Achieving, on an enterprise-wide scale, the degree of long-term success to which we aspire requires some significant adjustments in the most fundamental common practices used to create both library and application software. This introductory chapter illustrates the high-level goals, thought processes, and design trade-offs that lead to large-scale solutions. This hybrid of classical and modern approaches forms a cohesive methodology — one that we believe to be the most effective one known for delivering high-quality applications over the long term.

0.1 The Goal: Faster, Better, Cheaper!

The business objective for developing software is three-dimensional, involving schedule, product, and cost. There is much pain associated with industrial software development today. The symptoms include the unpredictability of development, the dangers associated with reuse, the enormous build times and executable sizes of what should be modest programs, and the abject fear people experience when trying to make even trivial enhancements to existing products. The bottom line is that the trade-offs among schedule, product, and cost are not satisfactory.

To achieve gains along all three dimensions, we need to move the design space itself. To make that happen, some output of the development process (i.e., some portion of the software produced) must somehow *feed back* into that process. Only then can the efficiency of the development process grow without bound. The challenge is to find an organization and a process that admits such feedback through actual software reuse. Our solution is a process that addresses the organization of both the software and the developers who create it.

Without being too specific at first, we postulate the existence of such a process and its idyllic state after several years of use. Virtually every component or subsystem we might need is already available and waiting to be reused (e.g., see Figure 0-67, section 0.10). By that point, this "hypothetical" development process has evolved to the point where implementing an application means having to do little more than finding and assembling the needed pieces. We claim that this process is not only possible but, in the long term, optimal. We sometimes borrow the phrase *long-term greedy*[93] to characterize our approach. When it comes to developing software on a large scale, our experience tells us that being long-term greedy is good business.

0.2 Application vs. Library Software

We observe that application and library development are substantially different, each resulting from different goals and pressures. Application development is essentially top-down, whereas the development of library software is primarily bottom-up. In application development, there is a need to solve a specific problem, get the job done quickly, and perhaps change the code later if needed. In the case of library development, the goal is to get the job done right, solve the problem more generally, and avoid making subsequent changes. The people involved in developing these respective kinds of software typically have different motivations, different temperaments, and different skill sets.

---

[93] **lindskoog99**

Application developers are rewarded for getting their current job done as quickly and effectively as possible. Hence, it is easy to understand why application source code is less stable than library code. Given that the primary focus of application development is to solve a particular problem quickly, such software will typically evolve over time. With each successive iteration, source code, perhaps even functionality, will change. The best application code is designed to be malleable.

Good library writers, on the other hand, have a quite different mind-set. Because library developers are typically less proximate to the revenue stream, they can benefit from certain latitudes rarely enjoyed by their application counterparts. Library software tends to live a relatively long life, which — by definition — spans the lifetimes of all applications that depend on it. When writing a library component, a competent library developer does not opt for an easy implementation that results in an interface that is hard to use or otherwise inconveniences the client. To the contrary, a good library developer will always trade off ease of implementation for ease of use.

0.3 Collaborative vs. Reusable Software

Large software problems are routinely carved up into subproblems that, if solved independently and then recombined, would exactly solve the problem as originally posed. Such a minimal decomposition, however, often leads to brittle software, characterized by excessive irregularities across tightly interdependent interface boundaries ("cracked plate"), leaving little room for change. Simple modifications to monolithic application-level functionality ("toaster toothbrush") might require us to revisit the implementations below these interfaces, increasing cost and putting reliability at risk (see Figure 0-9, section 0.3).

Collaborative interfaces tend to have a large *surface-to-volume ratio*, making independent understanding — never mind reuse — of the behavior of individual subsystems more difficult than it need be. This tight semantic coupling forces changes in one module to be reflected in another, blurring modularity by distributing design decisions across module boundaries. If we instead emphasize dividing our system along more natural boundaries, we carve out more regular pieces of software. These simpler, more familiar subsystems are not only easier to explain and to understand but are also more likely to be reusable "as is" as higher-level requirements inevitably change.

Classical reuse involves the reuse of a particular type, container, subsystem, etc., without regard for any of the parts used to implement it. A cracked plate or a `ToasterToothbrush` is not particularly reusable. Constructing a `Toaster` with a hook and a `Toothbrush` with a hole is a lighthearted example of collaboration characterized by awareness of peer parts. Our ability to create reusable pieces that are easily described (e.g., `Semicircle`, `Rectangle`, `Square`, `Triangle`) increases our chances that such pieces can and will be used without modification. Still, this level of reuse is not sufficient.

0.4 Hierarchically Reusable Software

To achieve maximal reuse, we must insist on maximal factoring at both a logical and physical level. A `ToasterToothbrush` can be factored into a `Toaster`, a `Toothbrush`, and an `Adapter` used to affix the `Toothbrush` to the `Toaster`. Adding a bit of glue gives us back the desired custom part (see Figure 0-12, section 0.3). This first level of factoring, however, achieves only classical reuse. To achieve *hierarchical reuse*, we must proactively decompose the `Toaster`, `Adapter`, and `Toothbrush` into their respective constituent parts (`Case` and `Chassis`, `Arm` and `Joint`, and `Handle` and `Bristles`). Only then can we realize the benefit of creating a `ToasterScrubbrush` in terms of a `Toaster`, `Adapter`, `Handle`, `Bristles`, and glue (see Figure 0-20b, section 0.4).

0.5 Malleable vs. Stable Software

Good software is either *malleable* (the behavior is easy to change) or *stable* (the behavior does not change). The hierarchical composition of small physical modules, which we call *components*, is a key aspect of stability. Consistently achieving such small modules requires aggressive factoring. For example, if we create a function having six parameters, there is a good chance we missed one. To add a parameter later, we would be forced either to modify the existing function, thus potentially violating the *open-closed principle* (section 0.5), or to create an entirely new function from scratch (duplicating unnecessarily large bodies of code). Had we instead created six functions having just one parameter each, and composed them, we could subsequently easily add a seventh, without affecting clients of the other six.

It is imperative that we acknowledge that only stable software can be reusable. Stability is necessary to ensure that assumptions made at higher levels are not subsequently invalidated. Instead of incompatibly altering the behavior of a reusable component, it is sometimes better to create a similar one that operates side by side — either temporarily or permanently — along with the original. Mutable software (ideally designed to be *malleable*), on the other hand, most appropriately resides at the highest levels and must *not* be shared, or the problem becomes over-constrained (e.g., `FlattenedGreenToasterToothbrushWithFlag`; Figure 0-31, section 0.5). Note that software that is neither stable nor malleable is generally undesirable.

The need for fine-grained factoring goes beyond just stability and testability. To realize *hierarchical reuse*, we must make sure to package each of our individual solutions within separate physical modules. Recall that Dijkstra argued for a fine-grained hierarchical decomposition, Parnas for encapsulating individual design decisions behind well-designed interfaces that communicate information only via simple (e.g., scalar) data types, and Myers for ensuring that those interfaces are well documented to aid in human comprehension. It is only by limiting our functional content to small (finely graduated, granular, and well-documented) physical modules that we are able to achieve paying in link time and disk space for only what we need. Moreover, it is only through this aggressive factoring that we will be able to capitalize on reuse at every level of abstraction — i.e., other than just those widely advertised for public consumption.

There are two distinct but highly interrelated kinds of design: *logical design* and *physical design*. Logical design addresses the functional aspects of the software we develop. Physical design addresses how we package our source code into files and libraries (e.g., see Figure 0-15, section 0.4). Physical design plays a crucial role when contemplating software of any substantial size. In particular, poor physical design can quickly lead to software that has cycles among its physical modules, and cyclically interdependent modules are virtually unmaintainable on a large scale. Contrary to what you might believe, physical design is a prerequisite to logical design and must be considered from the moment the initial problem is decomposed into subproblems that will admit independent solutions that then combine to solve the initial problem (and perhaps others). The importance of sound physical design in large development efforts cannot be overemphasized.

0.7 Physically Uniform Software: The Component

In our methodology, sound physical design is predicated on organizing logical content into coherent physical modules, called *components,* that are both uniform in structure and relatively small. In addition, we want these modules to be both *finely graduated* and *granular*. By *finely graduated*, we mean that the (vertical) "distance" between levels of abstraction is kept small. By *granular*, we mean that the (lateral) "area" of domain functionality is kept small. This fine-grained physical factoring decreases the likelihood that any particular module would need to change in response to a change in requirements. Moreover, fine-grained modularity provides an efficient means of addition via recombination of existing pieces (compared with creating the entire subfunctionality from scratch). Lastly, when software is well-factored and packaged within components, thorough testing is facilitated.

A component, as we define it, is our fundamental atomic unit of both *logical* and *physical* design. In C++, a component consists of a header (.h) file and an implementation (.cpp) file and should always have an associated test-driver (.t.cpp) file. We require that a component be relatively small, comprising a manageable amount of *logical* content that can be thoroughly tested from a single standalone test-driver file. A component has a well-*defined* interface and ideally a well-*designed* (e.g., easy to understand and use) interface. Finally, a well-*designed* component is designed to be *testable*.

In many ways, components, like the bricks of a house, are more similar than different. Although, microscopically, each brick is *logically* unique, all of the bricks have the same macroscopic *physical* form. At a distance, the only characteristic that distinguishes one brick from another is its relative position in the physical hierarchy. Bricks at a higher level can do more, not because they are bigger or contain other bricks but because they *depend on* other bricks to which they may delegate. Hence, bricks at higher physical levels, like managers in a company, have greater scope than the individual contributors under them.

Variety might be the spice of life, but it has no place when it comes to rendering software. Providing a regular physical form to capture our logical content is essential. Requiring uniformity in the physical packaging of our logical content greatly simplifies human cognition, facilitates the creation of effective development and support tools, improves the interoperability of proprietary subsystems, and enhances *developer mobility* throughout the enterprise.

0.8 Quantifying Hierarchical Reuse: An Analogy

As an elaborate analogy, we likened software application development to an optimization problem involving the formatting of words of text onto a page of fixed width. A brute-force approach of recursively solving every left/right division of text (analogous to pure top-down design in software) would run in exponential time. We observed, however, that, despite first appearances, there are simply *not* an exponentially large number of unique (i.e., useful) sub-problems to solve. Similarly, we claimed that the number of distinct partial subsolutions in software is, or should be, quite small (relatively speaking).

We then observed several other refinements to the optimization problem that have parallels with our software development methodology. The first refinement illustrated the importance of the stability of solutions so that they can be used in place rather than copied (copy-and-paste reuse). The second refinement stressed the importance of lookup speed. Just as in a mature software environment, much of the work of application development will be in finding the appropriate prefabricated solution to use.

For this analogy to hold, we observed that software subproblems encountered in different parts of an application decomposition would need to be sufficiently similar that they would admit "as-is" reuse. Achieving this goal, at a minimum, requires fine-grained factoring, a uniform physical rendering, and a canonical interface. Moreover, software intended for reuse, in addition to other more objective quality metrics, must be "attractive" (e.g., have crisp documentation, be aesthetically pleasing) or developers will choose not to use it. Lastly, design for reuse should aim to cover the intended domain with a suite of discrete, distinct components as opposed to a continuum where one component is perhaps only subtly different from another — especially for *vocabulary types* (see Volume II, section 4.4). Maximizing the probability of reuse is covered in Volume II, section 5.7.

0.9 Software Capital

From an enterprise perspective, we would like as much application code as practicable pushed down into stable libraries where it can be factored, refined, made more robust, and reused independently by future applications. Although it is not always possible to ensure that reusable software is available from the outset, the goal is to ensure that potentially reusable software is, on a regular basis, refactored and *demoted* (see section 3.5.3) to lower levels in the physical hierarchy, where it can be shared more widely. This sort of continuous-refactoring approach to software development is regarded by many as the state of the art. Given that our express goal is reuse, it behooves us to become more *library-centric* and see where that emphasis leads us.

By isolating common knowledge into an easily accessible software repository, we enable current, future, and possibly even past projects to exploit our knowledge base and deliver new functionality far more quickly than would otherwise be possible. This proprietary software repository becomes a capital asset of the firm that pays increasing dividends over time. A collection of well-engineered proprietary software that facilitates development across one or more application domains or product lines is what we mean by the term *Software Capital*. The primary motivation for aggressively creating Software Capital is to reduce time to market for future applications and products (see Figure 0-54, section 0.9). Improving quality, while reducing development and maintenance costs, is a welcome collateral benefit.

0.10 Growing the Investment

The implicit goal of growing our Software Capital asset is to obtain a viable, finely graduated, granular partition of essentially all relevant subsolutions. What is important is that we consistently decompose our applications to arrive at precisely the same subsolutions and — over time — realize running software far more quickly and reliably than would otherwise have been possible. Software Capital is characterized by relevant, prefabricated components that are easy to understand, easy to use, high performing, portable, and reliable (see Figure 0-55, section 0.9). Routine peer review, along with thorough testing, is how we consistently achieve these dimensions of quality. Only a small fraction of proprietary software belongs in this enterprise-wide infrastructure, but that tiny fraction supplants what would otherwise be a much larger body of disparate, duplicative, and incompatible solutions having relatively low performance, poor reliability, and exorbitantly higher maintenance costs.

As it turns out, Software Capital handily improves on all three dimensions of the schedule/product/budget design space at once. Moreover, because a significant amount of faster/better/cheaper is inherited, applications assembled from Software Capital will enjoy nontrivial benefits in all three dimensions, regardless of how the importance of these respective dimensions are weighted.

The first few applications will derive relatively little benefit from the Software Capital being mined from these early efforts. Additional development of capital will be guided by observing recurring business needs. Over time, proportionally more and more of the development effort will focus on application-level functionality. We note that, in a well-designed and mature software-development enterprise, almost all code that is developed is unique to the application being implemented, with only a relatively minor ongoing reinvestment in extending this important firm-wide asset we call Software Capital.

0.11 The Need for Vigilance

Developers are often justifiably skeptical of software developed elsewhere. For reuse to be effective, the software to be reused must be known by all to be of "unreasonably" good quality. If the worst thing a disgruntled developer can say about our enterprise-wide repository of Software Capital is that it is "too good" and "not worth the effort to write" but — since it is already there — will (of course) use it, we know we have achieved an important aspect of the necessary level of quality for successful reuse.

Without viable Software Capital, however, the resulting explosion of duplicative code repeatedly created to replace the missing reusable software might dominate, and even overwhelm, the overall development effort (e.g., see Figure 0-68, section 0.11). Given that the costs of developing library software are amortized over the numerous versions of the applications that use it (see Figure 0-69, section 0.11), we can appreciate that the perceived cost to produce it is typically substantially higher as well. As it turns out, however, the actual cost of *not* producing Software Capital is far higher, and that does not even take into account its primary benefit, which is reducing time to market for future applications and products (see Figure 0-54, section 0.9).

Throughout this chapter, we have introduced some of the underlying engineering and economic realities that have motivated us to develop and use what is arguably the most effective approach available for developing high-quality software — quickly and economically — on an enterprise scale. The rest of the book simply describes in detail how to be successful. All of the design, implementation, and testing techniques presented throughout this three-volume book, apply to large-scale systems. We have also seen that consistent use of all of the practices we advocate produces enormous benefits (e.g., reliability, maintainability, performance) within systems of even modest size.

In short, this book is about how to be increasingly successful at developing applications in a production environment. In the chapters that follow, we will walk through the disciplines of a mature and proven process for C++ software development, with the understanding that the applicability is not limited to any particular standardized version of C++, or even C++ itself. Every programming language — especially those that assemble independently compiled units — can benefit from applying these essential software engineering principles.

1

Compilers, Linkers, and Components

This book is about developing software on a large scale and, in particular, about how our component-based software engineering methodology leverages the intrinsic properties of components (as we define them) to produce optimal software solutions. First and foremost, a component is a *physical* concept (section 0.6). No matter what kind of *logical* design we bring to bear on the solution to a given problem, we *must* render that logical design as C++ source code, stored in one or more *files*. These files will be converted, by the C++ compiler and linker, into executable code. From this perspective, all renderings of C++ designs are *physical* designs, whether the designer has considered that aspect or not. Our approach to design therefore necessarily addresses physical as well as logical design, along with their inherent tensions and serendipitous synergies.

To understand and benefit fully from our design methodology, one must be familiar with several background topics related to physical design, which we review in this chapter. In particular, we focus on the physical aspects of software, culminating with a characterization of several important fundamental physical properties. We explain in detail the process and tools (e.g., preprocessor, compiler, linker) involved in creating and building C++ programs. This knowledge will, in turn, enhance our ability to make sound physical design decisions affecting objectively measurable characteristics such as compile time, link time, run time, and program size. Along the way, we will introduce the terminology and minimal notation (see section 1.7) that we use routinely, both throughout this book and in our daily work.

Once we have a thorough knowledge of the essential tools of our trade, we will commence the transition from "unstructured" development to component-based development. Using the basics of the C++ language, we will learn to understand, appreciate, and instill, in familiar `.h`/`.cpp`[1] pairs, important properties that will give life to the *components* that power our high-performance, reliable, and immensely scalable solutions. Although it is possible, in some sense, to explain what we mean by a "component" in just a few sentences, any such definition, no matter how correct, would still be of only limited utility. Before providing a formal definition and exposition of components in their ultimate context (see section 2.6), we will spend the remainder of this chapter understanding the many ramifications of these most basic units of physical design. By the time we get to the formalities in Chapter 2, we will have the background needed to appreciate them.[2]

---

[1] C++ source files have the suffix `.cpp` by default on Windows platforms. We originally adopted `.cpp` for that reason and because many development organizations maintained significant amounts of C-language source code, which traditionally ends in a `.c` suffix.

[2] Although we go into considerable low-level detail early in this chapter, much of the higher-level background material concisely reprised in the latter half of this chapter is explained at greater length in the early chapters (especially Chapters 3 and 4) of **lakos96**.

1.1   Knowledge Is Power: The Devil Is in the Details

There is quite a lot of material to cover in this chapter; still, it's probably a good idea to start with something familiar and not particularly intimidating. We will therefore follow our C heritage and begin with what has become a long-standing traditional introductory example.

1.1.1   "Hello World!"

C++, like C, Ada, Fortran, and Cobol before it (and Java since), belongs to a class of languages where separately "compiled" discrete software modules are somehow "linked" together to form a runnable program. Even the most trivial C++ programs are created and assembled in this way. Consider the familiar "Hello World!" program shown in Figure 1-1.[3]

```
// main.cpp
#include <iostream>
int main(int, const char *[])
{
    std::cout << "Hello World!" << std::endl;
    return 0;
}
```

Figure 1-1: Familiar "Hello World!" program for the C++ language

---

[3] Although it always worked on vertically all platforms (early GCC being a noted exception), it was not until C++11 that std::endl was mandated by the standard to be declared when including (just) <iostream> (instead of also having to include <ostream>). Current wisdom, however, generally recommends using '\n' instead of std::cout to avoid forcing a flush in a context where it might be supererogatory.

Although one might be tempted to call this a single-file program, it is in fact composed of the tiny application part that you see in Figure 1-1 and a comparatively huge (reusable) library part, the latter being the `iostream` facility within the C++ Standard Library.[4]

Although we might have little control over a particular vendor's implementation of the Standard Library, a thorough understanding of how our software is built in contemporary programming environments will prove invaluable in the design and implementation of the applications and libraries we create when developing software on a large scale. This understanding will also help us to assess, in advance, the viability of depending on specific open-source and third-party libraries.

This book presents many techniques and guidelines that have evolved through our considerable experience with creating C++ libraries and applications in an industrial setting.[5] We feel strongly that being successful in architecting — let alone developing — large C/C++ systems requires a thorough understanding of the low-level details of the language. There is a big difference between "Hello World!" and large-scale software; to a large extent, that difference — and the devil — is in the details.

1.1.2   Creating C++ Programs

The first stop on our journey toward creating successful applications is in understanding the details of the language itself. Let us now consider the simple `main` function that calls the *free* (nonmember) function `op` defined in a separate file:

---

[4] To better understand quantitatively the relative contributions of the *application* (i.e., the user's `main.cpp`) and the reusable library software supplied by the C++ Standard Library (not to mention that of the underlying OS), let's walk through the various artifacts of compilation on a typical platform, such as my new (c. 2016) Toshiba laptop running Cygwin with GCC 5.4.0. The size of the application source text, `main.cpp`, is just 166 bytes. When the `#include` directive is incorporated, the intermediate text on my laptop (`main.i` file) expands to more than 443K bytes! The resulting `main.o` file, however, is just 2.5K bytes, which — by today's standards — is still fairly small. The resulting executable program, however, is far more substantial. There are two distinct ways to link executables — *statically* and *dynamically*. *Statically linked* means that *all* of the needed information is incorporated into a single executable file; *dynamically linked* means that there are wide swaths of code that can be shared across separate processes. For this example built on my Toshiba laptop, the dynamically linked executable was roughly 64K bytes, whereas the all-inclusive — statically linked — executable image was roughly 10 megabytes! A summary of this data, along with another, similar platform (GCC 6.2.1 on a VM running on a MacBook Pro) is provided here for reference (see also Figure 1-4, section 1.2.1):

Artifact	Toshiba Z30-C Laptop	MacBook Pro Laptop
`main.cpp`	126 bytes	126 bytes
`main.i`	443,892 bytes	641,974 bytes
`main.o`	2,715 bytes	2,704 bytes
`a.out` (shared)	64,958 bytes	9,084 bytes
`a.out` (static)	10,424,051 bytes	2,065,128 bytes

[5] Our core libraries have been open-sourced for some time now; see **bde14**.

```
// main.cpp                          // op.cpp
int op(int);  // BAD IDEA            double op(int arg)
int main(void)                       {
{
    int result = op(10);                 // ...
    // ...
}                                    }
```

To use `op()` in `main()`, a declaration for `op()` must be visible within `main.cpp`. In the illustration above, we provided that declaration by writing it directly (locally) in `main.cpp`, which, as we are about to see, is problematic. At the time we first contemplated `main.cpp`, the return type of `op()` was `int` but has since evolved to `double`, as reflected in `op.cpp` (above). We won't catch this inconsistency at compile time and are not guaranteed by the C++ Standard that such errors will be detected at link time either. Hence, we might be in for an unpleasant surprise the next time we rebuild and *run* `main`.

Had the function *signature*[6] (as opposed to just the return type) changed, we would have caught the problem at link time, thanks to *C++ linkage*[7]:

```
// main.cpp                          // op.cpp
int op(int);  // BAD IDEA            int op(double arg)
int main(void)                       {
{
    int result = op(10);                 // ...
    // ...
}                                    }
```

Functions having C linkage, however, would conceal even this inconsistency until run time.

There are other inconsistencies that, in C++, are almost certain to go undetected until run time. For example, consider a local declaration of a global variable, `q`:

---

[6] A function's signature refers to its name along with the sequence of parameter types (but not its return type).

[7] Note that C++'s "type-safe" linkage ensures that the linker has access to the name, the parameter types, and (for class members) the cv-qualifiers of all functions (including operators). This access is typically implemented by encoding these attributes into the (compiled) function's name at the object-code level.

For example, a function declared as
```
double myFunction(const char *string, int length);
```
might, at the object-code level, receive a name something like `_Z10myFunctionPKci`, which (unlike C) is in no way assured to be portable across compiler vendors.

Functions in C++ cannot be overloaded based on return type alone. Hence, functions (ignoring function templates for now) are not required to propagate their return type to the linker, although some platforms may do so in the name of increased *quality of implementation* (QoI) — e.g., as a means to assist developers in finding their bugs at link time, rather than run time.

```
// main.cpp                          // q.cpp
extern int q; // BAD IDEA            double q = 7.5;
int main(void)
{
    int val = q;
    // ...
}
```

Notice that the type of the variable q is declared as an int in main.cpp but defined as a double in q.cpp. The compiler of main.cpp never sees the definition of q (located in q.cpp) and, by the time the linker gets involved, the actual type of the object q (i.e., double) is typically no longer available.

1.1.3   The Role of Header Files

As professional software developers, we strive to catch errors early in the development process, especially when those on other teams will be using our software. Instead of relying on clients to guess the signatures of our functions or the types of our global variables, it is our responsibility as library developers to supply them with a header file having the corresponding function or variable declarations. By including this header, our clients will catch many common usage errors at compile time, which is clearly preferable to catching them at link time or — worse yet — at run time:

```
// main.cpp              // op.h              // op.cpp
#include <op.h>          int op(double);     int op(double arg)
int main(void)                               {
{
    int result = op(10);                         // ...
    // ...
}                                            }
```

Notice that the op.cpp file above (wrongly) makes no reference to the corresponding .h file. Given that clients are always going to access externally defined entities via declarations in our header file (see section 1.11.1), we, as the authors of op.cpp, must also ensure that the declarations in the header file are consistent with their corresponding definitions. Having created a header file that is entirely independent of the implementation file, we again leave open the possibility of the two files becoming out of sync:

```
// main.cpp              // op.h              // op.cpp
#include <op.h>          int op(double);     double op(double arg)
int main(void)                               {
{
    int result = op(10);                         // ...
    // ...
}                                            }
```

Had the header file been included in the implementation file, the problem (in this particular instance) would have been detected as soon as `op.cpp` was compiled, and long before the code is ever made available to any client. We shall see later how careful adherence to our design principles prevents this and other, similar problems (e.g., mismatched signatures as opposed to just return types) that might otherwise arise as a result of separate compilation, and ultimately gives rise to our notion of a *component* (see sections 1.6 and 1.11).

1.2   Compiling and Linking C++

The process of building a C++ program naturally divides into two *main* phases. The first phase, referred to as the *compilation phase*,[8] itself encompasses both (1) the preprocessing of each source (`.cpp`) file along with all included header (`.h`) files into an intermediate representation, and (2) the translation of that representation into relocatable machine code, which is then placed in an object (`.o`) file. The second (main) phase will then combine these object files to form a cohesive program.

1.2.1   The Build Process: Using Compilers and Linkers

Most compilers provide switches that allow the result of intermediate phases to be observed directly. For example, the compiler can be directed to produce the result of the preprocessing phase (`.i` files), which can be useful for diagnosing problems with include files and macro expansion. The compiler's initial rendering of the object code can then be optimized to produce substantially reworked object code often capable of executing many times faster than would have occurred without this optimization phase. A compiler can usually also be directed to produce a listing of the assembly code (`.s` files) that corresponds to the object file generated.[9]

Inspection at this very low level can be used to verify suspected compiler and optimizer bugs as well as to understand in detail the machine-level overhead resulting from the use of higher-level language constructs.

---

[8] The compilation phase comprises nine intermediate phases defined in the C++ Standard.

[9] For example,

```
gcc -S filename.cpp
```

produces a *filename*.s file containing the generated assembly code.

```
gcc -E filename.cpp
```

shows the result of applying the preprocessor on standard output. Note that, although a lot is added to the source code of the preprocessed translation unit, not a lot, comparatively, is added to the translated assembly, especially when compiler optimizations are enabled.

Figure 1-2 illustrates how the preprocessor independently scans various `.cpp` files (`x1.cpp`, `x2.cpp`, `x3.cpp`, `x4.cpp`), in turn, and then, among other things, incorporates the text from each included `.h` file as indicated by `#include` preprocessor directives. Each included `.h` file is similarly scanned and `#include` directives nested within these headers are processed recursively. Conceptually, the resulting text forms an intermediate, source-level module called a *translation unit*, represented in Figure 1-2 as a file with a `.i` suffix (note that this `.i` file is hypothetical and not likely to be produced by a compiler unless specifically requested). This intermediate representation is then fed to the C++ compiler, which compiles the translation unit and produces a corresponding `.o` file containing the resulting object code.[10]

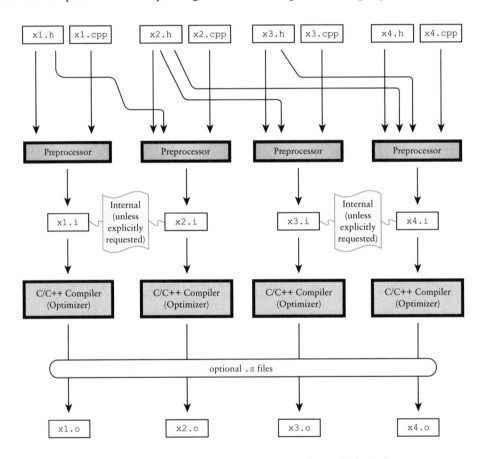

Figure 1-2: The compilation (preprocessor and translation) phase

---

[10] The `.o` suffix for object files is common in the POSIX family of operating systems, which includes Linux, Solaris, macOS, etc., which we will henceforth refer to collectively as *Unix platforms*. On Windows platforms, the `.obj` suffix is typically used.

In the second phase of the build process, known as the *link phase*, separately compiled .o files (some of which might be packaged into libraries) are fed to the linker to create an executable program. Figure 1-3 illustrates how each of the object files x1.o, x2.o, x3.o, and x4.o, generated in Figure 1-2, along with two additional libraries, namely, y.a and z.a, are linked to form an executable program.

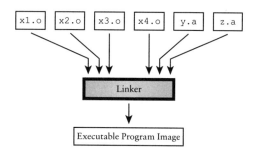

Figure 1-3: The link phase

An executable program image — *executable* for short — is derived from the function implementations in the .o files.[11] Each executable comprises (typically read-only) executable code (e.g., in the text segment[12]) and constant (i.e., immutable) data (e.g., in the rodata segment), both of which may be placed in read-only memory; it also provides space for mutable data of static storage duration (e.g., global variables) and, unless initialized explicitly, will (by default) be *zero initialized*[13] and then, typically, sequestered separately (e.g., in the

---

[11] The filename a.out is the default on Unix platforms, though typical executable names have no suffix. On Windows platforms, executable files have the .exe suffix by default.

[12] The precise terminology varies depending on platform (and we are admittedly showing a bias toward Unix). For example, sometimes this part of the executable is instead referred to as the .text *section*.

[13] What it means for an object to be *zero initialized* depends on the *kind* of type of that object: For fundamental numerical types, it means that the object receives the numerical value zero converted to that type; for pointer types, it means that it receives the pointer value corresponding to the literal 0 (and, as of C++11, that of nullptr). Note that, being a numerical type, the behavior of zero-initializing an enumeration — including one not having a named enumerator that would convert to the integer value zero — is defined and mirrors that of C.

bss[14] segment) where it can be more efficiently zeroed.[15,16] The memory to hold functions, constants, and global variables lasts for the entire duration of the execution of the program. For any reference to a function or global variable to refer correctly to its (one) definition, the entity must be assigned a unique (relocatable) address in the executable image. It is the responsibility of the linker, which builds the executable from separate object files, to assign these addresses, as the compiler does not have the global context necessary to make such assignments. On the other hand, the addresses for objects of all other storage durations are determined during the course of program execution and do not require linker involvement.

Throughout the compilation phase, the compiler processes a *single* translation unit for incorporation into a program. The use of header files provides a modular[17] way of informing the compiler of the existence of entities that might be shared across translation units. Many uses of such entities can be resolved locally by the compiler — especially those defined within the same translation unit as they are used. Other uses might refer to entities not defined within the same translation unit and, therefore, will need to be resolved later by the linker.

Each object file passed to the linker typically contains (1) definitions of symbols (e.g., functions, global variables) and (2) references to other symbols that are not defined within the translation unit. The linker attempts to resolve such undefined references in each object file by using definitions supplied by other object files. These definitions might, in turn, depend

---

[14] bss stands for *Basic Service Set, Block Started by Symbol*, or even *Better Save Space* (as some like to remember it by) since the bss segment (unlike the data segment) is not part of the executable image and therefore — apart from an indication of its numerical size — does not take up (proportional) space in the .o file.

[15] The memory "footprint" of a fundamental, pointer, or enumeration object that has been *zero-initialized* typically, but — due to the liberal discretion afforded compiler implementers by the C++ Standard — not necessarily, has a bit pattern consisting of all zero (0) bits. For example, in a typical (4-byte) int, the bit pattern in memory would be $0000...[24$ *more zeros*$]...0000$, which typically — e.g., in *two's complement* — corresponds to the integer value zero. For a typical (8-byte) double, the bit pattern would be $0000...[56$ *more zeros*$]...0000$, which typically — e.g., in the IEEE754/IEC559 Standard — corresponds to the floating-point value zero. In the cases of objects of pointer type, the bit pattern is typically, but not necessarily, $0000...[((pointer size, in bits) - 8)$ *more zeros*$]...0000$.
Favoring an all-zero bit pattern for zero-initialized fundamental, enumerated, and pointer types has the decided advantage that, when objects of those types are static and default initialized, instead of residing in the executable along with other, explicitly initialized objects (e.g., in the .data section), they can be kept separate (e.g., in the .bss section) where they can be more efficiently initialized at load time and without the redundancy of having also to store the separate (nonzero) initialization constants.

[16] For more information on executables, see **bovet13**.

[17] Note that we are deliberately using the term *modular* (in the classical sense) here to indicate that there is exactly one (unique) physically separable place to represent the information that governs the interface between the implementation and prospective clients and not the C++ modules facility available as of C++20.

on symbols defined in yet other object files, and so on. If, ultimately, a referenced symbol is not defined anywhere in the collection of object files presented to the linker, the linker reports an error.

Consider the simple multifile program shown in Figure 1-4.[18] The well-known entry point `main` is the C++ runtime interface to our program and must be defined in order to create an executable. If only `main.o` is supplied, the linker will report that the symbol `f()` is unresolved, e.g.,

```
$ g++ -I. main.cpp
/tmp/cctbI9g6.o:main.cpp:(.text+0xe): undefined reference to 'f()'
/tmp/cctbI9g6.o:main.cpp:(.text+0xe): relocation truncated to fit:
                        R_X86_64_PC32 against undefined symbol 'f()'
collect2: error: ld returned 1 exit status
$
```

If `main.o` and `f.o` are supplied, the linker will report that the symbol `g()` is undefined,[19] e.g.,

---

[18] Effective use of header files is discussed in section 1.4, and appropriate use of `#include` guards is discussed in section 1.5.

[19] Note that the Unix-platform `nm` command (or `dumpbin` on Windows platforms) can be used to list all undefined symbols and externally accessible definitions within a `.o` file:

```
$ g++ -I. -c f.cpp
$ nm f.o
0000000000000000 b .bss
0000000000000000 d .data
0000000000000000 p .pdata
0000000000000000 r .rdata$zzz
0000000000000000 t .text
0000000000000000 r .xdata
0000000000000000 T _Z1fv      // 'T' means: definition provided
                 U _Z1gv      // 'U' means: undefined
$
```

The additional challenge of name mangling, originally introduced in C++ to accommodate function overloading, is easily overcome by the use of programs such as `c++filt`:

```
$ g++ -I. -c f.cpp
$ nm f.o | c++filt
0000000000000000 b .bss
0000000000000000 d .data
0000000000000000 p .pdata
0000000000000000 r .rdata$zzz
0000000000000000 t .text
0000000000000000 r .xdata
0000000000000000 T f()        // 'T' means: definition provided
                 U g()        // 'U' means: undefined
$
```

```
$ g++ -I. main.cpp f.cpp
/tmp/ccq6leho.o:f.cpp:(.text+0x9): undefined reference to 'g()'
/tmp/ccq6leho.o:f.cpp:(.text+0x9): relocation truncated to fit:
                        R_X86_64_PC32 against undefined symbol 'g()'
collect2: error: ld returned 1 exit status
$
```

Not until all of `main.o`, `f.o`, and `g.o` are supplied does the link phase succeed, e.g.,

```
$ g++ -I. main.cpp f.cpp g.cpp
$
```

This final build command quietly succeeds.

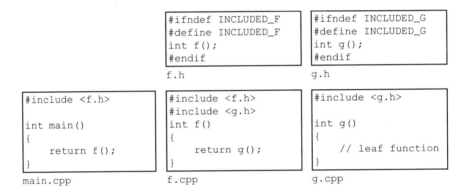

Figure 1-4: A simple multifile program

1.2.2   Classical Atomicity of Object (`.o`) Files

Object files have historically been atomic. That is, if an object file is incorporated into an executable, it is incorporated in its entirety. All externally accessible symbols defined within the `.o` file are now available to resolve undefined symbols in other `.o` files. By the same token, any unresolved symbols in that `.o` — whether or not they are used — must eventually be resolved or the link phase will fail.

As a result of needing to accommodate some of the more advanced language constructs (compared with C) in the initial version of the C++ language (such as implicit template instantiation and inline functions that don't inline), all modern platforms now support having multiple sections within a single .o file, such that each individual *section* can be incorporated (or not) independently of the rest of the .o, as we will discuss in full detail shortly. If and to what extent external symbol definitions reside in different sections of a .o file is both platform and build-configuration dependent, and certainly not something that should influence us during development (see section 2.15). To ensure portable, fine-grained control over our physical dependencies, we continue to design as if .o files — and *components* (section 0.7) — are atomic.

Now consider the slightly altered program in Figure 1-5. In this example, file f.cpp defines both f1() and f2(), but only f2() uses g(). Even though main() requires the definition of only f1() to link, incorporating f.o will have an unresolved reference to the symbol g(), requiring g.o — and any other .o files upon which g.o depends — to be gratuitously incorporated into our program. By instead placing the definitions of f1() and f2() in separate translation units (not shown), the unnecessary coupling and consequent link-time dependency on g.o are eliminated.

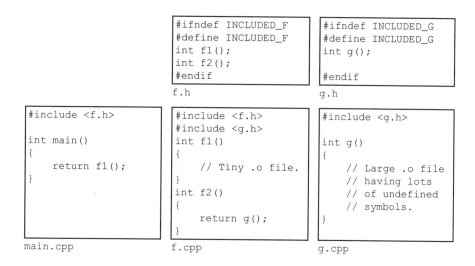

Figure 1-5: Extra link-time dependencies caused by colocation

When we misplace logical entities within our source files, we detract from the quality of our physical design. In addition to excessive dependencies among object files, it is also possible for two or more object files to be mutually dependent, as illustrated in Figure 1-6. After compiling all four `.cpp` files, it is necessary to link each of the two `.o` files containing `main()` with both of the remaining object files[20,21]:

```
$ CC main1.o x.o y.o
$ CC main2.o y.o x.o
$
```

```
#include <x.h>
int main()
{
    return a();
}
```
main1.cpp

```
#include <y.h>
int main()
{
    return c();
}
```
main2.cpp

```
#ifndef INCLUDED_X
#define INCLUDED_X
int a();
int b();
#endif
```
x.h

```
#ifndef INCLUDED_Y
#define INCLUDED_Y
int c();
int d();
#endif
```
y.h

```
#include <x.h>
#include <y.h>
int a()
{
    return d();
}
int b()
{
    return 10;
}
```
x.cpp

```
#include <y.h>
#include <x.h>
int c()
{
    return b();
}
int d()
{
    return 20;
}
```
y.cpp

Figure 1-6: Cyclic link-time dependencies among object files

---

[20] Each compiler vendor may have its own name for the compiler/linker driver program represented here as `CC` (e.g., `g++` for the GNU C++ Compiler, `cl` for the Microsoft Visual C++ Compiler).

[21] Note that the order in which object files are named explicitly on the command line is immaterial as each will be incorporated into the final program. Such is not the case for library archives, which we discuss in section 1.2.4.

For example, main1.o requires the symbol for a() defined in x.o, so we must link with x.o. However, a() has an unresolved reference to d(), which is defined in the other object file, y.o, so it too must be on the link line for main1.o. Now y.o has an unresolved reference to b(), which is satisfied by the definition found by the linker in x.o. Hence, x.o depends on y.o, which, in turn, depends back on x.o. A similar cyclic chain of dependencies occurs if we try to build a program with main2.cpp: main2.o depends on y.o, which depends on x.o, which — in turn — depends back on y.o. In fact, any use of either x.o or y.o in a program will necessitate linking with both of them.

In the example of Figure 1-6, the choice of which functions to place in which translation units was dubious. If we instead opt for the modularization depicted in Figure 1-7, each main can link successfully against a single .o file:

```
$ CC main1.o u.o
$ CC main2.o v.o
$
```

The .o files are now independent.

Figure 1-7: Alternate modularizations avoiding cyclic dependency

The lessons illustrated in Figures 1-4 to 1-7 underscore — at the most basic physical level — the potential consequences of colocating multiple functions within the same translation unit. For tiny (e.g., embedded) systems, there might well be affirmative value in placing each function within a separate translation unit. For larger systems, however, the value of doing so is offset by the advantage of colocating semantically related functions within a single physically cohesive unit. Such colocation of functionality is appropriate, especially when the functions are (1) logically cohesive and (2) share a common envelope of (allowed) physical dependencies (see section 2.2.14). The detailed rules (see section 2.6) and strategies (see section 3.3.1) governing colocation of classes within *components* (section 0.7) are driven by a desire to minimize this kind of physical coupling yet still encapsulate and hide each essential low-level design decision behind a single cohesive (logical and physical) *interface*, provided by a .h file (see section 1.4).

1.2.3   Sections and Weak Symbols in .o Files

So far we have considered, in detail, only the basic compiler/linker functionality needed over the years to implement commonly employed language constructs, such as those required by C. With the introduction of the C++ language, however, it has become common for compilers to generate certain kinds of function definitions[22] in multiple .o files and then rely on the linker to incorporate only one of the many (identical) copies in the final executable.

For this approach to work, the compiler must be able to achieve the effect of placing each such symbol definition in its own separate *section*, which can then be incorporated (or not) independently of any other object code within the .o file. It then becomes the responsibility of the linker to choose exactly one such definition from the possibly many (identical) definitions distributed across the .o files it encounters without (1) reporting multiple definitions of such isolated symbols or (2) dragging in any such segregated symbol definitions unless they satisfy some undefined reference, thus ensuring link-order independence.

Placing each symbol definition in its own separate physical section can result in additional build-time overhead. One way of achieving the same effect, without segregating definitions, is to mark definition symbols resulting from inline functions and function templates as *weak*, meaning that the symbol can be used to satisfy an undefined-symbol reference but will not cause a multiply-defined-symbol error to occur if incorporated into a program where another weak definition for that same undefined symbol has already been employed.

---

[22] E.g., for inline functions and function templates (see sections 1.3.12–1.3.14).

There are a variety of reasons, other than build-time performance (e.g., how exceptions are handled on certain platforms), that might lead to interdependencies among sections forcing a hybrid solution involving both distinct physical sections and annotating symbols as being *weak*. Note that if a typical linker were to attempt to incorporate both a weak and a (normal) *strong* symbol definition of the same name into a program (in either order), a multiply-defined-symbol error would result. Following commonsense software design practices (see Chapter 2) helps us satisfy fundamental language requirements, such as the ODR,[23] and thereby sidestep such troubling issues.

Keep in mind that all of this discussion of physical sections and *weak* versus *strong* symbol definitions is well beyond what is specified by the C++ Language Standard and is provided here as a foundation for understanding how low-level tools will be used to implement it. The only sure way to avoid having object code incorporated into your final executable program across all platforms is to keep it off the link line. Our fine-grained approach to software modularity (section 0.4) reflects this mind-set.

1.2.4   Library Archives

Listing each individual .o when linking a program is tedious and impractical, even for relatively small programs. Every compilation system includes a tool to combine several object (.o) files into a single physical entity called a *library* (or *archive*). By placing appropriately related object files into a library, we ease the process of building and distributing our software. Figure 1-8 illustrates how the archiver (ar on Unix platforms) creates a library from several .o files. These libraries (which, by convention, have a .a suffix on Unix platforms) can then be supplied to the linker.

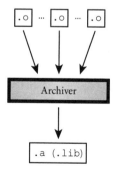

Figure 1-8: Creating a library file

---

[23] ODR stands for the *one-definition rule* (*see* section 1.3, especially sections 1.3.1 and 1.3.17).

The linker treats .o files that reside in libraries differently from those supplied directly. Every .o file supplied to the linker directly is incorporated into the resulting executable image regardless of whether it is needed, whereas .o files supplied via a library are incorporated only if needed. For example, consider the set of files shown in Figure 1-9. After compiling each of the respective .cpp files, we can create a working program by placing each of the .o files on the command line as follows:

```
$ CC main.o f.o g.o
$
```

Even though there is no need of g.o in order to link and run main, the linker will incorporate g.o into the executable program image, unnecessarily increasing its size. Moreover, if g.o happens to have any undefined symbols not resolvable by f.o or main.o, the link phase will fail.

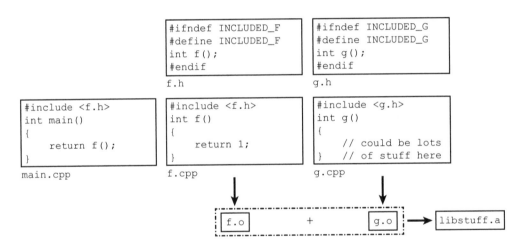

Figure 1-9: Colocating independent object files in a library

On the other hand, we can package the f.o and g.o files into a library as follows:

```
$ ar q libstuff.a f.o g.o
$
```

Now if we link main.o with the library, all is well — irrespective of any potentially undefined symbols in g.o:

```
$ CC main.o libstuff.a
$
```

The linker will resolve the undefined symbol `f()` referenced in `main.o` using the object file
`f.o` found in the supplied library, `libstuff.a`. Because there are no more undefined symbols,
the existence of another object file (`g.o`) in the library is ignored. This difference in behavior
between `.o` files placed on the command line and those found in library archives is important:
With libraries, clients pay (in terms of link time, disk space, and process memory size) only for
what they need. Treated naively, however, this difference can also become problematic.

1.2.5   The "Singleton" Registry Example

As a practical example, consider the implementation of a simple "singleton" — or more accurately, process-global — registry[24] of polymorphic objects derived from a common base-class
interface, `BaseEntry`, illustrated in Figure 1-10. Each concrete object that we intend to reside
in this registry must derive from `BaseEntry` and implement the virtual `clone` and `print`
methods, along with any other functions we decide are required of all registered objects.

```
// baseentry.h
// ...

class BaseEntry {

  public:
    virtual ~BaseEntry();
        // Destroy this object.

    virtual void clone(Handle<BaseEntry> *result) const = 0;
        // Allocate a dynamic copy of this object, and store
        // it in the specified 'result' handle.

    virtual std::ostream& print(std::ostream& stream) const = 0;
        // Identify the attributes of this object (primarily
        // for debugging purposes).

    // ...     (other methods common to all registered objects)
};
```

(a) Base class (interface) for registerable objects

---

[24] This registry is not itself an object of a C++ type that must be constructed at run time before it is used, as the
word *singleton* normally denotes (**gamma95**, Chapter 3, section "Singleton," pp. 127–136). Instead, the registry
is implemented by a data structure that is (1) unique within a process, and (2) *by design* "wakes up" in an empty
state at load time (**lakos96**, section 7.8.1.1, pp. 534–535) and, hence, requires no runtime initialization before it can
be used safely. In this way, we sidestep the almost insurmountable problems associated with the relative order of
runtime initialization of static objects across translation units, which we touch on in section 1.2.7 and elaborate on
more fully in Volume II, section 6.2.

```
// registry.h
// ...

class Registry {
    // ...

  public:
    static int enter(const char *name, const BaseEntry& exemplar);
        // Clone a copy of the specified 'exemplar' object, and associate
        // it with the specified 'name' in this registry.  Return 0 on
        // success, and a non-zero value (having no other effect) if 'name'
        // is already in use.

    static const BaseEntry *lookup(const char *name);
        // Return the address of the non-modifiable entry associated with
        // the specified 'name', or 0 if 'name' is not found.

    static std::ostream& print(std::ostream& stream);
        // List all entries in this registry on the specified output
        // 'stream' or emit "(* Empty Registry *)" if there are none.
};
```

(b) Static ("singleton") polymorphic object registry

Figure 1-10: A framework for registering polymorphic objects

Now suppose that we choose to be "clever" and have each concrete type derived from BaseEntry automatically self-register, as shown in Figure 1-11. Similar, derived concrete classes, DerivedEntry2, ..., are also written.

```
// derivedentry1.h
// ...

class DerivedEntry1 : public BaseEntry {
    // ...
  public:
    DerivedEntry1();
        // Create an empty instance of 'DerivedEntry1'.

    DerivedEntry1(const DerivedEntry1& original);
        // Create an instance of 'DerivedEntry1' having the
        // same "value" as the specified 'original' object.



    virtual ~DerivedEntry1();
        // Destroy this object.

    virtual void clone(Handle<BaseEntry> *result) const;
        // ...

    virtual std::ostream& print(std::ostream& stream) const;
        // ...

    // ...    (other methods common to all registered objects)
};
```

> The meaning of *value* is described in Volume II,
> section 4.1, but that notion doesn't really apply here.
> (We're just getting started, so please bear with us.)

(a) Header file for `DerivedEntry1`

```
// derivedentry1.cpp
// ...

#include <derivedentry1.h>
// ...

static DerivedEntry1 exemplar;  // BAD IDEA       (See Volume II, section 6.2.)
static int dummy = Registry::enter("DerivedEntry1", exemplar);
```

> Note that returning status is contrived solely to allow us to perform runtime
> initialization prior to entering main; apart from running out of memory, how
> could it fail? And if it could, why would we be ignoring the status? BAD IDEA!

```
// ...

DerivedEntry1::DerivedEntry1() /*...*/ { /*...*/ }

DerivedEntry1::DerivedEntry1(const DerivedEntry1& original) // ...

DerivedEntry1::~DerivedEntry1() { /*...*/ }

void DerivedEntry1::clone(Handle<BaseEntry> *result) const
{
    result->load(new DerivedEntry1(*this));
}

std::ostream& DerivedEntry1::print(std::ostream& stream) const
{
    return stream << "DerivedEntry1" << std::flush;
}
// ...
```

(b) Implementation file for DerivedEntry1

Figure 1-11: "Clever" self-registering concrete registry entry

To exercise the registry along with several such concrete derivations of the BaseEntry type, we might create the following main function that simply dumps each registry entry to stdout:

```
// main.cpp
#include <registry.h>
#include <iostream>
int main(void)
{
    std::cout << Registry::print(std::cout) << std::flush;
}
```

We would build the "test" program using the following link line:

```
$ CC main.o registry.o baseentry.o derivedentry1.o derivedentry2.o ...
$
```

When we run the program, our output might look as expected:

```
DerivedEntry1
DerivedEntry2
        ⋮
```

Now suppose that we are satisfied and distribute to our clients the `Registry` class, the abstract `BaseEntry` interface, and several useful derived entry types. We might naively try to package these objects into a library called `libreg.a` as follows[25]:

```
$ ar q libreg.a registry.o baseentry.o derivedentry1.o derivedentry2.o ...
$
```

A client might then opt to validate the utility of the `libreg.a` library using our `main.o` by building the test program with the following link line:

```
$ CC main.o libreg.a
$
```

But now, the output of the test program will look different:

```
(* Empty Registry *)
```

If this result is surprising, don't be discouraged. Many competent developers fall into this trap at some point in their professional careers. The problem is that, unlike `.o` files supplied directly on the linker command line, the incorporation of translation units from within libraries is not automatic but is instead on an *as-needed* basis. Invoking `Registry::print` causes an undefined symbol to be generated into `main.o`; hence, the linker will naturally pull in `registry.o` to resolve that reference to an external symbol. Since there are no more undefined symbols in `main.o` or `registry.o` for the library to resolve, none of the derived-entry `.o` files is incorporated into the program; hence, no entries are loaded into the registry.

---

[25] The name of the archiver program is typically `ar`, though compiler vendors are at liberty to call it whatever they like; e.g., Microsoft calls its corresponding program `lib`. Note that the `q` flag (shown here) is required by `ar`. Other flags, such as `c` and `v`, are commonly used along with `q` on Unix systems to, respectively, suppress warning when a library is created anew and provide verbose information about what is being archived.

Registries such as the one just described might have valid uses.[26] As professional software developers, however, we are well advised to resist the urge to rely on tenuous language constructs that exhibit different logical behavior depending on how they are deployed (see section 2.15). Additional reasons for avoiding any file-scope or namespace-scope variables requiring runtime initialization are touched on in section 1.2.7 and discussed further in Volume II, section 6.2.

1.2.6   Library Dependencies

Libraries may also depend on other libraries. Consider Figure 1-12 in which we have a file defining `main()`, `main.cpp`, and two components, **a** and **c**. In this example, the `main()` program calls `a()`, which, in turn, calls function `c()`. After compiling each of the three `.cpp` files, object file `a.o` is loaded into library `libx.a`, and object file `c.o` is loaded into `liby.a`. Now, the reference to the symbol for `c()` in `a.o` can be resolved by linking with the library `liby.a`, which contains `c.o` defining `c()`[27]:

```
$ CC main.o libx.a liby.a
$
```

---

[26] A common use of registries is to support Java-style serialization of polymorphic objects, though we assert that the value (pun intended) of such serialization is dubious (see Volume II, section 4.1).

[27] The details of how undefined symbols are resolved by library archives is not specified by the C++ Standard and, in practice, is highly implementation dependent. In the "classical" Unix-platform style, all `.o` files specified explicitly to the linker are incorporated immediately, whereas each library argument is scanned in order and used to satisfy any currently unresolved symbols before advancing to the next. Attempting to link the libraries above in the wrong order will fail:

```
$ CC main.o liby.a libx.a
Error: Undefined reference to 'a()'
ld returned 1 exit status
$
```

Most linkers can be instructed to rescan supplied libraries to resolve symbols referenced later in the argument list. Some linkers will do this rescan by default. Though this multipass approach renders the order in which libraries are supplied (apart from link time) immaterial, relying on this feature of a linker serves only to mask significant physical defects. Such cyclic dependencies across libraries also create a platform dependency with respect to deployment that makes porting more difficult. Fortunately, if we organize our software correctly at the physical level, we will never require the linker to perform a multipass scan, and this noisome platform-specific detail becomes one that we can quickly forget.

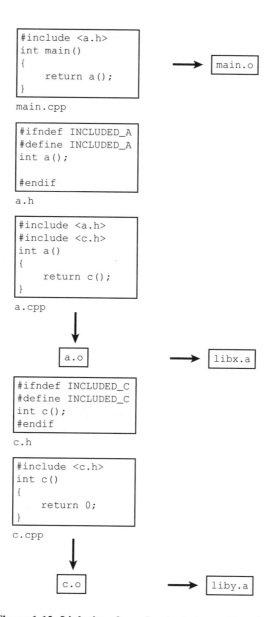

Figure 1-12: Link-time dependencies between libraries

A central principle of good physical design (section 0.6) is avoiding cyclic physical dependencies among physically distinct entities. We saw earlier how mutual dependencies can arise with object files. We shall now see how such bidirectional (cyclic) dependencies can occur with library archives as well.

Suppose we again have main() defined in main.cpp, but now we have two libraries x and y, each containing two object files, {a.o, b.o} and {c.o, d.o}, respectively, as illustrated in Figure 1-13. In this example, main() again calls a(), located in library x, which again calls c(), located in library y, but this time, c() calls b1() back in library x.

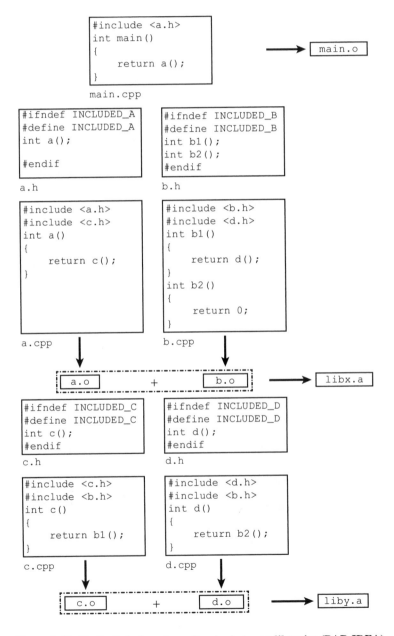

Figure 1-13: Cyclic link-time dependencies between libraries (BAD IDEA)

After compiling each of the five .cpp files, a.o and b.o are loaded into library libx.a; c.o and d.o are similarly loaded into liby.a. We can see that b.o and d.o are mutually dependent and, because they are incorporated into separate libraries, the libraries themselves are now mutually dependent. On some platforms — i.e., those that use single-pass linkers — if we try to link main.o with the two libraries

```
$ CC main.o libx.a liby.a
```

the link will fail.

When the linker examines main.o, it finds the symbol for a() undefined. The linker then looks at libx.a and finds that a.o defines the symbol for a(), but also requires the definition of c(). Since main.o does not define the symbol for c(), the linker looks in the current library for another .o file that defines c(). Finding none, the linker moves on to the next library, liby.a, where it finds the symbol for c() defined in c.o. The linker incorporates c.o where it observes that b1() is undefined. Since neither main.o nor a.o defines b1(), the linker searches the current library for another .o in the hope of resolving the undefined symbol for b1(). Finding none, and having no more libraries to search, the link phase ends in failure, reporting that b1() is undefined.

Repeating libx.a after liby.a on the command line

```
$ CC main.o libx.a liby.a libx.a
```

allows the linker to rescan libx.a where it finds the definition for b1() in b.o and finds the symbol for d() undefined there. Since d() is not defined in any of main.o, a.o, or c.o, the linker again searches libx.a looking for the definition of d(). Finding none, the linker reports d() as being undefined. If we now decide to repeat liby.a at the end,

```
$ CC main.o libx.a liby.a libx.a liby.a
$
```

all is well. The linker rescans liby.a and finds the symbol d() in d.o where b2() is undefined locally, but this time b2() is already defined in one of the previously incorporated object files, namely, b.o. There are no unresolved symbols remaining, and the link phase succeeds!

These difficulties with building libraries having cyclic link-time dependencies with single-pass linkers are a symptom of a much more profound problem: the inability to implement, test, and use such physically cyclic software hierarchically. Had we chosen instead to package a.o and c.o from Figure 1-13 in, say, libu.a, and b.o and d.o together in, say, libv.a as shown in Figure 1-14, no repetition of libraries would have been necessary:

```
$ CC main.o libu.a libv.a
$
```

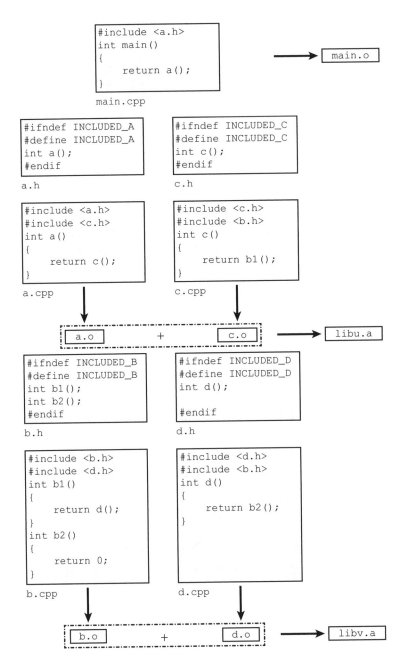

Figure 1-14: Acyclic link-time dependencies between libraries

More generally, we are almost always better off avoiding mutual dependencies among any entities — logical or physical. If mutual dependency is (for whatever reason) deemed necessary, we are well advised to package such mutually dependent entities — whether they be functions, classes, or (in the vanishingly rare case discussed here) translation units — together, rather than separately. Additional reasons for colocation are discussed in section 3.3.[28]

1.2.7   Link Order and Build-Time Behavior

The C++ Standard does not address the (platform-specific) details of how we package .o files within libraries, yet failing to understand how libraries generally behave in practice can lead to substantial problems during development and deployment. For starters, once a .o in a library is incorporated into a program, that .o is treated as if it were supplied directly on the command line. The entire .o is incorporated into the program, and any needed undefined symbols that cannot be resolved by previously incorporated object files will necessitate the incorporation of additional .o files or the link phase will fail.

Providing .o files having duplicate definitions of symbols to the linker directly is a fatal error, but it is quite possible to inadvertently supply one or more libraries containing separate .o files defining the same symbol. On platforms where the link phase occurs in two passes, the first (or last) occurrence of a needed symbol typically dictates which .o file is incorporated. Another approach, common on Unix platforms, is to scan each library in turn, incorporating all .o files that resolve currently undefined symbols before advancing to the next library. In any case, there is no practical way to control which of the multiple definitions is used.

Even if the two symbol definitions are identical, the respective .o files in which these symbol definitions reside might not be. Depending on which .o is chosen, other definitions might be dragged in that might conflict with yet other definitions, causing multiply-defined-symbol errors.[29] By the same token, additional undefined symbols resulting from the colocated definitions might not be able to be resolved. Even if the link is successful, the size and makeup of the resulting executable on disk might be different depending on link order. Ensuring that there is

---

[28] Note that cyclic physical dependencies among .o files within a single library — even on a system with a single-pass linker — might go unnoticed when testing the library as a whole; it is (in part) for this reason that we make it a point, during development, to test each library component separately, supplying access to only those other components (including their respective header files) on which the component under test is intended to depend (see sections 2.2.14 and 2.14.3, and Volume III, section 7.5).

[29] This same problem can occur when the compiler deposits multiple definitions within the same physical section of a .o file, giving rise to the need for *weak* symbol definitions (section 1.2.3).

just a single definition for each linker symbol and thereby avoiding such link-order idiosyncrasies is essential for the build process to be stable — i.e., repeatable and reliable.

1.2.8   Link Order and Runtime Behavior

There are other, even more subtle ways in which the order in which the .o files are processed can affect the runtime behavior of the resulting executable. In particular, the relative order in which file-scope static objects (such as those used to automatically initialize our registry in Figure 1-11, section 1.2.5) are constructed is implementation and link-order dependent. There is simply no reliable way in C++ to ensure that file-scope static objects in one translation unit are initialized before or after those in another. The only guarantee C++ provides across translation units is that a file-scope static object will be initialized before its first use *after* main has been entered.[30]

Relying on relative order of runtime static initializations across translation units can lead to unexpected and often catastrophic behavior. Consider, for example, the situation shown in Figure 1-15. The success of the client code depends on the static objects in server.o being initialized at startup prior to those in client.o. If that order is reversed, the value of key in client.o is likely to be a (non-null) pointer to an empty string, but the behavior is undefined nonetheless. Placing the static object inside a function[31]

```
const char *getKey()
{
    static std::string key("xyzy");
    return key.c_str();
}
```

solves the creation problem but cannot guarantee that the object remains valid until all potential clients are destroyed. Dynamically allocating (and never freeing) the memory would solve that problem, but we would then incur a memory leak that verification tools (such as Purify) would be obliged to report. If the singleton happens to control external resources (say, a database connection), then a "leak" could be even more problematic. Avoiding runtime initialization at file/namespace scope is the subject of Volume II, section 6.2.

---

[30] Use of static for declaring an object at namespace scope was deprecated (C++98/03) but later undeprecated (C++11) and made equivalent (both logically and physically) to declaring it in the unnamed namespace. Note also that the constexpr construct, first introduced in C++11, can sometimes be used to sidestep the runtime aspect of such initializations.

[31] **meyers97**, "Miscellany," Item 47, pp. 219–223

```
// client.h
// ...
```

```
// server.h
#ifndef INCLUDED_SERVER
#define INCLUDED_SERVER

const char *getKey();

#endif
```

```
// client.cpp
#include <client.h>
#include <server.h>

static const char *key = getKey();

//...
```

```
// server.cpp
#include <server.h>
#include <string>

static std::string key("xyzy");

const char *getKey()
{
    return key.c_str();
}
```

Figure 1-15: Relying on order of static initializations (BAD IDEA)

1.2.9   Shared (Dynamically Linked) Libraries

Finally, we should note that the use of "shared objects" or "dynamically linked libraries" (as they are called on Unix and Windows platforms, respectively) only increases the need to observe physical dependencies and package our logical content properly. These types of libraries tend to behave more like monolithic .o files than library archives as they are brought into a process atomically — i.e., all or nothing. The intricacies related to use of dynamic libraries are inherently platform-specific, and little more will be said about them here. Statically linked libraries, however, will serve as a good mental model for further analysis and discussion.

1.3   Declarations, Definitions, and Linkage

Much of what occurs when we build a program involves the association, by the compiler and sometimes the linker, of the use of named entities — such as templates, types, functions, and variables — with their corresponding *definitions*. The resolution of the use of a named entity to a unique definition within the program occurs indirectly through the use of *declarations*. That is, the use of a name by the compiler is enabled based on an explicit declaration, and the language rules determine how each declaration is associated with its corresponding (unique) definition. The extent to which a name may refer to an entity in a different scope or across translation units is governed by what is called *linkage*.

1.3.1   Declaration vs. Definition

Because a program can consist of multiple translation units and because these translation units are almost always compiled separately, the linkage rules for each C++ entity have been carefully specified in the language to coincide with the present-day capability of typical build tools, especially linkers. The physical realities of separate compilation and the limitations of typical build tools, however, mean that, if one is not careful, it is easy to allow inconsistencies to crop up — inconsistencies that might not be caught at compile or even link time and can result in difficult-to-find crashes at run time.

Many of the rules governing the construction of components are designed specifically to avoid such problems. To understand the motivation for these design rules, however, it is first necessary to understand the basic C++ concepts of *declarations*, *definitions*, and *linkage*, as well as how our build tools interact with them. Understanding how the underlying tools work will also help make what might seem like arbitrary linkage designations among different constructs in the standard more intuitive.

DEFINITION: A *declaration* is a language construct that introduces a name into a scope.

DEFINITION: A *definition* is a language construct that uniquely characterizes an entity within a program and, where applicable, reserves storage for it.

A *declaration* introduces a name[32] into a scope. That name may subsequently be used anywhere the declaration is visible to refer to the corresponding entity:

---

[32] More correctly, a declaration introduces something into a scope, and typically that something includes a name. Hypertechnically, however, there exist a few inconsequential logical constructs, such as *anonymous union*, that —according to the grammar of the C++ language, at least — are (1) considered *declarations*, and (2) do not necessarily introduce a name. Such "nameless" declarations are sufficiently rare and unimportant that they can, for most practical purposes, be safely ignored. Throughout this book, we will assume our approximate definition of *declaration* expressed here as opposed to the one implied by the C++ grammar.

```
typedef int Int;    // 'typedef' declaration of an alias for 'int'33
class Foo;          // pure (a.k.a. "forward") class declaration
enum E : int;       // 'int' enumeration declaration (new as of C++11)
int f(int x);       // function declaration (the name "x" is ignored)
```

A *definition* characterizes an entity, reserving storage where appropriate:

```
int a;                          // variable definition
class Foo { };                  // class definition
enum E { X };                   // definition of both 'E' and 'X'
int f(int x) { return x + 1; }  // definition of both 'f' and 'x'
```

Most[34] definitions also serve as their own declarations,[35] as is the case with each of the definitions above. Unfortunately, self-declaring definitions can also lead to subtle problems. Consider what can happen when a function defined at namespace scope is also separately declared — e.g., in a header file as shown in Figure 1-16.

```
// xyza_foo.h                        // xyza_foo.cpp      BAD IDEA
namespace xyza {                     namespace xyza {
int foobar(int x, double y);         int fooabr(int x, double y) { /*...*/ }
int foobaz(int x, double y);         int foobaz(double y, int x) { /*...*/ }
}                                    }
```

Figure 1-16: Defining free functions within their declared scope (BAD IDEA)

Do you see the two problems? In the first case, `foobar` is misspelled; in the second, the name `foobaz` is unintentionally overloaded. Including the `xyza_foo.h` header in the `xyza_foo.cpp` file will not expose this problem: The compiler will see each of the functions defined in the `.cpp` file as distinct entities from those declared in the corresponding `.h` file. Such mismatches in signatures between declaration and definition will go undetected at compile time (and, if these pure declarations go unused, at link time as well). We can, however, ensure that the compiler will report such defects — simply by defining the entity from outside of the scope in which it is declared — as shown in Figure 1-17.

---

[33] As of C++11, we *could* spell it
  `using Int = int;`

[34] But, by no means, all, as we will demonstrate shortly.

[35] It might come as a surprise (it did to me) that — according to the C++ language grammar, at least — every definition is also considered a *declaration*. We find this terminology to be most unfortunate, as it doesn't reflect the important notion that many definitions are also *self-declaring* (e.g., `int x;`), while others, such as those residing outside of the namespace in which they must also be separately declared (e.g., `int ns::x;`), are not. Throughout this book, when we use the term *definition only*, we mean that the definition itself is explicitly *not* self-declaring.

```
// xyza_foo.h

namespace xyza {

class Foo { /*...*/ };

bool operator==(const Foo& lhs,
                const Foo& rhs);

// ...

}
```

```
// xyza_foo.cpp

#include <xyza_foo.h>
                                     GOOD IDEA

bool xyza::operator==(const Foo& lhs,
                      const Foo& rhs)
{
    // ...
}
// ...
```

Figure 1-17: Defining free functions outside their declared scope (GOOD IDEA)

Such non-self-declaring definitions require that the name used in the definition be qualified with the name of the scope containing the corresponding declaration — irrespective of whether that scope is a namespace, struct, or class:

```
class Bar {
    static int s_count;  // declaration only
};
int Bar::s_count; // This definition will fail to compile if 's_count'
                  // is not already declared within the scope of 'Bar'.
```

Most declarations that are not also definitions can be repeated any number of times within a given scope:

```
class Foo;        // Class declarations may be repeated within a
class Foo;        // scope without causing an error.


typedef int Int; // Remember that a 'typedef' is considered a
typedef int Int; // declaration, and not a definition.


int f();          // This is a function declaration, not a definition;
int f();          // it can therefore be repeated any number of times.
```

Notable exceptions are member functions and `static` member data, which are declarations nested within a `class` or `struct` definition and cannot be repeated. Having two identical `typedef` declarations within the same class definition (unlike file, namespace, or function scope) also doesn't work; however, repeating a nested `class`, `struct`, or `union` declaration within a class definition is legal C++:

```
class Bar {
    static int s_count;   // static data member declaration
    static int s_count;   // Error!

    int f();              // member function declaration
    int f();              // Error!

    typedef int Int;      // typedef decl. nested within class scope
    typedef int Int;      // Error!

    class Baz;            // A class decl. can be repeated anywhere.
    class Baz;            // Fine.
};
```

By contrast, definitions must never be repeated:

```
class Foo { };  // class definition
class Foo { };  // Error!

enum E { };      // enumeration definition
enum E { };      // Error!

void f() { }     // function definition (reserves storage)
void f() { }     // Error!

int i;           // data definition (reserves storage)
int i;           // Error!
```

In fact, the C++ language requires that there be exactly one definition of each distinct entity that is used[36] within a program. This rule, known as the *one-definition rule* (ODR), is interpreted and realized in different ways, depending on the kind of entity in question (see below). To help specify the *logical* "sameness" of entities across different scopes and translation units, the C++ Standard defines the notion of *linkage*, which is summarized in Figure 1-18.

Linkage

The *declaration* of a name is said to have (logical) linkage when it might denote the same object, reference, function, type, template, namespace, or value as a name introduced by a declaration in another scope:

External Linkage — The entity that a declaration of a name denotes can be defined in a different translation unit or scope (or both).

Internal Linkage — The entity that a declaration of a name denotes can be defined in a different scope but not in a separate translation unit.

No Linkage — The entity that a declaration of a name denotes cannot be defined in a different scope or translation unit.

Figure 1-18: C++11 Standard definition of (logical) linkage

The C++ linkage rules allow us to determine whether two names that are declared in different scopes or translation units logically denote the same entity. For example, the name of a type or non-`static` function declared at file scope (or within any other named namespace scope) has *external* linkage, which means that this name would refer to the same entity as would the name in a similar declaration appearing in the same scope in a different translation unit.

As a more concrete example, consider Figure 1-19 depicting two separate files, `f.cpp` and `g.cpp`. Each file declares a class `Foo` and a function `bar(Foo *)` and also defines a unique function (named after the `.cpp` file) that invokes `bar` (on a null pointer). Since class `Foo` — having been declared at file scope in both files — has external linkage, both declarations of `Foo` denote the same C++ type. Similarly, `bar(Foo *)` also has external linkage, and therefore both of these declarations denote the same function. Hence, the language guarantees that `f()` and `g()` must (behave as if they) invoke the same function definition.

---

[36] That is, ODR-used; see **iso11**, section 3.2.2, p. 36.

```
// f.cpp
class Foo;

void bar(Foo *);

void f()
{
    bar(0);
}
```

```
// g.cpp
class Foo;

void bar(Foo *);

void g()
{
    bar(0);
}
```

Figure 1-19: Declarations referring to the same external-linkage entities

Suppose we were to declare function `bar(Foo *)` in either file of Figure 1-19 to be `static`[37]:

```
static void bar(Foo *);
```

Doing so would change the linkage of the name `bar(Foo *)` in that file to be *internal*, which would mean that the definition of `bar(Foo *)` could no longer reside outside of the translation unit in which it was used, and therefore `f()` and `g()` could no longer invoke the same function definition.

Suppose that instead of declaring `bar(Foo *)` to be `static`, we were to move the declaration of `Foo` (in either file of Figure 1-19) into the unnamed namespace:

```
namespace { class Foo; }
```

Now the declared class name `Foo` will itself have *internal* linkage, causing it to be logically local to the translation unit, which would make defining `bar(Foo *)` from outside that translation unit impossible. Hence, `f` and `g` would again be unable to invoke the same function definition.

1.3.2   (Logical) *Linkage* vs. (Physical) Linking

Historically, compiler and especially linker technology has strongly influenced the linkage rules and semantics of C and, in turn, C++. Nonetheless (logical) *linkage* and (physical) *linking* are two distinct concepts,[38] which should not be confused: *Linking* refers to the physical act of binding the use of a name to its definition (or meaning), whereas *linkage* is used to determine whether a given declaration and definition refer to the same logical entity.

---

[37] Declaring a function at namespace scope to be `static` in C++98 is logically (but not physically) equivalent to placing it in the unnamed namespace (see below); as of C++11, they are (both logically and physically) equivalent.

[38] And, of course, we don't mean the C++20 language feature bearing this name (see section 1.7.6 and Volume II, section 4.4).

1.3.3   The Need for Understanding Linking Tools

In an effort to abstract the language specification from any particular implementation choice, *linkage* has deliberately been defined entirely in terms of its logical effect, rather than any physical manifestation. Still, understanding the low-level details of "linking" — e.g., whether the compiler, linker, or both might ultimately be used to associate a particular use of a declared name with its corresponding definition (or meaning) — is essential (1) for gaining insight into the motivation for the C++ Standard's choice of "tool-independent" rules for (logical) linkage, and (2) as a foundation for understanding if and when the C++ Standard's ODR can be violated benignly in practice.

1.3.4   Alternate Definition of Physical "Linkage": *Bindage*

It is worth noting that the term *linkage* has also at times been used, albeit less formally, to refer directly to the kind of physical apparatus generally employed for linking a given C++ construct on typical platforms. While the C++ Standard's (logical) definition of *linkage* must, of course, take precedence, we continue to find this alternate, *physical* meaning conceptually useful — particularly in spoken communications. Moving forward, we will consistently refer to this informal, physical meaning of "linkage," instead, as *bindage*.[39,40,41]

It turns out that (physical) *bindage* for C++ comes in not two, but three, distinct (disjoint) flavors: *internal*, *external*, and *dual*!

DEFINITION: A C++ construct has *internal bindage* if, on typical platforms, use of a declared name of that kind of construct and its corresponding definition (or meaning) is *always* effectively bound at compile time.

---

[39] "The linker is the program that binds together the separately compiled parts." See **stroustrup85**, section 4.1, pp. 103–104, specifically p. 404.

[40] JC van Winkel, in his review of this manuscript, explained that the "linker" on the Burroughs B7700 system was called the *binder* (**unisys87**, bottom of p. 7, right column):

> The System Software Facility for the A 15System includes the Master Control Program/Advanced System (MCP/AS) operating system, Microcode, Utilities, an Algol compiler, a DC Algol compiler, a Program Binder, the SMF II Site Management, the Work Flow Language (WFL), Menu Assisted Resource Control (MARC), and Cross Reference Symbolic.

[41] To emphasize the logical/physical distinction explicitly, we may at times choose to refer to the C++ Standard's definition of *linkage* (redundantly) as (logical) *linkage* and as (physical) *bindage*.

Language constructs having *internal bindage* require both the definition (or associated meaning) and the use of the construct to be visible to the compiler within the same translation unit as no artifacts are introduced into the .o file for binding purposes. Examples of language constructs for which the use of declared names and their associated meanings are resolved always at compile time on typical platforms include alias (e.g., `typedef`) declarations, enumerators, class definitions, non-`static` class member data, and file-scope `static` functions and variables.[42]

> **DEFINITION**: A C++ construct has *external bindage* if, on typical platforms, a corresponding definition must not appear in more than one translation unit of a program (e.g., in order to avoid multiply-defined-symbol errors at link time).

Language constructs having *external bindage* do not require the use of the construct to be in the same translation unit in which it is defined; hence, the compiler will, on typical platforms, introduce artifacts into the .o file to be used subsequently by the linker to complete the binding of the use of the name to its (globally unique) definition. (Note that when the use of any construct occurs within the same translation unit as its definition, the compiler is at liberty to perform the complete binding at compile time — including that of functions that have not been declared `inline`.) Examples of language constructs that are generally bound at link time on typical platforms include non-`static` file-scope (or namespace-scope) data and functions, `static` and non-`static` class member functions, and `static` class data members. Figure 1-20 contrasts a few important definitions having internal and external bindage.

```
class Foo {
    Foo();                Declarations (only)
    static int s_defaultSize;
    // ...
};

static int local;

static double f() { /*...*/ }

typedef int Int;

enum Color { RED, GREEN };
```

```
Foo::Foo()
{
    // ...
}


int Foo::s_defaultSize = 10;

int global;

double g() { /*...*/ }
```

(a) Internal bindage definitions   (b) External bindage definitions

Figure 1-20: *Internal* versus *external* (physical) *bindage*

---

[42] While `static` variables and free functions may be assigned specific address offsets by the linker, the association is necessarily local to the translation unit and therefore (at least conceptually) the binding is performed by the compiler.

> **DEFINITION**: A C++ construct has *dual bindage* if, on typical platforms, (1) a corresponding definition can safely appear in more than one translation unit of the same program, and (2) use of a declared name of that kind of construct and its corresponding definition can be bound at link time.

Language constructs having *dual bindage* allow the compiler to generate definitions that can be both (a) reached from, and (b) duplicated in multiple translation units within a program. Having a definition (e.g., of a function) visible in multiple translation units increases the opportunities for binding to occur at compile time — e.g., via inlining (at the discretion of the compiler). The two primary examples for which use of a language construct and its corresponding definition may generally be bound at either compile or link time (at the discretion of the compiler) are inline functions and implicitly instantiated function templates.[43] We will further discuss additional physical properties of inline functions as well as those of class and function templates (including `extern` templates) starting in section 1.3.12.

1.3.5   More on How Linkers Work

A fully (statically) linked executable program image consists entirely of functions and data, which have *static* storage duration. (Other kinds of storage, available only to a running program, include *automatic* storage, which resides on the program stack, and *dynamic* storage, which must be allocated explicitly on the heap.) Whenever an entity having static storage duration is *defined* in a translation unit, a *symbol definition* for the entity is placed in that translation unit's resulting `.o` file. Whenever an entity having static storage duration that is not bound at compile time is *used* in a translation unit, a *symbol reference* representing that entity is placed in the translation unit's resulting `.o` file. Note that a declaration alone never introduces any artifacts into a `.o` file; it is only by *using* the declaration that a reference to a symbol may be generated:

```
void f(int x);          // No symbol reference generated.

struct Foo {
    static int d_bar;  // No symbol reference generated.
};
```

---

[43] As of C++17, there is a third such language construct, *inline variables*, which, although useful for streamlining common template metaprogramming idioms, are of dubious benefit when used to facilitate the introduction of global state (e.g., in header-only implementations).

```
// ...

f(3);                      // Symbol reference generated.

int y = Foo::d_bar;        // Symbol reference generated.
```

In the case of a function template, however, an implicitly instantiated definition is routinely generated as well.

When the program is built, it will be up to the linker to assign each undefined-symbol reference to a unique definition of an entity having static storage duration and then resolve all references to them — i.e., fill in the missing address information. Not surprisingly, it is these same entities — i.e., those having *external* (or *dual*) bindage — for which the language provides syntax that allows them to be declared separately from their definitions. At the same time, these declarations alone are sufficient for the compiler to generate code that makes full use of the entity without ever seeing its definition.[44]

1.3.6   A Tour of Entities Requiring Program-Wide Unique Addresses

As a simple, illustrative example, suppose our entire program consists of exactly two files, each of which is compiled separately:

```
// file1.cpp                    // file2.cpp
int g();                        int f()          // external linkage
int f();                        {
                                     return 5;
int main()                      }
{
    return f() * g();           int g()          // external linkage
}                               {
                                     return f() + 3;
// 'main' returns 40.           }
```

---

[44] Although we assert that locally declaring a construct having other than *internal bindage* and not also providing its definition in the same translation unit (or more precisely, .h/.cpp pair) is bad practice (see section 1.6.3), it is not an outright error with respect to the C++ language so long as a suitable definition for each use can, if needed, be found in some other translation unit's .o file at link time.

In both files, there is a declaration for the function `f()` at file scope (the definition in `file2.cpp` is self-declaring). Because of the linkage rules, `f()`, which is defined at file scope, has external linkage; hence, the name `f()` denotes the same entity in both declarations, and the call of `f()` in `main` must result in the invocation of the function `f()` defined in `file2.cpp` at run time. What's more, if we were to attempt to print the *address* of `f` from both translation units, the displayed address value would be the same[45]:

```
#include <iostream>

// ...

std::cout << reinterpret_cast<void *>(f) << std::endl;

// e.g., 0x401170
```

Now consider what happens if we declare the function `f()` `static` in `file2.cpp`:

```
// file1.cpp                    // file2.cpp
int g();                        static int f()   // internal linkage
int f();                        {
                                        return 5;
int main()                      }
{
    return f() * g();           int g()          // external linkage
}                               {
                                        return f() + 3;
// This program doesn't build!   }
```

The program will no longer build. The object file `file1.o` contains an undefined reference to a function `f()` that is not defined anywhere: The function `f()` defined in `file2.cpp` has internal linkage and, therefore, according to the language specification, can *never* be referenced *by name* outside of the translation unit. We can, however, take the address of a function having internal linkage, and that address can be returned to (and invoked from) a separate translation unit:

---

[45] Note that we could equivalently have replaced `f` with `&f` in the cast.

```
// file1.cpp                                    // file2.cpp
int g();                                        static int f()
int (*h())();  // function returning            {
               // the address of a                  return 5;
               // function returning            }
               // an integer
                                                int g()
int main()                                      {
{                                                   return f() + 3;
    int (*f)() = h();                           }
    return f() * g();
}                                               int (*h())()
                                                {
                                                    return &f;  // The '&' is
// 'main' again returns 40.                     }              // optional.
```

We can also introduce a new, separate definition for f into file1.cpp:

```
// file1.cpp                                    // file2.cpp
int g();                                        static int f()
                                                {
static int f()                                      return 5;
{                                               }
    return 10;
}                                               int g()
                                                {
int main()                                          return f() + 3;
{                                               }
    return f() * g();
}
```

```
// 'main' now returns 80.
```

Both of the two static declarations of f() have internal linkage and hence do not refer to the
same logical entity. At the physical level, the compiler marks each definition symbol as local,
so it is not visible (to the linker) from .o files other than the one in which it resides (internal

bindage). Hence, the `main` function will use the definition of `f()` defined in `file1.cpp`, and `g()` will use the one defined in `file2.cpp`.

It is worth pointing out that, because the source for the definitions of `f()` in their respective files are visible (in their own translation units), the compiler is at full liberty to suppress the generation of both definitions of `f()` and substitute each call to `f()` with its corresponding body, just as if the functions had also been explicitly declared `inline`.[46] In fact, we could remove the `static` keyword from either definition of `f()` (but not both) without conflict, as at least one would be local to its translation unit (thus having internal linkage and bindage), be logically and physically distinct from the other, and, therefore, not violate the ODR.

1.3.7   Constructs Where the Caller's Compiler Needs the Definition's Source Code

The physical implications of what it means to have just one *logical* definition within a program depends on the kind of entity being defined. While it is true that all definitions must (in some sense) be unique within a program and that names having external linkage can denote the same logical entity across translation units, it is only functions and objects having static storage duration that manifest themselves in the executable program image produced by the linker. For all other kinds of entities, the compiler will need to have access to the source code of an entity's definition to make full use of that entity. Hence, for these other kinds of entities, what it means for a definition to be "unique" throughout a program is interpreted somewhat differently.

For constructs where the compiler needs (or might need) access to the source code of the definition of an entity in order to use it substantively, the ODR permits more than one textual occurrence of the definition of the same entity in a program provided that (1) the source for each definition appears at most once in any translation unit, and (2) each occurrence of the definition means the same thing (i.e., has the same token sequence, all the tokens are interpreted in the same way, etc.). Provided these conditions hold, the program behaves *as if* there were just a single physical definition of the entity.

---

[46] Note that declaring a function `inline` — while still considered a strong hint by many compilers — is no guarantee that the definition will in fact be substituted at the call site.

Let's now consider just one example of a construct, such as an inline function, whose definition typically needs to be seen by a client's compiler. Figure 1-21 shows three global inline functions, max, min, and half, each of which are defined (explicitly) in both file1.cpp and file2.cpp. The linkage for all three inline functions — min, max, and half — is external. If we were to compile each of these source files and link the resulting object files together into a single program, the result would be ill-formed.

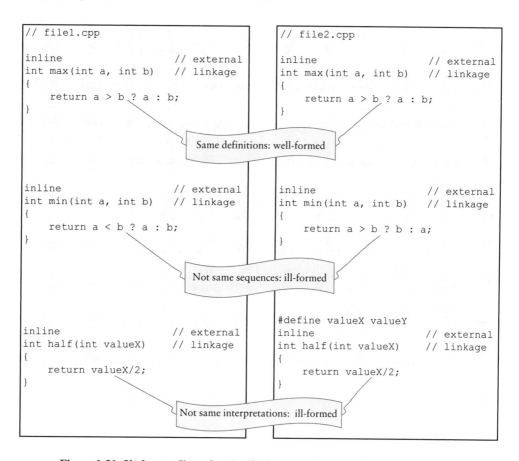

Figure 1-21: Understanding what the ODR means for inline-function definitions

Figure 1-21 illustrates what the ODR requires in order for inline function definitions to be "unique" across translation units. In the case of `max`, the sequence of characters is the same in both files, and the corresponding tokens in the two definitions have the same meaning: So far so good. In the case of `min`, however, such is not the case: Although the logical behavior might be identical, the sequences of tokens in the text files are not; hence, the program would be considered ill-formed, although no diagnostic is required by the C++ Standard. Finally, even though the compiled code would almost certainly be identical, the interpretation of `valueX` in the source text is not the same in both files; hence, even this tiny difference would (hypertechnically) cause the program to be considered ill-formed (with no diagnostic required).

Note that the example in Figure 1-21 is meant to convey the requirements of the ODR in C++ for constructs whose definitions might need to be seen by the compilers of clients in separate translation units. Achieving identical token sequences across multiple source files, however, is best achieved through the disciplined use of header files (see section 1.4). We will address the low-level physical implications of inline function definitions (among others) further (see section 1.3.12).

1.3.8   Not All Declarations Require a Definition to Be Useful

The declaration of an entity must always be visible for its name to be used. Some declarations, however, are useful in their own right. For example, a `typedef` declaration is a structural alias that requires no corresponding definition at either compile or link time in order to be fully usable.[47] How a declaration is used can affect whether the definition of the entity also needs to be visible. For example, a declaration of a user-defined type (e.g., `class`, `struct`, or `union`) can be used to create pointers and references to objects of the named type and even enable the *by-value* use of that name[48] in function prototypes without the client's compiler ever seeing the corresponding definition of that type:

```
class Opaque;
static Opaque *p = 0;
Opaque f(const Opaque& x);   // 'Opaque' is returned by value!
```

---

[47] Note, however, that the aliased type might itself need to be known — just as it would have been had it been used directly.

[48] Note that, as of C++11, the language capabilities were extended to provide support for *incomplete* types as template arguments (e.g., for containers), and as of C++17, two library containers — `std::vector` and `std::list` — are now required to do so. As with the C++ Standard itself, templates should not be assumed to support incomplete type arguments unless they are explicitly documented to do so.

By placing just the declaration of a class — where feasible (see section 1.7.5) — within a component's header file, rather than always `#include`-ing its definition, we can often substantially reduce unnecessary compile-time coupling (see section 3.10 and Volume II, section 6.6).

1.3.9   The Client's Compiler Typically Needs to See Class Definitions

A class declaration alone, however, does not provide sufficient information to create an object of that user-defined type, invoke the type's methods, inherit from that type, nest an object of that type in another user-defined type, or even know the `sizeof` (an object of) that type. Within a class definition typically resides other declarations and definitions. In particular, class member functions and static class data members are themselves just declarations of entities having external linkage — any use of which might have to be resolved at link time. When more than just the name of a user-defined type is needed, the corresponding definition of that type must have already been seen by the client's compiler:

```
struct Point {      // visible definition of type 'Point'
    int d_x;
    int d_y;
};


Point q;            // type definition required for size computation

int getX(const Point& p)
{
    return p.d_x;  // type definition required for offset computation
}
```

In the code snippet above, the compiler requires having seen the definition of the user-defined `Point` type in order to create object `q` because the compiler needs to be able to compute the `sizeof(Point)` to reserve the appropriate amount of storage for `q`. Similarly, the definition of `Point` is needed to compile the function `getX` because the compiler needs to be able to determine the offset of the data member `d_x` within the object referred to by `p`. And, because the compiler might need access to a type's definition from within multiple translation units that will ultimately be incorporated into a single program, the ODR allows for the definition of each distinct user-defined type to be repeated (once) in each translation unit, as illustrated in Figure 1-22.

```
// getx.cpp                          // gety.cpp

struct Point {                       struct Point {
    int d_x;                             int d_x;
    int d_y;                             int d_y;
};                                   };

int getX(const Point& p)             int getY(const Point& p)
{                                    {
    return p.d_x;                        return p.d_y;
}                                    }
```

Figure 1-22: Unique definition of type `Point` spanning translation units

Again, we are not advocating such source-code repetition as a design practice but rather just explaining the "nuts and bolts" of the underlying platform. There will be plenty of advice on how to achieve sound, usable, and maintainable software later in this volume (e.g., see Chapter 3).

1.3.10   Other Entities Where Users' Compilers Must See the Definition

There are many other uses of entities for which the compiler must be able to see the source code of the definition in order to generate code for the usage. In practice, the compiler simply generates code as if the program will comply with all of the requirements of the ODR. If the program does not, it is ill-formed and the behavior is undefined, and yet neither the compiler nor the linker is obliged by the C++ Language Standard to diagnose the problem.

1.3.11   Enumerations Have External Linkage, but So What?!

It is relatively common in practice to run afoul of the ODR. For example, consider the two elided `.cpp` files illustrated in Figure 1-23. If the `.o` files resulting from these two translation units are ever linked into the same program, that program would technically be ill-formed, as each translation unit contains a definition of the external-linkage entity named `Status` at file scope, yet the two definitions are clearly not the same.

```
// file1.cpp                         // file2.cpp
// ...                               // ...

enum Status { GOOD, BAD, UGLY };     enum Status { SUCCESS, FAILURE };

// ...                               // ...
```

Figure 1-23: An `enum` has external linkage and internal bindage

On the other hand, both enumeration names and the enumerators have internal *bindage*. Hence, on almost all relevant platforms, such subtle ODR violations will typically go undiagnosed and have no ill effects as there is simply no way for conventional compilers to detect the inconsistency across translation units, and no vestige of type `Status` would normally wind up in a `.o` file to give the linker the slightest chance to opine. These latent defects can, however, become problematic. Even a minor enhancement, such as adding external-linkage output operators overloaded on these physically secluded enumeration definitions, might well introduce artifacts into the `.o` file that could cause the build to fail or, worse, the program to misbehave at run time.

Cavalierly creating named enumerated types at file scope and risking a technically ill-formed program (though usually harmless in practice) is not recommended. As always, sequestering a named entity within an unnamed namespace is guaranteed to strip it of any external linkage and thereby ensures that it cannot collide directly or indirectly (logically or otherwise) with entities in other translation units.

1.3.12   Inline Functions Are a Somewhat Special Case

Inline functions are somewhat of a special case in that the definition (1) must be available in every translation unit in which it is invoked, and (2) can be repeated across translation units at both the source-code and object-code levels. Because the caller's compiler necessarily has access to the definition source, such functions might be "linked" by either the compiler or the linker, depending on whether the compiler decides[49] to substitute the function body at the point of call. If not, the compiler will need to deposit an out-of-line version of the function in the current translation unit to ensure that the linker has at least one definition to find. For that reason, we say that functions declared `inline` have *dual* bindage.

Modern compilers generate a definition of the inline function in the `.o` file in such a way that (1) only one of possibly many (identical) definitions found by the linker in separate `.o` files will be incorporated into the final executable program, and (2) incorporating such a definition serves to satisfy that one undefined symbol without necessarily dragging in other portions of the current `.o` file (except indirectly so as to satisfy additional undefined symbols associated with that one inline function definition).[50]

---

[49] The compiler's choice of whether to do the binding itself might be influenced by heuristics, such as trying to minimize run time or the amount of object code generated — e.g., whenever substitution of the function body in place would result in less object code than would be needed to invoke a non-`inline` version of the function.

[50] As discussed in section 1.2.3, linkers now provide for separate *sections* within a `.o` file that behave as if they were each a separate `.o` file within a library archive. That is, each separate section of the `.o` file is searched for needed symbol definitions. If such a section is incorporated (which occurs solely to resolve an undefined reference), only the code and associated undefined-symbol references for that particular section become part of the program. The compiler places each needed inline function definition into the `.o` file (at least conceptually) exactly one per section. Hence, incorporating one of the (identical) inline function definitions from the `.o` files corresponding to any of the translation units in the program has precisely the same effect (logical and physical) on the final executable.

If the address of an inline function is needed, that address is required to be unique throughout the program.[51] Taking the address of a function declared `inline` might result in an out-of-line copy of the compiled function definition being placed in the current translation unit's `.o` file but does not preclude that function's body from being substituted inline everywhere that it is invoked directly.[52] Moreover, the address of an inline function[53] is relevant only if it is taken within a given translation unit; if not (and the compiler successfully inlines the function wherever it is used locally), no definition of that inline function need appear in the `.o` file for the benefit of the current translation unit.[54]

1.3.13   Function and Class Templates

Templates are another complex feature of the C++ language whose logical and physical properties warrant considerable discussion. Templates, like classes and functions, have external linkage at file scope. That is, two class or function templates declared identically within the same (named) namespace in separate translation units refer to the same entity. Templates, however, are distinct from both classes and functions in that they are not used directly but instead are used to instantiate classes and functions that are.

1.3.14   Function Templates and Explicit Specializations

Let's start by examining the properties of function templates. As a simple yet practical example, consider the generic homogeneous comparison function, `compare`, illustrated in Figure 1-24. This function returns a negative, 0, or positive integer value depending on the relative values of its arguments of a conforming[55] type.

---

[51] Historically, due primarily to limitations of the tool chain, inline functions had *internal* (physical) *bindage* and, therefore, effectively *internal* (logical) linkage. That is, two inline functions having the same signature declared in the same scope in separate translation units were treated as if they referred to distinct logical entities. Early C++ compilers would make the equivalent of an independent file-scope `static` copy of the function in every translation unit in which a non-inline version of the function was needed. Taking the address of the inline function subsequently produced inconsistent results across translation units. This behavior was considered a bug since declaring a function `inline` is required to have absolutely no effect on logical behavior. Defining `static` data within inline functions was similarly problematic. Note that *inline variables*, adopted in C++17, address a physically similar (albeit dubious) need.

[52] Note that calling an inline function recursively is another way of encouraging an out-of-line copy of the definition to be generated.

[53] An inline function having static data might necessitate additional consideration.

[54] On some platforms, however, the non-`inline` definition is generated locally wherever an inline function is invoked — even when it is substituted inline by the compiler. In this case, the copy of the definition would remain a viable candidate for the linker to choose when resolving undefined symbols in other translation units.

[55] The notion of what makes a type *conforming* with respect to a template parameter (partially characterizable using a highly anticipated facility of C++20 known as *concepts*; see section 1.7.6) is the compile-time, structural analog of the function declarations (and contracts; see Volume II, Chapter 5) of a pure abstract base class (or *protocol*; see section 1.7.5); see section 1.7.7.

```
template <class TYPE>56,57
int compare(const TYPE& a, const TYPE& b);
    // Return a negative, 0, or positive integer indicating whether the
    // value of the specified 'a' object is less than, equal to, or
    // greater than that of the specified 'b' object.  The 'TYPE'
    // parameter must have an associated homogeneous operator '<'
    // consistent with the desired notion of value.
```

(a) Declaration and contract

---

[56] There are two schools of thought on whether to use `typename` versus `class` for template type parameters. Those who teach students learning C++ for the first time typically agree that `typename` is less confusing given that fundamental types, such as `int`, are valid type arguments, as are `struct`, `union`, and `enum` types. On the other hand, `typename` is *required* in only very special circumstances within templates (see the next footnote), and we believe that knowing exactly where, when, and why it is required leads to a deeper understanding of the complexities of the language, whereas just using it universally belies these details. Understanding the word `class` to mean "any type at all" is admittedly a bit of a "speed bump" for a novice, but it is hardly insurmountable. Note also that the C++ Standard itself has always been written in terms of `class`, not `typename`, for template parameters, which means that folks will need to know these details to access the Standard effectively. Finally, the keyword `class` is three characters shorter than the keyword `typename`, which can be a real benefit when trying to collect meaningful parameter names in a fixed line length of, say, 79 characters (which just happens to be our convention). So although `typename` was there in C++98, we have opted for the shorter `class` over the longer `typename` to introduce our template *type* parameters — fully acknowledging that this choice is purely one of style.

[57] The genesis of `typename` (having nothing whatsoever to do with the discussion above) was in discovering the need to distinguish a nested name of a template parameter — a.k.a. a *dependent* name — as representing a type as opposed to a value. For a nondependent name, what the name represents is known at the point a template is declared (or defined), whereas dependent names cannot be resolved until the point of instantiation, because the entity to which it refers depends on the actual argument supplied for the template parameter. If it is the intent that the dependent name is to represent a type, then it must be preceded by `typename`; otherwise, it will be presumed, by the compiler, to be a value — even if that would lead to a syntax error. E.g.,

```
template <class A, class B = typename A::value_type>
struct something_having_a_default_type_template_parameter;
```

Here, B is a template *type* parameter, but its default is a *dependent* type (with respect to A), which requires `typename` to precede it. Now consider a similar, yet a subtly different case:

```
template <class A, typename A::value_type V>
struct something_having_a_non_type_template_parameter;
```

In this case, V is a template *value* parameter of a *dependent* type (again with respect to A), so we must again use *typename* to make that known.

Keep in mind that the `typename` keyword is prohibited outside of template declarations and definitions, which include total specializations (discussed later in this subsection) as they — by definition — never have any unresolved template parameters.

One final note is that template template parameters (a construct we have never once found useful in practice) have historically not been permitted to use `typename` (instead of `class`) to introduce their own parameters. A template template parameter means that the parameter must itself be a template having a specified number of template parameters. E.g.,

```
template <template<class> class H, class S>
void f(const H<S>& value);
```

In this case, the first template argument to f must itself be a template having a single template parameter. Note that the first use of `class` in that example cannot be replaced with `typename` (although, as of C++17, it can); see **driscoll**. See also **abrahams05**, Appendix B, pp 307–321.

```
template <class TYPE>
int compare(const TYPE& a, const TYPE& b)        Note that, for the purposes of this
{                                                example, we have deliberately not
    return a < b ? -1 : b < a;                   declared this function inline.
}⁵⁸
```

(b) Definition

Figure 1-24: Free (i.e., nonmember) `compare` function template

To invoke `compare` on two objects of such a type, the compiler must have already seen a declaration of the `compare` template (Figure 1-24a), which (like other nonmember declarations) may be repeated within a translation unit:

```
template <class TYPE>
int compare(const TYPE& a, const TYPE& b);
```

Clients are now free to invoke `compare` on objects of arbitrary type so long as that type supports a suitable (i.e., *conforming*) definition of a < operator:

```
int result = compare(5, 3);  // result > 0
```

Upon seeing the statement above, the compiler implicitly generates an internal[59] declaration of an explicit specialization of the `compare` function template for objects of type `int`:

```
int compare(const int&, const int&);  // compiler generated
                                       // (internal)
```

Assuming no template definition source is available, the compiler has no choice but to generate (in the `.o` file) an external undefined symbol corresponding to the function signature of the explicit specialization.

---

[58] There are those who, in the name of readability, might reasonably prefer to see a body such as

```
        if (a < b) return -1;
  else if (a > b) return  1;
  else            return  0;
```

arguing that, for most modern compilers at even modest optimization levels, the generated object code will likely be the same — a claim that we have since corroborated using GCC 5.4.0 at optimization level -o1.

[59] The generated function name would need to be appropriately "mangled" so as not to conflict with an overloaded function having the same signature.

Notice that, primarily for didactic reasons, we have chosen *not* to declare the tiny function in Figure 1-24 `inline`, although we typically would have done so in practice (just as we would have for a tiny nontemplated one). There is, however, no real need for our declaring a function template `inline` as, unlike a regular non-`inline` function (which has external bindage), the C++ language already allows a function template's definition to be repeated in each translation unit — irrespective of whether it was declared `inline`. Moreover, once the source code of a function is visible (for whatever reason), the compiler is at full liberty to substitute the body of that function inline.

An unqualified function template definition, like an unqualified function definition, also serves as a declaration. When a function template definition (which must be unique within a translation unit) is visible, the compiler emits a separate instantiation of that function template's definition corresponding to each distinct implicitly generated instantiation of its declaration within that translation unit. And, just like an inline function, any explicit specialization of a function template whose definition is generated by the compiler — implicitly or otherwise (see below) — has dual bindage. Hence, when the compiler generates the definition for an explicit function template specialization in the `.o` file of the current translation unit, it does so in a way such that only one of possibly many (identical) definitions found by the linker in separate `.o` files will be incorporated into the final executable program.

There are times when knowing the explicit type of a function template parameter allows us to implement the resulting function more efficiently.[60] Let us now consider the important special case of our generic `compare` function template, i.e., when the function template's parameter type is `char`. According to the contract for `compare`, the requirement is that the integer returned to indicate relative size be either negative, 0, or positive, but the precise values are not specified. This latitude in the generic contract allows us to provide a more optimal implementation for the explicit specialization for `char`, as shown in Figure 1-25.

---

[60] We assert that, in almost any real-world application, performance — not variation in essential (logical) behavior — should be the sole reason for explicit specialization, and (where applicable) overloading is to be preferred (with functions "overloaded" on return type — e.g., "factory functions" — being a notable and common exception). By the same token, we might want to partially specialize a family of functions (e.g., on, say, the first parameter), but — given that C++ supports *partial specialization* for class templates only — we are forced to emulate this feature using appropriate function overloads instead.

```
template <>                                        // not a template
int compare<char>(const char& a, const char& b);
```

(a) Declaration

```
template <>                                        // not a template
int compare<char>(const char& a, const char& b)
{
    return b - a;
}61
```

(b) Definition

Figure 1-25: Explicit specialization of `compare` for type `char`

Declaring an explicit specialization, as in Figure 1-25a, tells the compiler that we will be supplying the definition for it as well and to use that definition (e.g., Figure 1-25b) rather than implicitly instantiating one from the template. It is therefore critical that the *declaration* of any explicit specialization follow that of the general function (or class) template but precede any use of the template for that specific type[62]:

```
template <class TYPE>
int compare(const TYPE& a, const TYPE& b);          // general template

// ...

template <>
int compare<char>(const char& a, const char& b);  // explicit
                                                    // specialization

// ...

int result = compare('a', 'b');                     // result < 0
```

---

[61] Note that both a and b are first *value-preserving integral* promoted to int — irrespective of whether char is signed or unsigned — as `sizeof(char) == 1` and `sizeof(int) > 1` on all conforming platforms.

[62] The importance of doing so consistently cannot be overstated, giving rise to the only limerick (actually part of the normative text) in the C++ Language Standard (**iso11**, section 14.7.3.7, pp. 375–376, specifically p. 376):

> When writing a specialization,
> be careful about its location;
> or to make it compile
> will be such a trial
> as to kindle its self-immolation.

Note, however, that an explicit specialization of a function template is not itself a template. Unless generated by the compiler (implicitly or otherwise), the definition has external bindage and therefore must not be present in more than one translation unit within a program:

```
template <>                                                 // external bindage
int compare<char>(const char& a, const char& b)  // not a template
{
    return b - a;                    Must be unique
}                                    throughout a
                                     program
```

That is, of course, unless the user-supplied explicit specialization is declared `inline`:

```
template <>
inline                                                      // dual bindage
int compare<char>(const char& a, const char& b)  // not a template
{
    return b - a;           Can be repeated
}                           in each translation unit
```

Historically, we have been told that the purpose of declaring a function `inline` is to give a hint to the compiler that it should try to replace the body of the function at the point of call in order to improve performance. The time for this sort of human suggestion is fading, just as it has for the `register` keyword many years back. These days, compilers are almost always far better equipped than human beings at determining whether inlining a function to which it has source-code access will improve runtime performance. We anticipate that the day will come when the only bona fide reason for ever declaring a function `inline` when using modern compilers[63,64]

---

[63] There are, however, popular compilers that will attempt to inline much more aggressively in template code if the `inline` keyword is present on the function definition, albeit often leading to more bloated, less-runtime-efficient code. For example, we tested this assertion on the `compare` function above using GCC 5.4.0; it didn't inline even with the `inline` keyword unless we used an optimization level of `-O1` or higher; without the `inline` keyword, it didn't inline at all — even with `-O4`!

[64] More recently, we tried compiling

```
extern "C" int printf(const char *, ...);
template <int N> inline int f(int i)
{
    return printf("%d\n", i) + printf("%d\n", i) + printf("%d\n", i);
}
template <int N> int g(int i)
{
    return printf("%d\n", i) + printf("%d\n", i) + printf("%d\n", i);
}
int main(int c, const char **v) { return f<1>(c) + g<2>(c); }
```

and observed, using https://godbolt.org, that the compiler had inlined the call to `f` (above) but not the call to `g`.

will be to allow us, under the ODR, to place its source in multiple translation units, thereby granting the compiler the opportunity to choose whether to inline that function's body (i.e., *dual* as opposed to *external bindage*).

There are, however, situations in which one might prefer, for reasons unrelated to run time or code size (see section 3.10), that the compiler not inline certain functions. Declaring a function in every translation unit in which it is used but defining it in only one .cpp file is the best way to ensure that conventional compilers will be unable to inline it outside the translation unit in which it is defined. Note that declaring a nonmember inline function static makes it local to the translation unit, both logically (internal as opposed to external linkage) and physically (internal as opposed to dual bindage).

Before moving on to class templates, it is worth noting that, unlike member function template instantiations and ordinary functions, each free (i.e., nonmember) function template instantiation is required to encode its return type (along with its signature)[65]:

```
int compare<int>(const int& a, const int& b); // template instantiation
```

Moreover, the symbol must be distinct from the symbol corresponding to an ordinary (nontemplated) function having the same signature (and return type):

```
int compare(const int& a, const int& b);      // ordinary free function
```

Both entities can co-exist and be accessed within a single scope in the same translation unit:

```
int r1 = compare(3, 4);        // If overloaded, invoke ordinary free
                               // function.
int r2 = compare<int>(3, 4);   // always invoke template specialization
```

---

[65] Why encoding the return type is required for function templates, but not regular functions, might not be obvious to some, so we asked (via private email) Alisdair Meredith, former Library Working Group (LWG) chair for the C++ Standards Committee (c. 2010–2015), for an off-the-cuff explanation (*n.b.*, SFINAE stands for Substitution Failure Is Not An Error):

> Think of two overloads of the same function name, constrained to trigger SFINAE under mutually exclusive circumstances. The same set of parameters might invoke different overloads, determined only by the SFINAE constraints on the result type. Hence, result type is part of the signature for function templates but not for regular functions that can never get into these confusing SFINAE situations.

The statements above are illustrative of both the similarities and subtle distinctions between function overloading and explicit specialization. In addition, note that, for normal functions, the standard conversion rules apply, whereas for function templates, there must be an exact match:

```
int compare_nontemplate(const long& a, const long& b);


template <class TYPE>
int compare_template(const TYPE& a, const TYPE& b);


compare_nontemplate(3, 5L);      // normal function, 3 promoted to 3L


compare_template(3, 5L);         // function template, compile error


compare_template<long>(3, 5L);  // function template, 3 promoted to 3L
```

Also note that we would *never* choose to use `long` as an interface (a.k.a. *vocabulary*) type (see Volume II, section 4.4).

1.3.15   Class Templates and Their Partial Specializations

Class templates are yet more sophisticated, allowing for what's known as *partial specialization*. As an illustrative but purely academic[66] example, consider a generic "utility" struct `FooUtil`, parameterized by `TYPE`. This utility contains a single `static` member function, `max`, having two parameters, `a` and `b` (of the specified parameter `TYPE`), which returns the "larger" of its two arguments, for the following (compile-time recursive) definition of *larger*:

1. If `TYPE` is not a pointer, apply the `<` operator and return `a` (by reference), unless `a < b`, in which case return `b`.

2. If `TYPE` is a pointer to `char`, return `a` unless the (presumably) null-terminated string at `b` is lexicographically larger than the one at `a`, in which case return `b`.

3. Otherwise, recursively apply the `max` function to the respective objects at addresses `a` and `b`, and return the address of the *larger* object.

Understand that this particular problem is shamelessly contrived to allow us to illustrate concisely yet intuitively the physical properties of declarations, definitions, and linkage of class

---

[66] Again, we consider all forms of template specialization as primarily an implementation detail; hence, we would avoid the use of partial or explicit specialization to vary (documented) *essential behavior* in practice. Moreover, this sort of design is simply "too cute" for production use, and yet it does provide valuable insight into how C++ compilers and linkers cooperate. For more advice on proper interface design, see Volume II, Chapter 5.

templates along with their various levels of specialization. Figure 1-26 illustrates how one *could* implement such a generic `struct` using a general class template, a partial specialization for pointer types, and an explicit specialization specifically for pointers to `char` (but please don't do anything like this in practice).

```
template <class TYPE>        // declaration of class template
class FooUtil;

template <class TYPE>        // declaration of partial specialization
class FooUtil<TYPE *>;            This is not a template!

template <>                  // declaration of explicit specialization
class FooUtil<char *>;
```

(a) Class template (and class) declarations

```
template <class TYPE>
struct FooUtil {
    static const TYPE& max(const TYPE& a, const TYPE& b);
};

template <class TYPE>
struct FooUtil<TYPE *> {
    static const TYPE *max(const TYPE *a, const TYPE *b);
};
                                  This is not a template!
template <>
struct FooUtil<char *> {
    static const char *max(const char *a, const char *b);
};
```

(b) Class template (and class) definitions; member function declarations

```
template <class TYPE>
const TYPE& FooUtil<TYPE>::max(const TYPE& a, const TYPE& b)
{
    return a < b ? b : a;
}

template <class TYPE>
const TYPE *FooUtil<TYPE *>::max(const TYPE *a, const TYPE *b)
{
    return !a ? b : !b ? a : FooUtil<TYPE>::max(*a, *b) == *a ? a : b;
}
                                  This is not a template!
template <>
const char *FooUtil<char *>::max(const char *a, const char *b)
{
    return !a ? b : !b ? a : std::strcmp(a, b) < 0 ? b : a;
}
```

(c) Definitions of member functions of a class template and its specializations

Figure 1-26: Class template `FooUtil` and its specializations

For example, for integers, `max` returns a reference to the larger `int`:

```
int ia = 3, ib = 5;
const int& r1 = FooUtil<int>::max(ia, ib);          // reference to 'ib'
```

For pointers to `char`, `max` returns the address of the first character in the lexicographically larger null-terminated sequence:

```
const char *sa = "abc", *sb = "def";
const char *r2 = FooUtil<char *>::max(sa, sb);   // address of 'd' in
                                                 // "def"
```

For pointers to `int`, `max` returns the address of the larger `int`:

```
int *pia = &ia, *pib = &ib;
int *r3 = FooUtil<int *>::max(pia, pib);            // address of 'ib'
```

For pointers to pointers to `int`, `max` returns the address of the pointer to the larger `int`:

```
int **ppia = &pia, **ppib = &pib;
int **r4 = FooUtil<int **>::max(ppia, ppib);        // address of 'pib'
```

The result is similar for pointers to pointers to `char`:

```
const char **psa = &sa, **psb = &sb:
const char **r5 = FooUtil<char **>::max(psa, psb);  // address of 'sb'
```

Figure 1-26a shows just the declarations of the `FooUtil` class template and its specializations, each of which may be repeated any number of times within a given scope. Figure 1-26b shows their corresponding definitions. The first definition is of the class template `FooUtil` itself. The second definition is for the partial specialization of `FooUtil` for arbitrary pointer types. A partial specialization is also a template, as the compiler, when called upon to do so, will need to infer the definition of a class — in this case one corresponding to the particular type of pointer supplied. The third definition, however, is of a class, not a class template, as the explicit specialization of `FooUtil` for the case of a pointer to `char` leaves nothing for the compiler to infer.

Both classes and class templates are meaningful to the compiler but are of no relevance to the linker. That is, no artifacts of either are deposited in a translation unit's `.o` file, as there are no memory addresses to be shared across translation units. Recall that such is not the case with respect to the distinction between functions and function templates or — in this case — between the definition of a member function of a class template (or its partial specialization) and that of a member function of its explicit specialization.

Now consider the three definitions shown in Figure 1-26c. The first definition is that of the member function corresponding to the general `FooUtil` class template and is itself a template. After seeing (just) the declaration of the general `FooUtil` template, when client code invokes

```
FooUtil<SomeType>::max(someObjectA, someObjectB)
```

the compiler will either (1) inline the function body or (2) generate an undefined-symbol reference unique to the class `FooUtil`, the template parameter *SomeType*, and the function `max` (including its signature):

```
FooUtil<SomeType>::max(const SomeType&, const SomeType&)
```

Unless instructed otherwise (see section 1.3.16), the compiler will also deposit a definition of the explicit instantiation of this member function template into the `.o` file, and — just like an implicit instantiation of a free function template (or inline function) — the compiler will do so in a way that at most one definition will be linked into the program. That is, any such function definition generated by the compiler will wind up having *dual bindage*.

The second definition in Figure 1-26c, corresponding to the member function in the partial specialization of `FooUtil` on a pointer type other than `char *`, is also a template. Client code invoking

```
FooUtil<SomeType *>::max(somePtrA, somePtrB)
```

where *SomeType* is anything other than `char`, will cause the compiler to generate an undefined symbol:

```
FooUtil<SomeType *>::max(const SomeType *, const SomeType *)
```

Again, the compiler will (by default) generate a definition (having dual bindage) for the particular specialization, which is suitable for the linker to use to resolve the undefined symbol yet will not cause the linker to automatically drag in any other definitions in this `.o` file nor conflict with other (identical) definitions in any other `.o` files.

Finally, the third definition in Figure 1-26c implements a member function of the explicit specialization of type `FooUtil` for the parameter type `char *`. Since the template specialization is explicit, rather than partial, there is nothing for the compiler to generate. Whenever the compiler generates an explicit specialization, its bindage is, by default, external; hence, unless the function template is declared `inline`, its definition is required by the ODR to appear at most once throughout the entire program.

1.3.16   `extern` Templates

As a potential physical optimization, we might want to direct the compiler not to generate into the `.o` file of every calling translation unit the (dual bindage) function definitions associated with certain frequently used explicit specializations of function or class templates, yet we still expose, to the caller's compiler, the source of the definition of the general template — e.g., for inlining purposes. A convenient mechanism[67] to achieve this specific goal is to place the keyword `extern` at the beginning of the identifying "declaration" of the explicit specialization, following the *declaration* (and typically also the definition) of the corresponding general template:

```
// xyza_compare.h

// ...                               Declaration and
                                       definition
template <class TYPE>                                    // general
int compare(const TYPE& a, const TYPE& b)                // template
{
    return a < b ? -1 : b < a;
}

extern template                                          // commonly used
int compare<double>(const double& a, const double& b);  // specialization

// ...                    "Declaration" only
                          (note: special-purpose syntax)
```

Then, in the (normally) one translation unit where you want the compiler to generate the definition from the general template, repeat that definition (typically via including the corresponding header) and then explicitly repeat the specialized "declaration" — this time without the `extern`:

---

[67] Note that this common extension for C++03 was not formally standardized until C++11.

```
// xyza_compare.cpp

#include <xyza_compare.h>

// ...

template                                              // commonly used
int compare<double>(const double& a, const double& b);  // specialization

// ...
```

"Declaration" only
(note: special-purpose syntax)

Now only the `xyza_compare.o` file will have the instantiation of the general definition of the `compare` function template specialized for type `double`. Notice that, if implemented using a header file as shown above, the compiler of the `xyza_compare.cpp` translation unit will wind up seeing the general template definition and *both* declarations of the explicit specialization, with the non-`extern` declaration overriding the previous one.

It is worth noting that the client's compiler — even with classical tool chains — remains capable of (and at full liberty to) inline the code for the identified common specialization at the call sight. The `extern template` declaration merely suppresses generation of function definitions into the calling translation unit's `.o` file for that specialization but doesn't prohibit the caller's compiler from generating the code inline (just as it would have done before) if appropriate. What makes such possible is that the only way to implement the common specialization in a `.o` file is to ask the compiler to do it by instantiating the general template there. Hence, whether the compiler generates the definition inline (implicitly) or in a given `.o` file (by explicit request), that definition is guaranteed (by the compiler) to be the same.[68]

Class templates behave similarly. Placing `extern template` in front of the declaration of an explicit specialization prevents the compiler from generating any of the member definitions locally into the `.o` file, though all instantiations of the general template — including those singled out as described here — will still be inlined at the call site (just as before) if the compiler chooses to do so:

---

[68] Note that, with GCC 5.4.0, the `compare` function did not inline at all for any optimization level up to `-O4`. Even after declaring it `inline`, it required an optimization level of at least `-O1` before inlining would occur, which suggests that the `inline` keyword might continue to carry some advisory weight with some compilers, especially when used within templates, as it has essentially no other purpose there.

```
// xyza_foo.h
// ...
template <class TYPE>              // general template
class Foo {
  public:
    static int compare(const TYPE& a, const TYPE& b)
    {
        return a < b ? -1 : b < a;
    }
};
extern template                    // common specialization
class Foo<double>;
// ...
```

Only the `.o` file of the translation unit containing the corresponding non-`extern` directive winds up having (all of) the member functions instantiated:

```
// xyza_foo.cpp
#include <xyza_foo.h>
template                           // common specialization
class Foo<double>;
```

Notice again that, when a header file is used (as it would be in practice; see section 3.3.4), the compiler of `xyza_foo.cpp` will see both "declarations" of the explicit specialization following the general template definition, and, again, the final, non-`extern` version will prevail.

1.3.17   Understanding the ODR (and Bindage) in Terms of Tools

When it comes to inline functions and function templates, understanding when a definition must be unique throughout an entire program versus being unique merely within each translation unit is made less daunting when you think about it from the point of view of the build tools that implement it. Whenever the compiler generates the definition of an explicit specialization from a general template definition — whether implicitly or by explicit request — each such definition will necessarily be identical. Knowing that, the compiler may also decide to inline the function, because doing so will always result in the same logical behavior as would linking to the externally accessible function it generated.

Given that all these definitions must be consistent and interchangeable, there is no harm in allowing more than one physical definition to reside in a single program. However, when the programmer is specifying a *custom* definition of an explicit specialization (i.e., not merely instructing the compiler where to generate one from the general definition), that definition (which could easily be different from the specialized definition generated by the compiler) must be unique throughout the entire program — that is, of course, unless the custom specialization is declared `inline`.

In particular, the user-defined specializations of `compare` for type `char` in Figure 1-25, section 1.3.14, and of `Foo` for type `char *` in Figure 1-26, section 1.3.15, must be unique throughout the entire program, whereas the common specializations of `compare` and `Foo` for type `double` (section 1.3.16) do not. This and other considerations (e.g., bindage) — from the point of view of the tools — are what provide insight and guidance in order to better appreciate the inherent complexities of the ODR, which tries its best to be tool-chain agnostic.

1.3.18   Namespaces

Opening a named namespace introduces the namespace name into the enclosing scope and is therefore a kind of declaration:

```
namespace xyza {  // introduce the namespace name 'xyza'
    // ...
}
```

There is no definition (or meaning) corresponding to this declaration apart from the name itself, and therefore there is no notion of bindage for namespaces themselves. Use of external- or dual-bindage constructs declared within a namespace might, however, generate (in the current translation unit's .o file) undefined-symbol references that incorporate the namespace name and are therefore treated as distinct from entities having the same declaration at file scope or in a different namespace:

```
void g();
namespace xyza { void g(); }
namespace xyzb { void g(); }

void f()
{                       // For example (GCC 6.3.1):
    ::g();              // U: _Z1gv
    xyza::g();          // U: _ZN4xyza1gEv
    xyzb::g();          // U: _ZN4xyzb1gEv
}
```

The unnamed namespace is intended to provide a scope that is logically local to a translation unit; hence, declarations of entities within an unnamed namespace have internal linkage. In theory, one would expect that bindage would also be internal; however, subtle technical idiosyncrasies in the standard, not corrected until C++11, forced the bindage to be external. Even if the implementation of entities in an unnamed namespace uses bindage that is technically external, the compiler converts it to be effectively internal, just as it does for declarations of functions and variables declared static at file or namespace scope.

```
namespace {
class Guard {
    // ...
  public:
    Guard();  // internal linkage and (effectively) internal bindage
    // ...
};
// ...
}  // close unnamed namespace
```

Older platforms, the actual bindage of entities nested within the unnamed namespace was external; a long and obscure symbol name (unique to the translation unit) is generated and used to qualify symbols within that namespace, thereby simulating internal bindage:

```
// file.cpp
namespace {        // unnamed namespace
    void g();
}


void f()
{                  // for example (GCC 3.4.4)
    g();           // U: __ZN37_GLOBAL__N_file.cpp_00000000_B874665C1gEv
}
```

On more recent platforms, the implementation has changed to reflect the evolving standard:

```
void f()
{                       // for example (GCC 6.3.1)
    g();                // U: _ZN12_GLOBAL__N_11gEv
}
```

We can also simulate internal bindage — purely by convention — through careful, systematic naming (see section 2.7.3).

1.3.19   Explanation of the Default Linkage of `const` Entities

Finally, it is worth noting that variables at file (or namespace) scope have *external* linkage by default, whereas variables that are declared `const` — unlike the C Language — have *internal* linkage:

```
int h;              // external linkage (and bindage)
const int i = 0;    // internal linkage (and bindage)

const int *j;       // external linkage (and bindage)
int *const k = &h;  // internal linkage (and bindage)
```

Notice that the pointer variable itself, and not the object to which it refers, must be `const` for the default linkage (and bindage) to be `internal`.

1.3.20   Summary of Declarations, Definitions, Linkage, and Bindage

As the detailed discussion above suggests, understanding abstractly how to distinguish pure declarations,[69] definitions that also act as declarations,[70] and definitions that don't is difficult at best. Figure 1-27 provides a fairly comprehensive list of illustrative examples of declarations versus definitions including their (logical) linkage as well as their (physical) bindage.

---

[69] Pure declarations are sometimes called *forward declarations* because they come *before* (as opposed to *along with*) the definition. Note that, especially for constructs having external *bindage*, it might well be that a compiler making use of a *local* declaration never gets to see its corresponding definition, rendering the use of the term "forward" suspect. With the exception of a very few internal-bindage constructs (e.g., `class`), we will require that a declaration corresponding to its external-linkage or dual-linkage definition reside in — and be used via — a header file (see section 1.4) that is included by the translation units of both implementer and client of that declaration.

[70] By "act as declarations" here we mean definitions that are *self-declaring*, and we, as needed, refer to definitions that aren't as "definition-only."

Construct at File Scope	declaration/ DEFINITION	(Logical) Linkage	(Physical) Bindage
`int i;`	DEFINITION	EXTERNAL	EXTERNAL
`const int M = 5;`	DEFINITION	internal	internal
`extern int j;`	declaration	EXTERNAL	EXTERNAL
`static int k;`	DEFINITION	internal	internal*
`void f();`	declaration	EXTERNAL	EXTERNAL
`static void f();`	declaration	internal	internal*
`inline void f() { }`	DEFINITION	EXTERNAL	Dual
`static inline void f() { }`	DEFINITION	internal	internal*
`typedef int Int;`	declaration	— NA —	internal
`enum A { };`	DEFINITION	EXTERNAL	internal
`enum { X };`	DEFINITION	EXTERNAL	internal
`enum { } e;`	DEFINITION	EXTERNAL	EXTERNAL
`class U;`	declaration	EXTERNAL	internal
`class V { };`	DEFINITION	EXTERNAL	internal
`struct W { };`	DEFINITION	EXTERNAL	internal
`class MyClass {`	DEFINITION	EXTERNAL	internal
`    int d_a;`	DEFINITION	EXTERNAL	internal
`    const int d_b;`	DEFINITION	EXTERNAL	internal
`    static int s_c;`	declaration	EXTERNAL	EXTERNAL
`    static const int s_d;`	declaration	EXTERNAL	EXTERNAL
`    typedef double Float64;`	declaration	— NA —	internal
`    enum Status { GOOD, BAD };`	DEFINITION	EXTERNAL	internal
`    void f() const;`	declaration	EXTERNAL	EXTERNAL
`    static void g();`	declaration	EXTERNAL	EXTERNAL
`    inline void h();`	declaration	EXTERNAL	Dual
`    static inline void i();`	declaration	EXTERNAL	Dual
`} x;`	DEFINITION	EXTERNAL	EXTERNAL
`int MyClass::s_c;`	DEFINITION-only	EXTERNAL	EXTERNAL
`const int MyClass::s_d = 0;`	DEFINITION-only	EXTERNAL	EXTERNAL
`void MyClass::f() const { }`	DEFINITION-only	EXTERNAL	EXTERNAL
`void MyClass::g() { }`	DEFINITION-only	EXTERNAL	EXTERNAL
`inline void MyClass::h() { }`	DEFINITION-only	EXTERNAL	Dual
`inline void MyClass::i() { }`	DEFINITION-only	EXTERNAL	Dual

* As of C++11, the desired semantics of (and consequently underlying mechanisms for) representing functions and data declared `static` converged with those of being declared in the unnamed namespace.

(continues)

(continued)

Construct at File Scope	declaration/ DEFINITION	(Logical) Linkage	(Physical) Bindage
`namespace { void f() { } }`	DEFINITION	internal	EXTERNAL*
`namespace Foo {`	DEFINITION	EXTERNAL	internal
`    int i;`	DEFINITION	EXTERNAL	EXTERNAL
`}`			
`template<class T> class Stack;`	declaration	EXTERNAL	internal
`template<class T> class Stack { };`	DEFINITION	EXTERNAL	internal
`template<class T> T max(T x, T y);`	declaration	EXTERNAL	internal
`template<>`			
`    int min<int>(int x, int y);`	declaration	EXTERNAL	EXTERNAL
`template <class T> class vector {`	DEFINITION	EXTERNAL	internal
`    void push_back(const T&);`	declaration	EXTERNAL	EXTERNAL
`};`			
`void vector<int>::push_back() {...}`	DEFINITION-only	EXTERNAL	EXTERNAL
`template <class T> struct X {`	DEFINITION	EXTERNAL	internal
`    friend void f(const X&);`	declaration	EXTERNAL	EXTERNAL
`};`			

* As of C++11, the desired semantics of (and consequently underlying mechanisms for) representing
functions and data declared `static` converged with those of being declared in the unnamed namespace.

Figure 1-27: Declaration, definition, or both; linkage; and bindage

In the following section, we illustrate how header files are commonly used to share definitions (where the binding might be done by the compiler), as well as pure declarations (where the binding must be done by the linker). In sections 1.6 and 1.11, we introduce the fundamental properties of components that (1) differentiate them from merely a pair of similarly named .h and .cpp files, and (2) help us to address many of the subtle issues discussed above.

1.4   Header Files

As engineers, we strive to catch errors early, especially when developers on other teams will be using our software. Figure 1-28 illustrates a familiar physical idiom: Instead of relying on clients to guess the signatures of our external-linkage functions (Figure 1-28c), it is our responsibility as library developers to supply a header file (Figure 1-28b) having the corresponding function (and global-variable) declarations. By including this header, our clients (Figure 1-28a) will catch many common usage errors at compile time that might not otherwise be caught until link time or — worse yet — run time.

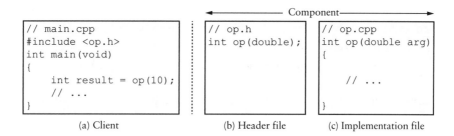

(a) Client   (b) Header file   (c) Implementation file

Figure 1-28: Using external-linkage function definitions

Historically, C language header files were used to facilitate the sharing of `typedef` declarations and `struct` definitions as well as to enable functions and variables having external linkage (and bindage) to interact across translation units. The one-to-one pairing of `.h` and `.c` files was, however, far less common in classic C than it is with `.h` and `.cpp` files in C++ today.

In vintage C programs, the procedural nature of the language seduced many early developers into excessive use of global data. Header files served primarily as "common" areas, as illustrated in Figure 1-29. In these unstructured programs, the implementation files tended to be monolithic and sometimes quite large (many thousands of lines) — the almost arbitrary partitioning of source code being governed by how much could be compiled at once in a "reasonable" amount of time.

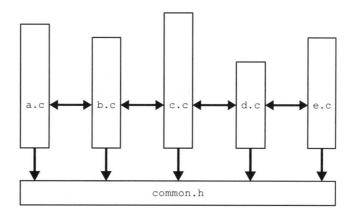

Figure 1-29: An unstructured program

Good modular design, on the other hand, encourages us to actively partition our implementations, colocating related implementation decisions (e.g., data) and hiding those details behind carefully crafted procedural interfaces (see section 3.11.7). In well-structured C programs, `.h` files are

often associated with declaring interfaces to conceptual modules, while their implementations
are relegated to .c files. Used properly, C headers (consisting almost exclusively of function and
`typedef` declarations, and `struct` and `enum` definitions) are of comparatively lighter weight,
contributing little (if anything) in the way of implementation to clients' resulting .o files.

Consequently, it is not uncommon in C to find a single, tersely commented .h file backed by
numerous "beefy" .c files, as illustrated in Figure 1-30, with a couple of *private* header files
thrown in to facilitate sharing across physical boundaries within logical modules. As we shall
see shortly, this more coarse-grained, less-regular physical structure was, in part, due to limitations imposed by the C language itself.

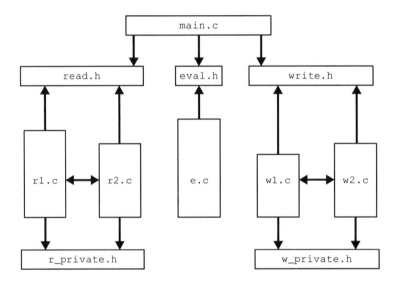

Figure 1-30: A coarse-grained modular C program

Beyond modules, the object-oriented paradigm encourages us to group useful functionality
around efficient, self-contained data structures, which can then be instantiated any number of
times. These so-called *abstract data types* (ADTs) naturally lend themselves to a more fine-
grained decomposition, with the potential for abundant intermediate interfaces and no need for
back-door access via private header files. Because these objects tend to be more self-contained,
we begin to think of them as separate entities, with each ADT being granted a separate header
file to hold its interface.

Our ability to create ADTs in C, however, is impeded by inadequate support for the efficient
encapsulation and (logical) hiding of data. Although C enables us to allocate a data structure in
the .c file and pass it back opaquely (via its address), C does not enable us to restrict access to

a data structure created as an automatic variable (on the program stack).[71] We can, of course, hide the details of the implementation by relegating them to the .c file, but — to hide the implementation — we are forced to pay the price of pointer indirection and a function call on every operation (no matter how tiny or trivial that operation might be).

With the advent of inline functions and `private` access in C++, many such inefficiencies were eliminated entirely. It is now common to find a single class definition in a .h file with the necessary implementation distributed appropriately (and more evenly) across that .h file and a corresponding .cpp file (having the same root name), such as those shown in Figure 1-31.

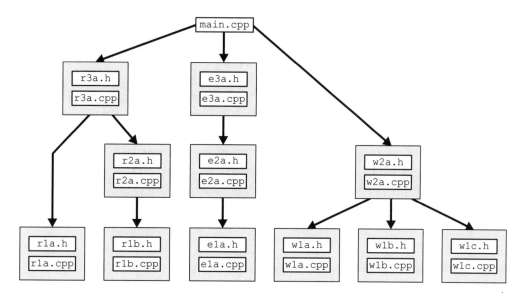

Figure 1-31: A fine-grained modular program

It is also common to find many details of the implementation in a header file — the justification, again, being runtime efficiency. The ability of C++ to allow a client's compiler to incorporate certain implementation details directly into its translation unit often enables us to bypass pointer indirections and costly function calls (let alone expensive dynamic memory allocation/de-allocation for the creation/destruction of every object). These efficiencies, however, do come at a price: Now, changes to the implementation of an ADT might force clients not only to relink but also to recompile! We will more fully discuss the ramifications of this compile-time

---

[71] To create a variable of a user-defined type (UDT) on the program stack, the compiler has to know the size of the variable; to know its size, the compiler has to have seen the definition of the data structure. In C (unlike C++), seeing the definition of a UDT necessarily implies being able to access its fields directly.

exposure (see section 3.10), as well as how to avoid it completely (see section 3.11) or at least partially (see Volume II, section 6.6).

Strictly speaking, we do not need header files to create multifile programs. Recall from section 1.3.1 that the C++ language requires only that there be at most one definition of any entity within a program. For entities having external linkage and bindage, the compiler will enforce uniqueness by generating a strong symbol definition, which if repeated will cause the linker to report multiply defined symbols. For other definitions having external linkage, however, it is our responsibility to ensure that each such definition is replicated identically (exactly once) in every translation unit that needs it. We must also ensure that declarations corresponding to each needed external- and dual-bindage definition are similarly incorporated. Header files provide a natural, convenient, and modular mechanism for fulfilling these obligations, as well as for sharing other useful constructs having internal bindage (e.g., `typedefs`).

Certain kinds of structural declarations, such as a `typedef` or a preprocessor constant (which are not subject to linkage as defined in the C++ Standard), have internal bindage and therefore need not be consistent from one translation unit to the next. As illustrated in Figure 1-32, we can declare `Number` to represent the type `int` at file scope in `file1.cpp` and `double` in `file2.cpp` with impunity. Having `DEFAULT_VALUE` represent `3` in one `.cpp` file and `4.5` in another is also fine. If, however, we repeat such constructs in the same context, they must of course be consistent.

```
// file1.cpp                        // file2.cpp

typedef int Number;                 typedef double Number;
typedef int Number;                 typedef double Number;

#define DEFAULT_VALUE 3             #define DEFAULT_VALUE 4.5
#define DEFAULT_VALUE 3             #define DEFAULT_VALUE 4.5

// ...                              // ...
```

Figure 1-32: Structural aliases may differ across translation units

On the other hand, if we want to share useful aliases (such as the signature of a callback function) with clients, a header file is our only option:

```
// myevent.h
class MyEvent {
    // ...
  public:
    typedef void (*EventCallback)(const char *, int, MyEvent *);
    // ...
```

```
    int registerInterest(EventCallback userSuppliedFunction);
    // ...
};
```

External-linkage definitions having internal- or dual-bindage must be replicated exactly across all translation units that need them. Even slight inconsistencies from one translation unit to the next, such as those shown in Figure 1-33, will violate the ODR and render programs ill-formed, with potentially dire consequences. Even if the meaning of two definitions are logically identical, as in Figure 1-33e, having two different token sequences to represent the definition of an entity within a program across translation units is nonetheless considered ill-formed. Note that an ODR violation that does not result in unexpected behavior on any relevant platforms is said to be *benign*. In Volume II, section 6.8, we will see how such benign ODR violations can be exploited when combining various subsystems built with different levels of *defensive programming* checks (see Volume II, sections 5.2 and 5.3).

```
// file1.cpp                                 // file2.cpp

      enum Status {                                enum Status {
(a)       GOOD,                                        BAD = -1,
          BAD                                          GOOD
      };                                           };

      union Scalar {                               union Scalar {
          int       d_integer;                         int       d_integer;
(b)       double    d_real;                            float     d_real;
          char      *d_string_p;                       char      *d_string_p;
      };                                           };

      struct Point {                               struct Point {
(c)       int d_xCoord;                                int d_yCoord;
          int d_yCoord;                                int d_xCoord;
      };                                           };

      class Box {                                  class Box {
          static int s_useCount;                       Point     d_origin;
          Point      d_lowerLeft;                      int       d_length;
          Point      d_upperRight;                     int       d_width;
(d)   public:                                      public:
          Box(const Point& lowerLeft,                  Box(const Point& origin,
              const Point& upperRight);                    int length, int width);
          // ...                                       // ...
      };                                           };

      enum Answer {                                enum Answer { // (typically
(e)       YES = 0,                                     YES = 0,    // benign) ODR
          NO                                           NO  = 1     // violation across
      };                                           };              // translation units
```

Figure 1-33: Inconsistent definitions yielding ill-formed programs

Sharing data and functions having external linkage can also be accomplished without header files, but this is ill-advised. Although it is highly unlikely that someone would opt to retype an entire class just to access the public methods (or static data) it declares, it is not unheard of (albeit a bad idea) to retype the declaration for externally defined free functions or variables.

For example, the files in Figure 1-34 contain inadvertent inconsistencies between the declarations of x and g() (in client.cpp) and their definitions (in provider.cpp), yet both files in the figure will compile. They might even link successfully, as the C++ Standard does not require the return type of an ordinary function to be encoded in its link-time symbol, nor does type-safe linkage apply to data. Instead, these latent defects will go unnoticed until run time.

```
// client.cpp

extern int x;     // BAD IDEA
extern int g();   // BAD IDEA
// ...
void client()
{
    x = 1;
    int y = g();
    // ...
}
```

```
// provider.cpp

double x;

double g()
{
    // ...
}
```

Figure 1-34: Inconsistent external-linkage declarations are ill-formed

The time-honored, prescribed way of ensuring consistency of a declaration with its corresponding definition and use by prospective clients across translation units in C, and now C++, is to place the declaration in a header file and then require that the header file be included by all clients (i.e., translation units that make use of the defined entity), as well as the .cpp file containing the definition — as the first substantive line of code (see section 1.6.1). As Figure 1-35 illustrates, inconsistencies between the declarations contained in provider.h and the definitions residing in provider.cpp are now exposed when provider.cpp is compiled. When client.cpp includes provider.h, the potential inconsistency that can occur when a declaration is retyped is eliminated. This practice of using header files to share information across translation units is essential for current static-analysis tools to perform effective local verifications of correctness on arbitrarily large code bases.[72]

---

[72] See **lippencott16a;** see also **lippencott16b** and **lippencott16c.**

```
// client.cpp                 // provider.h              // provider.cpp

#include <provider.h>         extern double x;          #include <provider.h>

void client()                 double g();               double x;
{
    x = 1;    Narrowing                                 double g()
                                                        {
    int y = g();                                            // ...
    // ...                                              }
}
```

Figure 1-35: Using header files to guarantee declaration consistency

When using free (i.e., nonmember) functions, even the inclusion of a header file is not sufficient to guarantee correctness. For example, both files shown in Figure 1-36 will compile: client.cpp compiles because it sees a valid declaration for f that it can use; provider.cpp compiles because the function definition for f(double) serves as its own declaration. The function declaration for f(int) is seen by the compiler simply as a permissible overload, not as an inconsistency.[73] When we try to link the program, however, the link will fail because there is no definition for the function f(int).

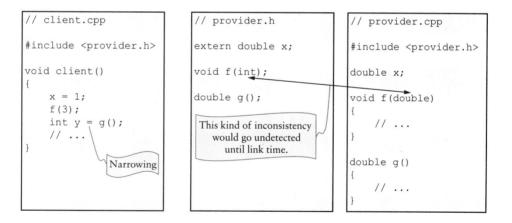

Figure 1-36: Even header files alone cannot guarantee consistency

---

[73] Note that signatures that are not identical yet do not produce distinct overloads (e.g., due to "too similar" parameter types) will, of course, be reported as errors during compilation.

Though effective at catching an omitted definition, even linking will be unable to detect the presence of an extra, undesired one. Our aim is to validate our intent (i.e., that there exists a declaration in the header file for every externally consumable definition in the associated implementation file) and to do so as early as possible. We can enforce our intent by adopting the convention (see section 2.5) that we always define our functions using the qualified-name syntax, as discussed at the beginning of section 1.3 (see Figure 1-17, section 1.3.1). Because a definition using qualified-name syntax does *not* implicitly also serve as a declaration, the compiler will require that there be a corresponding declaration directly within the named scope and report an error if there is not.

The C++ language provides us with a couple of alternatives for qualified naming: Either a named namespace or class can be used for this purpose. As Figure 1-36 shows, the client code is exactly the same — irrespective of whether a struct (Figure 1-36a) or a namespace (Figure 1-36b) is used. There are, however, numerous compelling reasons to prefer a struct[74] (see Figure 2-23, section 2.4.9).

```
// client.cpp

#include <myutil.h>

void client()
{
    float x = MyUtil::PI;

    MyUtil::count = 1;

    MyUtil::f(3);



    int y = MyUtil::g();
                  Narrowing
}
```

```
// myutil.h

#ifndef INCLUDED_MYUTIL
#define INCLUDED_MYUTIL

struct MyUtil {

    static const float PI;

    static int count;

    static void f(double);



    static double g();

};

#endif
```

```
// myutil.cpp

#include <myutil.h>



const float MyUtil::PI
                  = 3.14;
int MyUtil::count;

void MyUtil::f(double)
{
    // ...
}

double MyUtil::g()
{
    // ...
}
```

(a) Using a struct (GOOD IDEA)

---

[74] In this particular instance, the fundamental truths provided in this chapter are (perhaps prematurely) accompanied by some specific design guidance.

```
// client.cpp                    // myutil.h                      // myutil.cpp

#include <myutil.h>              #ifndef INCLUDED_MYUTIL         #include <myutil.h>
                                 #define INCLUDED_MYUTIL

                                 namespace MyUtil {


                                     extern const float PI;

      (same as above)                extern int count;                  (same as above)

                                     void f(double);

                                     double g();


                                 }

                                 #endif
```

(b) Using a namespace "properly" (*not* a very good idea)

```
// client.cpp                    // myutil.h                      // myutil.cpp

#include <myutil.h>              #ifndef INCLUDED_MYUTIL         #include <myutil.h>
                                 #define INCLUDED_MYUTIL
                                                                                     // BAD
                                 namespace MyUtil {             namespace MyUtil {   // IDEA

                                     extern const float PI;          const float PI = 3.14;

      (same as above)                extern int count;               int count;

                                     void f(double);                 void f(double)
                                                                     {
                                                                         // ...
                                                                     }

                                     double g();                     double g()
                                                                     {
                                                                         // ...
                                                                     }


                                 }                               }

                                 #endif
```

(c) Misusing a namespace (BAD IDEA)

Figure 1-37: Scoping free functions and global data (GOOD IDEA)

It is worth noting here that a namespace can be "misused" in a way a struct cannot, as illustrated in Figure 1-37c. As a syntactic convenience, the developer opens the namespace in the .cpp file, rather than using the qualified declarator syntax. Yet, as we saw earlier (Figure 1-36), inconsistencies between the declarations and the definitions will not be caught. By using a struct instead of a namespace for the purpose of scoping free functions and global data, there is no temptation to take this shortcut, and there is no loss of (useful) functionality in doing so.[75]

A namespace is the only construct in C++ that is (deliberately) nonatomic in nature. Unlike a struct, the definition of a namespace can be closed and later re-opened. For example, by using a namespace in place of a struct, someone else can unilaterally extend the logical module MyUtil (Figure 1-37b) from any corner of our physical universe (BAD IDEA), as illustrated in Figure 1-38.

```
// neptune.h                          // neptune.cpp
#ifndef INCLUDED_NEPTUNE             #include <neptune.h>
#define INCLUDED_NEPTUNE
                                      double MyUtil::op2(int arg)
namespace MyUtil {  // BAD IDEA       {
    static double op2(int arg);           // ...
    // ...                            }
}
                                      // ...
#endif                                // ...
```

Figure 1-38: Usurping the MyUtil namespace from a physically remote location

In this context, the nonatomic, nonmodular nature of namespaces runs counter to our much broader purpose of providing a well-defined logically and physically coherent atomic unit of design. For what it's worth, namespace aliases can be used to qualify a name but (unlike the namespace itself) cannot be used to re-open one[76]; still — by design — we have no use for namespace aliases in our methodology (see section 2.4). We will return to the quintessential issue of ensuring logical/physical coherence for components (see section 1.6.3), and again for larger aggregates (see section 2.3).

---

[75] There are times when we will need to define free functions at namespace scope. In our methodology, however, such functions are exclusively operators and application-independent *aspect* functions (such as swap) that are intended to act like operators — e.g., with respect to ADL (argument-dependent lookup); see section 2.4.9.

[76] **stroustrup00**, section 8.2.9.3, p. 184–185

Finally, any perceived advantage of the namespace construct hinges on the ability to employ `using` directives or declarations — a syntactic expedient we do not endorse. A valid conventional use of the `namespace` construct within our methodology, however, is to group aggregated logical content within a larger physical cohesive unit (see sections 2.4.6 and 2.4.7).

In summary, header files are not required for correctness, yet — when properly included by *both* the client and library translation unit — they are effective in achieving early detection of common errors and facilitate the use of practical (localized) static analysis tools. Header files are the prescribed way of sharing definitions of logical entities having internal and dual bindage as well as pure declarations for those having external and dual bindage. Defining free functions outside the scope in which they are declared further avoids errors caused by self-declaration (and we assert that `structs` are strictly better than namespaces for that purpose).

1.5   Include Directives and Include Guards

The details of how we import — exactly once — common artifacts such as those having internal and dual bindage evolved considerably during the pair of decades following my previous book. Spoiler alert: We now use angle brackets instead of double quotes in our include directives, and (redundant) external included guards are deprecated.

1.5.1   Include Directives

The syntactic mechanism by which we incorporate a header file is the preprocessor `#include` directive. The contents of the file named in the directive are substituted textually for the line containing the directive itself. The manner in which a header file is located is determined by the compiler implementation.[77] Typically, the sequence of directories in which to search for each file is determined by command-line arguments supplied to the compiler as well as the environment in which the compiler is invoked. The directory-search sequence is also affected by the form of the `#include` directive used of which there are two[78]:

```
#include "my_headerfile.h"   // BAD IDEA
#include <my_headerfile.h>   // GOOD IDEA
```

---

[77] **iso11**, sections 16.2.2–16.2.3, p. 414

[78] Note that the names of the components shown here add the prefix `my_` corresponding to a unique namespace in which all of the classes depicted in this section are presumed to reside. The naming strategy used in our methodology is described in detail in section 2.4.

Unfortunately, the C++ Language Standard does not specify any meaningful distinction between the two, other than to say that if the search using the implementation-defined procedure for the quoted ("") form fails, then it must fall back to the implementation-defined procedure for the form using angle brackets (<>). In some sense, this gives the latter form a more primitive meaning.

A typical compiler will, for the quoted form (""), search in the same directory as the file that contains the #include directive before searching the paths specified through other means, whereas, for the angle-bracket form (<>), the search in the same directory is skipped. The (typical) behavior for the former approach can be convenient and also serves two important purposes:

1. Facilitating the building of simple programs that are compiled and linked directly on the command line, by not requiring the user to specify additional command-line arguments (e.g., -I. on Unix platforms) to identify the (current) directory containing the header file

2. Avoiding ambiguity when potentially nonunique (especially short) header-file names are included locally (i.e., from the same directory as the .cpp file) within a subsystem

For larger development efforts, however, where header-file-name uniqueness can be assured (see section 2.4), use of double quotes ("") for correctly selecting a local header file over another, identically named one is unnecessary, just as is the implementation-dependent expedient of searching the local directory first by default. Although some compilers (e.g., gcc) provide switches that force the compiler to treat double quotes ("") as angle brackets (<>), there is no generally supported way to do so. When using angle brackets (<>), on the other hand, it will always be possible to achieve a result that is equivalent to having used double quotes ("") on a platform where that syntax means to first search the directory (say, package_dir) of the source file containing the #include by adding package_dir explicitly as the first directory to search.

Exclusive use of angle brackets (<>) as opposed to double quotes ("")[79] gives the development and build tools greater control in determining from where local headers are — or, more accurately, are not — to be extracted. By standardizing on angle brackets (<>), we can be sure that, given

---

[79] Note that this exclusive use of angle brackets (<>) — even for components within the same package — is one of a very few departures from the practices recommended in **lakos96**.

files `xyza_foo.c` and `xyza_bar.h`, the `#include  <xyza_bar.h>` in `xyza_foo.c` unambiguously means the same thing on all platforms irrespective of where `xyza_foo.c` happens to be located on the file system. Moreover, angle brackets provide greater flexibility during both development and deployment (see section 2.15) by allowing us to override the typical behavior imposed by double quotes ("") to select a header file *other* than one in the same directory as a source file that includes it. This additional capability afforded by the build tools when using angle brackets (`<>`) drives our decision to shun the use of the double-quote ("") syntax for `#include` directives in our large-scale development efforts.

1.5.2   Internal Include Guards

Once we start including header files, we must address how to avoid the duplication of definitions resulting from repeated header-file inclusion. It is not uncommon for a given header file to wind up being included in a translation unit multiple times. Consider the case shown in Figure 1-39 where both a `Point` and a `Box` are used directly in the implementation of a `Widget`. Because a `Box` embeds two `Point` objects, attempting to compile class `Box` requires having first seen the definition of class `Point`. We are therefore encouraged (see sections 1.6 and 1.11) and, by our methodology, required (see section 2.6) to have `my_box.h` itself include `my_point.h`. Since the noninline `move` method of `Widget` makes direct substantive use of both `Box` and `Point`, we are also required (see section 2.6) to include each of their respective header files directly in `my_widget.cpp`.

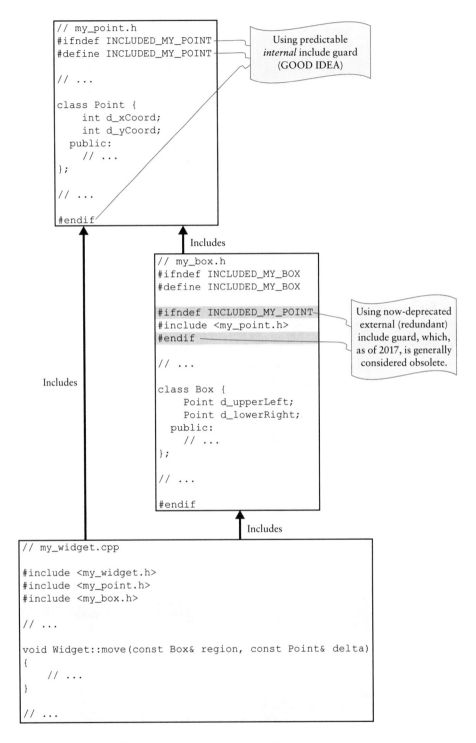

Figure 1-39: Reconvergence in the include graph

As we know from section 1.2.1, compiling first requires forming the translation unit by incorporating header files as specified by `#include` directives. When we compile `widget.cpp`, the preprocessor first replaces the `#include <my_point.h>` directive with the body of the `my_point.h` header file. The preprocessor then proceeds to do the same for `my_box.h`. During the processing of `my_box.h`, the preprocessor will again encounter a directive to `#include <my_point.h>`, which it will do. Absent any include guards, the repeated definition of class `Point` would cause the translation of `widget.cpp` to have two definitions of class `Point` and would therefore fail to compile.

Unlike C, C++ header files almost always contain one or more definitions (e.g., class definitions). Since definitions can never be repeated within a translation unit, it is standard practice to employ unique (and predictable) *internal* preprocessor include guards, similar to the ones shown in Figure 1-40, to ensure that the content of the header file is seen only once.

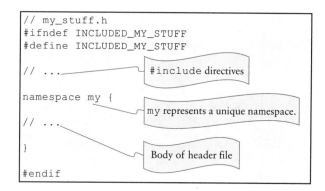

Figure 1-40: (Predictable) internal include guards

The first time a translation unit includes `my_stuff.h`, the guard symbol `INCLUDED_MY_STUFF` will be undefined, and the rest of the header file will be incorporated. To avoid repeated definition, the first thing we do after testing the guard symbol is to define the guard symbol. On any subsequent inclusion of the same header file in this translation unit, the unique guard symbol associated with this header will have already been defined and the entire body of the file will be skipped.

1.5.3   (Deprecated) External Include Guards

As of 2017, we no longer recommend use of (redundant) *external* include guards; we have, however, provided the discussion below for historical reference. Although internal include guards prevent duplication, the preprocessor might nonetheless open, read, and actively ignore repeated definitions and other debris contained in each repeatedly included header. Such needlessly repeated reprocessing has (historically) squandered significant resources during the compilation phase, especially for systems where there is substantial reconvergence in the include graph.[80] Figure 1-41 illustrates a worst-case (yet potentially valid) design wherein a client depends on a number of screen objects, and each screen header includes headers for the same set of widgets. With only *internal* include guards, the preprocessor could have ended up opening and scanning each widget's header as many times as there are screens. This problem, when it occurred, was exacerbated if the information was not available locally — e.g., if it was reread over a network file system (NFS) as opposed to a local hard drive.

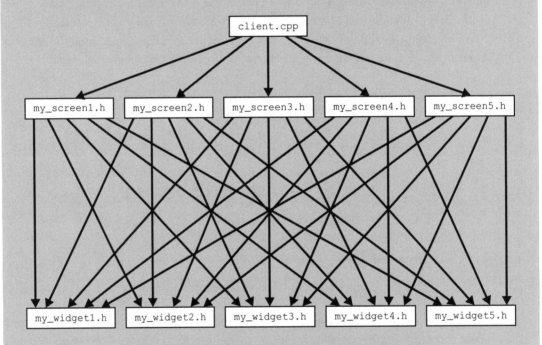

Figure 1-41: Potentially quadratic preprocessor behavior

The pathological reconvergence in Figure 1-41 is illustrative, but the very real (and painful) effects of repeated inclusion had continued to resurface (albeit much less frequently) until well into the 2010s. What might otherwise have been wasted time spent in preprocessing could, in such cases, have been markedly reduced by placing *redundant* external include guards around each #include directive nested in a header file, as shown in Figure 1-42.[81]

---

[80] **lakos96**, section 2.5, pp. 82–88

[81] Poorly implemented client applications that tended to include copious unneeded headers directly in other header files often also benefited.

With redundant include guards, `screen1.h` is effectively *guaranteed*[82] to include each of the widget headers exactly once.[83] That is, when `screen2.h` is included, the external guards suppress any possibility of reopening the widget headers.

```
// my_stuff.h
#ifndef INCLUDED_MY_STUFF      // internal/essential
#define INCLUDED_MY_STUFF      Still GOOD IDEA

#ifndef INCLUDED_HIS_STUFF     // external/redundant
#include <his_stuff.h>
#endif                         Now BAD IDEA

#ifndef INCLUDED_HER_STUFF     // external/redundant
#include <her_stuff.h>
#endif

#ifndef INCLUDED_CSTRING       // external/redundant
#include <cstring>
#define INCLUDED_CSTRING        Look here: extra line!
#endif

namespace my {

// ...
// ...                   (body of header file)
// ...

}

#endif
```

Figure 1-42: (Now deprecated) external ("redundant") include guards (BAD IDEA)

---

[82] Note that compilation systems that always incorporate a given header file into a translation unit at most once are technically nonconforming. Absent explicit syntax (e.g., `#include_once`) to make our intentions clear, any attempts by the compilation system to avoid rereading (or at the very least re-evaluating) headers would invariably be heuristic in nature. Note that `#pragma once` is a popular and widely supported albeit nonstandard feature intended for precisely this very purpose.

[83] In his 2014 review of a prior version of the manuscript that became this volume, JC van Winkel wrote, "I think compilers should *not* be smart about double inclusion. It should do what I ask it to do. If there were a standardized command like `#include_once` that would be fine, but the compiler should not decide it does not need to include a file again. People may have played tricks giving a second inclusion of the file different semantics. As an example (and a very dirty one at that), see the program that was packaged with the source of `gcc`: `enquire.c` that determines the word width of the host system: [van Winkel then quotes **pemberton93**, line 467]:

This file is read three times (it `#includes` itself), to generate otherwise identical code for each of `short+float`, `int+double`, `long+long double`. If `PASS` isn't defined, then this is the first pass. Code bracketed by 'PASS0' is for stuff independent of all three, but is read during the first pass."

Having predictable internal include-guard symbols was certainly desirable when employing (redundant) external guards but was not absolutely necessary. For headers that fell outside our influence, such as those associated with vendor-supplied or third-party libraries (e.g., `cstring` in Figure 1-42), we would have added a fourth line (*after* the `#include` directive) to set the uniform external guard symbol ourselves.

Many had claimed that use of redundant include guards was "tedious," "error-prone,"[84] and not worth the effort, especially given "today's compilers."[85] Yet others, who routinely work professionally developing commercial systems, correctly asserted that "...in some cases their use can improve compilation times of large applications considerably."[86] As of 2005, only the GCC compiler had addressed this issue; all four of our production platforms' native compilers continued to demonstrate a profound benefit from having redundant include guards.

In 2012, the experiment described in section 2.5 of my first book[87] for headers of 100 (and also 1,000) lines each was repeated on several platforms (1) using a local hard drive, and (2) over a network file-system. Both CPU and "wall" times were recorded. Unlike the factor of 25 speedup originally observed, in no case was the CPU-time speedup as much as a factor of 2, and in most cases it was close to 1.0. The wall-time speedup was more often significant, in some cases exceeding a factor of 4. In a separate experiment, we measured the compile-time of several of our low-level component-based libraries — with and without redundant include guards — on each of our four production platforms. On all but one platform, there was no measurable difference; on that one platform, however, we saw an overall compile-time speed-ups ranging from 45 percent to 65 percent.

Since they were first proposed, advances in technology (e.g., processors, networks, operating systems) and optimizations designed to address this specific problem had, to a large extent, mitigated the urgency of using redundant include guards. Moreover, the relative compile-time cost attributed to processing templates (see Volume II, section 4.5) in typical applications

---

[84] We found it easy enough to use a simple (e.g., Perl) script to check that the internal guard corresponds to the current file name and (at the same time) that each external guard corresponded to the header file being included, thereby eliminating all such potentially nasty copy-and-paste errors.

[85] **sutter05**, item 24, p. 43

[86] **dewhurst05**, item 62, pp. 229–230

[87] **lakos96**, section 2.5, Figure 2-5, p. 80

had, in many cases, come to dominate the overall cost of building software. As (selfless) reusable-library developers, however, we remained steadfast in our resolve to employ redundant guards in keeping with our library mind-set (section 0.2), which compels us to pull burdensome and even error-prone coding practices inward in order to maximize convenience, efficiencies, and robustness for clients — even if only marginally or in rare cases.[88]

More recently, however, we began to see that various open-source tools were becoming confused by these redundant guards, and hence their continued use in our hierarchically reusable libraries was deemed to have become a net negative. In late 2017, we safely and accurately removed all of these redundant guards wholesale (via a tiny script) with no disruption to our code base.

Redundant include guards were admittedly ugly. Fortunately, they were not needed when including headers in .cpp files, as reconvergence there was never an issue. The ugliness of redundant include guards did, however, have one important redeeming benefit: Their aesthetically displeasing nature in header files served to remind us that nesting #include directives within headers should occur only with good reason — i.e., when needed to ensure that the header file is self-sufficient with respect to compilation (see sections 1.6.1 and 2.6).

In short, internal (ideally predictable) include guards are required for all header files. External ("redundant") include guards are now deprecated, but until comparatively recently they were optional, did no real harm, and (for many years) helped to significantly reduce compile time (and also "gently" remind us to minimize including a header from within another header).

1.6   From .h / .cpp Pairs to Components

As we saw in section 1.4, the evolution of physical design (culminating in Figure 1-31, section 1.4) has led to the practice of placing one or more intimately related classes (see section 3.3.1), along with their associated free operators, in a single .h and corresponding .cpp file. These .h/.cpp pairs, or *components* (section 0.7) as they will be defined formally (see section 2.6), comprise the atomic units of physical design.

---

[88] Note that application clients of our library software need not have implemented redundant include guards themselves in order to have derived benefit from our having them within our libraries.

For now, we will assume any `.h`/`.cpp` pair we refer to as a *component* satisfies at least the following minimal properties:

1. The `.cpp` file incorporates its corresponding `.h` file as the first substantive line of code.

2. Logical constructs having external linkage defined in a `.cpp` file — and not otherwise effectively rendered externally invisible — are declared in the corresponding `.h` file.

3. Logical constructs having external or dual bindage that are declared within the header file of a component, if defined at all, are defined within that component only.

The fourth essential property of components will be presented in section 1.11.1.

1.6.1   Component Property 1

> The `.cpp` file incorporates its corresponding `.h` file as the first substantive line of code.

This first property helps to ensure that any declarations in the `.h` file are at least consistent with definitions in the `.cpp` file, as discussed in section 1.4. For definitions that can also act as declarations (section 1.3.1), such as those for free functions and global data, achieving consistency is not automatic: We must take additional pains to ensure that consistency — e.g., by locating such definitions outside of the namespace in which they are declared (see Figure 1-17, section 1.3.1). For definitions that are never themselves declarations, such as those for member functions not defined directly within the scope of the class and static member data, failing to include the class definition conveniently prevents the compilation phase from succeeding.

Moreover, by requiring that each `.cpp` file include its corresponding `.h` file as *the first substantive line of code*, we ensure that every header file will compile in isolation, forever eliminating problems associated with the order of includes. For example, consider the four files shown in Figure 1-43. Component **mything** satisfies part of the requirement of Component Property 1 in that it includes `mything.h` (Figure 1-43a) prior to defining anything in `mything.cpp` (Figure 1-43b). But, because the component does not include its own header first, the prior `#include` of `iostream` masks the omission of the forward declaration of type `ostream` (via a `#include <iosfwd>` directive) in `mything.h`. The situation is the same when we attempt to test the component (Figure 1-43c). When it comes to `client.cpp` (Figure 1-43d), the defect might or might not be exposed, depending on what has already been seen in that translation unit. If the defect is exposed, `client.cpp` will abruptly fail to compile; otherwise, the latent include-order defect will persist.

```
// mything.h
#ifndef INCLUDED_MYTHING
#define INCLUDED_MYTHING

                    ┌─────────────────────────────────────────────────┐
                    │ Oops! Missing forward declaration of ostream via <iosfwd> │
                    └─────────────────────────────────────────────────┘
class MyThing {
    // ...
  public:
    MyThing();
        // ...
};

std::ostream& operator<<(std::ostream& lhs, const MyThing& rhs);

#endif
```

(a) mything header file

```
// mything.cpp
#include <ostream>     // BAD IDEA: Should not be first.
#include <mything.h>   // BAD IDEA: Should be first.

MyThing::MyThing() { /*...*/ }

std::ostream& operator<<(std::ostream& lhs, const MyThing& rhs)
{
    return lhs << /*...*/;
}
```

(b) mything implementation file (ill-advised include order)

```
// mything.t.cpp
#include <iostream>
#include <mything.h>────┐ The defect will not
                        │ be detected here.
// ...

int main(int argc, char *argv[])
{
    // ...
}
```

(c) mything test driver

```
// client.cpp
#include <client.h>    // GOOD IDEA: Should be first!

#include <mything.h>───┐ The defect might or
#include <ostream>     │ might not surface here.

// ...
```

(d) myclient implementation file (correct include order)

Figure 1-43: Problems associated with relying on #include order

Ensuring that every header file can compile without relying on any previously included declarations or definitions is highly desirable, especially given that diagnosing such problems is not easy. Self-sufficiency of a header with respect to compilation can be enforced, provided that there is at least one translation unit where the header is guaranteed to be parsed before any other declarations or definitions has a chance to mask such defects. By simply requiring each component to include its own header as the very first substantive line of code, we ensure that its header will compile in isolation, and therefore can always be included safely[89] in any order by clients.[90]

1.6.2   Component Property 2

> Logical constructs having external linkage defined in a `.cpp` file — and not otherwise effectively rendered externally invisible — are declared in the corresponding `.h` file.

This second property helps to prevent inadvertent violations of the ODR by making any global names visible in the source code of the physical interface of the component.[91] By "effectively rendered externally invisible" we mean the linker symbol (resulting from a construct having external or dual bindage) is not legitimately reachable from (nor could it possibly collide with any symbol defined in) another component. Recall from section 1.3.18 that constructs in the unnamed namespace may have external bindage but are effectively unreachable from outside of the component, just as are entities having special names that — by convention only (see section 2.7.3) — are effectively local to a component.[92]

As a rule, we should always place within the unnamed namespace local types defined in the `.cpp` file that are not guaranteed to have globally unique names and ensure that any local functions or variables defined there at file scope are declared to be `static`. For example, consider

---

[89] Note that errant macros defined in previously included headers can inevitably be the undoing of otherwise sound header files.

[90] We could, of course, achieve our goal of ensuring the self-sufficiency of header files in other ways — e.g., by incorporating such isolated compilation tests into our build tools; the stated approach, however, works without having to assume such an extra compilation step in a customized build tool, making our preferred solution inherently more robust.

[91] These declarations may then be textually included, as needed, in other components, applications, or test drivers (see section 1.11.1).

[92] Constructs having internal bindage defined entirely within a `.cpp` file are also effectively private to a component and — at least as far as Component Property 2 is concerned — need not be declared in the header. Yet if such an internal-bindage entity — say, an `enum` (see the text surrounding Figure 1-23, section 1.3.11) — were used as a parameter or return type of a function having external linkage, that internal-bindage entity would nonetheless wind up having to be declared in the header in order to allow the function to be declared there as required by Component Property 2.

the .h/.cpp pair illustrated in Figure 1-44. All of the member functions of class MyCookie, as well as any static member data of that class, must be declared within that class, or those definitions will simply fail to compile. However, classes (e.g., Guard) and free functions (e.g., min) intended to be local to the component and hence defined entirely within the .cpp file could nonetheless inadvertently violate this property. Also problematic are free functions (e.g., operator!=) whose declarations are not automatically required in order for their corresponding definitions to compile (see Figure 1-16, section 1.3.1). Again, this specific problem is effectively addressed when free operators are defined outside of the namespace in which they are declared (see Figure 1-17, section 1.3.1).

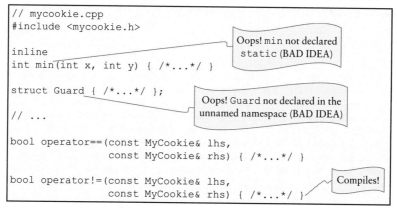

Figure 1-44: Declare *all* externally accessible definitions in the .h file!

Without Component Property 2, we leave open the possibility that an unpublished externally accessible definition could be accessed by crafting explicit `extern` declarations embedded in our clients' source code. Any use of such backdoor access would adversely affect our ability to develop and maintain stable software (section 0.5). The lack of a clear and complete interface would hinder our ability to document (see Volume II, section 6.17) and verify (see Volume III) intended behavior. Such backdoor access would also make ascertaining actual physical dependencies within existing systems inordinately more difficult (see section 1.11), substantially undermining the benefits of fine-grained modularity (section 0.4).

1.6.3   Component Property 3

Logical constructs having external or dual bindage that are declared within the header file of a component, if defined at all, are defined within that component only.

From a modularity standpoint, this property is perhaps the most obvious of the three, yet it's technically the most subtle. Simply stated, the definition of any logical construct having external or dual bindage that is advertised, via a declaration in the header file, as being unique will not reside anywhere other than in this `.h`/`.cpp` pair.[93] Figure 1-45 illustrates a complete disregard for the proper placement of logical constructs within the physical entities that hold them. In particular, the member functions `push` and `pop` declared in `intstack.h` are not implemented anywhere in `intstack.h` or `intstack.cpp` as would be expected but instead implemented in `intset.cpp` — and even in `main.cpp` of all places! Without this third property, the very notion of a `.h`/`.cpp` pair as being a coherent unit (see section 2.3) of fine-grained modular design (section 0.4) is meaningless.

---

[93] Explicit instantiations of templates using the `extern template` feature (section 1.3.16) will require the `extern template` statement (causing the code for instantiation to be suppressed) to reside in a single component's `.h` file, and then be generated by that same component's `.cpp` file. Such specialized instantiations — particularly for fundamental types — typically occur in the same component as the one defining the overall template. For a user-defined type (UDT), however, the instantiation of the template might instead reasonably need to occur in the component defining the UDT, thus creating a dependency from that component to the one defining the general template (instead of vice versa). Placing this explicit instantiation in an entirely separate (higher-level) component is problematic in that it runs the risk of being overlooked, thereby failing to provide the build-time optimizations intended.

Having a third component contain the explicit instantiation also increases the possibility of consuming both explicitly and implicitly instantiated versions of a template having the same type. While this inefficiency too would be undesirable, it would not be fatal: As with inline functions, the two forms of instantiation produce the same result with respect to the ODR; however, an explicit instantiation, unlike implicit ones, will typically not result in a "weak" symbol and therefore must be limited to just one per program. It is this latter observation that is the compelling one for not allowing such "optional" code to reside in a separate physical unit, lest it inadvertently reside in more than one within the same program; this same caution pertains to free operators that act on types from multiple components (see section 2.6).

```
// intset.h                          // intstack.h
#ifndef INCLUDED_INTSET              #ifndef INCLUDED_INTSTACK
#define INCLUDED_INTSET              #define INCLUDED_INTSTACK
class IntSet {                       class IntStack {
    // ...                               // ...
  public:                              public:
    // ...                               // ...
    // ...                               void push(int item);
    // ...                               void pop();
};                                   };
#endif                               #endif

        intset.h                             intstack.h
```

```
// intset.cpp                 // intstack.cpp              // main.cpp
#include <intset.h>           #include <intstack.h>       #include <intset.h>
#include <intstack.h>         // ...                       #include <intstack.h>
void IntStack::push(
                int item)     // ...                       void IntStack::pop()
{                             // ...                       {
    // ...                    // ...                           // ...
}    // BAD IDEA             // ...                       }    // BAD IDEA

// ...                        // ...                       // ...

  intset.cpp                    intstack.cpp                 main.cpp
```

Figure 1-45: Grossly improper modularization of logical constructs

Even subtle irregularities in the placement of logical constructs can have a significant practical impact. Consider the scenario depicted in Figure 1-46. File client.cpp includes date.h and makes substantial use of Date, but nothing else in the library. File date.h declares the free operator

```
std::ostream& operator<<(std::ostream&, const Date&);
```

having external bindage, but date.cpp fails to define it. File date.o is part of a library that provides much "weightier" types than Date. The implementer of the Calendar class, realizing that the output operator for dates is missing, decides to implement it in calendar.cpp. Clients that include date.h do not necessarily depend on calendar.o unless they invoke the date's operator<<. The .o file for **calendar**, being a substantial piece of machinery, quietly drags in many more .o files from the library, none of which is needed by Client. Users of this library might be completely unaware that any of this misappropriation is happening. Fortunately, a sound, hierarchical component-level testing strategy — one that physically isolates components from other, supposedly unrelated ones during testing — will detect these and other similar structural defects (see section 2.14 and Volume III, section 7.5).

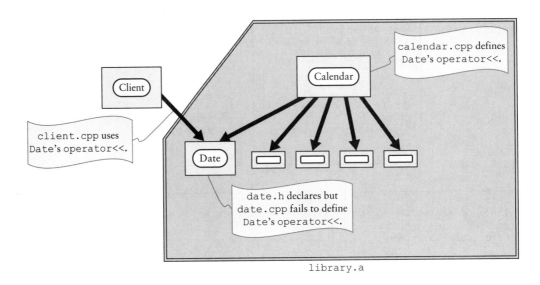

Figure 1-46: Subtly improper modularization of logical constructs

The three fundamental properties discussed in this section are essential for distinguishing a casual .h/.cpp pair from the atomic unit of design that we refer to as a *component*: (1) The header must be included in the first substantive line of code, (2) each external linkage definition must be declared in the header file, and (3) each external or dual bindage entity declared in a component's header file must not be defined anywhere other than in the same component. A fourth fundamental property for components, which will turn out to be especially useful for visualization and maintainability, is discussed in section 1.11.1.

1.7   Notation and Terminology

Object-oriented design lends itself to a rich set of notations.[94] Their elaborate nature derives from a desire not only to express a design before it is realized but also to capture many of the details of an existing implementation as part of a reverse-engineering analysis. Most of these notations denote relationships among the logical entities of a design, with surprisingly little attention paid to physical implications.

---

[94] **booch94**, Chapter 5, pp. 171–228

1.7.1   Overview

Even UML,[95,96] although useful for communicating logical designs, is somewhat bulky for our purposes and lacks succinct expressive power at the logical/physical boundaries. In our experience, the notations commonly needed to produce sound physical designs are strikingly few, as illustrated in Figure 1-47. If there is ever a need for additional notation, a labeled arrow explicitly identifying the relationship will usually suffice, but see also Figure 1-50, section 1.7.6.

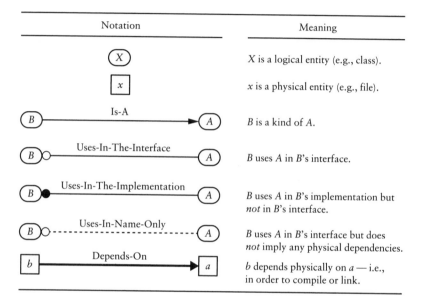

Figure 1-47: Summary of our basic logical/physical design notation

We will consistently identify logical entities (e.g., classes, structs, free operators) with *capsule*-like shapes (for types) or *ellipse*-like shapes (for functions)[97]:

(Car)

```
class Car {
    // ...
};
```

---

[95] **fowler04**

[96] **booch05**

[97] We represent Types in UpperCamelCase and functions in lowerCamelCase.

and use a rectangle for physical entities[98]:

```
// car.cpp
#include <car.h>
// ...
```

(car.cpp)

For our purposes, notation delineating the following four kinds of logical relationships will usually suffice:

Car —— Is-A ——▶ Vehicle

```
class Car : public Vehicle {
    // ...
};
```

Car ⊙—— Uses-In-The-Interface —— Gas

```
class Car {
    // ...
  public:
    // ...
    void addFuel(Gas *);
    // ...
};
```

Car ●—— Uses-In-The-Implementation —— Engine

```
class Car {
    Engine d_engine;
    // ...
};
```

Vehicle ⊙·········· Uses-In-Name-Only ·········· Gas

```
class Gas;
class Vehicle {
  public:
    // ...
    virtual void addFuel(Gas *) = 0;
    // ...
};[99]
```

Note that each of the four relationships shown above are necessarily between logical entities (depicted as ellipses). The notation for Depends-On — our sole relationship between physical entities (depicted as rectangles) — is typically shown only between icons representing physical entities:

[car.cpp] —— Depends-On ——▶ [car.h]

```
// car.cpp
#include <car.h>
// ...
```

---

[98] We consistently represent physical entities, such as files, components, and libraries, using all-lowercase names (see section 2.4.6).

[99] The important difference in *physical* implication between Uses-In-The-Interface and Uses-In-Name-Only is elucidated below.

Here the *file* car.cpp depends on the *file* car.h at compile time. If we treat (as we will throughout this book) a .cpp file and its corresponding .h file as a single unit, we can express the combined compile- and/or link-time dependency as

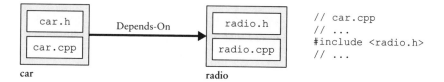

or even more concisely as simply

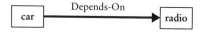

We'll talk more about the Depends-On relation for .h/.cpp pairs in section 1.8.

1.7.2   The Is-A Logical Relationship

Ⓓ ➝ Ⓑ means that "*D* is a kind of *B*" and that "*D* inherits publicly from *B*." The direction of the arrow is significant: It points in the direction of physical dependency implied by the inheritance relationship (see section 1.9). Because *D* is derived from *B*, the definition of class *B* must have already been seen in order for *D* to name *B* as a base class[100]:

```
class B { /*...*/ };
class D : public B { /*...*/ };
```

1.7.3   The Uses-In-The-Interface Logical Relationship

Ⓑ○—Ⓐ means "*B* uses *A* in the interface (of *B*)" and implies a physical dependency of *B* on *A* (see section 1.9). We will sometimes be "sloppy" and say, "*B* uses *A* in *its* interface" or "*B* uses *A* in *the* interface" (without qualification), but we will always mean "*B* uses *A* in *B's* interface," and never "*B* uses *A* in *A's* interface."

---

[100] In some older texts, you might see the arrow pointed in the opposite direction, which can be misleading. An arrow shows an asymmetric relationship between two entities denoted by its label (in this case Is-A). To draw the arrow the other way, we would logically have to call the relation something else, such as Derives or Is-A-Base-Class-Of:

This alternative notation is less desirable because the arrow points in the direction opposite to that of implied dependency (see section 1.9).

> **DEFINITION**: A type is *used in the interface of a function* if that type is named as part of the function's signature or return type.

Whenever a function declaration names a type in its parameter list or as part of the type of the value returned, the function is said to use that type in its interface. For example, the free (i.e., nonmember) function

```
bool operator==(const Date&, const Date&);
```

clearly makes use of class `Date` in its interface. This function happens to return a `bool`, so the `bool` type also would be considered part of this function's interface. Fundamental types are, however, ubiquitous; hence, their use will never induce physical dependencies, and therefore they are not considered further.

> **DEFINITION**: A type is *used in the (public) interface of a class* if the type is used in the interface of any (public) *member* function of that class.

If any class *member* function (friends don't count[101]) depends on a type in its interface, we say that the class depends on that type in its interface. For example, the `addHoliday` method of `Calendar`

```
void Calendar::addHoliday(const Date& holiday);
```

uses class `Date` in its interface; hence, `Date` is used in the interface of `Calendar`.

You can think of the "o———" symbol as an arrow with its tail at the bubble and the head missing or as a conductor's baton pointing at a member of the orchestra. The orientation of the arrow is important: It points in the direction of *implied dependency*. That is, if *B* uses *A*, then *B* depends on *A*, and not vice versa.

---

[101] Although there is no direct implication of dependency based on a logical "uses" relationship for a friend, in our methodology, friendship (see section 2.6) is not permitted to extend beyond the boundaries of a component (section 1.6). Hence, in our methodology, a logical *uses* relationship for a friend F of a type T in (the same) component c will always have the same physical implications for c as would that of a logical *uses* relationship for T itself (see section 1.9).

1.7.4   The Uses-In-The-Implementation Logical Relationship

$\boxed{B}$•———$\boxed{A}$ means "*B* uses *A* in the implementation (of *B*)." Like its interface-oriented counterpart, Uses-In-The-Implementation implies a *physical* dependency of *B* on *A* (see section 1.9)
but explicitly denies any use of *A* in *B*'s public (or protected) interface.[102]

> **DEFINITION: A type is *used in the implementation of a function* if that type is
> referred to anywhere in the definition of the function but not named in its public (or
> protected) interface.**

If a function names a type in its implementation, but not in its parameter list or as part of its
return type, the function is said to use that type in its implementation. Figure 1-48a shows
the logical view of class `Calendar`, its free (non-member) equality comparison (operator)
functions, `operator==` and `operator!=`, and an iterator, `CalendarHolidayIterator`,
which — emulating the style of the C++ Standard Library — returns by value.

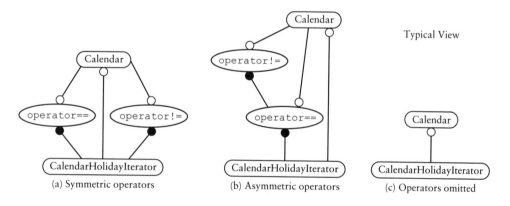

(a) Symmetric operators   (b) Asymmetric operators   (c) Operators omitted

Figure 1-48: Different logical views of a `calendar` component

---

[102] We generally discourage use of the `protected` keyword as its use almost always conflates two distinct
audiences: the public client and the derived-class author (see Volume II, section 4.7). See also **stroustrup94**,
section 9.1, pp. 301–302.

From Figure 1-48a alone, we can infer that the equality-comparison operator `operator==` uses class `Calendar` in its interface and class `CalendarHolidayIterator` in its implementation:

```
int operator==(const Calendar& lhs, const Calendar& rhs)
{
    CalendarHolidayIterator lit = lhs.beginHolidays();
    CalendarHolidayIterator rit = rhs.beginHolidays();
    // ...
}
```

Moreover, because the *uses* relationship shown is *in the implementation*, we can also infer from that diagram that `operator==` does *not* use `CalendarHolidayIterator` in its interface. Although Figure 1-48a shows `operator!=` implemented symmetrically to `operator==`, `operator!=` could instead have been implemented (e.g., inline) *in terms of* `operator==`[103]:

```
inline
int operator!=(const Calendar& lhs, const Calendar& rhs)
{
    return !(lhs == rhs);
}
```

A logical diagram corresponding to this alternative (asymmetric) implementation of `operator!=` is shown in Figure 1-48b.

Finally, because the implementations of free operators are typically lightweight and their physical dependencies virtually never exceed those of the class of objects on which they operate, we would normally omit their explicit representation, implicitly treating free operators as part of the class (as shown in Figure 1-48c). Note that our design methodology requires that the homogeneous operators reside in the same component that defines the class on which they operate (see section 2.6).

---

[103] Note that, as a rule, we would prefer asymmetric (i.e., not independent) implementations of the equality comparison operators *only* if `operator==` were sufficiently bulky as to make implementing it as an inline function inappropriate.

Looking ahead, it will turn out that our testing methodology (see Volume III) channels the added redundancy into an affirmative advantage that helps us to mechanically verify the complementary contract for `operator!=` — each providing an "oracle" for the other (see Volume III, section 8.6). What's more, at sufficiently high levels of optimization, the generated object code is often the same either way. In any event, we consistently document the essential behavior of the two equality comparison operators independently (see Volume II, section 6.17).

Layering (see section 3.7.2) is the process of building upon smaller, simpler, or more primitive types to form larger, more complex, or more sophisticated ones. Layering often occurs through composition — e.g., embedding an instance of a simpler type in the footprint of another (Has-A) or managing a dynamically allocated instance of that type via an embedded pointer (Holds-A) — but any form of substantive use, such as that which would induce a compile- or link-time dependency, would qualify as layering.

The particular way in which a class uses a type will affect not only how the class depends on that type but also to what extent *clients* of the class will be forced to depend on that type (see section 3.10.1). Here, we merely enumerate the different ways in which a class can use a type in its implementation.

DEFINITION: A type is *used in the implementation of a class* if that type is not used in the public (or protected) interface of the class, but is (1) used in a member function of the class, (2) referred to in the declaration of a data member of the class, or (3) [rare] derived from privately (i.e., is a private base type of the class).

Although a class can use another type in its implementation in several ways (see Figure 1-49), the notation used to represent each of the variations is the same.

Uses (E.g., `Date` "Uses" `DateImpUtil`)

The class has a member function that names the type in its implementation:

```
// date.cpp
#include <date.h>
#include <dateimputil.h>
// ...
```
                                                           (See Volume II, sections 5.2–5.3.)

```
Date::Date(int year, int month, int day)
: d_serial(DateImpUtil::ymd2serial(year, month, day))
{
    assert(DateImpUtil::isValidSerialDate(d_serial));
```
                                                           (See Volume II, section 6.8.)
```
}
```

Has-A (E.g., `Calendar` "Has-A" `BitArray`)

The class embeds an object (instance) of the type:

```
// calendar.h
// ...

#include <bitarray.h>
// ...

class Calendar {
    BitArray d_holidays;
    // ...
};
```

(continues)

(continued)

Holds-A (E.g., `BitArray` "Holds-A" `int` and an `Allocator`)

The class embeds a pointer (or reference) to an object (or the beginning of a contiguous sequence of objects) of the type. The class might or might not *own* (i.e., control the lifetime(s) of) the object(s) it holds.[104]

```
// bitarray.h
// ...

class Allocator;
// ...

class BitArray {
    int      *d_array_p;       // owned          [And held]
    int       d_capacity;
    int       d_length;                          [But not owned]
    Allocator *d_allocator_p;  // held
    // ...
};
                    // bitarray.cpp
                    #include <bitarray.h>
                    #include <allocator.h>
                    // ...

                    BitArray::BitArray(Allocator *basicAllocator)
                    : d_array_p(0)
                    , d_capacity(0)
                    , d_length(0)
                    , d_allocator_p(basicAllocator)
                    {
                    }
```

Was-A

The class privately inherits from the type. In practice, we rarely encounter a legitimate need to use private inheritance in well-designed code, preferring to employ the "Has-A" and "Holds-A" relationships instead.[105] Note that we never use the Is-A arrow notation to depict private inheritance, preferring instead the Uses-In-The-Implementation notation, which more accurately reflects its purpose.

Figure 1-49: Ways in which a class can use a type in its implementation

---

[104] Note that the constructor's `Allocator` (address) parameter, shown here to illustrate the form of the Holds-A relation in which the held object is *not* owned, differs considerably from the original allocator model set forth in C++98. It is the impetus for the new *scoped allocator model* introduced in C++11 and, ultimately, the far more flexible and effective Polymorphic Memory Resource (PMR) adopted in C++17. After identifying critical defects in the original model — specifically, a lack of interoperability (see Volume II, section 4.4) due to the use of template implementation policies (see Volume II, section 4.5) — we will explore the performance and other, collateral benefits of this profoundly superior approach to memory allocation (see Volume II, sections 4.10).

[105] One rare bona fide advantage of private inheritance over layering occurs when we can legitimately benefit from the empty-base-class optimization. Another even rarer use of private inheritance in C++03 (obviated in C++11) is to enable a data member to be initialized before it is passed as an argument to the constructor of a (now secondary) base class.

1.7.5   The Uses-In-Name-Only Logical Relationship and the Protocol Class

(B)o-----(A) means the name A is used in the interface of B but denies any implied physical dependency of B on A (see section 1.9). Note that here we use a "dashed" (nonsolid) line to explicitly denote the *absence* of any physical implications that could result in a component defining B necessarily having to #include the header of a (separate) component defining A.

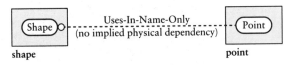

Occasionally, a class will name a type in its interface (collaboratively) via a local declaration but make no substantive use of the type in its implementation that would require having seen the definition of that type in order to compile, link, or even thoroughly test the class. Such restricted (nominal-only) use for concrete classes is contrived — achieved only by deliberate design, e.g., *opaque pointers* (see section 3.5.4), but occurs naturally for abstract ones, especially those that act as pure interfaces, such as Shape above. We will often refer to such a pure abstract interface class as a *protocol*.[106,107]

> **DEFINITION**: A *protocol class* is a class that (1) has only pure virtual functions except for a non-inline virtual destructor (defined in the .cpp file), (2) has no data members, and (3) does not derive from any other class (directly or indirectly) that is not itself a protocol class.

A protocol class is the quintessential example of one that uses types in its interface *in name only*. A component defining a protocol class forward declares (or, if necessary, #includes) the declaration of every relevant interface type but need not #include their definitions in either its .h or .cpp file. Note that we will sometimes choose to underline the name of a

---

[106] **lakos96**, section 6.4.1, pp. 386–398

[107] Historical background: Classical C++ compilers, to avoid creating static copies of virtual tables (along with compiler-generated virtual function definitions) in every translation unit in which such a class is used, typically place external bindage definitions in only the one translation unit implementing the first noninline virtual function declared within a class. Consequently, our practice has always been to order the declaration of the destructor prior to other instance methods within the class (see Volume II, section 6.14).

With the advent of advances in compiler/linker technology — e.g., to support dual bindage (section 1.3.2) — we could consider relaxing our long-standing requirement that the ("no-op") destructor of a protocol be (1) nonpure, and (2) defined (empty) in a unique translation unit (i.e., that of its component). Doing so, however, would result in (at least some) additional compile- and link-time overhead, with *at most* a minuscule improvement in runtime performance.

protocol class (e.g., class `Shape` above) to distinguish its pure-abstract nature (e.g., see Figure 0-51, section 1.7.7) from other categories of classes (see Volume II, section 4.2).

For example, consider a component defining a pure abstract `Shape` protocol that declares a pure virtual `origin` method:

```
// shape.h
// ...
class Point;
// ...
class Shape {
  public:
    virtual ~Shape();
        // Destroy this object.

    virtual Point origin() const = 0;
        // Return the coordinates of the origin of this object.
};

// shape.cpp
#include <shape.h>
// ...
Shape::~Shape()
{
}
```

Even though the `origin` method of `Shape` returns a `Point` *by value*, there is no substantive use of `Point` unless the client of `Shape` invokes the `origin()` method, in which case the client will be obliged to `#include` the definition of `Point` directly to avoid the possibility of relying on *transitive includes* (see section 2.6). The motivation for keeping abstract interfaces pure is the subject of Volume II, section 4.7. In Volume III, Chapter 7, we will explore *why* one might want to test a pure abstract class itself, and, in the remainder of Volume III, Chapters 8–10, *how* one might do so.

1.7.6 In-Structure-Only (ISO) Collaborative Logical Relationships

In addition to in-name-only usage, there is another category of purely collaborative logical relationships — i.e., ones that do not imply any physical dependencies — which are highly analogous to (yet distinct from) the logical relationships involving (pure) interface inheritance (see Volume II, section 4.7).

This separate category of purely collaborative logical relationships — which we refer to here as *In-Structure-Only* — was made possible by the original template facilities standardized in C++98 and forms the basis for generic programming and the Standard Template Library (STL).[108]

In our classical notation (see Figure 1-47, section 1.7.1), there was no standard symbology for representing In-Structure-Only (ISO) relationships. We have therefore made do with *ad hoc* labeled arrows, where needed, or otherwise omitted such relationships from our class diagrams entirely. As the occurrence of such relationships continued to expand beyond just those few identified in the C++ Standard, we found that there was an increasing need for consistent notation to capture them diagrammatically. Figure 1-50 describes a few additional symbols, which were deliberately constructed through the *hierarchical reuse* (section 0.4) of the various piece parts of the original symbols.

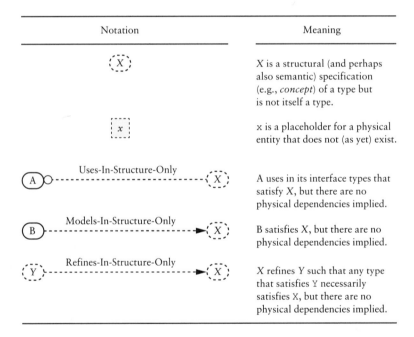

Notation	Meaning
X	X is a structural (and perhaps also semantic) specification (e.g., *concept*) of a type but is not itself a type.
x	x is a placeholder for a physical entity that does not (as yet) exist.
A — Uses-In-Structure-Only — X	A uses in its interface types that satisfy X, but there are no physical dependencies implied.
B — Models-In-Structure-Only — X	B satisfies X, but there are no physical dependencies implied.
Y — Refines-In-Structure-Only — X	X refines Y such that any type that satisfies Y necessarily satisfies X, but there are no physical dependencies implied.

Figure 1-50: Summary of additional, structurally collaborative logical notation

In keeping with long established meaning, we will consistently identify logical entities with an ellipse-like bubble but replace a solid perimeter with a broken one to indicate that the logical entity is a *specification* for a type rather than a type itself:

---

[108] **austern98**

EqualityComparable

Specifies that a given type, **T**, must, e.g., have a homogeneous equality-comparison function of the form
bool operator==(const T&, const T&)
that is *reflexive*, *symmetric*, and *transitive*.

Such a *type specification* (i.e., set of requirements on a type) is referred to in C++ as a *concept*.[109] We will also continue to use a rectangle to denote physical entities, again replacing the solid perimeter with a broken one — this time to indicate that the physical entity does not (as yet) exist:

equalitycomparable.h

Serves as a placeholder for a header file that might (someday) delineate the requirements of a type that is *EqualityComparable*.

The notation denoting the three kinds of In-Structure-Only (ISO) logical relationships, illustrated next, should address just about any relevant situation:

Uses-ISO

Date o- - - - - - - - - - - *Stream*

```
class Date {
    // ...
    template <class STREAM>
    STREAM& streamOut(STREAM& s, int version);
        // ...
        // The supplied 'STREAM' type is
        // required to satisfy the type
        // specification indicated by Stream.
        // ...
    // ...
};
```

Models-ISO

TestStream - - - - - - - - -▶ *Stream*

```
class TestStream {
    // ... This class satisfies the
    // type specification indicated
    // by Stream. ...

        // ...
};110
```

---

[109] **austern98**, section 2.2, pp. 16–19

[110] Under "Requirements and Concepts" (pp. 16–17) in section 2.2 of his 1998 book (**austern98**), Austern uses the phrase "is a model of" (p. 16) rather than the term *Models*, which we have adopted. Note that the use of the term *model* in Austern's book — as it is here — is in the mathematical sense, which is somewhat different than what we might be accustomed to from the physical sciences. See also **stepanov15**, section 6.6, pp. 102–104.

```
                       Refines-ISO                           // Every type that
┌ ─ ─ ─ ─ ─ ─ ─ ─ ┐                   ┌ ─ ─ ─ ─ ─ ─ ─ ┐      // satisfies the type
  ForwardIterator  ─ ─ ─ ─ ─ ─ ─ ▶     InputIterator         // specification
└ ─ ─ ─ ─ ─ ─ ─ ─ ┘                   └ ─ ─ ─ ─ ─ ─ ─ ┘      // indicated by
                                                             // ForwardIterator
                                                             // satisfies the type
                                                             // specification
                                                             // indicated by
                                                             // InputIterator.111
```

1.7.7   How Constrained Templates and Interface Inheritance Are Similar

Observing similarities (and differences) between interface inheritance and template parameters can be instructive as well. Let us begin by considering the fairly common design pattern suggested in Figure 1-51. In both implementations, we have a concrete server, `MyServer`, that requires the services of an abstract channel, which in Figure 1-51a is the protocol class, `Channel`, and in Figure 1-51b is some sort of specification, *Channel*, characterizing what requirements a supplied concrete channel type is expected to satisfy but which need not exist physically as part of the source code of any program.

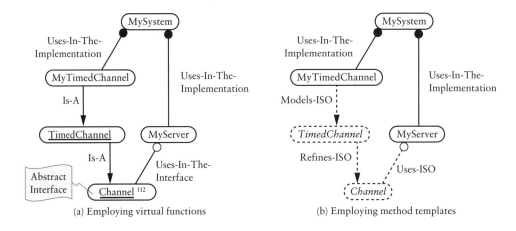

Figure 1-51: Contrasting inheritance and templates for a common design pattern

---

[111] The term *Refines* was similarly adapted from **austern98**, section 2.4, pp. 29–31.

[112] Especially during development, we sometimes underline a class name within a diagram to indicate that it serves as a (usually pure) abstract interface (see Volume II, section 4.7).

A timed-channel abstraction is a kind of channel abstraction. A type that implements a timed-channel abstraction should be usable wherever a type implementing a channel abstraction is required. This substitutability property is captured explicitly in Figure 1-51a by having the `TimedChannel` protocol publicly inherit from the `Channel` protocol. In Figure 1-51b, the dashed (nonsolid) Refines-ISO arrow suggests that the type requirements indicated by a *Timed-Channel* are a superset of those indicated by *Channel*, yet — unlike the *protocol hierarchy* of Figure 1-51a — there need be no physical manifestation of either specification embodied in the source code of any program (see section 3.5.7.5).

In each of the system implementations shown in Figure 1-51, `MyTimedChannel` is a concrete type satisfying requirements set forth for any timed channel. In Figure 1-51a, that property is made explicit in the source code by publicly inheriting from the `TimedChannel` protocol class; in Figure 1-51b, however, the diagram tells us that `MyTimedChannel` is expected to have the syntax (and semantics) common to every other acceptable timed-channel type — even though there might well be nothing in the source code to delineate the details of what is expected (but see below).

At the highest level, it is the `MySystem` class that finally unites the concrete channel with the client, though the underlying mechanisms for doing so differ substantially between the two designs depicted in Figure 1-51. In the case of Figure 1-51a, we could imagine a snippet of code that creates a `MyTimedChannel` and then passes the address of that channel to the constructor of `MyClient`, which then squirrels it away for later use — e.g., when sending or receiving messages — all without affecting the C++ type of the client object, `mc`:

```
class MySystem {
    // ...
    int someFunction()
    {
        MyTimedChannel mtc;
        MyClient mc(&mtc);
        // ...
    }
};
```

Moreover, using virtual functions, it is possible for the association between client and concrete channel to be deferred until run time. In the case of Figure 1-51b, however, the analogous design would require instantiating the composite C++ type at compile time:

```
class MySystem {
    // ...
    int someFunction()
    {
        MyClient<MyTimedChannel> mcmtc;
        // ...
    }
};
```

Note also that `MyClient<MyTimedChannel>` represents a distinct C++ type from, say, `MyClient<YourTimedChannel>` — the ramifications of which will be taken up in Volume II, sections 4.4 and 4.5.

1.7.8   How Constrained Templates and Interface Inheritance Differ

Given the analogy above, one might conclude that the use of constrained templates (see Volume II, section 4.5) and interface inheritance (see Volume II, section 4.7) are, from a patterns perspective, isomorphic and therefore interchangeable — differing only in the degree of closeness in the bindings. Such is not the case in general, however, and each has specialized uses where the other is simply not appropriate.[113]

1.7.8.1   Constrained Templates, but Not Interface Inheritance

For example, consider a type concept *Assignable*, which (among other things) requires a given concrete type, `T`, to be *EqualityComparable*, as described above (near the beginning of section 1.7.6), and also to implement an assignment operator of the syntactic form

```
T& operator=(const T&);
```

such that, given any two objects `a` and `b` of (the same) type `T`, after assigning the value of `b` to `a`, both objects compare equal, as in:

---

[113] **austern98**, section 2.4, pp. 29–31

```
template <class T>
    // Requires: 'T' satisfies Assignable.
void assign(T& a, const T& b)
{
    a = b;
    assert(b == a);
}
```

Now suppose we try to model the same code using an abstract base class:

```
class Assignable {
  public:
    virtual ~Assignable();  // Empty definition resides in '.cpp' file.
    virtual Assignable& operator=(const Assignable& rhs) = 0;
};
```

How are we supposed to implement the `assign` function in the example above? Suppose we were to try to implement it in terms of the base class as in:

```
void assign(Assignable& a, const Assignable& b)
{
    a = b;
    assert(b == a);
}
```

The C++ type system does not even guarantee that the two concrete derived types are the same, and if they are not, the very notion of assignment is dubious (see Volume II, section 4.3). Note also that C++ enables fundamental types to participate as types in constrained templates, but not so in inheritance relationships.

1.7.8.2   Interface Inheritance, but Not Constrained Templates

On the other hand, sometimes the use of constrained templates is strongly counter-indicated. Consider again the use of an abstract service, such as a communication channel like the one shown in Figure 1-51, section 1.7.7. By selecting the abstract-base-class approach, we have a natural way of holding on to (and later using) the supplied communication mechanism (i.e., via a pointer to its *protocol* base class). Had we instead used a constrained template, we would have had to parameterize the entire channel class based on this relatively minor implementation detail.

The C++98 design of the STL made the wrong choice for memory allocators, which has arguably been a huge impediment to more widespread memory-allocator adoption.[114]

1.7.9   All Three "Inheriting" Relationships Add Unique Value

All three different forms of "inheriting" relationships — Is-A, Models, and Refines — are necessary, each serving different, albeit sometimes overlapping, purposes. *Is-A* is the classical relationship between two (named) C++ classes (either or both of which may be abstract), *Models* is a relationship between a concrete type and a set of types, and *Refines* is a relationship between two sets of types. We need to understand the proper use of all three of these distinct forms if we are to be maximally effective with their use.

1.7.10   Documenting Type Constraints for Templates

As suggested above, there is some reason for concern regarding how we maintain software having such In-Structure-Only (ISO) relationships — especially when those requirements go beyond what is already documented in the standard. C++98 has essentially no support for enforcing type specifications on template arguments, so the best we can do with that original subset of C++ is to provide clear, complete documentation (somewhere) delineating our custom specifications (i.e., type requirements) that will need to be satisfied.[115]

Figure 1-52a shows a (pure) logical diagram (absent any physical entities) depicting a client type, `MyClient`, that uses types in its interface that model (i.e., satisfy the type requirements indicated by) the concept *Service*. Figure 1-52b shows the same subsystem, but this time as a component-class diagram — the rectangle with the nonsolid border explicitly denoting that no physical component delineating the detailed properties of `Service` exists. Assuming we have some central location that we can use to catalog the various type specifications by name, it might be sufficient to simply name those concepts in the form of an adjacent comment.[116]

---

[114] See **austern98**, section 9.4, 166–171. This fatal flaw was not properly addressed until the introduction of the polymorphic memory resource version of the STL containers in C++17 (see Volume II, section 4.10). See also **lakos17b, lakos17c**, and **lakos19**.

[115] There have been, historically, open-source implementations, such as Boost's C++98 concepts library, which enable type specifications and their enforcement. Extensive language-level support for concepts is available in C++ as of C++20.

[116] Alexander Stepanov, in his book *The Elements of Programming*, chose to indicate the type requirements for a template argument directly in the source code itself using a "`requires` clause" applied to the name of the concept indicating those requirements. Using the C++ preprocessor, he then created a `requires` macro that — from the point of view of the compiler — caused the entire clause to be treated the same as if it were a comment. See **stepanov09**, section 6.2, pp. 90–92, specifically p. 91:

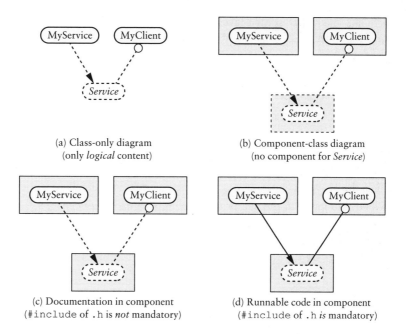

(a) Class-only diagram
(only *logical* content)

(b) Component-class diagram
(no component for *Service*)

(c) Documentation in component
(#include of .h is *not* mandatory)

(d) Runnable code in component
(#include of .h *is* mandatory)

Figure 1-52: Subtly different notations for in-structure relationships

```
#define requires(...)

template <typename I>
    requires(Iterator(I))    // This is precisely how Stepanov rendered it on p. 91 of stepanov09.
void increment(I& x)
{
    // Precondition: successor(x) is defined.                    (See Volume II, section 6.8.)
    x = successor(x);
}
```

Later, in his book *From Mathematics to Generic Programming*, Stepanov chose to depict this same information in the code itself by again using the C++ preprocessor, but this time aliasing the C++ keyword typename to the name of the concept indicating the type requirements. See **stepanov15**, Appendix C.2, pp. 266–267, specifically p. 267:

```
#define Iterator2 typename

template <Iterator2 I>    // This is how Stepanov would have rendered the previous example in stepanov15.
void increment2(I& x)
{
    // Precondition: successor(x) is defined.                    (See Volume II, section 6.8.)
    x = successor(successor(x));
}
```

Note that in neither case shown does the compiler perform any form of static verification to ensure that the supplied type is conforming; the additional effort is intended solely to document the requirements for the benefit of the human programmer.

Much like any other source-level information that is to be shared across translation unit boundaries in C/C++, a header file seems like an obvious place to capture a detailed type specification — even if it doesn't contain any "compilable" (i.e., noncommentary) source code. Figure 1-52c suggests a physical component that delineates the full complement of primitive requirements needed to characterize the concept of a *Service* (as opposed to merely referencing it in some centralized catalog).

Just as in the situation depicted in Figure 1-52b, it would again be the responsibility of the author of the component defining the concrete `MyService` type to ensure that it properly models the *Service* concept and so advertise that fact in its own client-facing documentation. It would also be up to the author of `MyClient` to name *Service* as a type requirement where appropriate. Last, but not least, it would be the responsibility of external users not to attempt to supply, to `MyClient`, an object of a type that did not claim to model *Service* where explicitly required (by `MyClient`).

Even when the English specification delineating all of the details of the *Service* concept is spelled out in its own physical component (as suggested in Figure 1-52c), there remains no inherent implied physical dependency on that component. That is, there is nothing needed from the component describing *Service* in order to compile or link either of the respective components defining `MyService` or `MyClient` (nor would there be in the case of refinement). For that reason, we continue to use the dashed-line variant to reflect (all of) these In-Structure-Only relationships.

We can easily imagine a development methodology (or language) in which every nonstandard concept is characterized fully in its own component and that components defining logical entities that *refine*, *model*, or *use* such concepts are required to `#include` *directly* (see section 2.6) the `.h` file of the component that characterizes them.[117] Given that all such In-Structure-Only (ISO) relationships also come with a mandated `#include` of the header used to characterize that concept, the implied physical dependency (in the implementation) is restored. Hence, the dashed lines in the ISO relationships would be replaced with solid ones, as illustrated in

---

[117] The desire to incorporate some notion of concepts into the C++ language has been around since before C++98 was standardized. Throughout the first decade of this century, the C++ Standards Committee worked to develop a version of concepts based on features found in Haskell (type classes) and Standard ML (signatures); see **siek10**. Due to several technical and usability concerns, however, the feature was withdrawn from C++11. A seminal meeting in Palo Alto (August 2011) involving Bjarne Stroustrup (the creator of C++), Alexander Stepanov (the creator of the STL), and many others, renewed interest in language-level support for concepts. The output of that meeting was a technical report, N3351 (**stroustrup12**), that used "usage-based" requirements to constrain the generic algorithms of the C++ Standard Library. Andrew Sutton was responsible for transforming the report into WG21 proposal N3580 (**sutton13**), "Concepts Lite," which formed the basis for the version of concepts finally adopted in C++20.

Figure 1-52d. Notice, however, that the *Service* concept's ellipse retains its dashed perimeter as it is still a type *specification* rather than a type itself.[118]

1.7.11   Summary of Notation and Terminology

To summarize, a function or (class) method uses a type in its interface if it names that type in its signature or return type. A user-defined type uses another type in its interface, **Uses-In-The-Interface**, if one (or more) of its member functions (methods) uses that type in the interface. A class uses a type in its implementation, **Uses-In-The-Implementation**, if it uses that type substantively yet does not expose that use (programmatically) in its interface. A type is a kind of some other type, **Is-A**, if it (properly) publicly inherits from it (see Volume II, section 4.6). A class (almost always a protocol) uses a class in name only, **Uses-In-Name-Only**, if the name, but not the definition, of that type is needed in order to compile, link, or test that class. Finally, we saw that analogous (and other) use of templates have given rise to some additional, purely collaborative In-Structure-Only (ISO) logical relationships: **Uses-In-Structure-Only**, **Models-In-Structure-Only**, and **Refines-In-Structure-Only**. We anticipate that each of these relationships involving concepts will come to imply a physical dependency after all, and so all but one of the new symbols — the ellipse having a dashed perimeter indicating the concept itself — will, in time, become obsolete.

1.8   The Depends-On Relation

The physical dependencies among the components that make up our software will profoundly affect development, testing, deployment, maintenance, and (hierarchical) reuse (section 0.4). In the previous section, we focused primarily on *logical* relationships (between logical entities). In this section, we will focus on the different aspects and properties (among physical entities) of dependency itself. As we shall see in the next section, logical relationships between logical entities, such as classes and free (operator) functions, imply predictable physical dependencies among the physical entities, such as components (section 1.6), in which those logical entities reside.

---

[118] As language support for verifying (at compile time) that arbitrary types satisfy named concepts comes into wide use, the need for `#include`-ing the header codifying the concept will be required not only by management fiat, but also by the same commonsense engineering that requires us to `#include` the bodies of templates and inline functions, rather than foolishly trying to keep their disparate definitions the same after copying their source code by hand. Template types will be expected to be constrained by named concepts, thus requiring physical inclusion of their headers, just as a component that purports to model a given concept actually does so via a static assertion (e.g., in its `.cpp` file). Even the *Refines* relationship will naturally mandate a physical dependency, since — by construction — the refined concept is a set of type requirements, one of which is the named concept that it refines. Hence, the notion of *In-Structure-Only* relationships should be considered just a useful transient artifact of an actively evolving C++ language.

> **DEFINITION**: A component **y** Depends-On a component **x** if **x** is needed to compile or link **y**.

The Depends-On relation is quite different from the other relations we have discussed. Is-A and Uses are logical relations because they apply to logical entities, irrespective of the physical components in which those logical entities reside. Depends-On is a physical relation because it applies to components as a whole, which are themselves physical entities.

The notation used to represent the dependency of one physical unit on another is a (fat) arrow. For example, the diagram in Figure 1-53 denotes that component **plane** depends on component **wing**. That is, component **plane** cannot be used (i.e., it cannot be compiled and linked into a program) unless component **wing** is also available. Recall from section 1.7.1 that, unlike logical entities, such as Classes and functions (where we use UpperCamelCase and lowerCamelCase, respectively), we consistently name physical entities, such as files, components, and libraries, using all lowercase (see section 2.4.6).

Figure 1-53: Component `plane` Depends-On component `wing`

As is our convention (section 1.7.1), logical entities are represented by ellipses, and physical entities are represented by rectangles. Notice that the arrow used to indicate physical dependency is drawn between components (rectangles) and not individual classes (ellipses). The (fat) arrow notation used to denote physical dependency should never be confused with the arrow notation used to denote logical relationships such as public inheritance. An inheritance arrow depicting the Is-A logical relationship always runs between (elliptical) logical entities, such as classes or structs; a Depends-On arrow always connects (rectangular) physical entities, such as files, components, and libraries (and also packages and package groups as described in sections 2.7 and 2.8, respectively).

Let us now consider the skeleton header file for the simple `polygon` component shown in Figure 1-54. There is just enough information visible for us to see that class `Polygon` has a data member of type `PointList`.[119] If a class has an instance of a user-defined type as a data member, it will be necessary to know the size (and layout) of that data member even to compile the definition of the class.

```
// polygon.h
#ifndef INCLUDED_POLYGON           Ignoring package
#define INCLUDED_POLYGON           names for now
                                   (See section 2.4.6.)
#include <pointlist.h>

// ...

class Polygon {
    PointList d_deltas;  // Has-A
    // ...
  public:
    // ...
};

// ...

#endif
```

Figure 1-54: Skeleton header file `polygon.h`

DEFINITION: A component **y** exhibits a *compile-time dependency* on component **x** if **x.h** is needed to compile **y.cpp.**

We say that a logical entity makes *substantive use* of a class if it is necessary for the compiler to have seen the definition of that class to compile the component defining that entity. More specifically, it is not possible to compile any file that needs the definition of `Polygon` without first including `pointlist.h`. In keeping with the rationale of Component Property 1 (section 1.6.1), it is appropriate to place the directive `#include <pointlist.h>` directly in the header file of the **polygon** component. Figure 1-55 illustrates the detailed compile-time dependencies among the files in components **polygon** and **pointlist**.

---

[119] For illustration purposes, we have chosen to implement our own linked-list type, `PointList`, that pools `Point` objects; a more general solution would be to implement a generic container template, parameterized by the type of elements it contains, and, unlike `PointList`, such a generic container would be entirely independent of class `Point`.

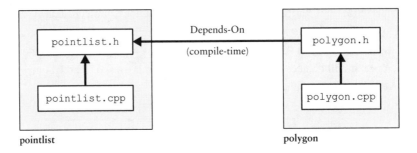

Figure 1-55: Compile-time dependency of `polygon.cpp` on `pointlist.h`

According to Component Property 1, a component's `.cpp` file must always depend on its own `.h` file at compile time. Since `polygon.cpp` will not compile without (the compiler having seen the contents of) `polygon.h` and since `polygon.h` will not compile without `pointlist.h`, `polygon.cpp` has an (indirect) compile-time dependency on `pointlist.h`. Notice again that the arrow used to indicate the physical dependency is drawn between two physical entities (in this case, files). A more abstract representation of physical dependency (i.e., at the component level) is shown in Figure 1-56.

Figure 1-56: Abstract representation of component dependency

> **DEFINITION**: A component **y** exhibits a *link-time dependency* on component **x** if the object file **y.o** (produced by compiling **y.cpp**) contains an undefined symbol for which **x.o** is required by the linker to resolve that symbol.

That is, if a component **y** needs the definition of a symbol and there is but one component **x** whose `.o` file could provide that definition, then **y** Depends-On **x** at link time. Note that dual bindage symbols, such as those generated for inline and implicitly instantiated function templates (sections 1.3.12 and 1.3.14, respectively), do not (typically) constitute a link-time dependency as they are (typically) repeated in multiple `.o` files — any one of which, especially including the one that uses it, is equally capable of resolving the undefined symbol.[120]

---

[120] Academically, we could contrive a situation in which just a small constant number (i.e., two or more) components supply a dual-bindage definition; however, we see no practical value in doing so (hence, we shall not discuss it further).

A component need not be dependent on another at compile time for it to be dependent on that component at link time. Consider the implementation for component **region** and the *alternate* implementation of component **polygon** shown in Figure 1-57.

```
// region.h
#ifndef INCLUDED_REGION
#define INCLUDED_REGION

#include <polygon.h>

// ...

class Region {
    Polygon d_polygon;  // Has-A
    // ...
  public:
    // ...
};

// ...

#endif
```

```
// polygon.h
#ifndef INCLUDED_POLYGON
#define INCLUDED_POLYGON

class PointList;

// ...

class Polygon {
    PointList *d_list_p;  // Holds A
    // ...
  public:
    // ...
};

// ...

#endif
```

```
// region.cpp
#include <region.h>

// ...
```

```
// polygon.cpp
#include <polygon.h>
#include <pointlist.h>

// ...
```

Figure 1-57: Link-time-only dependency of region on pointlist

Compiling pointlist.cpp of course requires pointlist.h. Both polygon.h and pointlist.h are needed to compile polygon.cpp. Finally, both region.h and polygon.h are needed to compile region.cpp. Notice that pointlist.h is *not* needed to compile region.cpp. There is no (direct or indirect) compile-time dependency of component **region** on component **pointlist** (a useful property discussed in section 3.10 and also in Volume II, section 6.6). However, **region** still exhibits an indirect *link-time* physical dependency on **pointlist**, which would become obvious were we to try to link region.o to its (unique, standalone) test driver (see Volume III, section 7.5) without providing pointlist.o as well.

Observation

A compile-time dependency often results in a link-time dependency.

If a component **x** must include another component's header y.h to compile, then it is reasonable to expect that the use of declarations therein might well generate undefined symbols at the object-code level (in x.o) that would then need to be resolved at link time (by y.o). A link-time dependency (section 1.3) will typically result whenever we use a declaration of (1) a noninline, non-templated function, (2) an explicit function-template specialization defined uniquely in a separate translation unit, or (3) external (including class) data having static storage duration. Even in those instances where a compile-time dependency does not introduce an actual dependency at link time, we dare not rely on such details as they are subject to change without notice.

Observation

The Depends-On relation for components is transitive.

If component **x** depends on component **y**, and **y**, in turn, depends on component **z**, then **x** depends on **z**. This transitive property of dependency among components makes no mention of which file in one component is dependent on which file in the other. Any such file-level dependency is sufficient to produce a physical dependency for the component as a whole. As Figure 1-58 shows, region.cpp includes external declarations in polygon.h that potentially introduce undefined symbols in region.o that must be resolved by polygon.o. By the same token, polygon.cpp includes external declarations in pointlist.h that potentially introduce undefined symbols in polygon.o that must be resolved by pointlist.o. Although region.o does not depend on pointlist.o directly, the (direct) compile-time dependencies of **region** on **polygon** and of **polygon** on **pointlist** have produced the (potential) indirect (link-time) physical dependency of **region** on **pointlist**.

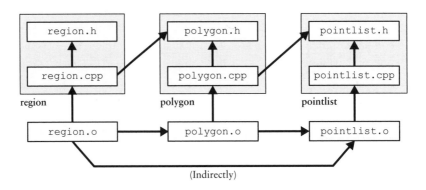

Figure 1-58: Indirect link-time dependency of region on pointlist

An important consequence of this transitivity is that we can exploit it to simplify our dependency diagrams without misrepresenting the essential physical nature of the subsystem they depict. Assuming the alternate implementation of **polygon** in Figure 1-57, the direct compile-time dependency graph for all four components in the subsystem topped by **region** is shown in Figure 1-59a.

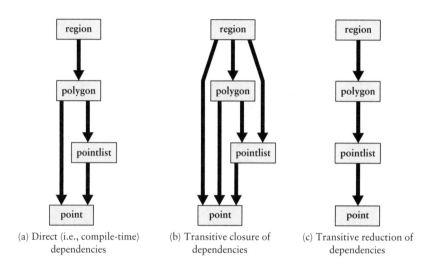

(a) Direct (i.e., compile-time)   (b) Transitive closure of   (c) Transitive reduction of
dependencies   dependencies   dependencies

Figure 1-59: Essentially equivalent physical dependency graphs

By transitivity, since **polygon** depends directly on **point**, and **region** depends directly on **polygon**, we could augment the dependency graph by adding (redundant) arrows from **region** to **pointlist** and **point** (Figure 1-59b) without affecting which components can be tested or reused independently of the others. More productively, however, we can reduce unnecessary clutter by eliminating the arrow representing the direct (compile-time) dependency of **polygon** on **point** (Figure 1-59c) since that dependency is already implied by transitivity anyway.

1.9   Implied Dependency

Abstract logical relationships are known to have certain physical implications among the components in which these logical entities reside. In the third edition of *The C++ Programming Language*, Stroustrup writes[121]:

---

[121] **stroustrup00,** section 23.4.3.3, pp. 106–107, specifically p. 107

The need to consider inheritance and use relationships at the design stage (and not just during implementation) follows directly from the use of classes to represent concepts. It also implies that the component (§23.4.3, §24.4), and not the individual class, is the unit of design.

In particular, substantive logical relationships such as Is-A and Uses that span component boundaries necessarily imply physical dependencies.[122] For example, Figure 1-60 shows a component/class diagram of a simple geometric subsystem (with component names temporarily omitted).[123]

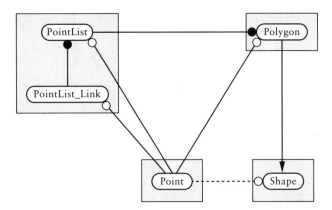

Figure 1-60: Logical relationships among classes defined in various components

The logical notation (section 1.7) in Figure 1-60 indicates that `Polygon` Is-A `Shape`. That is, class `Polygon` publicly inherits from class `Shape`. Without knowing anything more, we can conclude that the component defining `Polygon` has a direct (compile-time) physical dependency on the component defining `Shape`. This implied Depends-On relationship (between components) is illustrated in Figure 1-61. Note that, as a consequence of Component Property 1 (section 1.6.1), the component defining `Polygon` *must* `#include` the header of the component defining `Shape` in its `.h` file; otherwise, the `.cpp` file of the component defining `Polygon` would fail to compile.

---

[122] Note that Stroustrup's definition of component here is different from ours in that, by his definition, a component is primarily logical in nature.

[123] The use of an underscore in `PointList_Link` indicates, by convention only, that it is not intended for use outside the component in which it is defined (see sections 2.7.1 and 2.7.3).

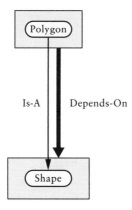

Figure 1-61: Is-A implies physical dependency

Figure 1-60 also indicates that class `Polygon` uses class `Point` in its interface (and substantively in its implementation), which in itself is sufficient to infer a physical dependency from the component defining `Polygon` on the component defining `Point`. Separately, both class `PointList` and its local helper class, `PointList_Link`, use `Point` in their respective interfaces. Either of these logical relationships would alone be sufficient to conclude that the component defining `PointList` (and `PointList_Link`) Depends-On the component defining `Point`; taken together, the implication is the same. The resulting physical dependencies implied by the Uses-In-The-Interface relationships among the components in Figure 1-60 are shown in Figure 1-62.

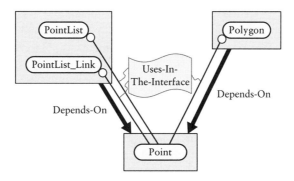

Figure 1-62: Uses-In-The-Interface implies physical dependency

In this particular case, all of the physical dependencies implied by the Uses-In-The-Interface relation happen to be direct, and therefore it will turn out that, according to our methodology for component design (see section 2.6), each of the two components using `Point` in the interface will be required to `#include` (in either its `.h` or `.cpp` file, as appropriate) the header of the component defining `Point`.

We could, however, imagine a slightly different situation, illustrated in Figure 1-63, in which a component defining, say, `YourPolygon` (corresponding to `Polygon` above) delegates *all* substantive use of `Point` (i.e., any use that would require the compiler to have seen the definition of `Point`) to the component defining `YourPolygonImp` (corresponding to `PointList` above). In that case, the physical dependency implied by using `Point` in the interface of `YourPolygon` would *not* be direct (nor necessarily even a compile-time dependency) as the Uses-In-The-Interface relation often suggests. Hence, there would be no reason to `#include` the definition of `Point` in either the `.h` or `.cpp` file for the component defining `YourPolygon` — that is, a local (forward) declaration of class `Point` in the header file defining your `YourPolygon` would suffice.

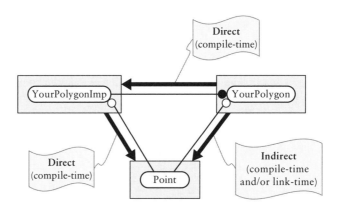

Figure 1-63: The dependency implied by a Uses-In-The-Interface might be indirect.

The component defining `YourPolygon` would, however, make substantive use of `YourPolygonImp`, which implies a direct (compile-time) dependency and an obligation to `#include` the definition of `YourPolygonImp` in either the `.h` or `.cpp` file (again as appropriate) of the component defining `YourPolygon`. Similarly, `YourPolygonImp` makes direct substantive use of `Point`. Hence, the physical dependency implied by the Uses-In-The-Interface relationship between `YourPolygon` and `Point`, although not direct, would nonetheless be correct due to transitivity.[124]

Returning to our original example, Figure 1-60 indicates that class `Polygon` uses class `PointList` in its implementation. Without any further analysis, we can be sure that the component defining `Polygon` depends physically on the component defining `PointList`, as illustrated in Figure 1-64. The figure also indicates a component-internal Uses-In-The-Implementation relationship between `PointList` and the local (component-private) helper class (see section 2.7), `PointList_Link`. Although `PointList` makes substantive use of `PointList_Link`, there is no additional implied physical dependency in this case, as these two logical entities are already physically coupled by virtue of their being colocated within the same component.

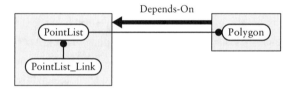

Figure 1-64: Uses-In-The-Implementation implies physical dependency.

Unlike the Uses-In-The-Interface relationship, physical dependency implied by Uses-In-The-Implementation is *always* direct. We could, however, construct a somewhat different scenario, illustrated in Figure 1-65, in which the component defining `YourPolygon` does not make any direct use of `PointList` but instead uses (in its implementation) `YourPolygonImp`, which, in turn, similarly uses `PointList`. Again, by transitivity, there would be an indirect (possibly compile-time) dependency of the component defining `YourPolygon` on the one defining `PointList`.

---

[124] Note that this example of Uses-In-the-Interface is not equivalent to Uses-In-Name-Only, which has no physical implications (direct or indirect) whatsoever.

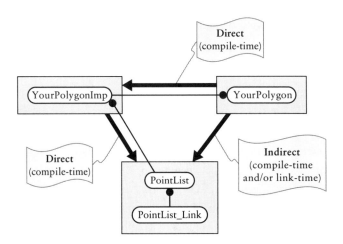

Figure 1-65: The dependency implied by Uses-In-The-Implementation is always direct.

Lastly, we consider the one logical relationship shown in the diagram of Figure 1-60, Uses-In-Name-Only, that does not imply *any* physical dependency. According to this notation, repeated in isolation in Figure 1-66, class Shape uses class Point in name *only* — e.g., its size is not relevant. From this information, we can conclude that — while there is nominal collaboration — there is no (direct or indirect) physical dependency implied by this logical relationship and therefore no implied need to #include the definition of Point anywhere in the component defining Shape (nor in any component on which Shape might directly or indirectly depend).

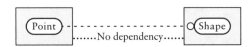

Figure 1-66: Uses-In-Name-Only implies no (direct or indirect) dependency.

The important difference between Uses-In-The-Interface (even where the implied dependency turns out to be indirect and only at link time) and Uses-In-Name-Only (which has no implication whatsoever on physical dependency) is often confused, but the distinction remains clear: A component using a type defined in another component *in name only* can be compiled, linked, and tested independently of that component, while a component using that same type *in the interface* cannot.

Although there can be at most one *uses* relationship between any two logical entities, a Uses-In-Name-Only relationship does not suppress a physical dependency implied by another relationship on a separate logical entity whose definition is colocated in the same component. For example, if a component defines two classes — one of which is used "in name only" and the other is used "in size" — a physical dependency will be implied (and a #include will be required), as illustrated in Figure 1-67.

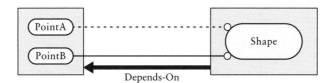

Figure 1-67: Uses-In-Name-Only does not suppress other implied dependencies.

Finally note that, although uncommon, it is not unheard of for two logical entities to have both an Is-A and a Uses-In-The-Interface relationship — especially when both relationships imply physical dependency in the same direction. For example, consider adapting a standard concrete type to a local abstract interface (protocol)[125] as illustrated in Figure 1-68. A MyPolygon Is-A StdPolygon (see Volume II, section 4.6) and can be used in (most) situations (see Volume II, section 5.5) in which an StdPolygon is expected. By the same token, some methods (e.g., constructors) defined on MyPolygon (which has no additional data members) will naturally take objects of type StdPolygon in the interface. The pair of logical relationships captures this dual intent, while implying the correct physical dependency.

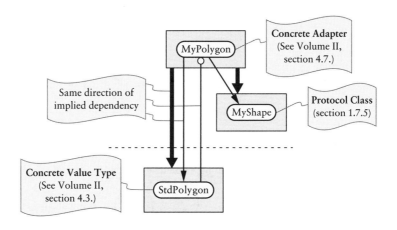

Figure 1-68: Uses and Is-A are not necessarily mutually exclusive.

---

[125] **lakos96**, Appendix A, pp. 756–758

The complete set of physical dependencies implied by the logical relationships shown in Figure 1-60 is presented in Figure 1-69a.[126] Once we have determined all of the physical dependencies, the diagram can be simplified by removing the logical entities, leaving only the physical relationships among the components, as illustrated in Figure 1-69b. Note that the numbers in the upper-right corners of the components are called *level numbers*, which are explained in the following section.

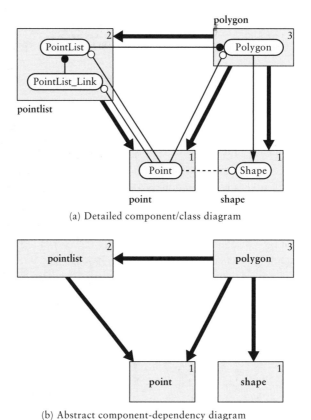

(a) Detailed component/class diagram

(b) Abstract component-dependency diagram

Figure 1-69: Physical dependencies implied by logical relationships

Inferring physical dependencies at the design stage enables us to ensure a sound physical architecture much earlier in the development process. Most of our small subsystem designs originate with the kind of simple component/class diagrams we've seen throughout this section. We deliberately

---

[126] Recall from section 1.7.1 that, in our methodology, component names, being physical entities, are always entirely lowercase (see section 2.4.6).

exploit the implication of logical relationships to predict the physical dependencies among the components in which they reside — long before the design is ever implemented. Undesirable physical characteristics will force us to alter — sometimes entirely rework — our logical designs. It is precisely this tight feedback that guides us toward becoming better, more effective architects.[127]

To summarize, our three substantive logical relationships, Is-A, Uses-In-The-Interface, and Uses-In-The-Implementation (sections 1.7.2–1.7.4), imply physical dependency when these relationships extend across component boundaries, while Uses-In-Name-Only (section 1.7.5) does not.

- **Is-A** induces a direct compile-time dependency that, in our methodology, requires placing a `#include` of the `.h` file defining the base class in the (distinct) `.h` file defining the derived one (section 1.7.2).

- **Uses-In-The-Interface** implies a (possibly indirect) dependency that (conceivably) might not require `#include`-ing the used type's definition in either the `.h` or the `.cpp` of the component using it but — by transitivity of physical dependency — nonetheless implies a bona fide physical dependency (section 1.7.3).

- **Uses-In-The-Implementation**, on the other hand, always induces a direct compile-time (and perhaps also a link-time) dependency that requires placing a `#include` of the `.h` defining the used type in either the `.h` or the `.cpp` (as appropriate) of the component using it (section 1.7.4).

- **Uses-In-Name-Only** indicates logical collaboration, but — unlike Uses-In-The-Interface — implies no physical dependency whatsoever (section 1.7.5), and similarly for the other purely collaborative ISO (In-Structure-Only) logical relationships (section 1.7.6); these purely collaborative relationships are compared (section 1.7.7) and contrasted (section 1.7.8) at the end of section 1.7.

By considering implied dependencies at design time, we can readily evaluate and ensure the physical quality of our software architecture long before any code is written.

1.10   Level Numbers

We now describe a method for partitioning components based on their physical dependencies into equivalence classes called *levels*. Each level is associated with a non-negative integer index, referred to as the *level number*. If the component dependencies in a software subsystem — e.g., a *package*

---

[127] Design rules, including those pertaining to external-linkage logical constructs, can be found in section 2.6.

(see section 2.8) — happen to form a directed acyclic graph (DAG), we can define the *level* of each component within that subsystem as the number of components along the longest path of physical dependencies between that component and a local *leaf* component.

DEFINITION: Acyclic physical dependencies admit the canonical assignment of (non-negative) level numbers:

Level 0: A non-local component.

Level 1: A local component not depending physically on any other local component (a.k.a. a *leaf component*).

Level *N*: A local component that depends physically on at least one local component at level $N - 1$ (for $N \geq 2$), but none at level N or higher.

In this definition, we assume that components (e.g., `iostream`) outside our current project directory (or *package*) to have already been tested and are known to function properly. These components are treated as given and have an assigned level of 0. A local component having no physical dependency on any other local component is called a *leaf* component and is defined to have a level of 1. Otherwise, each local component is defined to have a level number that is one more than the maximum level of the components upon which that component depends.

DEFINITION: A software subsystem rendered in terms of components that can be assigned level numbers is said to be *levelizable*.

Each node of every component-based subsystem whose physical dependencies form a DAG (directed acyclic graph) has, by our definition, exactly one possible level number; a node that participates in a cycle does not. That is, the notion of level for a node that is part of a cyclically dependent subsystem has no similar such natural, obvious, and intuitive meaning.[128]

---

[128] To enable software tools to accommodate dependency graphs having cycles, we can generalize the notion of level numbers by treating each cyclically dependent subset of *M* components as a single composite node spanning *M* levels, and with each component marked as having the highest level spanned by that composite. For example, given 5 local components — **a**, **b**, **c**, **d**, and **e** — where **b**, **c**, and **d** form a cycle of $M = 3$, and where **e** depends (directly) on **c**, and **c** depends (directly) on **a**, the assignment for the *extended level numbers* would be **a** $\rightarrow$ 1, **b** $\rightarrow$ 4, **c** $\rightarrow$ 4, **d** $\rightarrow$ 4, and **e** $\rightarrow$ 5. For more on this generalized definition of level numbers that, for the purposes of writing analysis tools, admits graphs with cycles, see **lakos96**, Appendix C.1, pp. 780–793, especially starting after the listing on p. 788.

For example, the diagram shown in Figure 1-60, section 1.9, had no dependency cycles and hence was *levelizable*. Figure 1-69b, section 1.9, shows the level number of each component displayed in the upper-right corner of the box depicting that component. The **point** component has no dependency on any other local component, so it is at level 1. Component **shape**, having just a Uses-In-Name-Only relation between class Shape and class Point, is also at level 1. Hence, both **point** and **shape** are considered *leaf* components of this subsystem. Component **pointlist** defines two classes, PointList and PointList_Link, both of which make substantive use of class Point; hence, component **pointlist** depends physically on leaf component **point** (only) and therefore is at level 2. Finally, the **polygon** component, which depends on components **point** and **shape** (both at level 1), also depends on component **pointlist** (at level 2) and hence is at level 3.

Note that the term *levelizable* applies to physical, not logical, entities. While an acyclic logical dependency graph might admit one or more testable physical partitions, the level numbers of (physical) components, along with the component properties set forth in section 1.6, imply a viable order for effective testing. Moreover, levelizable systems can be reused hierarchically as needed. The various partial subsystems of Figure 1-69, section 1.9, that can potentially be reused independently of other components are listed in Figure 1-70.

To Test or Use	At Level	You Also Need
point	1	
shape	1	
pointlist	2	point (level 1)
polygon	3	shape (level 1), point (level 1), pointlist (level 2)

Figure 1-70: Independently reusable partial subsystems

Another significant advantage of *acyclic* physical designs is that they are easier to comprehend incrementally compared to those having cycles, which becomes more and more obvious with increasing system size. The process of understanding a levelizable design can proceed in an orderly manner (either top-down or bottom-up). Not all subsystems formed by hierarchical physical design are reusable, but, to be maintainable, each component in a subsystem must be understandable (testable) in terms of other components that have already been understood (tested) — irrespective of how general their applicability might turn out to be — as we will advocate further (see section 2.14).

Of course, not every design is levelizable. Suppose we have a tiny subsystem consisting of just two components modeling, respectively, a manager and the employees in the group being managed. In order to manage (e.g., the lifetimes of) the employees, the component defining `Manager` will need to depend on the one defining `Employee`. We also plan to use `Employee` in the interface of `Manager` — e.g., for iteration purposes. Suppose further that we want to be able to ask an employee directly, "How many people are in your group?" This last requirement imposes a Uses-In-The-Implementation dependency of `Employee` back on `Manager`, which induces a cyclic physical dependency as illustrated in Figure 1-71a.

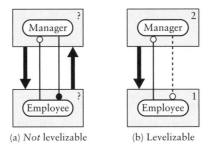

(a) *Not* levelizable   (b) Levelizable

Figure 1-71: Not every design is levelizable.

The original requirements, as stated above, lead us to a design that is not levelizable; however, all is not lost. If, instead of asking the employee detailed questions that only the manager knows, we simply ask the employee, "who is your manager?" (which the employee object stores as an opaque `Manager` pointer data member that requires just a pure `class` declaration), there is no corresponding upward physical dependency implied, as illustrated in Figure 1-71b. The requester can then use this address in a context where the `Manager` type's definition is visible to pose the original (or any other substantive) question to the `Manager` object directly — all this without inducing any cyclic physical dependencies.

The general technique illustrated in Figure 1-71 (see also section 3.5.4.1) for untangling physical dependencies is characterized by having one object use another in name only and is referred to as *Opaque Pointers*; it (see section 3.5.4) and eight other such *levelization techniques* are discussed in detail in section 3.5.

Whether a design *is* levelizable is not immediately obvious from a logical diagram. Consider the component/class diagram of Figure 1-72.[129] Can you tell from this diagram whether or not the components in this design are levelizable?

---

[129] This authentic design is reprinted verbatim from **lakos96**, section 4.7.2, Figure 4-13, p. 172.

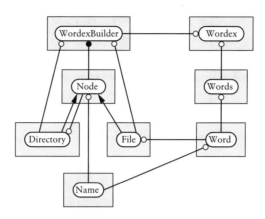

Figure 1-72: Is this design levelizable?

As it turns out, the indicated logical relationships in this design do *not* imply a cyclic physical dependency among any of the components shown; however, the component/class diagram is cluttered and contains more information than is needed to understand the physical structure of the subsystem. If we rearrange the placement of the components and eliminate the logical detail, we obtain the strikingly lucid component-dependency diagram of Figure 1-73.[130]

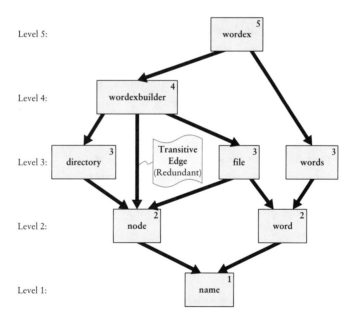

Figure 1-73: Implied component dependency diagram

[130] **lakos96**, section 4.7.2, Figure 4-15, p. 174

There is, however, one redundant edge in the diagram of Figure 1-73. Component **wordexbuilder** depends directly on components **directory**, **file**, and **node**. As we know from section 1.8, the Depends-On relation is transitive. Since **directory** (and **file** also) depends on **node**, the indicated dependency of **wordexbuilder** on **node** is implied and can be removed without affecting level numbers. The diagram in Figure 1-73 is clearly acyclic and typical of those for subsystems that address a specific application. At this level of abstraction, the physical structure of the design appears to be sound.

One of the great benefits of this analysis is that, after untangling the component dependency diagram, we were able to make a substantive, qualitative comment about the integrity of the physical design without even the tiniest discussion of the application domain. An inability to assign level numbers provides a clear and objective indication that the current design is unsound before it is ever implemented. Simple tools to help automate this analysis are easy to write, and have proven to be invaluable for the development of large systems.[131]

1.11   Extracting Actual Dependencies

Suppose that we have designed a large project, guided by the implied dependencies of logical relationships across component boundaries (section 1.9). Now that the design stage is largely complete and development is under way, we would like to have a tool that extracts the *actual* physical dependencies among our components so that we can track and compare them with our initial design expectations.

Although it is possible to parse the source for an entire C++ program or library to determine the exact component dependency graph, doing so is both difficult and relatively slow — so slow, in fact, as to be considered non-scalable.[132] We can, however, readily deduce the component dependency graph directly from the components' source files (`.h` and `.cpp`) simply by parsing only their C++ preprocessor `#include` directives. Such processing is relatively fast (and scalable), and is commonly done by a number of standard, public-domain dependency analysis tools.[133]

---

[131] **lakos96**, Appendix C, pp. 799–813

[132] More generally, what we advocate in this book assumes what is achievable today using a conventional tool chain (compiler, linker, etc.). Claims that there exist compilers that support special features, such as whole program optimizations, that might obviate practices suggested here are also summarily dismissed as not scalable now (nor are they likely to be in the foreseeable future).

[133] E.g., `gmake`, `scandeps` (from PVCS), `makedepend`, and Kythe.

In order for this dependency-analysis strategy to work, however, we will need to add a fourth property of `.h`/`.cpp` pairs to the three discussed in section 1.6 for well-formed components.

1.11.1   Component Property 4

> There are no local "forward" declarations for a logical construct having external or dual bindage defined (uniquely) by another component; instead, the `.h` file of that component is `#include`-ed to obtain the needed declaration.

The previous three properties (sections 6.1–6.3) ensured that every logical entity having other than internal bindage is declared in a component's `.h` file and that the compiler will have the opportunity to verify that the entity's definition is consistent with its declaration. This fourth property ensures that clients of the component use the validated declaration and do not create their own (perhaps erroneous) version of it.

For example, if we wanted to use the standard C Library function `pow` in one of our components, we would always include the corresponding header file containing the declaration of `pow` as in Figure 1-74a, and never attempt to declare it ourselves as in Figure 1-74b. Similarly, we would include the header file of the component providing the declaration of any global variable, rather than repeating its `extern` declaration explicitly.

(FINE)

(BAD IDEA)

```
// mycomponent.cpp
// ...
#include <cmath>

#include <cerrno>

#include <your_stuff.h>



// ...
```

```
// mycomponent.cpp
// ...
extern "C" double pow(double, double);

extern int errno;  // could be a macro!

namespace your { class Stuff; }

bool operator==(const your::Stuff&,
                const your::Stuff&);
// ...
```

(a) By including the header

(b) By repeating the declaration explicitly

Figure 1-74: Accessing nonlocal entities having external bindage

Component Property 4 appropriately forces a conspicuous compile-time dependency whenever one component makes use of a logical construct having external or dual bindage defined in another. Apart from the engineering justifications discussed earlier, Component Property 4 also makes it possible for developers to deduce *all* direct dependencies of a component at glance, simply by inspecting the #include directives at the tops of the two files. Satisfying any of the four properties for .h/.cpp pairs required of proper components has obvious benefits in terms of modularity and maintainability, but collectively they lead to a seminal observation:

Observation

C++ preprocessor #include directives alone are sufficient to deduce *all* actual physical dependencies among the components within a system, provided the system compiles.

Component Property 4 requires that, for a component **x** to make substantive use of any logical entity in component **y**, **x** must include y.h in either x.h or x.cpp. Hence, direct substantive use of one component by another always implies a compile-time dependency. The contrapositive (that if **x** does *not* include y.h, then **x** does *not* make substantive use of **y**) is certainly true given Component Property 4, provided **x** compiles.

Conversely, the only legitimate reason for component **x** to include y.h is if component **x** does in fact make direct substantive use of component **y**. Otherwise, the inclusion itself would be superfluous and introduce unnecessary compile-time coupling. The contrapositive (that if **x** does *not* make substantive use of component **y**, then **x** does *not* include y.h) should also be true, though occasionally, due to human oversight, it is not.[134]

DEFINITION: A component, x, *Includes* another component, y, if the contents of y.h are ultimately incorporated into the translation unit corresponding to x.cpp at compile time (for *any* of the supported build targets).

---

[134] Writing tools to detect and remove (or restructure) unnecessary #include directives is more difficult than it might first appear. Prior to writing his seminal *Effective C++* programming books, Scott Meyers set out to write software to mechanically detect such design suboptimalities but quickly found that many fell short of unambiguous objective solution. Decades later, research (**felber10**) leading to a tool integrated into an IDE called Cevelop (www.cevelop.com) that automates the reduction/removal of unnecessary #includes was conducted under the auspices of Professor Peter Sommerlad (Peter.Sommerlad@hsr.ch) at IFS Institute for Software at FHO-HSR Hochschule für Technik, a university of applied sciences in Rapperswil, Switzerland.

The `#include` directives embedded within source code quite accurately indicate link-time as well as compile-time dependencies among proper components. Knowing that any substantive use of a component is flagged by including its header file guarantees that the *transitive closure*[135] of the *Includes* relation indicates all possible physical dependencies among components. A dependency graph extracted in this manner might indicate additional, spurious dependencies brought on by unnecessary `#include` directives (which should be removed). But, given that our four essential component properties of `.h` / `.cpp` pairs hold, the Includes relation will never omit any actual component dependencies.

The ability to extract actual physical dependencies from a potentially large collection of components quickly and accurately allows us to verify — throughout the development process — that these dependencies are consistent with our overall architectural plan.[136] Such tools have, over the years, continued to prove invaluable in the development and maintenance of large systems.[137]

1.12   Summary

1.1 Knowledge Is Power: The Devil Is in the Details

Many would tell you that design is independent of (1) the language used to express it and (2) the tools used to build and render it. We disagree. The details of what the language supports and what it can express subtly, yet pervasively, shape the way we talk and even think about design. Without a thorough understanding of how the source code we write with our editors is translated and assembled into runnable programs, we lack the *physical* foundation necessary to create large systems that scale. In fact, without a solid understanding of what's going on beneath the source code, even small programs can exhibit nontrivial correctness and maintenance issues.

1.2 Compiling and Linking C++

C++ programs are built in two main phases. In the *compilation phase* (see Figure 1-2, section 1.2.1): (1) Each implementation (`.cpp`) file is preprocessed to incorporate any header (`.h`)

---

[135] The definition of *transitive closure* on a binary relation is as follows: Given a square boolean matrix A(I, J) in which each element $A(i, j)$ $[0 \le i < I$ and $0 \le j < J]$ denotes whether element i is related to element j in one step, then the transitive closure denotes the binary relation that indicates whether element i is related to element j in 1 or more steps.

[136] A complete specification of a suite of tools to extract physical dependencies is provided in **lakos96,** Appendix C, pp. 779–813.

[137] With the relatively recent advent of Clang, tooling requiring full-on parsing of C++ has been greatly facilitated, and still it does not now, nor can it ever, compare with the raw speed afforded by straightforward pattern matching of `#include` directives.

files indicated by `#include` directives, appearing either directly (in the `.cpp` file) or recursively (in an included `.h` file), into a single intermediate representation called a *translation unit*; (2) this source-level representation is then translated (compiled) into a binary (machine-readable) representation and stored in an object (`.o`) file.

During the *link phase* (see Figure 1-3, section 1.2.1), each of the `.o` files to be incorporated into the program are examined in order to determine what undefined symbols must be resolved externally by definitions provided in other `.o` files. Each external symbol reference must be resolved uniquely or the link will fail. If successful, the resulting program containing the well-known entry point `main` will be stored as an executable file (e.g., `a.out`).

The common capabilities of tools, especially those of the linker, are an artificially limiting factor as to what can be achieved in a language such as C++. Historically, object files were always necessarily incorporated into programs atomically. Moreover, all undefined symbols residing within each such `.o` file had to be resolved, regardless of whether they were used. Hence, even logically related functions have sometimes been placed in separate translation units as colocation can lead to dependencies on otherwise unneeded `.o` files and, therefore, result in unnecessarily large programs.

To support more advanced language features, such as implicit instantiation, as well as inline functions, all modern platforms now support the ability of a compiler to generate duplicate function definitions in multiple `.o` files and then rely on the linker to incorporate exactly one of many (identical) copies in the final executable. For this approach to work, however, the compiler/linker technology must ensure that each such definition acts as if it resides in its own *segment* within a `.o` file, such that it can be incorporated (or not) independently of any other code within that `.o` file — i.e., use of that definition does not drag in any others. Nonetheless, because any such details are heavily platform (and deployment) dependent (see section 2.15), we continue to design as if `.o` files are always incorporated atomically.

Library archives help make building software easier and facilitate its distribution. Instead of linking against individual `.o` files, we might choose to use the archiver (e.g., `ar` on Unix platforms) to place an appropriate set of `.o` files in a library (e.g., `.a`) file (see Figure 1-8, section 1.2.4). Unlike `.o` files supplied directly, `.o` files supplied to the linker via a library are incorporated only if needed to resolve previously undefined symbols. Once a `.o` is incorporated, however, it is treated subsequently as if it had been supplied directly. Note that care must be taken not to allow this kind of difference to alter the intended behavior of library software (e.g., via runtime initialized file-scope static variables) as was the case in the "Singleton" registry example (see Figure 1-11, section 1.2.5).

The way in which library archives are processed depends on the platform. On Unix platforms, for example, the libraries are scanned in sequence; each library in turn is used to resolve any symbol references before moving on to the next. Carelessly colocating object files within an archive so as to cause mutual dependencies across libraries makes them harder for human beings to understand and maintain. Among the many other undesirable consequences, having mutual dependencies across library archives can (on some platforms) require having to repeat one or more libraries on the link line — the order and frequency of which being subject to change with even minor enhancements to those libraries.

1.3 Declarations, Definitions, and Linkage

A *declaration* (typically) introduces a name into a scope and — for the most part — can be repeated within a translation unit. On the other hand, there can be at most one definition of any object, function, or type within a program, as governed by the one-definition rule (ODR). In C++, there are pure (e.g., forward) declarations, definitions that can also act as declarations (i.e., they are self-declaring), and those that can't. Distinguishing among these kinds of constructs is not easy and is, perhaps, best introduced by example (see Figure 1-27, section 1.2.20).

Pure declarations are typically of types used as function parameters or return types. In almost all cases, the compiler using such a forward declaration will ultimately see the corresponding definition (when it comes time to use it substantively). In rare (and almost always contrived) scenarios, a class declaration may be used when no corresponding definition appears anywhere in the program (see the Uses-In-Name-Only relation, section 1.7.5); pure abstract interfaces — which we call *protocols* — are the only natural way for such relationships to occur in practice. By resorting to forward class declarations instead of `#include` directives in header files where appropriate (sections 1.6 and 1.11), we can often substantially reduce unnecessary compile-time coupling (see Volume II, section 6.6).

For named entities whose use might be resolved by the linker, the declaration serves to describe to the compiler everything it needs to know to make full use of the entity — everything, that is, except its address in the memory of the final executable program. If any substantive *use* of such an entity is made via its declaration, and assuming no corresponding definition is visible locally within the translation unit, a reference to the symbol associated with that entity will be placed in this translation unit's resulting `.o` file. It will then be up to the linker to find a (unique) definition of this entity and fill in the missing address information at link time.

The ODR applies to both individual translation units and the program as a whole. Within a given translation unit, "one" means a single instance of the source-code definition[138]:

> No translation unit shall contain more than one definition of any variable,
> function, class type, enumeration type, or template.

When we are talking about a program, what is and isn't considered multiple definitions depends on the nature of the entity being defined and is closely tied to the physical bindage of that entity. For example, variable and noninline function definitions at file or namespace scope having external linkage (and bindage) must be globally unique throughout all translation units within a program.[139] On the other hand, it is permissible for the definitions of logical entities having external linkage and internal or dual bindage to be repeated in separate translation units, provided that each such definition (1) is rendered using the same sequence of tokens, and (2) means essentially the same thing.[140]

As designers of hierarchically reusable software, it behooves us to fully understand the implications of the declarations and definitions we write. According to the C++ Standard, if a name can denote an entity declared in another scope, that name is said to have *linkage*. If a name can denote an entity defined in another *translation unit*, the name is said to have *external linkage*; by contrast, a name that can denote an entity within only the same translation unit is said to have *internal linkage*, as summarized in Figure 1-75.

no linkage	The logical entity cannot be referenced outside of the local scope in which it is defined.
internal linkage	The logical entity can be referenced across different scopes but within only the same translation unit.
external linkage	The logical entity can be referenced across translation units.

Figure 1-75: The three categories of (logical) *linkage*

---

[138] **iso11**, section 3.2.1, p. 36
[139] **iso11**, section 3.2.3, pp. 36–37
[140] **iso11**, section 3.2.5, pp. 37–38

For any use of a name, the compiler must be able to determine the entity to which the name refers. To do so, a declaration of the name must be visible to the compiler at the point of its usage in the translation unit. Linkage is what allows separate declarations in different contexts to refer to the same entity. Within a translation unit, linkage makes it possible to forward declare a type whose definition will eventually be seen by the compiler. External linkage makes it possible to declare a function or object whose definition will not be seen by the compiler and whose full use must be enabled by its declaration and then later bound to its definition by the linker.

The physical mechanisms on typical platforms employed to associate the use of types, data, and functions with their corresponding definitions has, on occasion, also been referred to as (physical) *linkage*. Instead, we will consistently refer to such typical physical association mechanisms as *bindage*, as summarized in Figure 1-76.

internal bindage	The definition of the entity may be repeated in every translation unit; the use of the entity is always resolved by the compiler, never by the linker (e.g., class, `struct`, `typedef`, or preprocessor macro).
dual bindage	The definition of the entity may be repeated in every translation unit; the use of the entity may be resolved by the compiler (assuming it can see the definition source and elects to do so) or otherwise by the linker (e.g., inline function or implicitly instantiated explicit specialization of a function template).
external bindage	The definition of the entity cannot occur in more than one translation unit within a program and must be resolved by the linker.

Figure 1-76: The three categories of (physical) *bindage*

Note that, unlike the definitions of constructs having *internal bindage*, those having *external* or *dual bindage* are not needed to be seen by a client's compiler in order for them to be used. That is, the use can be resolved entirely by the linker. Thus, local declarations of non-internal-bindage entities — in particular — are especially problematic: Instead of being a compile-time error, an erroneous local declaration becomes at best a link-time error, if not a runtime one.

Declarations using the same name in the same namespace — even across translation units — logically refer to the same entity within the program. The ODR requires that the definition of each such entity be unique. Hence, creating, for example, two enumerations having the same name in separate translation units at file scope but with different definitions is a violation of the ODR. Types such as an enumeration (having internal bindage), however, are simply not directly accessible from other translation units; hence, on typical platforms, these types are effectively private to their translation unit even though the C++ Standard defines them as having external linkage.

Absent, say, an external-bindage function using this type in its interface (thereby allowing the definition to escape its translation unit), this ODR violation would likely go undetected on most platforms. Compilers that are aware of multiple translation units at a time would, however, be entirely within their rights to reject any such code that they can determine to be noncompliant with the C++ Standard. As a rule, we are well advised to avoid even such so-called *benign* violations of the ODR unless, of course, there is a compelling engineering reason to do otherwise (see Volume II, section 6.8).

On typical platforms, when the compiler of a translation unit does not have access to the source code of a definition, the linker will be required to resolve use of the name of a function to its definition; when it does, the compiler may choose to link the use of a name with its definition by itself — irrespective of whether that function was declared inline. Understanding the capabilities and limitations of the underlying tools on typical platforms (e.g., in terms of *bindage*) better enables us to model, and thereby comprehend and reason about, the complexities of the C++ language (e.g., with respect to linkage).

1.4 Header Files

Header files in both C and C++, though not strictly necessary, are intended to facilitate the sharing of common source code across translation units. C, being a procedural language, enables, but does not effectively support, abstract data types (ADTs). Consequently, modular programming in C evolved into relatively large and somewhat irregular physical units. With the advent of private data and inline functions in C++, efficient objects of ADTs could be created as automatic variables (directly on the program stack). These smaller (atomic) units of design, with their implementations more evenly distributed between the `.h` and `.cpp` files, became independently useful, leading to the informal organization of software, often characterized as `.h`/`.cpp` pairs.

Note that either a `struct` or `namespace` could be used to scope what would otherwise be free (nonmember) functions or global variables. If a `namespace` is used for this purpose, care must be taken to be sure to implement the *qualified* definition *outside* of the namespace (just like we would be forced to do with a `struct`). In this way, inconsistencies between the declaration and definition of a function's signature or the name of a global variable are automatically detected by library developers at compile time (rather than hit-or-miss by their clients at link time). For this and other engineering reasons (see Figure 2-23, section 2.4.9), we prefer to use `struct` for scopes limited to a single physical module (component) and to use `namespace` for scopes that span them.

We use header files as a modular mechanism for sharing definitions having internal or dual bindage, such as those of classes, inline functions, and templates, as well as structural aliases such as `typedef`s and preprocessor macros. We also use headers for dispensing consistent declarations of shared external-bindage constructs such as functions (or variables) having static storage duration.

1.5 Include Directives and Include Guards

Include guards are required in header files to ensure that any definitions contained in a header file that is `#include`-ed by a single translation unit more than once are parsed by the compiler exactly once. *Internal* include guards achieve this goal but alone had (for many years) continued to lead to excessive time spent during compilation on some industry-standard platforms.

External ("redundant") include guards in headers, now deprecated, were used to prevent compilers (especially older ones) from even opening header files more than once, historically improving build-time performance. More recently, however, their vestigial benefit on more modern platforms, if any, was that — being truly ugly — redundant guards served to remind us that we should `#include` a .h file in a header *only* to ensure that the header is self-sufficient with respect to compilation, and for no other reason.

1.6 From .h / .cpp Pairs to Components

Our software development methodology is predicated on the existence of atomic building blocks that we call *components*, consisting of .h / .cpp pairs, each having certain basic physical properties (sections 1.6 and 1.11), as summarized in Figure 1-77.

Component Property 1	The .cpp file incorporates (includes) its corresponding .h file prior to defining any logical constructs and, in fact, as the first substantive line of source code (section 1.6.1).
Component Property 2	All logical constructs having external linkage, except where rendered effectively internal by convention (see section 2.7.3), that are defined in a .cpp file are declared (somehow) in the corresponding .h file (section 1.6.2).
Component Property 3	All logical constructs having external or dual bindage that are declared in the .h file of a component are defined, if needed, within that component — i.e., in either its .h or .cpp file — and nowhere else (section 1.6.3).
Component Property 4	There are no pure (forward) declarations of any logical construct having external or dual bindage residing outside the (unique) component that defines it; instead, the appropriate .h file is included to obtain the needed extern declaration (section 1.11.1).

Figure 1-77: The four essential properties of components

Component Property 1 enables the compiler to help ensure consistency between the physical interface and implementation (at compile time). Making the component include its own header effectively and forever eliminates include-order-dependent defects. Component Property 2 ensures that all exported symbols are represented at the source-code level and can be accessed via including the header file (obviating the proscribed creation of any local extern declarations). Without Component Property 3, any modularity implied by the association between .h and .cpp files having the same root name would be vacuous. Component Property 4, discussed separately (section 1.11), not only ensures that changes to function names, signatures, and return types in library code will be detected by clients at compile time (rather than at link time, or worse, run time) but also enables us to extract physical dependencies orders of magnitude faster than would otherwise be possible (e.g., by parsing the C++ source code), via a simple (e.g., Perl) script inspecting just the #include directives in the combined .h and .cpp files.

1.7 Notation and Terminology

Throughout this book we will use our own minimal notation (see Figure 1-47, section 1.7.1). Logical entities (e.g., classes and functions) are surrounded by capsule-like and ellipse-like bubbles, respectively; physical entities (e.g., files) are surrounded by rectangles. The symbol "(D) —Is-A→ (B)" indicates (public) inheritance: D is a B. A type is used in the interface of a function (or method) if that function names the type either in its signature or to describe the value returned. A type is used in the interface of a class if it is used in a member (not friend) function of the class. The symbol "(B)o—Uses-In-The-Interface—(A)" denotes that B uses A in this way. If a class (or function) B names a type A in its implementation but doesn't use A in the interface, we depict the relationship as "(B)●—Uses-In-The-Implementation—(A)." In the event private inheritance is ever used, we would annotate it with this symbol, rather than an arrow (which would mean public inheritance). Finally, if B uses A in the interface by name, but not substantively (i.e., not requiring the definition of A to compile, link, or thoroughly test B), we express that special case of the Uses-In-The-Interface relation as "$\widebrace{B}\overset{\text{Uses-In-Name-Only}}{\cdots\cdots\cdots\cdots}\widebrace{A}$." Additional symbols used to depict other, purely collaborative — *In-Structure-Only* (ISO) — logical dependencies are summarized in Figure 1-50, section 1.7.6.

1.8 The Depends-On Relation

In addition to the logical relationships reprised above, we defined one physical relationship, Depends-On, which necessarily occurs, and is depicted between, only *physical* entities. The notation "$\boxed{y} \xrightarrow{\text{Depends-On}} \boxed{x}$" denotes that **x** is required to compile or link **y**. A compile-time dependency often results in a link time dependency, since any undefined symbols created by accessing extern declarations in a .h file must be satisfied by definitions residing in the corresponding .cpp file. Since .o files are presumed to be incorporated atomically, given three components **a**, **b**, and **c**, if a.cpp includes b.h and b.cpp includes c.h, it is likely that c.o will be needed to resolve undefined symbols in b.o, which in turn will likely be needed to resolve undefined symbols in a.o. Hence, a.o indirectly depends on c.o, and the Depends-On relation for .h/.cpp pairs conforming to the component properties delineated in this chapter is transitive.

1.9 Implied Dependency

Substantive logical relationships (e.g., public inheritance or use in either the interface or implementation) that span physical boundaries imply physical dependencies. By considering the physical consequences of implied dependencies *as we design*, we can preemptively avoid mistakes that, if not detected up front, might later force us to substantially rework our code. We will exploit the fourth property of conforming .h/.cpp pairs to automatically validate our dependency assumptions among components throughout the development process.

1.10 Level Numbers

The primary purpose of *level numbers* is to help us detect cycles early and eliminate them. Component *levelization* involves assigning deterministic level numbers to components within a subsystem based on their positions in a local (acyclic) physical hierarchy. Components that have no physical dependencies on other local ones, called *leaf components*, are naturally at level 1. Every other local component **c** has a level number that is one more than that of the local component having the largest level number upon which **c** depends. By this definition, assigning level numbers to components within a software subsystem is possible if and only if there are no cyclic physical dependencies. Avoiding such physical design cycles dramatically improves our ability to understand, test, and maintain software.

Finally, in this chapter we have described how best to envisage the underlying mechanisms that govern highly complex compiled languages such as C++. Armed with this mental model, we are now better prepared both to interpret the C++ Standard as worded and to reason about critical design decisions impacted by implementation details that might otherwise fall between the cracks. The four essential properties of components described here (sections 1.6 and 1.11) serve to characterize our fundamental atomic unit of logical and physical design. The practical benefit of this fourth property — i.e., never redeclaring locally any construct having *external* or *dual* bindage and instead always including the (unique) header file from the component that defines it — is the ability to extract from the `#include` directives alone the envelope of (physical) component dependencies without having to parse the C++ source code itself. Together, these properties ensure that conforming `.h`/`.cpp` pairs are logically and physical coherent atomic units of design, which can then be packaged into larger coherent entities suitable for independent release. How components (along with other, nonconforming software) are packaged and deployed is presented in detail in the following chapter.

2

Packaging and Design Rules

The term *software engineering* means different things to different people. Some smart, passionate, and individually productive developers consider the creation of software to be a form of art, upon which any imposed constraints, however beneficial to the whole, would stifle personal creativity. This attitude breeds gratuitous irregularity that, in turn, undermines the overall effectiveness of our software development process. Instead, we believe that certain fundamental rules (and even a few arbitrary conventions) must be adhered to if, as an organization, we are to reach the highest levels of software productivity. It is with that understanding that the material in this chapter is offered.

C++ provides an enormous degree of freedom in expressing ideas both logically and physically. Left unchecked, our ability to comprehend arbitrary and varied physical structure wanes with increasing system size. Yet neither the compiler nor the linker knows or cares what our source code does, so long as it follows their organizational rules. All these tools see is the *physical* structure of our code. We can therefore choose to organize the source code independently of the domain functionality that it embodies. Our intent here is to provide some general structure to frame the potentially vast quantities of software we develop. By design, this organizational structure is physically uniform and independent of the task at hand. In short, this chapter defines "the rules of the game."

What we are about to motivate and then present is a fairly small set of architectural design rules that collectively provide a proven physical framework for organizing component-based software (along with non-component-based legacy, open-source, and third-party software) in a way that enables effective design, development, testing, and deployment on an enterprise scale. Unlike typical naming conventions or mere coding standards, however, these architectural rules transcend language features and focus on what is important, with a distinct emphasis on achieving development scalability and effective reuse. Certainly, the organization of software we recommend here is not the only plausible one, but it is one that we have used successfully in practice for many years and one that has withstood the test of time.

2.1   The Big Picture

The way in which software is organized governs the degree to which we can leverage that software to solve current and new business problems quickly and effectively. By design, much of the code that we write for use by applications will reside in sharable libraries and not directly in any one application. Our goal, therefore, is to provide some top-level organizational structure — such as the one illustrated in Figure 2-1 — that allows us to partition our software into discrete physical units so as to facilitate finding, understanding, and potentially reusing available software solutions.

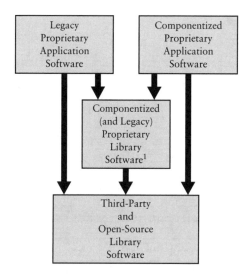

Figure 2-1: Enterprise-level view of software organization

As Chapters 0 and 1 describe, most of what we do with respect to creating new library and application software involves components as the atomic units of design. But components alone, as depicted in Figure 2-2a, are too small to be effective in managing and maintaining software on a large scale. We will therefore want to aggregate logically related components having similar physical dependencies into a larger physical entity that we refer to as a *package*, which can be treated more effectively as a unit. These larger logically and physically cohesive

---

[1] Open-source code that has been augmented (or forked) to achieve some particular purpose would also fall into this category (e.g., third-party software adapted to use our (polymorphic) memory-allocator model — see Volume II, section 4.10).

entities can then, in turn, be further aggregated into a yet larger body of software, which we call a *package group*, comprising packages having similar physical dependencies[2] that, taken as a whole, are suitable for independent release, as illustrated in Figure 2-2b.

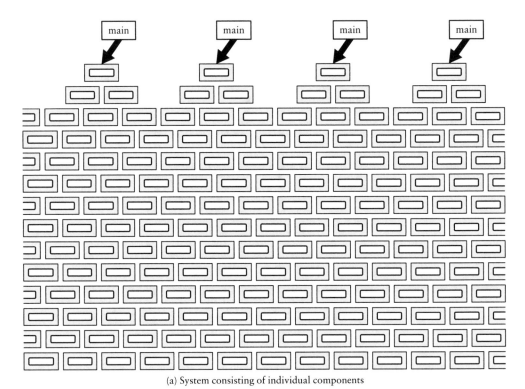

(a) System consisting of individual components

---

[2] Note that, while the packages within a group are themselves necessarily internally logically cohesive, such need not be the case for a package group as a whole (see sections 2.8 and 2.9, respectively).

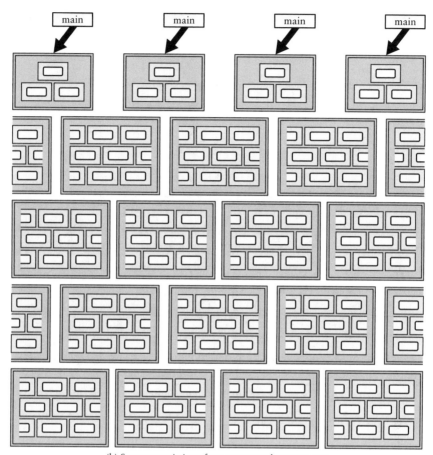

(b) System consisting of pre-aggregated components

Figure 2-2: Individual components do not scale up.

In addition, some of the software that we might need to use could be organized quite differently. For example, we may want to take advantage of certain third-party and open-source libraries, which might not be component-based. We might have our own legacy libraries to use that are also not component-based. These software libraries, of necessity, must come together at a level of aggregation larger than components, as depicted in Figure 2-3.

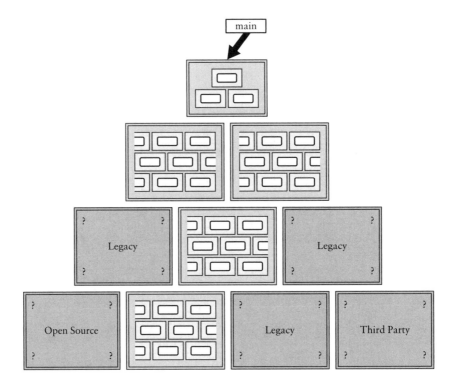

Figure 2-3: Integration with non-component-based (library) software

We generally think of a top-level unit of integration within a large system informally as a "library" whose interface typically consists of a collection of header files in a single directory (e.g., /usr/include) and a single library archive (e.g., libc.a, libc.so) depending on the target platform. We might uniquely refer to this particular *architectural* entity as a whole as "The C Library" although its internal structure (i.e., how logical content is partitioned among its .o files) is entirely *organizational* (i.e., not part of its specification or *contract;* see Volume II, section 5.2) and might vary from one vendor platform to another.

Integration with legacy, open-source, and third-party libraries is important and will be addressed. Our purpose in the next few sections, however, is first to identify desirable characteristics of library software and then to provide a prescriptive methodology for packaging our own. After that, we will return to the issues of integrating with non-component-based software (see section 2.12) and then focus on the custom (nonshareable) top-level application code surrounding main() (see section 2.13).

2.2   Physical Aggregation

In the preceding chapters, we talked about the atomic unit of physical design, which we call a component, and also the physical hierarchy created by their (acyclic) physical dependencies. Scalability demands hierarchy, and the hierarchy imposed by physical dependency, while of critical importance, is only one architectural aspect of large-scale physical design. Separately, we must also consider how related components can be packaged into larger cohesive physical units. We refer to this other hierarchical dimension of component-based design as *physical aggregation*.

2.2.1   General Definition of Physical Aggregate

> **DEFINITION**: An *aggregate* is a cohesive physical unit of design comprising logical content.

The purpose of aggregation is to bring together logical content (in the form of C++ source code) as a cohesive physical entity that can be treated architecturally as an atomic unit. At one end of the physical-aggregation spectrum lies the component. Each individual component aggregates logical content. Figure 2-4 illustrates schematically a collection of 15 components having 5 separate levels of physical dependency that together might represent a hierarchically reusable subsystem.

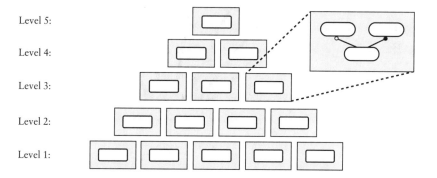

Figure 2-4: Logical content aggregated within 15 individual components

2.2.2   Small End of Physical-Aggregation Spectrum

> **DEFINITION**: A *component* is the innermost level of physical aggregation.

By design, each component embodies a limited amount of code — typically only a few hundred to a thousand lines of source[3] (excluding comments and the component's associated test driver). A single component is therefore too fine-grained (section 0.4) to fully represent most nontrivial architectural subsystems and *patterns*.[4] For example, given a protocol (section 1.7.5) for, say, an (abstract) memory allocator (see Volume II, section 4.10), we might want to provide several distinct components defining various concrete implementations, each tailored to address a different specific behavioral and performance need.[5] Taken as a whole, these components naturally represent a larger cohesive architectural entity, as illustrated in Figure 2-5. To capture these and other cohesive relationships among logically related components — assuming they do not have substantially disparate physical dependencies — we might choose to colocate them within a larger physical unit (see sections 2.8, 2.9, and 3.3). In so doing, we can facilitate both the discovery and management of our library software.

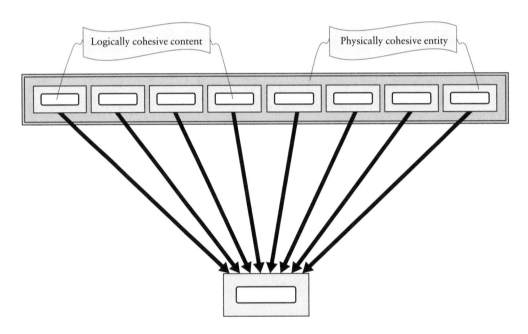

Figure 2-5: Suite of logically similar yet independent components

---

[3] Note that complexity of implementation, coupled with our ability to understand and *test* a given component — more than line count itself — governs its practical maximum "size" (see Volume III, sections 7.3 and 7.5).

[4] See **gamma94**.

[5] E.g., `bdlma::MultipoolAllocator`, `bdlma::SequentialAllocator`, and `bdlma::BufferedSequentialAllocator` (see **bde14**, subdirectory `/groups/bdl/bdlma/`).

2.2.3   Large End of Physical-Aggregation Spectrum

> **DEFINITION:** A *unit of release* (*UOR*) is the outermost level of physical aggregation.

At the other end of the physical-aggregation spectrum is the *unit of release* (UOR), which represents a physically (and usually also logically) cohesive collection of software (source code) that is designed to be deployed and consumed in an all-or-nothing fashion. Each UOR typically comprises multiple separate smaller physical aggregates, bringing together vastly more source code than would occur in any individual component. Even so, we should expect our library software will in time grow to be far too large to belong to any one UOR. Hence, from an enterprise-wide planning perspective, we must be prepared to accommodate the many UORs that are likely to appear at the top level of our inventory of library source code.

2.2.4   Conceptual Atomicity of Aggregates

Guideline

Every physical aggregate should be treated atomically for design purposes.

Even though a UOR may aggregate otherwise physically independent entities, it should nonetheless always be treated, for design purposes, as atomic.[6] Like a component (and every physical aggregate), the granularity with which the contents of a UOR are incorporated into a dependent program will depend on organizational, platform-specific, and deployment details, none of which can be relied upon at design time. Hence, we must assume that any use of a UOR could well result in incorporating all of it — and everything it depends on — into our final executable program. For this reason alone, how we choose to aggregate our software into distinct UORs is vital.

---

[6] The assertion that a library may not be organizationally atomic is true for conventional static (.a) libraries (section 1.2.4), but not generally so for shared (.so) libraries. Even with static libraries, regulatory requirements (e.g., for trading applications) may force substantial retesting of an application when relinked against a static library whose timestamp has changed, even when the only difference is an additional unused component. In such cases, we may — for the purpose of optimization only — choose to partition our libraries into multiple regions (e.g., multiple .so or .a libraries) as a post-processing step during deployment (see section 2.15.10). Again, such organizational optimizations in no way affect the architecture, use, or *allowed dependencies* (see section 2.2.14) of the UOR.

2.2.5   Generalized Definition of Dependencies for Aggregates

> **DEFINITION:** An aggregate **y** Depends-On another aggregate **x** if any file in **x** is required in order to compile, link, or thoroughly test **y**.

This definition of physical dependency for aggregates intentionally casts a wide net, so that it can be applied to aggregates that do not necessarily follow our methodology. For aggregates composed entirely of components as defined by the four properties in Chapter 1,[7] the definition of direct dependency of **y** on **x** reduces to whether any file in **y** includes a header from **x**.

> **Observation**
>
> **The Depends-On relation among aggregates is transitive.**

Given the atomic nature with which physical aggregates must be treated for design purposes, if an aggregate **z** Depends-On **y** (directly or otherwise) and **y** in turn Depends-On **x**, then we must assume, at least from an architectural perspective, that **z** Depends-On **x**.

2.2.6   Architectural Significance

> **DEFINITION:** A logical or physical entity is *architecturally significant* if its name (or symbol) is intentionally visible from outside of the UOR in which it is defined.

Architecturally significant entities are those parts of a UOR that are intended to be seen (and potentially used) directly by external clients. These entities together effectively form the *public interface* of the UOR, any changes to which could adversely affect the stability of its clients. The definition of *architectural significance* emphasizes deliberate intent, rather than just the actual physical manifestation, because it is that intent that is necessarily reflected by the architecture.

---

[7] Component Properties 1–3 (sections 1.6.1–1.6.3) and Component Property 4 (section 1.11.1).

A suboptimal implementation might, for example, inadvertently expose a symbol (at the .o level) that was never *intended* for use outside the UOR. If such unintentional visibility were to occur within a UOR consisting entirely of components, it would likely be due to an accidental violation of Component Property 2 (section 1.6.2) and not a deliberate (and misguided) attempt to provide a secret "backdoor" access point. Repairing such defects would not constitute a change in architecture — especially in this case, since any use of such a symbol would itself be a violation of Component Property 4 (section 1.11.1).

2.2.7   Architectural Significance for General UORs

In our component-based methodology, all the software that we write outside the file that implements main() is implemented in terms of components. Unfortunately, not all UORs that we might want or need (or be compelled) to use are necessarily component-based (the way we would have designed them). We will start by considering the parts of a general UOR that are architecturally significant irrespective of whether or not they are made up exclusively of components. Later we will discuss the specifics of those that fortunately are.

2.2.8   Parts of a UOR That Are Architecturally Significant

In a nutshell, each externally accessible .h file,[8] each nonprivate logical construct declared within those .h files, and the UOR itself are all architecturally significant. To make use of logical entities from outside the UOR in which they are defined, their (package-qualified) names (see section 2.4.6) will be needed. In addition, the .h files declaring those entities must (or at least should) be included (section 1.11.1) — by name — directly (see section 2.6) for clients to make substantive use of them. Finally, to refer to the particular library comprising the .o files corresponding to a UOR (e.g., for linking purposes), it will be necessary to identify it, again, by name.

2.2.9   What Parts of a UOR Are *Not* Architecturally Significant?

While .h files are naturally architecturally significant, .cpp files and their corresponding .o files are not. If we were to change the names of header files or redistribute the logical constructs declared within them, it would adversely affect the stability of its clients; however, such is not the case for .cpp or .o files. Assuming the UOR is identified in totality by its name, the internal

---

[8] Some methodologies allow for the use of "private" header files (e.g., see Figure 1-30, section 1.4) that are not deployed along with the UOR; our component-based approach (sections 1.6 and 1.11) does not (for good reasons; see section 3.9.7), but does provide for subordinate components (see section 2.7.5).

organization of the library archive that embodies the .o files (corresponding to its .cpp files) comprised by that UOR will have absolutely no effect on client source code. What's more, changing such *insulated* details (see section 3.11.1) will not require client code even to recompile.

2.2.10   A Component Is "Naturally" Architecturally Significant

For UORs consisting of .h/.cpp pairs forming components as defined in Chapter 1, both the .h and .cpp files will each have the component name as a prefix (see section 2.4.6), making components architecturally significant as well. To maximize hierarchical reuse (section 0.4), all components within a UOR and all nonprivate constructs defined within those components are normally architecturally significant. There are, however, valid engineering reasons for occasionally suppressing the architectural significance of a component. Section 2.7 describes how we can — by conventional naming — effectively limit the visibility of (1) nonprivate logical entities outside of the component in which they are defined, and (2) a component as a whole.

2.2.11   Does a Component Really Have to Be a .h/.cpp Pair?

What ultimately characterizes a component architecturally is governed entirely by its .h file. In Chapter 1, we arrived at the definition of a component as being a .h/.cpp pair satisfying four essential properties. In virtually all cases, this phrasing serves as *the* definition of a component in C++.[9] For completeness, however, we point out that, though this definition is sufficient and practically useful, it is not strictly necessary. The true essential requirement for components in C++ is that there be *exactly one* .h file and one[10] (at least) *or more* (see below) .cpp files that together satisfy these four essential properties.

2.2.12   When, If Ever, Is a .h/.cpp Pair Not Good Enough?

In exceedingly rare cases,[11] there might be sufficient justification to represent a single component using multiple .cpp files. Unlike header files, .cpp files in a component, and especially the resulting .o files in a statically linked library (.a), are not considered *architecturally significant*. For example, a component **myutil** defining three logically related, but physically independent functions might reasonably be implemented as having a single header file

---

[9] More generally, for any given language that supports multiple units of translation (e.g., C, C++, Java, Perl, Ada, Pascal, FORTRAN, COBOL), the physical form of a component is standard and independent of its content.

[10] We require that the component header be included in at least one component .cpp file so that we can observe, just by compiling the component, that its .h file is self-sufficient with respect to compilation (section 1.6.1).

[11] E.g., to further reduce the size of already tiny programs (such as embedded C) or to break hopelessly large (particularly computer-generated) components into separate translation units of a size manageable for the compiler.

myutil.h and multiple implementation files — e.g., myutil.1.cpp, myutil.2.cpp, and myutil.3.cpp — each uniquely named, but all sharing the component name as a common prefix. Consequently, a program calling only one of the three functions *might*, under certain deployment strategies (see section 2.15), wind up incorporating only the one .o file corresponding to the needed function. Such nuanced considerations are not relevant to typical development and are most usually relegated to the subdomain of embedded systems.

2.2.13   Partitioning a .cpp File Is an Organizational-Only Change

It is important to realize that the aggressive physical partitioning discussed above is permissible only because it is *organizational* and not *architectural*. That is, our view and use of the component, its logical design, and its physical dependencies are left unaffected by such architecturally *insignificant* optimizations. Introducing (or removing) such optimizations has no effect on the client-facing interface (including any need for recompilation) or logical behavior, only on program size. By contrast, introducing multiple .h files for a single component would represent an architectural change manifestly affecting usage; hence, a component — in all cases — *must* have exactly one header file, whose root name identifies the component *uniquely* (see section 2.2.23).

2.2.14   Entity Manifest and Allowed Dependencies

> **DEFINITION**: A *manifest* is a specification of the collection of physical entities — typically expressed in external metadata (see section 2.16) — intended to be part of the physical aggregate to which it pertains.

> **DEFINITION**: An *allowed dependency* is a physical dependency — typically expressed in external metadata (see section 2.16) — that is permitted to exist in the physical hierarchy to which it pertains.

Observation

> The definition of every physical aggregate must comprise the specification of (1) the entities it aggregates, and (2) the external entities that it is *allowed* to depend on *directly*.

To be practically useful, every aggregate (from a component to a UOR) must, at a minimum, somehow allow us to specify contractually the entities it aggregates, as well as the other physical entities upon which those contained entities are *allowed* (i.e., explicitly permitted) to depend directly. Much of our design methodology is anchored in understanding the physical dependencies among the discrete *logically and physically cohesive* (see section 2.3) entities within our software. Given a dependency graph, without knowing the specific (outwardly visible) entities at its nodes or its (permissible) edges, there is simply no good way to reason about it.

For any given component, as illustrated in Figure 2-6a, the manifest of aggregated entities is implied by the accessible logical entities declared within its header file. The *allowed* direct dependencies are implied by the combined `#include` directives embedded within the `.h` and `.cpp` files of that component (section 1.11). For the second and successive levels of physical aggregation, the manifest of member aggregates and list of *allowed* dependencies is an essential part of the architectural specification and must somehow be stated explicitly (Figure 2-6b).

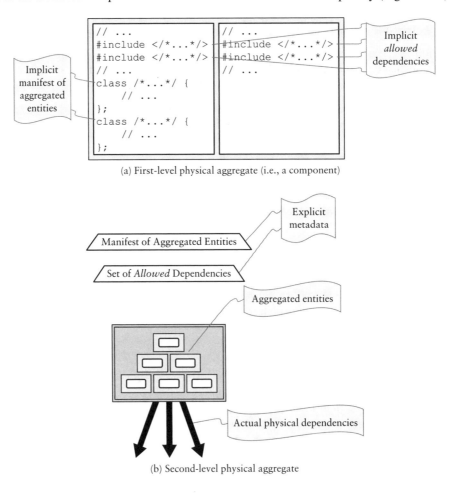

(a) First-level physical aggregate (i.e., a component)

(b) Second-level physical aggregate

Figure 2-6: Specifying members and *allowed* dependencies for aggregates

Unfortunately, the C++ language itself does not support any notion of architecture beyond a single translation unit.[12] Hence, much of the aggregative structure we discuss in this chapter will have to be implemented alongside the language using metadata (see section 2.16). This metadata will be kept locally as an integral part of each aggregate to help guide the tools we use to develop, build, and deploy our software.[13] An abstract subsystem consisting of four second-level aggregates forming three separate (aggregate) dependency levels is illustrated schematically in Figure 2-7.

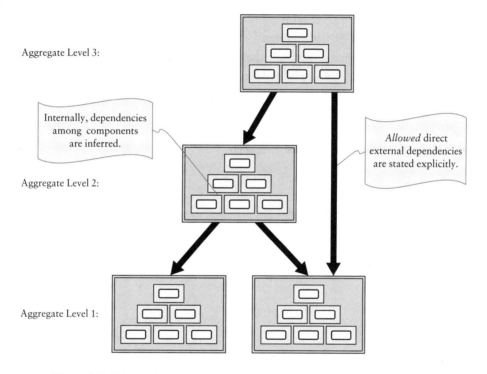

Aggregate Level 3:

Internally, dependencies among components are inferred.

Allowed direct external dependencies are stated explicitly.

Aggregate Level 2:

Aggregate Level 1:

Figure 2-7: Schematic subsystem built from second-level physical aggregates

---

[12] As of this writing, work was progressing in the C++ Standards Committee to identify requirements for a new packaging construct called a `module` (see **lakos17a** and **lakos18**), and a preliminary version of this long-anticipated *modules* feature was voted into the draft of the C++20 Standard at the committee meeting in Kona, HI, on February, 23, 2019.

[13] A detailed overview of this architectural metadata along with its practical application and how build and other tools might consume it is provided for reference in section 2.16.

2.2.15   Need for Expressing Envelope of Allowed Dependencies

Expressing the envelope of *allowed* dependencies for aggregations of components explicitly might, at first, seem redundant and therefore unnecessary. As noted in section 1.11, there are numerous dependency-analysis tools available that can be used to extract actual dependencies from the aggregated components and produce the envelope of those dependencies across physical aggregates automatically, but to do so misses the point: The purpose of stating *allowed* dependencies is to be anticipatory, not reactive. Characterizing a set of proposed aggregations and then supplying an envelope of *allowed* dependencies among those aggregations enables us to express our physical design (intent) *before* any code is written. As new functionality is added, unexpected physical dependencies can be detected and flagged as implementation errors. Without specifying *allowed* dependencies *a priori*, there is no physical design to implement, let alone verify. Hence, explicitly specifying — and verifying — *allowed* dependencies is necessary at every level of physical aggregation.

2.2.16   Need for Balance in Physical Hierarchy

Observation

> **To maximize human cognition, peer entities within a physical aggregate should be of comparable physical complexity (e.g., have the same level of physical aggregation).**

Between a component and a UOR, we might imagine that there could (in theory) be any number of intermediate levels of physical aggregation, each of which might or might not have architectural significance. Some physical aggregation hierarchies are better than others. In particular, an unbalanced hierarchy, such as the one illustrated schematically in Figure 2-8, is suboptimal.

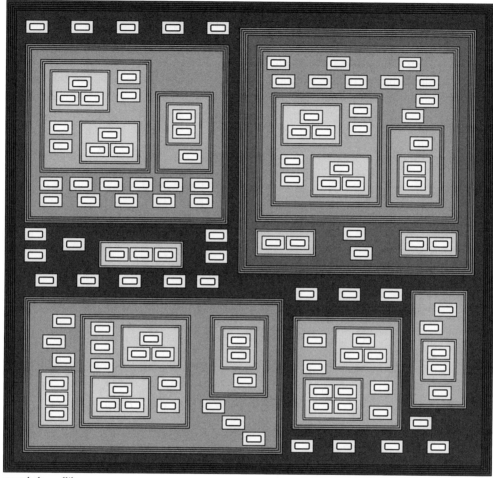

myunbalancedlib

Figure 2-8: UOR having unbalanced levels of physical aggregation (BAD IDEA)

2.2.17   Not Just Hierarchy, but Also Balance

Effective regular decomposition of large systems requires not only hierarchy, but also balance. We choose to model our software development accordingly. Although not strictly necessary, we want each aggregate to comprise entities having similar physical complexity. In particular, we deliberately avoid placing components alongside larger aggregates within a UOR. We find that entities having comparable complexity at each aggregation depth improves comprehension and facilitates reuse.

At each increasing level of physical aggregation, we strive to bring together a significant, but not overwhelming amount of information and engineering at a uniform level of abstraction such that it can be understood and used effectively. As a rule, we would like the relevant schematic detail to correspond to what might reasonably fit on a single 8 1/2 × 11 inch piece of paper[14] as suggested by the complexity of each of the individual diagrams in Figure 2-9. By achieving this balance — much like the chapters and sections within this book — we provide fairly uniformly chunked content, which makes it more convenient to analyze and discuss.

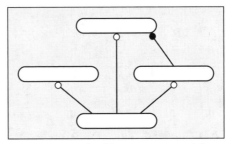

(a) Aggregation level I: component containing
related logical content

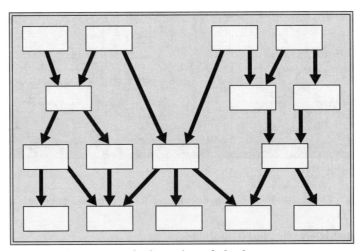

(b) Aggregation level II: package of related components

---

[14] Being an American, I have chosen the most common loose-leaf paper size in the United States, as opposed to ones conforming to ISO 216 used by other countries where A4 is the most common (and similar) size (see http://www.papersizes.org/).

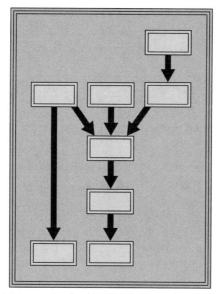

(c) Aggregation level III: group of related packages

Figure 2-9: Balancing complexity at each level of physical aggregation

2.2.18   Having More Than Three Levels of Physical Aggregation Is Too Many

Observation

More than three levels of appropriately balanced physical aggregation are virtually always unnecessary and can be problematic.

While components (being deliberately fine grained) are too small to be practical to release or deploy individually, having more than three appropriately balanced levels of physical aggregation (as illustrated schematically in Figure 2-10) is not especially useful and can be impractical due to the sheer magnitude of the code involved. There are limits as to what we can reasonably fit into a single physical library and what typical development and build tools can accommodate. There are also design and deployment issues that would tend to discourage physically aggregating such massive architectural entities.

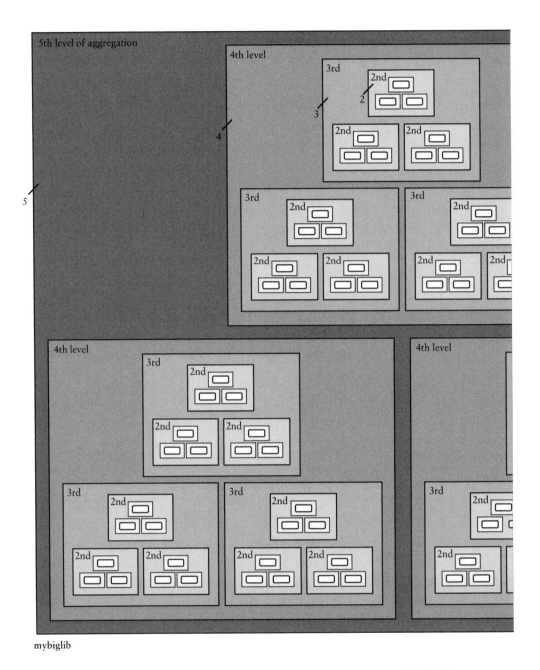

Figure 2-10: More than three levels of physical aggregation (BAD IDEA)

2.2.19   Three Levels Are Enough Even for Larger Systems

In our experience, we find that three appropriately balanced, architecturally significant levels of physical aggregation have been sufficient to represent very large libraries. When there are three architecturally significant levels, we will consistently refer to each entity at the second level of architecturally significant aggregates within the UOR as a *package*[15] (see section 2.8) and the UOR itself as a *package group* (see section 2.9).

For example, using even the modest size estimates for a component, package, and package group illustrated in Figure 2-11, each UOR would, on average, support a couple of hundred thousand lines of noncommentary source code — excluding, of course, the corresponding component-level test drivers (see Volume III, section 7.5). Thus, an enterprise-wide body of library software consisting of 10 million lines of source code could fit comfortably within fifty such UORs, with yet larger code bases requiring only proportionately more.

$$500\,\frac{\text{source lines}}{\text{component}} \times 20\,\frac{\text{components}}{\text{package}} \times 20\,\frac{\text{packages}}{\text{package group}} = 200{,}000\,\frac{\text{source lines}}{\text{UOR}}$$

Figure 2-11: Modest size estimates of components, packages, and package groups.

2.2.20   UORs Always Have Two or Three Levels of Physical Aggregation

Hence, in our methodology, the number of appropriately balanced, architecturally significant levels of physical aggregation within our library software will always be at least two (i.e., the individual components and the UOR that comprises them), but never more than three.

There might, in rare cases, be valid reasons — e.g., to accommodate a large, monolithic, externally designed interface[16] — to introduce, purely for organizational purposes, an additional, intervening level of physical aggregation. Any such organization-based partitioning of the implementation of an architecturally significant aggregate — just like with that of a component — should, of course, never be architecturally significant (see section 2.11).

---

[15] Note that a UOR can also be an isolated package, but there should be a compelling engineering reason for preferring to do so over a package group, especially for (hierarchically reusable) library software.

[16] The C++ Standard Library residing entirely in the `std` namespace, is itself an example of such a monolithic specification.

2.2.21   Three Balanced Levels of Aggregation Are Sufficient. Trust Me!

The "artificial" constraints on physical aggregation suggested here do not in any way stop individual developers from being creative; rather, this regularly structured physical aggregation model helps to focus creativity where it will be most effective — the functionality, not the packaging — thereby making our software developers as a whole more successful. It will turn out that having a regular, balanced, and fairly shallow architectural structure also lends itself to an economical notation for identifying every architecturally significant logical and physical entity within our proprietary library software (see section 2.4).

2.2.22   There Should Be Nothing Architecturally Significant Larger Than a UOR

We deliberately avoid creating anything architecturally significant that is larger than a single (physical) UOR.[17] Treating such expansive *logical* units atomically, as illustrated in Figure 2-12a, would increase our envelope of allowed dependencies without providing any concrete encapsulation of logical functionality within a cohesive physical entity (see section 2.3). Instead, we choose to model such coarse architectural policy more articulately as individual *allowed* physical dependencies among UORs (Figure 2-12b). The more that we can encapsulate each logical subsystem within a single (architecturally significant) physical aggregate, the more we will be able to infer useful physical dependencies (section 1.9) from logical relationships across those entities.

---

[17] Having a single, enterprise-wide namespace in which to guard the names within *all* of the components we collectively write is (1) independent of any aspect of specific designs, and (2) a good idea (see section 2.4.6).

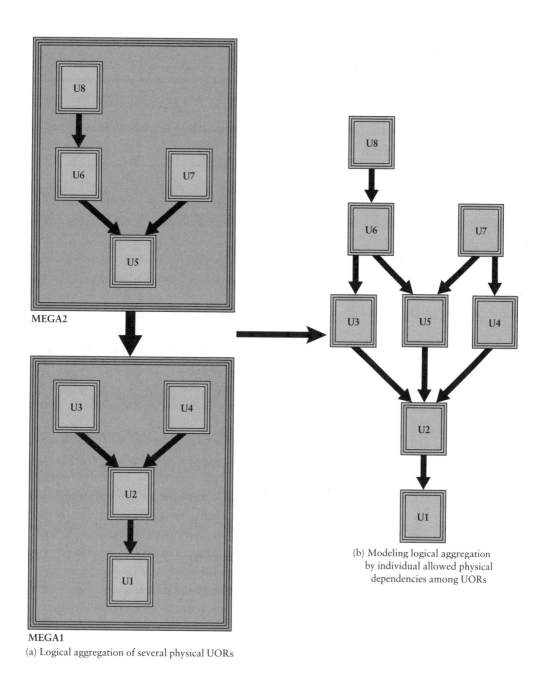

MEGA2

MEGA1

(a) Logical aggregation of several physical UORs

(b) Modeling logical aggregation
by individual allowed physical
dependencies among UORs

Figure 2-12: Supplanting logical aggregation with allowed physical dependency

2.2.23   Architecturally Significant Names Must Be Unique

Design Rule

The name of every architecturally significant entity must be unique throughout the enterprise.

The C++ language requires that the name of every logical entity visible outside of the translation unit in which it is defined must be unique within a program (section 1.3.1). We need more. We require that the names of all externally accessible logical entities within our library identify each entity uniquely because, with reuse, a combination of those logical entities might one day wind up within the same program (see section 3.9.4). For the same reason, the names of all UORs (package groups and packages) and components — each also being visible to external clients — must be globally unique as well.

Even without our cohesive naming strategy (see section 2.4), there remain compelling advantages (e.g., see sections 2.4.6 and 2.15.2) to ensuring that component filenames are themselves guaranteed to be globally unique throughout the enterprise — irrespective of directory structure.[18]

> The benefit of unique filenames is uniqueness. When one sees a filename (such as `xyza_context.h`) anywhere in the system — be it in a log message, an assertion, an email, or a tab in a text editor – one knows, uniquely, the component to which it refers. Unique filenames also make the rendering of include directives in source code orthogonal to the physical placement of headers on a filesystem. A lack of unique filenames does not break any one thing, but makes a large collection of tasks more difficult because the filename itself is no longer a unique identifier. In a large-scale organization with hundreds of thousands of components (among which there will inevitably be many having the *base name* "context"), maintaining the filename as a unique identifier has been, and will continue to be, a very valuable property indeed!
>
> — Mike Verschell

---

[18] On April 1, 2019, Mike Verschell became the manager of Bloomberg's BDE team, replacing its founder (John Lakos) after nearly eighteen rewarding years of applying the methodology described in this book to developing real-world large-scale C++ software. Mike provided the quoted synthesis of his position on unique filenames via personal email.

2.2.24   No Cyclic Physical Dependencies!

Design Imperative

Allowed (explicitly stated) dependencies among physical aggregates must be acyclic.

Cyclic physical dependencies[19] among any physical entities — irrespective of the level of physical aggregation — do not scale and are always undesirable. Such cyclically interdependent architectures are not only harder to build, they are also much, much harder to comprehend, test, and maintain than their acyclic counterparts. In fact, to help improve human cognition, we almost always structure our source code to avoid forward references to logical entities even within the same component. Whenever the physical specification of a design would allow cyclic dependencies among architecturally significant physical aggregates, we assert that the design is unacceptably flawed. Even if, for some unusual (organizational) reason, we were to choose to partition an outwardly visible aggregate into subaggregates that were *not* architecturally significant (e.g., see section 2.11), we would nonetheless insist that the allowed dependencies among those subaggregates be acyclic as well (see also Figure 2-89, section 2.15.10).

2.2.25   Section Summary

In summary, a physical aggregate is a physically cohesive unit of logical content and a necessary abstraction in any development process. The organizational details of a physical aggregate will likely vary from one platform, compiler/linker technology, and deployment strategy to the next; hence, each physical aggregate is treated, at least architecturally, as atomic. Our logical designs must also, therefore, always be governed by the envelope of architecturally *allowed* (rather than actual) physical dependencies specified for the aggregate. Balancing complexity at each successive level of aggregation facilitates human cognition and potential reuse. The use of three balanced levels of architecturally significant physical aggregation has been demonstrated to be sufficient (and in fact optimal) to describe even the largest of systems. We do, however, want to avoid architecturally significant logical entities (other than an enterprise-wide namespace) that span UORs.

---

[19] A collection of interdependent (connected) entities is cyclically dependent if the transitive closure of the binary relation matrix representing direct dependencies between any two entities is not antisymmetric.

2.3   **Logical/Physical Coherence**

When developing large-scale software, it is essential that our logical and physical designs coincide in several fairly specific ways at every level of packaging. Perhaps the most funda-mental property of well-packaged software is that all logical constructs advertised within the collective interface of a physical module or aggregate — e.g., component, package, UOR (section 2.2) — are implemented directly within that module. Software that does not have this property generally cannot be described in terms of a graph where the nodes represent cohesive *logical* content and the directed edges represent (acyclic) dependencies on other *physical* modules. We refer to such undesirable software as *logically and physically incoherent*.

For example, Component Property 3 (section 1.6.3) states that if a logical construct having external bindage is declared in a component's header, then that component is the only one per-mitted to define that construct. Recall from section 1.9 that, knowing the logical relationships among classes contained within separate components having Component Property 3, we can reliably infer physical dependencies among those components. Arbitrary `.h`/`.cpp` pairs that do not fully encapsulate the definitions of their logical constructs unnecessarily make reasoning about the design (and organizational) dependencies substantially more complicated (e.g., the misplaced definition of the output operator for the `Date` class in Figure 1-46, section 1.6.3). We therefore require that whatever logical constructs a component advertises as its own are defined entirely within that component, and never elsewhere.

Guideline

Architecturally cohesive logical entities should be tightly encapsulated within physical ones.

The same benefits of logical/physical coherence that we derive from individual components apply also to library software at higher levels of aggregation. Imagine, for example, that we have two fairly large logical subsystems that we call **buyside** and **sellside**. Each subsys-tem is composed of several classes. For this discussion, let us assume that each of the classes is defined in its own separate component, and that the dependency graph of the unbundled components is acyclic. Figure 2-13 shows what often happens when subsystems conceived from only a logical perspective materialize. Although the logical and physical aspects of these systems coincide, the cyclic physical nature of the aggregate design does not scale, and is therefore unacceptable (section 2.2.24).

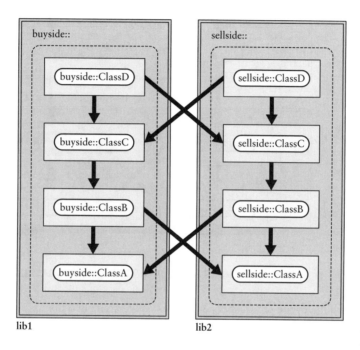

Figure 2-13: Cyclic physical dependencies (BAD IDEA)

Avoiding cyclic physical dependencies across aggregate boundaries is not only for the benefit of build tools, it also facilitates human cognition and reasoning. If all that were needed was to have two libraries where the envelope of component dependencies across aggregates was acyclic, then it would suffice to mechanically repartition these components as shown in Figure 2-14. But for software packaging to facilitate human cognition, in addition to being physically acyclic, the logical and physical aspects of a design must remain *coherent*.

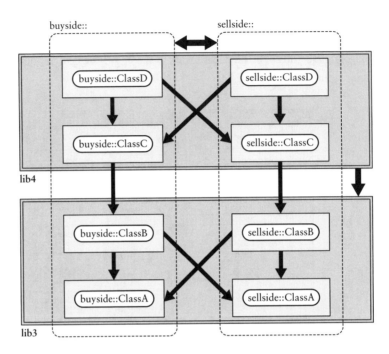

Figure 2-14: Logical/physical *incoherence* (BAD IDEA)

Although the cyclic physical dependencies between the two libraries have been eliminated, the logical and physical designs have diverged. Now, neither logical subsystem is encapsulated by either physical library. As a result, our ability to infer aggregate physical dependencies from abstract logical usage — i.e., at the subsystem level — is lost. That is, if a client abstractly uses *either* the **buyside** *or* **sellside** logical subsystems, we must either know the details of that usage or otherwise assume an implied physical dependency on *both* libraries. Just as with cyclic physical dependencies, our ability to *reason* about logically and physically incoherent designs does not scale; hence, such designs are to be avoided.

Uniting the logical and physical properties of software is what makes the efficient development of large-scale systems possible. Achieving an effective modularization of logical subsystems is not always easy and might require significant adjustment to the logical design of our sub-systems (see Chapter 3). As Figure 2-15 suggests, the reworked design might even yield a somewhat different logical model. Achieving designs having both logical/physical coherence and acyclic physical dependencies early in the development cycle requires forethought but is far easier than trying to tweak a design after coding is underway. Once released to clients, however, the already arduous task of re-architecting a subsystem will invariably become qualitatively more intractable, often insurmountably so.

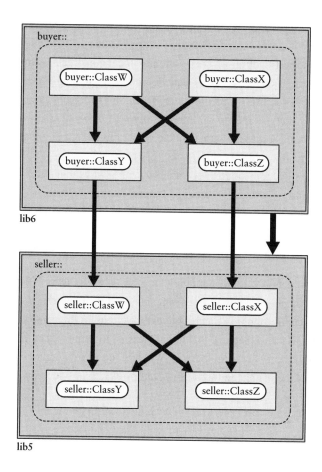

Figure 2-15: Acyclic logical/physical *coherence* (GOOD IDEA)

Achieving logical and physical coherence along with acyclic physical dependencies across our entire code base is absolutely essential. In addition to ensuring these important properties, however, we will need a strategy that guarantees not just that the name of each architecturally significant logical and physical entity is unique throughout the enterprise, but that it can also be identified (and its definition located) just from its point of use, without having to resort to tools (e.g., an IDE). The following section addresses how we realize these additional goals in practice.

2.4   Logical and Physical Name Cohesion

The ability to identify the physical location of the definition of essentially every logical construct — directly from its point of use — is an important aspect of design that distinguishes our methodology from others used in the software industry. The practical advantages of this aspect of design, however, are many and are explored in this section.

2.4.1   History of Addressing Namespace Pollution

Global namespace pollution — specifically, local constructs usurping short common names — is an age-old problem. All of us have learned that naming a class `Link` or a function `max` at file scope — even in a `.cpp` file — is just asking for trouble. Left unmanaged, the probability of name conflicts increases combinatorially with program size. Developers have traditionally responded to this problem with ad hoc conventions for naming logical constructs based on what are *hopefully* unique prefixes (e.g., `ls_Link`, `myMax`, `size_t`). When the use of a logical construct is confined to a single `.cpp` file, we can always make individual functions `static` and nest local classes within the unnamed namespace. The problem of name collisions, however, extends to header files as well.

2.4.2   Unique Naming Is Required; Cohesive Naming Is Good for Humans

Recall from section 2.2.6 that a logical or physical entity is *architecturally significant* if its name (or symbol) is intentionally visible from outside of the UOR that defines it. To refer to each architecturally significant entity unambiguously, we require the name of each such entity to be globally unique. How we achieve this uniqueness is, to some extent, an implementation detail — at least from the compiler's perspective. When it comes to human beings, however, cohesive naming, as we will elucidate in this section, has proven to provide powerful cognitive reinforcement.

Suppose we want to implement an architecturally significant type, say one that represents a *price* — e.g., for a financial instrument. How should we ensure that the name of this type is globally unique? In theory, there are many ways to achieve unique naming. We could, for example, maintain a central registry of logical names. The first developer to choose `Price` gets it! The next developer implementing a similar concept (there are many ways to characterize a price) would be forced to choose something else (e.g., `MyPrice`, `Price23`). The same approach could just as easily be used to reserve unique filenames.

2.4.3   Absurd Extreme of Neither Cohesive nor Mnemonic Naming

Taking this approach to the extreme, we could even have the registry generate unique type names based on a global counter — e.g., `T125061`, `T125062`, `T125063`, and so on. We could do similarly for component names (e.g., **c05684**, **c05685**, **c05686**) and even for units of release (e.g., **u1401**, **u1135**, **u1564**), as illustrated in Figure 2-16. It all works just fine as far as the compiler and linker are concerned. Moreover, physically moving a component from one aggregate to another would have no nominal implications. Human cognition, however, is not served by this approach.

```
// c27341.h              // component defining our "date" class

#include <c11317.h>      // Declares T161459 implementing day-of-week.

// ...

class T121056;           // Local Declaration of In-Stream Facility
class T121059;           // Local Declaration of Out-Stream Facility

class T121547 {          // definition of our "date" class

    static bool isYearMonthDayValid(int year, int month, int day);

    // ...

    T121547();
    T121547(int year, int month, int day);
    T121547(const T121547& original);
    ~T121547();

    // ...

    T121547& operator=(const T121547& rhs);

    // ...

    void setYearMonthDay(int year, int month,int day);
    int setYearMonthDayIfValid(int year, int month, int day);

    // ...

    int year() const;
    int month() const;
    int day() const;
    T161459::Enum dayOfWeek() const;

};

// ...

T121056& operator>>(T121056&  inStream,       T121547& date);
T121059& operator<<(T121059& outStream, const T121547& date);
```

Figure 2-16: Absurdly opaque, noncohesive generated unique names (BAD IDEA)

Maintaining a central database to reserve individual class or component names is not practical and clearly not the best answer. Instead, we will exploit hierarchy to allocate multiple levels of namespaces at once. This hierarchy, however, is neither ad hoc nor arbitrary; with the exception of an overarching enterprise-wide namespace (see below), each namespace that we employ in our methodology will correspond to a coherent, *architecturally significant*, logically and physically cohesive aggregate.

2.4.4   Things to Make Cohesive

For every architecturally significant logical entity there are at least three related architectural names:

1. The name (or symbol) of the logical entity itself

2. The name of the component (or header) that declares the logical entity

3. The name of the UOR that implements the logical entity

Ensuring that these names are deliberately cohesive will have significant implications with respect to development and maintenance. Hence, how and at what physical levels we achieve nominal cohesion is a distinctive and very important design consideration within our methodology.

2.4.5   Past/Current Definition of Package

> **DEFINITION:** A *package* is the smallest architecturally significant physical aggregate larger than a component.

> **COROLLARY:** The name of each package must be unique throughout the enterprise.

A package (see section 2.8) is an *architecturally significant* — i.e., globally visible — unit of logical and physical design that serves to aggregate components, subject to explicitly stated, *allowed dependency* criteria (section 2.2.14). A package is also a means for making related components physically and, as we are about to see, nominally cohesive. In these ways, packages enable designers to capture and reflect, in source code, important architectural information not easily expressed in terms of components alone.

Historically,[20] a package was defined as a collection of components organized as a (logically and) physically cohesive unit (see section 2.8.1). Although every package we write ourselves

---

[20] **lakos96**, section 7.1, pp. 474–483

will necessarily be implemented exclusively in terms of components, other kinds of well-reasoned architecturally significant physical entities comprising multiple header files, yet not aggregating components, are certainly possible.[21]

With the definition as worded above, the word *package* can serve as a unifying term to describe any architecturally significant body of code that is larger than a component, but without necessarily being component-based. We will, however, consistently characterize packages that are not composed entirely of components adhering to our design rules — especially those pertaining to our cohesive naming conventions delineated throughout the remainder of this section (section 2.4) — as *irregular* (see section 2.12).

Suppose now that we have a logical subsystem called the *Bond Trading System* (referred to in code as `bts` for short). Suppose further that this logical subsystem consists of a number of classes (including a price class) that have been implemented in terms of components, which, in turn, have been aggregated into a package to be deployed atomically as an independent library (e.g., `libbts.a`). How should we distinguish the `bts` *bond* price class from other price classes, and what should be the name of the component in which that price class is defined?

2.4.6   The Point of Use Should Be Sufficient to Identify Location

---

Guideline

The *use* of each logical entity declared at package-namespace scope should alone be sufficient to indicate the component, package, and UOR in which that entity is defined.

Whenever we see a logical construct used in code, we want to know immediately to which component, package, and UOR it belongs. Without an explicit policy to do otherwise, the name

---

[21] Robert Martin is the only other popular author we know of to describe in terms of C++ (previous to **lakos96** or otherwise) an even remotely similar concept. In his adaptation of Booch's *Class Categories*, which originally were themselves just logical entities (**booch94**, section 5.1, "Essentials: Class Categories," pp. 581–584), Martin's category unites a cluster of classes related by both logical and physical properties. Based on personal (telephone) correspondence (c. 2005), his augmented categories were intended to be significantly larger than a component, but somewhat smaller than a typical package (see Figure 2-11, section 2.2.19), virtually always sporting exactly one class per header (see section 3.1.1); see **martin95**, "High-Level Closure Using Categories," pp. 226–231.

of a class, the header file declaring that class, and the UOR implementing that class might all have unrelated names, as illustrated Figure 2-17. Clients reading `BondPrice` will not be able to predict, from usage alone, which header file defines it, nor which library implements it; hence, global search tools would be required during all subsequent maintenance of client code.

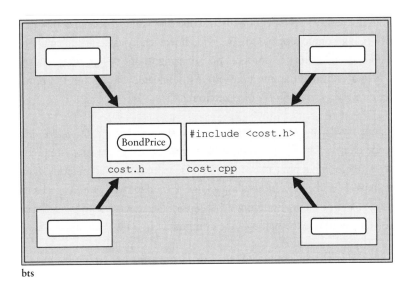

bts

Figure 2-17: Noncohesive logical and physical naming (BAD IDEA)

By the same token, other components packaged together to implement this logical subsystem might well have names that are unrelated to each other, obscuring the cohesive physical modularity of this subsystem. Although not strictly necessary, experience shows that human cognition is facilitated by explicit "visual" associations within the source code. This nominal cohesion, in turn, reinforces the more critical requirement of logical/physical coherence (section 2.3). Hence, logical and physical name cohesion across related architecturally significant entities is an explicit design goal of our packaging methodology.

Design Rule

Component files (`.h`/`.cpp`) must have the same root name as that of the component itself (i.e., they differ only in suffix).

By their nature, components implemented as `.h`/`.cpp` pairs naturally already exhibit some degree of physical name cohesion. Note that as recently as the writing of my first book (1996), however, such was not the case. Due to unreasonable restrictions on the length of names that could be accommodated to distinguish `.o` files contained in library archive (`.a`) files of the day, `.o` files often had to be shortened; hence, an external cross-reference needed to be maintained in order to reestablish the cohesive nature of components.[22]

> **COROLLARY: Every library component filename must be unique throughout the enterprise.**

Recall from section 2.2.23 that every globally visible physical entity must itself be uniquely named. Since library component headers are at least potentially (see section 3.9.7) clearly visible from outside their respective units of release, and their corresponding `.cpp` file(s) derive from the same root name and yet are distinct among themselves, they too must be globally unique. Note that, unlike library components, the names of components residing in application packages (see section 2.13) do not have to be distinct from those in other application packages so long as their logical and physical names do not conflict with those in our library as, in our methodology, no two such application packages would ever be present in the same program.

Design Rule

Every component must reside within a package.

Components, which are intended to address a highly focused purpose and are tailored to bolster hierarchical reuse (section 0.4), are invariably too fine grained to be practical to be released individually (section 2.2.20). Hence, in our methodology, each component is necessarily nested within a higher-level, architecturally significant aggregate, which (by definition) is a *package*. Although the benefits of physical uniformity — enhanced understandability and facilitation of automation tools — as outlined in section 0.7 alone are compelling, mindless adherence to this

---

[22] **lakos96**, Appendix C, pp. 779–813 and, in particular, Appendix C.1, pp. 180–193

rule, however, will fall far short of the potential benefit it seeks to motivate. The intent here is not just to provide a uniform and balanced physical representation of software, but also to craft a hierarchical repository where the contained elements, from a logical as well as a physical perspective, are cohesive and synergistic (see section 2.8.3). Moreover, we want to ensure that each library component we write has a natural and obvious place in the physical hierarchy of our firm-wide repository (see sections 3.1.4 and 3.12).

Design Rule

The (all-lowercase) name of each component must begin with the (all-lowercase) name of the package to which it belongs, followed by an underscore (_).

A first step toward ensuring overt visible cohesion between architecturally significant names is making sure that the component name reflects the name of the package in which it resides, as shown in Figure 2-18. Just by looking at the name of the **bts_cost** component, we know that there exist two component files named bts_cost.h and bts_cost.cpp, which reside in the **bts** package.[23,24]

---

[23] In our methodology, packages (see section 2.8) are either aggregated into a group (see section 2.9) or else released as standalone packages, with these two categories each having its own distinct (nonoverlapping) naming conventions (see section 2.10). Packages that belong to a group have names that are four to six characters in length with the first three corresponding to the name of the package group, which serves as the unit of release (UOR). Typical standalone packages have names that are seven or more characters in order to ensure that they remain disjoint from those of all grouped packages. In rare cases, particularly for very widely used (or standard) libraries, we may choose to create a package-group sized package having just a single three-character prefix, such as **bts** (or **std**). Although having a single ultra-short namespace name across a very large number of components can sometimes enhance productivity across a broad client base, such libraries typically demand significantly more skill and effort to develop and maintain than their less coarsely named package-group-based counterparts. The use of (architecturally insignificant) subpackages to support such nominally monolithic libraries is discussed in section 2.11.

[24] This nomenclature stems from way back before standardization, and we had to use logical package prefixes to implement logical namespaces — e.g., bget_Point instead of bget::Point. Even with the advent of the namespace construct in the C++98 Standard, we continue to exploit this approach to naming of physical entities and, occasionally, even logical ones — e.g., in procedural interfaces (see section 3.11.7).

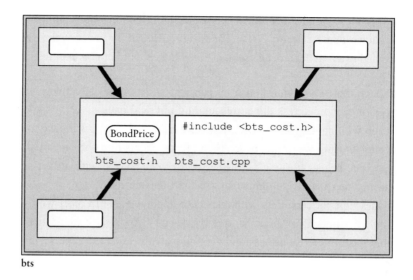

Figure 2-18: Component names always reflect their enclosing package.

Our preference that the names of physical entities (e.g., files, packages, and libraries) not contain any uppercase letters (section 1.7.1) begins with the observation that some popular file systems — Microsoft's NTFS, in particular — do not distinguish between uppercase and lowercase.[25] Theoretically, it is sufficient that the *lowercased* rendering of all filenames be unique. Practically, however, having any unnecessary extra degree of freedom in our physical packaging, thereby complicating development/deployment tools, let alone human comprehension, makes the use of mixed-case filenames for C++ source code suboptimal.[26]

Separately, and perhaps most importantly, we find that having class names, which we consistently render in mixed case (section 1.7.1) — being distinct from physical names, which we render in all lowercase — is notationally convenient and also visually reinforces the distinction

---

[25] With the intent of improving readability (and/or nominal cohesion), it is frequently suggested that we change to allow uppercase letters in component filenames and require them to match exactly the principal class or common prefix of contained classes (see section 2.6), instead of the *lowercased* name as is currently required. We recognize that the readability of multiword filenames can suffer (ironically providing a welcome incentive to keep component base names appropriately concise).

[26] Insisting that our component filenames be rendered in `all_lowercase` also effectively precludes "overloading" on case for logical names, e.g., having both `DateTimeMap` and `DatetimeMap` in separate components — which, from a readability standpoint, is something we would probably want to avoid anyway. Imagine trying to communicate such a distinction over a customer-service telephone hotline!

between these two distinct dimensions of design, e.g., in component/class diagrams such as the one shown above (Figure 2-18). The utility afforded by this visual distinction within source code and external documents, such as this book, should not be underestimated.

Although the `namespace` construct can and will be used effectively with respect to *logical* names, it cannot address the corresponding physical ones — i.e., component filenames. That is, even with namespaces, having a header file employing a simple name such as `date.h` is still problematic. We could, as many do, force clients to embed a partial (relative) path to the appropriate header file (e.g., `#include <bts/date.h>`) within their source code; however, ensuring enterprise-wide uniqueness in the filename itself (e.g., `#include <bts_date.h>`) provides superior flexibility with respect to deployment.[27] In other words, by making all component filenames themselves unique by design (irrespective of relative directory paths), we enable much more robustness and flexibility with respect to repackaging during deployment (see section 2.15.2).

Taking a software vendor's perspective, an early explicit requirement of our packaging methodology was the ability to select one component, or an arbitrary set of specific components, from a vast repository, extract (copies of) them along with just the components on which those components depended (directly or indirectly), and make these components available to customers as a library having a single ("flat") include directory and a single archive. Had we allowed our development directory structure to adulterate our source files, we would be forced to replicate a perhaps very large and sparsely populated directory structure on our clients' systems. Similarly, nonunique `.cpp` filenames would make re-archiving `.o` files from multiple packages into a single library archive anything but straightforward.

This unnecessarily sparse directory structure would be exacerbated by a third level of physical aggregation. For example, the same header that resided within the package-level `#include` directory during development can co-exist (i.e., within a single group-level `#include` directory) alongside headers from other packages grouped together within the same UOR, which can be more convenient (and also more efficient[28]) for use by external clients. Having this superior flexibility in deployment — especially for library software — trumps any arguments based on aesthetics or "common practice."

---

[27] We assert (see section 2.10.2) that this approach is viable for even the largest of source-code repositories. For example, see **potvin16**.

[28] **lakos96**, section 7.6.1 (pp. 514–520), and, in particular, Figures 7-21 and 7-22 (p. 519 and p. 520, respectively)

There are other collateral benefits for ensuring globally unique filenames. Having the file-name embody its unique package prefix also simplifies predicting include-guard names. As illustrated in Figure 1-40, in section 1.5.2, the guard name is simply the prefix `INCLUDED_` followed by the root filename in uppercase (e.g., for file `bts_bondprice.h` the guard symbol is simply `INCLUDED_BTS_BONDPRICE`). Compilers often make use of the implementation filename as the basis for generating unique symbols within a program — e.g., for virtual tables or constructs in an unnamed namespace. Hard-coding the unique package prefix in the file-name also means that its globally unique identity is preserved outside the directory structure in which it was created — e.g., in `~/tmp`, as an email attachment, or on the printer tray. Con-sistently repeating the filename as a comment on the very first line of each component file, as we do (see section 2.5), further reinforces its identity. Knowing the context of a file simply by looking at its name is a valuable property that one soon comes to expect and then depend on.

Design Rule

Each logical entity declared within a component must be nested within a namespace having the name of the package in which that entity resides.

Before the introduction of the `namespace` keyword into the C++ language (and currently for languages such as C that do not provide a logical namespace construct), the best solution available was to require that (where possible) the name of every logical entity declared at file scope begin with a (registered) prefix unique to the architecturally significant physically cohe-sive aggregate immediately enclosing them, namely, a package.[29] Attaching a logical package prefix to the name of every architecturally significant logical entity within a component, albeit aesthetically displeasing to many, was effective not only at avoiding name collisions, but also at achieving nominal cohesion, thereby reinforcing logical/physical coherence. A reimple-mentation of the physical module of Figure 2-17 (above) using logical package prefixes (now deprecated) is shown for reference only in Figure 2-19.

---

[29] **lakos96**, section 7.6.1, pp. 514–520, and in particular Figure 7-21, p. 519

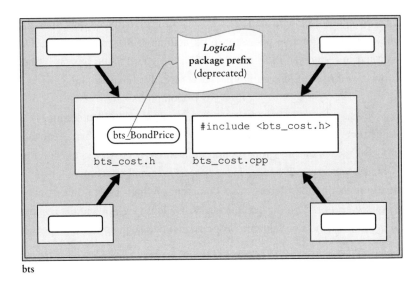

Figure 2-19: (Classical) logical package prefixes (deprecated)

Now that the `namespace` construct has long since been supported by all relevant C++ compilers, there has been an inculcation toward having concise, unadulterated logical names. Hence, we now (since c. 2005) nest each logical entity within a namespace having the same name as the package containing the component that defines the construct, as shown in Figure 2-20. Our use of logical package namespaces is isomorphic to our original use of logical package prefixes, and therefore consistent with our continued use of physical package prefixes for component filenames to preserve logical and physical name cohesion.

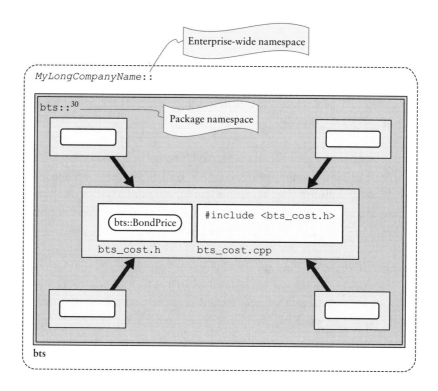

Figure 2-20: (Modern) logical package and enterprise namespaces

2.4.7   Proprietary Software Requires an Enterprise Namespace

Notice how Figure 2-20, section 2.4.6, anticipates that we now also recommend an overarching enterprise-wide namespace as a way of enabling us to disambiguate (albeit extremely rare in practice) collisions with other software that might follow our (or a similar) naming methodology.

Design Rule

Each package namespace must be nested within a unique enterprise-wide namespace.

By shielding all of our proprietary code (other than application `main` functions, see section 2.13) behind a single enterprise-wide name, e.g., our full company name (as illustrated in

---

[30] Note that when namespaces are not appropriate (e.g., functions having `extern "C"` linkage), we revert back to the use of logical package prefixes (see section 3.11.7).

Figure 2-20, section 2.4.6), we all but eliminate any chance of accidental external collision. And, since all of our components reside within the same enterprise namespace, there is no need or temptation to employ `using` declarations or directives.[31] In the very unlikely event that a collision with external software occurs — even in the presence of `using` directives — all that is required to disambiguate the collision is to prepend (1) the firm-wide symbol, (2) the third-party product's symbol, or (3) `::` if the third-party code failed to take this precaution.

Having, instead, each individual package represented by a namespace at the highest level would lead, at least conceptually, to myriad short global symbols, combinatorially increasing the probability of collision with vendors adopting a similar strategy (see the birthday problem in Volume III, section 8.3).[32] In any event, having a single (somehow unique) enterprise-wide "umbrella" namespace for our own code serves to mitigate risk and is therefore desirable.

The next step in achieving logical and physical name cohesion is to formalize how logical entities defined within a component are named so that their use alone identifies the component in which they are defined. To simplify the description, we provide the following definition of a component's base name.

> **DEFINITION**: The *base name* of a component is the root name of the component's header file, excluding its package prefix and subsequent underscore.

For example, the *base name* of the component illustrated in Figure 2-20, section 2.4.6, is **cost**. This name, however, fails to achieve nominal cohesion with the class `BondPrice`, which it defines.

---

[31] Note that for large code bases that make significant use of templates, having a long enterprise namespace name can prove prohibitive with respect to the size of the debug symbols that the compiler generates, which may force us to go for a much shorter name — e.g., our stock ticker.

[32] Decentralized registration of packages via package groups (see section 2.9.4) is effective at managing naming conflicts within a single organization. We can, however, easily envisage a world in which source code from multiple enterprises having distinct naming regimes (consistent with our methodology) needs to co-exist within a single code base. Under those circumstances, there might be affirmative value in preventing accidental header-file collisions by proactively adding a very short (e.g., exactly *two*-character) mutually unique *physical* prefix (e.g., "bb_") to each organization's component names corresponding to (but not necessarily the same as) their respective unique enterprise-wide (logical) namespace names (see sections 2.4.6, 2.4.7, and 2.10.2).

2.4.8   Logical Constructs Should Be Nominally Anchored to Their Component

> **DEFINITION:** An *aspect function* is a named (member or free) function of a given signature having ubiquitously uniform semantics (e.g., `begin` or `swap`) and, if free, behaves much like an operator — e.g., with respect to argument-dependent lookup (ADL).

Design Rule

The name of every logical construct declared at package-namespace scope — other than free *operator* and *aspect* functions (such as `operator==` and `swap`) — must have, as a prefix, the base name of the component that implements it; macro names (`ALL_UPPERCASE`), which are not scoped (lexically) by the package namespace, must incorporate, as a prefix, the entire uppercased name of the component (including the package prefix).

> **COROLLARY:** The fully qualified name (or signature, if a function or operator) of each logical entity declared within an architecturally significant component header file must be unique throughout the enterprise.

Naming a component after its principal class or `struct` (but in all lowercase), as shown in Figure 2-21, usually resolves most potential ambiguity. For example, we would expect that class `bts::PackedCalendar` would be defined in a component called **bts_packedcalendar** (or conceivably, **bts_packed**, if the component defined other intimately related "packed" types). Note that in our methodology, however, we tend to have a single (principal) class per component unless there is one of four specific countervailing reasons to do otherwise (see section 3.3.1). Whenever there is more than one class defined at package-namespace scope within a single component, each such class name will incorporate that component's base name (albeit in "UpperCamelCase") as a prefix.[33]

---

[33] Note that this rule may not apply when the external ("client-facing") component headers are already specified otherwise — e.g., standardized interfaces or established legacy libraries.

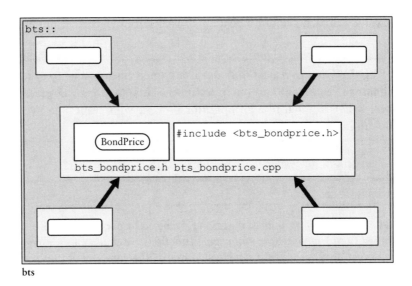

bts

Figure 2-21: Nominally cohesive class and component (GOOD IDEA)

Where appropriate, we routinely define outwardly accessible ("public") auxiliary classes, such as iterators, in the same component either by appending to the name of the primary class (e.g., `bdlt::PackedCalendarHolidayIterator`), or else by nesting the auxiliary class within the principal class itself (e.g., `PackedCalendar::HolidayIterator`).[34] Note, however, that some detective work might be unavoidable when operators, inheritance, or user-defined conversion are involved. The rules surrounding the placement of free operators within components are discussed below.

2.4.9   Only Classes, `structs`, and Free Operators at Package-Namespace Scope

---

Design Rule

Only classes, `structs`, and free operator functions (and operator-like *aspect* functions, e.g., `swap`) are permitted to be *declared* at package-namespace scope in a component's `.h` file.

---

[34] In practice, the nested iterator type, `PackedCalendar::HolidayIterator`, would likely be a `typedef` to the non-nested auxiliary iterator class, `bts::PackedCalendarHolidayIterator`, which grants the container private (`friend`) access (e.g., see section 3.12.5.1). The mandatory colocation of two classes where one grants private access to another is discussed in section 2.6.

To minimize clutter, we have consistently avoided declaring individual functions as well as enumerations, variables, constants, etc., at namespace scope in component header files, preferring instead always to nest these logical constructs within the scope of an appropriate `class` or `struct`.[35] In so doing, we anchor these less substantial constructs within a larger, architecturally significant logical entity, that, unlike a namespace (section 1.3.18), is necessarily fully contained within a single component (section 0.7). We understand that this rule, like the previous one, might not be applicable when there are valid countervailing business reasons such as an externally specified ("client-facing") interface.[36]

Having modifiable global variables at namespace scope is simply a bad idea. Nesting such variables within a class as `static` data members and providing only functional access is also generally a bad idea, but at least addresses the issue of nominal cohesion. On the other hand, nesting compile-time-initialized constants along with `typedef` declarations[37] within the scope of a class or `struct` is perfectly fine. Requiring that enumerations be nested within a class, `struct`, or function ensures that all of the enumerators are scoped locally and cannot collide with those in other components within the same package namespace.[38]

---

[35] lakos96, section 2.3.5, p. 77–79, in particular p. 77

[36] Sometimes it might be useful to *know* that the name of a class is itself unique throughout the enterprise. For example, if for some reason we were to implement *streaming* (a.k.a. *externalization* or *serialization*) of polymorphic objects outside of our process space (see Volume II, section 4.1), it would be important that we identify uniquely the concrete class that we are streaming. One common and effective approach is to prepend the stream data with the character string name of the concrete class whose value we are transmitting. As with the include guard symbols for files (section 1.5.2), this process is reduced to rote mechanics, provided we are assured that the name of every potentially streamable concrete class in our organization is guaranteed to be unique. Logical package prefixes (now predicated) addressed this issue directly, but we can still achieve the same effect by streaming the (ultra-concise) package name (section 2.10.1) followed by that of the class, along with a (single-character) delimiter (of course).

[37] `typedef` declarations, although often useful (e.g., to specify an *aspect*, as in `SomeContainer::iterator`), obscure the underlying types in code and, consequently, can easily detract from readability. In particular, one would not typically use a `typedef` to alias a fundamental type to one more specific to its application — e.g.,

```
typedef int NumElements;
```

would be a BAD IDEA. Separately, there would ideally be a single C++ type to represent each truly distinct *platonic* type used widely across interface boundaries (see Volume II, section 4.4).

[38] C++11 provides what is known as an `enum class`, which addresses the issue of scoping the enumerators, as well as providing for stronger type safety. Note that all enumerations in C++11 allow their underlying integral type to be specified and, unlike C++03, thereby form what is known as a *complete type*, enabling them to be declared and used locally (i.e., without also specifying the enumerators). The ability to elide enumerators can constitute what is sometimes referred to in tort law as an "attractive nuisance" in that, unless the elided enumeration is supplied by a library in a header separate from the one containing its complete definition, a client wishing to insulate itself from the enumerators would be forced to declare the enumeration locally in violation of Component Property 3 (section 1.6.3).

The justification for avoiding free functions, except operator and operator-like "aspect" functions, which might benefit from argument-dependent lookup (ADL), derives from our desire to encapsulate an appropriate amount of logically and physically coherent functionality within a nominally cohesive component. While classes are substantial architectural entities that are easily identifiable from their names, individual functions are generally too small and specific for each to be made nominally cohesive with the single component that defines them, as in Figure 2-22a.[39]

Creating components that hold multiple functions in which there is no nominal cohesion (Figure 2-22b) makes human reasoning about such physical nodes much more difficult and is therefore also a bad idea. Forcing the name of each function to have, as a prefix, the initial-lowercased rendering of the base name of the component (Figure 2-22c) achieves nominal cohesion, but is awkward at best, and fails to emphasize logical coherence (section 2.3). We could employ a third level of namespace (Figure 2-22d), but for reasons discussed below (Figure 2-23) and also near the end of section 2.5, we feel that would be suboptimal.

```
// xyza_roundtowardzero.h

namespace xyza {

double roundTowardZero(double value);

}   // close package namespace
```

(a) Nominally cohesive function at package-namespace scope (BAD IDEA)

```
// xyza_mathutil.h

namespace xyza {

double roundTowardZero(double value);

double factorial(double value);

}   // close package namespace
```

(b) Nominally noncohesive functions at package-namespace scope (BAD IDEA)

---

[39] Given that we virtually always open and close a package namespace exactly once within a component (see section 2.5), we choose not to indent its contents, thereby increasing usable real estate given a practical maximum line length (e.g., 79) suitable for efficient reading, printing, side-by-side comparison, etc. (see Volume II, section 6.15).

```
// xyza_mathutil.h

namespace xyza {

double mathUtilRoundTowardZero(double value);

double mathUtilFactorial(double value);

}   // close package namespace
```
(c) Nominally cohesive functions at package-namespace scope (AWKWARD)

```
// xyza_mathutil.h

namespace xyza {

namespace MathUtil {

    double roundTowardZero(double value);

    double factorial(double value);

}   // close local namespace

}   // close package namespace
```
(d) Nominally cohesive namespace containing functions (NOT OPTIMAL)

```
// xyza_mathutil.h

namespace xyza {

struct MathUtil {

    static double roundTowardZero(double value);

    static double factorial(double value);

};

}   // close package namespace
```
(e) Nominally cohesive utility `struct` containing functions (WHAT WE DO)

Figure 2-22: Ensuring nominal cohesion for free functions and components

We therefore generally avoid declaring free *(nonoperator)* functions at package-namespace scope, and instead achieve both nominal logical and physical cohesion by grouping related functionality within an extra level of namespace matching the component name using `static` methods within a `struct` (Figure 2-22e), which we will consistently refer to as a *utility* (see section 3.2.7) and so indicate with a `Util` suffix (e.g., `xyza::MathUtil`).[40] Additional, collateral advantages for preferring a `struct` (e.g., Figure 2-22e) over a third level of `namespace` (e.g., Figure 2-22d) for implementing a *utility* are summarized in Figure 2-23.[41]

There are many advantages of using a `struct` (e.g., Figure 2-22e) over a third level of namespace (e.g., Figure 2-22d) for aggregating related (what would otherwise be *free*) functions into a single *utility* component.

(1) The distinct syntax and atomic nature of a `struct` having `static` methods makes its purpose as a component-scoped entity clearer than would yet another, nested `namespace`, leaving namespaces for routine use at the package and enterprise levels exclusively.

(2) The self-declaring nature of functions and data defined at namespace scope (section 1.3.1) are necessarily eliminated when they are instead nested (as `static` members) within a `struct`.

(3) Unlike a `namespace`, a `struct` does not permit `using` directives (or declarations) to import function names into the current (e.g., package) namespace, thereby preventing any consequent loss in readability.[42]

(4) Unlike a `namespace`, a `struct` can support private nested data — e.g., as an optimization for accessing *insulated* (external bindage) table-based implementation details, residing in the `.cpp` file, by one or more inline functions, residing in the `.h` file (see Volume II, section 6.7).

(5) Unlike a `namespace`, a `struct` can be passed as a template parameter — e.g., as a cartridge of related functions satisfying a concept (e.g., see Figure 3-29, section 3.3.7).

(6) Unlike a `namespace`, a C-style function in a `struct` does not participate in Argument-Dependent Lookup (ADL), thereby avoiding potentially large overload sets, which could needlessly affect compile-time performance and possibly introduce unanticipated (perhaps even latent) ambiguity, or — much worse — invoke the wrong function.[43] By placing our "free" functions in a `struct`, we make our design decision not to employ ADL explicit.

(7) Except for a few very stylized cases, such as `std::placeholders` (e.g., `_1`, `_2`, `_3`) and `std::literals`, use of namespace declarations are generally ill-advised. Should we subsequently discover a rare valid engineering reason for enabling local `using` declarations, we can easily migrate a `struct` to a `namespace` by creating a new component-private `struct` (see section 2.9.1), e.g., `MathUtil_Imp`, and forwarding calls to it from the new nested (e.g., `MathUtil`) namespace. Note that, except when used as in (5), it is always possible to migrate from a `struct` to a `namespace` without forcing any clients to rework their source code, but, given the possibility of `using` directives/declarations, not vice versa (see Volume II, section 5.5).

Figure 2-23: Prefer `struct` to `namespace` for aggregating "free" functions.

---

[40] Note that it is not possible to have partial specializations for static method templates in a `struct` the way you can for free-function templates.

[41] Because only free (i.e., non-member) functions participate in ADL, extending the C++ language to accommodate new features, e.g., redeclaration (**voutilainen19**), for such functions (as opposed to `static` members of a `struct`) is considered by some to be substantially more technically difficult to implement in relevant C++ compilers. For more on why such extensions might be practically useful in future incarnations of the C++ language, see Volume II, section 6.8.

[42] Although `using` declarations can be used to import declarations of overloaded functions of a given name from a private (or protected) base class into a public one, we generally discourage such use, as it would require a public client to view otherwise private (or protected) detail; instead, we prefer to create (and document) an inline forwarding function. Note that a similar issue arises with forwarding constructors as of C++11.

[43] Titus Winters of Google has recently (c. 2018) expressed increasing concerns as to the scalability and stability of such overload sets (**winters18a**, "ADL"); see also **winters18b**, particularly starting at the 11:30 time marker.

Design Rule

A component header is permitted to contain the declaration of a *free* (i.e., non-member) operator or *aspect* function (at package-namespace scope) only when one or more of its parameters incorporates a type defined in the same component.

In our methodology, operators, whether member or free, are by their nature fundamental to the type(s) on which they operate. Every unary and homogeneous binary operator — i.e., one written in terms of a single user-defined type, e.g.,

```
bool operator==(const BondPrice& lhs, const BondPrice& rhs);
```

is declared and defined within the same component (e.g., **bts_bondprice**) as the type (e.g., `bts::BondPrice`) on which it operates. Note that, except for forms of assignment (e.g., =, +=, *=), we will always choose to make a binary operator free (as opposed to a member) to ensure symmetry with respect to user-defined conversions (see Volume II, section 6.13). For conventionally heterogeneous operators such as

```
std::ostream& operator<<(std::ostream&   stream,
                         const BondPrice& price);
```

the motivation to make them free is born of extensibility without modification, as in the open-closed principle (section 0.5). In any event, the place to look for the definition of an operator (entirely consistent with ADL) is within a component that defines a type on which that operator operates.

If we were to allow free operators to be defined in arbitrary components, how could we even know if they exist? If we saw one being used, how would we track down its definition? Even more insidious is the possibility that a client unwittingly duplicates such a definition locally. The resulting latent incompatibilities, manifested by future multiply-defined-symbol linker errors, would threaten to destabilize our development process.

As an important, relevant example, consider the standard template container class, `std::vector`, for which no standard output operator is defined. Referring to Figure 2-24, suppose that the author of component **my_stuff** finds outputting a vector to be generally useful, and so "thoughtfully" provides

```
template <class TYPE>
std::ostream& operator<<(std::ostream&            lhs,
                         const std::vector<TYPE>& rhs);
```

(along with an appropriate definition) in its header for general use by clients. It is not hard to imagine that component **your_stuff** might do so as well. Now consider what happens when their_stuff.cpp includes both my_stuff.h and your_stuff.h. The inevitable result is multiply defined symbols![44]

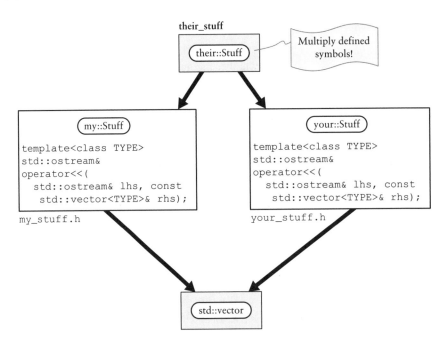

Figure 2-24: Problems with defining operators in unexpected components

Instead, the functionality should have been implemented as a static member function of a utility struct (see section 3.2.7) in a separate component, as illustrated in Figure 2-25.

---

[44] Because the offending operator is a template, which has dual bindage (section 1.3.4), it is entirely possible that the duplicate definitions will go unnoticed by either the compiler or the linker for quite some time — that is, until the compiler can see the two template definitions side-by-side in a single translation unit. Had the construct instead had external bindage, such as an ordinary function or an explicit instantiation, merely linking the two components into the same program would have been sufficient to expose the incompatibility.

```
// xyza_printutil.h

// ...

namespace xyza {

// ...

struct PrintUtil {

    // ...

    template<class TYPE>
    static std::ostream& print(std::ostream&     stream,
                               const std::vector<TYPE>& object);

    // ...
};

// ...

}  // close package namespace

// ...
```

Figure 2-25: Avoiding free operators on nonlocal types

As illustrated in Figure 2-26, providing an output operator on a type `my::Type` — or conceivably even on a `std::vector<my::Type>` — in component **my_type** is perfectly fine. The general design concept being illustrated here is to follow the teachings of the philosopher Immanuel Kant and avoid doing those things that, if also done by others, would adversely affect society (see section 3.9.1). By adhering to this simple rule for operators, we ensure that (1) we know where to look for each operator, and (2) operator definitions will not be duplicated (and therefore cannot conflict at higher levels in the physical hierarchy).

```
// my_type.h
// ...

namespace my {

class Type {
    // ...
};

std::ostream& operator<<(std::ostream& stream, const Type& object);          Correct

std::ostream& operator<<(std::ostream&          stream,    Not wrong
                         const std::vector<Type>& object);

}  // close package namespace

// ...
```

Figure 2-26: Overloading free operators on types within the same component

If a single free operator refers to two types implemented in separate components, where one depends on the other, the operator would of course be defined in the higher-level component. If, however, the components are otherwise independent (as illustrated Figure 2-27a), we have two alternatives:

1. [Suboptimal] Arbitrarily choose one of the components to be at a higher-level and place the free operator there, as in Figure 2-27b (thus introducing additional physical dependency for one of the components).

2. [Preferred] Create a utility class in a separate component, as in Figure 2-27c, and define one or more nonoperator functions nested within a `struct` that serves the same purpose (see section 3.2.7). Note that it is *never* appropriate to *escalate* (see section 3.5.2) co-dependent free operators to a separate component.

Use of operators for anything but the most fundamental, obvious, and intuitive operations (see Volume II, section 6.11) are almost always a bad idea and should generally be avoided; any valid, practical need for operators across otherwise independent user-defined types is virtually nonexistent.[45]

---

[45] We note that the C++ streaming operators and Boost.Spirit are (rare) arguably plausible counter-examples; still, we maintain that heterogeneous equality comparison operators across disparate user-defined value types (see Volume II, section 4.1), such as `Square` and `Rectangle` (Figure 2-27), remain invariably misguided for entirely different reasons (see Volume II, section 4.3).

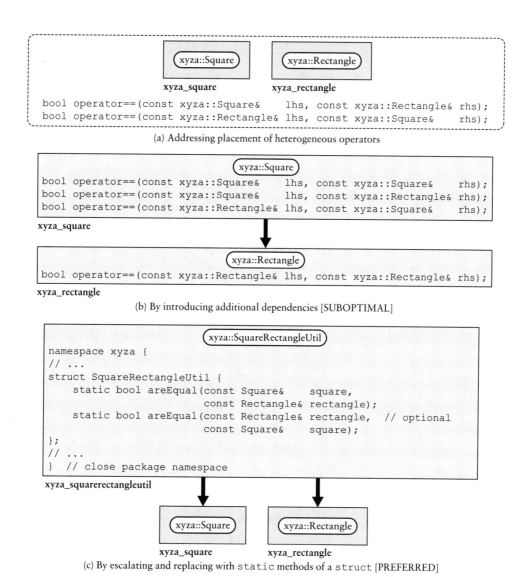

(a) Addressing placement of heterogeneous operators

(b) By introducing additional dependencies [SUBOPTIMAL]

(c) By escalating and replacing with `static` methods of a `struct` [PREFERRED]

Figure 2-27: Implementing "free operators" referring to multiple peer types

2.4.10   Package Prefixes Are Not Just Style

Make no mistake, how packages are named is not just a matter of style; package names have profound architectural significance. As an example, consider Figure 2-28, which shows a hierarchy of components whose dependencies form a binary tree. Clearly these components are levelizable (section 1.10) and, hence, have no cycles. However, it is not in general possible to assign components of a multipackage subsystem to arbitrary packages without introducing package-level cycles. In this example, the packages containing these components (as implied by the package prefixes embedded in the component names) would be cyclic and therefore *not* levelizable.

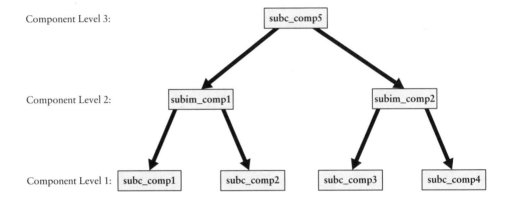

Figure 2-28: Implied cyclic package dependencies (BAD IDEA)

The problem, identified by Figure 2-29, can easily arise in practice. Consider the design of a single package that is intended to contain everything that is directly usable by clients of a multipackage subsystem. If this presentation package (**subc**) defines both protocol (i.e., pure abstract interface) classes (which are inherently very low level) and wrapper components (which are inherently very high level), it will not be possible to interleave components from a separate implementation package (**subim**).[46]

---

[46] For complex subsystems, the implementation components represented here as a single package **subim** may appropriately span many packages at several different levels; however, the basic idea remains the same.

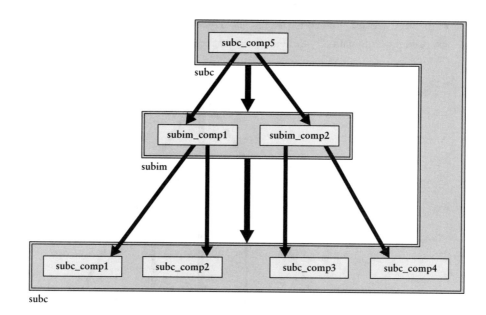

Figure 2-29: Acyclic component hierarchy; cyclic package hierarchy (BAD IDEA)

COROLLARY: Allowed (explicitly stated) dependencies among packages must be acyclic.

Allowing cyclic dependencies among packages, like any other aggregate, would make our software qualitatively more complicated. Ultimately, *all* cyclically involved packages would have to be treated as a unit. A general solution to this common problem, illustrated in Figure 2-30, is simply to provide two separate client-facing packages. One package (**subw**) will reside at the top of the subsystem and contain components that define only wrappers[47] (e.g., **subw_comp1**); the second will reside at the bottom of the package hierarchy and incorporate components

---

[47] A *wrapper* is a *facade* that allows clients to manipulate objects (typically of some other type) without providing direct programmatic access to those objects (see sections 3.1.10 and 3.11.6).

(e.g., `subv_comp1`) that define protocol and other *vocabulary* types (see Volume II, section 4.4) exposed programmatically through the wrapper interface.[48]

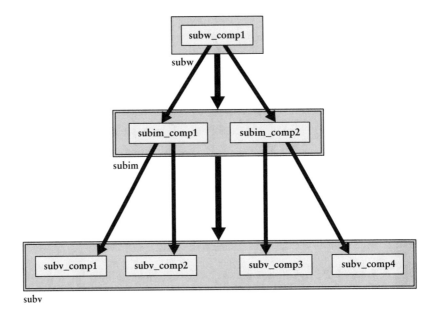

Figure 2-30: Repackaging of components to avoid cyclic package dependencies

Components that are used in the interface of the wrapper components (`subw`), and also *in name only* by low-level protocols, typically reside either in the same package as the protocols (e.g., `subv` in Figure 2-30) or in a separate, lower-level package, as illustrated in Figure 2-31b, as opposed to at the same level (Figure 2-31a), in order to enable concrete test implementations of the protocols to properly reside along with them (e.g., in `subp`), yet allow such test implementations to depend on the actual concrete vocabulary types (e.g., in `subt`) rather than having to mock them.

---

[48] See the *escalating encapsulation* levelization technique (section 3.5.10).

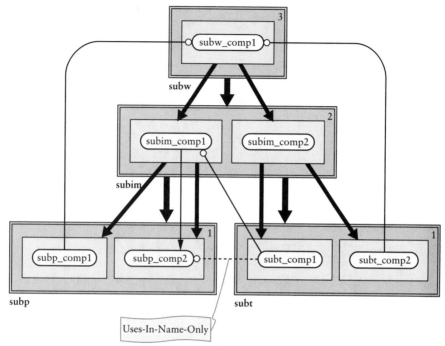

(a) Parallel protocol and concrete vocabulary-type packages (BAD IDEA)

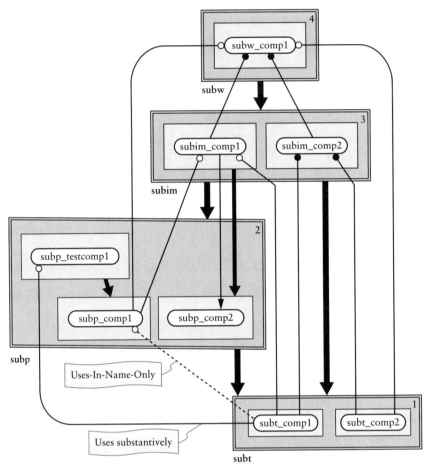

(b) Subordinate local vocabulary-type package (GOOD IDEA)

Figure 2-31: Alternative packaging strategies

2.4.11   Package Prefixes Are How We Name Package Groups

Although packages, being architecturally significant aggregates, have unique names (and namespaces), it is often advantageous to bundle packages having similar purposes and/or similar envelopes of physical dependency into a larger, logically and physically coherent, nominally cohesive aggregate. We could make a big deal about this issue (and perhaps we should, given its importance). Instead we will avoid the drama and just make our point: The first three letters of a package name identify the physically cohesive package group in which a grouped package resides.

The reason for this simple approach is, well, simple (see section 2.10.1): We simply must have an ultra-efficient way to specify the package group and package of each component and class in order to obviate noisome and debilitating `using` directives and declarations (see section 2.4.12). The choice of three letters (as opposed to, say, two or four) is simply an engineering trade-off. This simple, concise, and effective approach to naming package groups is illustrated in Figure 2-32. We will revisit our package-naming rules (in much greater depth) in section 2.10.

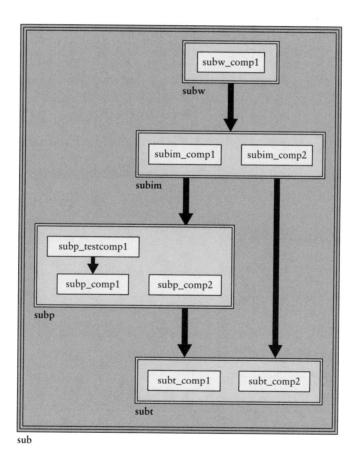

Figure 2-32: Logically and physically cohesive package group

2.4.12   `using` **Directives and Declarations Are Generally a BAD IDEA**

Let us now take a closer look at our use of the C++ `namespace` construct to partition logical entities along package boundaries. One of the solid benefits of package namespaces is that access to other entities local to that package does not require explicit qualification. This advantage is particularly pronounced at the application level, where much of the code that interoperates is defined locally (see section 2.13). Absent `using` directives and declarations, an unqualified reference is as informative as a qualified one: An unqualified reference implies that the entity is local to *this* package.[49]

In the code example of Figure 2-33, we cannot simply look at the definition of the `insertAfterLink` helper function and know which `Link` class we are talking about without potentially having to scan back through the entire file for preceding occurrences of `using`.

---

[49] There is still, however, one pragmatic reason to prefer the inflexibility of the hard-coded logical package prefix that continues to give us pause even though we have fully embraced package namespaces in our day-to-day work. Unfortunately, any use of `using` directives and declarations render case-by-case explicit use of the package namespace "tag" for remotely defined types optional, at the expense of nominal cohesion. Occasionally, library developers will need to "search the universe" for all uses of some class or utility. When we consider the possible use of `using` directives and declarations, any hope of relying on a simple search and replace (e.g., in the event a component "moves" from one package to another) is lost. Instead, we are forced to parse every line of source code. Even when we have such an elaborate tool (e.g., Clang), it, like the compiler itself, runs many orders of magnitude slower than a simple search engine looking for a fixed identifier string. We saw this same kind of speed issue with respect to determining the envelope of direct physical dependencies by scanning for just the `#include` directives nested within a component (section 1.11). Hence, use of the `namespace` construct, at least in this particular respect, is not *as* scalable as the classical, albeit archaic (and now deprecated), logical package prefix.

```
// my_link.cpp
#include <my_link.h>

// ...

#include <your_list.h>  // defines class 'Link'

// ...

namespace Foo {
    class Link { /*...*/ };  // another definition of 'Link'
}

// ...           ┌─────────────────────────────┐
// ...           │  Cannot determine which Link is │
// ...           │  being used without looking at  │
// ...           │      prior using directives      │
// ...           └─────────────────────────────┘
// ...

inline
static void insertAfterLink(Link *node, Link *newNode)
{
    BSLS_ASSERT(node);                    (See Volume II, section 6.8.)
    BSLS_ASSERT(newNode);

    newNode->next = node->next;
    newNode->prev = node;
    node->next = newNode;

    if (newNode->next) {
        newNode->next->prev = newNode;
    }
}

// ...
```

Figure 2-33: Nonlocal namespace names are optional! (BAD IDEA)

What's worse, it might be that `using` directives or declarations are not even local to the implementation file, but are instead imported quietly in one or more of many included header files
as illustrated in Figure 2-34. And, unlike the C++ Standard Library (or `std` in code), which is
comparatively small, unchanging, and well known, we cannot be expected to know every class
within every component of every package throughout our enterprise. Still worse, nesting a variety of `using` directives and declarations within header files risks making relevant the relative
order in which these headers are incorporated into a translation unit![50]

---

[50] **sutter05**, item 59, pp. 108–110

```cpp
// my_app.cpp
#include <my_app.h>
#include <cdel_log.h>
#include <ddet_swap.h>
#include <ddet_table.h>
#include <ddeu_isma30360.h>
#include <dteal_technology.h>
#include <emeg_protocol.h>
#include <emem_list.h>
#include <etef_fizzbin.h>
#include <etet_trade.h>
#include <eteu_semiannual.h>
#include <fmeec_transport.h>
#include <fteem_balloon.h>
#include <ftet_account.h>
#include <ftet_position.h>
#include <ftex_prepayment.h>
// ...
// ...
// ...
#include <pcst_client.h>
#include <otem_config.h>
#include <tdep_render.h>
#include <ynot_evenmore.h>

// ...
// ...
// ...
// ...
// ...
// ...
// ...
```

> Cannot determine which `Relay` is being used even after looking at every statement in this file — using directives/declarations or otherwise!

```cpp
static void communicate(Relay *relay)
{
    static Callback myCallback;

    if (relay->isOperational()) {
        relay->setForwardCallback(&myCallback):
    }
    else {
        Log::singleton().write("Life is like a box of chocolates...");
    }

    // ...
}

// ...
```

Figure 2-34: `using` **directives/declarations can be included! (BAD IDEA)**

Design Rule

Neither `using` directives nor `using` declarations are permitted to appear outside function scope within a component.

No matter what, we must forbid any `using` directives or declarations in header files outside of function scope.[51,52,53,54] Perhaps some advocates of `using` in headers might not yet have realized that the incorporation of names from one namespace, A, into another, B, does not end with the closing brace of B into which names from A were imported, but remain in B until the end of the translation unit. Consequently, `using` directives or declarations are sometimes used (we should say horribly misused) in header files when declaring class member data and function prototypes to shorten the names of types declared in distant namespaces

---

[51] And, in library code, `using` is generally best avoided altogether. If used there at all, a `using` *declaration* (not *directive*) — whether employed to enable ADL (e.g., for a free *aspect* function, such as `swap`), or merely as a compact alias (e.g., as an entry into a dispatch table) — should appear only within a very limited lexical context, i.e., function (or block) scope.

[52] In C++98, `using` declarations replaced *access declarations* (which were deprecated intermediately and, in C++11, finally removed) for the purpose of promoting all overloads of a given (named) member function from a base class into the current scope while potentially increasing its level of access, e.g., from private to public. As we will discuss shortly, we avoid any use of class-scope `using` declarations, especially those that might force public clients to refer to less-than-public regions of a class's implementation.

[53] C++11 introduced other contexts in which the `using` keyword is valid (e.g., as an *alias declaration* used to replace `typedef`) having nothing to do with either `using` declarations or `using` directives.

[54] Alisdair Meredith notes (via personal email, 2018) that, when a base class is a template, the set of overloads to forward is an open set. Accidental breakage can occur when a design requires that each of the overloads be exposed manually. When the intent is to *perfectly forward* an overload set from a base class, a `using` declaration is a clear statement of that design intent.

Nonetheless, our recommended approach is to avoid such uses of (typically *structural*) inheritance (see Volume II, section 4.6), preferring the more compositional *Has-A* (section 1.7.4) approach to *layering* (see section 3.7.2) instead.

That said, exceptional cases do exist. Alisdair Meredith further points out (again, via personal email, 2018) that we ourselves have, on occasion, been known to introduce a base class having fewer template parameters, and then use *structural* inheritance and `using` declarations to expose that functionality as the public interface. If we were now to replace `using` declarations with, say, `inline` forwarding functions, we would negate the intended effect of reducing template-induced code bloat (see Volume II, section 4.5).

(BAD IDEA).[55] Instead, we must use the package-qualified name of each logical entity not local to the enclosing package. For this reason, we will want to ensure that widely used ("package") namespace names, like std, are very short indeed.

The use of using declarations for function forwarding during private (never mind protected) inheritance is also to be avoided because (1) our ability to document and understand such functionality in the derived header itself is compromised, and (2) inheritance necessarily implies compile-time coupling (section 1.9; see also section 3.10). We generally prefer to avoid private inheritance, in favor of layering (a.k.a. *composition*), and explicit (inline) function forwarding.

Finally, using namespaces to define a logical "location" independent of its physical location, say, to avoid changing #include directives (should some class be logically "repackaged") is — in our view — misguided. If we change the *logical* location of a class then — in our methodology — that class must be moved to its proper *physical* location as well. Unless logical and physical locations coincide, many of the advantages of sound physical design — e.g., reduced compile time, link time, and executable size (not to mention organization and under-standability) — are compromised.

Adhering to these cohesive naming rules does, however, impose some extra burden on library developers. That is, if a logical construct were to "move" from one *architectural location* to another, its address (i.e., its component name), and therefore some aspect of its fully qualified logical name, *must* necessarily change as well. This "deficiency" is actually a feature in that it allows for a reasonable deprecation strategy: During refactoring, it is possible for two versions

---

[55] Local typedefs have historically been effective at addressing long names in data definitions and function prototypes due to specific template instantiations:

```
class Book {
    // ...
    typedef std::map<std::string, std::string>      StrStrMap;
    typedef std::map<std::string, std::vector<int> > StrIntarrayMap;
    // ...
    StrStrMap      d_glossary;
    StrIntarrayMap d_index;
    // ...
};
```

We recognize that C++11 offers using as a syntactic alternative, and that thoughtful (discriminating) use of auto can also help eliminate redundant (or otherwise superfluous) explicit type information in source code. See **lakos21**.

of the same logical entity to co-exist for a period of time as clients rework their code to refer to the new component before the original one is finally removed.[56]

2.4.13   Section Summary

In summary, our rigorous approach to cohesive naming — packages, components, classes, and free (operator) functions — not only avoids collisions, it also provides valuable visual cues within the source code that serve to identify the physical location of all architecturally significant entities. Experience shows that human cognition is facilitated by such visual associations. In turn, this nominal cohesion reinforces the even more critical requirement of logical/physical coherence (section 2.3). Hence, logical and physical name cohesion across related architecturally significant entities is an integral part of our component-based packaging methodology.

2.5   Component Source-Code Organization

In this section, we describe the general, high-level layout of source code within components. Recall, from section 0.7, our goal of representing all of our proprietary software in relatively small, atomic, uniform physical modules. We assert that *components*, as characterized in Chapter 1 (sections 1.6 and 1.11), are the optimal atomic building blocks of scalable systems. Moreover, we contend that the *component*, and not the *class*, is the appropriate unit of logical as well as physical design.

From a distance, every component in a system looks the same, regardless of its logical content. Essentially the same structural design shown in Figure 0-33, section 0.7, is repeated in Figure 2-35, but now each name incorporates its corresponding package prefix (section 2.4.6), illustrated here with the package name **xyza**.[57] Without hindering conventional class-level design, components provide the "real estate" on which to encapsulate closely related logical entities while admitting consideration of essential physical issues that routinely impact design decisions at the class level (see Volume II, Chapter 5).

---

[56] For those auspicious environments where the entire universe of affected code is known (e.g., all of the enterprise source code resides in a single source-code repository and there are no outside clients), it is vastly preferable to invest heavily in tooling to automate this continuous-refactoring process and thus avoid the tedious and error-prone effort of moving code incrementally by hand.

[57] Having a package named **xyza** implies that it is a member of the package group **xyz** (section 2.4.11).

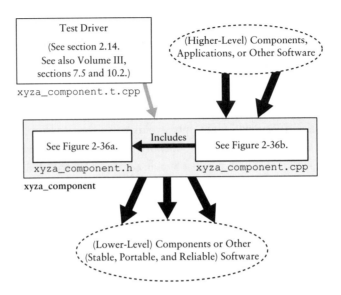

Figure 2-35: Canonical distant view of every packaged component

When we zoom in closer, we will find that the organization of each component is also standard and largely independent of logical content from one component to the next. Figure 2-36 illustrates the canonical "boilerplate" that accompanies the essential logical content of every component we write. The header file (Figure 2-36a) begins with a single line that is reserved for use by the development environment to tag a component as needed for identification. Then comes the required predictable include guard, followed by the detailed component-level documentation and usage examples as discussed in Volume II, sections 6.15 and 6.16, respectively.

Next, we place in the header only those `#include` directives needed to compile the header itself.[58] The remaining needed `#include` directives are properly relegated to the `.cpp` file. The order in which we include headers is governed by physical hierarchy. Headers for components that reside in the same package are included first. Then we include components in other packages within the same package group. Next, we include components within other package groups. Finally, we include standard headers. Within each of these four subsections, include directives are arranged alphabetically.

It is at this point that we open up the enterprise-wide namespace. We will need to tuck any local ("forward") declarations to classes outside the current package in the enterprise namespace, which we do one per line. We then open the package-level namespace, and place all local declarations of types defined in the current package there, again, one per line.

---

[58] Note that these nested includes are *not* surrounded by what are now deprecated *external* (a.k.a."redundant") include guards as discussed in section 1.5.3.

We now proceed to declare every piece of logical content we intend to provide in this header. We typically format this content as a sequence of one or more classes (or, for utilities, as a single `struct`), with each class immediately followed by the declarations of any associated free operators.[59] We generally avoid declaring free nonoperator functions entirely; however, we are sometimes compelled to make exceptions for standard ("aspect") functions, such as `swap`, that — by convention — have universally consistent syntax and semantics, and thus act as if they were operators. If we do declare such a free aspect function, we do so immediately following any free operators for the associated class. A detailed discussion of how we organize logical content within each class can be found in Volume II, section 6.14.

For readability, and to separate the notions of contract and implementation, we consistently[60] place the source code of any definitions that must be shared across translation units outside the lexical scope of the class and below the entire public interface of the component. Once the public interface of the component is complete, we delimit the logical interface and implementation with a prominent banner[61]:

```
// ============================================================================
//                            INLINE FUNCTION DEFINITIONS
// ============================================================================
```

---

[59] Historically, some compilers required free functions be declared using `inline` at the point of declaration for them to be inlined. We have observed that this is no longer an issue on any relevant platform.

[60] There are some very rare exceptions that might compel us to do otherwise, invariably involving templates:

1. When we have copious regular template structures (e.g., prior to variadic templates in C++11), separating out the declaration from its (inline) definition would entail duplicating most of the code in an already massive component, yet the individual declarations aren't meant to be read by human beings.

2. There is also the classic case in C++ where a local declaration of a template's non-templated `friend` function having a parameter of the same type as the class template cannot be generally redeclared (and defined) outside the lexical scope of the class, although it would be possible to provide a limited set of definitions for a limited set of instantiations (should that ever be desired). E.g.,

    ```
    template <class T>
    class MyType {
        int d_data;
        friend bool operator==(const MyType& lhs, const MyType& rhs);
    };
    // Crazy case -- we can compare only 'MyType<int>' and not any other
    // type, as the linker will never find the definition.
    bool operator==(const MyType<int>& lhs, const MyType<int>& rhs)
    {
        return lhs.d_data == rhs.d_data;
    }
    ```

[61] Several descriptive banner titles have been proposed throughout the years (see the next page):

All inline *member* function and *member* function template definitions follow in the same relative order in which they are declared[62]; free functions, however, are organized separately. Recall from section 1.3.1 that a free function defined at namespace scope can also serve as its own declaration. If the signature of an unqualified function definition fails to match a previous declaration, the definition itself introduces a new declaration. This suboptimal behavior can be suppressed by defining a previously declared free function outside of the namespace in which it was declared. Free operators (like any other free functions) defined within a namespace are also self-declaring (in that namespace). We therefore opt first to close the package namespace, and then package-qualify each of these free operator definitions, followed by the definitions of any necessary (operator-like) free (aspect) functions as illustrated near the bottom of Figure 2-36a.

In the case of type traits (see Volume II, section 4.5), it might be necessary to specialize templates defined in other packages. Though the trait itself serves as a vocabulary type (see Volume II, section 4.4), such specializations are often optimizations, and — unless specifically documented as essential behavior (see Volume II, section 5.2) — are (i.e., should be) considered implementation details and subject to change without notice. We therefore choose to implement such specializations in the implementation portion of the header file. Since these specializations must be implemented within the same namespace as the definition, the current package namespace must be closed; hence, we find it convenient to place these specializations after all inline-function and function-template definitions that reside beyond the close of the package namespace.[63] Finally, we close the enterprise-wide namespace and terminate the (internal) include guard, unambiguously signifying the end of the header file.

```
[ ]    IMPLEMENTATION

[ ]    INLINE DEFINITIONS

[X]    INLINE FUNCTION DEFINITIONS                                    (original)

[ ]    INTERNAL AND DUAL BINDAGE DEFINITIONS

[ ]    INLINE FUNCTION AND FUNCTION TEMPLATE DEFINITIONS

[ ]    INLINE-FUNCTION, FUNCTION-TEMPLATE, AND TRAIT DEFINITIONS
```

After more than two decades of thoughtful deliberation, we now believe that our original banner
```
INLINE FUNCTION DEFINITIONS
```
remains the best compromise between simplicity, accuracy, clarity, and stability. We have therefore adopted that original banner — ideally centered (starting in column 27) within our fixed (79-character) maximum line length — as our permanent standard, irrespective of what other kinds of header-file-bound implementation artifacts (e.g., **voutilainen19**) might someday come to reside below it (see Volume II, section 6.3).

[62] Historically, we had to be concerned that, when one inline function was implemented in terms of another, the definition of the called appeared first in the source code. We have observed that, for several years now, the relative ordering of interdependent inline function definitions has not been an issue on any relevant platforms.

[63] Note that traits are typically not used by the current component, but rather by (the compilers of) clients of that component; hence, having traits come last in the header file does not present any problems in practice.

```
// xyza_component.h              -*-C++-*-
```
← The filename is always first along with any other fields or tags needed for identification.

```
#ifndef INCLUDED_XYZA_COMPONENT
#define INCLUDED_XYZA_COMPONENT
```
← Internal include guard.

```
//@PURPOSE: This is a one-line sentence.
//
//@CLASSES:
//  xyza::Class1: one-line phrase
//  xyza::Class2: one-line phrase
//  ...
//
//@DESCRIPTION: This component ...
// ...
///Usage
///-----
// ...
```
← This section holds general information about the component, such as its purpose, the entities it implements, and a comprehensive, detailed description of the component as a whole.

← Ideally, each component will provide one or more examples, illustrating how the component can be used profitably in practice (see Volume II, section 6.16).

```
#include <xyza_component1.h>
#include <xyza_component2.h>
#include <xyza_component3.h>
// ...

#include <xyzb_component1.h>
#include <xyzb_component2.h>
#include <xyzc_component1.h>
#include <xyzc_component2.h>
#include <xyzc_component3.h>
#include <xyzd_component1.h>
// ...

#include <qrsx_component1.h>
// ...
#include <qrsz_component3.h>
// ...
#include <zyxq_component3.h>

#include <iosfwd>
// ...
```
← This section holds all `#include` directives required by this header file in order to make it self-sufficient with respect to compilation; all other relevant `#include` directives properly reside in the `.cpp` file. Note that the order is first components in the same package, then the same package group, then different package groups, and finally standard headers (ordered alphabetically within each subsection). Note the consistent use of angle brackets (<>) for the `#include` directives (section 1.5.1).

```
namespace MyLongCompanyName {
```
← Begin adding to our enterprise-wide namespace.

```
namespace abcz { class ClassA; }
namespace qrsy { class ClassA; }
namespace qrsy { class ClassB; }
```
← All local declarations of types defined in other packages go here (one declaration per line).

```
namespace xyza {
```
← Begin adding to our package-level namespace.

(continues)

(continued)

```
class ClassA;
class ClassB;
```

← All local declarations of types defined in the current package go here.

```
class Class1 {
    // ...
  public:
    Class1();
    // ...
    int func1(qrsy::ClassA *object);
    // ...
    int func2(qrsy::ClassB *object);

    // ...
};
```

← What comes next is typically a sequence of classes, with each class immediately followed by any associated free operators (see Volume II, section 6.14 for more details on class organization).

← Inline member functions are declared within class scope, but are defined near the bottom of the header file (after the component's logical interface).

```
bool operator==(const Class1& lhs,
                const Class1& rhs);
// ...
```

← At least one type in the signature of each operator must be defined locally (i.e., within the same component).

```
std::ostream&
operator<<(std::ostream& stream,
           const Class1& object);
// ...
```

← The output operator is usually defined in the `.cpp` file.

```
void swap(Class1& a, Class1& b);
```

← Any standard (operator-like) free-function declarations go here.

```
class Class2 {
    // ...
};
```

← This begins the second class, followed by its associated free operators...

```
// ...
        ⋮
```

← ... and so on.

(continues)

(continued)

```
// ===================================
//     INLINE FUNCTION DEFINITIONS
// ===================================
```
← Banner delimiting the logical interface of this component from its implementation.

```
inline
int Class1::func2(qrsy::ClassB *object)
{
    // ...
}

// ...
```
← All `inline` member function (and function template) definitions (see Volume II, section 6.3) whose source is accessible from outside this component come next. Note that the relative order of these definitions mirrors that of their declarations above.

```
}  // close package namespace
```
← End adding to our package-level namespace.

```
inline
bool xyza::operator==(const Class1& lhs,
                      const Class1& rhs)
{
    // ...
}

// ...
```
← In order to avoid (unsafe) self-declaration, define any `inline` free operators outside of the namespace in which they were declared (and in the same relative order).

```
inline
void xyza::swap(Class1& a, Class1& b)
{
    // ...
}

// ...
```
← Any necessary `inline` (operator-like) free function definitions follow in turn.

```
namespace abcmf {
template <>
struct IsBig<xyza::Class1>
                     : std::true_type {};
}  // close namespace abcmf

// ...
```
← Specializations of any templates (e.g., type traits) defined in other packages that involve types defined in this component (see Volume II, section 4.5) go dead last.

```
}  // close enterprise namespace
#endif
```
← End adding to our enterprise-wide namespace and close the (internal) include guard.

```
xyza_component.h
```

(a) Header file format

```
// xyza_component.cpp              -*-C++-*-
```
← The filename is always first.

```
// ...
// ...    (implementation overview)
// ...
```
← Provide any general overview (text, diagrams, etc.) that facilitates cognition.

```
#include <xyza_component.h>

#include <xyzb_component4.h>
#include <xyzb_component5.h>
// ...
#include <qrsx_component2.h>
// ...
#include <iostream>
// ...
```
← The header file for this component is always included as the first substantive (i.e., non-commentary) line of code. This include is followed by the inclusion of lower-level headers, again in hierarchical order using brackets (<>).

```
namespace MyLongCompanyName   {
namespace xyza {
```
← Begin adding to our enterprise-wide and package namespaces.

```
namespace {
    // ...
}   // close unnamed namespace
```
← Any (otherwise) "external-linkage" constructs intended to be local to this translation unit belong here.

```
int Class1::func1(qrsy::ClassA *object)
{
    // ...
    // ...
}
// ...
```
← Any other logical content, except for free (operator) function definitions, goes here.

```
}   // close package namespace
```
← End adding to our package-level namespace.

```
std::ostream&
xyza::operator<<(std::ostream& stream,
                 const Class1& object)
{
    // ...
}
// ...
```
← Define any exported noninline free operators outside the package namespace (in order to prevent self-declaration).

```
}   // close enterprise namespace
```
← End adding to our enterprise-wide namespace.

```
xyza_component.cpp
```

(b) Implementation file format

Figure 2-36: Standard "boilerplate" format for every component

Turning to the implementation file (Figure 2-36b), we again find the first line reserved for administrative use, followed by an optional description of the idiosyncrasies of the implementation in whatever format suits our purpose. The next section is necessarily the `#include` directives headed by the one incorporating our own component's interface and followed by those of progressively lower-level components (each, respectively, in alphabetical order): same package, lower-level packages, other package groups, and those in system-level headers.

Next, we open the enterprise and package namespaces together (as there is nothing that ever belongs between them)[64] and place there all remaining logical content, except for any remaining `extern` free (operator or aspect) function definitions, which, as in the `.h` file, should be implemented just after the close of the package namespace. The definitions in the `.cpp` file of any functions declared in the `.h` file should again appear in the same relative order. Any logical content whose linkage we wish to remain local to this translation unit — whether by declaring it `static`, in an unnamed namespace, or by convention (see section 2.7.3) — is implemented first. Finally, the enterprise-wide namespace is closed along with the commentary annotation, serving to indicate unambiguously the logical end of the `.cpp` file.

Guideline

Avoid architecturally significant use of the C++ `namespace` construct except for the enterprise-wide namespace and directly nested package namespaces.

The C++ `namespace` construct makes sense for partitioning names that span component boundaries. Within a single component, however, we nest all other logical content within either a `class` or `struct` (section 2.4.9), which better serves the role of a component-local namespace.[65] By limiting the architecturally significant use of the C++ `namespace` construct

---

[64] As of C++17, the alternate syntax

```
namespace MyLongCompanyName::xyza {
    // ...
}
```

is available, but we would not use it as we will typically close the respective package and package-group namespaces at different points in the source text.

[65] Note that there might be cases, e.g., involving versioning or to enable ADL, where other uses of namespaces (especially nonarchitectural ones) could be justified.

to just these two specific roles, we make clear our intent to enforce uniform and balanced levels of coherent logical and physical aggregation.

Given this uniform and limited use of C++ namespaces, we productively omit the two extra levels of indentation that might otherwise be associated with code nested within them, documenting the corresponding closing braces with simply

```
// close package namespace
```

and

```
// close enterprise namespace
```

respectively (using the generic "package" and "enterprise" in the comments ubiquitously primarily to avoid likely copy-and-paste errors).

In this section, we have provided a detailed sketch of the layout of top-level content within a component. While certainly not the only possible organization, this format has proven to be sufficient for essentially all of the software we write. In the following section, we present a series of fundamental component design rules that govern their physical characteristics and logical content. Adhering to this layout and subsequently discussed design rules enables us to fully realize the benefits of our component-based methodology.

2.6   Component Design Rules

All of our fundamental rules surrounding sound component-based software design — like the organization of the component content itself — is entirely independent of subject domain (i.e., the topic of logical functionality being implemented). Some of the practices we require — e.g., following certain specific layout and style rules (designed to minimize gratuitous inconsistency in rendering; see Volume II, Chapter 6) — can be fairly characterized as arbitrary; others cannot. In this section we delineate a concise, coherent, and important set of essential, objectively verifiable logical and physical design rules, which over the years have demonstrably improved the understandability, testability, and maintainability of our software.

Design Rule

**A component must comprise exactly one .h file and (at least) one corresponding
.cpp file having the same root name, which together satisfy the four fundamental
properties (sections 1.6 and 1.11) of components.**

As discussed in section 0.7, ensuring physical regularity is essential to exploiting many of the
benefits of our component-based development strategy. In Chapter 1 (sections 1.6 and 1.11),
we discussed four fundamental properties that differentiate components from mere (nominally
cohesive) .h / .cpp pairs. These four properties form the basis for such physical regularity as
well as the essential modularity that results, which we reprise here, cast as design rules.

Design Rule

**COMPONENT PROPERTY 1: A component's .cpp file includes its corresponding
.h file as the first substantive line of code.**

The goal here is that each component header file be self-sufficient with respect to compilation.
By including the .h file in a component's corresponding .cpp file we not only expose, during
translation, any syntax errors within the header itself, we also catch inconsistencies between
the .h and .cpp files — especially when we avoid definitions implemented directly within the
package namespace (section 2.5).

Moreover, when a second (separate) translation unit, such as a component-level test driver
(see Volume III, section 7.5), also includes the header file during testing, we have the added
opportunity (at link time) to catch bugs resulting from improper *strong* (section 1.2.3) external-
linkage symbol definitions — a defect that including the header in just a (single) test-driver file
alone would fail to detect.

By further requiring that this include directive be the first *substantive* (i.e., noncommentary) line of code (Component Property 1, section 1.6.1), we ensure that the header will compile cleanly in isolation and, thereby, forever eliminate any problems associated with include order.

Finally, recall from section 1.5.1 that all such `#include` directives are best implemented using angle brackets (`<>`), rather than double quotes (`""`), in order to increase flexibility during deployment (see section 2.15.1).

Design Rule

COMPONENT PROPERTY 2: Each logical construct effectively having external linkage defined in a component's `.cpp` file is declared in that component's `.h` file.

We assert that it is the job of the component writer to ensure that no truly external-linkage symbol definition is exported from a component's object (`.o`) file *unless* a corresponding declaration exists in that component's header file (Component Property 2, section 1.6.2). By exporting an unpublished symbol from a component's `.cpp` file, we run the risk of (1) having the definition collide with other symbols within a program, and (2) tempting clients to access the definition via a local declaration, thereby introducing an unnecessarily hard-to-trace ("backdoor") dependency. For classes that are logically "local" to a component, such as those that might otherwise be found in the unnamed namespace, but must be *locally declared* within the `.h` file, we may elect to simulate internal bindage by choosing — purely by convention (see section 2.7.3) — a class name that, like a nested class, is guaranteed not to collide with names outside the component. The method declarations within such classes — i.e., the class definitions themselves — having external or dual bindage are therefore exempt from this rule.

Design Rule

COMPONENT PROPERTY 3: Each logical construct effectively having external bindage declared in the `.h` file of a component (if defined at all) is defined within that component.

Providing a definition separate from the one component in which it is principally declared and documented (e.g., see Figure 1-45, section 1.6.3) induces coupling in ways that are not reflective of the apparent logical decomposition as required for modularity (Component Property 3, section 1.6.3). By "effectively" we mean that this rule also applies to a dual-bindage construct (section 1.3.4) that is deliberately declared, but not defined (e.g., using an `extern` template declaration; section 1.3.16) within the header of a component, and then defined explicitly in just a single `.cpp` file, thereby enabling a *unique* link-time dependency (section 1.8). Note, however, that member functions declared `private` purely to suppress unwanted behavior (refer to Figure 2-37) — such as (a) copy construction or copy assignment,[66] or (b) an undesirable conversion[67] — may be left unimplemented; that they are declared private makes any external attempt to invoke them futile.

```
class Foo {

    // ...

    private:
        Foo(const Foo&);             // (a) not implemented
        Foo& operator=(const Foo&);  // (a) not implemented

        Foo(int);                    // (b) not implemented

    public:
        Foo(char);                   // (b) implemented in this component

    // ...
};
```

Figure 2-37: (Classical) use of `private` to suppress generated behavior

---

[66] C++11 allows us to use the preferred syntax
```
Foo(const Foo&) = deleted;
```
and
```
Foo& operator=(const Foo&) = deleted;
```
instead.

[67] C++11 allows us to use the preferred syntax
```
Foo(int) = deleted;
```
instead.

Design Rule

COMPONENT PROPERTY 4: A component's functionality is accessed only via a #include of its header file and never by a local extern declaration.

A change to the logical interface of one component ought to trigger recompilation of any component that uses it. As discussed in section 1.4, substituting local `extern` declarations for the appropriate `#include` directive (see Figure 1-35, section 1.4) short circuits this safeguard and turns compile-time errors into more expensive link-time or runtime ones. What's more, as we saw in section 1.11, the welcome by-product of always following this rule (section 1.11.1) is that we can efficiently deduce the complete set of a component's physical dependencies simply by inspecting the `#include` directives in its combined `.h` and `.cpp` files.

Design Rule

Every logical construct we write outside of a file that defines main must reside within a component.

Insisting on packaging *all* of our source code in uniform physical modules ensures that the form of each (physical) component is independent of its logical content. Still, we routinely encounter suggestions for "optimizations" based on what individual developers feel are "compelling" reasons. Requiring a `.cpp` file for every component might initially sound like an unnecessary burden on the developer. For example, it might seem like it is "no big deal" to omit the `.cpp` file for the day-of-week enumeration shown in Figure 2-38.[68] After all, what would go in it?

---

[68] Recall from section 2.4.9 that we prefer to use a `struct` (see Figure 2-22, section 2.4.9) to implement a third level of namespace in which to nest constants, `static` data, functions (see Figures 2-22 and 2-23, section 2.4.9), `typedef`s, and `enum`s (see Figures 2-38 and 2-39, below) declared within a component.

```
// bdlt_dayofweek.h

// ...

#ifndef INCLUDED_BDLT_DAYOFWEEK
#define INCLUDED_BDLT_DAYOFWEEK

namespace MyLongCompanyName {
namespace bdlt {

struct DayOfWeek {
    enum Enum {
        SUN = 0,
        SUNDAY = SUN,
        MON
        MONDAY = MON,
        TUE,
        TUESDAY = TUE,
        // ...
    };
};

}  // close package namespace
}  // close enterprise namespace
#endif
```

Syntax error: missing comma

Figure 2-38: `.h` file with no corresponding `.cpp` file (BAD IDEA)

Now consider keeping the structure of a component intact by having a trivial implementation file that merely includes the header as in Figure 2-39. The component can now be compiled independently (like any other component), thereby exposing immediately many common compilation errors. Consider also that the original nonuniform physical structure consisting of just a `.h` file introduces a subtle bias that might influence some as to whether a subsequently added helper function (e.g., `toAscii`) is implemented as an `inline` function — i.e., entirely in the (preexisting) header or in the (not-yet-created) `.cpp` file. By the same token, allowing the physical structure to be affected by logical changes as simple as altering the `inline` status of a single function is also something we very much want to avoid.

```
// bdlt_dayofweek.h                    // bdlt_dayofweek.cpp
#ifndef INCLUDED_BDLT_DAYOFWEEK        #include <bdlt_dayofweek.h>
#define INCLUDED_BDLT_DAYOFWEEK

// ...

namespace MyLongCompanyName {
namespace bdlt {

struct DayOfWeek {
    enum Enum {
        SUN = 0,
        SUNDAY = SUN,
        MON,   // Bug fixed!
        MONDAY = MON,
        TUE,
        TUESDAY = TUE,
        // ...
    };
};

}  // close package namespace
}  // close enterprise namespace
#endif
```

bdlt_dayofweek

Figure 2-39: "Trivial" component implementing a day-of-week enumeration

What might seem like a simple nested enumeration that barely deserves a header file of its own could very well evolve into a mature component supporting a variety of (value-semantic) operations (see Volume II, sections 4.1 and 4.3), many of which (e.g., printing, streaming) would result in gratuitous compile-time coupling if implemented in the `.h` file (see section 3.10). Figure 2-40 shows a more fully developed component for enumerating days of the week.[69] This pattern can then be used to quickly produce other enumeration components along with their associated test drivers (see Volume III, Chapter 10).

---

[69] C++11 introduced the notion of an *enumeration class*, which affords many of the desirable properties achieved by nesting an enumeration in a class.

```
// bdlt_dayofweek.h                                             -*-C++-*-
#ifndef INCLUDED_BDLT_DAYOFWEEK
#define INCLUDED_BDLT_DAYOFWEEK

//@PURPOSE: Provide support for enumerating the seven days of the week.
// ...

#include <iosfwd>

namespace MyLongCompanyName {
namespace bdlt {

struct DayOfWeek {
    // This 'struct' provides a namespace for enumerating the ...

    // TYPES
    enum Enum {
        e_SUN = 1, e_SUNDAY    = e_SUN,
        e_MON,     e_MONDAY     = e_MON,
        e_TUE,     e_TUESDAY    = e_TUE,
        e_WED,     e_WEDNESDAY  = e_WED,
        e_THU,     e_THURSDAY   = e_THU,
        e_FRI,     e_FRIDAY     = e_FRI,
        e_SAT,     e_SATURDAY   = e_SAT
    };

    // CLASS METHODS
    template <class STREAM>
    static STREAM& bdexStreamIn(STREAM&           stream,
                                DayOfWeek::Enum&  variable,
                                int               version);
        // Assign to the specified 'variable' the value read from the
        // specified 'stream' using the specified 'version' format, ...

    template <class STREAM>
    static STREAM& bdexStreamOut(STREAM&          stream,
                                 DayOfWeek::Enum value,
                                 int             version);
        // Write the value of the specified 'value', using the specified
        // 'version' format, to the specified output 'stream', and ...

    static std::ostream& print(std::ostream&   stream,
                               DayOfWeek::Enum value,
                               int             level         = 0,
                               int             spacesPerLevel = 4);
        // Write the string representation of the specified enumeration
        // 'value' to the specified output 'stream', and return ...

    static const char *toAscii(Enum dayOfWeek);
        // Return the abbreviated character-string representation of the
        // enumerator corresponding to the specified 'dayOfWeek'.  ...
```

(continues)

(continued)

```
};

// FREE OPERATORS
std::ostream& operator<<(std::ostream&    stream,
                         DayOfWeek::Enum dayOfWeek);
    // Write the string representation of the specified enumeration
    // 'value' to the specified output 'stream' in a single-line format,
    // ...

// FREE FUNCTIONS
template <class STREAM>
STREAM& bdexStreamIn(STREAM&            stream,
                     DayOfWeek::Enum& variable,
                     int               version);
    // Load into the specified 'variable' the 'DayOfWeek::Enum' value
    // read from the specified input 'stream' using the specified
    // 'version' format, ...

template <class STREAM>
STREAM& bdexStreamOut(STREAM&                stream,
                      const DayOfWeek::Enum& value,
                      int                    version);
    // Write the specified 'value', using the specified 'version' format,
    // to the specified output 'stream', and return a reference to
    // 'stream'.  ...

// ========================================================================
//                      INLINE FUNCTION DEFINITIONS
// ========================================================================

// CLASS METHODS
template <class STREAM>
STREAM& DayOfWeek::bdexStreamIn(STREAM&            stream,
                                DayOfWeek::Enum& variable,
                                int               version)
{
    // ...
    return stream;
}

template <class STREAM>
STREAM& DayOfWeek::bdexStreamOut(STREAM&            stream,
                                 DayOfWeek::Enum value,
                                 int             version)
{
    // ...
    return stream;
}

}  // close package namespace
```

(continues)

(continued)

```
// FREE OPERATORS
inline
std::ostream& bdlt::operator<<(std::ostream&   stream,
                               DayOfWeek::Enum value)
{
    return DayOfWeek::print(stream, value, 0, -1);
}


// FREE FUNCTIONS
template <class STREAM>
STREAM& bdlt::bdexStreamIn(STREAM&          stream,
                           DayOfWeek::Enum& variable,
                           int              version)
{
    return DayOfWeek::bdexStreamIn(stream, variable, version);
}


template <class STREAM>
STREAM& bdlt::bdexStreamOut(STREAM&                stream,
                            const DayOfWeek::Enum& value,
                            int                    version)
{
    return DayOfWeek::bdexStreamOut(stream, value, version);
}


}  // close enterprise namespace
#endif
```

```
// bdlt_dayofweek.cpp                                             -*-C++-*-
#include <bdlt_dayofweek.h>

#include <iostream>
#include <cassert>

namespace MyLongCompanyName {
namespace bdlt {

// CLASS METHODS
std::ostream& DayOfWeek::print(std::ostream&   stream,
                               DayOfWeek::Enum value,
                               int             level,
                               int             spacesPerLevel)
{
    // ...
    stream << toAscii(value);
    // ...
    return stream;
}
```

(continues)

(continued)

```
const char *DayOfWeek::toAscii(DayOfWeek::Enum dayOfWeek)
{
#define CASE(X) case(e_ ## X): return #X
    switch (dayOfWeek) {
      CASE(SUN);
      CASE(MON);
      CASE(TUE);
      CASE(WED);
      CASE(THU);
      CASE(FRI);
      CASE(SAT);
      default:
        assert("Invalid Day Of Week" && 0);
    }
#undef CASE
}

}  // close package namespace
}  // close enterprise namespace
```

Note rare but occasionally valuable *local* use of the C++ preprocessor.

Always clean up after yourself!

bdlt_dayofweek

Figure 2-40: Library component implementing full-featured day-of-week type

Note that even a component implementing a single *protocol* (i.e., pure abstract interface) class (section 1.7.5) must have a .cpp file (1) to ensure that the header compiles in isolation, and (2) to hold the noninline destructor. Moreover, it will also have an associated .t.cpp file to implement the component-level test driver, which — as with a component defining an enumeration — is there to provide the needed *redundancy* (see Volume III, section 7.2) to ensure that the component is, *and remains*, implemented properly.

The perceived need for "private" header files is another oft-heard reason to deviate from our established norm. Private headers are undesirable because, like inter-component friendship (see below), they grant privileged access beyond the standard public contract (see Volume II, section 5.2) to physically separate modules. As discussed in section 1.4, however, full support for private *data* coupled with the ability to have intermediate interfaces without having to compromise performance in a language such as C++ obviates all use of private headers. Additional reasons to avoid selectively hiding component header files (other than as a pure deployment optimization, see section 2.15) are discussed in section 3.9.7.

Regularity alone is sufficient to justify the strict physical form of components.[70] Regardless of how seemingly harmless a proposed deviation might appear, the time and effort it takes to consider the efficacy of each physical irregularity (often repeated with each new set of eyes that sees it) should make it clear that, for large-scale systems, it is simply *never*[71] a good idea to deviate from the one fixed and regular component structure.

Design Rule

The `.h` file of each component must contain a unique and predictable include guard: INCLUDED_*PACKAGE_COMPONENTBASE* (e.g., `INCLUDED_BDLT_DATETIME`).

Unique *internal* include guards are required to avoid duplicate definitions resulting from reconvergence in the include graph of a single translation unit. Requiring these include guards to be mechanically predictable (i.e., from the component name alone) enables us to verify them with automated tools:

```
// bdlt_datetime.h                                          -*-C++-*-
#ifndef INCLUDED_BDLT_DATETIME
#define INCLUDED_BDLT_DATETIME
// ...
#endif
```

This predictability also enabled the use of (now deprecated) *external* ("redundant") include guards (section 1.5.3).

---

[70] David Sankel, one of our more well-known and outspoken team leaders at Bloomberg, put it this way (in his review of this manuscript):

> More generally, regularity in rendering enables future changes to be applied more uniformly (and therefore more likely automatically) throughout the code base. If there is, say, a change in convention or an enhancement to the C++ language itself that should be applied everywhere, a regular code base makes this possible with minimal cost, whereas unnecessary diversity frequently implies that every component must be updated "by hand," with a differential in cost that can be staggering.

[71] Note that, purely as a deployment optimization (e.g., for very low-level components in, say, the C Standard Library), we do acknowledge the potential benefit of distributing the functionality implemented within a single component across multiple `.c` files (section 2.2.12), but never across multiple `.h` files (see also section 2.15.10).

Design Rule

Logical constructs having other than internal bindage (e.g., inline functions) that are exported by a component must be first declared (within the header file) and then defined separately (within the same component), with all free (e.g., operator) functions defined outside the namespace in which they were declared.

In particular, this design rule requires that inline functions (which have dual bindage) not be defined in class scope to ensure that there is an interface that is separate from implementation (see Volume II, section 5.2). For reasons elucidated in section 1.3.1, free operators, as well as any other free (aspect) functions, are to be defined outside the package namespace in which they are declared. By simply following our prescribed component layout (see Figure 2-36, section 2.5), we go a long way toward ensuring that this important rule is satisfied.

Design Rule

Runtime initialization of file- or namespace-scope static objects is not permitted.

Runtime initialization of file- or namespace-scope static variables, especially in files that don't also contain `main`, has been and, unfortunately, continues to be a perennial source of software defects, as illustrated by the singleton-registry (section 1.2.5). There are, however, several other compelling reasons for ardently avoiding such misguided initializations (see Volume II, section 6.2).

COROLLARY: The `.h` file of each component must compile in isolation.

This requirement is assured to be satisfied simply by adhering to Component Property 1 of section 1.6.1 as required above, but we state it here explicitly for emphasis.

Guideline

The `.h` file should contain only those `#include` directives (or, where appropriate, local ["forward"] class declarations) necessary to ensure that the header file compiles in isolation.

At the same time, we want to avoid any unnecessary `#include` directives (or even local declarations) in header files. As it turns out, there are just a few common cases where it would be necessary or appropriate to `#include` another header within a header. The five most common (by far) reasons for properly including a header within a header are summarized in Figure 2-41.[72]

Justifying a `#include` directive within a header file:

(a) **Is-A** (or any form of inheritance)

(b) **Has-A** (an embedded object but *not* Holds-A or Uses-In-The-Interface)

(c) **Inline** (any object used substantively in an inline definition)

(d) **Enum** (i.e., enumerated values)

(e) **Typedef** (to an explicit template specialization — e.g., `std::string`)

Figure 2-41: Common situations in which one header properly includes another

When deriving a class, `Bar`, from another class, `Foo` (defined in a separate component, **xyza_foo**), it is always necessary for the compiler to have already seen the definition of `Foo` in order to compile `Bar`. Hence, it is essential that we place a `#include <xyza_foo.h>` directive in the header, `pqrs_bar.h`, defining `Bar` (Figure 2-41a):

```
// pqrs_bar.h
#include <xyza_foo.h>          // included definition
// ...
class Bar : public xyza::Foo { // Is-A
    // ...

};
```

---

[72] There are, to be sure, other circumstances that would dictate inclusion of a header in another header in order to ensure self-sufficiency with respect to compilation as required by Component Property 1, section 1.6.1. Covariant return types are one such example. Another reason would be when employing something from the C++ Standard Library, for which local declarations are explicitly disallowed.

The same is true for embedded objects (Figure 2-41b):

```
// pqrs_bar.h
#include <xyza_foo.h> // included definition
// ...
class Bar {
    xyza::Foo d_foo;  // Has-A
    // ...

};
```

But *not* so for objects that are held (i.e., via their address):

```
// pqrs_bar.h
// ...
namespace xyza { class Foo; } // local ("forward") declaration73
// ...
class Bar {
    xyza::Foo *d_foo_p; // Holds-A
    // ...

};
```

Contrary to what some might think, it is not necessary to `#include` the type of an object in a component's header just because the type is used in the interface (section 1.7.3) of a function in that header. As Figure 2-42 illustrates, this assertion is true even if objects of that type are passed[74] and returned[75] by value.

---

[73] Keeping such local declarations in sync can be facilitated either by automated static-analysis tools, or by dint of forwarding headers, implemented as their own components using the same component-based design rules (presented in this section) as apply to the underlying component itself.

[74] Note that we consistently pass user-defined types (as arguments) by reference-to-`const` rather than by value (see Volume II, section 6.12).

[75] Even in modern C++ (C++11 and later), we would continue to return objects by value only when they do not allocate memory (see Volume II, section 4.10).

```
// pqrs_bar.h

// ...

namespace xyza { class Foo; }   // local ("forward") declaration

// ...

class Bar {
    // ...
                         ┌─────────────────────────┐
                         │  Returned by Value       │
    public:              │  (BAD IDEA for UDTs      │
                         │  that allocate memory)   │
    // ...               └─────────────────────────┘
                                          ┌──────────────────────┐
                                          │  Passed by Value      │
                                          │  (BAD IDEA for UDTs)  │
                                          └──────────────────────┘
    xyza::Foo someFunction(xyza::Foo foo);   // Uses-In-The-Interface

};

// ...
```

Figure 2-42: Uses-In-the-Interface does *not* imply a `#include` directive in the header.

When a type is used substantively in an `inline` function, the compiler must have already seen the definition of this type in order to compile it. The same is true for a type used substantively in an (implicitly instantiated) function template. Although some compilers might not detect the missing definition until the function is invoked (instantiated), including the header is the right thing to do to ensure that (1) the header file compiles in isolation with all compilers, and (2) client code always compiles when invoking the function. It is therefore necessary to `#include`, in the header file defining an `inline` function (or function template), the header defining any class used substantively within the body of that function's definition (Figure 2-41c):

```
// prqs_bar.h

#include <xyza_foo.h>

// ...

class Bar {

    // ...

   public:

    // ...

    void function();

    // ...

};

// ...

inline

void Bar::function() { Foo obj; /* ... */ }  // used substantively

// ...
```

> Note that this declaration does *not* need to be specified using the `inline` keyword in conforming implementations of the C++ Language Standard.

Historically, variables of enumerated types could never be locally (i.e., "forward") declared.[76] For the same reason (among others) that we choose never to "forward declare" global variables (section 1.11), we also choose never to declare variables of enumerated type locally[77] and instead always access the (complete) definition via its associated header file (Figure 2-41d):

```
// pqrs_bar.h
#include <xyza_foo.h>              // defines enumerated type
// ...
class Bar {
  // ...
  public:
    // ...
    xyza::Foo::Enum function();  // non-inline function
    // ...
};
```

---

[76] That changed somewhat in C++11; however, such a "forward declaration" would be for some fixed integral type having external bindage (section 1.3.4).

[77] Especially in C++11, where we might be tempted to do so ("attractive nuisance") in order to elide our compile-time dependency on the specific enumerators when we don't need to know them.

Finally, when a type is not a class, but instead a `typedef` to an explicit specialization of a class template,[78] such as `std::string` or `std::ostream`, we cannot use the conventional approach to locally declare the class. In the case of `std::ostream`, we can `#include <iosfwd>` to "forward declare" `std::ostream`; unfortunately, no similar mechanism exists for `std::string`, and so we are forced to `#include <string>` itself, even if its definition is not needed (Figure 2-41e)[79]:

```
// pqrs_bar.h
#include <string>              // included template definition
// ...
class Bar {
    std::string *d_string_p;  // Holds-A ('string' is a type alias)
    // ...
};
```

Except for the five specific cases outlined in Figure 2-41, it is almost always a mistake to `#include` a header within a header. There are other, rare situations, such as *covariant return types*, in which including a header in a header may be warranted; fortunately, the compiler will always warn you of such cases, provided of course that you adhere assiduously to Component Property 1 (section 1.6.1).[80]

DEFINITION: A *transitive include* implies that a client is relying on the use of one header to include another in order to make direct use of the functionality afforded indirectly via the nested include.

Design Rule

Any *direct* substantive use of one component by another requires the corresponding `#include` directive to be present *directly* in the client component (in either the `.h` or `.cpp` file, but not both) unless indirect inclusion is implied by intrinsic and substantial compile-time dependency — i.e., public inheritance (nothing else).

---

[78] Commonly referred to as a *type alias*.

[79] Note that it is invalid to declare anything in the C++ Standard Library locally.

[80] The use of forwarding headers to facilitate code migration, particularly involving templates, is another entirely separate motivation for including headers within headers. Note that the purpose of a forwarding header can be realized through the use of an additional component following the same rules as described in this section.

> **COROLLARY: Transitive includes are not permitted, except to access a public base class of a type whose definition is included directly.**

As ever, we are well advised to avoid depending on behavior that is merely an artifact of a particular implementation choice. That the artifact is a necessary physical consequence of a logically encapsulated implementation detail does not release us from this important responsibility. Hence, relying on one component header to indirectly include another, which we refer to as a *transitive include*, is seldom wise. Of all the common circumstances listed in Figure 2-41 for properly including a header within a header, only Is-A — i.e., specifically *public* inheritance, as illustrated in Figure 2-43 — provides sufficient indicia that the desired #include directive will necessarily always be present in the included header.

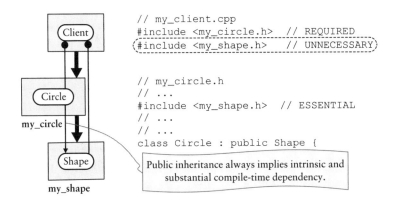

Figure 2-43: Public inheritance implies intrinsic compile-time dependency.

In all other cases, even a minor change to the component could eliminate the need for it to nest an include directive for a lower-level component in the higher-level component's header. With private inheritance or Has-A, even a minor change to the implementation of the higher-level component could eliminate any need for it to include the header of the lower-level one in its header. For example, given that Point in Figure 2-44 is not used in the interface, any dependency on it could be removed entirely, and replaced with a pair of raw integers without causing any change to the logical (programmatically accessible) interface.

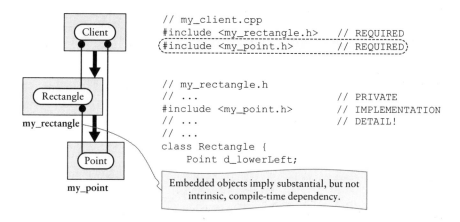

```
                        // my_client.cpp
                        #include <my_rectangle.h>     // REQUIRED
                        #include <my_point.h>         // REQUIRED


                        // my_rectangle.h
                        // ...                         // PRIVATE
                        #include <my_point.h>          // IMPLEMENTATION
                        // ...                         // DETAIL!
                        // ...
                        class Rectangle {
                            Point d_lowerLeft;
```

Embedded objects imply substantial, but not intrinsic, compile-time dependency.

Figure 2-44: Uses-In-The-Implementation (e.g., Has-A) is never intrinsic.

Even if `Point` *were* used in the interface, it would not be difficult to *insulate* (see section 3.11.1) its use by replacing the Has-A relationship with Holds-A (section 1.7.4), and substituting any `inline` functions (Figure 2-41c) that accept or return `Point` in the interface with noninline ones. Clients of both components that did not include the lower-level component's header directly would then be forced to *rework* their code. Hence, the header file of any component included by another for implementation purposes alone must not be relied upon to include that (lower-level) header.

Logical relationships such as Uses-In-The-Interface are also *not* sufficient to justify physical reliance on nested includes, even when the type is an enumeration (Figure 2-41d) or a `typedef` to an explicit template specialization (Figure 2-41e), which historically could not (or, in C++11, should not[81]) be declared locally. As illustrated in Figure 2-45, even minor interface modifications such as replacing an enumerated return type with an `int` (often a good idea), or escalating a seldom-used, nonprimitive function to another, higher-level (e.g., utility) component (see section 3.2.7), might eliminate the physical dependency, and obviate having the nested `#include` directive — again with potentially little (if any) reworking of client code, provided this rule is followed.

---

[81] Enumerations as of C++11, as with `static` data, should not be declared locally, to avoid type mismatches due to external bindage (section 1.3.4).

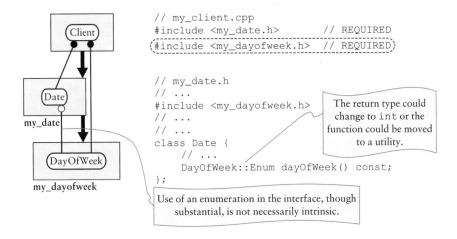

Figure 2-45: Even Uses-In-The-Interface is not necessarily intrinsic.

Hence, with the sole exception of public inheritance, whenever one component substantively uses the functionality provided in another *directly*, it should also always include that component's .h file *directly*.

Design Imperative

Cyclic physical dependencies among components are not permitted.

A component, by definition, is the smallest unit of physical aggregation, and the allowed dependencies of all physical aggregates must be acyclic (section 2.2.24). Two components are cyclically dependent if compiling, linking, or even testing either one necessarily requires the presence of the other.

For example, suppose that we have two components, **xyza_array1** and **xyza_array2**, each of which defines a user-defined type that represents an array of arbitrary type — the only difference being the way in which memory for contained objects is organized: in-place versus out-of-place.[82] Now suppose that each of these two array types provides a constructor to convert from the other type. That is, there is a constructor in class xyza::Array1 that

---

[82] While xyza::Array1 (like std::vector) provides optimal access to contained elements, xyza::Array2 trades an extra level of indirection when accessing array elements for significantly improved performance during arbitrary insert and remove operations for heavy-weight object types, as well as preserving the address of a given array element, even when the underlying array resizes or its index position changes.

takes a reference to a `const xyza::Array2`, and vice versa. Notice that the implied cycle-inducing `#include` directives shown in Figure 2-46a happen to be placed directly within the `.h` files of these components. Moving the `#include` directives to the respective `.cpp` files (Figure 2-46b) affects the character of that coupling from a client's perspective — i.e., makes it link-time instead of compile-time (see section 3.10) — but in no way mitigates the mutual physical dependency (section 1.8).

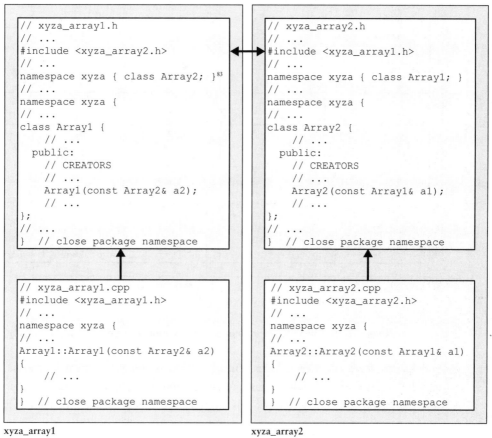

```
// xyza_array1.h
// ...
#include <xyza_array2.h>
// ...
namespace xyza { class Array2; }83
// ...
namespace xyza {
// ...
class Array1 {
    // ...
  public:
    // CREATORS
    // ...
    Array1(const Array2& a2);
    // ...
};
// ...
}  // close package namespace
```

```
// xyza_array2.h
// ...
#include <xyza_array1.h>
// ...
namespace xyza { class Array1; }
// ...
namespace xyza {
// ...
class Array2 {
    // ...
  public:
    // CREATORS
    // ...
    Array2(const Array1& a1);
    // ...
};
// ...
}  // close package namespace
```

```
// xyza_array1.cpp
#include <xyza_array1.h>
// ...
namespace xyza {
// ...
Array1::Array1(const Array2& a2)
{
    // ...
}
}  // close package namespace
```

```
// xyza_array2.cpp
#include <xyza_array2.h>
// ...
namespace xyza {
// ...
Array2::Array2(const Array1& a1)
{
    // ...
}
}  // close package namespace
```

xyza_array1   xyza_array2

(a) Mutual `#include` directives exposed in `.h` files (BAD IDEA!)

---

[83] This seemingly redundant class declaration following the (cyclic) `#include` is necessary. Attempting to compile this code as elided here will result in infinite recursion. Adding the requisite internal `#include` guards (section 1.5.2) will manage the recursion but now, without this unguarded forward class declaration, when we compile `xyza_array2.cpp`, it will `#include xyza_array2.h`, which will immediately `#include xyza_array1.h`, which in turn will immediately (again) `#include xyza_array2.h`, which this time is a no-op! Now, unless we have also forward declared `Array2` to be in the **xyza** namespace before the class definition of `Array1`, the compiler will not (yet) know that `Array2` is a type and the member function declaration `Array1(const Array2& A2)` will fail to compile. **tl;dr**: Never allow cyclically dependent headers (and ignore this footnote).

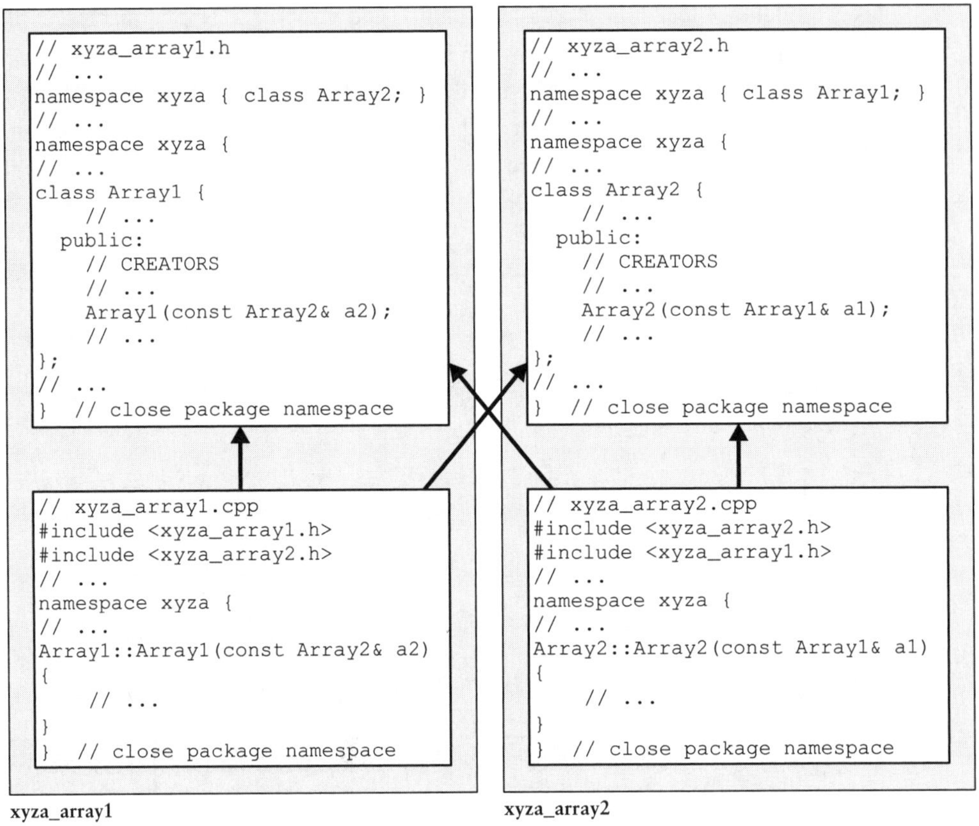

```
// xyza_array1.h
// ...
namespace xyza { class Array2; }
// ...
namespace xyza {
// ...
class Array1 {
    // ...
  public:
    // CREATORS
    // ...
    Array1(const Array2& a2);
    // ...
};
// ...
}  // close package namespace
```

```
// xyza_array1.cpp
#include <xyza_array1.h>
#include <xyza_array2.h>
// ...
namespace xyza {
// ...
Array1::Array1(const Array2& a2)
{
    // ...
}
}  // close package namespace
```

xyza_array1

```
// xyza_array2.h
// ...
namespace xyza { class Array1; }
// ...
namespace xyza {
// ...
class Array2 {
    // ...
  public:
    // CREATORS
    // ...
    Array2(const Array1& a1);
    // ...
};
// ...
}  // close package namespace
```

```
// xyza_array2.cpp
#include <xyza_array2.h>
#include <xyza_array1.h>
// ...
namespace xyza {
// ...
Array2::Array2(const Array1& a1)
{
    // ...
}
}  // close package namespace
```

xyza_array2

(b) Mutual #include directives buried in .cpp files (BAD IDEA!)

Figure 2-46: Cyclic physical dependencies among components (BAD IDEA!)

Anticipating *levelization* techniques, elucidated in section 3.5, we might choose to eliminate the cycles in Figure 2-46 by making one component fully independent of the other. For
example, Figure 2-47 shows the perhaps arbitrary decision to enable efficient construction of
xyza::Array1 from xyza::Array2, but not vice versa. To enable conversion in the other
direction, xyza::Array1 provides a by-value conversion operator. Of course, we could just
as easily have chosen to go the other way, with **xyza_array2** depending on **xyza_array1**.
Either way, we would fail to achieve the full flexibility of independent reuse, not to mention
running afoul of tight control over memory allocation (see Volume II, section 4.10).

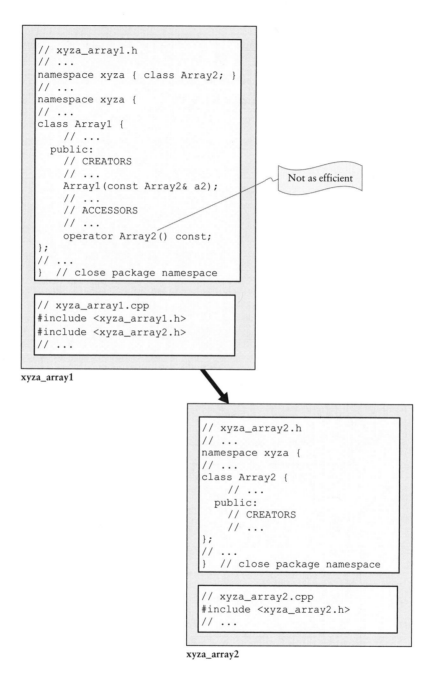

Figure 2-47: Arbitrary levelization, sacrificing performance (BAD IDEA!)

Any need for implicit conversion here is dubious. A more flexible, efficient solution is achieved by *escalating* (see section 3.5.2) the cyclically interdependent conversion routines to a third component (and making them explicit) as shown in Figure 2-48. Instead of returning the converted object by value, the value is loaded into a preexisting object passed in (by address) as the first argument (see Volume II, section 6.12). Now, both `xyza::Array1` and `xyza::Array2` can be used independently of each other. Clients that depend on just one of these classes do not *pay* in any way (e.g., compile time, link time, or executable size) for the other. Only those clients that (1) use both arrays, and (2) also need to convert between them, link in all the code.

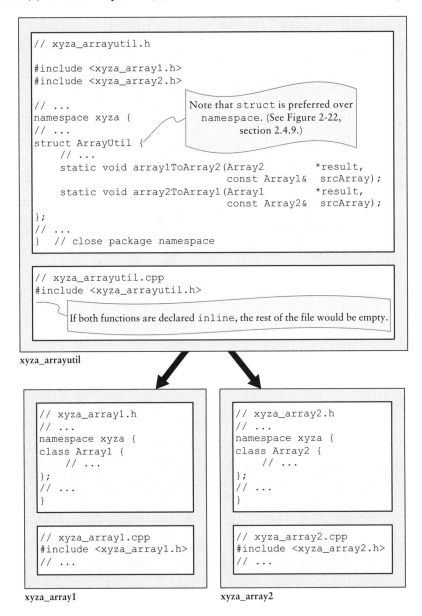

Figure 2-48: Proper levelization introducing third ("utility") component

The *levelization* technique illustrated here, namely, *escalation* (see section 3.5.2), is but one of many discussed in section 3.5 that can be used for eliminating cyclic, excessive, or otherwise undesirable link-time dependencies. In Chapter 3 we will explore a variety of ways in which to express our designs so that they can be realized in terms of highly modular components while minimizing both compile- and link-time physical dependencies.

Design Imperative

Access to the private details of a logical construct must not span the boundaries of the physical aggregate in which it is defined — e.g., "long-distance" (inter-component) friendship is not permitted.

Perhaps the most fundamental and well-known principle of modular programming (section 0.4) is that of hiding each low-level design decision behind a single, clear, and well-defined inter-face. Not coincidentally, it has been observed that code that is likely to change together should reside in close physical proximity within a system (see section 3.3.6). The component, being our fundamental unit of both logical and physical design (section 0.7), serves to encapsulate and hide these low-level details. Having both logical and physical modularity coincide is what enables a new version of a component to replace the previous one independently of any other component (see Volume II, section 5.5). Note that exposing implementation details through the use of protected access is similarly problematic (see section 3.11.5.3).

Consider the **xyza_hashtable** component in Figure 2-49. An xyza::HashtableIter class provides read-only access to all key-value pairs in a given xyza::Hashtable object. The xyza::HashtableManip class, in addition to iteration, provides the ability to selectively remove entries from a modifiable xyza::Hashtable. The implementations of both the iterator and the manipulator will naturally be strongly influenced by (if not *depend on*) the private details of the container (see section 1.7.4).[84] Clearly, all three classes necessarily share knowledge of private details and therefore should be encapsulated within a single atomic physical module (i.e., a component).

---

[84] In this contemporary iterator pattern (elucidated in section 1.7.4), the constructors of both xyza::HashtableIter and xyza::HashtableManip are declared private, with each class declaring xyza::Hashtable as a friend.

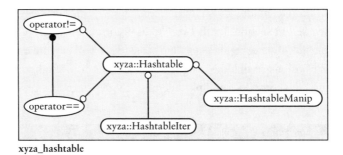

xyza_hashtable

Figure 2-49: Logical view of the `xyza_hashtable` component

For argument's sake, consider instead placing each of these classes in separate components as illustrated in the component/class diagram of Figure 2-50. Now, even an ostensibly compatible change to a local implementation detail of `xyza::Hashtable` might force a corresponding change in either or both lower-level components. By the same token, making any changes to the private implementation (e.g., private constructor) of either `xyza::HashtableIter` or `xyza::HashtableManip` could outright break the container in the higher-level component unless it too is updated in lockstep.

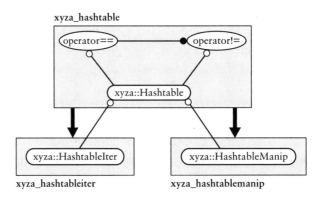

Figure 2-50: "Long distance" (i.e., inter-component) friendship (BAD IDEA!)

Granting nonlocal logical entities private access often leads to unexpectedly severe inflexibility and needless expense. The more physically distant the "privileged" software, the greater the burden. Maintainability alone justifies colocating an iterator with its container, but consider that, whenever an object in a higher-level component has private *modifiable* access, our ability to test the lower-level component hierarchically is lost (see Figure 2-79, section 2.14.3).

Giving friend access to a class in a separate component also happens to make it easy for a rogue implementation sporting the same name to be inadvertently granted (or steal) privileged access.[85] By insisting that private access not extend beyond component boundaries, we are able to substitute one valid implementation of a component's published *contract* (see Volume II, section 5.5) for another — irrespective of the private details of every other component. Not surprisingly, this notion of ensuring fine-grained physical *substitutability* is among the most fundamental in our development methodology.

Guideline

Aim for one (public) class per component unless there is an engineering justification to do otherwise.

The *size* of a component, its *complexity*, and its overall *quality* affect our ability to understand, maintain, and test it effectively (see Volume III, section 7.3). Moreover, preserving a fine-grained physical structure (section 0.7) helps us to minimize physical dependencies and thereby facilitates independent reuse. We therefore strive to limit (ideally to one) the number of classes in any given component unless there is a compelling engineering reason to do otherwise. The need for colocation will manifest if placing classes in separate components would result in either (1) *long-distance* (i.e., inter-component) friendship, or (2) a cyclic physical dependency (which, in practice, *very* rarely[86] arises).[87] We must therefore avoid any design that might contain a large or, worse, unbounded cluster of such tightly coupled classes (see section 3.1.9).

In this section we presented several important, objectively verifiable design rules that make our software measurably more understandable, testable, and maintainable. Each component has at least one .cpp file (and possibly more[88]), but always exactly one .h file, all having the same root name. Together, these files satisfy the four properties of components delineated in Chapter 1 (sections 1.6 and 1.11): (1) include — using angle brackets (<>) rather than double quotes (" ") — the .h file first in the .cpp file, (2) declare all external-linkage definitions in the .h file,

---

[85] **lakos96**, section 3.6.2, pp. 144–146

[86] All known practical use cases effectively requiring cyclic dependencies among classes involve mutual compile-time recursion (see Volume II, section 4.5). We always prefer acyclic logical solutions — e.g., see Figure 2-54, section 2.7.4.

[87] Two other engineering reasons for colocating outwardly accessible classes defined at package-namespace scope (as opposed to component-private ones, see section 2.7.1), along with these first two (primary) criteria, are discussed in detail in section 3.3.1.

[88] E.g., we might opt for more than one (similarly named) .cpp file for a given component to enable statically linked programs to drag in less than all of a needed component's object code (see section 2.2.12). Recall that the .cpp files of components, along with the resulting .o files comprised by, say, a static library archive (.a), are not *architecturally significant* (section 1.2.6).

(3) never define external bindage constructs outside of the component in which they are declared, and (4) access functionality in other components only via `#include` directives, again using angle brackets (<>).

Every logical construct that we write outside of a file that defines `main` — even code written exclusively for a single application — belongs in a proper component, including enumerations and protocols, which traditionally do not require any external bindage definitions. We require that the `.h` file compile in isolation, but we try to minimize the number of `#include` directives (and local class declarations) in component header files, except that we must not rely on unsafe *transitive includes* — i.e., for anything other than public inheritance.

Cyclic physical dependencies (compile- or link-time) among components are never necessary nor appropriate. Long-distance friendship — i.e., affording private access across any physical (e.g., component) boundaries — is also proscribed, as such access would vitiate independent substitutability of one conforming component implementation for another. Finally, we strive to avoid having more than one (public) class within a component absent compelling engineering reasons (by far the most common of which is friendship) to do otherwise.

2.7   Component-Private Classes and Subordinate Components

A prominently advertised benefit of our component-based approach is that of hierarchical reuse (section 0.4). In order to maximize that benefit, we want to avoid making private those stable implementation details that might prove valuable in other contexts. Inevitably, however, there are circumstances when hierarchical reuse is ill-advised. This section addresses such (infrequent) situations.

2.7.1   Component-Private Classes

Recall from section 0.7 that we consider the component our fundamental atomic unit of design. Generally speaking, we want each component we write to provide one or (with good reason) more (see section 3.3.1) appropriately named classes or a single utility `struct` (see section 3.2.8), each of which is intended to be stable and directly usable from outside the component in which it is defined. There are, however, situations where we will want to define classes used within a component that are potentially unstable implementation details of that component and (at least for now) unsuitable for direct public consumption. We will therefore want to designate such classes as being *private* to the component in which they are defined, and, as such, unavailable for direct use from outside it.[89] A related topic, subordinate components, is discussed below (see section 2.7.5).

> **DEFINITION**: A *component-private* class (or `struct`) is one defined at package-namespace scope that must not be used directly by logical entities located outside of the component in which it is defined.

2.7.2   There Are Several Competing Implementation Alternatives

There are several ways to prevent a class from being used outside the component in which it is declared, each having its own associated benefits and drawbacks.[90] One possibility is to isolate the class entirely within the `.cpp` file (e.g., within an unnamed namespace), which — when feasible[91] — is usually preferable. The C++ language also provides explicit syntax for declaring (private) nested classes. We have found, however, that nesting a class (privately or otherwise) within another class in most cases has undesirable consequences that, as we are about to show, render such designs suboptimal (see Figure 2-52, section 2.7.3).

2.7.3   Conventional Use of Underscore

Design Rule

Avoid the use of an underscore character (_) purely as a separator in logical names except between two all-uppercase words or for established (lowercase) single-character prefixes and suffixes (i.e., `d_`, `s_`, `e_`, `k_`, and `_p`).

In our methodology, we have chosen to treat the valid identifier-character underscore (_) specially, reserving its use for a higher purpose than mere word separation, for which we use

---

[89] The introduction of C++ modules (C++20) might well lead to a better implementation of component-private classes than is available with classical translation units — e.g., with regard to *transitive includes* (section 2.6).

[90] **lakos96**, section 8.4, pp. 572–579, in particular Figure 8-12, p. 577

[91] It is typically feasible to sequester a helper class entirely within the unnamed namespace of a component's `.cpp` file when there are no methods within the helper class that will benefit from inlining by external clients, and when there is no compelling need to test the implementation class directly (as opposed to indirectly, via the public interface of the principal class).

camelCase or CamelCase in most logical names as appropriate (section 1.7.1). We do, however, continue to use the underscore purely as a separator for words in what are (historically) ALL_UPPERCASE_SYMBOLS such as macros, macro arguments, template parameters, and compile-time constants (e.g., enumerators), and also for established (lowercase) single-character prefixes and suffixes serving as syntactic descriptors — e.g., d_dataMember, s_staticDataMember, d_pointerDataMember_p, s_staticPointerDataMember_p, e_ENUMERATOR, k_COMPILE_TIME_CONSTANT, s_STATIC_COMPILE_TIME_CONSTANT_DATA_MEMBER, or s_STATIC_COMPILE_TIME_CONSTANT_POINTER_DATA_MEMBER_p.[92] The conventional use of an extra underscore in *subordinate* component names is discussed in section 2.7.5.

Design Rule

A logical entity declared in a component header at package-namespace scope whose name contains an *extra* underscore — i.e., other than as required (1) as a valid separator (e.g., between all-uppercase words or as part of an established prefix/suffix), or (2) for nominal cohesion (e.g., in *subordinate* components) — is considered to be local to the component that defines it and must not be accessed directly from outside that component; the lowercased name up to the (first) *extra* underscore must match exactly the component's *base name*.

Any logical construct whose given name freely incorporates an extra underscore is — purely by convention — considered *private* to the component that defines it, and must not be used directly by any logical constructs located outside that component. Recall from section 2.4.7 that the *base name* of the component is the part of the component name following the underscore delimiting the package prefix, and typically matches the lowercased name of the principal class defined, at package-namespace scope, in the header file of that component.

As Figure 2-51 illustrates, we can use this convention to avoid having to declare private helper classes (such as Link or a nontrivial iterator) within the lexical scope of a principal class (such as List) and instead declare them at package-namespace scope, just like every other class.[93]

---

[92] Note that the k_ notation is entirely redundant, as the all-uppercase symbol itself implies the compile-time-constant nature clearly, yet it avoids any potential problems with rogue #defines emanating from poorly designed (e.g., legacy) code. Given a static, compile-time-constant data member, we would naturally prefer an s_ prefix for an otherwise ALL_UPPER_CASE_SYMBOL to communicate all of the syntactic information.

[93] We have chosen to make the first letter of component-local class names uppercase to be consistent with the UpperCamelCase convention we use generally to render type names; note that components defining local classes typically also define a public class whose name exactly matches the component's base name.

```
// xyza_list.h

// ...

namespace xyza {

class List_Link {          // component-private class
    List_Link *d_next_p;
    // ...
  public:
    // ...
};

class List_Iterator {      // component-private class
    // ...
  public:
    // ...
};

class List_ConstIterator {  // component-private class
    // ...
  public:
    // ...
};

class List {               // component-public class
    List_Link *d_head_p;
    // ...
  public:
    // ...
    typedef List_Iterator      iterator;        // public alias
    typedef List_ConstIterator const_iterator;  // public alias
    // ...
};

// ...

}  // close package namespace
// ...
```

Figure 2-51: Example of employing component-private classes (GOOD IDEA)

Guideline

Avoid *defining* a nested class within the lexical scope of its enclosing class.

Where compile-time access from outside the component in which the definition of a nested class is required, we have found that rendering multiple levels of public and private access in the lexical scope of a single parent class to be unacceptably difficult to comprehend, as suggested in Figure 2-52. Except for the most trivial ones, we ardently avoid *defining* a class within the lexical scope of another.

```
// xyza_list.h

// ...

namespace xyza {

class List {                  // component-public class

    class Link {              // private nested class definition
        Link *d_next_p;       // (BAD IDEA)
        // ...
      public:
        // ...
    };

    Link *d_head_p;

    // ...

  public:

    class iterator {          // public nested class definition
        // ...              // (BAD IDEA)
      public:
        // ...
    };

    class const_iterator {  // public nested class definition
        // ...              // (BAD IDEA)
      public:
        // ...
    };

    // ...
};

// ...

}  // close package namespace

// ...
```

Figure 2-52: Example of employing nested class definitions (BAD IDEA)

Guideline

Avoid *declaring* nested classes altogether.

Deliberately steering clear of a useful language feature that enforces encapsulation where such is appropriate might, at first, seem wrong-minded. There are, however, valid software engineering reasons that transcend the C++ language for doing so.[94] We contend that keeping all nontrivial classes at a uniform depth — just as we do for components, packages, and package groups — significantly improves human cognition. Given that we have adopted the component, and not the class, as the fundamental atomic unit of logical as well as physical design (section 0.7), we have earned the freedom to expand encapsulation, just as we have done with friendship, to the boundaries of the component, thereby eliminating all unnecessary complexity that frequently results from nested classes.[95]

Long before the C++ language supported forward declarations of nested classes,[96] we were successfully employing the extra-underscore convention in logical names — e.g., to implement fully insulating concrete classes[97] (see section 3.11.6). Even now with the ubiquitous ability to forward declare nested classes reliably, there remain substantial drawbacks to doing so. Unlike the conventional (nominally distinct) component-private peer classes that we advocate, every nested class (public as well as private) automatically has access to the private details of its enclosing class as illustrated in Figure 2-53a.[98] In our methodology, we find that this private access is never desired as it encourages intimate cyclic interdependencies between the parent and nested classes (which we will discuss in more detail below). What's more, the C++ language does not allow us to define an instance of the nested class in the parent until the definition of that nested class has been seen by the compiler, thereby requiring not just its declaration,

---

[94] As always, we strive to focus on the underlying objectives, and use (or, when necessary, create) the right tools to achieve those objectives. That a given language feature happens to be designed for a particular purpose does not automatically imply that its use is appropriate. On the other hand, any coding standard that outright forbids the use of a particular C++ construct without presenting a compelling justification and universally better alternative is, if not wrong, likely overstated.

[95] According to Nathan Burgers, one of the newer members (c. 2018) on our BDE team and a modules specialist, "The new modules feature (available as of C++20) provides the ability to create component-private classes through its export facility. Modules may either export a class (to make it available to importers) or not export a class to hide it from importers (thereby making it truly component-private)" (via personal conversation).

[96] See **stroustrup94**, section 13.5, pp. 289–290.

[97] **lakos96**, section 6.4.2, pp. 398–405, in particular, `Example_i` in Figure 6-51, p. 403

[98] Note that, unlike some other popular languages, the constructor of a nested class object in C++ is *not* automatically given a pointer to the object of its enclosing class.

but also its definition to reside within the lexical scope of the parent (Figure 2-53b). Finally, employing a private nested type means that file-scope `static` helper functions, along with all constructs defined in the unnamed namespace within the component's `.cpp` file, would be unable to know of, let alone process, a private nested type (Figure 2-53c) — that privilege being reserved exclusively for members and friends of the enclosing class.

```
class Wrapper {

    class Imp;  // private nested class declaration

    int d_x;     // private imp. details of 'Wrapper' to which 'Imp' is
    // ...        // automatically granted private access (BAD IDEA)

  public:
    // ...
    void f();
    // ...
};

class Wrapper::Imp {
    // ...
  public:
    // ...
    void g(Wrapper *p);  // cyclic private access  (BAD IDEA)
};

void Wrapper::f()
{
    Imp imp;
    // ...
}

void Wrapper::Imp::g(Wrapper *p)
{
    p->d_x = 0;  // exploiting private access to parent class (BAD IDEA)
    // ...
}
```

(a) Private access to peer implementation details is automatic.

```
class Wrapper {
    class Imp;  // private nested class declaration

    Imp d_imp;  // error: field 'd_imp' has incomplete type

    // ...
};
```

(b) Cannot create an instance in parent without nesting the definition

```
// xyza_wrapper.h

// ...

class Wrapper {
    class Imp;  // private nested class declaration

    // ...
};
```

```
// xyza_wrapper.cpp

// ...

static void fileScopeStaticFunction(Wrapper::Imp *p)  // Error: Class
{                                                     // 'Wrapper::Imp'
    // ...                                            // is private.
}
```

(c) Cannot pass to `static` functions isolated within the `.cpp` file

Figure 2-53: Undesirable "features" of private nested classes

Using our methodology's extra-underscore convention, a (non-nested) component-private `Wrapper_Imp` class can be treated internally to the component just like any other class: It (a) is *not* automatically granted friend access to any other class, (b) *can* be used to define a nested object in what would have been the parent `Wrapper` class, and (c) *can* be freely passed to constructs confined entirely to the `.cpp` file, yet, by convention (and enforced by tools) be unavailable to client code that resides outside of the component in which it is defined.[99] Despite its language-enforced encapsulation benefits, we assert that public as well as private nested classes are generally a bad idea.[100] While it is clear that cyclic dependencies across component boundaries are never a good idea, we strive, both for readability and also pedagogy, to organize logical constructs within even a single component so as to avoid forward declarations that (if located in separate components) would lead to cyclic physical dependencies among them (e.g., see Figure 2-54, section 2.7.4). Having a class reside within another adds complexity that simply isn't needed, which by itself would make nested classes undesirable. That nesting a class provides additional superfluous access to its parent, requires it to be complete before use within the parent, and tends to degrade readability only makes matters worse.

---

[99] Note that a class that is intended to be entirely local to the `.cpp` file can take advantage of this extra-underscore convention to effectively achieve internal linkage (section 1.3.2) and therefore need not be declared in the corresponding `.h` file (section 1.6.2) — and without having to be placed in the unnamed namespace (section 1.3.18) — thereby substantially improving both the size and readability of the debug symbols generated on most platforms.

[100] We leave our view of the advisability of protected nested classes to the imagination of the reader.

2.7.4   **Classic Example of Using Component-Private Classes**

Consider the practical example of implementing a container and its STL-style iterator within a single component. Figure 2-54a illustrates an implementation that makes the container and its iterator cyclically dependent, which, though not wrong, we consider (as a matter of style) to be suboptimal. We assert that avoiding logical cycles — even within a single component — both improves clarity and conditions developers to think logically in more physically sound ways. Using component-private classes as illustrated in Figure 2-54b, we can implement the component such that there would be no cyclic physical dependencies implied (section 1.9) among the classes defined within that component.

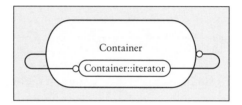

```
// ...

class Container {
    // ...
  public:
    class iterator;
    // ...
    iterator begin();
    iterator end();
    // ...
};

class Container::iterator {
    // ...
  private:
    friend class Container;  // Parent class is not an implicit 'friend'.
    iterator(Container *container);
  public:
    // ...
};

// ...

Container::Iterator Container::begin()
{
    return Iterator(this);
}

// ...
```

(a) Private-nested-class-based container implementation (BAD IDEA)

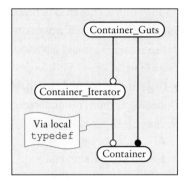

```
// ...

class Container_Guts {                          // component-private
    // ...
};

class Container_Iterator {                       // component-private
    // ...
  private:                                       // redundant:
    Container_Iterator(Container_Guts *guts);    // private constructor,
    friend class Container;                       // "slave" of 'Container'
  public:
    // ...
};

class Container {
    Container_Guts *d_guts_p;
    // ...

  public:
    typedef Container_Iterator iterator;         // public nested alias
    // ...
    iterator begin();
    iterator end();
    // ...
};

// ...

Container::iterator Container::begin()
{
    return Container_Iterator(d_guts_p);
}

// ...
```

(b) Component-private-class-based container implementation (GOOD IDEA)

Figure 2-54: Private-nested versus component-private classes

Notice that, in Figure 2-54b, we have chosen to define the iterator class, `Container_Iterator`, to be component-private, so that it is used from outside the component only by its idiomatic nested `typedef` alias, `iterator`. We could have instead defined the iterator class to be accessible directly (e.g., `ContainerIterator`); doing so, however, would unnecessarily expose implementation details (e.g., its name, and that it is a user-defined-type, not a fundamental pointer type), thereby impeding certain (re)implementation options (e.g., renaming or changing it to a `Container::value_type *`).

Also notice that we have seemingly redundantly declared the iterator's constructor `private` and `Container` a `friend` — even though the type of the only constructor parameter, `Container_Guts *`, is itself a pointer to a component-private class. First, consider that these additional constraints are consistent with intended use, and serve to document, as well as enforce, the single unit of logical encapsulation typically shared by a container and its iterator. Although perhaps not appropriate in this example, we can easily imagine a design in which the `Container_Guts` class is replaced by a more reusable data type, made public, and, perhaps, even relocated to its own component, in which case the private constructor and friendship would become absolutely mandatory.

Finally, consider that relying on a component-private class to achieve logical encapsulation between other (public) classes within the same component is a distant cousin of the highly undesirable practice of hiding header files to achieve logical encapsulation across classes in separate components (see section 3.9.7). As a matter of style, therefore, we avoid exposing private types in the public interface of components except via a public nested alias — e.g., `iterator`, as in Figure 2-54b.[101]

Taking such matters a step further, suppose that there are multiple independent "public" classes within some component, each making use of the same private helper class. To use the nested-class feature of C++ to hide that class from prospective clients outside the component, we would have to declare that type (perhaps arbitrarily) within one of several public types with all other public types now artificially (1) depending on that type, and (2) having private access to it. This unfortunate dependency and friendship, though "legal" (section 2.6), is suboptimal. We could instead create yet another public class having no public methods, whose sole purpose is

---

[101] A similar rule might apply to unexported types defined in (C++20) modules.

to hide our implementation type, and then require this dubious extra class to befriend all other interested classes within the component, but why bother? As Figure 2-55 illustrates, the conventional use of an extra underscore in the logical name of a shared component-private class more effectively and generally addresses this and all other related issues.[102]

```
// xyza_facility.h

// ...

class Facility_SharedImpDetail {   // component-private class
    // ...
};

class Facility1 {
    // ...
};

class Facility2 {
    // ...
};

class Facility3 {
    // ...
};

// ...
```

Needs access to
Facility_SharedImpDetail

Figure 2-55: Illustrating general advantage of component-private classes

2.7.5   Subordinate Components

We have also observed that, in rare circumstances, especially those that require implementing some externally specified interface (e.g., the C++ Standard Library), attempting to place all of the source code that is intended for exclusive use by an outwardly facing component in that same component might be suboptimal, yet we do not want to encourage unbounded direct access to a "less than public" component either — even within just a single package. Hence, we have invented the notion of a *subordinate component*.

---

[102] Notice how choosing *not* to make any public class match the base name exactly emphasizes our design intent not to logically associate the component-private class with any one of the public classes over the rest; see also section 3.3.3.

> **DEFINITION:** A *subordinate component* is one that must not be `#included` (or used) directly by any component other than the one (located within the same package) to which that component has been explicitly designated as being subordinate; a component can be subordinate to at most one nonsubordinate one.

As we are at liberty to specify how to designate one component as being *subordinate* to another, we have chosen — in the spirit of reusing keywords in C++ — to employ the overloaded use of the underscore (_) character for this purpose.

Design Rule

A component, `c`, having an underscore in its base name is reserved to indicate that the component is *subordinate* to another component (in the same package) whose name is a prefix all the way up to (but not including) an underscore in the base name of `c`.

Any component whose base name contains an underscore (e.g., **`xyza_base_name`**) is — again, purely by convention — considered *subordinate* to a component in the same package (e.g., **`xyza_base`**) whose name exactly matches the characters up to an underscore in its base name, and (as illustrated in Figure 2-56a) may be included (and used) directly by such a component, but no other.

```
// xyza_base.cpp

#include <xyza_base.h>
#include <xyza_base_name.h>
#include <xyza_base_name_guts.h>

//...

    //...

    Base_Name_Guts guts;

    //...

    Base_Name name(&guts);

    //...
```

```
// xyza_base_name.cpp

#include <xyza_base_name.h>
#include <xyza_base_name_imputil1.h>
#include <xyza_base_name_imputil2.h>

//...

    // ...

    Base_Name_ImpUtil1::someFunc();

    // ...

    Base_Name_ImpUtil2::someFunc();

    // ...
```

(a) Indirect subordinate components   (b) Subordinates of subordinates

Figure 2-56: Illustrating syntactic use of subordinate components

Note that the wording in the design rule deliberately allows for the possibility that a component base name may have multiple underscores (e.g., **xyza_base_name_imputil2**), thereby allowing for a hierarchy (tree not DAG) of subordinate components as suggested in Figure 2-56b, and yet explicitly permits direct inclusion/use of a "grandchild" component (e.g., **xyza_base_name_guts**) by its "grandparent" (**xyza_base** in Figure 2-56a). Also note that this convention intentionally precludes allowing more than one "public" component from depending directly on any one component that is "private" to the package (see section 3.9.7). Finally, note that a component-private class within a subordinate component — e.g., xyza::Base_Name_ImpUtil in component **xyza_base_name** — would not be directly accessible outside of that component (i.e., even to **xyza_base**); however, a class having the (not component-private) name xyza::Base_NameImpUtil would be, but only to **xyza_base**.

As stated earlier, the "extra underscore" convention for designating subordinate components is most commonly used when the specification of the component is not under our control, and it is not practical or possible to make the required implementation and/or test apparatus stable/reusable. Such large intimate dependencies can arise when testing heavily compile-time parameterized, complex containers such as std::unordered_map. We will therefore sometimes factor out the "guts" and "iterators" into separate subordinate components to facilitate independent testing. The need for subordinate components also arises when implementing platform-dependent (e.g., networking or thread-related) software. Hence, we might consider naming the subordinate components after the relevant platforms (perhaps hierarchically organized):

```
bdlmt_threadpool

bdlmt_threadpool_win32
bdlmt_threadpool_win64

bdlmt_threadpool_unix32
bdlmt_threadpool_unix32_sun
bdlmt_threadpool_unix32_hp
bdlmt_threadpool_unix32_ibm
bdlmt_threadpool_unix32_linux

bdlmt_threadpool_unix64
bdlmt_threadpool_unix64_sun
bdlmt_threadpool_unix64_hp
bdlmt_threadpool_unix64_ibm
bdlmt_threadpool_unix64_linux
```

We used this approach for our initial implementation of C++11-style atomics. See also section 3.3.8.

2.7.6   Section Summary

To summarize: There are occasions where the interface of a helper class is unstable and subject to change without notice. In order to improve readability, flexibility, and uniformity, while avoiding the drawbacks of nested classes delineated above, we continue to reserve the use of an underscore in a logical name declared at package-namespace scope to denote constructs that are private to a component, preferring instead to declare each "helper" class directly in package-namespace scope, thereby obviating use of all but the most trivial of nested classes and `struct`s. Similarly, we reserve the use of underscores in the base name of a component to indicate that it is not only local to the package in which it resides, but also private to a unique tree of components rooted in a single publicly accessible one, and must not be included/used by any component (within the package) other than ones to which it is subordinate.

2.8   The Package

A large program can span many developers, several layers of management, and even multiple geographic sites. The physical structure of our system will reflect not only the logical structure of the application, but also the organizational structure of the development team that implements it. Large systems require physical organization beyond what can be accomplished by a levelizable hierarchy of individual components alone. In order to encompass more complex functionality, we need to exploit units of physical design at higher levels of abstraction. We begin here with the smallest unit of physical abstraction larger than a component, which we refer to in our methodology as a *package*.

2.8.1   Using Packages to Factor Subsystems

When designing a system from the highest level, there are almost always large pieces that make sense to talk about as individual units. Consider the design of an interpreter for a large language (such as C++) shown in Figure 2-57. Each of the subsystems described is likely to be too large and complex to fit appropriately into a single component. Each of these larger units (indicated in Figure 2-57 with a "double box") must be implemented as a collection of levelizable components.[103]

---

[103] We do allow for the possibility that one or more packages may not follow our component-based methodology (see section 2.12).

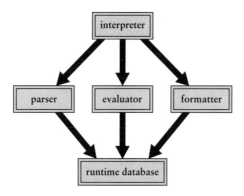

Figure 2-57: High-level interpreter architecture

The dependencies in Figure 2-57 among these larger units represent an aggregation of the dependencies among the components that make up each subsystem. For example, the runtime database is an independent subsystem; it has no dependencies on components other than those found in standard or otherwise generically reusable libraries. Each of the parser, evaluator, and formatter subsystems has components that depend on one or more components in the runtime database, but none of the components in any of these three parallel subsystems depends on any components in the other two. The top-level interpreter consists of components that depend on components within each of the three parallel subsystems (and perhaps even directly on components within the runtime database).

Carefully partitioning a system into large units and then considering the aggregate dependencies among these units is critical when distributing the development effort for projects across multiple individuals, development teams, or geographical sites. Although we would not characterize the development of the subsystem shown in Figure 2-57 as a *large* project, it could easily be assigned to more than one developer. This natural partitioning of components makes it relatively straightforward for several developers to work on this project concurrently. After the runtime database is designed, there would be an opportunity for three concurrent development efforts to begin work on the parsing, evaluating, and formatting functionality, respectively. Once these pieces start to fall into place, the implementation and testing of the top-level interpreter by a fourth developer (or team) could move into full swing.

Recall that a package is an *architecturally significant* (i.e., globally visible) unit of physical design that serves to aggregate logical content at a level larger than that of an individual component (see Figure 2-9b, section 2.2.17). A package is also a means for making related components nominally cohesive (section 2.4.5). In these ways, packages enable designers to capture and reflect — directly within source code — important architectural information not easily expressed in terms of components alone. Let's now reintroduce the term *package*, which — unless explicitly specified as *irregular* (see section 2.12) — denotes a collection of logically and physically cohesive components.

DEFINITION: A *package* is an architecturally significant collection of components (1) organized as a physically cohesive unit, and (2) sharing a common package namespace.

A typical package comprises a set of components organized as part of a single unit of release whose logical constructs, defined within a common (unique) package namespace (typically within an enterprise namespace), together serve a focused semantic purpose. A package might consist of a loosely coupled collection of low-level, reusable components, such as the C++ Standard Library.[104] Alternatively, a package might embody a special-purpose subsystem intended for use by just a single client. Either way, a well-designed package encapsulates a cohesive collection of components that fulfill some focused charter.

The degree to which parts of the system are likely to be reused as a unit also plays a role in factoring a subsystem. In the example of Figure 2-57, the runtime database might be used widely, while the three parallel subsystems are used only once. Even if the runtime database were very small in comparison to these other parts of the subsystem, it could well make sense to place this low-level functionality in its own separate package to avoid tying its reusable functionality to any of the other less-often-used ones (e.g., see Figure 3-60, section 3.5.6).

Packaging also reflects the development organization. Typically, a package will be owned/authored by a single developer or team. The impact of a change within a package can be well understood by its owner and dealt with both consistently and effectively. Changes across package boundaries typically affect other development teams and can be highly disruptive. We therefore strive to locate tightly coupled or collaborative parts of a subsystem that are likely to change within a single package (see sections 3.3.2–3.3.6), and ideally within a single component (section 2.7.1) or, failing that, within a subordinate component hierarchy (section 2.7.5).

---

[104] Note that the C++ Standard Library was not originally designed with our definition of components or strict avoidance of acyclic dependencies in mind.

The physical structure of the development view of a package is intentionally identical to every other package — irrespective of whether or not it happens to be a member of a package group (see section 2.9). We have historically represented each package as a directory in our file system bearing the package name. Figure 2-58a illustrates the top-level layout of the contents of our (hypothetical) isolated **evaluator** package.[105,106] The source files of each contained component reside side-by-side along with their associated component-level test-driver programs (see Volume III, section 7.5), as illustrated in Figure 2-58b.

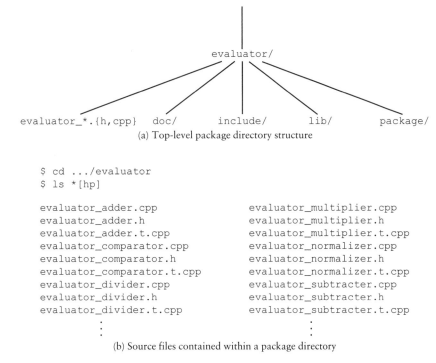

(a) Top-level package directory structure

```
$ cd .../evaluator
$ ls *[hp]

evaluator_adder.cpp              evaluator_multiplier.cpp
evaluator_adder.h                evaluator_multiplier.h
evaluator_adder.t.cpp            evaluator_multiplier.t.cpp
evaluator_comparator.cpp         evaluator_normalizer.cpp
evaluator_comparator.h           evaluator_normalizer.h
evaluator_comparator.t.cpp       evaluator_normalizer.t.cpp
evaluator_divider.cpp            evaluator_subtracter.cpp
evaluator_divider.h              evaluator_subtracter.h
evaluator_divider.t.cpp          evaluator_subtracter.t.cpp
            ⋮                                 ⋮
```

(b) Source files contained within a package directory

Figure 2-58: Physical layout of standalone package (evaluator)

---

[105] Note that the names of isolated packages must be at least seven alphanumeric characters in length or somehow otherwise kept distinct from all names for grouped packages (section 2.4.11); see section 2.10.3.

[106] Isolated packages require less forethought than grouped ones (see section 2.9) and are easy to overuse. Upon reviewing an early draft of this book, David Sankel opined:

> Isolated packages, in practice, are problematic: We tend to get too many of them, and it becomes difficult to comprehend the system. A package group initially having just one package within it should not be shied away from.

Also residing at the same level as the component and test-driver source code are four standard subdirectories: `doc`, `include`, `lib`, and `package`. The `doc` and `package` subdirectories contain, respectively, the package-level documentation (see Volume II, section 6.15) and metadata (see section 2.16) describing allowed dependencies on other UORs as discussed below.[107] Use of the `include` and `lib` subdirectories — during both development and at deployment — is discussed further in section 2.15.3.

The hierarchy implied by the dependencies among components within a package is a distinctly softer and more malleable concept than the harsh stratification of packages (e.g., within a group). Under certain circumstances, we might choose to impose additional *internal* (i.e., not architecturally significant) aggregate component structure within a package (see section 2.11); attempting to reflect all the individual component dependencies within the physical structure of a package using subdirectories, however, is simply a bad idea.[108]

Notationally, we represent a package as in Figure 2-59a — the double box reflecting the second architecturally significant level of physical aggregation. We denote package dependencies atomically, as illustrated in Figure 2-59b. That is, if any component in a package depends on something, the package as a whole depends on it as well. Conversely, if something depends on a particular component within a package, we assume that something depends on everything in the package. Although the granular nature of static libraries makes the actual physical dependencies among packages far from atomic (section 1.2.2), that technology might not be the one with which we deploy (see section 2.15.9). Using metadata (see section 2.16), we are even able to restrict the allowed direct dependencies on a package to one or an arbitrary subset of components within a package, and still we must assume that the entity depends on the entire package. Hence, we design as if package dependency is atomic.

---

[107] Note that for grouped packages, these dependencies will typically be limited to the names of other packages within this UOR (see section 2.16).

[108] Note that it may sometimes be desirable to create a "view" on a package that contains the component under development, its test driver, and only those components (but not test drivers) local to the package upon which the component under test depends (directly or otherwise) to ensure that there are no accidental physical dependencies outside those explicitly allowed by the embedded `#include` directives (see section 2.15.5).

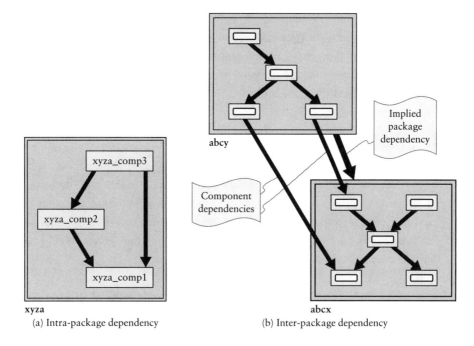

xyza_comp3

xyza_comp2

xyza_comp1

xyza
(a) Intra-package dependency

abcy

Implied package dependency

Component dependencies

abcx
(b) Inter-package dependency

Figure 2-59: Package notation

Consequently, the details of inter-package component dependencies are typically omitted from dependency diagrams among completed packages (e.g., Figure 2-57); however, highlighting intra-package component-level dependencies — and sometimes even class-level logical relationships, such as Is-A and Uses-In-the-Interface (section 1.7.2) — are often helpful during the design phase. Interactive tool support for extracting various views of intra-package component-level dependencies has proven extremely effective at allowing developers to "visualize" and eliminate unnecessary, excessive, or otherwise inappropriate component dependencies.

Design Rule

Anticipated *allowed* (direct) *dependencies* of each package must be stated explicitly.

Much more so than an individual component, the dependencies of each package — whether on other packages within a package group (see section 2.9) or, for isolated packages, on other UORs — exist by design, not by accident. Isolated or not, the *allowed* direct dependencies of packages are treated as an architectural specification, and are stated up front. That is, a package architect explicitly *declares* (in a file located in the `package` subdirectory) the envelope of other entities on which the package is *allowed* to depend.

As an initial instructive example, consider a high-performance, configurable engine such as one used to perform program trading. A well-designed trading engine will be a complete subsystem unto itself, providing a high-performance, but lexically neutral, *programmatic* interface. Any number of applications or libraries can use the trading engine directly with no need for lexical interpretation. By the same token, any number of human-facing interfaces might be contrived to control the engine — no one of which is necessarily any more special than the other.

Before we begin to think seriously about implementation, we know that the parser will depend on the engine and perhaps other text-processing utilities that are entirely independent of the engine. We also know that the components that implement the engine will *not* depend on any of those used within the package housing the parser, never mind the generic low-level parser-utilities library. To make these architectural-level intentions clear, we state *up front* (within the respective `package` subdirectories) that our first trading-parser package, **tparse1**, is allowed to depend on the trading-engine package, **tengine**, and the generic parser-utilities package, **parseutil**, as illustrated in Figure 2-60.

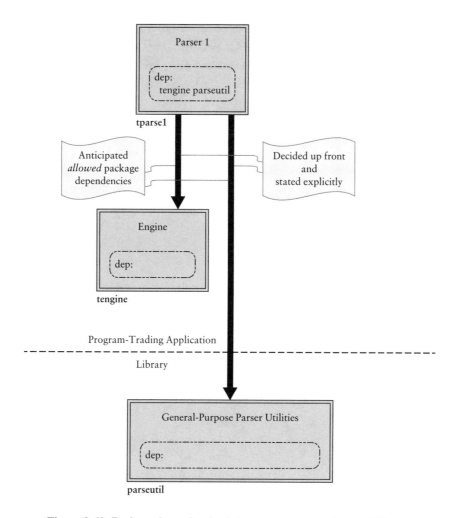

Figure 2-60: Package dependencies between a parser, engine, and library

More generally, granting a package *q* the right to depend directly on a package *p* conveys to development tools and developers alike the express intent that any component header names from *p* are *allowed* to be used in #include directives embedded in source files (.h or .cpp) comprising one or more components in *q*. Additionally, any component-level test driver (.t.cpp) files associated with components in *q* are also permitted to include headers in *p* directly.

Figure 2-61 illustrates (a) explicitly stated *allowed* package dependencies, and (b) several actual component dependencies for each of five packages. For example, Figure 2-61a reflects the architect's intent to have packages **package1** and **package2** depend on no other packages — i.e., these packages are each intended to be at the lowest local level[109] (i.e., level 1) and are therefore necessarily independent (section 1.10).

package5: package3 package2

package4: package3

package3: package1 package2

package2:

package1:

(a) (Abstract) specification of *allowed* direct package dependencies

---

[109] Note that, like components, the level of a package (e.g., see Figure 2-7, section 2.2.14) is with respect to our current view. If these are isolated packages, then each of them forms a unit of release (UOR), and therefore each has an absolute level within the overall physical hierarchy. On the other hand, if we are looking at packages within a package group, all packages (and UORs) outside that group are considered to have a level of 0. Within the group, all leaf packages — i.e., packages that don't depend on any other packages within the group — are defined to have a level of 1. Package groups are discussed in detail in section 2.9.

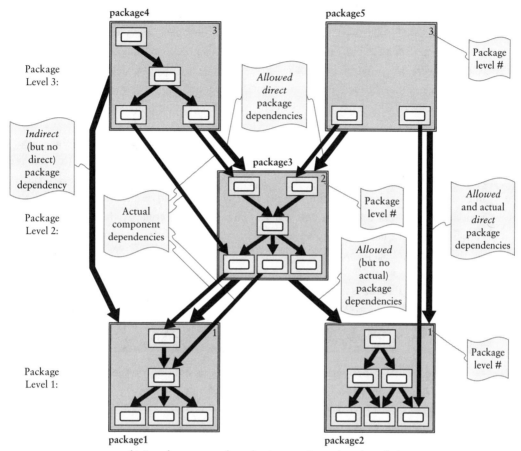

Package Level 3:

Package Level 2:

Package Level 1:

package4

package5

Package level #

Allowed direct package dependencies

Indirect (but no direct) package dependency

package3

Actual component dependencies

Package level #

Allowed and actual direct package dependencies

Allowed (but no actual) package dependencies

Package level #

package1

package2

(b) Actual component dependencies spanning package boundaries

Figure 2-61: Direct *allowed* and actual dependencies among packages

According to the specification in Figure 2-61a, components in **package3** are permitted to depend directly on components within either **package1** or **package2**. As shown in Figure 2-61b, however, the *allowed* dependencies of **package3** are consummated with actual dependencies on **package1**, but not as yet on **package2**; the architectural declaration informs component developers that they are *allowed* to create such actual dependencies should the need arise. From a physical perspective, however, the actual dependency is irrelevant: The *allowed* dependency on **package2** alone would force **package3** to level 2. It is the *allowed* dependency that serves as the specification for the physical design; the actual dependency is merely an implementation detail governed by that specification.

The declaration of a package's *allowed* dependencies is for *direct* dependencies only and is not transitive. That is, if package **p3** is allowed to depend *directly* on package **p2**, and **p2** is allowed to depend *directly* on package **p1**, that does not mean that **p3** is necessarily allowed to depend *directly* on **p1**. Each allowed *direct* dependency must be stated explicitly. Note that nested headers (i.e., headers included by other headers) do not constitute direct dependencies; the client will, of course, need access to all such headers in order to compile.

For example, Figure 2-61b shows packages **package4** and **package5** at level three. Package **package4** is allowed to depend directly on **package3**, but even though headers from **package1** might be needed in order for components in **package4** to compile, no #include directive for the header of a component residing in **package1** is permitted to be embedded directly in a component source file or test driver belonging to **package4**. By contrast, the dependency specification of Figure 2-61a does allow **package5** to depend directly on components belonging to **package2** as well as **package3**.[110]

2.8.2   Cycles Among Packages Are BAD

Design Imperative

Cyclic physical dependencies among packages, as defined by their (explicitly stated) *allowed dependencies*, **are not permitted.**

---

[110] Note that, although the abstract notation described here is not, by default, transitive, transitivity is often what is desired. Instead of having to provide all transitive dependencies explicitly, a simple flag stating that transitivity should apply can be added to the abstract allowed-dependency specification, and any specific unwanted dependencies can then be "blacklisted" — e.g.:

```
TRANSITIVITY = TRUE
package5: package3 package2
package4: package3
package3: package1 package2
package2:
package1:
!(package4 : package1)
```

An example of not wanting to allow transitive dependency might involve a dependency on an implementation-only package. Also note that the modules language feature (first available as of C++20) might eventually turn out to be a better implementation choice, as it could, through its use of exports, potentially capture the allowed/disallowed direct access in the source code itself.

Two or more packages are cyclically dependent if their explicitly stated *allowed* direct dependencies form a cycle, even if the actual dependencies do not. For example, the *allowed* dependencies between components in the three packages in Figure 2-62 induce a package-level cycle even though no component-level cycle exists: Component c_w (in package *c*) depends on component b_x, which, in turn, depends on a_y, which, depends on c_z (back in package *c*). Even if the dependency of component a_y on c_z were removed, explicitly authorizing such a potential cycle is itself a violation, as it invites the dependency of a_y on c_z.

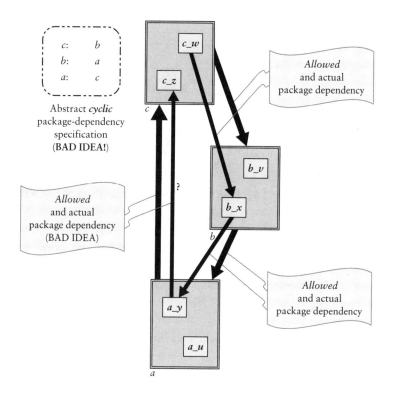

Figure 2-62: Cyclic *allowed* package dependencies (BAD IDEA)

2.8.3   Placement, Scope, and Scale Are an Important First Consideration

Failing to consider early where a component belongs is at the root of numerous problems. In our methodology, we explicitly preclude placing individual components as peers alongside packages in our library software; doing so would dilute our balanced regular organization (section 2.2.16). Yet creating packages solely as vessels for holding unrelated components is arguably worse. This type of artificial or *coincidental* cohesion[111] (see section 3.2) inevitably produces packages that have no clear purpose or common logical properties, resulting in physical dependencies that are formed by coincidence, rather than deliberate design, as illustrated in Figure 2-63.

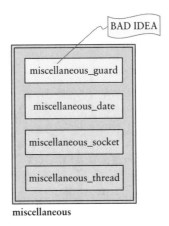

miscellaneous

Figure 2-63: Insufficiently specific package scope (BAD IDEA)

Determining the appropriate location to add new functionality is admittedly a challenge (see section 3.1.4). Both logical and physical factors must be satisfied in order for the placement to be considered successful. Even with the best of intentions, we frequently observe nascent architects struggling to identify the scope of a new package in which a particular component belongs.

For example, consider a component that is to implement Base64 encode/decode functionality.[112] Such a component might[113] provide separate pure functions, nested within a `struct` (see section 3.2.7), to encode and decode an arbitrary number of bytes to and from a character string (`char *`), and perhaps one or more additional pure functions, say, to determine if a given

---

[111] **booch94**, "Measuring the Quality of an Abstraction" in section 3.6, pp. 136–138 (specifically the middle of p. 137)

[112] **freed96**, section 6.8, pp. 24–26

[113] Note that, in practice, encoder/decoder designs such as these are inherently not scalable in that the entire message must be encoded as a block before it can be sent (and then decoded). A more robust approach is to implement the encoder (and decoder) as a finite-state machine that accepts incremental input and emits incremental output. The indicated stateless "convenience" functions could then be implemented easily in terms of these more powerful underlying stateful mechanisms. (Factoring out appropriate subfunctionality is the subject of Volume II, section 6.4.)

string was a valid encoding or the maximum size of an encoded string as a function of the number of input bytes.

Ignoring packaging for the moment, we might well choose to name this component something long and descriptive like **base64encoderutil** in order to both (1) characterize the domain of functionality, and (2) emphasize the stateless nature of the functions it implements. Even with this mind-set, an inexperienced architect might still be tempted to place such a component in a new **base64encoder** package, as illustrated in Figure 2-64.

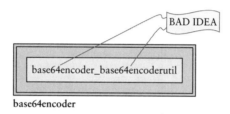

Figure 2-64: Overly specific package scope (BAD IDEA)

Unless encoders themselves are our business, having an entire package dedicated to Base64 encoders is absurd (as would having an entire package group dedicated to encoders, see section 2.9). We must resist our natural tendency to form overly specific packages, especially when contemplating a new component that does not seem to fit the profile of any existing package. Such narrowly focused packages run counter to our desire to achieve *balanced* aggregation (section 2.2.17) in that such specificity all but guarantees that no future components — e.g., implementing related encodings — would be appropriate to this package[114]:

```
Base85EncoderUtil
BinhexEncoderUtil115
UuEncoderUtil
YencEncoderUtil
```

---

[114] Macintosh binhex 4.0 (**faltstrom94**), base85 is from Level 2 PostScript, and yEnc (**helbing02**).

[115] Note that the "h" of "BinHex" is intentionally set lowercase in the name of the encoder utility `BinhexEncoderUtil` because the `Binhex` (representing "BinHex") acts as a compound adjective modifying `EncoderUtil`. Also note that acronyms, such as "FSM" (finite-state machine), would be treated similarly – e.g., `FsmEncoderUtil`. For more on utility types, see section 3.2.7.

Given that a Base64EncoderUtil is a kind of reusable encoder and that there are many potentially useful kinds of low-level encoders, encrypters, translators, etc. — each with essentially
the same (minimal) physical dependencies — we might choose to create a package for all of
our encoders and decoders and call it **encoder**[116] whose scope, at least for now, encompasses
all such encoder-like utilities. Although this package might initially contain only a single component[117] (**base64encoderutil**), we can now reasonably expect that more components will
follow as the package matures, as illustrated in Figure 2-65.

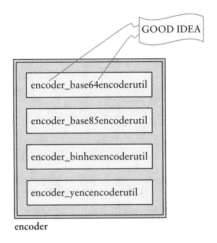

Figure 2-65: Appropriately specific package scope (GOOD IDEA)

The partitioning of software into separate packages should ideally be natural and intuitive to
clients, especially for widely reusable software. Segregating similar components having subtly
different logical or physical properties in distinct packages can present a barrier to reuse. In the
worst case, the package name can seem almost like a cryptic password needed to unlock
the functionality already fully delineated by the component name. Even with well-defined criteria, separating closely related components — such as one implementing a type that represents

---

[116] In our methodology, individual isolated package names are required either to be at least 7 characters, or prefixed
with a single character followed by an underscore — e.g., **encoder** or **a_dc** (see section 2.10).

[117] In practice, we would probably implement this functionality as two separate components — one to encode and
the other to decode — with the decoder depending on the encoder for testing purposes only (see Figure 2-82e,
section 2.14.3; Figure 3-25, section 3.3.6; Volume II, section 4.9; and Volume III, section 8.6).

a value (see Volume II, section 4.1) from those that implement nonprimitive (see section 3.2.7) yet widely useful "utility" functionality on that type — in distinct packages can make finding that functionality unnecessarily difficult.

Careful packaging should aid in finding and understanding provided functionality, not impede it. Ideally, the package name itself will be the name commonly used to refer to the cohesive collection of components that it embodies. A properly designed package will typically consist of (1) a subsystem that, as a whole, provides a particular service (e.g., a logging facility), (2) a variety of components that each serve a similar specific function (e.g., memory allocators), or (3) a larger, more loosely related collection of functionality that addresses some general level of abstraction (e.g., the C++ Standard Library).

2.8.4   The Inestimable Communicative Value of (Unique) Package Prefixes

Finally, the encoding of the unique physical "address" of virtually every architecturally significant logical entity goes far beyond what can be dismissed as mere "style." This nominal cohesion forces us to be reverent of the physical properties that the logical name connotes — something naming conventions alone will never do. Given that it is generally not possible to assign arbitrary package prefixes to subsets of otherwise acyclic components without introducing cycles among the packages (section 2.4.10), it is imperative that we consider the larger issue of packaging along with low-level details of component-based logical and physical design at every stage of the development process.

There is yet one more benefit to consistent use of explicit package names that one learns to appreciate more and more over time. Initially, a particular package name might seem obscure, arbitrary, and useless from a logical perspective. Yet each prefix carries a dimension of meaning not conveyed by the component name alone. Consider the three packages shown in Figure 2-66, belonging to a fairly low-level package group **dm2** for an actual IC CAD system. Initially, the package names (i.e., **dm2t**, **dm2p**, and **dm2e**) are entirely meaningless.

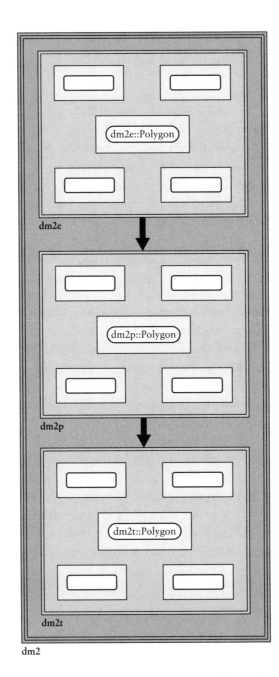

Figure 2-66: Package prefixes add substantive orthogonal meaning to class names.

As we start to work with these packages, we begin to notice certain similarities and patterns. Each of the types defined in **dm2t** are high-performance, concrete, value-semantic types with absolutely no virtual functions. By contrast, each of the types defined in **dm2p** inherit from the protocol class defined in **dm2p_primitive**. Moreover, each of these types also inherits[118] from a corresponding type in **dm2t**. We soon come to expect that every type in **dm2p** is a kind of dm2p::Primitive adapter for the high-performance equivalent in **dm2t**. The **dm2e** package defines the kind of elements that can be put in a cell. Each component in **dm2e** defines a type of element. Every element type in **dm2e** derives from the protocol class dm2e::Element that, among other things, accepts arbitrary attributes provided that they implement the dm2p::Primitive protocol.

What's the point? The point is that when we see a new package-qualified class name, the first thing we consider is *not* the class-name part, but rather the package-name part — the part which by now we've seen many times before. If we see dm2t::Polygon, we think high-performance, stand-alone data structure. If we see dm2p::Polygon, we think "potential attribute for a dm2e::Element." If we see dm2e::Polygon, we think "concrete type derived from dm2e::Element" suitable for incorporation into a cell. The other point is that when we see dm2p::GrimblePritz, we know that it is *neither* a high-performance standalone data structure *nor* a kind of dm2e::Element that can be added to a cell, but instead is a primitive (of some kind) that adapts a type defined in **dm2t** for use as an attribute in a dm2e::Element.

2.8.5   Section Summary

In summary, determining the appropriate physical location at which to add new functionality is a challenge. Both logical and physical factors must be considered. The content of each package must be both logically cohesive and also share the same (tight) envelope of allowed physical dependencies. Given our predilection for a balanced physical hierarchy (section 2.2.17), we must assess carefully the scope of each package we create. Just as creating packages of unrelated components is ill-advised, so is creating a package that is too specific to ever admit more than just a couple of components. By taking a step back and planning for the long term, we are much more likely to make the right component packaging choices with respect to the location, characterization, dependency, and scope.

---

[118] See Volume II, section 4.6, for details on how to adapt value-semantic types (see Volume II, section 4.3), such as those in **dm2t**, to a protocol class (section 1.7.5), such as dm2p::Primitive. See also **lakos96**, Appendix A, pp. 737–768, in particular the two figures on p. 756 and p. 757, respectively.

2.9   The Package Group

Our ability to aggregate components effectively is essential to our development process. Packages are an important architectural entity but alone are not sufficient for truly large development efforts. If a package were our only means of physical aggregation, then every component in each UOR would reside in the same namespace. By introducing a third level of aggregation — the *package group* — we facilitate the bundling of much larger quantities of physically similar logical content, while preserving vital logical boundaries. What's more, the administration of grouped package names, as introduced in section 2.4.11, can be readily decentralized.

2.9.1   The Third Level of Physical Aggregation

> **DEFINITION**: A *package group* is an architecturally significant collection of packages, organized as a physically cohesive unit.

> **COROLLARY:** The name of each package group must be unique throughout the enterprise.

Package groups dovetail with other UORs (e.g., isolated packages and third-party libraries) to support arbitrarily large applications, systems, and products throughout an enterprise. Every package group consists of a set of packages, each governed by the same (common) set of physical dependencies on other UORs. Because package groups are very large and well known, they intentionally have very short (i.e., exactly 3 character) names (section 2.4.11). We construct package groups out of packages for essentially the same reasons that we construct packages out of components: Thoughtful aggregation facilitates both human understanding and build efficiencies. Having lots of individual packages residing outside of package groups is a symptom of poor planning and tends to complicate understanding and maintenance on an enterprise scale.

Consider again the encoder/decoder package, `encoder`, depicted in Figure 2-65, section 2.8.3. Suppose now that we had also envisioned other packages such as primitive parsing utilities, command-line and configuration-file interpreters, and a logging facility, which together would make up a set of related packages that we think of as our "basic application library." Assuming they share the same envelope of physical dependencies, it might make sense to group these packages together into a single package group, which we might call **bal**. The names of the packages contained in the package group might then become **baled** (encoders/decoders), **balpu** (parsing utilities), **balcm** (configuration management), and **ball** (logging), respectively (section 2.4.11). With this physical grouping of packages, the much more substantial **bal** package group becomes the physical aggregate whose name is visible at the highest level of our software repository.

At first, such terse package "names" (really just tags) within a group might appear to be overly cryptic, making discovery of reusable software problematic. The main goal of these names is, however, to make clear from the point of use (1) exactly what is being used, and (2) the precise location of where it lives in our global repository of software. Even if we used more descriptive package names, we would still have to provide the same extensive documentation (see Volume II, sections 6.15–6.17) and effective search tools for finding these solutions in the first place. Also, longer package names, especially for packages that are used frequently, would no doubt lead to using declarations/directives in violation of our design rules (section 2.4.12), which, in turn, would impede our ability to identify immediately — from the point of its use — the unique package that defines a given logical construct along with the component that implements it.

A package group, like an isolated package, is a unit of release, which, when deployed, in principle takes the form of a library[119] (i.e., a .a, .so, .lib, or .dll file) and a directory of header files. In development, the physical structure of a package group, as illustrated in Figure 2-67, mirrors that of a package (Figure 2-58, section 2.8.1). That is, we represent each package group in our file system as a directory bearing the package group's name. This directory, like a package, contains four standard subdirectories (Figure 2-67a): doc, include, lib, and group.[120] The top-level package-group directory also contains subdirectories corresponding to each individual package within the group as illustrated in Figure 2-67b. By design, the physical layout of each grouped package is identical to that of every isolated package (Figure 2-58, section 2.8.1).

---

[119] In practice, each library will have several translated variants created using distinct build settings (see sections 2.15 and 2.16).

[120] We have, historically, used group to indicate the directory in which the group-level metadata resides. Ideally, instead of group, one might use, say, packagegroup in order to keep the former name outside of the four- to six-character range to which we restrict our grouped package names (section 2.4.11). Thus, the **up** package suffix within the **gro** package group would not be an exception for people or tools (see section 2.16).

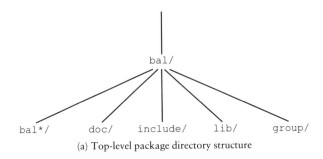

(a) Top-level package directory structure

```
$ cd .../bal
$ ls -d bal*
baladm    balcm    baled    ball     balrgx   baltm
balalg    baldb    balext   balm     balsys   balu
balc      baldbu   balgph   balpu    balt     balxml
```

(b) Sample listing of package directories contained within a package group

Figure 2-67: Physical layout of fairly low-level package group `bal`

Note that, while perhaps clever, it is almost always wrong to create a (grouped) package whose name is a valid English word such as **group**. People are not machines, and they would be fighting an almost impossible battle to keep from parsing the token atomically. In general, we advocate that grouped package names should be chosen deliberately to *avoid* having them turn out to spell words, especially distasteful ones.

As our second example, Figure 2-68a illustrates the top-level layout of the **bsl** (BDE Standard Library) package group. The doc subdirectory holds overview documentation material that applies to the package group as a whole (see Volume II, section 6.15). Similarly, the group subdirectory holds the bsl.dep file, which specifies the envelope of allowed dependencies for this package group (as a whole) on other UORs. The discussion of how both the include and lib subdirectories might be used during development and deployment for package groups is again deferred until section 2.15.3.

Just like **bal**, the **bsl** package group also contains a separate directory corresponding to each package within the group, with each package having the package-group name as a prefix. Figure 2-68b illustrates several distinct package directories corresponding to the packages residing within the package group; those having a + sign in their names are *irregular* (see section 2.12) in that, due to externally defined interface constraints, they do not reside in their own separate package namespaces as are required (section 2.6) for *regular* packages. Note that, for package groups whose design is entirely under our control, such as **bal**, no such irregular packages (and therefore package names) are needed.

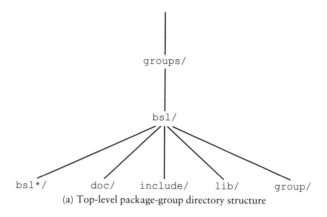

(a) Top-level package-group directory structure

```
$ cd .../bsl
$ ls -d bsl*
bsl+bslhdrs   bslalg   bslh    bslma   bslmt   bslscm   bsltf
bsl+stdhdrs   bsldoc   bslim   bslmf   bsls    bslstl   bslx
```
(b) Sample listing of package directories contained within a package group

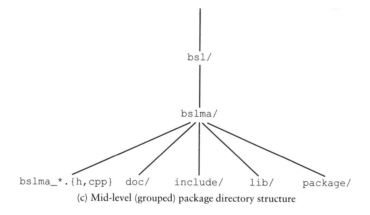

(c) Mid-level (grouped) package directory structure

```
$ cd .../bsl/bslma
$ ls *[hp]
bslma_allocator.cpp            bslma_default.cpp
bslma_allocator.h              bslma_default.h
bslma_allocator.t.cpp          bslma_default.t.cpp
bslma_autodeallocator.cpp      bslma_newdeleteallocator.cpp
bslma_autodeallocator.h        bslma_newdeleteallocator.h
bslma_autodeallocator.t.cpp    bslma_newdeleteallocator.t.cpp
bslma_autodestructor.cpp       bslma_testallocator.cpp
bslma_autodestructor.h         bslma_testallocator.h
bslma_autodestructor.t.cpp     bslma_testallocator.t.cpp
        ⋮                              ⋮
```
(d) Elided sample listing of source files contained within a grouped package

Figure 2-68: Physical layout of package `bslma` in package group `bsl`

Among the packages in **bsl** is the one that pertains to memory allocators, **bslma**. Figure 2-68c reflects the standard package structure, first introduced in Figure 2-58a, section 2.8.1, for isolated packages. The `doc` and `package` subdirectories serve the same purpose as for an isolated package, except that dependencies defined in the `package` subdirectory are limited to (the names of) other packages within the same group. Discussion of how the `include` and `lib` directories might be used during build and deployment is once again deferred until section 2.15.3. The elided component source files, along with their associated test drivers — each bearing the package name as a prefix — are illustrated in Figure 2-68d.

Notationally, we represent a package group as in Figure 2-69a, using a triple box to indicate the third architecturally significant level of physical aggregation.[121] When component dependencies span package-group boundaries, they introduce external dependencies, as illustrated in Figure 2-69b.

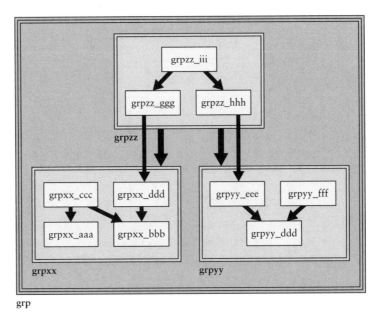

(a) Intra-package-group dependency

---

[121] We have, on occasion (e.g., see Figure 2-10, section 2.2.18), adopted an electrical-engineering-like short-hand notation consisting of just a single box with a "slash 2" or "slash 3" through it (see right).

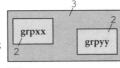

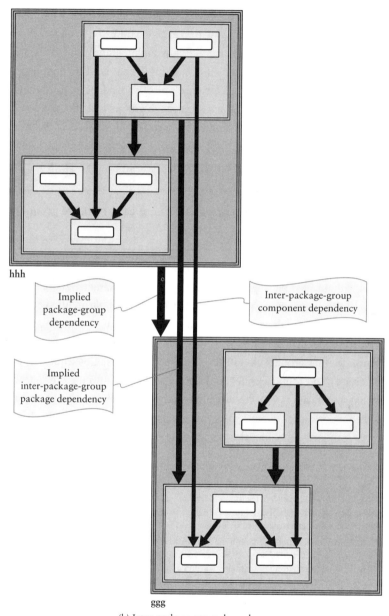

hhh

Implied
package-group
dependency

Inter-package-group
component dependency

Implied
inter-package-group
package dependency

ggg

(b) Inter-package-group dependency

Figure 2-69: Package group notation

DEFINITION: A package group *g* Depends-On another UOR *u* if any package in *g* Depends-On *u*.

We denote direct dependencies between package groups similarly to the way we denote dependencies between packages. Just as with packages, transitivity of actual physical dependencies across package groups is by no means certain; architecturally, however, we consider the dependency of a package group to be "all or nothing." That is, if a client depends on any part of a package group, that client inherits the envelope of dependencies for the entire group. Hence, the details of package dependencies across package groups and any mention of individual components are, in practice, typically omitted from package-group-level diagrams.

Design Rule

Anticipated *allowed* **(direct)** *dependencies* **of each package group must be stated explicitly.**

Just as with isolated packages, an integral part of the characterization of a package group is the set of UORs upon which that package group as a whole is allowed to depend.[122] Whereas the functionality and dependencies of individually-released isolated packages are crafted separately, the dependencies of each of the packages within the group are governed by, and must conform to, that group's overall physical specifications. Consequently, package-group dependencies are of profound architectural significance and — even more so than packages — require up-front specification. It is therefore imperative that each package group identify at its inception precisely upon which other UORs (i.e., package groups, isolated packages, and legacy, open-source, and third-party libraries) its member packages are *allowed* to depend directly.[123]

---

[122] Note that allowed dependencies for an individual package on other packages within the group are specified in metadata directly within the `.dep` file in the `package` directory for that package, while allowed dependencies on other UORs are centrally located in a like-named file in the `group` directory (see section 2.16).

[123] Note that we might choose, through the use of metadata and supporting tools (see section 2.16), to restrict the allowed direct dependency of some UOR v as a whole to a subset of the packages and/or components of some other UOR u. (This augmentation in notation is permitted because it amounts only to a voluntary narrowing of privilege.) Our development tools would then report when direct use exceeded what was explicitly allowed. Despite this architectural restriction, v would continue to inherit *all* of the physical dependencies of u.

On the other hand, the overall dependencies for each aggregate on another must *always* be treated architecturally as atomic. E.g., if *any* component in package group v is allowed to depend on some other UOR, u (or part thereof), then so must every other component in v. Failing to treat the external dependencies of aggregates atomically runs counter to our desire to achieve logical and physical cohesion (section 2.3), and invites coupling our architecture to both our technology and deployment strategy (see section 2.15.9); the benefit of denoting allowed aggregate physical dependencies abstractly would be lost.

For example, consider how we might form the dependencies between the package groups used in building a typical trading system. We assume the following firm-wide (software-infrastructure) package groups will be needed:

odl - *Our Development Library*
otl - *Our Transport Library*
oal - *Our Application Library*
ogl - *Our Graphical-user-interface Library*
obl - *Our Business Library*

Next, trading systems has its own department-wide library of domain-specific reusable software:

tde - *Trading-systems Development Environment*

Finally, the trading application itself has its own package group:

ta1 - *Trading Application-specific* functionality for system *one*

The *allowed* direct physical dependencies among these package groups are specified abstractly in Figure 2-70a, and illustrated in Figure 2-70b. Note that these allowed dependencies would, in practice, reside in a separate *groupname*.dep file located in the respective group subdirectories.

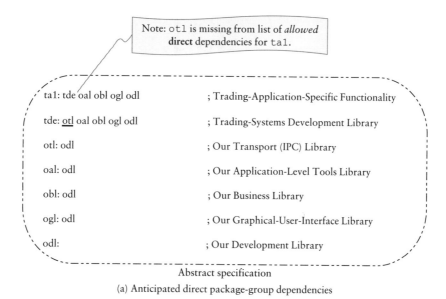

(a) Anticipated direct package-group dependencies

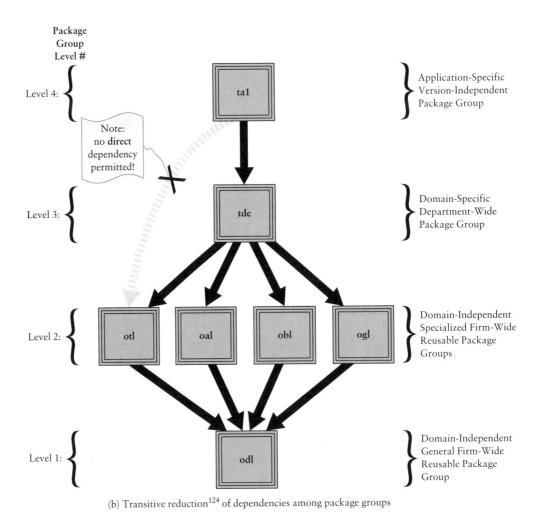

(b) Transitive reduction[124] of dependencies among package groups

Figure 2-70: Dependencies among a trading application's package groups

Note the deliberate architectural decision to proscribe the functionality implemented in the package group **ta1** from directly using the functionality implemented in the package group **otl**. According to the specification, the **tde** package group is permitted to depend *directly* on every package group that it depends on indirectly (e.g., **odl**), whereas components defined in **ta1** are *not* allowed to directly include headers from components defined in **otl**. Whether it is appropriate or not for a package group to use a subordinate package group directly is an

---

[124] See Figure 1-59, section 1.8.

architectural decision, and we are not advocating the prohibition of direct use on subordinate UORs as a part of our design philosophy. What is important is that the decision to allow direct use of one UOR on another can be a conscious one, and need not always default to the (coincidental) envelope of transitive physical dependencies.

Design Imperative

Allowed (explicitly stated) dependencies among UORs must be acyclic!

Recall that two or more UORs (e.g., packages and package groups) — being physical aggregates (section 2.2.1) — are cyclically dependent if their explicitly stated *allowed* direct dependencies (section 2.2.14) form a cycle, even if the actual component dependencies do not. Mechanically, the concept is virtually identical to that of cyclic package-level dependencies, illustrated in Figure 2-62, section 2.8.2. Given that package groups are typically an order of magnitude larger than packages and always independent units of release, the consequences of cyclic dependencies involving package groups are dire. In particular, we lose the ability to release libraries in levelized order (section 1.10). If any design imperative should be immune to mitigating circumstances and followed scrupulously without question, we nominate this one (section 2.2.24): Avoid any possibility of cycles among UORs!

Consider again the trading system application architecture of Figure 2-70. Figure 2-71a recreates the essential acyclic dependencies among the package groups. Now suppose that we discover that we have inadvertently "misplaced" some functionality (say, atomic instructions, scoped guards, etc.) in `otl` that is determined to be "needed" by one or more components in `odl`. As serious as this situation might be, the prospect of duplicating these mechanisms[125] in `odl` and perhaps eventually obsoleting the redundant code in `otl` is viable; allowing components in `odl` to depend on `otl`, however, is not.

---

[125] The problem is made qualitatively more complicated when the misplaced functionality involves vocabulary types (see Volume II, section 4.4).

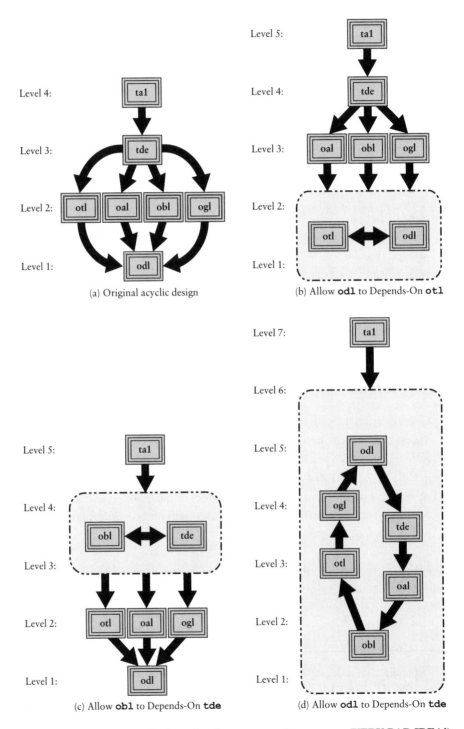

(a) Original acyclic design

(b) Allow **odl** to Depends-On **otl**

(c) Allow **obl** to Depends-On **tde**

(d) Allow **odl** to Depends-On **tde**

Figure 2-71: Allowing cyclic dependencies among package groups (VERY BAD IDEA!)

As Figure 2-71b illustrates, allowing `odl` to depend on `otl` would create a cyclic dependency between these two package groups. Now, from a maintenance perspective, neither library can be built, tested, or released independently of the other. More importantly, applications or other libraries wanting to make use of the most basic functionality would also be forced to depend on our elaborate interprocess communication software, even though `otl` is not relevant for a large class of applications. Relevance aside, there is no longer an order in which these library files are guaranteed to link successfully; on many platforms, clients will be forced to fiddle with their link lines, repeat libraries, and suffer considerable inefficiencies in their own build process (section 1.2.6).

Similar difficulties would arise if we were to allow our generally applicable basic business functionality `obl` to depend on a package group such as `tde` belonging to another department (Figure 2-71c). The organizational ramifications of such a decision would be truly unfortunate. Now two departments would be forced always to collaborate in order to release – in lockstep — the two package groups involved. Other departments (e.g., accounting or analytics) that would otherwise be interested in `obl` might be deterred if they knew that they would be inseparably tied — both in software and in schedule — to an unrelated peer department. That having been said, the low-level cycle of Figure 2-71b might be even more troubling in that it could affect many more potential clients, and also dramatically increase the cost of maintenance.[126]

Finally, we could discover that the core team for trading systems has just created a package in `tde` that provides precisely the functionality needed to solve a number of urgent business problems important to many clients of `odl`. No matter how tempting, the urge to allow `odl` to depend on `tde` (Figure 2-71d) must be suppressed. Our well-designed hierarchical repository of software could, with one such blow, be converted to a cyclically dependent "Big Ball of Mud" (section 0.2). If not rectified immediately, the damage could quickly grow to become, for all practical purposes, irreparable.

2.9.2   Organizing Package Groups During Deployment

From an organizational perspective, however, we may choose to treat a cluster of package groups as a single unit for deployment purposes. Consider again the five firm-wide package groups shown in levels 1 and 2 of the dependency diagram in Figure 2-70, section 2.9.1. In theory, we should be able to release the lowest-level group, `odl`, and then release each of

---

[126] See also **lakos96**, section 5.2, Figure 5-18a–d, pp. 225–228.

the other four groups, `obl`, `otl`, `oal`, and `ogl`, at once, or individually, in any arbitrary order. For very large systems, however, this incremental deployment approach would be grossly inefficient, as all of the (higher-level) software that depends on it would, in principle, have to be rebuilt (and redeployed to every production machine) each time any single group is released.

Assuming that the same core team is responsible for maintaining these package groups, especially if each group is under active development, significant build-time and other deployment efficiencies can be realized by treating all of these physical groups as a single *organizational* unit of deployment,[127] which is subject to change without notice (see section 2.15.10). For developer convenience, these core package groups might even be organized as part of a single source-code repository. Any such organization, however, must have no architecturally significant artifacts, thereby allowing the source to be repartitioned, and the deployment strategy to evolve, with absolutely no change to the source code of either the library or its clients.

2.9.3   How Do We Use Package Groups in Practice?

Having discussed what constitutes a package group, let us now explore the different ways package groups are used routinely in practice.

Observation
_____

Package groups support logically and physically cohesive library development.
_____

There are two distinct ways in which we use package groups effectively in large-scale development to achieve logically and physically cohesive subsystems. The first use — generally reusable or infrastructure libraries — is to capture widely consumable functionality that, while addressing different logical topics in separate packages, share a common anticipated audience as well as a common envelope of physical dependencies. Packages in a reusable group will often consist of *horizontal*[128] packages, where all of their components are intended for direct use by clients outside the group. Typical packages in an infrastructure group will often

---

[127] Any such *organizational* cluster of UORs would, of course, necessarily have to be chosen so as to avoid cyclic physical dependencies among clusters.

[128] **lakos96**, section 4.1.3, Figure 4-26c, p. 195

represent generally reusable *tree-like*[129] subsystems, such as a logger, where only some of their components are intended for direct use by external clients, but are not entirely subordinate to other packages in the group.

The second use — application libraries — is to partition a cohesive, complex subsystem having a well-understood logical design and purpose into interface and implementation packages. In these kinds of package groups, only a potentially small subset of the packages within the group will be used directly by external clients. Hence, clients will identify use of such a group with the appropriate wrapper and/or interface packages (e.g., see Figure 2-30, section 2.4.10, and Figure 2-32, section 2.4.11). From the implementer's perspective, however, the separate packages provide convenient, internal boundaries of the design that are immediately visible from the source. These visible package boundaries, in turn, encourage the development of acyclic, logically and physically coherent sub-subsystems, that can be readily understood and maintained.

Each package group, when fully populated, is intended to represent a substantial body of software. Possible candidates for having sufficient complexity for implementation as a physically oriented application package group include a programming language compiler/interpreter, a CAD circuit simulator, a portfolio manager, and so on. Upon completion, the package group becomes the logically and physically coherent rendering of a cohesive and typically substantial application subsystem.

Just as with packages, determining the scope of a package group is a critical design issue. An overly specific package group containing just a single package would serve to clutter the global design space. By the same token, creating a package group with an overly general charter (e.g., business logic) could lead to units of release having unbounded size. Until one has considerable experience, it is not uncommon to misestimate the magnitude of a particular subsystem.

For example, suppose we wanted to create reusable library software to perform serialization (a.k.a. externalization, byte streaming, marshaling) of in-process data values via an abstract base class (runtime polymorphism).[130] Is this functionality best implemented as (a) a component, (b) a few components, (c) a package, (d) several packages, or (e) a package group?

---

[129] **lakos96**, section 4.1.3, Figure 4-26b, p. 195

[130] As it turns out, the use of method templates and *concepts* to achieve compile-time polymorphic byte streaming, though perhaps theoretically somewhat less flexible, still satisfies all practical requirements, and — for this particular functionality — has been demonstrated to have significantly higher runtime performance than the (now obsolete) runtime-polymorphic variant (see Volume II, section 4.1). Nonetheless, this example provides ample pedagogical value on multiple levels.

Without more information, it is hard to know for sure. Figure 2-72 gives a rough sense of the relative sizes implied by each. Keep in mind that these are only modest order-of-magnitude estimates consistent with those depicted in Figure 2-11, section 2.2.19; a complete component containing less than a hundred lines of source (excluding comments) or a well-factored package group containing over a million noncommentary lines of source are certainly plausible.

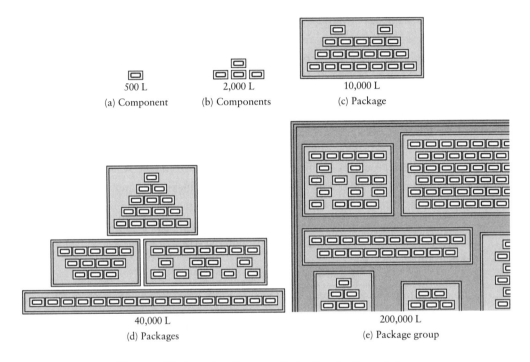

Figure 2-72: Assessing the magnitude of an implementation

Is serialization a component? No. Runtime polymorphic byte streaming will involve at least two pure abstract interfaces[131] (one for input and one for output) and *at least* four concrete implementations (two for production and two for testing). Is serialization a package in its own right? Perhaps. Or perhaps serialization shares a package with other similar functionality. Is serialization two (or more) packages? Perhaps. We might want to distinguish between interfaces that transform content to and from a canonical wire format and a cross-stream capability that enables byte streaming to and from a foreign host in the target machine's configuration — i.e., sizes, alignments, and endianness.

---

[131] A.k.a. *protocols* (section 1.7.5).

The relative placement of packages is another critical aspect of high-level library design. If our streaming functionality resides in two or more packages, should it still reside in the same package group? Perhaps. We might call the cross-stream package **xyzxc**, which could easily reside at a significantly higher level in the **xyz** package group than does its abstract interface (e.g., **xyzx**) and thereby depend on functionality provided by packages that themselves depend on **xyzx**. Alternatively, this separate cross-streaming package could be located in a less frequently used, higher-level package group geared toward our basic transport (**obt**) or, perhaps, a more general and eclectic one for our basic applications (**oba**).

Is serialization a package group? No. If this simple streaming functionality winds up being even close to what should populate a mature package group (i.e., something like two hundred thousand lines of noncommentary source code), the implementation is almost surely worse than useless.[132] Given that we plan to have only one canonical production format for an invasive facility to externalize all of our low-level types, and that the package name will likely be used exclusively to identify it, we would elect to place all such related components in their own appropriately named package near the bottom of the lowest-level package group in our system.[133]

Observation

Package groups allow acyclic application libraries to evolve over time.

Another subtle, yet powerful benefit of package groups in large development organizations comes from the observation that most individual projects are not particularly large, yet — over time — result in massive amounts of code that ideally will reside side-by-side in a well-organized infrastructure. Anticipating where in the physical hierarchy the next ten years of project code will go is not even remotely possible. What we can do, however, is anticipate some coarse levels of significant physical dependency. We can then use package groups to carve out some separate pieces of "real estate" — each characterized almost entirely by the envelope of dependencies governing member packages. The libraries that result will have the properties that (1) each

---

[132] See Figure 3-29, section 3.3.7, for another instructive example of package sizing involving concepts (section 1.7.6) and utilities (section 3.2.7).

[133] In reality, the open-source compile-time polymorphic analog to the object-oriented streaming package described here resides in the **bslx** package of our open-source **bsl** package group (repository **bde14**, subdirectory `/groups/bsl/bslx/`).

individual package is itself logically cohesive and (2) each package shares the same envelope of physical dependencies as every other package in the group. Absent total omniscience, this result is the best we can reasonably hope for, and — in practice — it's not at all bad either.

As a simple illustration, suppose a new development group is starting up in the Equity Derivatives department of our company and plans to employ the component-based methodology advocated in this book. After sufficient discussion with the firm-wide core team (whose members are thoroughly familiar with our methodology), it is determined that the general kinds of projects on which these specialized application developers will be working involve a mixture of coarse dependencies. The anticipated dependencies turn out to group into three basic categories, as illustrated in Figure 2-73.

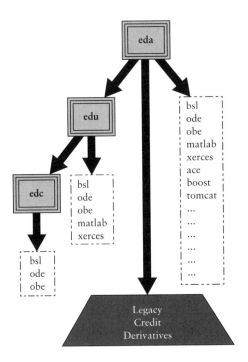

Figure 2-73: Predefining coarse dependency with package groups

The most primitive development — Equity Derivatives Core (**edc**) — will rely on only Our (firm-wide) Development Environment (**ode**) and Our (firm-wide) Business Environment (**obe**) proprietary libraries, which of course depend on foundation open-source libraries such as **bsl**. Mid-level infrastructure — Equity Derivatives Utilities (**edu**) — will leverage **edc** and, in addition to **bsl**, **ode**, and **obe**, will be permitted to depend on a short list of approved third-party products. Finally, only the highest level of equity derivatives infrastructure — Equity Derivatives Applications (**eda**) — will be allowed to depend on the legacy infrastructure, which brings with it a much wider list of open-source and third-party products.

Over time, common code that must depend on legacy software will necessarily have to be located in packages of the **eda** package group, while cleaner subsystems with more limited physical dependencies might be able to reside in the lower-level **edu** package group. Very clean components, having minimal dependencies that are likely candidates for department-wide reuse, would properly reside in the lowest department-level package group, **edc**. The application packages that result, though perhaps somewhat logically diverse, lead to package groups that are nonetheless physically cohesive and acyclic. With sufficient forethought and up-front design effort, many packages will find their proper place in some well-scoped package group within our firm's acyclic physical hierarchy of software.

Note that, as a vital part of the ongoing maintenance process, we advocate employing what's called *continuous refactoring*, whereby generally useful components in an application library are extracted, refined, generalized, and moved lower in a department's UOR dependency graph, where they will become more obvious candidates for an infrastructure team to further refactor and place at yet a lower level in the firm-wide repository, thereby enabling even wider reuse.

Guideline

Each package should, if possible, be part of an appropriate package group.

While designing in terms of standalone (isolated) packages might require less up-front effort initially, it will — over time — invariably increase costs in terms of physical complexity, human understanding, maintenance, and usability. To the extent possible, we are well advised to design in terms of package groups, and make every effort to place each new component within a package suitably located within an appropriate package group, unless there is a compelling reason to do otherwise (see below).

Guideline

Allowed package-group dependencies should be (1) minimal, and (2) seldom increased.

A well-designed package group will consist of packages that share a tight common envelope of physical dependencies, while being logically cohesive. Ideally, each package would belong to a package group having these properties, yet not every package that is logically cohesive with other packages within a package group properly belongs there. Those that do not are almost always anchored by some substantial physical dependency — e.g., on legacy, open-source, or third-party software (see section 2.12).

For example, consider the package group **xyz** in Figure 2-74, which is currently allowed to depend on only the firm-wide core package group **ode** and the open-source foundation library **bsl**. Within **xyz**, packages **xyza**, **xyzb**, and **xyzc** are independent, while package **xyze** depends on packages **xyzb** and **xyzc**. Because these packages are grouped, use of **xyze** implies that clients will need to link against **xyza** (and vice versa), yet, because all of these packages have essentially the same physical dependencies, there is no reason not to aggregate them.

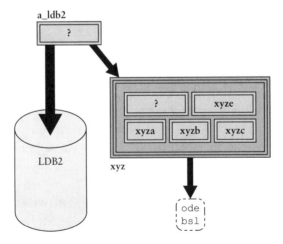

Figure 2-74: Isolating heavy-weight dependencies with standalone packages

Now consider another package, **a_ldb2** (see section 2.10.3), that is logically cohesive with all of the packages currently in the **xyz** package group and happens to depend on the **xyza** and **xyzb** packages, but also wraps (or adapts, see Volume II, section 4.6) access to a large legacy database, **LDB2**. If we were to choose to make this new package part of the **xyz** package group (and rename it to **xyzd**), then anyone wanting to use *any* of the packages in **xyz** would be forced to depend on the heavy-weight **LDB2** legacy database. Placing this package in any other group that did not already depend on **LDB2** would have a similar effect. So, even though **a_ldb2** might be logically cohesive with the **xyz** package group, we deliberately choose *not* to burden the **xyz** package group with the dependency on **LDB2**, and keep **a_ldb2** as an *isolated* (or "standalone") *package*.

2.9.4   Decentralized (Autonomous) Package Creation

Observation

Package groups support decentralized package creation.

Package groups, being architecturally significant, must have names that are unique throughout the enterprise. Such unique naming is typically accomplished in practice by actively maintaining a centralized enterprise-wide registry of package-group names. Since the package-group name automatically reserves the namespaces for all the names of packages it contains (section 2.4.11), once a package group name is dispensed, package group owners are free to create as many packages as needed without having to consult the central registry, thus decentralizing package creation.

2.9.5   Section Summary

In summary, package groups are our third and highest level of architecturally significant *physical* aggregation. While packages always serve to aggregate both logically and physically related components, package groups provide a vehicle for aggregating packages that may not be logically cohesive, yet still necessarily share the same envelope of allowed physical dependencies.

Ideally, the charter of a well-designed library package group will be broad enough to attract a somewhat logically diverse suite of packages, yet (1) address a common purpose and/or serve a particular class of clientele, (2) be sufficiently scoped so as not to grow over time to become excessively large, and (3) share a very narrow envelope of allowed physical dependencies.

Package groups that are owned and populated by multiple (e.g., application) teams over long periods of time will likely lack the tighter logical cohesion of those centrally owned and managed by a single (e.g., infrastructure) team, yet will still achieve profound benefits by providing an organized framework ensuring that like dependencies of colocated components are enforced and that no cyclic physical dependencies among UORs will creep in over time.

Finally, we generally want library UORs to be represented as package groups, with isolated packages being the occasional exception, used primarily to accommodate heavyweight dependencies on typically open-source or third-party libraries. In this way, we can decentralize the creation of individual packages, allowing package group owners to create them independently as needed.

2.10   Naming Packages and Package Groups

Having a sound naming strategy for widely visible entities is essential for large-scale software development. In this section, we delineate our overall approach for naming architecturally significant logical and physical entities. In particular, we offer industry-proven, concise naming rules for package groups, packages that reside within package groups, and those that do not.

2.10.1   Intuitively Descriptive Package Names Are Overrated

When creating a package group, one might initially assume, as many do, that its name should be allowed to be of arbitrary length, sufficient to be immediately comprehensible and illuminating to the unfamiliar, and similarly so for the names of packages they contain. Thus, a `Calendar` class located in the package associated with time-related types in one of our most basic package groups could have an eminently descriptive qualified logical name:

> `our_development_library::time::Calendar` *(VERY BAD IDEA)*

Sadly, the level of pain associated with using such admittedly "literate" namespace names will give way to `using` directives (section 2.4.12) that will collect and grow like a cancer as they are carted about as a block from one source file to the next, eradicating any descriptive advantage such names might have once afforded.

We could employ extreme abbreviations and still maintain syntactically delimited namespaces:

> `odl::t::Calendar` *(BAD IDEA)*

But to what end? Fortunately, package-group names form a natural prefix for enterprise-wide unique package names. By simply merging the fixed-length group name with a one- or two- (at most three-) character package suffix, we arrive at the unique package name `odlt` (pronounced "oh-delt"):

```
odlt::Calendar (GOOD IDEA)
```

By instead opting for compact yet unique package names, such as **std**, though initially cryptic, they quickly become part of our vocabulary, reinforced through repeated use.[134]

Given our fervent need for concision in package names, systematically achieving uniqueness is again brought to the forefront. Recall that, in our methodology, only classes, structures, and free operators (and operator-like *aspect* functions) are permitted to be declared at file or namespace scope (section 2.4.9). Nominal logical/physical cohesion is then achieved by having the component name match the lowercased leading characters of each `class` or `struct` defined at package-namespace scope within that component. Following these guidelines, the unique-naming problem for all logical constructs then reduces to avoiding collisions among component names in the global *physical* namespace, which we accomplish by ensuring that package names themselves are unique throughout the enterprise.

For a UOR that is just a single package, the package name is automatically both the logical namespace and also the physical prefix of each component that it comprises. For a UOR that aggregates multiple packages, we employ the notion of a package group, which, by definition, is *architecturally significant* (section 2.2.6) and, therefore, must have a globally unique name. This name, of uniform length, will form a prefix for the name of every package in the group. Note that we must also ensure that the respective authorized namespaces for grouped and isolated ("standalone") packages do not overlap.

2.10.2   Package-Group Names

Design Rule

The (all-lowercase) alphanumeric name of every package group must be exactly three characters and form a valid identifier:

\<Package Group Name\> ::= [a-z] [a-z0-9] [a-z0-9]

---

[134] The ability to unambiguously parse a name in isolation benefits tools and people alike. If the group names were not of fixed length, inferring the group name from the package name — absent an explicit and costly delimiter — would require a registry (i.e., database) lookup, which has severe practical disadvantages. Notice that, in our approach, the group is immediately obvious irrespective of whether or not it has been registered (see section 2.10.3).

Short cryptic names admittedly have their drawbacks. Nonetheless, whatever space can be afforded for descriptive purposes is far better invested in the component's "given" name rather than the parental "tag" used to identify its enclosing package and thereby its (unique) location in the physical hierarchy. Being that package groups, like other major libraries such as the C++ Standard Library (namespace `std`), are relatively few and well known, we have chosen — albeit perhaps ruthlessly — to limit package-group names to exactly three characters in length, yielding $26 \times 36 \times 36 = 33{,}696$ distinct package-group names.

Understand that the specific length of three characters advocated here is less important than that package-group names be very short and that they all have exactly[135] *the same* length (to obviate an extra delimiter).[136] A centrally administered, enterprise-wide registry of allocated UOR names (see section 2.10.3) erases any fear that such names will collide, and brevity here breeds productivity. We also have built-in escape provisions[137] should they someday be needed.

2.10.3   Package Names

Design Rule

The (all-lowercase) name of each package within a package group must begin with the name of the group, followed by one, two, or three lowercase alphanumeric characters that uniquely distinguish the package within its group.

<Grouped Package Name> ::= <Package Group Name> [a-z0-9] ([a-z0-9] ([a-z0-9])?)?

---

[135] The word "exactly" — used here for emphasis — in the context of mathematical values, such as integers, is (at best) entirely redundant (see Volume II, section 4.1).

[136] We reserve the right to prepend to any package group name (e.g., **xyz**) a **z_** prefix (e.g., **z_xyz**) to form the valid five-character name of a package group that serves as the C-language compatible procedural wrapper interface for the corresponding lower-level, C++-only (three character) package group (see section 3.11.7.8).

[137] E.g., all **two-character prefixes** are currently reserved for future use. In particular, to minimize accidental header-file name collisions (section 2.9.4) across organizations having similar methodologies, each organization *exporting* libraries might consider adding, to each of its own header names, a consistent (hopefully) unique two-character *physical* prefix (e.g., **bb_**) corresponding to its (longer) unique enterprise-wide namespace name. Alternatively, each company *importing* eclectic libraries might choose to anchor (and refer to *in its own source code*) the components in these respective code bases via their new (distinguishing) *local* directory names (or equivalently local unique header-file prefixes). The `#include` directives contained in the source code of the exported header files of each (imported) library would also need to be updated (as part of its deployment; see section 2.15) to reflect the now locally unique identity of its headers.

For example, it is easy to see by inspection that the **bdlt**, **bdlma**, and **bdlb** packages all belong to the same **bdl** package group:

```
bdlt_datetime                          // time-related types

bdlma_bufferedsequentialallocator  // special purpose memory allocators

bdlb_bitutil                           // general low-level functionality
```

Thanks to logical and physical name cohesion (section 2.4), given the declaration of an object of class bdlt::PackedCalendar, we can quickly determine that the class belongs to the **bdlt_packedcalendar** component in the **bdlt** package of the **bdl** package group. And, because the locations of package groups are (comparatively) few and (ideally) well-known, finding these files and the logical entities contained therein is automatic and mechanical for human beings and tools alike.

In order to separate the namespaces of standalone packages from those that may be part of a package group, we exclude four to six character names for standalone packages and also provide a single character escape sequence. Note, however, that we reserve the single character escape sequence **m_** for application packages (see section 2.13) and **z_** for the exclusive use of C-language-compatible procedural interfaces (see section 3.11.7.8). Finally, in rare cases, such as the C++ Standard Library (**std**) itself, we might opt to have a package-group-sized standalone package (i.e., having a single namespace), in which case its name (and corresponding namespace) would have exactly three characters (see sections 2.10.3 and 2.11).

Design Rule

The (all-lowercase) name of each standalone package must begin with a lowercase alphabetic character and either (1) consist of more than six (or exactly three, which is RARE) alphanumeric characters, or (2) be followed by an underscore, a letter, and then zero or more alphanumeric characters (note that the prefix "z_" is treated specially; see Figure 2-75, section 2.10.3).

<Ungrouped Package Name> ::= <Package Group Name> ([a-z0-9] $)^4$ ([a-z0-9])*

| <Package Group Name>   *VERY RARE*

| [a-y] _ [a-z] ([a-z0-9])*   *z_ is special.*

For example, Figure 2-75 illustrates a variety of package names that, by inspection, immediately imply standalone packages. In particular, any package name that is more than six characters is known not to be part of any group. Having a single-character prefix, followed by an underscore (except **z_**, see section 3.11.7.8) also indicates that the package is not grouped. In truly exceptional cases, such as the C++ Standard Library, we would entertain having just a single, very large package with a very short (i.e., exactly three-character) name, such as **std** (see section 2.11). In such cases, one would not generally be able to tell from the (three-character) name alone whether it refers to a group or an oversized standalone package. In the case of the latter, however, one would invariably recognize (in code) a ubiquitous package prefix (e.g., std) as such in practice.

```
z234567::Cryptograph     // more than 6 characters

mystandalonepackage::Foo  // way more than 6 characters

m_mailserver             // uses 'm_' ("main" application) prefix
                         // (e.g., see Figure 2-77, section 2.13)

a_xml                    // uses 'a_' ("adapter") prefix
                         // (e.g., see Figure 2-74, section 2.9.3)

z_a_xml                  // C-compatible wrapper for the above adapter
                         // (e.g., see Figure 3-147, section 3.11.7.8)
```

Figure 2-75: Various naming conventions identifying standalone packages

---

Guideline

The name of each (sharable) UOR within an enterprise should be registered (and reserved) with a central authority *before* it is used.

Just as in multithreaded programming (see Volume II, section 6.1), we want to avoid race conditions that might compromise the integrity of our architecture. Before a group in an enterprise makes extensive use of a UOR name that is capable of being referred to by external clients (i.e., other than an **m_**...), it is only prudent to reserve that name so that other, like-minded people don't inadvertently choose a similar name. Ultimately, the centralized nature of our package-based organization will force the issue. The saying "An ounce of prevention is worth a pound of cure" pertains here.

Observation

Choosing package names within a package group is automatically decentralized.

One of the great collateral benefits of our grouped-package nomenclature is that, once a package group name is reserved, there is never any need to go back and reregister at the component or package level (section 2.9.4). That all just works. Even though each package within the package group must also have a globally unique name, within this limited scope, just one or two additional characters is usually sufficient to get the job done.

2.10.4   Section Summary

In summary, having an effective naming strategy is important when developing software on a large scale. To avoid enticing client use of `using` directives and declarations, the names clients use to refer to entities outside their own package must be kept *extremely* short. Given that we have adopted a maximum of three levels of architecturally significant physical aggregation (section 2.2.19), we are able to exploit a highly compressed nomenclature to readily access software in other packages, and equally so those in other package groups. Left to chance, having such short package names could easily lead to accidental duplication and collisions. Having a thoughtful, comprehensive hierarchical naming convention as well as an enterprise-wide registry of UOR names handily addresses this issue. Moreover, registered package group names allow for the process of naming new individual packages within a group to be decentralized. The autonomy afforded by this naming strategy is in part what enables our development process to scale to accommodate extremely large software-development organizations.

2.11   Subpackages

We maintain that three architecturally significant levels of physical aggregation are sufficient for any situation. We also understand the occasional need to represent an unusually large collection of components within a single namespace — i.e., when mandated by an externally defined specification. Such foreign specifications (e.g., the C++ Standard Library), in which large numbers of independently reusable components are intended for direct use by clients, might not have been designed in a way that optimally incorporates architecturally significant subaggregate dependencies within the UOR.[138]

---

[138] Libraries, such as the STL, having few interdependencies are sometimes characterized as being *horizontal*. See **lakos96**, section 7.4, Figure 7-16a, p. 504.

Absent sufficient forethought and proper factoring, having separate packages (and therefore namespaces) within a unit of release could even prove problematic. For example, ill-conceived partitioning forcing clients to have to remember which cryptic package variant is arbitrarily associated with a particular component name (e.g., **xyza_bitarray** versus **xyzt_date**) could easily impede usability. It is therefore critical that the package name itself properly characterize the package. Ideally, the package name will be the commonly used *spoken* name used to refer to the facility or subsystem it represents — e.g., **bslma** (pronounced "be-sel-ma") is the name commonly used to refer to the memory-allocator-facility package located in the **bsl** package group.

Given a large and poorly factored UOR, having a single namespace also allows somewhat greater flexibility to its implementers in "moving" — i.e., substantially altering the relative physical (implementation) dependencies of — the components that reside within that UOR without forcing external clients to update their code. That said, we cannot overemphasize that any benefit from such physical flexibility to implementers is invariably more than offset by increased costs in terms of understandability, reliability, and maintenance resulting from insufficient up-front design and planning. In our experience, the practical value of having architecturally significant, logically cohesive, internal physical structure in large UORs is unequivocal.

In extremely rare cases, we — as library developers (section 0.2) — might ourselves choose to absorb the implementation complexity inward, forgo the proven ease of development and maintenance that the nominal cohesion of the fractal namespaces of package groups provides (section 2.4.11), and create a well-coordinated, physically sound, package-group-sized package having just a single namespace, such as std. Though far from ideal, at least now casual clients of this UOR need remember just the one package name, **xyz** (e.g., **xyz_bitarray** and **xyz_date**).[139]

The remainder of this short section, which for most should be entirely hypothetical, discusses how we might preserve the internal aggregation hierarchy without exposing it (or changes to it) to clients. Figure 2-76 illustrates two similar representations of a pedagogical UOR containing nine components. Figure 2-76a shows a package group **grp** containing three packages, each containing three components. In this purely didactic example, we assume that component names are (or can easily be made) unique across packages. Hence, requiring clients to match the component name with its corresponding package within a group could be eliminated.

---

[139] Note that, although such an enlarged package could, in theory, be a member of a package group, **xyz** (e.g., **xyza_bitarray** and **xyza_date**), doing so would violate our principle that aggregates at a given depth within an aggregate should have comparable physical complexity (see Figure 2-9c, section 2.2.17).

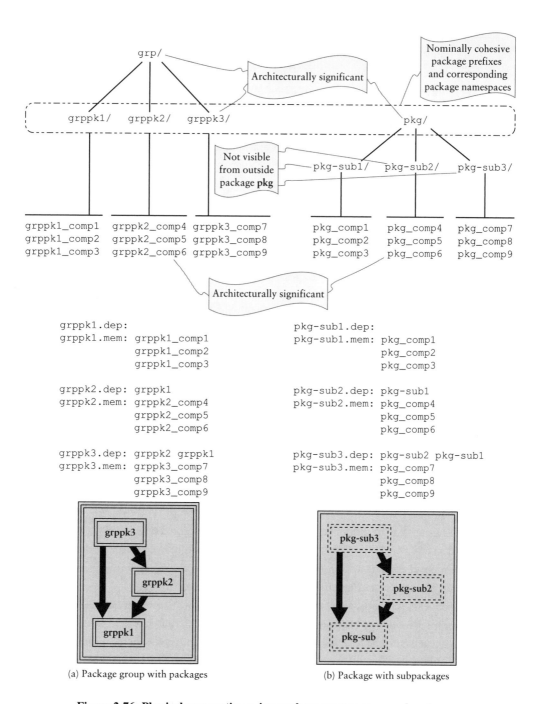

Figure 2-76: Physical aggregation using package groups versus subpackages

In some sense, what is needed is a single namespace for all the packages in the group, with all member-file prefixes matching that namespace (Figure 3-76b). The resulting transformation, however, is nothing other than to turn what would properly be a package group **grp** (Figure 2-76a) into an oversized (albeit otherwise *regular*) package **pkg** (see section 2.12), and yet retain three physical levels of aggregation (Figure 2-76b). According to our definition of a package (section 2.4.5), **pkg** would become the first *architecturally significant* level of aggregation larger than a component. Hence, a subpackage, which (by that same definition) is *not* architecturally significant, is entirely irrelevant outside of the package that defines it.

From an architectural perspective, "subpackages" are invisible; they can be changed or eliminated entirely without ever affecting any source code. The advantages provided by the use of subpackages within a large package are entirely organizational (i.e., for the benefit of the package author/maintainer). The extent to which they help is limited to expressing aggregate dependencies among clusters of logically and physically related components that do not enjoy the nominal cohesion afforded by packages within a group. By making explicit which components belong to which subpackages (via each subpackage .mem file) and upon what other subpackages that subpackage is permitted to depend (via each subpackage .dep file), we might be better able to enforce an internal organization that can be maintained, tested, and ported in the incremental and hierarchical way to which we are accustomed.

Let's now consider a vendor-supplied or open-source implementation of the C++ Standard Library. The interface is already specified (and happens not to conform to our canonical model of a package group). For reasons discussed throughout, the functionality in this widely reusable library is guarded by a single terse namespace std. Despite the homogeneous namespace, there is considerable potential for logically and physically coherent clustering when it comes to implementation.

For example, in a component-based rendering of the C++ Standard Library, the STL containers and std::string would almost certainly share a common envelope of dependencies on other component clusters within the library itself (e.g., low-level metafunctions, traits, exceptions, etc.). Streams would also be implemented as a cohesive collection of components with like dependencies. Our experience with maintaining various implementations of the C++ Standard Library[140] confirms that an absence of adequate internal physical structure obfuscates the design and can lead to unwanted cyclic physical dependencies (in the worst case involving public interfaces). Well-chosen subpackages can provide the physical structure needed to preserve the effective maintainability of such libraries.

---

[140] Including enhancements to support our polymorphic allocator model (see Volume II, section 4.10).

In summary, subpackages, as presented here, might be of value to maintainers of excessively large standalone packages. Since subpackages are explicitly not architecturally significant, they cannot be referred to as entities from outside of a package; hence, they are not relevant when it comes to deployment (see section 2.15.9). Subpackages are, however, physical aggregates (section 2.2.1) and, hence, cyclic dependencies among subpackages (as defined by the dependencies among the respective components they contain) are not permitted. Given the vanishingly rare utility of oversized packages, we conclude that subpackages do not warrant further consideration.

2.12   Legacy, Open-Source, and Third-Party Software

Following our methodology, all newly developed proprietary library software will take the form of components (sections 2.5–2.7) that have been properly aggregated into packages (section 2.8), and most usually package groups (section 2.9), all of which follow a consistent naming strategy (section 2.10). As Figure 2-3, section 2.1, illustrates, however, not all of our library software will necessarily be component-based. Some of it might well predate our consistent use of components, and some will likely come from other sources that use a different methodology. The atomic unit of integration for non-component-based software is, by default, a library and corresponding header files that can be deployed as an independent unit of release. The source for such software most closely resembles the definition of a package but will typically not comply with our cohesive source-code packaging nomenclature (sections 2.4 and 2.10).

> **DEFINITION**: A package is *irregular* if it is not composed entirely of proper components, each adhering to our design rules, especially those pertaining to cohesive naming.

Recall from section 2.2.7 that every UOR is architecturally significant and therefore requires a unique name. Legacy, open-source, and third-party libraries are no exception. To incorporate and refer to these libraries within our infrastructure, it will be necessary to assign each of them a globally unique name. Because these names are typically not reflected in their source code, the names are essentially arbitrary.

A legacy library can be treated as either a single irregular package or as a package group consisting of one irregular package. The latter approach allows for the incremental refactoring of the legacy library into a levelizable (section 1.10) set of regular packages over time (see sections 3.4 and 3.5). The names of irregular packages within a group are typically kept syntactically distinct from regular package names. For example, package group **xyz** might consist of packages **xyza** and **xyzb**, which are regular, and package **xyz+oldstuff**, which is not.[141] In the specific case of our **bsl** package group, a member package having a + in its name implies that logical content defined within that package resides in the bsl namespace in order to mirror the predefined C++ Standard Library specification. For open-source and third-party libraries, however, we will usually avoid any modification, as that would result in a code fork; hence, we will normally treat each such library as a single irregular isolated package.

We will need to state our dependency on irregular UORs by name in the .dep file of each UOR (e.g., isolated package or package group). It will be up to the build system and the people who maintain the irregular software to install it in such a way that it can be found and used by the build system for all supported targets on all relevant platforms. The information that describes the supported build targets (e.g., DEBUG_STATIC, OPTIMIZED_SHARED) and relevant platforms (e.g., SUN_STUDIO12, HP_UX, IBM_AIX) is beyond the scope of the C++ language, and must reside in metadata associated with the software — e.g., in capabilities (.cap) files (see section 2.16).

For example, suppose we find we have a need to parse XML and decide to incorporate the Xerces open-source library into our development environment for that purpose. We would probably adopt **xerces** as the name of the irregular UOR. Next, we would associate with **xerces** (in meta-data) the various platforms and targets for which it will be supported. It would then be necessary to build and deploy **xerces** (by hand if necessary) so that its outward interface (a collection of headers and a library archive) mirrored that of our proprietary *regular* software. Finally, we might want to wrap the Xerces functionality with a conforming interface so that the code that needs XML parsing functionality is not polluted by the use of irregular names.[142]

---

[141] Note that the choice of a + character was not entirely arbitrary — it was chosen from of a short list of punctuation characters identified (by Peter Wainwright at Bloomberg c. 2003) as being least likely to interact with typical file and operating systems.

[142] Wrapping the separate parts of a large subsystem, as discussed in sections 3.1.10.9, 3.6.10, and 3.11.6, is not always possible; even when it is technically practicable (e.g., see section 3.1.10.8), wrapping might not be the best business decision, as David Sankel explains (in his review of the manuscript for this volume):

> There are, however, some serious pitfalls with this approach that should be pointed out: Maintaining a wrapper of a library that is constantly changing is a burden and almost always becomes out of date. For this reason, 'biting the bullet' accepting the irregularity is frequently the right engineering choice.

Most production-ready, open-source libraries come with their own build/install scripts that release the source code into a specified location. Such software, when released, often includes a small hierarchy consisting of relative paths. Unlike our own *regular* proprietary software, we cannot count on the global uniqueness of the names of the files in which *irregular* software resides. For that reason, we will not, in general, be able to flatten that software or colocate it with other irregular software during deployment (see section 2.15.7). Such software might also depend on the platform-specific properties of `#include` directives (section 1.5.1) that use double-quotes (`""`) rather than angle brackets (`<>`). Finally, we will need to ensure that the software runs on all of our supported platforms (or characterize, in a `.cap` file, those on which it does). Hence, each nonconforming library will require at least some initial effort to fit it into our component-based framework.

In summary, integration with irregular software is largely one of deployment, and not design. Each legacy, open-source, or third-party library will be given a globally unique name that will be used to refer to it as a black box from other UORs. Once appropriate metadata is assigned to it, this irregular software can be treated just as if it were regular, except that it will likely not follow all of our strict naming conventions. We will talk more about deployment generally in section 2.15. What makes all of this software work seamlessly is the ability to describe its properties in metadata and then employ component-based tools that use this metadata to perform appropriately (see section 2.16).

2.13   Applications

In this section, we present a consistent framework for developing applications. Library development, in order to be maximally useful, must follow a disciplined approach that leads to a high-level of stability, interoperability, and, ideally, hierarchical reuse (section 0.4); application development, however, need not. As discussed in section 0.2, the goal of application development is primarily to deliver high-quality solutions as quickly as possible subject to a much more dynamic environment having ever-changing requirements. Since applications naturally reside at the highest level in the overall physical hierarchy of software, the need for stability (and especially reusability) is largely eliminated. Hence, developing applications reliably is not inconsistent with the goals of agility.[143]

---

[143] http://agilemanifesto.org/

Application developers are naturally application-centric. Given that each application is at the top of the physical hierarchy, it can be organized and built in any way that the application developer sees fit — entirely independent of other applications. In a large development organization, however, there are typically many applications being developed concurrently. These applications will, in turn, have many versions. Devising a framework that can be used to integrate all applications into a single methodology has compelling advantages when managing application software development on a large scale.

At the very highest level, we choose to organize our software into two branches of development: applications and libraries. As Figure 2-77 illustrates, conforming applications and library UORs would be placed in their respective branches. Applications developed outside of this organizational structure could still make use of the new regular library software via their own conventional build tools. Library software developed outside of our methodology would be integrated into this organization at the UOR level as discussed in section 2.10.

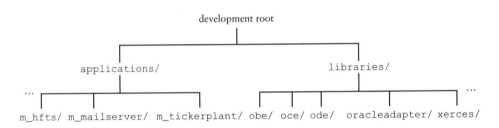

Figure 2-77: Development framework organized into applications and libraries

A conforming application should be a relatively small unit of release, having the same physical structure as a standalone package (section 2.8). Unlike library packages, however, application packages must not be depended upon by any other UOR, but are permitted to contain individual files (in addition to test drivers) that live outside the global namespace and contain a `main` routine. Consider the **m_mailserver** application package of Figure 2-78. This application contains a collection of files that conforms to the same isolated package structure (see Figure 2-58, section 2.8.1), but in addition has two distinguished files, `m_mailserver_server.m.cpp` and `m_mailserver_administrator.m.cpp`, that represent the two *programs* that this application supports.

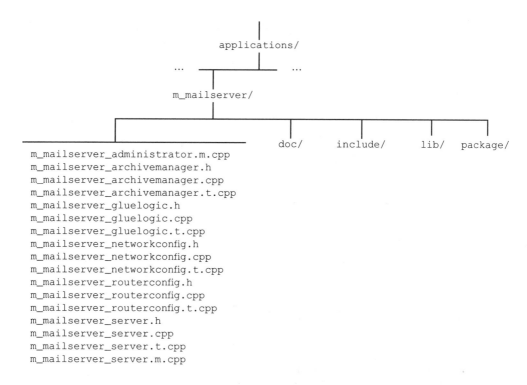

Figure 2-78: Directory structure for typical application package m_mailserver

Files that have an extra .m (for "main program") or .t (for "test driver") before the .cpp suffix indicate that they are source files that contain the definition of a main routine. All other source files in this package reside in standard components:

m_mailserver_archivemanager
m_mailserver_gluelogic
m_mailserver_networkconfig
m_mailserver_routerconfig
m_mailserver_server

A main-program file, one having a .m.cpp suffix, may or may not have the same root name as one of the components — e.g., m_mailserver_server.m.cpp does, and m_mailserver_administrator.m.cpp does not.

Strictly speaking, the only requirement about applications is that the names within an application do not conflict with any libraries that the application uses. If a conflict does occur, it is typically easy for the application developer to resolve. For small-scale development, this reactive resolution is adequate. On a larger scale, however, with potentially hundreds or even thousands of applications being built and deployed automatically, it is not optimal. Left to chance, we run the risk of accidental conflicts as new library components are added. Unless library and application namespaces are kept syntactically disjoint by design, conflicts will continue to be an issue as our code base matures.

Design Rule

The allowable names for applications (i.e., application-level "packages") must be disjoint from those of all other kinds of packages.

As you might have noticed, the name of each application package has an extra **m_** prefix. This choice is a purely arbitrary implementation detail of our naming rules (section 2.10), which ensures that no application name can ever conflict with a library name.[144] Moreover, since all application code (other than the code in `.m.cpp` files) must reside in a namespace matching the package name, there is no possibility that any application package symbol will collide with any library symbol either.

Design Rule

**All code within an application package must be local (private) to that package —
i.e., *nothing* outside the package is permitted to depend on software defined within
an application-level package.**

The code that resides at the top level of an application can be highly collaborative and must remain malleable (section 0.5). Given that the pressures to produce application code rapidly is justifiably far stronger than for reusable library code, it is crucial that we not allow other developers to impede this malleability by unilaterally placing expectations on the stability of software private to other applications. Application code may be shared among closely related `main` programs (i.e., `.m.cpp` files) residing within the same application package; however,

---

[144] Having application package names be disjoint from those of library packages ensures that there will never be potential latent conflicts with application code — e.g., as new packages are added to existing package groups over time (section 2.9.4).

if code is to be shared across application packages, it must be refactored and *demoted* (see section 3.5.3) into library software — no exceptions.

Having all of the top-level application logic reside in just a single package has some important advantages. The maintenance of application code, being malleable and yet highly collaborative, might involve making changes to several components at once. Because all of this collaborative code resides in a single package, it is far easier to change and release that code in lockstep. Moreover, because all of this code resides in a single namespace, we can avoid the pain of ever having to qualify our names with the annoyingly long and ugly application namespaces such as `m_mailserver`.[145] Since much of what application developers write and use is in their own package, writability (and also readability) are enhanced by dropping the application prefix (without any need for `using` directives or declarations).

Organizing all of our applications as isolated packages removes much of the creativity from the build process, allowing that creativity to be more profitably focused elsewhere. In a large organization having hundreds of ongoing projects, refocusing the creativity of our developers to the solutions they create, rather than on how they are packaged, built, and deployed, is an important part of achieving a higher throughput at a much lower cost of ownership. Given this very simple, very regular application structure, it becomes possible to automate much of the burden that heretofore has been a painful, tedious, and error-prone process. What constitutes an adequate external environment for building and deploying *regular* applications is discussed in terms of *metadata* in section 2.16.

2.14   The Hierarchical Testability Requirement

It is not uncommon for "an abstractly defined structure" to be based on *axioms* — i.e., statements or propositions that are "regarded as being established, accepted, or self-evidently true."[146] In our methodology, one such axiom is that cyclic physical dependencies among distinct physical entities are always undesirable. Yet, unlike some axioms in mathematics, we — as engineers — have multiple reasons to believe that allowing such design cycles is a bad idea. We

---

[145] Recall that reusable library software benefits from having short namespace tags; enterprise and application package namespaces, on the other hand, are protective in nature and typically not referenced in source code.

[146] www.lexico.com

have argued that cyclic designs are more difficult for human beings to comprehend than acyclic ones. What's more, cyclic physical dependencies (see section 3.4) can prevent (e.g., hierarchical) reuse (section 0.4) of even a tiny part of a subsystem without incorporating all of it. In this section, however, we will explore the need to avoid cyclic physical dependencies at every level of physical aggregation from an entirely different perspective — that of ensuring practical, thorough (hierarchical) testability.

2.14.1   Leveraging Our Methodology for Fine-Grained Unit Testing

Ensuring reliability for large-scale systems is possible only by up-front design. Our component-based methodology provides the leverage we need to achieve this important goal. Given the inherent complexity of large systems, however, we will need several dimensions of leverage: fine-grained modularity, hierarchy, feedback, and reuse. Insisting on small, well-factored, logically and physically coherent units of design, i.e., components (sections 0.7, 1.6, 1.11, and 2.6), is an essential first step. We then need to exploit the *dual* physical hierarchy (aggregation and dependency) of our component-based designs to first decompose them fully and then optimally order the verification effort. Next, we will associate with each component a unique standalone test driver program (see Volume III, section 7.5), which we will then use to establish the redundancy and focused immediate feedback necessary to verify every aspect of functionality on a component-by-component basis. Finally, we will reuse a uniform physical form, methodology, and interface that will standardize our testing approach, and thereby mitigate much of the collateral complexity associated with software verification.

2.14.2   Plan for This Section (Plus Plug for Volume II and Especially Volume III)

In this section, we address objectively verifiable rules necessary for scalable component-level testing. Later, in Chapter 3, we will discuss techniques for refining and improving our physical factoring — e.g., to avoid cyclic, excessive, or otherwise inappropriate dependencies. It will turn out that awareness of common class categories (see Volume II, section 4.2) to guide our component designs not only improves human cognition, but also further enhances the effectiveness of component-level testing. In Volume III, Chapter 7, we'll revisit the need for, and principles behind, component-level testing. In subsequent chapters in Volume III, we will elaborate on the methods for selecting appropriate input data (Chapter 8), implementation techniques for delivering test data (Chapter 9), and the overall organization of component-level test drivers in general (Chapter 10), which is then tailored to specific class categories. By the end of the three volumes, we'll have the knowledge needed to ensure our testing efforts are both thorough and efficient. For now, however, we start with the basics.

2.14.3   Testing Hierarchically Needs to Be Possible

Design Imperative

Hierarchical Testability Requirement: Every physical entity must be *thoroughly testable* in terms only of other physical entities that themselves have already been tested thoroughly.

Testability (or more generally, our ability to obtain feedback), as it is with any other engineering discipline, is a cornerstone of our methodology. If we cannot measure it, we cannot know if we got it right or adjust it to make it better. Attempting to obtain this feedback on a system of overwhelming complexity is, well, overwhelming. By insisting that our systems be decomposable into subsystems (e.g., package groups and packages) and finally into fine-grained atomic modular physical units (e.g., components), we enable the bare possibility of effective thorough testing. This decomposability property alone, however, is not sufficient! At each level of physical aggregation, there must be at least one order in which testing can proceed such that every physical entity at that level — be it a component, package, or package group — can be verified without having to depend on anything (1) other than what the entity already depends on, or (2) that is not independently verifiable (or somehow otherwise known to be correct).

The implications that flow from consideration of this all-important governance overlap several others we have already seen. For example, an immediate consequence is that cyclic physical dependency among components, or units of release (e.g., packages and package groups), is not allowed, as no member of such a cycle could ever be tested independently of the rest. This rule, however, encompasses far subtler forms of intractability. Consider again from Figure 2-50, section 2.6, the ill-advised long-distance friendship granted by a container to some nonlocal type with modifiable access. Figure 2-79a shows abstractly a higher-level *manip* component that can materially affect (and therefore potentially disrupt) the consistent internal (private) state defined within a lower-level *container* component in a way that, absent testing the *manip* component itself, is impossible to defend against. Since *manip* clearly depends on *container*, neither can be fully tested independently of the other.

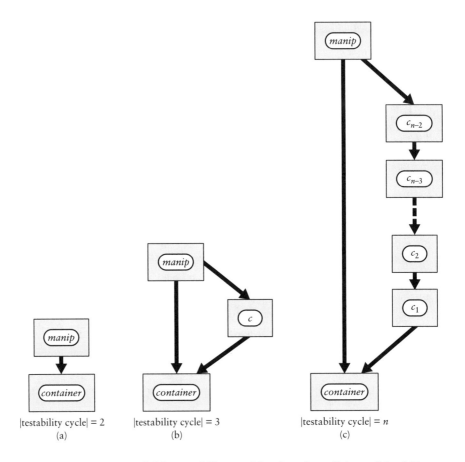

Figure 2-79: Unbounded intractability resulting from long-distance friendship

It might at first appear as though we should just test the two together and be done with it. Not so fast! If *manip* is a separate physical entity, what is to stop *manip* from depending on some other possibly substantial component c, which, as in Figure 2-79b, happens to depend on *container*. Our testability-induced cycle will have grown to involve not just the original two components, but now three! Having a testability cycle (or even an actual dependency cycle for that matter) is not necessarily intractable provided that the magnitude of that cycle is bounded (and small). Unfortunately, misguided long-distance friendship — ironically, often in the name of "safety" — can lead to unbounded involvement as in Figure 2-79c.

While *modifiable* private access across component boundaries is a clear violation of our hierarchical testability requirement, even *nonmodifiable* backdoor access violates another important principle: *physical substitutability* (see Volume II, section 5.6). That is, if we make a change to an encapsulated private implementation detail of a class, we will be unable to check that change back in to our system until we have made any needed corresponding changes to all of its friends, even if the outward-facing *public* interface and contract have not changed. Note that an analogous, unbounded breach of encapsulation results from protected access. By insisting that friendship not span our atomic units of physical design (section 2.6), and strongly discouraging almost any use of protected access (see section 3.11.5.3), we all but eliminate intimately interdependent implementations that span component boundaries, and thereby help to ensure substitutability as well as hierarchical testability.

Design Rule

Associated with every component (and having the same root name) must be a *unique*, physically separate test driver having a consistent suffix (e.g., `.t.cpp`).

The reasoning behind the need for testing (at all), testing at the component level, and (given our finely graduated, granular physical structure) testing using unique standalone test driver programs, as illustrated in Figure 2-80, is the subject of Volume III's Chapter 7. Here we simply delineate the prescribed organization.[147] Figure 2-80a illustrates the factored implementation of the `bdlt_datetime` component and its test driver in terms of two lower-level components, `bdlt_date` and `bdlt_time`, each having its own independent standalone test driver. The directory structure for the `bdlt` package is standard (Figure 2-80b), with constituent component and test driver files as shown in Figure 2-80c.

---

[147] We are, of course, aware that there exist widely used testing frameworks that facilitate the testing effort and that organize the testing process differently.

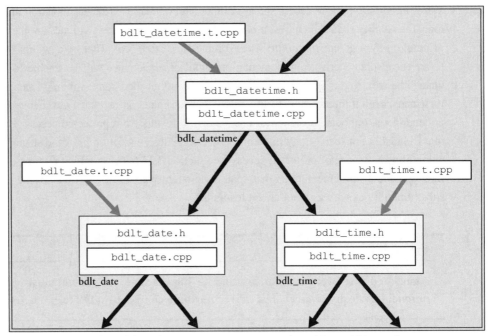

(a) Physical dependencies among components and test drivers within a package

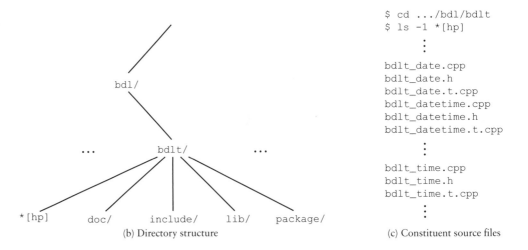

(b) Directory structure

(c) Constituent source files

Figure 2-80: Associated unique test drivers for each component in a package

Figure 2-81a, much like Figure 2-80a, shows (albeit abstractly) a hierarchy of three components, each properly associated with its own unique test driver. For example, any testing deemed necessary to ensure that *u* is behaving as intended is accomplished entirely by the test driver `u.t.cpp`. The test driver `v.t.cpp` performs the same service for component *v*. Ensuring that component *w* is implemented correctly is likewise accomplished entirely by test driver `w.t.cpp`, which is, however, allowed to presume that components *u* and *v* have already been independently tested thoroughly.

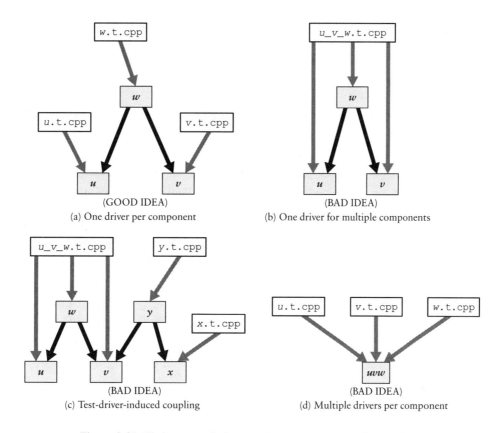

Figure 2-81: Various associations among components and test drivers

Consider instead the scenario in Figure 2-81b, where a single test driver `u_v_w.t.cpp` is used to verify all three components. Even though the driver has direct access to each of the three components, there is a strong likelihood that the quality of testing will be compromised (see Volume III, section 7.3). Apart from our general aversion to irregular physical structure, the amount of testing that *must* now "fit" within a single file (see below) has increased threefold. Experience shows that the testing code itself will tend to be both less regular and less maintainable, and also far less thorough, than if the test cases had been properly distributed across multiple drivers, with each driver focused on just a single component (see Volume III, section 7.5 and Chapter 10).

Human nature notwithstanding, providing only a single driver `u_v_w.t.cpp` eliminates our ability to verify components *u* and *v* independently of *w*.[148] One might try to argue that neither *u* nor *v* is useful without *w*, so why bother to test them separately? The short answer for fully factored component-based designs is, "because we can." Not only is evenly distributing the testing effort more efficient and effective, we never know when we or someone else will justifiably extend our fine-grained architecture to exploit a stable[149] component — one that might have been assumed to be only a subcomponent (e.g., *u* or *v*) — in ways we could not have anticipated.[150]

Figure 2-81c illustrates an alternate version *y* of a critical component *w* that reuses a highly specific, yet stable implementation detail *v*, but substitutes use of the existing component *u* with that of a new component *x* (see Figure 0-65, section 0.10). Furthermore, suppose that this new subsystem, headed by *y*, came about because the implementation of *u* used by *w* would not build on the new platform to which we are currently porting. According to our hierarchical testing requirement, in order to test *y*, we must first test *v* and *x*. In order to test *v* on the new platform, however, we must *first* port and build *u* and *w*. Yet it was our inability to port *u* that motivated the creation of *x* and *y* in the first place![151] It is only by consistently factoring the testing effort with precisely the same granularity as that of the underlying component functionality that we are able to avoid unexpected and potentially costly coupling induced by testing.

Finally, we require that there be exactly one[152,153] *unique* standalone driver file alongside each component for the purposes of component-level testing. Given a sufficiently complex component, we might be tempted to distribute the testing effort across multiple test driver files as in

---

[148] Moreover, the implicit private knowledge of the implementation of a component extended to its corresponding test-driver's author (see below) is simply not available to authors of higher-level component test drivers.

[149] For those rare cases where we choose to distribute unstable implementation details across components within a package, we would naturally employ the purely conventional use of *subordinate components* (section 2.7.5).

[150] For analogous reasons, we choose not to put more than a single class within a component unless there is a compelling engineering reason to do otherwise (see section 3.1.1).

[151] We would probably also then want to deprecate any further use of *u* and *w*.

[152] There might be some potential exceptions (e.g., involving concurrency) in which custom test apparatus creating multiple processes will need to be invoked. Although having a single program spawning multiple processes is usually sufficient, such customization must be supported, or at least tolerated by the build system.

[153] It should also be mentioned that occasionally it is important that certain code *not* compile, especially when working with SFINAE, which might also require more complex test apparatus.

Figure 2-81d. Again, apart from our desire for a regular structure, we require that the size and complexity of a component be kept within manageable limits.

Line count and other similar measures of size and complexity are fairly arbitrary. From an engineering perspective, however, our ability to test effectively must govern what we create; hence, the upper bound on component complexity we have adopted in our methodology is simply that which can be tested thoroughly *from a single test driver* (see Volume III, section 7.5). This particular choice of governor, having no arbitrary hard numerical limits, induces a healthy tension, and serves adequately to control component complexity.

Design Rule

The component test driver resides (physically) in the same directory as the component it tests.

The test driver is integral to the development and maintenance of a component. In our view, it is invariably the component author — and not a separate tester — who is ultimately responsible for the testability and inherent reliability of each component. Although a test driver does not have any special "private" programmatic access, the developer of the test driver will (and generally must) have intimate *white-box* knowledge of the implementation of the component under test (see Volume III, section 8.1). Moreover, the component author will sometimes make a somewhat stronger contract with the test driver than with the general client population, solely to facilitate testing. The typically intense and intimate collaboration between a component and its test driver, coupled with common ownership, argues strongly for the physical modularity of placing the test driver alongside its associated component in the same (e.g., package) directory as pictured in Figure 2-80c (above).[154]

Design Rule

The hierarchical *direct* (physical) dependencies of a test driver must not exceed those of the component under test.

---

[154] It should be mentioned that *black-box* (or acceptance) testing of components is also useful. Black-box (or even *gray-box*) tests (see Volume III, section 8.1) tend to have greater longevity, as the implementation can change (or evolve) and yet the tests remain relevant.

A test driver can be thought of as an extension of a particular component that shares its physical characteristics. Given the transitive nature of physical dependencies, a test driver will naturally inherit all of the dependencies of its associated component. Consider the two peer components *u* and *v* shown in Figure 2-82a. Neither of these components depends on any other (local) component. Hence (section 1.10), each of them is locally at level 1.

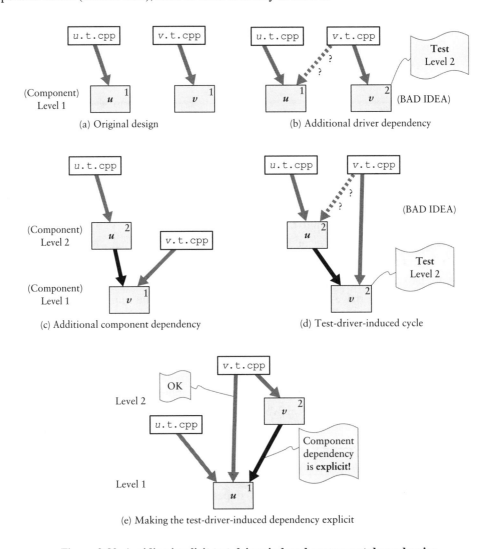

Figure 2-82: Avoiding implicit test-driver-induced component dependencies

Now consider, as illustrated in Figure 2-82b, the implication of allowing the test driver for *v* to depend also on *u*. Component *v* itself does not depend on component *u*, yet in order to satisfy our hierarchical testability requirement, we are compelled to test *u* before testing *v*. Instead of a test driver *reflecting* the physical relationships defined by the component that it tests, we now have a situation where the test driver *dictates* the allowable relationships among these components (BAD IDEA). In terms of testability, component *v* is now implicitly (and far too subtly) at level 2.

Now suppose for the moment that we instead decide to allow component *u* (itself) to depend on component *v*, as illustrated in Figure 2-82c. The effect is almost the mirror image of that in Figure 2-82b except that, unlike the test-induced dependency of *v* on *u*, the dependency of *u* on *v* here is explicit. The problem with implicit test-driver-induced dependency is crystallized when we combine the implicit dependency in Figure 2-82b with the explicit one in Figure 2-82c to form the combined test-driver-induced *cyclic* dependency illustrated in Figure 2-82d; now, neither *u* nor *v* can be tested independently of the other.

In order to ensure that situation (b) in Figure 2-82 never becomes that of situation (d), we would either rework the `v.t.cpp` to reestablish situation (a) or make the dependency explicit (with a "dummy" `#include <u.h>` directive in `v.cpp`[155]), leading to the situation in Figure 2-82e.

2.14.4   Relative Import of Local Component Dependencies with Respect to Testing

Use by a given component test driver of another component in the same package falls into one of three distinct categories based on the nature of use as summarized abstractly in Figure 2-83. We also provide three corresponding concrete examples in Figure 2-84. As Figure 2-84a illustrates, `odet::Time` uses `odet::TimeInterval` in its interface (and substantively in its implementation) openly implying that the preprocessor directive

```
#include <odet_timeinterval.h>
```

already appears somewhere in the source of component **odet_time**. Hence, we have no problem with repeating that directive in `odet_time.t.cpp`.

---

[155] As we'll illustrate shortly (below), when a `#include` is provided solely for testing purposes, we typically indicate it by a comment of the form:

```
// v.cpp
// ...
#include <u.h>  // for testing only
// ...
```

See also section 3.3.6; Volume II, section 4.9; and Volume III, section 8.6.

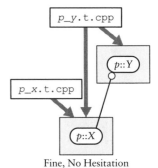

(a) **Interface Dependency** If a type *p::X*, defined in a local component *p_x*, is used in the interface[156] of the component under test *p_y*, we know that the physical dependency of component *p_y* on *p_x* is openly implied anyway (section 1.9) and, therefore, do not hesitate to include p_x.h in p_y.t.cpp.[157]

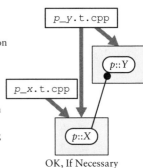

(b) **Implementation Dependency** If a type *p::X* does not appear in the interface of component *p_y*, but is used *directly* and substantively in the implementation of *p_y*, and, furthermore, we believe that using *p_x* in the test driver for *p_y* would significantly facilitate the testing effort, we may, purely for practical reasons, choose to use *p::X* to test *p_y*, knowing full well that a subsequent reimplementation of component *p_y* that is independent of component *p_x* might invalidate that decision, potentially leading to a complete reimplementation of p_y.t.cpp.

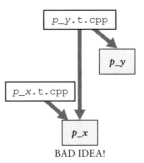

(c) **No Direct Dependency** If a component *p_y* does not depend on a component *p_x* (or if that dependency is indirect and therefore only coincidental), it is problematic to allow the test driver p_y.t.cpp to depend on *p_x*. Instead, we will either (1) rework the test driver (Figure 2-82a, section 2.14.3), or (2) opt to make that dependency explicit (Figure 2-82e, section 2.14.3).

Figure 2-83: Abstract use of local components in test drivers

---

[156] Unless, of course, this use is specifically designed to be In-Name-Only (section 1.7.5).

[157] Note that any use implied by the interface of a component is sufficient to justify allowing use by its test driver as the cost of reworking the test driver (in the relatively unlikely event that the interface changes) is potentially insignificant (e.g., compared to having to rework the entire client base) and, in any event, the cost of reworking the tests for that component is bounded (i.e., limited to that one test driver). Such is not the case for presuming transitive inclusion (section 2.6) where the bar is considerably higher — i.e., only public inheritance (Is-A) gives license to omit direct inclusion of the (base class's) header file by client components.

Next assume that `odlc::BitArray` is used in the implementation of `odlc::Calendar` as shown in Figure 2-84b. We might, for whatever reason, choose not to revisit the functionality associated with **odlc_bitarray**, but instead simply use it to verify its correct use internally within **odlc_calendar**. Since that use, albeit in the implementation only, is substantive, a *direct* dependency is — at least for now — necessarily established by a

```
#include <odlc_bitarray.h>
```

directive somewhere in either `odlc_calendar.h` or `odlc_calendar.cpp`. Our methodology therefore permits us to allow `odlc_calendar.t.cpp` to follow suit. If, however, the implementation of **odlc_calendar** were to change in such a way that it was no longer dependent on **odlc_bitarray**, our hierarchical testability requirement would require that the test driver itself would also have to be reworked.

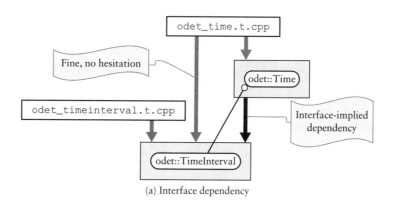

(a) Interface dependency

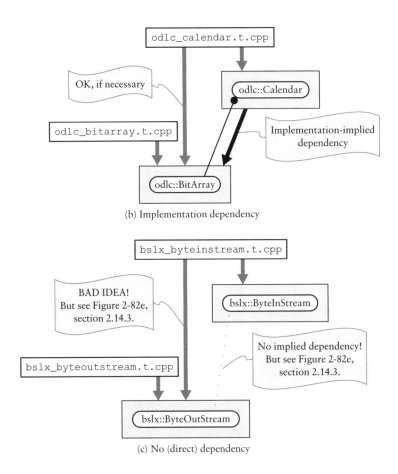

(b) Implementation dependency

(c) No (direct) dependency

Figure 2-84: Examples of use of local components in test drivers

Finally, consider two physically independent, yet highly semantically collaborative components, such as a concrete encoder/decoder pair. Like any other physically independent components, we are able to test each in isolation. We will want to ensure that the first component (the encoder) is working properly independent of the second (the decoder). We would then also want to test the second independently of the first.

After we have tested both independently, we all know we'll sleep better if we test the two collaborative components together. In the case of an encoder/decoder pair, that means also running a substantial amount of generated test data through the encoder, followed by the decoder, and verifying that the final resulting output matches the initial input (see Volume III, section 8.6).

Hence, we will therefore occasionally make an engineering decision to allow a test driver to depend on another local component even when the component under test does not itself need to depend on that other component physically. In such cases (e.g., Figure 2-84c), we will, owever, *own up* to the subtle implied inflexibility (e.g., Figure 2-82b, section 2.14.3) by introducing a line such as

```
// bslx_byteinstream.cpp
// ...
#include <bslx_byteoutstream.h>  // for testing only
// ...
```

to make that deliberate inflexibility explicit in the component itself (e.g., Figure 2-82e, section 2.14.3).[158] The mutual test would then be placed in the test driver for the (now) higher-level component, **bslx_byteinstream**. In this way, we ensure — with the help of our automated build system driven by metadata (see section 2.16) — that no subtle test-driver-induced component cycles accidentally find their way into our packages.

2.14.5   Allowed Test-Driver Dependencies Across Packages

When it comes to depending on components in other packages, the strict interpretation of "no additional dependencies" can be relaxed slightly. Recall that the dependencies of a package arc described either as being on other packages within a group (section 2.9), or — for standalone packages — on other UORs (section 2.8), and not on the specific components in those other packages. If a *direct* dependency of one package *q* on another *p* is — for whatever reason — explicitly allowed, then all of the components within package *p* will be available. We are therefore permitted to use every component in *p* in order to test any component in *q* — even if none of those specific components in *p* is actually depended upon by the component of *q* under test.

For example, consider that package **xyza** shown in Figure 2-85 supports a *protocol* (pure abstract interface) for a generic service, along with several concrete implementations of that service.[159] Let's assume that the protocol xyza::Service is defined in component **xyza_service**. Also provided in package **xyza** are several concrete implementations of this protocol, including xyza::TestService, which is designed especially for facilitating the testing of clients that make use of the xyza::Service protocol. Figure 2-85 also shows the higher-level package **xyzb**, which defines basic "client" components, some of which, such as xyzb::Client5, use xyza::Service in the interface.

---

[158] Note that by following our component design rules (section 2.6) and our stern proscription of runtime initialization of objects declared at file or namespace scope in library software, or any header file (see Volume II, section 6.2), such "unnecessary" include directives should never affect the resulting compiled translation unit or otherwise introduce any additional dependencies into the deployed software (e.g., see Figure 1-11, section 1.2.5).

[159] Note that even pure abstract interfaces require proper component-level test drivers (see Volume III, section 7.2 and Chapter 10).

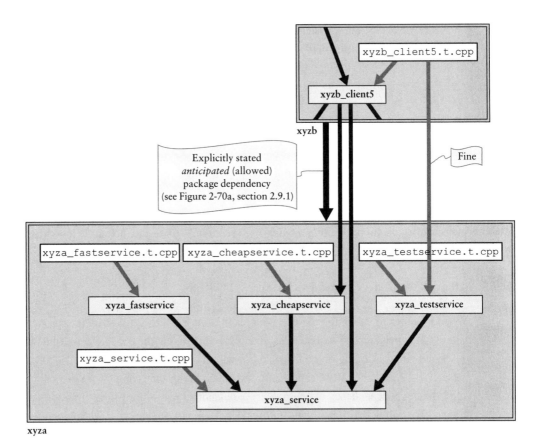

Figure 2-85: A test driver may *depend on any* component in an allowed package.

The general technique of consistently supplying, along with each abstract interface, an instrumented and easily controllable *dummy* (a.k.a. "mock") implementation thereof in order to factor and help orchestrate the effective testing of clients is discussed in Volume III, Chapter 9. Here, we simply observe that although the **xyzb_client5** component does not require any code from **xyza_testservice** in order to compile, link, or run, we *do* need it in order to test. Because of our somewhat coarser conceptual definition of dependency across package boundaries, such use of a factored test implementation by client test drivers is not only allowed, but encouraged! There is no need to make the component dependency across package boundaries explicit using for-testing-only #include directives; however, any use by test drivers of components in other packages, whose *direct* dependency is not explicitly sanctioned in metadata (see section 2.16), is, of course, still prohibited.

Similar to packages, dependencies on package groups are described as being on the entire group and not on the specific packages or components within the group. Hence, we do not hesitate to introduce new actual dependencies in the test driver on components in lower-level package groups, provided that the anticipated *direct* dependency has been stated explicitly (in metadata) for the current package group or isolated package. Figure 2-86 summarizes various allowable test driver dependencies across package groups.

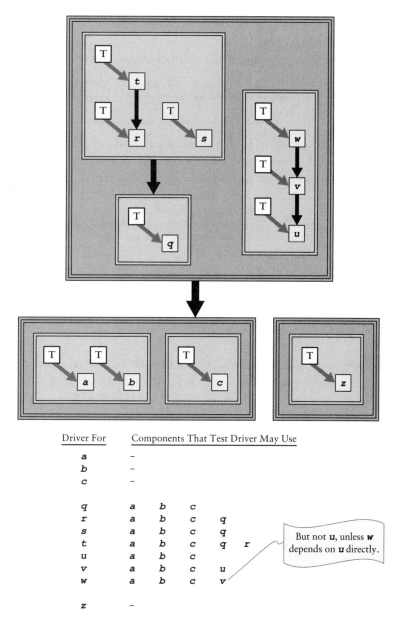

Driver For	Components That Test Driver May Use				
a	–				
b	–				
c	–				
q	*a*	*b*	*c*		
r	*a*	*b*	*c*	*q*	
s	*a*	*b*	*c*	*q*	
t	*a*	*b*	*c*	*q*	*r*
u	*a*	*b*	*c*		
v	*a*	*b*	*c*	*u*	
w	*a*	*b*	*c*	*v*	
z	–				

But not *u*, unless *w* depends on *u* directly.

Figure 2-86: Summary of *allowed* dependencies for component test drivers

Still more generally, when a component resides in an aggregate, the envelope of allowed dependencies for that aggregate must be stated explicitly. All components and test drivers in that aggregate share the same envelope of *allowed* dependencies. Hence, if any component in that aggregate is permitted to depend on an external architecturally significant piece of software (i.e., component, package, package group, or irregular UOR), then every component and every test driver in that aggregate is entitled to do the same.

2.14.6   Minimize Test-Driver Dependencies on the External Environment

---

Design Rule

The dependencies of a test driver on external data or other apparatus that is not explicitly part of our supported (portable) build environment must not exceed those of the component under test.

One of our goals in developing component-based software is to eliminate the burrs and thorns that might discourage a developer from continuing to use and actively maintain a component's test driver under varied and adverse circumstances. Even under normal conditions, test drivers that depend on external resources at run time — i.e., beyond those of the component under test itself — are often more difficult to understand and maintain than fully self-contained test drivers having no such external dependencies.

Now consider the additional complexity of maintaining a collection of components where test drivers might require ad hoc access to external resources such as environment variables, data files, remote processes, or persistent storage. Developers would have to maintain not only the test driver's interaction with those resources, but also the resources themselves. This task is often nontrivial and can easily (read that, "will") impede our testing effort. Furthermore, an inability to port one or more runtime testing resources to a new platform will likely undermine our ability to perform effective testing on that platform.

For example, suppose we are testing a calendar-cache component (e.g., see section 3.12.10) that uses, in the interface of its constructor, a calendar-loader protocol (section 1.7.5) to fetch new calendar information on demand, as illustrated in Figure 2-87. Use of a *protocol* (pure abstract interface) class by the cache is an important technique (see section 3.11.5.3) that (1) enables ultimate flexibility in how the cache is to be populated on demand, and (2) avoids even an indirect link-time dependency on any particular external resource.

Given that we have deliberately factored our component-based subsystem to avoid direct dependency on any particular data source, we must also make sure that the test driver (e.g., for the calendar-cache component) does not make use of a concrete "test" implementation (e.g., `TestFileCalendarLoader`) that directly or indirectly depends on an external data resource or any other nonportable environmental facility. Instead, we want to properly encapsulate the test implementation portably — either within the client test driver itself (e.g., `TestDataCalendarLoader`) or, ideally, within a separate, independently reusable component such as **bdlt_testcalendarloader** (not shown), which we encourage, especially for a widely used protocol such as one used for memory allocation (see Volume II, sections 4.4 and 4.7–4.10).

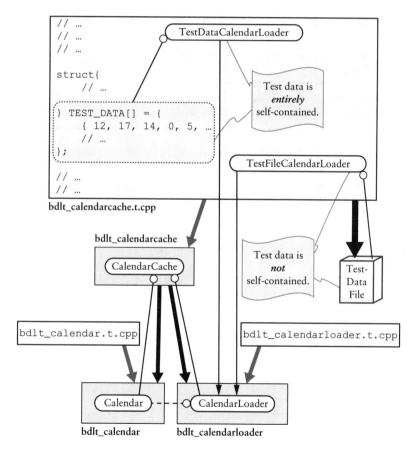

Figure 2-87: Avoiding additional test driver dependency on external resources

In our experience, the burden of manually maintaining and administering external resources deters effective, consistent use of component-level test drivers. Developers are swamped with mundane activities such as setting database permissions or scheduling remote processes. Over time, these administrative responsibilities are neglected, and poorly designed (irregular) test programs inevitably fall into disuse.

Hence, we make it a point *not* to depend on external data sources (e.g., flat files or databases) or any other external resources beyond those on which the component itself already depends — irrespective of how closely they might simulate the "real world" — unless we can assure ourselves that our test driver can reliably access them on all supported platforms.

2.14.7   Insist on a Uniform (Standalone) Test-Driver Invocation Interface

---

Guideline

There should be a well-defined subset of the invocation interface for each test driver that is standard across the enterprise.

An important goal of our testing effort is the seamless integration of component-level test drivers, used during development, to also form an automated regression test suite. We choose to organize our test drivers into separate, independently runnable test cases (see Volume III, section 10.2), both to improve human cognition and also to enable reduced test time through parallelism.[160,161]

To facilitate automation, not to mention developer mobility (section 0.7), we require that all test drivers adhere to a common standard invocation interface for use by regression test machinery. This interface must be sufficient to (1) run *all* test cases implemented by the test program, and (2) report how many errors were encountered in running each test case.

---

[160] Parallel processing can proceed in fixed-sized batches (e.g., 10 at a time) or, in logarithmic time, determine the total number of available test cases.

[161] The reader should be aware that, these days, more and more folks are electing to employ test drivers whereby there is just one executable that runs the tests for several components (e.g., all of those within, say, a package or UOR). These drivers (such as `Boost.Test` and `GTest`) have the capability to run tests in parallel. This strategy, while it has drawbacks due to global state corruption between tests, results in faster runs of the test suite, as it avoids the overhead of starting an entirely new process by instead just spawning a new thread.

Consider the following example of a standard invocation interface:

```
$ a.out [ 1 .. N ] [ ... ]
```

A single test program (a.out) supports N test cases with associated numbers starting at 1. When the test program is run with a case number that is outside the valid range of tests, a standard negative value (e.g., –1) is returned, except that 0 is an "alias" for test case N. Otherwise, the non-negative number of errors encountered is returned (up to some implementation-defined maximum), where a return value of 0 implies success. Given this interface, the simple Perl code shown in Figure 2-88 can be used by any regression machinery to run a suite of test drivers.[162]

```
#!/usr/bin/perl -w
#  ... Define 'sub run' ...
#  ... Define '@components' ...
foreach my $comp (@components) {
    my $total = 0;
    my $case  = 1;
    my $rc    = 0;
    do {
        $total += $rc;
        $rc = run($comp, $case);
        ++$case;
    } while ($rc >= 0);
}
#  ...
```

Figure 2-88: Trivial Perl script to consolidate test-driver results

The uniformity afforded by such a standard invocation interface enables the running of driver programs without any knowledge of the internals of either the test driver or the component under test. Although a given test program may have specific customizations for development purposes (see Volume III, section 10.1), the processing and interpretation of these arguments is outside the standard invocation interface, and must not be relied upon in order to validate the component during nightly (i.e., continuous) regression tests. In other words, the onus is on

---

[162] The Perl script shown in Figure 2-88 was written (c. 2006) for illustration purposes only; it was reviewed (c. 2019) by Mike Giroux of Bloomberg's BDE (after which it was compressed to make room for this tl;dr footnote). I created the very first version of this (Shell?) script (c. 1989) while I was at Silicon Design Labs (SDL), which ultimately was acquired by Mentor Graphics. The first Perl version, created for production use, was written (c. 1997) by Eugene Rodolphe of the F.A.S.T. (Financial Analytics and Structured Transactions) group at Bear Sterns & Co, Inc. The first Bloomberg production version (c. 2003), also written in Perl (currently about 623 lines), was authored by Peter Wainwright, then part of BDE. The first Python implementation was created (c. 2014) by Chen He, also a former member of BDE. An appropriately robust version of this script was then productized and made publicly available (c. 2015) by Oleg Subbotin, also of BDE; this version (**subbotin15**) has been used extensively in production throughout Bloomberg.

the test driver author to encode, in the driver program itself, the appropriate *default* inputs and parameters needed to definitively verify its associated component.

Guideline

The "user experience" for each test driver should (ideally) be standard across the enterprise.

By "user experience" we mean that, overall, developers will perceive the organization and operation of test drivers as more or less uniform and independent of the particular component-level functionality that they are testing, or package in which they were developed. The particular organization and developer-oriented operation we have used for decades, and continue to advocate for component-level test drivers, is described in detail in Volume III, Chapter 10. By adhering to a consistent layout and developer-oriented interface, we greatly facilitate understanding, as developers move from one project to the next, and from one development group to another.

2.14.8   Section Summary

In summary, the hierarchical testing requirement is all about ensuring that everything on which each and every component we write depends is independently tested thoroughly before we set about to test our component. The ability to test effectively and obtain feedback is an essential tool of engineering, and software engineering is no exception. To that end, we require that each component-level test driver be fully focused on just the single component with which it is uniquely associated. Given that each component-level test driver is afforded exclusive intimate knowledge of the component to which it is associated, each such test driver resides physically alongside that component (having the same root name) within its enclosing package directory.

Test driver dependencies (e.g., on an external database) that exceed those of the component under test undermine portability, and are therefore to be ardently avoided. With respect to other components within a package, intrinsic dependencies, such as those defined in the interface of the component under test, are of no concern, while those that exist only within the implementation should be more carefully considered. On the other hand, dependencies by test drivers on components within a given package that exceed those of the component under test are simply not permitted; if we decide that such test-driver dependencies are warranted, we consistently make that dependency explicit in the .cpp file of the component itself, via an appropriately documented #include directive. Allowed component-test-driver dependencies on nonlocal entities are, however, less strict — just as are those for the components themselves.

Finally, we must secure a way for our enterprise-wide build system to test each component. Such is possible only if we insist on a uniform subset of the invocation interface of every component-level test driver used to thoroughly test its corresponding component. Separately, we want to establish a standard organization along with a consistent look-and-feel of our component-level test drivers in order to allow for easy migration of our software developers from one development project or group to the next.

2.15   From Development to Deployment

As we endeavor to organize source code so as to minimize our own development burden, we must also ensure that we can deploy it in whatever ways most readily facilitate its consumption by all of its potential clients. How source code is organized during development and how it will eventually be deployed to production on all our various supported platforms are inherently separate issues. In order to maximize the flexibility of deploying our software, these two separate concerns must not be coupled unnecessarily. In this section, we discuss how we deliberately strive to keep our architecture separate from any subsequent implementation-only details of deployment, and how and why those deployment details might manifest.

We must anticipate that our own proprietary library software might eventually grow to be vastly larger than many other third-party libraries our application clients might use. We will therefore preemptively segment our library software into appropriately sized units of architectural design (section 2.2.20) on which both higher-level library and application clients may separately choose to depend. We therefore want to ensure that these UORs are constrained architecturally only by inherent physical dependencies implied by relationships among the logical entities they contain (section 1.9), and never by expedients predicated on how they are expected to be deployed.

2.15.1   The Flexible Deployment of Software Should Not Be Compromised

---

Design Rule

Neither relative nor absolute path names (i.e., no directory names) are permitted to be used when #include-ing a component header file.

Full flexibility in deployment requires that it be possible to install and use each of our library UORs from anywhere in the file system. In sharp contrast to the top-down directory organization employed by many popular libraries, we deliberately avoid having a singly rooted structure baked into our common, reusable library source code. Moreover, given that a library UOR is an entity on which multiple applications and other libraries may depend, we want to ensure that we can deploy each UOR as needed, including the ability to commingle header and object files, respectively, among arbitrary include directories and library archives.[163] Any hard-coded dependency on the development directory structure in our source code would impose that same structure at deployment, leaving our software unnecessarily inflexible, and — in particular — precluding the arbitrary repackaging of components for deployment purposes.

2.15.2   Having Unique .h and .o Names Are Key

For our avoidance of hard-coded directory paths to be viable, ensuring enterprise-wide unique filenames is essential. Software having not-necessarily-unique header filenames might require directory-pathname qualification or the use of (deprecated) implementation-dependent double quote ("") syntax for #include directives (section 1.5.1). Fortunately, as a consequence of our definition of a component (section 2.6) and its associated nomenclature (section 2.4), every component .h and corresponding .o file will naturally turn out to be unique throughout the enterprise (sections 2.8–2.10).

2.15.3   Software Organization Will Vary During Development

Depending on our precise development process, how we access our software for our own use during development might vary. As a classic (now mostly pedagogical[164]) example, suppose we are enhancing a component **xyza_foo** in package **xyza** of package group **xyz**, which we own. Components in other, higher-level packages within the same group may already be using this component, and so we won't want to affect them with intermediate changes until the component is validated (along with the others in the package). Hence, during development, higher-level packages within the group do not access the component source directly, but instead continue to look for the currently exported .h and .o versions located, respectively, within the individual package's include and lib directories. When all is deemed copacetic, the new snapshot of the package is pushed to these directories.

---

[163] On one very old (no longer supported) platform, we encountered moderate scalability issues when colocating *all* header files from a large enterprise in a single include directory; we know of no such limits on *any* other platforms.

[164] Although we no longer deploy our software within our source-code directory structure as part of our large-scale software development process, we feel strongly that doing so should in no way be precluded by our methodology.

Similarly, there are times when we might need to make substantial changes across packages within a group that, when complete, may have little or no practical impact on external clients of the group, yet during the upgrade would be disruptive. Once we again have a consistent set of packages within the group, each of the header files within the member packages' `include` directories are copied to the single `include` directory for the group, and each of the `.o` files are moved to a single group-level library archive under the `lib` directory. Absent a guarantee of (at least group-wide) unique component filenames, no such repackaging during development would be possible. Clearly this particular approach is simplistic and by no means the only (or even the best) way to structure a component-based software development process; we assert, however, that such a process must not be precluded by our source-code organization *a priori*.

2.15.4   Enterprise-Wide Unique Names Facilitate Refactoring

Over time, it not uncommon to choose to relocate a particular piece of functionality to a different (e.g., lower-level) UOR (e.g., so that it can be shared more widely).[165] Ideally, a new component will be created implementing the same (or equivalent) functionality as the original one, but having a new nominally cohesive name indicating its new physical position. The original component will then be deprecated, and after all clients have migrated to the new component (over some number of releases), the old component is removed.

In practice, however, there are times when the normal, multi-release deprecation process isn't feasible. For example, when a particular value or service is used widely in the interfaces of functions, it is almost always undesirable to have more than one C++ type (called a *vocabulary type*) to represent it (see Volume II, section 4.4). In such cases, it might be necessary to move the component that defines this type as-is — i.e., without immediately renaming it — and then, at some later convenient time (e.g., during a code freeze), make the global name change across all known clients. Without the initial assurance of unique filenames across all UORs, such temporary refactoring techniques would not be guaranteed to work, as a file in the source directory might collide with a file having the same name in the destination directory. Again, such (temporary) pragmatic deployment workarounds should not be precluded by how we have chosen to organize our software during development.

---

[165] This kind of refactoring is also a levelization technique called *demotion* (see section 3.5.3).

2.15.5   Software Organization May Vary During Just the Build Process

What is and is not accessible can even vary during just the build process itself. Suppose we are developing component **xyzb_bar** in package **xyzb** that depends on package **xyza** within package group **xyz**, and we want to test **xyzb_bar**. One approach would be to build the entire package group as a single UOR — the way it might typically be deployed — and build the test driver xyzb_bar.t.cpp against it. Doing so, however, could inadvertently allow the test driver — or even the component proper — to allow access to .h or .o files for components in higher-level packages within the same package group, and therefore allow rogue dependencies to go undetected. In fact, this same concern applies even to dependencies on higher-level components within the same package.

To guard against such dependency errors, we deliberately choose to build each lower-level package within the group separately. We then provide a local view of the current package that consists of only the subset of local components on which the current component is allowed to depend as defined by the #include directives of the component itself — i.e., deliberately excluding those in the test driver (section 2.14.3). In this way, we ensure beyond any doubt that only the components that are intended to be available are accessible. Hence, the ability to repackage our library software can be used to facilitate a robust build and test process that ensures only proper internal physical dependencies.

2.15.6   Flexibility in Deployment Is Needed Even Under Normal Circumstances

The form in which library software is consumed when routinely deployed to production will typically be substantially different from how it is organized for development and build purposes. In development, one of our primary goals is modularity; in production, it is efficiency. In development, we choose to organize our software into separate corresponding library and #include directories for each package and UOR. In production, however, as a compile-time optimization, we may choose to colocate all of our proprietary headers in one include directory (or a few), thus minimizing the number of required -I rules.[166] Such would not be possible without the firm-wide uniqueness of component filenames discussed earlier.

2.15.7   Flexibility Is Also Important to Make Custom Deployments Possible

The nature of our relationship with particular clients might also play a substantial role in how our software is deployed. For in-house consumption, we would typically expose everything in our suite of libraries. Given a special business relationship with an external client, however, we

---

[166] See **lakos96**, section 7.6.1, Figure 7-21, p. 519.

might find it profitable to provide only the highly selective subset of our vast hierarchically organized repository of library software needed to support a specific application, or category thereof.

Forcing our client to recreate our sprawling, firm-wide, package-group-based directory structure, only to receive this potentially sparse subset could be inconvenient. Given such customized distributions, it might turn out to be useful — either for mere convenience, or perhaps
even for security or legal reasons — to repackage this "thin slice" of our overall supported
functionality as a single library (e.g., .a or .so) and a single directory of header files (*.h),
none of which is possible without *enterprise-wide* unique component names.

2.15.8   Flexibility in Stylistic Rendering Within Header Files

There are yet other practical reasons why we might choose to deploy our code differently for
different clients. For example, our preferred commenting style historically has been to place
(e.g., function) contracts indented directly below the declaration:

```
bool isEven(int value);
    // Return 'true' if the specified value is evenly divisible by 2,
    // and 'false' otherwise.
```

In recent years, there has been a tendency for tools, likely influenced by other languages
that fail to separate pure declarations from definitions (section 1.3.1), to expect comments
documenting a function's contract to be located directly above and left-aligned with the function's declaration:

```
// Return 'true' if the specified value is evenly divisible by 2, and
// 'false' otherwise.
bool isEven(int value);
```

Presenting headers having an alternate commenting style could turn out to be a real productivity
enhancer for some clients. Yet many developers, especially those who work directly from source
(and hence have no use for such tools), tend to favor (some strongly) our preferred (below-and-
indented) commenting style. Irrespective of how we might choose to eventually deploy our libraries,
we naturally continue to develop in the manner to which we ourselves have become accustomed
and for arguably good reasons (see section 2.15.3). Adhering to our preferred development style,
however, does not prevent us from deploying our libraries in whatever equivalent forms our respective clients desire.

2.15.9   How Libraries Are Deployed Is Never Architecturally Significant

---
Observation

The coarse physical granularity of UORs that must be assumed (architecturally) during development often exceeds that of deployed software.

When designing portable, reusable software, we must be cautious when making any assumptions about the target platforms or how our software will ultimately be deployed, planning for the proverbial worst case. From an architectural perspective, therefore, we design as if every UOR is atomic — i.e., if we depend on a UOR, we must allow for the possibility that we depend on all of it. The actual granularity of these physical entities once deployed, however, might vary significantly, depending on the platform and technology. Hence, the ultra-conservative assumptions of physical granularity used during development is often much coarser than what is actually achieved after deployment.

For example, when we build our software as static libraries (.a), typically only those individual .o files that are needed from the .a are drawn into the final executable (section 1.2.4).[167] On the other hand, when we build our software as shared libraries (.so), all the code packaged within each shared library is typically dragged into an executable atomically. We may therefore choose to further partition our deployed libraries based on the library technology (e.g., static or shared), as well as the specific platform (e.g., hardware, operating system, and compiler). How we choose to deploy our software, however, must remain decoupled from its architecture.

2.15.10 Partitioning Deployed Software for Engineering Reasons

---
Design Rule

Any additional organizational partitioning employed solely for deployment purposes must not be architecturally significant.

---

[167] In fact, on some platforms, using appropriate compiler settings, only the individual symbol definitions needed from a given .o are incorporated.

There are two kinds of libraries: architectural and organizational. An *architectural* library is a UOR, e.g., package group (section 2.9), which is conceptually indivisible. Purely as an optimization, however, release and deployment engineers may choose to partition a given UOR into *regions* that are built and released independently. Such regions, much like subpackages (section 2.11), are inherently *organizational* and not architectural in nature; that is, they are an implementation detail of the deployment process. These regions must not be referred to explicitly as part of any design as they (1) are generally not unique, (2) can vary from one platform or technology to another, and (3) may change frequently and without notice.

For example, suppose we have a package group **xyz** that consists of four large packages, **xyza**, **xyzb**, **xyzc**, and **xyzd**, as shown in Figure 2-89. Suppose further that it is determined empirically that the overwhelming majority of clients need only the **xyza** and **xyzc** packages (and don't need either **xyzb** or **xyzd**). For static libraries (.a) there is no issue; only the needed component .o files from package group **xyz** will be incorporated into the final program. When deployed using typical shared-library technology, however, every component's .o in all four packages will automatically be incorporated into a running program.

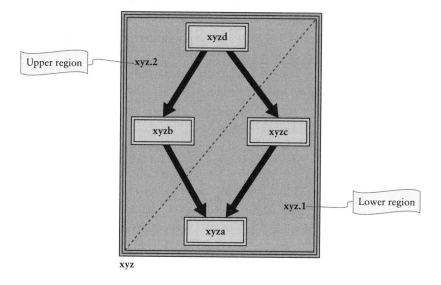

Figure 2-89: Organizational partition of package group xyz during deployment

As part of the deployment process, build and release engineers may choose to partition the package group of Figure 2-89 into two (or more) regions, e.g., **xyz.1** and **xyz.2** as shown. The only requirement is that these regions within the UOR (even if dividing components within a package) be levelizable: It will then be possible to substitute a contiguous (see below) sequence of unique region libraries in place of one representing the entire UOR. Even though these region libraries, e.g., xyz.1.so and xyz.2.so, exist as independent named physical entities,[168] there must be no way to refer to them architecturally. It is only by keeping the names of such organization-only entities private to the build system that we are free to (re)optimize our deployed software, as new empirical information becomes available.

It is worth reemphasizing that organizational partitions, created by build and release engineers during deployment, are — by definition — not architectural in nature. In particular, we must never attempt to use such organizational partitions as a means of avoiding cyclic or otherwise undesirable physical dependencies among UORs (which are again necessarily architecturally atomic). Referring again to Figure 2-89, consider the scenario in which an isolated package **a_xml** depends on package **xyza** in package group **xyz**. Suppose we later discovered that **xyzd** could benefit from depending on functionality implemented in **a_xml**, which would result in a cyclic physical dependency between UOR **xyz** and UOR **a_xml**. As we know from sections 2.2.24, 2.4.10, 2.8.2, and 2.9.1, such cyclic physical dependencies are emphatically forbidden.

One might naively try to argue that we can solve that problem by simply declaring that region **xyz.2** of package group **xyz** is permitted to depend on **a_xml**, which, in turn, is permitted to depend on only region **xyz.1** of package group **xyz**, and releasing the two regions separately. The internal link line might now appear as follows:

```
$ ld ... -lxyz.2 -la_xml -lxyz.1 ...  (BAD IDEA)
```

Notice, however, that an external library archive now unhappily resides *between* two organizational regions of the single architecturally atomic entity **xyz**. Appealing though this expedient might sound to the uninitiated, it is woefully ill-advised.

As soon as we allow partitions of UORs to be architecturally accessible, they naturally cease to be organizational. We can no longer change what constitutes a partition to optimize our deployment without affecting the correctness of our architecture or perhaps even the success of

---

[168] Recall, from section 2.2.12, that we are able to partition .cpp files in a similar way because .cpp files in a component, and especially .o files in a library archive (.a), are never considered *architecturally significant.*

our builds! It is precisely this difference between organizational and architectural entities that enables us to configure our deployment organization *independently* of our development architecture. No matter how tempting, we *must* resist allowing purely organizational entities to gain architectural status. The only architecturally significant physical entities in our component-based development methodology must remain components (sections 2.5–2.7), packages (section 2.8), package groups (section 2.9) and, of course, non-component-based UORs (section 2.12).

2.15.11 Partitioning Deployed Software for Business Reasons

Finally, stability might also play a significant role in our deployment strategy. Imagine, for a moment, that there are regions of some architectural piece of our infrastructure that are inherently stable and have not changed for years. Imagine now that new related functionality, which is logically part of that architectural unit, but implemented in separate components, is under active development. Clients that are satisfied with the current "version" of the library should not have to rebuild, and perhaps not even be forced to retest[169] because something "close by" on which they do not actually depend has changed.

Any new components — even if they logically reside within the same packages as other stable ones within a given UOR — necessarily reside (physically) above all existing stable software. In fact, for deployment purposes, build and release engineers may choose to flatten all of the packages of a given package group before partitioning, based solely on component-level dependencies, and using stability as the criteria.

For example, consider initial packages **xyza** and **xyzb** in package group **xyz** as shown in Figure 2-90a. Clients of this package group currently consume libxyz.a, some of whom have no desire (or cannot afford) to upgrade. Now imagine that two new components **xyza_comp3** and **xyzb_comp3** are added, respectively, to packages **xyza** and **xyzb** as shown in Figure 2-90b. Rather than altering the currently deployed library libxyz.a to hold the new software (affecting its timestamp), we could instead deploy a second library libxyz.1.a representing the region of software that was added. Notice that it is not a coincidence that the two regions are levelizable, as none of the existing stable software could ever refer back (up) to the newly added components.

---

[169] For example, government agencies, such as the Securities and Exchange Commission (SEC), may require that certain exchange-related software be retested for a specified period of time whenever a library timestamp changes.

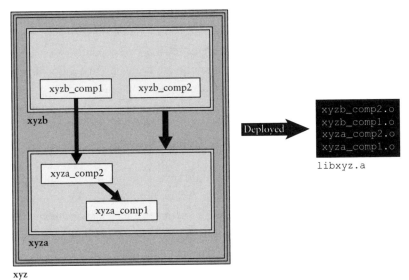

(a) Stable UOR released as a single physical library

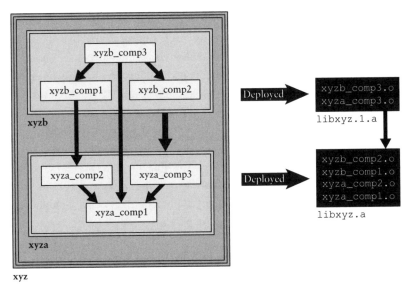

(b) Enhanced UOR released as two separate physical libraries

Figure 2-90: Repackaging for stability across package boundaries

The partitioning used here to achieve absolute, incontrovertible stability during deployment — as ever — is purely organizational, having no effect on the architectural design of the software under development. There are, of course, other, more traditional ways of ensuring that new versions of our deployed software do not break existing clients — e.g., via component-level testing (see Volume III). However, by deploying the stable and actively developed portions of an (architecturally atomic) UOR as separate physical libraries, we might — under certain special circumstances — be able to avoid, or at least defer, library changes that would otherwise be needlessly disruptive.

2.15.12   Section Summary

To recap: Generally speaking, the task of development is architectural, whereas the task of deployment is organizational. A sound development process must ensure that build and release engineers have the freedom to use additional situational and time-varying knowledge, involving platform, build targets, and usage, to configure the software for optimal consumption by all of its clients. To preserve such flexibility, however, it is essential that developers neither hard-code development directory structure in their `#include` directives nor attempt to depend on ephemeral deployment artifacts, or the ability to redeploy optimally will quickly evaporate. At the same time, developers should not abandon sound development practices due to a particular deployment configuration, such as commenting style (section 2.15.8). Unix man pages, for example, are organized with comments below. The function declaration is the headline, summarizing the story concisely. A well-designed declaration often suffices, and (especially flush-left) leading comments unduly obfuscate the declaration. And comments reference the declaration, not vice versa. Finally, the entire development, build, and release process should be supported by robust tools that can encapsulate (and hide) organizational entities (i.e., their names) so that such deployment-only details never become architecturally significant. Most importantly, though, the development process must govern the tools that support it, not the other way around.

2.16   Metadata

By Thomas Marshall, with Peter Wainwright

N.B.: The opinions presented in this section are those of Thomas Marshall, advised by Peter Wainwright: two seminal members of the original BDE team.

Architectural metadata allows a software engineer to define the design intent of a code base. It can be consumed by tooling, for the purposes of validation or enforcement, and read by programmers, to understand how to maintain a code base. The design can often be deduced directly from the code at the start of a project, but as code grows in complexity and sophistication, it is hard to keep all of the details in mind.

Architectural metadata also allows for planning ahead. An engineer can set out the intended dependencies and relationships among parts of a code base before it is fully built. As a project grows, the metadata can help maintain structural integrity, and avoid costly design errors that are much harder to fix when they are discovered later.

Many forms of packaging and dependency metadata exist, but most of these are aimed primarily toward consuming released artifacts, and are not declarations of design intent. The metadata discussed here can be translated into such forms, but is aimed at the capture of architectural intentions independent of build considerations. It can also allow declarations to be made about the internal structure of a UOR that are of architectural significance, but are not reflected in how it is built.

2.16.1   Metadata Is "By Decree"

It is important to understand that architectural metadata is a design input, and not a consequence of implementation. It might appear to some that metadata is "discoverable" by analyzing the source code being described, but this is not the case. Metadata is written by developers and is correct "by decree" (unless and until policy tools or a design review say otherwise). In other words, if the metadata and the code disagree, the code is wrong.

This mind-set has two useful consequences. As mentioned, code can appear sound and be without an obvious design flaw, but violate the architectural intentions of the code base. Analysis tools can discover this, so the metadata can enforce high-level design choices. While this might at first seem punitive, developers are human and can make mistakes, and discovering a design error early allows the developer to correct the code quickly, while it is still inexpensive to do so. Metadata is therefore a cost-effective way to assist developers in meeting specifications while maintaining productivity.

Less obviously, metadata allows developers to declare an intent or impose restrictions that are not yet reflected in the *current* code base, but which are anticipated by the design to be important for future releases, as features are added. Code changes can thus be prevented, even though they are well designed when considered against the current code base, because they would cause difficulties for planned future features. Architectural metadata, in other words, can help prevent technical debt from burdening a project before it is even written.

2.16.2 Types of Metadata

Architectural metadata can be divided into four distinct categories:

1. Dependency hierarchy

2. Build requirements

3. "Manifest" of entities (membership metadata)

4. Enterprise-specific policies that restrict or augment standard rules

Of these, only dependency metadata is unambiguously 100 percent architectural. The other three types do have architectural aspects but are grouped as much by functional cohesion as by the strict definition of "architectural."

2.16.2.1 Dependency Metadata

On a practical day-to-day basis, dependency metadata is the most important category of metadata. Dependency metadata specifies allowed dependencies among peer levels of aggregation: components within a package, packages within a package group, units of release within an enterprise, and, in large code bases and or ones using, e.g., multiple open-source software projects, among enterprises.

At the highest level of abstraction, the statement that "entity A depends on entity B" denotes that there is an edge in the hierarchy graph from A to B, and nothing more. This edge in turn precludes adding edges that would cause a cycle in the dependency graph, and that is in fact its defining purpose.

In the vast majority of cases, the "dependency" also means that all code in A can access all code in B freely, but this is not part of the definition, and access must be granted (logically) as a separate metadata entry.

There are a few reasons why this seemingly pedantic formality is also practical. One reason is that, in some cases it is desirable to allow only partial access from A to B. For example, it might be the wish of the client A that everything in A can access only a single package in B, because other functionality that B has chosen to provide is deemed problematic, perhaps only in the context of a single task, or perhaps for broader reasons. Though far less likely in practice, it might be the wish of the client A that only a portion of A can access B.

The most general case is that A can specify (logically) an entire matrix whereby each component in A is granted or denied access to each component in B depending on the corresponding matrix element. This level of granularity is almost never needed in the real world, but to accommodate needed use cases, it is cleaner to implement the general case and then use it only if and when need arises.

Note that the notation used to represent metadata is free to afford user convenience in the typical case while still retaining the ability to express the most general case if and as needed (see below). Also note that dependency metadata in all cases expresses the intent of the *client*. (See the section below on policy metadata where similar restrictions are imposed by the library provider.)

A second, perhaps less obvious, reason to separate establishing an edge in the graph from actually granting access to code is that the owner of library A may wish to express, in a tools-enforceable manner, that some other library B cannot become a client of A, even when A expressly can't access the code of library B. This kind of dependency prohibition can be expressed in metadata by (1) creating an edge from library A to library B, and (2) denoting that every element in the access matrix be turned off. Indeed, such choices are a hallmark of sound design.

Use cases for this feature include new libraries, where the designer of A knows where in the hierarchy A belongs, but doesn't (yet) want developers working on A to use certain code or features in (now-enforced) lower-level libraries. This feature might to some appear unnecessary to the point of being silly, but, as discussed above, metadata allows tools to "remember" what human developers can (and do) forget. A similar but distinct use case arises in large code bases with legacy code that is in the process of being deprecated. The dependency with no code access (here referred to as a "virtual dependency") imposes the intended hierarchy while forcing developers to avoid the "attractive nuisance" of the deprecated legacy code.

Weak Dependencies

Existing code bases may already violate an intended design if it is encoded into metadata only after development is under way. Even with declared dependencies, substantial refactoring could require a different organization that invalidates some existing dependencies. For these practical reasons, we can use a "weak" dependency.

A "weak" dependency is an illegal dependency — one that is not consistent with the directed acyclic graph formed by the ordinary (i.e., "strong") dependencies. Ideally, in a well-designed code base, weak dependencies should never exist. However, when an enterprise is migrating from its legacy development practices to a more orderly engineering methodology such as described in this book, they are very likely to be discovered.

The main purpose of a weak dependency is to document the existence of these "bad calls," isolating them at the symbol-to-symbol level even though they are (typically) documented at the UOR level. This in turn allows for an orderly, prioritized remediation, while reducing developer-facing delays as tools attempt to stop changes that will ultimately be permitted.

Weak dependencies are also preferable to "grandfathering," where tools (silently) recognize that a specific illegal symbol-to-symbol call already exists. In short, the declared weak dependency (complete with its symbol-to-symbol specification) documents a problem while postponing the need to fix it — that fix potentially being very expensive.

Dependency Metadata for Different Levels of Aggregation

In our discussion of metadata above, we focused on intra-enterprise dependencies among units of release. Such metadata at this level is essential for a code base of any size at all, and failing to implement library-level metadata is a serious engineering deficiency. The reason is simple enough: In a large organization, with many (perhaps thousands) of UORs available for potential reuse, it is not always practical or even possible for any one designer to have a good working knowledge of the entire code base. Having enterprise-wide dependency metadata readily available provides valuable information to the designer as to what "useful" code might or might not in fact be usable by the UOR under development. Perhaps of comparable importance, the dependency metadata can often motivate design discussions with potential clients of the UOR earlier in the development process. Such discussions can inform the design choices of teams that might not otherwise have had reason (or, simply, sufficient insight) to consider.

Having said that, documenting dependencies at other levels of aggregation is also sound engineering practice. For libraries that are package groups, it is strongly advised that the dependencies among packages in the group be rendered in metadata exactly analogously to library metadata. Failing to do so, while less problematic than not having library metadata, is not without cost, for the same reason (if on a smaller scale) as is the case for libraries: Developers can express their design intent and tools can enforce the intent, eliminating the risk that an undetected design violation will force an awkward, perhaps expensive, workaround at a later date.

One could make the same argument for having package-level metadata where the hierarchy of components within the package is specified explicitly. In practice, this has not proven cost-effective. One reason is that the "designer" of the package is typically much closer to the rendering, and so mistakes are less likely. Another reason is that, because of the smaller scale, mistakes are less costly. Perhaps the most compelling reason, however, is that the intra-package dependencies of components are far more fluid and subject to change — especially during initial development — than those at higher levels of aggregation. The include directives within a component provide a natural mechanism for specifying direct dependencies on a per-component basis (Property 4, section 1.11), and it is extremely easy to extract the current hierarchy from a very simple analysis of the `#include` directives of the components within the package (section 1.11), so "self-policing" of local component dependencies is in practice more cost-effective.

Looking in the other direction (toward the very large scale), and given the increasing use of open-source software within our enterprise-wide code base, it is also useful to support scoping the enterprise namespace in the metadata. This feature is necessary because, in the most general case, it is not possible to preclude duplicate library names in, e.g., one's own enterprise and an open-source code base being used. For this reason, metadata entries for libraries in other enterprise namespaces should be qualified with the enterprise name. As an example only, the `foo` library in the `SpiffyCode` enterprise might have an entry of the form `SpiffyCode::foo`, which would avoid a collision with a library `foo` in one's own enterprise. Note that open-source and other third-party software will also require build metadata, which can be extracted from the hierarchy metadata.

A Few Words on Dependency Metadata Implementation

As we've discussed, separating the existence of an edge in the dependency graph from the (possibly finely granular) granting of access to code is a valuable feature of the expressivity of the metadata. As we also mentioned, however, the overwhelmingly most common use case is that a dependency will also grant full access to the code. It is therefore advisable that, in the human-facing interface to update metadata, that a request/entry that simply denotes "A depends on B" also grants full access to code, and that the less commonly used variants be given the burden of making their intent explicit.

As illustrative examples only, an entry such as `virtual:B` in the metadata for A can be used to indicate that there is a dependency from A to B, with no code access. This choice leaves the simple unaugmented entry B to indicate the most common use case of allowing A access to all code in B. Similarly, entries of the form

```
B::foo
B::bar
```

can denote that A depends on B, and that all of A can access only foo and bar within B.

There is considerable freedom to render more complex dependency restrictions in a form that meets the use cases of an organization. As mentioned above, there is value in the rendering being uniform across an organization, but that's not a requirement so long as everyone can view and understand the meaning in a common language — e.g., in terms of the underlying fully general (matrix-access) representation.

2.16.2.2   Build Requirements Metadata

Building software is a complex engineering task in its own right, and a discussion of those complexities is well beyond the scope of this section. Instead, we'll simply describe the three distinct classifications of build metadata that are necessary to be maintained across an enterprise. Each UOR must provide its own build metadata; moreover, in some situations it is appropriate for a package within a package group to provide its own build metadata, but such situations are not common, and are best avoided unless they are absolutely necessary, in which case the need will soon enough become clear. In the discussion below we'll address UOR-level metadata, and any generalizations will be obvious enough at the level of detail that we present.

Local Definitions

Local build definitions specify the sequence of build flags for each platform, compiler, and linker that are needed to build a UOR. They are (in principle) not visible to build tools other than those building that UOR.

Global Definitions

Global build definitions specify the sequence of build flags for each platform, compiler, and linker that are needed to build a UOR and any client code. Global build definitions are visible to all potential clients of a UOR.[170]

---

[170] Note that the highly anticipated new language feature of C++20 known as *modules* will undoubtedly need to somehow encode its own form of metadata in order for client compilers to build inline functions and function templates uniformly — i.e., with the same (e.g., assertion-level) build options — across disparate translation units.

Capabilities

Capabilities metadata are statements in the form of assertions, both positive and negative, documenting combinations of platforms and build types that can and cannot be supported by a UOR. Capabilities, like global build definitions, are visible to all potential clients of a UOR.

Whereas global and local definitions are used to generate actual builds, the primary purpose of capabilities metadata is for use by developer-facing discovery and documentation-rendering tools.

2.16.2.3   Membership Metadata

Membership metadata — which declares what physically present entities are and are not to be considered by build and test tools — is a very useful construct for an active development team. A developer can check code into the local development repository/branch while it is still a work-in-progress and toggle that new code in and out of visibility as needed. For example, teams that have a "dashboard" that reports nightly build issues can see a reassuring sea of green status flags, since still-buggy code under active development is ignored. Mechanisms such as these that reduce "noise" in status-reporting tools can be far more valuable than some might assume.

Conversely, membership metadata in a production repository is affirmatively a net negative. In production, there are two separate issues. First, having to update a manual membership metadata registry every time new code is checked in is simply error-prone. In the vast majority of cases, it will be the metadata that is "wrong" and the checked-in code that is "right." Second, there is the added complication that analysis tools — often initiated ad hoc by a developer — will have to consult the metadata rather than just the checked-in code, and will have no basis to question any discrepancy between the repository and the metadata. In short, for a production repository, the principle of one fact in one place has far more value than any redundant checking that membership metadata might afford.

2.16.2.4   Enterprise-Specific Policy Metadata

Enterprise-specific policy metadata is a safety valve from the one-size-fits-all regularity that is, for the most part, a hallmark of sound engineering practice. Whereas dependency and build metadata are generally relevant and familiar in all development contexts, policy metadata can express constraints that could be meaningless to other organizations.

An example of such "locally meaningful" metadata is the OFFLINE ONLY tag, which might be totally mysterious to anyone outside the organization, but every developer in that firm would recognize that an "Offline" is a kind of executable used in production, and a library so marked may not be linked into any executables that are not commonly recognized as being "Offlines." (There would then also need to be metadata identifying different kinds of tasks.)

Policy metadata typically provides assertions (i.e., boolean predicates) that govern commits to the source repository, and usually apply to commits of source code within the UOR, but can also apply to other metadata in that UOR, or to metadata referencing the declaring UOR. An example of policy metadata that in turn governs dependency metadata is a declaration of PRIVATE DEPENDENCY, mechanically preventing any prospective client from gaining access to the code within the declaring UOR. (See below for more on this specific type of policy metadata.)

Policy metadata is virtually unbounded in its content, so long as each entry constitutes a criterion that can be unambiguously evaluated as either true or false for every commit to the repository. As such, policy metadata may be, but need not be, "architectural" in the sense that dependency metadata is architectural.

Examples of (unexplained and intentionally potentially cryptic) policy metadata flags are:

```
BUSINESS LOGIC LEVEL
G++ WARNINGS ARE FATAL
GCC WARNINGS ARE FATAL
GUI LIBRARY
INITIALIZATION UOR
NO NEW DEPENDENCIES
NO NEW FILES
OFFLINE ONLY
PRIVATE DEPENDENCY
RAPID BUILD
SCREEN LIBRARY
STRAIGHT THROUGH
```

Note that we don't actually advocate "cryptic" metadata flags, but we do acknowledge that, in a large enterprise, the need for very specific policy may arise, and sometimes in only small pockets of the code base. So long as tools can process each flag correctly in each context, it is acceptable (if not obviously optimal) to have as part of the enterprise culture that, if you don't understand a policy metadata flag, you probably don't need to worry about it. Other choices are of course possible.

PRIVATE DEPENDENCY Policy Metadata

The main distinction between policy metadata and dependency metadata is that dependency metadata represents the wishes and intent of the *client* (subject to mechanical policy enforcement), while policy metadata represents the design intent of the library developers providing the dependency. As such, the PRIVATE DEPENDENCY policy metadata flag can (and should) be implemented with a notion of granularity similar to that described for dependency metadata. Such granularity allows for truly private "implementation" packages (and, where necessary, components), where the intent is that absolutely nothing outside the library should ever use the implementation software. This use case contrasts with the softer case where the metadata flag is intended to engender a discussion between potential clients and the library developers; after a successful discussion, a manual override of the prohibition is a distinct possibility.

2.16.3   Metadata Rendering

Architectural metadata may be rendered in many different ways, and there is no strict requirement that there be a single uniform rendering format. There *is*, however, a requirement that all tools, both developer-facing and otherwise, be aware of all metadata as if it were uniformly rendered. This requirement in turn favors an enterprise-wide uniform rendering, for the obvious reason of tool simplicity and ease of maintenance and extension.

It is important, however, that architectural metadata is defined separately from strict build metadata, since the latter must define how builds take place, and might be generated, while the former is a declaration of intent that must be authored. As noted above, build metadata can contain details that are not architectural, and should not contain intended dependencies that are not yet reflected in the implementation. For these reasons, do not convolve them.

Our preferred rendering is to have each type of metadata in its own text file, colocated with the entity being governed by the metadata. In this way, the concept of logical-physical cohesion extends not just to code but to the metadata that describes the code as well. It also makes it trivial to implement validation on file changes, as the syntax of each file is narrow and specific. So, every source repository that contains the code of (and named for) a package will contain a directory named package in which live the metadata files (section 2.8). (Note that this convention is followed whether the package is part of a package group or is its own UOR.) Similarly, every package group will have a directory named `group` containing the metadata files for that UOR (section 2.9).

Our preferred naming convention for the individual files (e.g., within the `group` directory) is to have the root name be the name of the entity (e.g., the package group) and have different file type extensions for the different metadata files. For example, we use the `.dep` file type for the dependency metadata and the `.mem` file type for the membership metadata file. In both of these files, the format is for each entry (dependency or member) to be entered one per line, in alphabetical order.

In the case of virtual and weak dependencies, the entries are prefixed with `virtual:` and `weak:`, respectively, and are alphabetized separately below the normal (or "strong") dependencies.

2.16.4   Metadata Summary

In summary, software metadata is as much an engineering work product as the code that the metadata describes; metadata is written by developers and is explicitly *not* discoverable from the code. Metadata captures the design, policy, and build intents and requirements in a compact form that is both human readable and readable by tools that variously enforce and act on the design rules in the metadata. For large code bases, metadata is not only cost effective, but its relatively small cost returns enormous value, both in routine developer productivity and in safeguarding the value of the software assets.

Of the various kinds of metadata, by far the most important is the dependency metadata. It ensures cycle-free design (vital for both human understanding and for testing) and facilitates communication on design ideas across development teams in large organizations, where daily collegial interactions may not be possible.

Dependency metadata allows clients to specify exactly what they do — and do not — wish to depend on, at any needed level of granularity, and to have tools guarantee that their intentions are enforced.

Policy metadata allows an organization to integrate its specific needs on scales ranging from global across the enterprise to the parochial purview of small teams whose requirements may differ from the enterprise as a whole.

Policy metadata takes the form of boolean predicates that must be satisfied by all code throughout the enterprise, although, as alluded to above, any given policy may apply to an arbitrarily small amount of code. A key example of policy metadata is the explicit specification of the public and private portions of a library.

Build metadata can be partially machine-extracted from dependency and policy metadata (not from the code), and can also be augmented by manually maintained entries. The net result is that even irregular, problematic code can be built with fully automated build tools with a high likelihood of success.

> **Tom Marshall** was the first person I hired (from my previous company, Bear Stearns) after joining Bloomberg back in December, 2001. Tom initially served as a senior developer on my original BDE team (from 2001 to 2005) before moving on to become the founder and leader of the Architecture Office (AO) in Software Infrastructure (SI). The AO coordinates the physical structure of the software that powers the Bloomberg (Professional) Terminal, implementing existing processes, and contributing to the design of new policies that aid in governing that software. Under Tom's direction, his team manages physical dependencies among discrete software entities, and assists developers in creating, reorganizing, and refactoring new and existing libraries. Separately, Tom has developed numerous software tools used by the AO and its customers to analyze, maintain, and improve the hierarchy, restructure/refactor production code, and facilitate routine operations. Finally, the AO has a strong educational component to its mission: (1) formal training, and (2) informal collaboration and consulting.

> **Peter Wainwright** joined the BDE team (c. 2003) as its first tools developer. Seeded with the basic ideas presented in this chapter, Peter began to design a data model (consisting of several file formats), along with a modular suite of tools to consume them, thus enabling developers to easily capture, express, and exploit physical properties characterized in terms of extra-linguistic information that we now refer to collectively as *metadata*. An established Perl expert, presenter (e.g., in C++ and Physical Design), and repeat author (e.g., *Professional Apache* and *Professional Perl* — both from Apress), Peter proceeded to implement the first validation tools to regulate the relationships between C++ components and packages, giving birth to what has grown into our current-day, component-based development process. Peter later moved on to become the leader of SI's build and deployment team, overseeing the transformation of development environments to adopt advanced source control, static analysis, code quality assessment and validation, and reproducible builds. Separately, Peter continues to develop advanced technical and training content to promote best practices and effective developer workflows throughout Bloomberg's software-developer community.

2.17   Summary

2.1 The Big Picture

The structural organization of software is prerequisite to any discussion of design. Much as the format of compiled code is independent of the functionality it encodes, so (we feel) should be the physical organization of our proprietary source code. In our approach, the vast majority of the code base lies in libraries as opposed to being tied inseparably to any one application. It will therefore be necessary to partition our proprietary libraries into separate architectural modules, each of which can be released independently. We also acknowledge that our (component-based) methodology is not the only one; hence, we must allow for integration with legacy software as well as thoughtfully selected open-source and third-party libraries.

2.2 Physical Aggregation

Physical dependency is one important aspect of physical hierarchy; physical aggregation is another. The component is the smallest unit of physical aggregation. Components alone, however, are not sufficient for large development efforts. At the outermost level of the physical spectrum lies the unit of release (UOR). Each successive level of physical aggregation brings together a manageable, but not overwhelming, amount of content at a uniform level of abstraction. The name of every UOR, like that of every (nonsubordinate) library component, is visible from outside the UOR. We refer to such globally visible entities as *architecturally significant*. In our methodology, we require that the name of every *architecturally significant* entity be unique throughout the enterprise.

Dependency across separately released (physical) module boundaries is *architectural*, not *organizational*. Although physical dependency might appear to be an implementation detail to the end user of a program, it is not so from the perspective of an application developer attempting to build it. In order to assemble a program, the build system must know all about these dependencies along with all the physical entities to which they apply. Any such explicitly stated dependencies must always be acyclic.

Physical dependencies are an essential aspect of design at every level of physical aggregation (see Figure 2-9, section 2.2.17). While dependencies among components within an aggregate are inferred directly from `#include` directives embedded within that component (but not its test driver), the envelope of anticipated dependencies at each successive level of aggregation should be stated — in metadata (section 2.16) before any coding commences. These *allowed* dependencies become part of the physical design specification to be followed during development and subsequently verified.

Having a uniform depth of physical aggregation is an essential aspect of our development process. Although any number of levels of aggregation are possible, our experience suggests that two or three levels is sufficient to describe even the largest of library UORs. Insisting on at most three *architecturally significant* levels of aggregation helps to enforce a welcome degree of balance and planning, which has been demonstrated empirically to support development efforts encompassing tens of millions of lines of source code. For larger subsystems, we simply employ multiple UORs and represent the physical relationships among them individually.

2.3 Logical/Physical Coherence

Library software should be modular to isolate clients from the low-level design decisions used to implement the functionality it provides. For us to reason about our software effectively, however, logical encapsulation *must* be reflective of physical reality. Effective modularity, therefore, requires that logical and physical design coincide at every level of architectural aggregation. We refer to this property as *logical and physical coherence*.

Logically and physically coherent designs ensure that the direct implementation of each logical construct advertised by an *architecturally significant* physical aggregation is embodied within that physical module. Each module may then, in turn, delegate, as permitted by *allowed dependencies*, to other (lower-level) physical units. In this way, we are able to achieve hierarchically modular units of library software in which both logical and physical encapsulation coincide.

2.4 Logical and Physical Name Cohesion

We define a *package* as being the lowest globally visible level of physical aggregation within a UOR that is greater than a component. Being architecturally significant, every library package name must be unique. Historically, we used package prefixes to associate all global logical constructs and component filenames with the package in which they reside. Coherent use of package namespaces and package prefixes now serve the same purpose, with all component-based source code residing within a single enterprise-wide namespace.

Having unique package prefixes and namespaces is important, not only as a means to avoid conflicts, but also as a systematic approach to locating software within the physical hierarchy of our enterprise. Insisting that it be a syntactically trivial, mechanical matter for either a person or tool to immediately identify — from client usage alone — the source files defining any logical construct within our proprietary libraries is, in our view, essential to organizing arbitrarily large-scale software effectively.

Component files share the same root name as the component itself. Every component resides within a package and its name has, as a prefix, the name of that package; hence, the name of every component (along with the names of the files it comprises) are, like the package name itself, unique throughout the enterprise. In order for logical and physical units of software to be nominally cohesive, each global logical entity defined within our software should be unambiguously tied *in name* to exactly one of the components that make up the larger architectural units. Each packaged component is nominally associated with a unique UOR. We refer to this systematic nominal association as *logical and physical name cohesion*.

Being able to know where a logical construct is implemented directly from use facilitates the ability to understand and maintain our code base. For example, just by looking at the use of a class such as `bdlt::Date`, we can readily infer that there exist two component files, named `bdlt_date.h` and `bdlt_date.cpp`, and that these reside in the **bdlt** package of the **bdl** package group. Given that package group locations are few and well known, finding these files and the logical definitions contained therein is trivial for human beings and tools alike.

To achieve full-on logical and physical cohesion at the component level, however, we also require that, apart from operators (and operator-like *aspect* functions, e.g., `swap`), the lower-cased name of every logical construct defined within a component at package-namespace scope has the defining component's base name as a prefix (see Figure 2-22, section 2.4.9). Macro names (all-uppercase), not being scoped by the package namespace, are required to have the entire uppercased name of the component as the prefix.

To reduce clutter, we further require that only classes, `struct`s, and free operator (or *aspect*) functions be defined at package-namespace scope. In particular, we consistently implement what would otherwise be free (nonmember) functions as static members of a `struct`. Any free operator (or *aspect*) functions that are defined within a component must have at least one parameter whose type is defined within that same component (see Figure 2-26, section 2.4.9).

Package prefixes and namespaces are more than mere naming conventions — they reflect the reality of the physical architecture. To promote an ordered, hierarchical, and incremental understanding of the parts that make up our system, we disallow cyclic physical dependencies among packages — a stronger condition than merely disallowing cyclic dependencies among their constituent components. That is, given a collection of components with acyclic dependencies, it is not generally possible to assign these components to arbitrary packages without introducing cycles in the package dependencies (see Figure 2-29, section 2.4.10).

Substantial use of `using` directives and declarations work against nominal cohesion, thereby impeding readability and therefore understandability and maintainability. Any use of `using` in components outside function scope in a `.h` or before a `#include` directive in a `.cpp` could result in include-order dependencies. Hence, we require that use of `using` in components (declarations are preferable to directives) be limited to the body of a single function, and recommend that it be reserved for truly special cases (e.g., `std::function` or to enable ADL locally). To make avoidance of `using` practicable, it is paramount that we keep all of our package names — like **std** — blissfully short.

Failure to enforce cohesive logical and physical naming of our proprietary software allows our physical designs to diverge from their logical intent and thereby cease to reinforce it, and ultimately detract from it. Moreover, the absence of coherent logical and physical naming impedes human cognition; no longer could we refer to the logical and physical aspects of a design as a single coherent entity. Furthermore, our ability to create effective development and analysis tools, etc. would be crippled. Achieving nominal cohesion leads, in practice, to better logical/ physical coherence, which, in turn, facilitates our ability to reason about our software.

There is, however, additional burden placed on library developers to satisfy these extra naming constraints in that moving a logical entity from one physical location to another will necessarily require clients to rework their code. The good news is that this approach allows refactoring to occur over a period of time as it is possible for two versions of an entity to coexist at different architectural locations within the same version of a library.

2.5 Component Source-Code Organization

Components (see Figure 2-35, section 2.5), being fundamental units of logical and physical design, are required to satisfy a cohesive suite of design rules, along with addressing a variety of other, sometimes competing concerns. In order to maximize human comprehension, however, it is highly desirable that — to the extent possible — the contents of components be organized uniformly as well. Many organizations are viable. Figure 2-36, section 2.5, provides a schematic diagram of how we consistently arrange top-level content within components. Note that we deliberately avoid use of namespaces other than those used to implement the enterprise-wide and immediately nested package namespaces, which (coincidentally) facilitates source-code rendering. Note also that we deliberately avoid *defining* free operator (and aspect) functions within the package namespace (in which they are *declared*), thereby necessarily detecting — at compile time — accidental mismatches between corresponding declarations and definitions.

2.6 Component Design Rules

Our component-based design rules, like the top-level arrangement of component content, are subject-domain independent. Each component consists of exactly one `.h` file and (at least) one `.cpp` file. Together, these header and implementation files, which share the same root name, satisfy four fundamental properties:

Component Property 1: The `.cpp` file — even if otherwise empty — includes its own `.h` file as the first substantive (i.e., noncommentary or source-control-related) line of code.

Component Property 2: Each external-linkage construct defined in the `.cpp` file that is not rendered (or effectively rendered — e.g., via private classes, section 2.7.3) invisible outside of the component must be declared in the `.h` file.

Component Property 3: Each construct having external or dual bindage is never defined outside the component whose header file declares it; for constructs that have (or effectively have — e.g., via use of `extern` templates, section 1.3.16) external bindage, the definition resides in the `.cpp` file.

Component Property 4: Any functionality defined within a component is accessed via a `#include` of the header in which that functionality is declared, not via local declaration.

Apart from files that define `main`, every logical construct that we write resides within a component. All of our components contain unique and predictable include guards: `INCLUDED_PACKAGE_COMPONENTBASE`. To promote the separation of exported interfaces (and contracts) from any one implementation choice, we deliberately avoid defining inline function bodies within class scope in header files. Further ensuring that free function and function-template definitions reside outside of the package namespace in which they are declared provides substantial compile-time consistency checking at no cost. Runtime initialization of file-/namespace-scope static objects in components is not permitted.

While every component header must compile in isolation, including other headers from within a component header should be minimized (e.g., through local class declarations), but without resorting to inappropriate use of transitive includes (see below). The five common cases that

necessitate a header to include another in order to ensure self-sufficiency with respect to compilation are: (a) Is-A, (b) Has-A, (c) Inline, (d) Enum, and (e) Typedef (see Figure 2-41, section 2.6).
There are a few other edge cases (e.g., covariant return types), but these rarely occur in practice.

Whenever we use a logical entity defined outside our translation unit, we make sure to
`#include` the corresponding header directly rather than relying on some other header we
might have included to do so (sometimes referred to as a *transitive include*) — the sole exception being a publicly inherited base class (see Figure 2-43, section 2.6) because the dependency
is intrinsic. What might start out as an implementation that Has-A or inline-uses a given type,
each of which mandate the nested includes of its header, could all too easily be reworked to one
imposing no compile-time dependency on that type, and the nested include removed.

Even when a type is used in the interface of a function, if not *primitive* (see section 3.2.7), that
function might wind up being *escalated* (see section 3.5.2) to a higher level, possibly eliminating
any need for the component to include the one defining the desired (transitively included) type.
Unless the logical implications are both *intrinsic* and substantial (i.e., Is-A), we are obliged to
use `#include` directives to make our own direct, independent physical requirements explicit.

Cyclic physical dependency among components is not permitted. We further require logical and
physical encapsulation to coincide. Hence, access to private details of any logical entity (e.g.,
a class) does not extend beyond the boundaries of the physical module (i.e., the component)
that implements it. In particular, friendship may not be granted to logical entities outside of the
component defining the type granting the friendship. (Similar problems arise from protected
access, which is also generally to be avoided.)

Given our desire to facilitate fine-grained hierarchical reuse (section 0.4), we strive for a single
(public) class per component unless there is a compelling engineering reason to do otherwise.
Friendship is by far the most common reason for colocating outwardly accessible classes.
Cyclic interdependency is virtually always unnecessary; two other occasional justifications for
colocation are discussed in section 3.3.1.

2.7 Component-Private Classes and Subordinate Components

A component-private class (or `struct`) is one that is defined at package-namespace scope,
but is not to be used directly from outside the component in which it is defined. Although there
are mechanisms in the C++ language itself for achieving this objective (e.g., private nested

classes), we often find them to be suboptimal (see Figure 2-53, section 2.7.3). We avoid defining nested classes within the lexical scope of a parent class and, in fact, generally avoid declaring nested classes altogether.

In our methodology, by convention, a logical entity having an underscore in its name indicates that it is local to the component that defines it. Practical advantages for using this unorthodox "underscore" approach are captured in Figure 2-56, section 2.7.5.

In rare cases, we will find it appropriate to make an entire component private to a hierarchy of components (within a package). A subordinate component is one that has an extra underscore in its name and — purely by convention — must not be #included directly except by another component (in the same package) whose name forms a proper prefix of that component.

2.8 The Package

Any substantial software development requires units of physical design larger than a component. A *package* serves as the second level of architecturally significant aggregation. In our methodology, every component resides within a package. The purpose of a package is to unite a substantial amount of semantically related functionality sharing the same envelope of physical dependencies that can be referred to abstractly and maintained effectively. These larger physical entities naturally reflect the logical structure of the software they embody, but inevitably also that of the organization that created it.

A *regular package* is a collection of components organized as a physically cohesive unit. A well-designed package consists of components that serve a common purpose and naturally share the same envelope of physical dependencies. The physical structure of every *regular* package is the same — irrespective of whether it is part of a larger UOR (i.e., package group).

We organize *regular* package source code within a file system under a directory having the same name as the package, and containing the constituent component source files along with a few distinguished subdirectories (see Figure 2-58, section 2.8.1). Note that the files implementing standalone component-level test drivers reside side-by-side along with those of the corresponding components on which they operate.

Characterizing components as being "similar" will necessarily require analyzing what each component will need to Depends-On (section 1.9), yet is also essential. Such terse, often cryptic, but always visible tags quickly come to connote common logical and physical traits and properties among the constituent components they represent — sometimes even rivaling the semantic value of the component name itself (see Figure 2-66, section 2.8.4). This feature of our methodology has — over literally decades of experience — proven to be immensely useful in practice.

2.9 The Package Group

Judiciously colocating logically related components having similar physical dependencies into larger discrete physical units makes both understanding and reasoning about our software easier. Even the added structure afforded by packages, however, is not sufficient for truly large development efforts. We therefore introduced the *package group* — a collection of packages organized as a physically cohesive unit — as our third (and highest) level of *architecturally significant* physical aggregation.

A package group, like an isolated package, forms the basis for a unit of release; hence, each package group's name must be unique throughout the enterprise. A package group depends directly on another UOR if any file in the package group includes a header from that UOR. Even more so than with packages, the dominant criteria that characterizes a package group is the envelope of allowed dependencies for which all constituent packages must subscribe. The anticipated envelope of allowed dependencies for the entire group must be stated explicitly in metadata — e.g., within the `group` subdirectory within the group directory structure (see Figure 2-67, section 2.9.1). Cyclic physical dependencies involving package groups and other UORs are not permitted.

Package groups serve at least two important purposes. The first of these is to provide visible internal boundaries that developers can use to partition large, well-understood, cohesive library subsystems. A mature package group can contain hundreds of thousands of lines of source code (not including test drivers). The internal packages and their explicitly stated dependencies form the architectural blueprint as the package group matures. When writing reusable infrastructure, packages enable us to carve out and reserve a place for each of the various suites of related components that we plan eventually to create (see Figure 2-72, section 2.9.3). The use of packages also makes finding components having related functionality easier. We must, however, guard against our natural temptation to create overly specific packages (and package groups). By thoughtfully characterizing both the logical scope and physical properties of each package — like a sound zoning ordinance — we provide guidance for the proper incorporation of new components into initially sparse packages as the package group matures over the fullness of time.

The second important use of package groups is to provide the "real estate" needed to support the cumulative infrastructure resulting from a sequence of eclectic smaller projects. In this scenario, several package groups are created a priori, characterized entirely by their coarse physical dependencies. In this second scenario (see Figure 2-73, section 2.9.3), the terse hierarchical naming strategy enables the decentralization of package creation, providing package group owners a certain degree of autonomy to create and name new packages on demand. It is important, however, never to introduce any packages into a package group that do not conform to its overall envelope of allowed physical dependencies. That is, all packages within a group are characterized and governed by the same set of allowed physical dependencies, the extension of which should never be undertaken lightly as it would affect all existing clients.

Not every package is a candidate to be a member of a group. For example, a package that wraps or, more generally, *adapts* a particular open-source or third-party product will typically (1) be comprised of relatively few components and (2) have that product as its dominant dependency. Aggregating this package with others that do not share this substantial physical dependency would significantly increase physical coupling, with no significant countervailing benefit. By contrast, effective package groups house packages that naturally share the same envelope of physical dependencies. Hence, adapter packages with their highly specialized and often substantial dependencies are best kept isolated and released as separate libraries (see Figure 2-74, section 2.9.3).

2.10 Naming Packages and Package Groups

We want to keep names short to avoid temptation for using using. Although some might argue for what has sometimes been called "literate programming" (i.e., having long and descriptive namespaces names), we maintain that ultra-terse names (such as std) are much more likely to survive using directives and declarations, and are therefore to be preferred. By insisting that package names themselves be unique throughout the enterprise, we compress the nomenclature and pave the way for consistent treatment of packages, whether grouped or isolated.

A package group can be implemented as a directory having a unique three-character name matching the group name, and containing a collection of package directories. Each package directory name begins with the same three letters as the group followed by a unique suffix to form the globally unique package name. Package names that are longer than six letters indicate that the package is not grouped, as do any package names that begin with a single-letter prefix followed by an underscore (except **z_**). In very rare cases, a ubiquitous standalone package (e.g., **std**) may have a name that is exactly three letters (see Figure 2-75, section 2.10.3).

In order to avoid duplication of symbols, the name of each UOR within an enterprise must be registered with a central authority before it is used. One of the benefits of grouped packages is that the process of choosing names for new packages within existing package groups is automatically decentralized. By providing very short package namespace tags for libraries, especially when thoughtfully aggregated into package groups, we all but eliminate any need for `using` declarations, and thereby increase nominal logical and physical cohesion (section 2.4), which in turn aids in achieving logical/physical coherence (section 2.3).

2.11 Subpackages

In rare circumstances, such as when designing for broad reuse, one might elect to organize a substantial amount of *horizontal* functionality within a single package (e.g., `std`). Although we must sacrifice nominal cohesion, it might still be useful to constrain the physical structure of such large packages through internal partitioning that is not visible in the source. We refer to each resulting region as a *subpackage* (see Figure 2-76, section 2.11). Subpackages provide a constrained view of a package, are intended solely for the benefit of maintainers of that package, and, therefore, are not architecturally significant. Hence, any given subpackage partition can be altered or removed altogether with absolutely no effect on external clients.

2.12 Legacy, Open-Source, and Third-Party Software

The reality is that not all software is component-based. In order to integrate with legacy, open-source, or third-party libraries, each must somehow be assigned a globally unique name. Such names are typically not reflected in the code, and are, in some sense, arbitrary. These names are, however, architecturally significant and available during deployment. We refer to these structurally and/or nominally noncompliant libraries as *irregular*.

We often choose to model a legacy library as a package group containing a single package so that, over time, we can refactor the code into a levelizable collection of regular packages within the same group. On the other hand, for open-source and third-party libraries, we will typically want to avoid creating a code fork; hence, each of these kinds of libraries is typically modeled as a single irregular isolated package.

Open-source or third-party libraries, however, typically come with their own build/install scripts, often involving relative paths. Since there can be duplicate filenames emanating from different directories, we will generally be forced to preserve their hard-coded deployment structure along with any (deprecated) double-quote (`""`) syntax for `#include` directives (section 1.5.1).

2.13 Applications

In our methodology, library development follows a fairly rigorous process, while application software enjoys far more latitude. Nonetheless, having a structured reusable framework (along with extensive tool support) in which to develop a sequence of applications is entirely consistent with the common goal of developing high quality applications at reasonable cost as quickly as possible. At the highest level, we partition our UORs into two distinct flavors: applications and libraries. Well-factored applications are typically relatively small; hence, in our methodology, we model the highest level in the physical hierarchy — an application — as a package-sized UOR.

Application packages, however, have several distinguishing features: (1) Application packages have one or more `.m.cpp` files, which are the only files (other than test drivers) that are permitted to define a `main` function or to implement functionality outside the enterprise-wide namespace; (2) the names of application packages are syntactically distinct from all library packages (e.g., they begin with **m_**), mindful that the application namespace is declared, but seldom used in qualified references; and (3) because applications are inherently malleable, nothing defined within an application package may be referenced from outside of that package.

2.14 The Hierarchical Testability Requirement

Library or application, we require that every physical entity throughout our hierarchy be thoroughly testable, depending on nothing that has not already been tested thoroughly (or is otherwise known or presumed to be correct). In particular, there must be an order in which components can be compiled, linked, and tested in terms only of other components that have already been similarly tested.

This *hierarchical testability requirement* reinforces the need to avoid component cycles and *long-distance* (i.e., inter-component) friendships. Associated with every component is a unique, physically separate test driver having a consistent suffix (e.g., `.t.cpp`). Attempting to test more than one component using a single test driver is not generally practical. Requiring each component to be testable from a single test driver file naturally places a soft bound on the overall complexity of components.

Each test driver is located (physically) alongside the component source code (within the enclosing package). A component test driver is not permitted to depend on any component within the package other than those upon which the component under test depends directly. An interface dependency is preferred, but a direct and substantial implementation-only dependency might be acceptable. If any other test-driver dependency on local components is deemed necessary, that dependency must be made explicit by adding an appropriate "dummy" `#include` directive in the component's `.cpp` file (along with an appropriate comment). Test driver dependencies on software outside the package containing the component under test are governed by the envelope of allowed dependencies for that package and those of the enclosing group.

We discourage test driver dependencies on external apparatus, databases, text files, etc. on the grounds that they are not self-contained and might not be easily ported to new platforms. In order for our developer-implemented test drivers to participate in automated regression testing, we require that there be a well-defined subset of the invocation interface for each test driver that is standard across the enterprise. In order to enhance developer mobility, we recommend that the "look and feel" of using a test driver be made standard and therefore familiar to all developers within our organization.

2.15 From Development to Deployment

Preserving flexibility in deployment is an important physical consideration unique to librar-ies. The organizational structure of our software will typically vary as it is being developed. During the development of a package group, for example, each of the lower-level packages within the group may reside in separate libraries (to avoid exposure to unauthorized components), while packages in other groups may be rolled up and used as a single library. We might, on occasion, find ourselves moving a component (e.g., one representing a *vocabulary type*) to another UOR without necessarily being able to immediately change the name. Hence, having enterprise-wide-unique component filenames is key to ensuring flexibility during development.

How software is organized during development is often quite different from how it is deployed in production. We might, for example, have potential clients who would be even more eager to use our software if we, say, preprocessed it to be rendered in the more avant-garde "East const" style, instead of the more traditional "const West" rendering consistently shown throughout this book (but that would, of course, be a business decision and not a technical one). More practi-cally, separate archives may be merged to achieve better compile-time efficiency. Properly organized, complex libraries may be concurrently deployed to good advantage in a variety of different ways. For example, we might, for business reasons, opt to extract the essential subset of components for a particular client and supply a custom release in the form of a single header directory and library archive. Hence, regardless of our development directory structure, we must separately ensure our ability to repackage (e.g., flatten) our library software and, in particular, that the name of each of our component files is itself unique across the enterprise — irrespective of the directory in which the file happens to reside.

How software is deployed must never be allowed to become architecturally significant. Purely as an optimization, build and release engineers may take advantage of additional platform information, usage profiles, etc. in order to partition architecturally atomic UORs into arbitrary levelizable subregions (e.g., see Figure 2-89, section 2.15.10) that are deployed as separate physical (e.g., static or shared) libraries (e.g., to separate out the most commonly used or most stable portions of a UOR). In order to preserve full flexibility of deployment, however, developers must not depend on any such optimizations. As we have stressed throughout this chapter, we must make no assumptions during design and development about the atomicity of any UOR (or any aggregate for that matter) since that property is platform, technology, and customer dependent, by no means unique, and subject to change without notice.

2.16 Metadata

All dependencies on libraries (component-based or otherwise) within our development environment are specified the same way: The enterprise-wide unique names of each architecturally significant piece of library software upon which a given UOR depends is specified as metadata along with the source code in the directory structure of that UOR. Tool chains (e.g., Clang, LLVM, and our own custom tools) — and not just the compilers alone — are essential for achieving high-quality designs, and for reducing defects through both static and dynamic analysis.

In the words of Tom Marshal and Peter Wainwright, two principal members of the original BDE team that I founded at Bloomberg LP in December 2001, software metadata is an engineering work product written by developers; it is discoverable from the code. Metadata captures the design, policy, and build intents and requirements in a compact form that is both human readable and readable by tools that variously enforce and act on the design rules in the metadata. Metadata preserves and adds value to a code base by mechanically enforcing design intentions and by facilitating communications among disparate clients and library developers.

Dependency metadata is the most important type of metadata, ensuring cycle-free design and facilitating communication on design ideas, both of which contribute directly to the value of the software to its end users.

Policy metadata consists of a set of boolean predicates that express constraints on software that are specific to the needs of an organization or even a small group within an organization.

Build metadata is both extracted from dependency and policy metadata and manually maintained in, e.g., configuration files. Proper build metadata ensures the reproducible success of all builds.

3

Physical Design and Factoring

Software is *physical*. We cannot develop large-scale software systems successfully without addressing the physical aspects head on. Cyclic, excessive, or otherwise inappropriate physical dependencies must be avoided, as must friendship that spans physical boundaries. Good logical design is essential (see Volume II, Chapter 4), yet without incorporating physical considerations from the very inception of the design process, we will be unable to achieve our goal of maximizing productivity in the long term.

Location is critical. Knowing early *where* to locate specific functionality in the physical hierarchy is often as important to good software design as knowing *what* it does. Just as with knowing when to group related software, it is also important to know when any given subset of desired functionality best resides with the client software that inspired its initial implementation or at a lower level where it can be used (*reused*) more widely.[1] By proactively organizing our production software so as to maximize hierarchical reuse (section 0.4), we achieve economies of scale and also avoid many of its liabilities.

Factoring is important. Thorough factoring of our *physical* designs is also essential to long-term success. We must make sure not to encumber our fine-grained reusable solutions with unnecessary clutter. Each component and every package should have a clear and focused purpose or charter. Ideally, low-level design decisions will be isolated within individual components. At the same time, physical dependencies must be appropriately constrained. Adeptly factoring logically cohesive functionality into components and packages that share similar physical dependencies is the *essence* of what makes our component-based software design methodology so successful.

In this chapter, we address the topic of physical design from the developer's perspective and how physical considerations change the way we view software. We will look both at situations to avoid as well as goals for which to strive. In particular, we cover specific techniques that help to unite logical and physical design (section 2.3), while avoiding physical design violations (section 2.6) such as cyclic physical dependencies and long-distance (inter-component) friendships (see section 3.5). After that, we examine the benefits of *lateral* versus classical *layered* architectures (see section 3.7) and how to avoid pitfalls that would compromise physical interoperability (see section 3.9). We then explore architectural-level *insulation* techniques for avoiding unnecessary compile-time coupling (see section 3.11). Finally, as a comprehensive

---

[1] See, for example, **stroustrup00**, section 24.4, pp. 755–757, particularly p. 756:

> In most contexts, we need to have the actual wheels hidden to maintain the abstraction of a car (when you use a car you cannot operate the wheels independently). However, the `Wheel` class itself seems a good candidate for wider use, so moving it outside class `Car` might be better.

example, we exhibit a well-designed, thoroughly factored, complex subsystem, implemented almost entirely in terms of reusable components distributed over several packages and package groups (see section 3.12).

3.1   Thinking Physically

Physical design, as it pertains to C++ programming (and, later, programming in general), was first popularized in the mid-1990s.[2] An inscription can be found at the top of the back cover of my first book, *Large-Scale C++ Software Design*[3]:

> Developing a large-scale software system in C++ requires more than just a
> sound understanding of the logical design issues covered in most books on C++
> programming. To be successful, you will also need a grasp of physical design
> concepts that, while closely tied to the technical aspects of development, include
> a dimension with which even expert software developers may have little or no
> experience.
>
> — John Lakos (c. 1996)

A quarter of a century later, these prescient words continue to ring true. With the benefit of considerable cumulative experience at applying these ideas at scale, we are in an even better position to elucidate the thought processes surrounding this important newer (but no longer new) dimension known as *physical design*.

3.1.1   Pure Classical (Logical) Software Design Is Naive

Classical software design is pure *logical* design. In this model, software is naively perceived to reside in a single seamless space. Having just one monolith of software renders any notion of physical dependency meaningless. In a monolith, there is also no concept of direction: all logical modules are mutually accessible. And, because there are no physical boundaries, the *size* of any logical unit of encapsulation is essentially unbounded. Moreover, arbitrary friendships allow what should be private access to local implementation details to extend to distant and potentially vast amounts of software. Hence, pure logical design, unadvised by physical realities, is often suboptimal if not impractical and typically does not scale.

---

[2] **martin95**, Chapter 3, section "Cohesion, Closure, and Reusability," pp. 231–257. See also **martin03**, Chapter 11, pp. 127–134.

[3] **lakos96**, back cover

3.1.2   Components Serve as Our Fine-Grained Modules

Sound physical design naturally governs good logical design in practice. In our methodology, components serve as our fine-grained modules. Components (section 0.7) are the atomic unit of both logical and physical design. As such, private details must not span component boundaries (section 2.6), the size of which are, in turn, governed by our ability to test them from a single test-driver file (section 2.14.3). Hence, the extent to which local (private) information can be shared is intentionally kept quite small. Moreover, these fine-grained modules are forbidden from exhibiting cyclic physical dependencies. While these additional physical constraints provide many tangible benefits, they also pose new and interesting design challenges that must be addressed.

3.1.3   The Software Design Space Has Direction

Physical design plays a central role in providing a welcome dimension of structure to our software. In particular, the physical design space of software is not isotropic — that is, it has direction! There is a crisp notion of up and down. Software at higher levels in the physical hierarchy may depend on lower-level software, but not vice versa. Moreover, two components, packages, or package groups may be entirely independent, giving way to a notion of *lateral* software as well (see section 3.7.5). Hence, we typically use these directional terms to convey the relative physical locations of the components a component-based software subsystem comprises.

3.1.3.1   Example of Relative Physical Position: Abstract Interfaces

A good illustration of thinking physically is the appropriate use of pure abstract interfaces (see Volume II, sections 4.6 and 4.7). Such interfaces, or *protocols* (section 1.7.5), introduce an aspect of physical *position* that might, at first, seem unnatural to those grounded in procedural languages, such as C, and yet are both powerful and very useful. Traditionally, we tend to think of an implementation as somehow being at a lower level than its interface. For *concrete* classes, as illustrated abstractly in Figure 3-1a,[4] the client always resides *above* the concrete implementation of the interface and necessarily depends on that implementation at compile and/or link time. We say that the client is *layered* (see section 3.7.2) on that concrete component. Any *compatible* changes — i.e., those not affecting syntax or essential behavior

---

[4] Recall that we consistently use *pseudo* package names (section 2.10.3), such as **my**, **your**, and **their**, to indicate abstract or "toy" examples, and we use conventional nondescript names, such as **xyza** and **abcx**, to indicate more realistic implementations in grouped packages, where absolute position is not especially relevant.

(see Volume II, section 5.6) — that we make to that implementation, such as to alter performance characteristics, are destructive in that the old characteristics are no longer available (at least not within the same process).

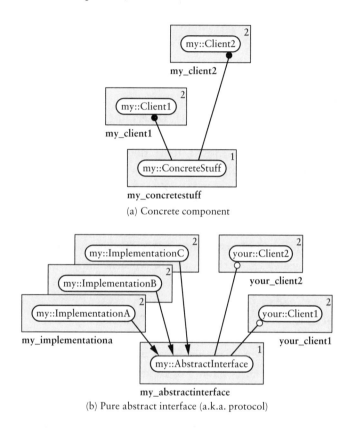

(a) Concrete component

(b) Pure abstract interface (a.k.a. protocol)

Figure 3-1: Relative *physical* position of interface versus implementation

By contrast, an implementation of a (pure) *abstract* interface, like each of its clients, necessarily resides *above* the component in which the interface class is defined. As Figure 3-1b suggests, a client of an abstract interface does not typically participate in a physical dependency relationship (either way) with any of the implementations. We say that the relative positions of the components implementing and using the interface are *lateral*. Moreover, new implementations may be added at any time without having to modify any existing components, leading to increased stability (section 0.5). It will turn out that pure abstract interfaces will play a crucial role in eliminating physical dependencies through the use of *lateral* architectures (see section 3.7.5).

3.1.4   Software Has Absolute Location

Absolute position is another important aspect that pure logical design completely sidesteps. When one considers building a new home, it is often said that the three most important considerations are location, location, and location. That same consideration also applies to the construction of new software. The absolute position of a component within the physical hierarchy of an enterprise will necessarily determine both the software on which that entity is allowed to depend as well as what software is able to use that component.

3.1.4.1   Asking the Right Questions Helps Us Determine Optimal Location

An important goal as an enterprise is to distribute our software throughout the physical hierarchy so as to maximize its utility through hierarchical reuse (section 0.4). In making the correct determination of proper location, we will want to ask ourselves many important questions. Does the software belong to a specific application, or should it be part of a more generally reusable library? If in a library, does that software belong at a high level (i.e., close to the application that first motivated it) so that it can be modified more easily, or at a lower level where it can be used more widely? Properly placed, the physical entity will have the appropriate trade-offs between visibility, stability, and dependency that will maximize its utility for the long term.

3.1.4.2   See What Exists to Avoid Reinventing the Wheel

Whenever we are solving a problem, we will want to look in our repository of (hierarchically) reusable software (section 0.4) to avoid reinventing what is already there (e.g., see Figure 0-56, section 0.9). Ideally, each individual component we design will have a well-focused purpose that aims to maximize its applicability (see Volume II, section 5.7). When we do find that we need to create a new reusable solution, we will look within our software infrastructure to (1) determine where the pinnacle — i.e., the highest-level component (or components) — of that solution should reside, and (2) how the remainder of the implementation of that subsystem should be distributed among the (lower-level) packages and package groups within our enterprise. In a mature hierarchically reusable infrastructure, many of the components we might need will already exist and, in fact, some of which *must* be used in order to make our new component-based solution interoperable with others (see Volume II, section 4.4).

3.1.4.3   Good Citizenship: Identifying Proper Physical Location

In the process of designing our new subsystem, we may find it necessary to introduce several new components, perhaps some new packages, and (though unlikely) possibly even new package groups to satisfy needs not yet adequately addressed. Part of our responsibility as "good citizens," however, is to identify the proper location for reusable entities in the enterprise-wide repository of Software Capital (section 0.9), determine a charter that characterizes software entities in that region, and design those entities accordingly.

3.1.5   The Criteria for Colocation Should Be Substantial, Not Superficial

How logical content is best aggregated is typically governed by substantive and enduring properties (e.g., cohesive semantics, similar essential physical dependencies, or anticipated dependencies by clients) rather than by superficial characteristics (e.g., having similar syntactic properties such as being of the same class category; see Volume II, section 4.2) or by comparatively insignificant or ephemeral qualities like having similar levels of alias-, exception-, or thread-safety guarantees (see Volume II, section 6.1).

For example, primitive functionality — i.e., functionality that requires private access to the internal representation of an object to be implemented efficiently — must belong to the same component as the definition of its class (e.g., `xyza_something`). Functionality that can be implemented without private access but is still closely semantically related can (and should) be implemented in a separate component (see section 3.2.7). That distinct *utility* component can reside either alongside the associated component in the same package (e.g., `xyza_somethingutil`) or with other similar utility components in a higher-level *utility package* (e.g., `xyzau_something`).

3.1.6   Discovery of Nonprimitive Functionality Absent Regularity Is Problematic

Experience has shown that placing nonprimitive (see section 3.2.7) yet semantically related and generally useful functionality having similar physical dependencies in a separate package — e.g., consisting (exclusively) of "utility" components having corresponding names — to be an obstacle to discovery by prospective clients (see section 3.2.9.1). Unless we have an established framework in which either the nonprimitive functionality is dead regular (e.g., see Figure 3-29, section 3.3.7) or some specific aspect of it induces substantial additional physical dependencies (e.g., as with the **a_lib2** package of Figure 2-74, section 2.9.3), it is usually better to colocate such nonprimitive yet semantically cohesive "utilities" (see Volume II, section 4.2) in components within the same package as their corresponding (typically value) types (see Volume II, section 4.1) on which they operate.

3.1.7   Package Scope Is an Important Design Consideration

Scope (see Figure 2-72, section 2.9.3) is an important consideration when it comes to designing packages and package groups. Packages, unlike components, are not closed entities and will typically grow over time. This property is particularly true of *horizontal packages* (e.g., see Figure 3-113, section 3.7.4.1), such as **bdlma**, that aggregate similar yet independent library components implementing a common protocol base class, in this case bslma::Allocator (see Volume II, section 4.10). Characterizing a package such that it will likely never properly accommodate more than one or a few components runs counter to our goal of creating a balanced physical hierarchy (section 2.2.17). In such circumstances, we say that the scope of the package fails to produce sufficient physical *fanout*. On the other hand, failure to anticipate significant expansion could lead to disproportionately (even unworkably) large packages in the long run. Our goal therefore must be to characterize our packages and package groups so as to reach the "right size" in the long-term steady state.

3.1.7.1   Package Charter Must Be Delineated in Package-Level Documentation

To know where to put new components, as well as find those that we need that might already exist, it is important that we fully characterize each new package we create (section 2.8). We call this characterization the package *charter*, which must be thoroughly delineated explicitly in package-level documentation (see Volume II, section 6.15). We will also need to choose a (very) short but unique name that will serve as the prefix for the name of each component file that resides within that package. This prefix, which also serves as the package name, is at best a tag, but it is in no way a substitute for a well-articulated charter.

3.1.7.2   Package Prefixes Are at Best Mnemonic Tags, Not Descriptive Names

A package prefix, especially one within a group, is typically chosen to be somewhat mnemonic but is otherwise largely arbitrary, except that shorter prefixes (e.g., **xyza**) tend to indicate more generally useful (or interface) packages while longer prefixes (**xyzabc**) sometimes suggest less widely applicable (or implementation) packages. Ideally, the trailing letter or letters distinguishing packages within a group will represent a meaningful word or phrase, such as **t** (for "time") or **ma** (for "memory allocation"). Sometimes, short names (e.g., **s** for "system"), along with their associated meaning (e.g., components used, in part, to encapsulate platform-dependent functionality), are reused from group to group. Creative conventional use of related package prefixes, such as sharing the first letter — e.g., **f** (functor), **fr** (functor representation), **fri** (functor representation implementation), and **fu** (functor utility) — after the group name (e.g., **bde** as in **bdef**, **bdefr**, **bdefri**, and **bdefu**; see Figure 3-37, section 3.3.8.3) can effectively indicate local relationships among closely collaborating package subsets within a package group.[5]

3.1.7.3   Package Prefixes Force Us to Consider Design More Globally Early

Package prefixes and namespaces (section 2.4.9) play a crucial role in the design process on many levels. For one thing, these tags are part of the name of every global logical and physical entity. We cannot even edit a file, let alone write a class, without being forced to think about its package prefix, which in turn forces us to think about *where* this class belongs. In this way, package prefixes gently steer our thought processes toward considering design from a much more global perspective much earlier in the development process.

3.1.7.4   Package Prefixes Force Us to Consider Package Dependencies from the Start

Package prefixes also force us to think about the envelope of package-level dependencies from its inception. By forcing a component into an absolute position, package prefixes quickly have designers facing the reality that entire clusters of components must continue to remain physically (if not conceptually) independent of others. The package serves as an abstract physical characterization of each component with which the component itself must comply. The explicit tagging of every global logical and physical entity with its corresponding package name further reinforces its absolute *physical* location. This visible tagging is especially useful when a component is viewed out of context (e.g., when a library component is used in application code).

---

[5] Note that shorter names, such as **bdef**, that have just a single letter distinguishing the package within a group (**bde**) are typically reserved for public-facing packages, whereas packages having names that employ all three available letters are almost always relegated to supporting packages that, though not private, are not generally expected to be used outside the group. Choosing widely used group names carefully (e.g., **ode**, as we did back at Bear Stearns, c. 1997, for "our development environment"), coupled with just a single trailing consonant (e.g., **s**, **t**) and sometimes even a vowel (e.g., **u**), makes for names that are delightfully pronounceable: **odes** ("o-des"), **odet** ("o-det"), **odeu** ("o-dew").

3.1.7.5   Even Opaque Package Prefixes Grow to Take On Important Meaning

Once a prefix is identified, it carries significant meaning (section 2.8.4): Not only does a package prefix uniquely identify the physical home address of that software, it also typically serves to identify logical as well as physical characteristics shared across multiple components within that package.

Consider, for example, the component **bdlma_pool** and in particular its (principle) class `bdlma::Pool`.[6] The name `Pool` indicates that this class performs some sort of pooling; however, the **bdlma** prefix (and corresponding namespace) tells us that this class resides in a component alongside others that together support generalized memory allocation and, in particular, are interoperable with the base-level interface `bslma::Allocator` in the **bslma_allocator** component (see Volume II, section 4.10). Taken together, the ten characters of **bdlma_pool** succinctly tell us much of what a `bdlma::Pool` does. Most importantly, though, the package name tells us — at a glance — in exactly what subdirectory (`bdlma`) of what package group (**bdl**) the source code for this globally accessible memory-pooling construct can be found (see Figure 2-77, section 2.13).

3.1.7.6   Effective (e.g., Associative) Use of Package Names Within Groups

As a second example, consider a relatively low-level, highly structured infrastructure framework package group **ote** (Our Transport Environment), illustrated (in part) in Figure 3-2, which provides fundamental inter-process communication functionality. The physical structure of **ote** consists of several packages, including **otec**, **oteci**, and **otecm**, whose names, related by a common leading **c** following the package group name, are used to suggest an especially tight semantic coupling within the group.

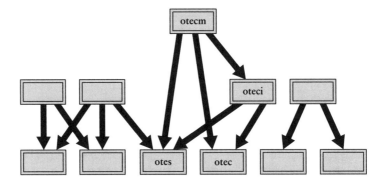

Figure 3-2: Highly structured transport framework package group, `ote`

---

[6] **bdlma_pool** is a component in the **bdlma** package of the **bdl** package group of Bloomberg's open-source distribution of the BDE (see **bde14**, subdirectory `/groups/bdl/bdlma/`).

Here, the **otes** package provides "system-level" services that are required by many of the components in this transport package group, such as the Unix `iovec` ("scatter/gather") buffer structure, but in a form that is platform-neutral. The **otec** package defines a variety of *channel* protocols for use in both stream- and message-based transport, each of which is available in blocking or nonblocking form; a separate *protocol hierarchy*[7] (see Volume II, sections 4.6 and 4.7) for each of these flavors, respectively, is used to broker corresponding implementations that either do or don't have timeout capability.[8] Standard concrete implementations of the protocols provided in the **otec** package reside in **oteci**. Finally, **otecm** provides a framework for managing multiple channels in both a single- or multithreaded environment. Notice that each package name carries with it a strong semantic connotation and, to varying degrees (e.g., see sections 3.2.9 and 3.3.7), may also suggest the component categories (see Volume II, section 4.2) that reside within.

3.1.8 Limitations Due to Prohibition on Cyclic Physical Dependencies

Thinking physically means organizing our software in ways that achieve our physical design goals. For example, our prohibition of cyclic physical dependencies in general (section 2.2.24), and among components in particular (section 2.6), will, at times, force us to phrase our software designs in ways that might not initially seem intuitive. Imagine, for example, a situation in which we have a manager class, `Manager`, that is responsible for the lifetimes of objects, of type `Employee`, in its charge. Suppose further that both the `Manager` and `Employee` types are substantial and reside in their own respective components as illustrated in Figure 3-3a. Now suppose, as depicted in Figure 3-3b, that it may be required for a client to learn the number of employees who report to a given manager at times when only one of the manager's employees is available (e.g., passed as the single argument to a function).[9]

---

[7] **lakos96**, Appendix A, pp. 737–768

[8] In practice, we will want to separate each of these semantically distinct abstract interfaces into three syntactically separate parts, based on the level of service they are expected to provide and the clients that will use them. The three general levels of abstraction are called "channel," "channel allocator," and "(channel) allocator factory." In our methodology, the terms "allocator" and "factory" are almost synonymous, with "allocator" being just slightly more low-level/primitive; we use different words here to avoid repetition. In its simplest form, "channel" abstracts the concept of an endpoint of a communication mechanism, providing appropriate "read" and "write" methods, while a "channel allocator" dispenses channels as resources and, hence, abstracts the concepts of creating and destroying channels. Finally, an allocator factory (for channels) is substantially a naming service capable of dispensing channel allocators, which will, in turn, dispense channels appropriately configured. Each triple of concrete implementation classes for these three physically separate protocols will, due to friendship, invariably reside within a single component (see section 3.3.3.1).

[9] Note that this same sort of architectural topology is a recurring pattern in software — e.g., with elements in a list or in rows in a table.

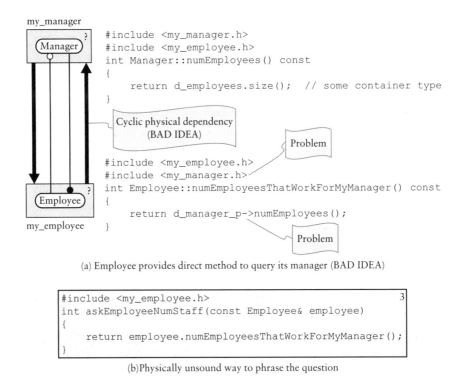

(a) Employee provides direct method to query its manager (BAD IDEA)

```
#include <my_employee.h>                                              3
int askEmployeeNumStaff(const Employee& employee)
{
    return employee.numEmployeesThatWorkForMyManager();
}
```

(b)Physically unsound way to phrase the question

Figure 3-3: Cyclic rendering of manager/employee functionality (BAD IDEA)

The client's implementation of its own `askEmployeeNumStaff` function, shown in
Figure 3-3b, expects the employee object to do all the work. Having a direct method such as
`numEmployeesThatWorkForMyManager` on the `Employee` object (Figure 3-3a) — or by
any other name — requires not only that each `Employee` object be imbued with the address
of its manager (e.g., at construction) but also that the component defining the `Employee` class
`#include` the header defining the `Manager` class, thereby inducing a cyclic physical dependency between the **my_manager** and **my_employee** components.[10] Such a design violates our
most important physical design rule (section 2.6): No cyclic physical dependencies!

---

[10] Again, given that every component must reside within a package (section 2.4.6), we will sometimes use silly
(pseudo) package names, such as **my**, to suggest (unrealistic) "toy" examples versus abstract (but valid) package
names, such as **xyza**, to indicate more realistic library examples, but in a package group (**xyz**) at an unspecified
location in the physical hierarchy.

Being a lower-level entity, an employee should not attempt to tell the manager what to do directly. An `Employee` is, however, allowed to identify its manager via an (opaque) address, as suggested by Figure 3-4a, without having to `#include` the `my_manager.h` header. With this small adjustment, we enable a higher-level client function such as `askEmployeeNumStaff` (Figure 3-4b) to rephrase the original question to (1) first ask the `Employee` object for its `Manager` object's address, and (2) then use that address (now in the context of the definition of the object to which it refers) to ask that specific `Manager` object directly for the number of `Employee` objects it manages.

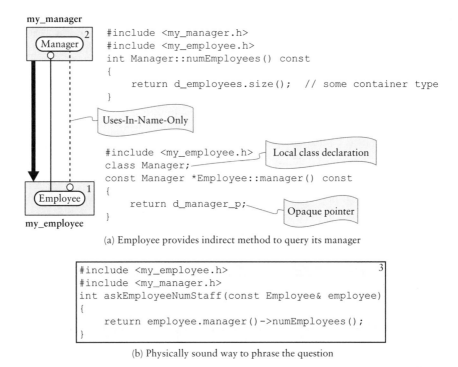

(a) Employee provides indirect method to query its manager

```
#include <my_employee.h>                                        3
#include <my_manager.h>
int askEmployeeNumStaff(const Employee& employee)
{
    return employee.manager()->numEmployees();
}
```

(b) Physically sound way to phrase the question

Figure 3-4: Acyclic rendering of manager/employee functionality (GOOD IDEA)

This simple, straightforward transformation, referred to as *opaque pointers*, makes use of a *local class declaration* (rather than a `#include` of the `Manager` class's definition) to break the "upward" physical dependency and is but one of nine classical *levelization techniques*[11] that we will cover in full detail in section 3.5.[12] Additional motivation for avoiding cycles is presented in section 3.4.

---

[11] **lakos96**, Chapter 5, pp. 203–325

[12] For an alternative explanation of this *opaque pointer* solution to this very same *levelization* problem, see Figures 3-53 and 3-54, section 3.5.4.1.

3.1.9   Constraints on Friendship Intentionally Preclude Some Logical Designs

The physical reality of components also imposes important constraints on the scope of local implementation details.[13] In our methodology, the primary vehicle for presenting encapsulating interfaces has been the *component*, the size of which is (deliberately) artificially limited by requiring that each component be testable from a single driver file (section 2.14.3). We explicitly forbid a unit of logical encapsulation from spanning physical (i.e., component) boundaries (section 2.6). This essential restriction along with a soft bound on component size is what encourages the kind of fine-grained modularity and finely graduated granular software designs that make both hierarchical reuse (section 0.4) and thorough testing (see Volume III) possible.

3.1.10   Introducing an Example That Justifiably Requires Wrapping

To illustrate some of the necessary design limitations that our physical encapsulation rules deliberately impose, let us suppose that we have decided that we need a special-purpose date-sequence type, which we will call a `TimeSeries`. Perhaps this (nontemplate) container type will have some built-in support for concurrency or impose additional policy (e.g., no two contained dates may be adjacent), or almost any number of other eccentricities. Since none of these peculiar features is offered by our core development library (**ode**), we'll need to implement this special-purpose date container type ourselves. Given that we already have a suitably customized, high-performance, and portable date-sequence class, `odet::DateSequence`[14] (defined in the **odet_datesequence** component), we will certainly want to reuse that functionality in the implementation of our new class, `my::TimeSeries` (defined in component **my_timeseries**). Figure 3-5 provides a *component/class diagram* illustrating the relevant pieces and identifying certain implementation options (discussed in section 3.1.10.1).

---

[13] Historically, the C++ language has not supported a unit of both logical and physical encapsulation larger than a translation unit. With the advent of C++ modules, however, it is not inconceivable that a corresponding — and perhaps even architecturally useful — higher-level notion of coherent logical and physical encapsulation might emerge. We will see an example of the potential benefit for language support for such a larger unit of logical/physical encapsulation at the end of section 3.5 in the context of the escalating-encapsulation *levelization* technique (see Figure 3-99, section 3.5.10.8).

[14] Assume that the **t** following the package-group name **ode** (for "our development environment") to form the **odet** package stands for "time."

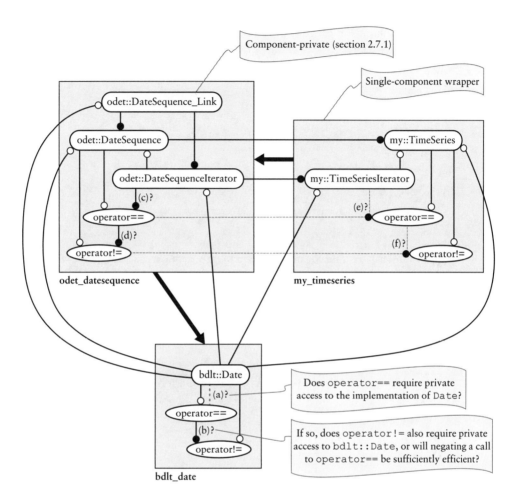

Figure 3-5: Creating a single-component wrapper (no problem!)

3.1.10.1   Wrapping Just the Time Series and Its Iterator in a Single Component

Our `odet::DateSequence` library class naturally uses, in its interface, the ubiquitous `bdlt::Date`[15,16] *vocabulary type* (see Volume II, section 4.4) as does its (`const`) iterator, `odet::DateSequenceIterator`, along with the component-private (section 2.7.1)

---

[15] **pacifico12**

[16] An open-source implementation of **bdlt_date** may be found in Bloomberg's open-source distribution of BDE (**bde14**, subdirectory `/tree/master/groups/bdl/bdlt/`).

implementation-only type `odet::DateSequence_Link`. As shown, **odet_datesequence** clearly *depends on* **bdlt_date** (sections 1.8 and 1.9). Our `my::TimeSeries` type will naturally also use `bdlt::Date` directly but will embed an instance of `odet::DateSequence` to do the actual work:

```
class TimeSeries {
    odet::DateSequence d_sequenceImp;
  public:
    // ...
    // ACCESSORS
    TimeSeriesIterator begin() const;
};
```

We will similarly treat its corresponding iterator, `TimeSeriesIterator`, whose definition we would locate textually ahead of that of the container (in the same header) to avoid having a forward declaration and a local logical cycle (e.g., see Figures 2-52 and 2-54, sections 2.7.3 and 2.7.4, respectively) — even though logical cycles within a component (see section 3.3.2) are technically permitted (section 2.6):

```
class TimeSeriesIterator {
    odet::DateSequenceIterator d_sequenceImpIterator;
  private:
    // CREATORS
    // ...
  public:
    // ...
};
```

To obtain a `my::TimeSeriesIterator` from a `my::TimeSeries` object, we invoke the `begin` method of the underlying `odet::DateSequence` data member, `d_sequenceImp`, and use the returned *in-process* value (see Volume II, sections 4.1–4.3) as a constructor argument:

```
inline
TimeSeriesIterator TimeSeries::begin() const
{
    return TimeSeriesIterator(d_sequenceImp.begin());
}
```

3.1.10.2   Private Access Within a Single Component Is an Implementation Detail

Within a single component, we have the freedom to access the private details of other logical entities. To begin our analysis, let's first consider the implementation of the (always free) equality-comparison operators (see Volume II, section 6.13) illustrated in Figure 3-5. The homogeneous `operator==` on `bdlt::Date` might not require private access to its implementation to achieve maximal efficiency (Figure 3.3a). Fortunately, because of our design rules prohibiting long-distance friendship, that information is necessarily private to the component, and any need for private access may change without notice to clients. These same privacy rules also allow us the freedom to implement (and alter at will) the implementation of the homogeneous `operator!=` in terms of either the corresponding `operator==` or, if determined (e.g., empirically through careful measurement) not to be sufficiently efficient, directly via local friendship.[17]

3.1.10.3   An Iterator Helps to Realize the Open-Closed Principle

Next, let's turn to the **odet_datesequence** component and examine the various logical parts it comprises. The `DateSequence` class, being a container, naturally provides an iterator, thereby enabling external clients to efficiently access its elements. In so doing, the iterator facilitates the *open-closed principle* (section 0.5), which allows clients to extend existing functionality, as we are endeavoring to do here, without having to change the source code of the (stable) reusable components being exploited. If the iterator is implemented completely optimally (on all supported platforms), there will be no need for the homogeneous equality-comparison operator, `operator==`, to have private access to the container, and so `operator==` can instead use the iterator [Figure 3-5; see (c)], but if not, there is always the option for `operator==` to access the container implementation directly (via local friendship). Most likely, `operator!=` can be implemented "efficiently enough" in terms of `operator==` [Figure 3-5; see (d)] — the other available options being to implement it using the supplied iterator directly or via direct (private) access to the container's implementation (again, via local friendship).

---

[17] Note that for a date implemented internally as a serial number of days from some epoch, both operators would typically be implemented as `inline` functions operating directly on the underlying implementation using the respective built-in `==` and `!=` operations on integers.

3.1.10.4   Private Access Within a Wrapper Component Is Typically Essential

Now, let's consider our new *wrapper* component,[18] **my_timeseries**, and its implementation options. In our methodology, we consistently use the terms *handle* and *wrapper* to delineate types that *do* and do *not*, respectively, provide programmatic access to the underlying objects upon which they depend. To preserve encapsulation (i.e., hide that my::TimeSeries is implemented in terms of odet::DateSequence), only the my::TimeSeries class is permitted to construct instances of my::TimeSeriesIterator, so my::TimeSeriesIterator declares its constructors private and grants my::TimeSeries friend status. (The only other obvious alternative would be to make the constructor of my::TimeSeriesIterator public, which would expose the underlying odet::DateSequence implementation.) Therefore, because our design rules require that friendship not span component boundaries (section 2.6), the definitions of both my::TimeSeries and my::TimeSeriesIterator *must* reside within the same component (see section 3.3.1.1).

3.1.10.5   Since This Is Just a Single-Component Wrapper, We Have Several Options

Finally, let's look at our implementation choices for the equality-comparison operators in our **my_timeseries** wrapper component. Because this is a single-component wrapper (i.e., one that wraps just a single component), we have several design alternatives [Figure 3-5; see (e)] of which we present just the most likely two: (a) rely on our local iterator, my::TimeSeriesIterator, to provide efficient access to a my::TimeSeries object without any friendship, or (b) access the underlying odet::DateSequence from the supplied my::TimeSeries via local friendship and then, because the wrapper ensures a restrictive subset, invoke the publicly accessible operator== defined in **odet_datesequence**.

If the delegating function is declared inline, the first alternative (a), suggested above, *might* achieve acceptable (perhaps even optimal) performance; however, the second alternative (b) will, in all conceivable circumstances, be at least as good if not better — e.g., due to implementation limits on the depth of inlining. Hence, because (by virtue of both being in the

---

[18] We have, historically, always used the term *wrapper* to indicate that there is *no* programmatic access to the underlying resource from outside the component that defines it and have consistently used the term *handle* to suggest otherwise; see **lakos96**, section 6.5.3, pp. 429–434.

same component) the operator happens to have access to the underlying representation (in the container), we would naturally opt to take advantage of that private access:

```
inline
bool my::operator==(const TimeSeries& lhs, const TimeSeries& rhs)
{
    return lhs.d_sequenceImp == rhs.d_sequenceImp;
}                                   // Use 'operator==' for 'DateSequence'.
```

The implementation options for the corresponding `operator!=` are similar, and there is also the possibility of defining that operator in terms of the negation of the corresponding `operator==` (above); but, given that we again happen to have private access, the direct implementation (which is effectively guaranteed to be runtime optimal) is clearly indicated:

```
inline
bool my::operator!=(const TimeSeries& lhs, const TimeSeries& rhs)
{
    return lhs.d_sequenceImp != rhs.d_sequenceImp;
}                                   // Use 'operator!=' for 'DateSequence'.
```

3.1.10.6 Multicomponent Wrappers, Not Having Private Access, Are Problematic

As we have said all along, enforcing relatively small units of encapsulation constrains our logical designs in nontrivial ways. For example, consider the *multicomponent*[19] *wrapper* illustrated in Figure 3-6a. In this example we have, for whatever reason, elected to wrap not only `odet::DateSequence` but also `bdlt::Date`, with each implemented in its own, separate component. We are now faced with the conundrum of how `my::TimeSeries` can access the private data in `my::Date` without anyone else doing the same. Unfortunately, creating multicomponent wrappers successfully is hard[20] as the separate wrapper components typically need "special" access to get to the very underlying representations that we are trying to hide, and, until relatively recently, there has been no known general, after-the-fact way of doing so consistent with our component design rules (section 2.6). We now have a general (albeit "hacky")

---

[19] Note that the term *multicomponent* used here refers to the wrapper itself, not what is being wrapped.

[20] **lakos96**, section 6.4.3.2, pp. 415–425

solution to this problem, which has become part of the escalating-encapsulation levelization technique discussed in section 3.5.10 (see, in particular, Figure 3-100, section 3.5.10.8).[21]

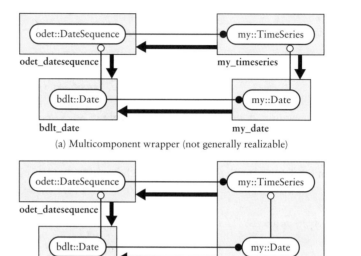

(a) Multicomponent wrapper (not generally realizable)

(b) Small single-component wrapper (fine if that's all and it fits)

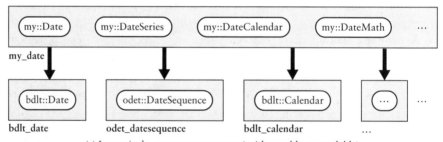

(c) Large single-component wrapper (neither stable nor scalable)

Figure 3-6: Architectural restrictions imposed by component design rules

---

[21] We hope that this recurring need for wrapping existing systems will eventually be much better addressed by the highly anticipated, new C++ language feature, *modules*, once it becomes widely available.

[22] Note, however, that according to section 2.2.4.8, the class name `my::Date` is a design-rule violation because it does not incorporate the base name of the component as a prefix.

3.1.10.7   Example Why Multicomponent Wrappers Typically Need "Special" Access

As a concrete example of the inherent difficulties in implementation that multicomponent wrappers impose, suppose that we have a client that is working exclusively with `my::Date` and `my::TimeSeries` "wrapper" objects and wants to create, within some function, a time series consisting of a particular sequence of dates. First, the client creates an empty time series:

```
my::TimeSeries importantDates;
```

Then, the client creates a date, say, Independence Day in the United States:

```
my::Date independenceDay(1776, 7, 4);
```

Now, the client adds `independenceDay` to the time series of `importantDates`:

```
importantDates.add(independenceDay);
```

But how do we implement the `my::TimeSeries::add` method to do that? Recall that `my::TimeSeries` has, as its only data member, an object named `d_sequenceImp` of type `odet:DateSequence`. This general date-sequence type has no knowledge of type `my::Date` and yet is quite capable of inserting a given value of type `bdlt::Date` at any valid position using an object of type `odet::DateSequenceIterator`. Because both `my::Date` and `bdlt::Date` so happen to approximate the same *mathematical* type, which is itself problematic (see Volume II, section 4.4), it is at least possible for the method

```
void my::TimeSeries::add(const Date& value);
```

to extract the individual values of the *salient attributes* (see Volume II, section 4.1), `year`, `month`, and `day`, of the `my::Date` object passed in; we can use those values to construct a temporary `bdlt::Date` object having the same overall value, which can then be passed to the `add` method of the underlying `my::DateSequence` data member, `d_sequenceImp`.

Not only is this approach horribly inefficient, it is even possible *only* because the underlying date object represents a *value* (see Volume II, section 4.1), which can be communicated independently of its C++ type. In all other cases, e.g., a *mechanism* type (see Volume II, section 4.2) such as a lock or memory allocator, no such extraction via the public interface is possible; hence, we would therefore need some sort of "privileged" access to extract a reference to the underlying (in-process) representation from cooperating wrapper components (typically residing within the same package).

3.1.10.8   Wrapping Interoperating Components Separately Generally Doesn't Work

Given our component-centric design rules, there are a couple of obvious alternatives, neither particularly appealing. We can either expose the underlying `bdlt::Date` in `my::Date` (making `my::Date` just a glorified *handle* for `bdlt::Date`)[23] or place both the `my::Date` and `my::DateSequence` in the same component, e.g., **my_date** (as illustrated in Figure 3-6b, section 3.1.10.6), thereby reverting to a single-component encapsulating wrapper. The former approach violates the intended encapsulation (or, more precisely, information hiding), with the latter potentially violating nominal cohesion (section 2.4).[24]

Even with appropriate logical naming adjustments, the single-component-wrapper approach is generally workable only if (1) the combined implementation does not exceed the complexity of what can reasonably be effectively verified from a single test driver, and (2) it is unlikely to require unbounded future extension in the way of additional classes, which is far from obvious here. As Figure 3-6c, section 3.1.10.6, suggests, both the size and instability could soon enough precipitate a redesign along with potentially unbounded implications.

3.1.10.9   What Should We Do When Faced with a Multicomponent Wrapper?

So what should we do when we believe we need a multicomponent wrapper? In our methodology, granting long-distance friendship (section 2.6) is simply not an option. Exposing encapsulated, and what should rightfully be hidden, design decisions (e.g., by converting the *wrapper* to a *handle*) would compromise our ability to change the underlying implementation in the future (see Volume II, section 5.5). Hiding the headers of the lower-level components in an effort to achieve pseudo-encapsulation is an even worse idea (see section 3.9.7). As it happens, there is now a relatively new incarnation of the *escalating-encapsulation* levelization technique (see section 3.5.10) that can be useful in wrapping large subsystems through the use of corresponding *shadow classes* implemented in separate components typically residing in a higher-level

---

[23] Developers familiar with system-level socket programming in pseudo object-oriented networking frameworks will be familiar with the concept of *almost encapsulating* — i.e., shamelessly exposing the native descriptor through the "wrapper" object's public API — because any such framework is inherently incapable of granting only the operating system privileged access to its internal representations.

[24] It has been suggested that one could, via naming convention, label certain functions as being for use only within the current package. Doing so, however, would violate encapsulation in an unbounded way within the package — even if the convention were fully respected by clients outside of that package. That said, occasional legitimate needs for such access (along with many more illegitimate ones; see section 3.9) do arise in practice (see the final examples of *escalating encapsulation* at the end of section 3.5.10).

wrapper package. Creating a procedural interface (see section 3.11.7) is always possible and could perhaps provide a viable alternative as well.

3.1.11   Section Summary

To summarize this introductory section, achieving good physical design makes us consider aspects of software that transcend traditional (pure) logical design. We are forced to consider, up front, where, in the physical hierarchy, each component will reside and upon what other software it will depend. We will need to think about how we organize and distribute our component-based solutions throughout our hierarchically reusable library software. Considering the relative positions of clients and implementations — e.g., when employing abstract interfaces — will enable us to achieve greater flexibility and stability where appropriate. Avoiding cyclic dependencies will sometimes make us rethink how we organize and package logical content. Finally, by restricting friendship to logical entities within the same component, we force developers to factor their software in ways that might, at times, seem frustrating and unwarranted. In so doing, however, we help to ensure, among other things, that our software is scalable and that the amount of testing effort required to validate any one component is bounded (section 2.14.3) — a feat whose worth is not to be underestimated.

3.2   Avoiding Poor Physical Modularity

Good modularity is accomplished by placing software that belongs together in physical proximity. The criteria used for modularization will govern its effectiveness. In this section, we begin by looking at ineffective modularization criteria and then grow our understanding to incorporate more effective ones. Aspects of modularity and class design including *completeness*, *minimalism*, and *primitiveness* are explored. This section concludes with an elaborate example — a "tunable" polygon component — comprising all of the above.

3.2.1   There Are Many Poor Modularization Criteria; Syntax Is One of Them

There are innumerable ways of achieving poor modularity — some obvious, others less so, but poor nonetheless. As a deliberately extreme but didactically useful first example, imagine choosing to partition logical content based on the kind of C++ construct used to implement it. That is, suppose we were to choose to place all the classes in one component or package, all the C-style functions in another, all the enumerations in yet another, and so on. Adhering to such an arbitrary, syntax-centric *modularization criteria* would clearly make achieving truly important architectural properties such as logical/physical coherence (section 2.3) or avoiding cyclic dependencies at every level of physical aggregation (section 2.2.24) hopelessly difficult if not impossible. As absurd as this initial example might sound, it is surprisingly easy to apply modularization criteria that is almost as suboptimal (e.g., see section 3.2.9.1), leading to unnecessarily inflexible, hard-to-understand, and hard-to-use designs.

3.2.2   Factoring Out Generally Useful Software into Libraries Is Critical

---

Guideline

Always try to factor and, when time allows, proactively *demote* generally useful functionality created for a specific application to its appropriate location in the physical hierarchy of our ever growing repository of *Software Capital*.

Identifying reusable pockets of functionality — and then properly factoring and *demoting* (see section 3.5.3) these generally useful units of software from applications into separate, lower-level libraries — is one of the most basic and critically important ways of achieving modularization (section 0.2). Hence, whenever we establish a new development environment and first begin to develop applications, we naturally commit to maintaining a centralized library of fine-grained modules (e.g., components) for inter-application use. As important as reuse is, however, it should not come at the expense of overly flexible interfaces (resulting from overly complicated designs). Rather, each component should have a well-focused purpose that is easy to understand and use (see Figure 0-55, section 0.9) yet aims to achieve wide-ranging applicability (see Volume II, section 5.7).

3.2.3   Failing to Maintain Application/Library Modularity Due to Pressure

During the early stages of application development, significant time and resources are invested in properly factoring out appropriate reusable functionality as suggested in Figure 3-7. As many of us know all too well, however, "the best-laid plans of mice and men oft go astray." Under pressure to deliver product, it is also common to suspend "temporarily" our avowed factoring efforts and subsequently colocate all of the code developed in the course of creating an application with that application. Use of this latter, "I need it now" criterion for modularization, though sometimes "the right answer" in short bursts, does not engender proper reuse across applications. If left unabated, however, more and more generally useful functionality becomes buried within a sea of irrelevant, application-specific code. In many real-world software development environments, the likelihood of introducing dependencies among the applications — perhaps even cyclic ones — becomes unacceptably high.

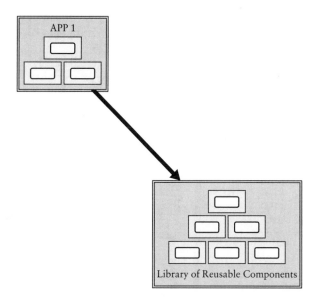

Figure 3-7: Separating generally useful software from applications (GOOD IDEA)

3.2.4   Continuous Demotion of Reusable Components Is Essential

The importance of continuously factoring out, in a timely fashion, generally useful functionality from collaborative and malleable application code and *demoting* it into widely available and stable libraries, where it can be readily and safely reused, cannot be overstated. Even when care has been taken to partition the logical elements within the application into discrete components, this software is often hard to find or even to know that it exists. What's more, applications must either depend on other ones (as illustrated in Figure 3-8), which is an explicit design-rule violation in our methodology (section 2.13), or duplicate the needed source code in their own private repositories. Either way, finding, using, and maintaining existing solutions is not facilitated.[25]

---

[25] Note that some service-oriented architectures (SOAs) might choose to address this problem somewhat differently. According to JC van Winkel (in his review of the manuscript for this volume), Google's way of resolving cyclic physical dependencies among application modules is by having multiple servers running in production offering RPC endpoints. Here, a server acts more or less like what's referred to above as an application. JC goes on to say, "Applications don't get too large because you 'just' have more of them, each housing one or more libraries. Yes, you pay by having the RPC overhead but that is relatively minor in Google's context (which serves almost everything over the network anyway)."

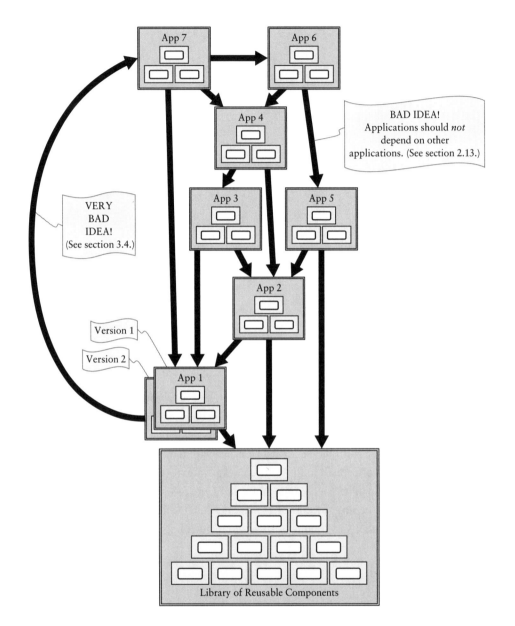

Figure 3-8: Tempting applications to depend on others (BAD IDEA)

Even with an SOA, implementing each service module by maximally leveraging a common pool of (hierarchically reusable) Software Capital (section 0.9) is invariably a wise strategy. For that matter, minimizing cyclic runtime dependencies (among services) is wise, too.

3.2.4.1 Otherwise, in Time, Our Software Might Devolve into a "Big Ball of Mud"!

Without active downward motion of generally useful functionality to stable libraries, buoyed by an ongoing affirmative effort to achieve hierarchical reuse, the motivation of application developers to modularize their code wanes, and we are likely to see more and more generally useful functionality becoming hopelessly intertwined with highly specific application code (as depicted in Figure 0-68, section 0.11).

For example, implementing a generally useful class such as `Base64Encoder` in the same application file as the one that defines `main` ensures that the `Base64Encoder` class will *not* be reused in any other application unless the text representing that class is surgically extracted and copied into a new translation unit, which — unless demoted there and then — would wind up continuing to be local to that same application.

Similarly, defining `Base64Encoder` in the same component as one that adapts an application to its GUI implies that anyone who wants to use `Base64Encoder` will, at the very least, also be forced to link in a significant body of GUI code that it cannot possibly use. At this point we are well on our way to devolving into "A Big Ball of Mud" (section 0.2).

3.2.5 Physical Dependency Is Not an Implementation Detail to an App Developer

Observation
Physical implementation dependencies strongly govern modularization.

Classical software design is quick to dismiss that which is not programmatically visible through a module's interfaces as mere "implementation details." Yet, ignoring physical design considerations — such as compile-time, and especially link-time, dependencies — can lead to significant problems for clients, who must ultimately build and deploy their software. Imagine that you need to staple a large number of documents currently sitting on your desk. You see a stapler on a table across the room and walk over to retrieve it. As you grasp the stapler, you discover that it is inexorably attached to the table.

Implementation detail? Perhaps. Acceptable? We think not. Hence, as suggested in Figure 2-74, section 2.9.3, we will invariably choose *not* to introduce a construct having excessive implementation dependencies into a UOR — even if it would otherwise (i.e., logically) be entirely cohesive.

Guideline

Avoid colocating more than one public class in a component unless there is a compelling *engineering* reason to do so.

Since its inception, one of the most fundamental principles guiding the design of the C++ language is that clients should pay (e.g., in terms of time and space) only for what they use. In that same spirit, we always strive to partition functionality into fine-grained components that can then be used *à la carte* (as opposed to all or nothing for unfactored software). We therefore generally limit a component to just a single (public) class unless there is a compelling *engineering* reason to do otherwise (see section 3.3.1). When the clients of two or more classes are known — let alone designed — to be disjoint (or nearly so), defining them in the same physically atomic module becomes especially contraindicated.

An important extreme case to which the above guideline applies occurs when we have taken the trouble to deliberately factor out, from a given type's implementation, a *stable*, lower-level abstraction — be it a suite of utility functions or an instantiable type that is not itself used in the interface (section 1.7.3) of the principal type defined in a component. In such cases, colocating this lower-level functionality in the same component necessarily exposes (at compile time) direct clients of the higher-level abstraction to details that they probably don't need.

What's worse, should the encapsulated (*use* of the) implementation (see section 3.11.1) of the principal class change to use a different lower-level type, either this (now legacy) implementation type would need to be dragged around by all clients in perpetuity or it would need to be excised and placed in its own, separate component (now having a new header file name), and therefore all direct clients of the old implementation type would then be forced to rework their code (i.e., change their `#include` directive to reflect the new component-header name).[26] Rather than allow the possibility for such to occur, it is far better to (physically) isolate stable, publicly accessible implementation-only (logical) entities from their principle client-facing types in the first place.

Observation

Anticipated client usage significantly influences modularization.

As an example of the need for physical modularization based on distinct client usage, consider the classical object-oriented pattern consisting of a protocol (section 1.7.5), one or more concrete implementations of that protocol, and one or more clients that use these implementations, but only indirectly (via the protocol). To help illustrate the specifics, let's assume we are dealing with the general domain of the high-rise building construction industry. Referring to Figure 3-9, suppose that the protocol class `Tool` represents an abstract mechanism designed to allow a specific concrete (i.e., instantiable) tool, derived from `Tool`, to be used indirectly. Suppose further that we have a family of *Worker* types, each of which knows how to operate any of a family of compliant *SpecificTool*, via the `Tool` protocol. Finally, imagine that there is a large family of overarching *Manager* types where each is responsible for selecting from a suite of various kinds of specific tool types and for "handing off" objects of those types to various kinds of worker objects in order to perform a specific kind of task.

---

[26] For a concrete example of the possible consequences of such inadequate factoring, see Figure 3-171, section 3.12.11.2.

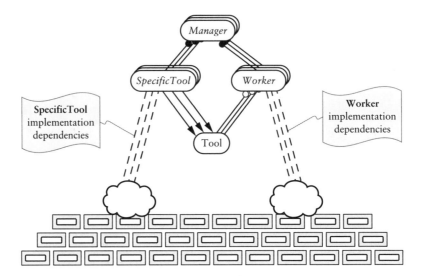

Figure 3-9: Classical protocol-based, object-oriented design pattern

---

Guideline

Especially avoid colocating classes expected to have largely disjoint clients.

The predominant reason for employing an abstract interface is to allow an external developer to extend the set of available behaviors (e.g., create a new *SpecificTool*) without having to alter client code (e.g., the source of any *Worker*). An important collateral benefit is that an abstract interface enables us to break *all* physical dependencies between the clients that consume it and the code that implements it (see section 3.11.5.3).

Defining a concrete implementation in the same component as the protocol it implements is almost always a resoundingly bad idea. Figure 3-10a illustrates the highly suboptimal (physical) modularization where we have colocated `SpecificToolX` with the `Tool` protocol. Notice that, with respect to those two classes, `Worker5` consumes only `Tool`, whereas `ManagerX5` operates on only `SpecificToolX`. By placing *SpecificTool* implementations within the same component as the `Tool` protocol, we lose much of the practical engineering benefit that abstract interfaces

afford. That is, we needlessly force worker components to again depend on specific tool implementations, with all of the compile- and link-time consequences physical dependency entails.

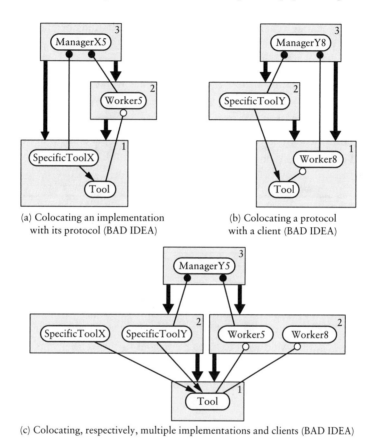

(a) Colocating an implementation
with its protocol (BAD IDEA)

(b) Colocating a protocol
with a client (BAD IDEA)

(c) Colocating, respectively, multiple implementations and clients (BAD IDEA)

Figure 3-10: Colocating classes having largely disjoint clients (BAD IDEA)

For similar reasons, defining a client in the same component as a protocol that it uses is
also generally a bad idea. As illustrated in Figure 3-10b, a typical concrete implementation,
SpecificToolY, will implement the protocol, Tool, but make no use of a colocated client,

`Worker8`.[27] Yet, by colocating `Worker8` along with `Tool`, we force all concrete tool implementations to depend on `Worker8` and also to inherit all of its external dependencies as well!

Finally, colocating otherwise independent implementations or clients within a single component is also ill advised — especially when it is known that only one will be used by any given client. In the scenario we have been considering, each of many manager types makes use of small subsets of the respective concrete tool and worker types. As Figure 3-10c illustrates, a typical manager, `ManagerY5`, is responsible for supplying (an object of) a particular type of client, `Worker5`, with (an object of) a particular type of tool, `SpecificToolY`. By colocating either implementations or clients, we artificially introduce physical dependencies on the other unused classes where none is warranted.

Guideline

Avoid colocating functionality expected to have largely disjoint clients.

As we know from section 2.5, each class must reside in its entirety within a single component. Given the prospect of a class that might over time grow to become relatively large and be used by different categories of clients, as shown very generally (in purely physical terms) in Figure 3-11a, we would want to at least consider further refinements leading to multiple classes consisting of widely used "core" functionality and then additional, higher-level functionality that tends to be used together, but only by distinct categories of clients, as suggested in Figure 3-11b.

---

[27] When the abstract interface is introduced solely to break an explicit cycle between two concrete classes (e.g., see Figure 3-75, section 3.5.7.4), it might be that there will be only a single derived class used in production (and possibly also a dummy test implementation), which necessarily depends on both the abstract interface (to implement it) and the unique client (to use it). Even so, placing the abstract interface in its own component does no harm and, for regularity, is strongly recommended. Another, even more common modern-day instance of introducing abstract interfaces is solely to enable what's called *mocking* of lower-level components during unit testing (section 2.14.5) — a practice we do not generally endorse (see Volume III).

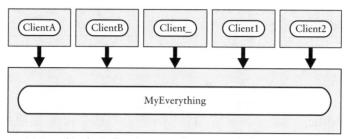

(a) Everything logically cohesive residing in a single class (or `struct`)

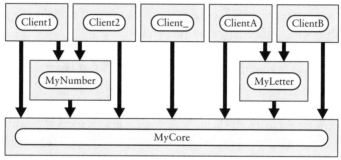

(b) Cohesive functionality distributed among several classes/`structs`

Figure 3-11: Factoring out cohesive functionality based on client usage

We are now ready to introduce a more specific yet extremely common and important application of this general principle, based on whether specific functionality is or is not considered *primitive*. Before we do that, however, we will first point out the general need for each component we author to have a cohesive, well-defined, focused purpose.

Guideline

Each component we design should have a tightly focused purpose.

When designing a component, our goal should be to identify a highly focused domain that can be readily explained and then provide appropriate publicly accessible functionality to accomplish the specific needs for which the component was first commissioned ("used") as well as other similar needs that are likely to occur in the future ("reuse"). Failing to establish a focused purpose is all too common and results in software that is unnecessarily hard to understand, use, and maintain, and harder still to reuse effectively (see Volume II, section 5.7).

Guideline

The functionality provided by a reusable component should be *complete* yet *minimal*.

Given such a focused domain, it is said[28] that a component is *sufficient*, with respect to a particular client, if the functionality it provides fully addresses the needs of that client within that focused domain. For example, consider an application that requires an integer stack component but makes use of only the `push`, `top`, and `length` methods. While a "stack" component providing just that functionality (but not, say, `pop`) might be *sufficient* for that application, it would certainly not be considered generally useful.

When it comes to fostering reuse, sufficiency for a first client is clearly not enough. We need to supply functionality that supports some natural notion of *closure* with respect to relevant (*primitive*) functionality (see below). A component that does somehow supply sufficient functionality for essentially all clients with respect to that focused domain is said to be *complete*. Such a component would naturally also satisfy the *open-closed* criteria (section 0.5).

At the same time, we want all of the functions that a component provides to be uniquely useful. That is, we want to avoid providing unnecessary or redundant functionality that might clutter the interface, making it less easy to understand how to use effectively. Components that, to a large extent, provide a single way to perform each essential operation are said to be *minimal*.

DEFINITION: Functionality that intrinsically requires private access to objects of a type on which it operates in order to be implemented efficiently is said to be a *primitive* operation of that type.

Any function that requires private access to a type on which it operates is *manifestly primitive*. Even if a function can be reasonably implemented without private access, if the performance of that implementation is not comparably efficient, that function is nonetheless primitive. Often, however, there are effective measures we can employ that dramatically reduce the kinds of functionality that would otherwise be considered primitive. It is only after those steps are taken that the remaining functionality can be considered *inherently primitive*.

---

[28] **booch94**, section 3.6, pp. 136–137 (especially p. 137)

3.2.6   Iterators Can Help Reduce What Would Otherwise Be Primitive Functionality

---

Observation

Iterators often dramatically reduce what would otherwise be considered *manifestly primitive* operations.

To perform nonprimitive operations on objects that aggregate others, it is often necessary to have efficient access to the underlying objects. For the relatively few containers, such as a standard `vector`, that provide efficient `inline` access (via an index) to each of the contained objects, it is at least possible to write arbitrary nonprimitive functionality — e.g., sorting, searching, partitioning — in a separate component (having no private access). Though no longer considered primitive, supporting the notion of an iterator for a `vector` is still beneficial (e.g., for generic algorithms).

When it comes to functions that need to operate on the many kinds of containers, such as a standard `list` or `unordered_set`, that do not provide direct `inline` access to each of their contained objects, there are basically two alternatives (section 0.5): (1) grant each such function private access, thereby forcing it to reside in the same component as the container (BAD IDEA), or (2) provide an efficient way of systematically visiting each member object in turn (GOOD IDEA). By consistently providing efficient `inline` access via iterators where appropriate, we significantly reduce what must be considered *inherently primitive* functionality.

3.2.7   Not Just Minimal, Primitive: The Utility `struct`

Guideline

Almost all of the (domain-specific) functionality implemented within a component that defines an instantiable type should be *primitive*.

As it turns out, unique usefulness alone is not sufficient justification to incorporate functionality into a component. Not all useful operations are useful to all clients. Insisting that every potentially useful operation on an instantiable type be a method of its class — whether or not it requires private access — encourages instability (section 0.5) and is utterly nonscalable. With this "method-only" mind-set, a simple component might, over time, grow to become unworkably large and impractical, impeding its comprehensibility and therefore reducing its value.

Guideline

Most nonprimitive functionality that operates on an instantiable type should be implemented in a higher-level utility `struct`.

Our goal with each instantiable type that we write should be to provide a subset of functionality that is *complete* yet *minimal*. Any additional useful functionality that we can arrange to be implemented efficiently without private access should be located in a separate, higher-level "utility" component. In so doing, we not only improve stability for the flagship type, we also keep crisp its essential purpose (see Volume II, section 4.2), such as representing a *value* (see Volume II, section 4.1).

3.2.8   Concluding Example: An Encapsulating Polygon Interface

As a final instructional illustration of what is and is not inherently primitive functionality, suppose we are asked to design a low-level, high-performance, general-purpose class for representing arbitrary closed polygonal shapes on an integer Cartesian grid. In this context, a polygon is most commonly thought of as a sequence of absolute coordinates that represent adjacent vertices, implicitly connected by edges. After concluding that each object of such a polygon class naturally represents a *value* (see Volume II, section 4.1) and that the type we've been asked to design should be a (concrete) *value type* (see Volume II, section 4.2) having proper *value semantics* (see Volume II, section 4.3), the next issue we must consider will be about the types our `Polygon` class will use in its interface (section 1.7.3).

3.2.8.1   What Other UDTs Are Used in the Interface?

Given that several of our polygon's intrinsic operations are likely to involve vertices, which are conveniently represented as integer coordinate pairs, we will quickly realize that our polygon class, call it `our::Polygon`, should use the appropriate (concrete) value-semantic *vocabulary type*, call it `the::Point`,[29] in its interface (see Volume II, section 4.4). Hence, the component that defines `our::Polygon` (let's assume it is **our_polygon**) will necessarily reside, in our physical hierarchy, somewhere above the one defining `the::Point` (e.g., **the_point**).

3.2.8.2   What Invariants Should `our::Polygon` Impose?

Let's now take a moment to consider some specifics of our class `Polygon`, residing in the pseudopackage **our**. There are many interesting issues that one can ponder. For example, is the `origin` of a polygon (i.e., when placed at a geographic position) synonymous with `vertex[0]`, or is it a separate attribute? If synonymous, what happens if a polygon has no vertices? What then is its origin? What are the fewest number of vertices in a valid polygon? Can a polygon ever be invalid, or are all polygons, like integers,[30] necessarily valid? Is a polygon permitted to cross itself — i.e., are the edges allowed to form, say, a figure eight? Is a polygon permitted to have coincident edges? How about identical consecutive vertices? Should repeated vertices be coalesced automatically? The answers to such sophisticated design questions are often highly application-specific. Imposing specific, detailed invariants on the value type itself — such as no crossing edges — can easily lead to more complications than are solved (see Volume II, section 5.9).

3.2.8.3   What Are the Important Use Cases?

There are several basic, low-level design alternatives for a polygon class. How `our::Polygon` will be used will dictate how it is best implemented and, in turn, what operations are inherently primitive. For example, we might at first reason that, being the most frequent operation, minimizing the cost of accessing a vertex should take precedence over, say, moving the entire polygon. Storing the absolute positions of each vertex value directly in the polygon would minimize the runtime cost of randomly accessing individual vertices. As it turns out, however, most real-world applications will seldom want to access a single vertex without accessing the rest in consecutive order. These same sorts of applications, however, will often want to move an arbitrarily large collection of polygons efficiently.

---

[29] Again, we are using pseudopackage names (section 2.10.3) **our** and **the** here because (1) physical position is not at issue, and (2) the components as described here are not being proposed for inclusion in any actual package groups comprising our Software Capital.

[30] Accessing an uninitialized `int` is technically *undefined behavior* — even though every `int` state represents a unique and valid value — and is therefore to be frowned upon even if no actual harm would result.

As is often the case, we might not know at the outset the overall optimal implementation strategy for our component and, therefore, design our interface to allow for experimentation. To preserve substantial flexibility in the internal representation of a polygon value, the vertices of an `our::Polygon` object should themselves be accessible only *by value*[31] from any publicly accessible functionality of the component in which the `our::Polygon` class is defined.

We might, for example, want to consider representing each of the N vertices internally as a delta (vector difference) from the previous one, with the first being absolute — i.e., a delta from $(0,0)$. In so doing, we could reduce from $O[N]$ to $O[1]$ the runtime cost to move (*all* of the vertices of) an `our::Polygon` and, so long as we provide an efficient mechanism (e.g., an iterator) to re-create the vertices in turn, the cost of retrieving all N vertices *in order* would remain $O[N]$. The cost of randomly accessing an individual vertex, however, would now be increased from $O[1]$ to $O[N]$.

3.2.8.4   What Are the Specific Requirements?

It turns out (see below) that it can sometimes be convenient, even if not absolutely necessary, to be able to efficiently obtain an arbitrary vertex via its index. Fortunately, efficient random access to vertices and efficient bulk moves need not be mutually exclusive. If we represent each absolute vertex as an offset from a single reference vertex (say, the first one), instead of the previous one, we can both access an arbitrary vertex value[32] *and* move the entire polygon (with maximum efficiency) in constant (i.e., $O[1]$) time! To do so, however, we will need to relax the requirement of being able to move *every* individual vertex (including that one reference one) efficiently — a price we might well be willing to pay. A partial set of functional and (readily achievable) performance requirements for `our::Polygon` is provided in Figure 3-12.

---

[31] It is reasonable to assume that the type `the::Point`, used to represent the value of a vertex for a `Polygon` object, will not require dynamic memory allocation; hence, there are no concerns (arising from the potential use of local memory allocators) with returning such an object by value (see Volume II, section 4.10).

[32] Albeit at the (hopefully inconsequential) constant-factor cost of an extra arithmetic operation.

Let N be the number of vertices.

Regular Value-Semantic Operations:
    - default construction $O[1]$
    - copy construction $O[N]$
    - destruction $O[N]$
    - copy assignment $O[N]$
    - swap $O[1]$ (same allocator)
    - equality comparison $O[N]$
    - iteration step $O[1]$ (where applicable)

Domain-Specific Requirements:
    - append vertex $O[1]$ (amortized)
    - insert vertex at index $O[N]$
    - remove vertex at index $O[N]$

    - get number of vertices $O[1]$

    - access vertex (e.g., value) at index $O[1]$ or $O[N]$ (significant)
    - set/move vertex at index $O[1]$ or $O[N]$ (significant)
    - move entire polygon $O[1]$ or $O[N]$ (significant)

    - calculate perimeter $O[N]$
    - calculate area $O[N]$

    - determine if rotationally similar $O[N^2]$

    - determine topological number $O[?]$ ☺

Figure 3-12: Initial performance requirements for `our::Polygon`

3.2.8.5   Which Required Behaviors Are *Primitive* and Which Aren't?

Next, we need to determine which of these required behaviors are inherently primitive and which can (and should) be implemented efficiently outside of the component. Fundamental operations, such as construction, destruction, and (where applicable) copy assignment, are obviously an intimate part of an object's implementation. What's more, the C++ language requires that such integral functionality not be declared outside the lexical scope of the class on which it operates; hence, according to Component Property 3 (section 1.6.3), this functionality *must* be implemented within that same component.

Other operations such as equality comparison, which are a natural part of any typical (*regular*) value type (see Volume II, section 4.3), should also be implemented in the same component — whether or not their implementation requires private access (see item 4, Figure 3-20, section 3.3.1). Iterators, whose main purpose is to isolate, and thereby make malleable, specific details of an implementation while preserving stability, yet still allow efficient implementation of new functionality *outside the component*, will (or someday might) also require private access. Hence, iterators are prime candidates to be defined within the same component as a container type (see section 3.3.1.1), but not necessarily within the lexical scope of the container class itself (section 2.7.4).

Let us now turn to the domain-specific requirements for `our::Polygon`. We are being asked to enable a vertex to be appended to a polygon in *amortized constant time,*[33] as well as insert or remove one, given an integer index, in linear time. We also need to be able to determine the number of vertices in a given polygon immediately, i.e., in $O[1]$ time. To avoid exposing the details of the underlying representation, we will obviously need to supply functions to perform these operations. Such functions will, of course, require private access to `our::Polygon` and so, again, they will necessarily (section 2.6) be implemented in the same component.

3.2.8.6   Weighing the Implementation Alternatives

Guideline

Strive for an interface that affords maximum runtime efficiency while keeping implementation options as open and flexible as practicable.

Requirements on three critical behaviors will strongly influence the possible range of implementation choices for this component:

1. Access vertex (e.g., value) at index $O[1]$ or $O[N]$ (significant)

2. Set/move vertex at index $O[1]$ or $O[N]$ (significant)

3. Move entire polygon $O[1]$ or $O[N]$ (significant)

---

[33] The term *amortized constant time* means that we can perform an arbitrarily large number, N, of consecutive operations of this kind in time proportional to N while accounting for the (comparatively rare) $O[\log(N)]$ times we need to resize the capacity of any underlying data structure having a geometric growth.

As it turns out — much like trying to optimize product, schedule, and budget (section 0.1) — we can choose any two of these to be bounded by constant time without affecting a carefully designed interface for this component: If we were to choose the first and second behaviors to be performed in constant time, we would represent the vertices as absolute coordinates; if we were to choose the second and third behaviors, we would represent the values at each vertex as a *delta* from the previous one, with only the initial vertex being absolute; and, if we were to choose the first and the third behaviors to be $O[1]$, we would represent each of the vertices as an *offset* relative to a consistent (but unspecified) relative *reference* vertex (e.g., the first one).

3.2.8.7   Achieving Two Out of Three Ain't Bad

Demanding that *all three* behaviors be achievable in constant time would require having each of the vertices be defined relative to an independent reference point. To achieve proper value semantics (see Volume II, section 4.3), we would need either (1) to make this relative reference point a separate *salient* attribute (e.g., `origin`), which would necessarily contribute to the overall *value* of the polygon object, or (2) to define our `the::Point` class in terms of an unbounded integer class that cannot overflow[34] — neither one of which are we prepared to entertain at this time.

3.2.8.8   Primitiveness vs. Flexibility of Implementation

Observation

The degree of flexibility in the implementation might affect what can be considered *primitive*.

What should be considered primitive will sometimes depend on how much flexibility in the implementation we are attempting to preserve. Suppose, for just a moment, we were prepared to make *all* of the data members of a class *public* (BAD IDEA!). In that case, all of the functionality on the class would necessarily be nonprimitive and, unless otherwise constrained by the language itself, could be implemented in a separate utility component, but naturally at the cost

---

[34] Otherwise, two polygon objects that outwardly appear to have the same *value* might not be able to accommodate the same sequence of *salient operations* without one (but not the other) causing an internal overflow (see Volume II, section 4.3).

of having essentially zero flexibility to make changes to the implementation. In the real world, however, we will want to preserve at least some flexibility in the implementation — especially when doing so introduces essentially zero runtime overhead. Hence, we look to provide sufficient primitive functionality to allow us to change the details of implementation (within appropriate limits) without forcing clients to rework their source code.

3.2.8.9   Flexibility of Implementation Extends *Primitive* Functionality

Preserving flexibility of the implementation is a perennial design goal of interfaces. Consider, for example, the operation to `move` the entire polygon. If we knew that the polygon is represented in terms of absolute vertex coordinates, there would be no advantage to making `move` primitive, and an $O[N]$ version could be implemented efficiently in a separate component. On the other hand, if either of the other two implementations suggested above were employed, the `move` operation could be implemented in constant time, but only if it has access to the private details of the implementation. Even if absolute coordinates are used today, in order to preserve the option to change to either of the other two implementation alternatives in the future, we should prefer making the `move` functionality primitive.[35]

3.2.8.10   Primitiveness Is Not a Draconian Requirement

As the section title suggests, *primitiveness* is not absolute. Given that we have primitive operations to access and set (via index) the absolute values of individual vertices with maximal efficiency, a separate function to *move* a vertex at a given index by a *delta* might not be considered truly primitive. Still, having a

```
void moveVertex(std::size_t index, const the::Point& delta);
```

function be a member could well prove useful, not just as a user convenience, but perhaps also affording modest (i.e., constant factor) efficiency gains, depending on the low-level details of the implementation. Hence, in addition to the absolutely primitive and necessary

```
the::Point vertex(std::size_t index) const;
```

and

```
void setVertex(std::size_t index, const the::Point& vertex);
```

---

[35] To be fair, David Sankel correctly points out (in his review of the manuscript for this volume) that, though not ideal, "the option to change to a member-function move operation exists: It just means that you might end up with a redundant utility function that is implemented in terms of the member function."

methods, we might also entertain having a member function such as

```
void moveVertex(std::size_t index, const the::Point& delta);
```

in our `Polygon` class. The criteria for properly incorporating nonprimitive functionality in a component implementing a value type, such as `our::Polygon`, is admittedly somewhat fuzzy (see section 3.3.1); astute engineering judgment will be required to avoid that infamous *slippery slope*.

3.2.8.11   What About Familiar Functionality Such as *Perimeter* and *Area*?

Next, let us consider the requirement that we be able to calculate both the perimeter and the area of a polygon in linear time. To some, the knee-jerk reaction might be that both *Perimeter* and *Area* are so familiar and fundamental to what a polygon represents that they must have private access to the internal representation of the polygon object. Yet it is here where the pendulum begins to swing the other way.

What is it that we really need in order to calculate the *Perimeter* or *Area* of a polygon efficiently? The fact is that algorithms for efficiently determining such quantities do not require private access so long as there is a way of accessing the needed information efficiently. Figure 3-13 illustrates how one can write efficient (nonprimitive) functions for calculating both *Perimeter* and *Area*, given just the public interface of an `our::Polygon` object, using vertex iterators, irrespective of which of the three proposed internal implementations is employed!

Linear-Time Operations on a Polygon

$$\text{Perimeter} = \sum_{i=0}^{N-1} \sqrt{\Delta x_i^2 + \Delta y_i^2}$$

$$\text{Area} = \frac{1}{2}\sum_{i=0}^{N-1} x_i \cdot \Delta y_i - y_i \cdot \Delta x_i$$

where

$$\Delta z_i = z_{(i+1)\bmod N} - z_i \quad z \in \{x, y\}$$

and

$$N = \text{Number of Vertices}$$

Figure 3-13: Some common nonprimitive operations on polygon types

In addition to providing asymptotic optimality, we — as reusable library developers — must also care about even small constant-factor optimizations. Providing constant-time access to just the absolute vertex values — though fully satisfying the asymptotic (Big-*O*) complexity requirements of Figure 3-12 — might, alone, fall short of being completely optimal. If our implementation happens to store absolute vertices, there is nothing to be gained. But suppose our::Polygon — now or in the future — is implemented in terms of sequential *deltas* or, let us assume for now, *offsets* from a particular reference vertex. There would then be a distinct advantage to exposing additional primitive methods.

For example, imagine that along with providing a method to return the vertex value

```
inline
the::Point vertex(std::size_t index) const
{
    return d_offsets[(index + 1) % d_numVertices] - d_reference;
}
```

we also provide a member function to supply the forward difference:

```
inline
the::Point delta(std::size_t index) const;
{
    return d_offset[(index + 1) % d_numVertices] - d_offset[index];
}
```

In so doing, we are able to eliminate one *modulo* and two *subtraction* operations from

```
the::Point delta = (d_offsets[(i + 1)% d_numVertices] - d_reference)
                 - (d_offsets[ i     % d_numVertices] - d_reference);
```

yielding

```
the::Point delta = d_offsets[(i + 1) % d_numVertices] - d_offsets[i];
```

Even if we know that the current implementation affords no advantage, there's no real harm either as we are doing no more than what would have been needed anyway; the upside to providing these additional primitive interface functions is that it allows us to optimize our implementation in the future without forcing our clients who have employed these methods to rework their code.

If maximal runtime performance is considered paramount (as it often is), we might even choose to provide a "raw" offset method[36] that returns vertices in the same relative positions, but with

---

[36] When we want to indicate to potential clients and maintainers alike that a particular function has "sharp edges" that fairly demand an unusually careful reading of the preconditions of the function's *contract* (see Volume II, section 5.2), we typically affix the suffix "Raw" to the function name (see Volume II, section 6.11).

each vertex presented relative to a consistent, but unspecified, "reference" point — analogous to the familiar, but nebulous, "... + C" in indefinite integral calculus:

```
inline
the::Point Polygon::offset(std::size_t index) const
{
    return d_offset[index];
}
```

Notice again that we deliberately return the offset *by value*, rather than by `const` reference in order to preserve flexibility in the implementation. By returning this carefully documented "raw" value, utility functions such as

```
struct PolygonUtil {
    // ...

    static double area(const Polygon& polygon);
        // Return the area of the specified 'polygon'.  The behavior ...

    // ...
};
```

that care about only relative positions of x and y can avoid an extra subtraction operation per vertex in the particular `our::Polygon` implementation currently under consideration, and with absolutely no additional overhead for the other two alternative implementations.[37]

Guideline

Prefer providing low-level, reusable primitive functionality rather than implementing primitive application-level functionality directly.

3.2.8.12   Providing Iterator Support for Generic Algorithms

Unlike many containers, the two most likely implementations of `our::Polygon` — i.e., the two that enable efficient random access via vertex index — do not require iterators in order to achieve

---

[37] It is worth noting that if, as shown, these accessor methods are declared `inline`, it is quite possible that, in an optimized build mode, many of these performance improvements could be accomplished by the optimizer automatically. Nonetheless, by specifically asking for *only* that which is truly needed, we provide the best chance for the compiler to perform optimally.

efficient extensibility. Nonetheless, consistently defining iterators to provide access to contained objects affords two distinct benefits: (1) clients who access vertices, deltas, or even "raw" offsets, but do so in only the natural sequence, should prefer to use iterators in order to pick up even the most minute optimizations that such restricted use of the underlying implementation can realize, and (2) interoperability is served by allowing generic algorithms to operate on `our::Polygon` correctly irrespective of which of these three viable implementation alternatives is employed. It therefore might make good engineering sense to provide separate standard *input* iterators for each of these distinct sequences: vertices, deltas, and raw deltas, even though to preserve full encapsulation such iterators will be forced to return elements *by value* as opposed to *by reference*.[38]

3.2.8.13   Focus on Generally Useful Primitive Functionality

To exact the last iota of performance, while protecting stability in the face of changing implementation, we might consider providing a nonstandard, iterator-like class that exposes direct access to all three current values (i.e., *vertex*, *delta*, and *offset*) so that only one variable need be advanced. An example of the use of such a compound iterator to calculate the area of an `our::Polygon` class object *optimally* and without private access — irrespective of which of the three different implementation choices discussed above is employed — is provided in Figure 3-14. Notice how we are going out of our way to provide only *reusable* primitive "helper" functionality rather than just implementing the needed application-level methods outright.

```
double PolygonUtil::area(const Polygon& value)
{
    double result = 0.0;

    for (Polygon::const_iterator it  = value.cbegin();
                                 it != value.cend();
                                 ++it)
    {
        result += it.offset().x() * it.delta().y()
                - it.offset().y() * it.delta().x();
    }

    return 0.5 * result;
}
```

Figure 3-14: Nonprimitive implementation of `area` for `our::Polygon`

---

[38] Because the outward representation of a vertex value (i.e., `the::Point`) is itself comparable in size to a pointer variable on most modern architectures, there may be no relative overhead in returning a copy as opposed to the address. Given that such accessor functions are almost certainly declared `inline`, the compiler is at full liberty to optimize across their boundaries, regardless.

3.2.8.14   Suppress Any Urge to Colocate Nonprimitive Functionality

Although some will find colocating relevant and useful nonprimitive functionality, such as finding the *Perimeter* or *Area*, hard to resist, resist we must. If returning either the *Perimeter* or the *Area* of a polygon is to be considered primitive, then the slippery slope begins. What about predicates such as `isConvex`, `areTouching`, and `isContainedBy`? There is no end to what can be asked of an `our::Polygon` object. The goal in designing a fully functional polygon component must be to make sure that we, along with our clients can write efficient, arbitrarily complex functions on objects of type `our::Polygon` *without* having to modify it! Hence, the primitive functionality of `our::Polygon` must be as *complete* as practicable.

3.2.8.15   Supporting Unusual Functionality

We now turn to somewhat more esoteric functionality. In some applications, in addition to knowing if two polygons represent (precisely) the same value (see Volume II, section 4.1), it will also be important to know whether they are, in some sense, similar. Two polygons are *rotationally similar* if the index labelings of the vertices of one can be rotated such that the vertex values at corresponding index positions are the same.[39] Figure 3-15 illustrates two *rotationally similar* polygons x and y, each having the same number of vertices and representing the same shape, but not having the same index labelings of their vertices: The leftmost lowest vertex of x is labeled 0, while the corresponding vertex in y is labeled 4. Rotating, in sequence, the vertex labels in x ahead by 2 (or back by 4) and then comparing the result with y using the one true equality comparator, `operator==`, on `our::Polygon` exhibits the similarity.

---

[39] Note that it would not be desirable to consider the reverse order since the opposite orientation would have different connotations, such as implying a negative area or "hole" (see below).

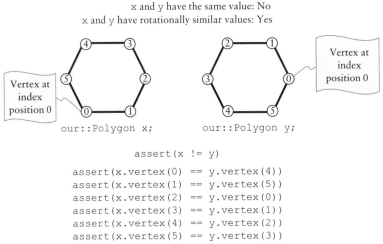

```
                          assert(x != y)
            assert(x.vertex(0)  ==  y.vertex(4))
            assert(x.vertex(1)  ==  y.vertex(5))
            assert(x.vertex(2)  ==  y.vertex(0))
            assert(x.vertex(3)  ==  y.vertex(1))
            assert(x.vertex(4)  ==  y.vertex(2))
            assert(x.vertex(5)  ==  y.vertex(3))
```

Figure 3-15: One of many useful notions of "equivalence" for two polygons

When equality comparison of object *values* (see Volume II, section 4.1) is determined to be appropriate, we are expected to declare both an `operator==` function and an `operator!=` function — each having behavior consistent with *value semantics* (see Volume II, section 4.3) — as *free* operators (see Volume II, section 6.13) in the *same* component as the value type on which they operate (see section 3.3.1.4). But where does functionality that determines whether two `our::Polygon` objects are rotationally similar belong? The answer is emphatically not in the same component as `our::Polygon`! Either a client can implement this functionality efficiently outside the component in which `our::Polygon` is defined, or we will again need to augment that component so that the client can.

As it turns out, the "are-rotationally-similar" functionality we seek can be implemented efficiently in terms of the primitive functionality we have already anticipated, provided that indexed access to vertex values is guaranteed to be $O[1]$; otherwise, we, as library developers, will need to work a bit harder. The interface for such a nonprimitive utility function is shown in Figure 3-16a. An efficient implementation requiring no private access to the implementation of `our::Polygon`, assuming that we do have constant-time indexed access to vertex values, is provided in Figure 3-16b.

```
struct PolygonUtil {
    // This 'struct' provides a namespace for a suite of pure functions that...

    static bool areRotationallySimilar(const Polygon& a, const Polygon& b);
        // Return 'true' if the specified 'a' and 'b' polygons are
        // rotationally similar, and 'false' otherwise.  Two polygons are
        // rotationally similar if there exists a sequential rotation of
        // their vertex values after which they would then compare equal.
};
```

(a) Interface

```
bool PolygonUtil::areRotationallySimilar(const Polygon& a, const Polygon& b)
{
    const std::size_t len = a.numVertices();

    if (len != b.numVertices()) {
        return false;  // Polygons had different vertex counts.      // RETURN
    }

    // For each offset from the starting vertex of 'a' ...

    for (std::size_t offset = 0; offset < len; ++offset) {

        std::size_t i = 0;

        for (; i < len; ++i) {

            if (a.vertex((offset + i) % len) != b.vertex(i)) {
                break;
            }
        }

        if (len == i) {
            return true;  // All vertices matched!                  // RETURN
        }

        // Rotate by one more, and try again.
    }

    return false;  // No matching rotation found.
}
```

(b) Random-access, index-based implementation

```
bool PolygonUtil::areRotationallySimilar(const Polygon& a, const Polygon& b)
{
    const std::size_t len = a.numVertices();

    if (len != b.numVertices()) {
        return false;  // Polygons have different vertex counts.      // RETURN
    }

    // For each starting vertex of 'a' ...

    for (Polygon::const_iterator sa = a.cbegin(); sa != a.cend(); ++sa) {

        Polygon::RotationalIterator ita(sa);      // *** custom iterator ***

        Polygon::const_iterator itb = b.cbegin();

        for ( ; itb != b.cend(); ++itb, ++ita) {

            if (ita.vertex() != itb.vertex()) {  // Same as: if (*ita != *itb)
                break;
            }
        }

        if (b.cend() == itb) {
            return true;  // All vertices matched!                    // RETURN
        }

        // Rotate by one more, and try again.
    }

    return false;  // No matching rotation found.
}
```

(c) Customized bidirectional-iterator-based implementation

Figure 3-16: Implementing `areRotationallySimilar` for `our::Polygon`

If it should turn out that we are not prepared to guarantee constant-time indexed access to
the absolute vertices of `our::Polygon`, we can nonetheless ensure optimal runtime performance for all three proposed implementations postulated above via a custom iterator,
`RotationalIterator`, as suggested in Figure 3-16c. This special-purpose iterator takes, at
construction, an initial position from a standard iterator and provides each subsequent vertex
on each iteration step, but wrapping around to the first when it reaches the last vertex. Note
that, to be completely optimal, this rotational iterator will naturally require private access to the
standard one as well as `Polygon` itself.

Guideline

Strive to provide sufficient primitive functionality to support the *open-closed principle* (section 0.5) by ensuring that each component's functionality is *complete*: Arbitrary application functionality should be implementable (e.g., by a client) in a separate, higher-level component.

It has been said, "Give a man a fish and you feed him for a day; teach a man to fish and you feed him for a lifetime." Notice above that we have again avoided making the needed specific application-oriented functionality primitive but instead elected to augment the underlying type with reusable "tools" (i.e., primitive machinery) that can then be used to implement the currently needed functionality efficiently along with similar application-level functionality in the future — without necessarily requiring direct private access resulting in additional modification of the underlying type.

The extent of useful, practical application-level functionality based on a simple value type, such as `our::Polygon`, is unbounded. Consider, for example, the decidedly nonprimitive `topologicalNumber` function whose interface and contract[40] is illustrated in Figure 3-17. It is only by proactively limiting the functionality in a component to what is not just *minimal*, but predominately *primitive*, yet sufficiently complete to be useful for implementing arbitrary application-level functionality that we preserve and keep stable the pure, unadulterated essence that *is* the focus of our user-defined type (see Volume II, section 5.7).

---

[40] Documenting complex functionality can sometimes benefit from artwork! :-)

```
struct TopologyUtil {
    // This 'struct' provides a namespace for a suite of pure functions used
    // to perform topological analysis of shapes represented by objects of
    // type 'our::Polygon'. ...

    static int topologicalNumber(const our::Polygon& shape);
        // Return the topological number (T#) of the specified 'shape' (i.e.,
        // 1 for a simple shape, 2 for a doughnut, 3 for a doughnut with an
        // island, etc.), and a negative value if 'shape' is invalid (i.e.,
        // its edges cross).  A sequence of edges that come together, are
        // coincident, and then eventually diverge from the same respective
        // sides as they converged are not considered crossing.  Note that
        // non-zero area in a region is required in order to contribute to T#
        // (e.g., a valid shape with zero area yields 0).
        //..
        //          ,--Zero Area       I---------<---------H
        //       L                     |                   |     Crossing__,
        // 2,0=======1                 |   D----->-----E    |       Edges   /
        //    T# = 0     B--<--A       |   |           |    |              /
        //              /       \      |   |   A-<-9   |    |             L
        //          C   5->-6  9       |   |   |   | F,5===2,G
        // 4---<---3 |   |   |   |      | C,6===7->-8  |    |      4-->--5
        // |       | D   4-<-3==2,8     |   | ,B        |    |      |    |
        // 5       2  \    ,7 /         |   5-----<-----4    |    7,3=<=<=2,6
        //  \     /    \   /            |                    |      |    |
        //  6,0->-1     E,0->-1     J,0--------->---------1  8,0-->--1
        //
        //    T# = 1      T# = 2             T# = 3           Invalid
        //..

    // ...

};
```

Figure 3-17: Some not-so-common nonprimitive operations on polygon types

Writing a simple, industrial-strength polygon class interface that hides significant implementation details is anything but simple. To make what we have discussed concrete, Figure 3-18 illustrates a superset of all primitive functionality for `our::Polygon` discussed in this section. The purpose of this interface is to suggest how we might encapsulate (and hide) various details of the implementation from a prospective client. Our goal is to allow external algorithms operating on `our::Polygon` — particularly those that access, but do not modify the polygon — to run as fast as if they had direct access to the underlying representation, yet shield them from its inward complexity. In particular, how memory is managed internally should not be relevant to how the *value* of a polygon is represented or manipulated.

```
// ...

namespace our {

// ...

class Polygon {                Wouldn't you
     // ...                    like to know? 😊

  public:
    // TYPES

                    // Compound Iterators

    typedef PolygonConstIterator   iterator;
    typedef PolygonConstIterator   const_iterator;[41]

    typedef PolygonRotationalIterator RotationalIterator;

                    // Generic Iterators

    typedef PolygonConstIterator      VertexIterator;
    typedef Polygon_DeltaIterator     DeltaIterator;
    typedef Polygon_OffsetIterator    OffsetIterator;
    typedef PolygonRotationalIterator RotationalVertexIterator;[42]

    // CREATORS
    explicit Polygon(bslma::Allocator *basicAllocator = 0);[43]

    template <class INPUT_ITERATOR>                (See Volume II, section 4.10).
    Polygon(const INPUT_ITERATOR&  begin,
            const INPUT_ITERATOR&  end,
            bslma::Allocator       *basicAllocator = 0);

    Polygon(const Polygon&    original,
            bslma::Allocator *basicAllocator = 0);[44]

    ~Polygon();

    // MANIPULATORS
    Polygon& operator=(const Polygon& rhs);

    void appendVertex(const the::Point& vertex);

    template <class INPUT_ITERATOR>
    void appendVertices(const INPUT_ITERATOR& begin,
                        const INPUT_ITERATOR& end);
```

(continues)

---

[41] Note that, because these iterators provide more than the minimal functionality needed to model the basic (input_iterator) *concept* (see section 1.7.6), they will need to be documented explicitly (see Volume II, sections 6.15–6.17), and hence cannot be treated merely as private details of this component.

[42] Note that because these iterators provide only the minimal functionality needed to model the basic (input_iterator) *concept*, they may be treated as private details of this component (e.g., see Figure 2-54, section 2.7.4).

[43] Note that, as of C++11, there is a general tendency in the Standard to prefer overloads to default arguments so as to avoid having the keyword explicit also apply to the default constructor.

[44] Note that, as of C++11, we would also naturally implement both move operations — i.e., move construction and move assignment.

548

```
    void insertVertex(std::size_t                    dstIndexPosition,
                      const the::Point&              vertex);
    void insertVertex(const VertexIterator&          dstIndexPosition,
                      const the::Point&              vertex);
    void insertVertex(const RotationalVertexIterator& dstIndexPosition,
                      const the::Point&              vertex);

    template <class INPUT_ITERATOR>
    void insertVertices(std::size_t                    dstIndexPosition,
                        const INPUT_ITERATOR&          begin,
                        const INPUT_ITERATOR&          end);
    template <class INPUT_ITERATOR>
    void insertVertices(const VertexIterator&          dstIndexPosition,
                        const INPUT_ITERATOR&          begin,
                        const INPUT_ITERATOR&          end);
    template <class INPUT_ITERATOR>
    void insertVertices(const RotationalVertexIterator& dstIndexPosition,
                        const INPUT_ITERATOR&          begin,
                        const INPUT_ITERATOR&          end);

    void moveVertex(std::size_t                    indexPosition,
                    const the::Point&              delta);
    void moveVertex(const VertexIterator&          indexPosition,
                    const the::Point&              delta);
    void moveVertex(const RotationalVertexIterator& indexPosition,
                    const the::Point&              delta);

    template <class INPUT_ITERATOR>
    void moveVertices(std::size_t                    indexPosition,
                      const INPUT_ITERATOR&          begin,
                      const INPUT_ITERATOR&          end);
    template <class INPUT_ITERATOR>
    void moveVertices(const VertexIterator&          indexPosition,
                      const INPUT_ITERATOR&          begin,
                      const INPUT_ITERATOR&          end);
    template <class INPUT_ITERATOR>
    void moveVertices(const RotationalVertexIterator& indexPosition,
                      const INPUT_ITERATOR&          begin,
                      const INPUT_ITERATOR&          end);

    void moveAllVertices(const the::Point& delta);

    void removeVertex(std::size_t                    indexPosition);
    void removeVertex(const VertexIterator&          indexPosition);
    void removeVertex(const RotationalVertexIterator& indexPosition);

    void removeVertices(std::size_t                    indexPosition,
                        std::size_t                    numVertices);
    void removeVertices(const VertexIterator&          indexPosition,
                        std::size_t                    numVertices);
    void removeVertices(const RotationalVertexIterator& indexPosition,
                        std::size_t                    numVertices);
```

(continues)

```
    void replaceVertex(std::size_t                   indexPosition,
                       const the::Point&             vertex);
    void replaceVertex(const VertexIterator&         indexPosition,
                       const the::Point&             vertex);
    void replaceVertex(const RotationalVertexIterator& indexPosition,
                       const the::Point&             vertex);

    template <class INPUT_ITERATOR>
    void replaceVertices(std::size_t               dstIndexPosition,
                         const INPUT_ITERATOR&     begin,
                         const INPUT_ITERATOR&     end);
    template <class INPUT_ITERATOR>
    void replaceVertices(const VertexIterator&     dstIndexPosition,
                         const INPUT_ITERATOR&     begin,
                         const INPUT_ITERATOR&     end);
    template <class INPUT_ITERATOR>
    void replaceVertices(const RotationalVertexIterator& dstIndexPosition,
                         const INPUT_ITERATOR&     begin,
                         const INPUT_ITERATOR&     end);

                        // Aspects
    iterator begin();

    iterator end();

    void swap(Polygon& a, Polygon& b);[45]

    // ACCESSORS
    std::size_t numVertices() const;

    the::Point delta(std::size_t                   indexPosition) const;
    the::Point delta(const VertexIterator&         indexPosition) const;
    the::Point delta(const RotationalVertexIterator& indexPosition) const;

    the::Point offset(std::size_t                  indexPosition) const;
    the::Point offset(const VertexIterator&        indexPosition) const;
    the::Point offset(const RotationalVertexIterator& indexPosition) const;

    the::Point vertex(std::size_t                  indexPosition) const;
    the::Point vertex(const VertexIterator&        indexPosition) const;
    the::Point vertex(const RotationalVertexIterator& indexPosition) const;

                        // Standard Iterators

    DeltaIterator      beginDeltas() const;

    OffsetIterator     beginOffsets() const;

    VertexIterator     beginVertices() const;

    DeltaIterator      endDeltas() const;
```

(continues)

---

[45] Note that, as of C++11, we have move operations, and this method becomes far less important. The standard `swap` algorithm is implemented with moves, which assuming class `Polygon` implements move semantics, should be sufficient. For illustrative purposes only, the resulting general algorithm, instantiated for `Polygon`, would act like this:

```
    OffsetIterator     endOffsets() const;

    VertexIterator     endVertices() const;

                        // Custom Iterators

    RotationalIterator beginRotational(const iterator& iterator) const;
    RotationalIterator beginRotational(int              index) const;

                        // Aspects

    bslma::Allocator *allocator() const;

    const_iterator cbegin() const;

    const_iterator cend() const;

    std::ostream& print(std::ostream& stream,
                        int           level = 0,
                        int           spacesPerLevel = 4) const;
};

// FREE OPERATORS
bool operator==(const Polygon& lhs, const Polygon& rhs);

bool operator!=(const Polygon& lhs, const Polygon& rhs);[46]

std::ostream& operator<<(std::ostream& stream, const Polygon& object);

// FREE FUNCTIONS
void swap(Polygon& a, Polygon& b);

// ==============================================================================
//                          INLINE FUNCTION DEFINITIONS
// ==============================================================================

// ...

}  // close package namespace

// ...
```

Figure 3-18: Overly encapsulating complete interface for `our::Polygon`

```
    void swap(Polygon& a, Polygon& b)
    {
        Polygon c(std::move(a));
        a = std::move(b);
        b = std::move(c);
    }
```

[46] Note that most clients expect these functions to operate (at least in the typical/expected case) in time that is proportional to the number of vertices (see Volume II, section 4.3).

Notice that several variants of iterators are provided, including compound iterators, each returning vertices, deltas, and offsets via appropriately named methods (as well as vertices via conventional operators). Also provided are individual iterators (specifically for `vertex`, `delta`, and `offset`) suitable for typical generic use. The `const`/non-`const` model used here is similar to that of `std::set` in which both `const` and non-`const` iterator `typedef` declarations appear in class scope, but the same component-private iterator type (having no non-`const` methods) is used to implement both. Given that references to individual vertices are possible for only one of the three alternative implementations, no provision to enable a future iterator allowing modifiable access (to be added) — e.g., via structural inheritance (see Volume II, section 4.6) — was considered.

Preserving all of our implementation options, as we have tried to do here, is not generally practical. Were we to decide to settle on a subset of viable implementation alternatives, we would then be able to eliminate some of the proposed interface of Figure 3-18, leading to a simpler, more readily understood component — perhaps with some marginal efficiency gains in the areas that are deemed most critical. It is hoped that — if nothing else — this example provides "food for thought" when designing *complete* yet *minimal* component interfaces.

3.2.9   Semantics vs. Syntax as Modularization Criteria

Guideline

Prefer semantics and physical dependency over syntax as a modularization criteria, especially at the package level.

3.2.9.1   Poor Use of u as a Package Suffix

Finally, as we indicated at the beginning of this section, it is sometimes tempting to characterize a package based on syntactic rather than semantic properties. For example, in the past we had chosen always to place the nonprimitive functionality for a given component implementing a value type (see Volume II, section 4.1), say **bdet_date**, in a separate component having a matching base name (section 2.4.7), but in a higher-level "utilities" package having a **u** suffix (e.g., **bdetu_date**), even when that nonprimitive functionality had no additional physical dependencies. We have observed in practice, however, that — unless the packages are, by design, dead regular (e.g., see Figure 3-29, section 3.3.7, and Figure 3-37, section 3.3.8.3) — banishing that nonprimitive functionality to a higher-level package impedes its discovery by perspective clients.

3.2.9.2   Good Use of `util` as a Component Suffix

On the other hand, commonly used nonprimitive functionality, such as `area` for `our::Polygon` — which does not contribute significant additional dependencies and, if not for our goal of minimality, would be part of the flagship component's interface itself — is more appropriately located within the same package but in a separate "utility" component (see Volume II, section 4.2) having a similar name. We use the **util** suffix (e.g., **our_polygonutil**) to denote such semantically related yet nonprimitive functionality. Not only does this approach significantly enhance discoverability by clients, other components within the same package as the flagship package are now able to use this nonprimitive functionality in their own implementations without violating package levelization rules (section 2.8.2).

3.2.10   Section Summary

To summarize this section, we want to make sure that we avoid putting into a component, package, or package group functionality that does not rightfully deserve to be colocated there. Failure to acknowledge up front what is (or could be) reusable functionality can (and typically does) result in valuable behavior being hopelessly mired in application-specific source code. Contrary to classical teachings, the "implementation details" — specifically, physical dependencies — strongly influence how we organize and aggregate the source code for the functionality our software provides.

Anticipated client usage also governs our choice of software modularization. In particular, whenever we envisage disparate clients referring to correspondingly separate parts of a single component or package, we should consider further factoring. Figure 3-19 summarizes and contrasts some of what would be considered good versus poor modularization criteria.

Good	Poor
Semantically related functionality	Syntactically related functionality
Application versus library Tightly focused functionally	Functionality needed here and now
Physical dependencies Different client categories Primitive versus nonprimitive	Written by same person/group

Figure 3-19: Modularization criteria summary

Well-designed (reusable) components are focused, complete, minimal, and primitive. Each component we write should have a tightly focused purpose. When designed for a particular application, a component must, of course, be *sufficient* for the specific needs of that application. On the other hand, a potentially reusable component will be considered *complete* only if it addresses not just the application for which it was commissioned, but also for all similar applications within that same narrow domain, and hence satisfies the open-closed principle (section 0.5).

Keeping components *minimal* — i.e., devoid of redundant (or irrelevant) functionality — makes them more readily understandable. To help ensure stability and scalability, however, we will also want to avoid incorporating *nonprimitive* functionality along with primitive functionality in the same components, particularly those defining value types. By *nonprimitive* we mean functionality that can be implemented efficiently (without privileged access) outside of the component that defines the type being used — e.g., in one of possibly several higher-level *utility* components.

If we discover that new application-level functionality on a type defined within a library component cannot be efficiently implemented externally (other than implementing it directly within the component that defines the type), the remedy should be to augment that component to provide low-level "helper" functionality (e.g., iterators) so that the required new (and also similar) functionality can be implemented externally (in the future). In this way, only a fraction of useful functionality on a class need be part of the component that implements it.

In particular, supplying a complete set of primitive functionality for `our::Polygon`, in terms of `vertex`, `delta`, `offset`, `index`, `VertexIterator`, and `RotationalVertexIterator`, allows us to implement virtually any application functionality (e.g., `perimeter`, `area`, `areRotationallySimilar`, `topologicalNumber`) without needing privileged access or causing any significant loss in runtime performance. Being able to implement new (nonprimitive) operations in terms of only a well-chosen set of primitive public interface functions affords both greater freedom to adjust the underlying representation as well as greater stability for existing clients of the class.

Finally, remember that good modularity is invariably governed by semantics, not syntax. Placing like components in a separate package just because they all have the same class category (see Volume II, section 4.2) is unwise. Except for very special cases where the syntax is an integral part of the semantics, it is wise to avoid letting syntactic form be a modularization criterion.

3.3   Grouping Things Physically That Belong Together Logically

The very definition of modularity involves careful grouping and also the hiding of lower-level design decisions behind well-defined interfaces. These "encapsulated" details can be at any level of abstraction — from the lowest levels of the operating system to the highest levels of an application. What is important is that — to the extent possible — each individual implementation choice is isolated within a single module.[47] So long as the contract (see Volume II, section 5.2) for that module is not violated, revisiting the implementation of one module should never mandate revisiting that of any other (see Volume II, section 5.5).

3.3.1   Four Explicit Criteria for Class Colocation

Guideline

Avoid defining more than one *public* class within a single component unless there is a compelling engineering reason to do so (see Figure 3-20, section 3.3.1).

The *component* (section 0.7) serves as our most basic and fundamental unit of physical modularity. Our goal of achieving finely graduated, granular software (section 0.4) encourages us to strive to place each *public* (i.e., externally accessible) class (or `struct`) within its own separate component unless there is a specific, compelling reason to do otherwise. In our experience, we have found exactly four compelling reasons for opting to colocate *public* classes, which are enumerated in Figure 3-20. Note that classes having an underscore in their name and/or those that reside entirely within the `.cpp` file of a component (e.g., defined within an unnamed namespace) are not considered public but will be discussed shortly (see sections 3.3.3–3.3.5).

---

[47] Classic C++ had no formal notion of a *module* — the closest approximation being a (library) *component* (section 0.7), typically rendered as a `.h`/`.cpp` pair satisfying certain fundamental properties (sections 1.6 and 1.11). Proper components in our methodology also subscribe to our approach to enterprise-wide unique naming (section 2.4) and essential design rules (section 2.6). There is, however, a new language feature, C++ modules (e.g., see **modules18**), that was adopted into the C++ draft standard (February 2019). The initial feature set, though not fully finalized as of this writing, will (of necessity) almost certainly satisfy the high-level "business" requirements set forth in **lakos17a** and also the technical ones needed to model components (see also **lakos18**).

---

1. **Private Access** — When one class grants `friend` access to another.

2. **Cyclic Dependency** — When placing two classes in separate components would result in a cyclic physical dependency. [*RARE*]

3. **Single Solution** — When placing otherwise physically independent, yet highly collaborative functionality in separate components would serve no useful purpose (i.e., with respect to independent reuse).

4. **Flea on an Elephant** — When there is a tiny class or function that
    (i) depends on a much larger *primary* class,
    (ii) adds no additional dependencies, and
    (iii) is an essential part of the *primary* class's common usage.

Figure 3-20: Justification for multiple *public* classes in a single component

3.3.1.1   First Reason: Friendship

The first, and overwhelmingly the most common, valid reason for colocation of classes within a single component is friendship. As we have already seen (e.g., with `our::Polygon` in section 3.2), providing one or more iterators, having or granting friend access to its associated container class, enables client software defined outside of a component to implement new functionality without having to touch the source code of the component defining that type. According to section 2.6, such friendship must not span component boundaries; hence, the iterators must reside in the same component as their associated container.

As another example of colocation due to necessary friendship, consider the abstract factory design pattern of Figure 3-21. Here, class `Widget` represents any abstract resource, and `WidgetFactory` is the abstract factory producing that resource. Being pure interfaces, there is no issue regarding friendship, and the two interface classes properly reside in separate components.

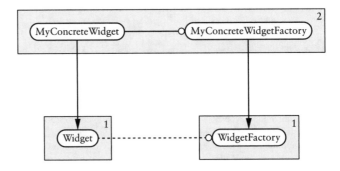

Figure 3-21: Friendship and the abstract factory design pattern

When we consider a paired implementation of these abstract interfaces, however, we must also consider friendship. By definition, a factory is responsible for creating (and reclaiming) resources (see Volume II, section 4.8). Just as with iterators and containers, the intimate knowledge a factory has when constructing an object is typically not something we want to expose, as it is likely highly sensitive to the encapsulated (private) implementation choice. At a minimum, the constructors of a concrete widget should be declared private and made available only to the corresponding concrete factory (i.e., via friendship). Hence, these two concrete implementation classes would properly reside in the same component.[48]

3.3.1.2 Second Reason: Cyclic Dependency

The second, and much rarer justification, for colocating classes occurs when defining them in separate components would result in a cyclic physical dependency among those components — a violation of one of our most important design rules (section 2.6). Although known to be very uncommon and very special (e.g., involving mutually recursive templated data structures, such as an abstract syntax tree, where tight, compile-time coupling forces the definitions of multiple class templates to reside within a single component), such "necessary" colocation to avoid cyclic physical dependencies almost always results from a poor logical design, perhaps mandated by some externally prescribed interface (see Figure 3-88, section 3.5.9).[49] Section 3.5 describes a suite of proven *levelization* techniques for refactoring logical designs to avoid any need for *mutual* or *cyclic* physical dependencies.

3.3.1.3 Third Reason: Single Solution

The third valid reason for colocation is one of practicality. Suppose we have a fairly regular set of relatively small logical entities (e.g., classes, functions, macros), each *peers* of the others (i.e., none depends physically on another), yet where no one of them is independently useful by itself — i.e., all of them are needed in order to address a single complete solution to a given problem as illustrated in Figure 3-22a. A classic example of the need for such a collection of

---

[48] Note that even if "friendship" is not explicit, if two classes' internals must coincide in some way and/or necessarily change in lockstep with each other beyond what is specified in their respective public contracts (see Volume II, section 5.2), then that kind of implicit logical coupling would also argue for colocation.

[49] Note that when classes otherwise reside within a single component, we nonetheless strive to avoid even cyclic logical relationships as we consider them bad form (i.e., they are inconsistent with just slightly larger designs that do not fit within a component), and with just a bit more effort they can essentially always be avoided (e.g., see Figure 2-54, section 2.7.4).

logical entities is to simulate variadic macros and templates.[50] In this unusual circumstance of independent yet highly collaborative peers, we reasonably elect to place all such classes in a single component to minimize needless physical clutter.[51]

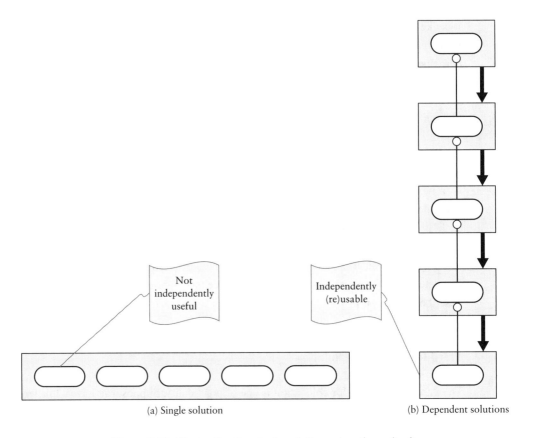

(a) Single solution   (b) Dependent solutions

Figure 3-22: Illustrating the *single solution* colocation criteria

If, however, the logical entities are not small and regular, if some depend (physically) on others, or if individual entities might be useful on their own, then separate components are indicated (Figure 3-22b).

---

[50] As of C++11, variadics are part of the C++ language, substantially reducing the applicability of this justification for colocation.

[51] This third criteria justifying colocation also happens to apply to components implementing C-compatible procedural interfaces (e.g., see Figure 3–147, section 3.11.7.3).

For example, suppose that we have five classes, `Coordinate`, `Point`, `Box`, `BoxCollection`, and `Garage`, each one depending on the previous. One might argue that a `BoxCollection` is useless without a `Box`, so it makes sense to have the `Box` defined in the same component as the `BoxCollection`. But that's not the criteria we use. Instead, we observe that a `Box` can be used independently of a `BoxCollection` and so we place the `Box`, on which the `BoxCollection` depends, in its own separate component. By the same token, placing the `Point` class in the same component as the `Box` class just because `Point` is small and needed to implement `Box` is not sufficient justification for colocation: Class `Point` is also an independently useful concept.

Placing a utility class containing just a few nonprimitive functions in the same component as the value type on which it operates defeats an essential purpose of separating primitive from nonprimitive functionality (section 3.2.7) — namely that it enables us to add or make changes to the interfaces of nonprimitive functions without forcing clients of just the primitive functionality to recompile. Again, in order for the definitions of multiple, externally accessible classes to properly reside in the same component, they must be physically independent, logically collaborative, typically small, regular, individually useless, and yet collectively comprise a cohesive solution to a single, indivisible problem.

3.3.1.4   Fourth Reason: Flea on an Elephant

The fourth valid reason for colocation of public classes allows some room for discretion. Suppose that we have a very large public subsystem such as a logger singleton that defines two public methods: `initSingleton` and `shutdownSingleton`. Suppose further that we provide a scoped-guard class, `LoggerScopedGuard`, that on construction calls `Logger::initSingleton`, and on destruction calls `Logger::shutdownSingleton`, where all functions are declared `inline`. Like a "flea on an elephant," the added weight of this purely syntactic, highly collaborative, all-inline class will go completely unnoticed from a physical perspective. Moreover, the usage-examples section (see Volume II, section 6.16) of the logger's component-level documentation (see Volume II, section 6.15) will want to promote usage of the `LoggerScopedGuard`. Were this trivial guard class escalated to a separate component, it might well go unnoticed (and unused).[52] Hence, colocating the two classes within a single component, as illustrated in Figure 3-23a, makes good practical sense.

---

[52] In our methodology, we avoid the cyclic nature of describing software at a higher level in our component-level documentation (see Volume II, section 6.15). What's more, components' (mandatory) usage examples (see Volume II, section 6.16) avoid any use of another component unavailable (section 2.14.3) to the component's standalone test driver (see Volume III, section 7.5) as it must test *all* such usage examples (see Volume III, Chapter 10).

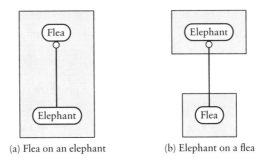

(a) Flea on an elephant   (b) Elephant on a flea

Figure 3-23: Illustrating the *Flea on an Elephant* colocation criteria

By contrast, if the roles were reversed — i.e., "an elephant on a flea" — we would not think twice about it: We would *always* implement the two classes in separate components (so as not to physically couple the lighter-weight class with the heavier-weight one unnecessarily), as illustrated in Figure 3-23b. Note that there can be a tendency toward abuse due to unjustifiable rationalization. A flea is a flea, and an elephant is an elephant: Goats, pigs, chickens, etc., need not apply. Note that another important illustration of this principle is the mandatory (section 2.6) colocation of nonfriend free operators, such as the homogeneous `operator==`, within the same component as a type on which they operate (section 2.4.9).

3.3.2   Colocation Beyond Components

Guideline

Colocate software that must change together.

Mutual collaboration is an important criterion for colocation. In particular, we want to colocate software that must naturally or practically change together.[53] Such mutual collaboration (section 0.3) typically occurs at the application level (section 0.2). In our methodology, such malleable (section 0.5) application software is deliberately located within a single package-sized unit of release (UOR). To enable software at the highest level of an application to change freely, we deliberately disallow external software from depending on it (section 2.13).

3.3.3 When to Make Helper Classes Private to a Component

Ideally, all highly collaborative changes to library software will be confined to a single component. It is then permitted (section 2.6) to use language features such as friendship to help ensure that external clients cannot gain access to unstable interfaces. Sometimes, particularly with generic programming, we will want to factor our class implementations into a number of subordinate classes whose interfaces are specific to the details of the parent's implementation, are subject to change, and are therefore not intended for use outside the component implementing the primary class. In such cases, we may want to employ the *extra underscore* convention (section 2.7.3) to indicate that use of the helper class is explicitly restricted to constructs within its defining component.

Figure 3-24 illustrates how a specialized generic container template class `HashTable2` might be implemented in terms of a number of private implementation classes (in this case `struct`s) colocated within the same component. The first nonpublic `struct`, `HashTable2_DefaultPolicies`, provides the set of default polices, which the client is free to override, but are specifically intended to change in response to empirical optimization over time. The second such `struct`, `HashTable2_ImpUtil`, provides a suite of `static` helper methods deliberately not parameterized by the types of the principle class, thus reducing both client compile time and code bloat.[54] The third component-private `struct`, `HashTable2_WorkArounds`, is used solely to isolate current compiler bugs and will presumably be removed as soon as the compiler vendor can be persuaded to accept a suitable patch. All of these classes provide useful factoring, yet none of them should be used outside of the one component defining the principal public class.

---

[53] See **martin95**, "The Cohesion of Common Closure," pp. 233–234.

[54] Reducing the amount of code involved in complex template instantiation — especially when implemented with external bindage in the `.cpp` file — can often substantially reduce both the time needed to compile and the resulting code size (see Volume II, section 4.5).

```
// bdec_hashtable2.h

// ...

namespace MyLongCompanyName {

// ...

namespace bdec {

// ...

struct HashTable2_DefaultPolicies;

// ...

                // ===============================================
                // class template HashTable2<KEY, VALUE, POLICIES>
                // ===============================================

template <typename KEY,
          typename VALUE    = bslmf::Nil,55
          typename POLICIES = HashTable2_DefaultPolicies>
class HashTable2 {
    // This class implements a hash table using a double-hashing algorithm. ...

    // ...

  public:

    // ...
};

// -------- Anything below here is implementation specific: DO NOT USE --------

                // =========================================
                // private struct HashTable2_DefaultPolicies
                // =========================================

struct HashTable2_DefaultPolicies {
    // This component-private 'struct' implements default policies for the
    // principle class, 'HashTable2'. ...

    // ...
};
```

(continues)

---

[55] **bslmf** represents the "metafunction" package in the **bsl** package group (see **bde14**, subdirectory `/groups/bsl/bslmf/`).

(continued)

```
                     // ==================================
                     // private struct HashTable2_ImpUtil
                     // ==================================

struct HashTable2_ImpUtil {
    // This component-private 'struct' implements non-templated helper
    // functions local to this component. ...

    // ...
};

                     // ===================================
                     // private class HashTable2_WorkArounds
                     // ===================================

struct HashTable2_WorkArounds {
    // This component-private 'struct' implements no additional logical
    // functionality; it is used only to isolate compiler bugs...

    // ...
};

// ============================================================================
//                          INLINE FUNCTION DEFINITIONS
// ============================================================================
// ...

}  // close package namespace

// ...

}  // close enterprise namespace

// ...
```

Figure 3-24: Factoring the implementation with component-private classes

It is worth noting that component-private classes are not, or should not be, a substitute for thinking through an architectural problem carefully with an eye toward hierarchical reuse (section 0.4), yet there are those in a hurry to "push on" that will often avoid making proper components out of perfectly reusable lower-level logical constructs because, in the short term (only), it will be faster or cheaper that way (section 0.1). This expedient, if not remedied quickly, once the emergent deadline passes, completely misses the point of always being "long-term greedy" (section 0.12).[56]

---

[56] David Sankel opines (in his review of the manuscript for this volume): "The immediate cost of being 'long term greedy,' whether that be developer fatigue or annoying management intervention, can be significantly reduced by providing automated tools that do the otherwise-manual work. . . . You're correctly outlining what 'the right thing' is, but it is just as important to, as much as possible, make the right thing the easy thing."

Packing potentially independently useful functionality into a single component makes it significantly harder to test. We have a mature testing methodology (see Volume III), which takes advantage of recurring patterns based on the *category* (see Volume II, section 4.2) of the principle class. Having multiple classes within a component means that the ordering of test cases (see Volume III, Chapter 10) would no longer be canonical, which in turn would significantly degrade our ability to create, understand, and maintain our component-level ("unit") test drivers.

Moreover, when such an inherently useful piece-part is needed for external use in the future, it will not be ready for immediate consumption and will then have to be extricated from its component, documented, retested, etc., or worse, duplicated in some other component as a private detail, where it will nonetheless have to be documented and tested. Component-private classes should be limited to only highly collaborative classes, classes that are likely to change, and where change will necessarily have to occur in lock-step with other colocated classes.

3.3.4   Colocation of Template Specializations

Template specializations are another common reason for colocation. Suppose we are creating a template class, such as a *metafunction*, that — for whatever reason[57] — requires one or more specializations. No one of these specializations is useful on its own, yet along with the general template class, they conspire to deliver a complete and efficient solution. In such cases, we declare the specialization, like inline functions, within the same component header below all public classes. Note, however, that any explicit specializations of function templates that are not declared `inline` will have external bindage (section 1.3.4), and therefore their definitions do properly reside within the corresponding `.cpp` file.

3.3.5   Use of Subordinate Components

Sometimes we will find that collaborative changes will reasonably extend beyond component boundaries. In such cases, it is often appropriate to restrict the use of an entire component. Our conventional use of the double-underscore convention for component names (section 2.7.3) allows us to make the use of a component subordinate to another component (within the same package) explicit (section 2.7.5). Recall that a common use of the convention is to allow for platform-specific implementations to reside in separate `.h`/`.cpp` pairs. We might, however, run across other situations in which the interfaces of lower-level components used to implement

---

[57] A template specialization is used primarily as an implementation detail (of a general template) that takes advantage of a specific type, typically for optimization purposes, and (generally speaking) should not be used to customize the semantics — i.e., contract (see Volume II, section 5.2) — of the general template.

a subsystem are simply too collaborative, unstable, or "half-baked" to be exposed for general consumption. Restricting the use of such subcomponents to a particular component (again, within a single package) is often the "right" solution in practice (at least in the short term).

3.3.6   Colocate Tight Mutual Collaboration within a Single UOR

Guideline

Limit tight mutual collaboration across public components to a single UOR.

Although less desirable, malleable interfaces (section 0.5) may need to be exposed at the library level. When the public interface of several collaborative components will need to change over time, colocating them within the same unit of release (UOR) greatly simplifies maintenance. Spreading these changes out over multiple parallel UORs often makes it necessary to release these libraries in lock-step. Such tight UOR collaboration across levels is worse still and can lead to always having to rebuild and release an unbounded number of libraries at once!

The problem with nonlocal collaboration is not so much in the production release process, which occurs relatively infrequently, but rather during development, where the software is recompiled, relinked, and exercised repeatedly throughout the day. When all of the software that is evolving together is kept to a single UOR, the cost of *turning the crank*, so to speak, is kept relatively small. Having to switch between separate UORs to make consistent edits and then having to rebuild and rerelease each intervening library in turn (to verify incremental enhancements) makes the task of development especially onerous: Development speed can suffer horribly — especially if other sound *physical-design* practices have also been ignored.

Imagine that we have a cryptographic streaming subsystem implemented across several UORs as shown in Figure 3-25. The "encrypt" facility, similar to an *encoder* (section 2.8.3), is located in one UOR, while the "decrypt" facility is in another, which — *for testing only* (see Figure 2.84c, section 2.14.4) — depends on the first (see Figure 2.82e, section 2.14.3); see also Volume III, section 8.6. Both of these UORs depend on an evolving set of enumerations and traits (specific to encryption) located in components way down at the bottom of the physical hierarchy. Each encryptable type distributed throughout this hierarchy also depends on the (low-level) traits component and might need to be recompiled (if not reworked) each time it's updated.

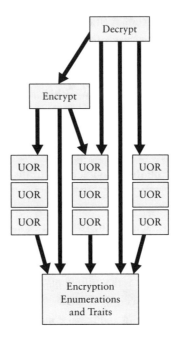

Figure 3-25: Tight collaboration across UORs (BAD IDEA)

As designed, the amount of effort needed to maintain this encryption subsystem is excessively large. Each time we go to change the collaborate parts of our malleable encryption subsystem together, we are forced to rebuild a tremendous amount of software. If instead we grouped all of the malleable machinery necessary to implement the subsystem within a single UOR, it would at least have the property that it can be developed and maintained without having to rebuild large parts of our code base on each edit-compile-link cycle. Once we have it right, we can then rerelease the subsystem as a whole and allow downstream modules to rework their code (in levelized order) as needed.

3.3.7   Day-Count Example

As a second, real-world example of colocating malleable library subsystems, consider day-count conventions introduced (historically) by the financial services industry to facilitate calculations involving the number of days between two dates. Instead of determining the actual number of days from one date to the next, the `difference` function will return an approximation whose precise value depends on the two dates; note, however, that moving each of the two argument dates up by one day will not necessarily produce the same result.

For instance, the *ISMA 30/360* day-count convention approximates calculations by assuming a 30-day month and a 360-day year: Let the earlier date be represented by $Y1/M1/D1$ and the later date by $Y2/M2/D2$. If $D1$ is 31, change it to 30. If $D2$ is 31, change it to 30. The difference is now given by $(Y2 - Y1) \cdot 360 + (M2 - M1) \cdot 30 + D2 - D1$.[58]

Such conventions are quite arbitrary. Another one, *PSA 30/360* (having an end of month adjustment), is described as follows. Let the earlier date be represented by $Y1/M1/D1$ and the later date by $Y2/M2/D2$. If $D1$ is the last day of February (29 in a leap year, else 28), then change $D1$ to 30; else if $D1$ is 31, change $D1$ to 30. If at this point $D1$ is 30 and $D2$ is 31, change $D2$ to 30. The difference is now the maximum of 0 and $(Y2 - Y1) \cdot 360 + (M2 - M1) \cdot 30 + D2 - D1$.[59] Note that the `max` function is required because $D2$ has no February adjustment and simple differences like (1999/02/28 − 1999/02/28) produce −2 without it.

Although they have long outlived their *computational* usefulness, there are literally dozens of these subtly different day-count conventions in production use today, and the set may continue to grow (albeit slowly). When evaluating a particular financial instrument, a specific arcane day-count convention is often prescribed. Given that such functionality is needed, where should it go?

Placing such highly specific and baroque functionality in our library date class (whether as an instance or `static` method) is decidedly ill advised. With each new convention added, the component implementing the widely used (value-semantic) date class (see Volume II, section 4.3) would have to be modified, which is contrary to our desire to ensure stability (see Volume II, section 5.6), especially for low-level *vocabulary* types (see Volume II, section 4.4). Moreover, such functionality is most likely not relevant to the vast majority of users of a date class; hence, such functionality would clutter the essential interface for the general audience. As there is typically no real performance advantage to having direct access to the underlying representation, this nonprimitive functionality (section 3.2.7) is best implemented outside the flagship component for dates.[60]

---

[58] **brown90**

[59] **fincad08**

[60] The one canonical date difference, *actual/actual*, naturally belongs within the library component implementing the date class itself (e.g., as `operator-` and `operator-=`). As it happens, this particular difference calculation can also benefit significantly from direct access to a *private* serial date value, which is our preferred implementation for our ubiquitously used-in-the-interface date objects (see Volume II, section 4.4).

Again, we ask ourselves, where should these weird day-count functions reside? One possible solution is to move all of these difference functions to a single higher-level component (perhaps not even in the same package) where each `static` method of the utility class takes two date arguments and is named to reflect the specific convention as illustrated in Figure 3-26a. In this rendering, there will be two functions for each convention — one for `daysDiff` and one for fractional year — for a total of $2N$ functions (N being the number of conventions).

```
struct DayCountUtil {
    // This 'struct' provides a namespace for a suite of pure functions used
    // to calculate date differences based on various day-count conventions.

    static
    int isma30360DaysDiff(const bdlt::Date& earlier, const bdlt::Date& later);
        // Return the number of days between the specified 'earlier' and
        // 'later' dates according to the ISMA 30/360 convention defined as
        // follows.  Let 'earlier' be represented by Y1/M1/D1 and 'later' by
        // Y2/M2/D2.  If D1 is 31, change it to 30.  If D2 is 31, change it to
        // 30.  The difference is now given by (Y2 - Y1) * 360 + (M2 - M1) *
        // 30 + D2 - D1.  The behavior is undefined unless 'earlier <= later'.
        // Note that this algorithm is documented in a published reference:
        // Formulae For Yield And Other Calculations (1992) ISBB 0-9515474-0-2.

    static
    double isma30360Term(const bdlt::Date& earlier, const bdlt::Date& later);
        // Return the fractional number of years spanned by the specified
        // 'earlier' and 'later' dates according to the ISMA 30/360 convention
        // defined as follows.  Let 'earlier' be represented by Y1/M1/D1 and
        // 'later' by Y2/M2/D2.  If D1 is 31, change it to 30.  If D2 is 31,
        // change it to 30.  The difference is now given by (Y2 - Y1) * 360 +
        // (M2 - M1) * 30 + D2 - D1.  In this convention, a year is defined as
        // having exactly 360 days -- irrespective of 'earlier' and 'later';
        // hence, the value returned is the same as that of the expression
        // '(isma30360DaysDiff(earlier, later) / 360.0)'.  The behavior is
        // undefined unless 'earlier <= later'.  Note that this algorithm is
        // documented in a published reference: Formulae For Yield And Other
        // Calculations (1992) ISBN 0-9515474-0-2.

    static
    int psa30360eomDaysDiff(const bdlt::Date& d1, const bdlt::Date& d2);
        // ...

    // ...
};
```

(a) Two separate functions for each convention

```
struct DayCountUtil {
    // This 'struct' provides a namespace for an enumerated set of day-count
    // conventions and a pair of pure procedures that can be used to obtain
    // the days difference and fractional year for any supported convention.

    enum DayCount {
        // Enumerated set of supported day-count conventions.  Assume that,
        // for each enumerated convention, the earlier date be represented by
        // Y1/M1/D1 and the later one by Y2/M2/D2.

        ISMA30360,      // If D1 is 31, change it to 30.  If D2 is 31,
                        // change it to 30.  The difference is now given
                        // by (Y2 - Y1) * 360 + (M2 - M1) * 30 + D2 - D1.
                        // Reference: Formulae For Yield And Other
                        // Calculations (1992) ISBN 0-9515474-0-2.

        PSA30360EOM,    // ...

        SIA30360EOM,    // ...

        SIA30360NEOM,   // ...
    };

    static
    int daysDiff(const bdlt::Date& earlier,
                 const bdlt::Date& later,
                 DayCount          convention);
        // Return the number of days between the specified 'earlier' and
        // 'later' dates according to the specified day-count 'convention'.
        // The behavior is undefined unless 'earlier <= later'.

    static
    double term(const bdlt::Date& earlier,
                const bdlt::Date& later,
                DayCount          convention);
        // Return the fractional number of years spanned by the specified
        // 'earlier' and 'later' dates according to the specified day-count
        // 'convention'.  The behavior is undefined unless 'earlier <= later'.
};
```

(b) Two basic functions, each parameterized by an enumeration

Figure 3-26: Single component implementing various day-count conventions

Equivalently, we could create an enumeration and a single pair of static functions that calculate the number of days difference and fraction of a year based on two dates and an enumerator (Figure 3-26b). This latter, more compact rendering is also more flexible, but it is significantly less efficient[61] when only one specific convention (often known at compile time) is needed. Note that the potential need for maximal runtime efficiency is, in part, why we did not initially just opt for a good "old-fashioned" pure abstract `DayCount` base class ("protocol") along with a suite of concrete implementations (in separate components, of course).[62]

Either of the solutions proposed in Figure 3-26 decouples this nonprimitive functionality from our underlying date class but still leaves all of the conventions implemented within a single component and therefore physically coupled to each other. Any program needing only a single convention is forced to bring in all of them, and any time a convention is added, all programs requiring any existing convention would be forced to recompile. Clearly this alternative modularization also leaves something to be desired.

Now consider that we could, instead, create an entire package of components dedicated to day-counts as in Figure 3-27a. We might call this package **bbldc** for *Basic Business Library Day Count*. This relatively lightweight package would naturally live in the **bbl** package group, which would depend on only our *Basic Development Library* package group, **bdl**, as well as **bsl**.[63]

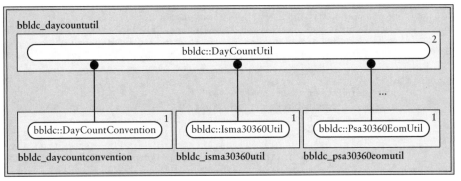

(a) The **bbldc** package structure

---

[61] Such a function is not reasonably `inline`-able and would have an additional runtime dispatch based on the supplied convention type.

[62] But please do be sure to check out our alternative of compile-time dispatch in Figure 3-28.

[63] These and other hierarchically reusable package groups can be found in Bloomberg's open-source distribution of BDE (see **bde14**).

```
// bbldc_isma30360util.h                                              -*-C++-*-
// ...

struct Isma30360Util {
    // This utility 'struct' provides a namespace for a pair of pure functions
    // used, respectively, to determine the number of days and fractional-year
    // difference according to the ISMA 30/360 day-count convention defined as
    // follows:
    //
    // Let the earlier date be represented by Y1/M1/D1 and later one by
    // Y2/M2/D2.  If D1 is 31, change it to 30.  If D2 is 31, change it to 30.
    // The difference is now given by (Y2 - Y1) * 360 + (M2 - M1) * 30 +
    // D2 - D1.  A year is defined as having exactly 360 days -- irrespective
    // of the specific values of the supplied earlier and later dates.
    //
    // Reference: Formulae For Yield And Other Calculations (1992)
    // ISBN 0-9515474-0-2.

    static
    int daysDiff(const bdlt::Date& earlier, const bdlt::Date& later);
        // Return the number of days between the specified 'earlier' and
        // 'later' dates according to the ISMA 30/360 convention, defined in
        // the class-level documentation.  The behavior is undefined unless
        // 'earlier <= later'.

    static
    double term(const bdlt::Date& earlier, const bdlt::Date& later);
        // Return the fractional number of years spanned by the specified
        // 'earlier' and 'later' dates according to the ISMA 30/360 day-count
        // convention, defined in the class-level documentation.  The
        // behavior is undefined unless 'earlier <= later'.
};

//...
```

(b) Typical leaf component **bbldc_isma30360util** in package **bbldc**

```
// bbldc_daycountconvention.h                                             -*-C++-*-
// ...

struct DayCountConvention {
    // This 'struct' provides a namespace for enumerating each of the
    // day-count conventions supported in the Basic Business Library
    // Day-Count ('bbldc') package.

    enum Enum {
        // Enumerated set of supported day-count conventions.

        ISMA30360,        // See the 'bbldc_isma30360util' component.

        PSA30360EOM,      // See the 'bbldc_psa30360eomutil' component.

        SIA30360EOM,      // See the 'bbldc_sia30360eomutil' component.

        SIA30360NEOM,     // See the 'bbldc_sia30360neomutil' component.

        // ...
    };

    // ...
};

// ...
```

(c) Separate component **bbldc_daycountconvention** to hold the enumeration

```
// bbldc_daycountutil.h                                                   -*-C++-*-
// ...

struct DayCountUtil {
    // This utility 'struct' provides a namespace for a pair of pure functions
    // used, respectively, to determine the number of days difference and
    // fractional year for any of the supported day-count conventions defined
    // in 'bbldc_daycountconvention'.

    static
    int daysDiff(const bdlt::Date&      earlier,
                 const bdlt::Date&      later,
                 DayCountConvention::Enum convention);
        // Return the number of days difference between the specified 'earlier'
        // and 'later' dates according to the specified day-count 'convention'.
        // The behavior is undefined unless 'earlier <= later'.

    static
    double term(const bdlt::Date&      earlier,
                const bdlt::Date&      later,
                DayCountConvention::Enum convention);
        // Return the fractional number of years spanned by the specified
        // 'earlier' and 'later' dates according to the specified day-count
        // 'convention'.  The behavior is undefined unless 'earlier <= later'.
};

// ...
```

(d) Top-level wrapper utility uniting all supported day-count conventions

Figure 3-27: Factoring day-count across the bbldc package

Each supported convention (e.g., ISMA 30/360) would be implemented in a separate "leaf" component as illustrated in Figure 3-27b. The `util` suffix is our convention for identifying a canonical "utility" component (see Figure 2-23, section 2.4.9) consisting of a single `struct` containing only public `static` methods, `typedefs`, and constants (and, rarely, private `static` data[64]). Clients requiring only a subset of the conventions need not incorporate the rest nor be affected as new day-count components are added. Since the amount of code used to implement any one `daysDiff` or `term` function is small, these functions can be productively inlined. Moreover, each such component (along with its test driver) serves as a blueprint for the next (see Volume III, Chapter 10).

The enumeration itself is also placed in its own leaf-level component (Figure 3-27c) consistent with our desire to fully factor our designs into canonical categories (see Volume II, section 4.2). Clients who need only to identify conventions without having to perform calculations can limit their dependencies to the one "enumeration" component, and avoid unnecessarily involving the rest. Finally, for systems that specifically require access to all supported day-count conventions, the top-level *wrapper* [65] component `bbldc_daycountutil` is provided (Figure 3-27d).

It might seem that we have paid a high price for this fine-grained flexibility in terms of the number of components required. Generally speaking, the more components we have, the more development work and physical complexity ensues. Notice here, however, that just the opposite is true. Certain constructs such as enumerations are significantly cheaper to factor out and treat as a separate unit. In fact, the auxiliary functional mechanisms needed to support an enumeration (e.g., conversion to ASCII, streaming) and their associated documentation and testing are prime candidates for a semi-automatic generation process we refer to as *duping*.[66] Once an archetypal enumeration component (e.g., `bdlt_dayofweek`) has been designed, implemented, documented, and tested (see Volume III, Chapter 10), the incremental cost of "duping" it — along with its component-level test driver — to another (e.g., `bbldc_daycount`) is tiny and far cheaper than inserting that functionality into some other kind of component (e.g., `bbldc_daycountutil`).

By the same token, once we have implemented, documented, and tested one of the many leaf components implementing a day-count, the incremental cost of duping it to others is also relatively small. The regularity of this design keeps the complexity of added components quite manageable.

---

[64] E.g., to implement fast insulated table lookup (see Volume II, section 6.6).

[65] Also known as a *façade*. See **gamma95**, Chapter 4, section "Facade," pp. 185–193.

[66] Note that this deliberate form of copying "exemplar" components to improve productivity and consistency while minimizing typing, is in no way intended to give license to less disciplined forms of copying and pasting of source code.

And, because all of the components implementing day-counts reside in the same package, we can conveniently refer to them collectively via the package name **bbldc**. It is by proactively factoring out regular patterns such as enumerations and day-count calculations into separate, similar components that we can substantially reduce both complexity and development cost, while achieving a maximally efficient, effective, and flexible fine-grained reusable architecture.

Furthermore, consider that all of these "duped" day-count components implement a consistent *structural protocol*, a.k.a. a *concept* (section 1.7.6), that can be used generically. That is, any compliant day-count utility `struct` can be used as a compile-time type argument for any templated class that is designed to operate on a type satisfying this *day-count concept*. Moreover, it is easy to adapt this (maximally efficient) compile-time polymorphism to more flexible[67] "runtime" polymorphism by creating a derived templated class, e.g., `DayCountAdapter`, that converts a conforming day-count `struct` to a derived type that implements a (unique) *vocabulary* (see Volume II, section 4.4) base-class protocol, e.g., `DayCount`, as illustrated in Figure 3-28.

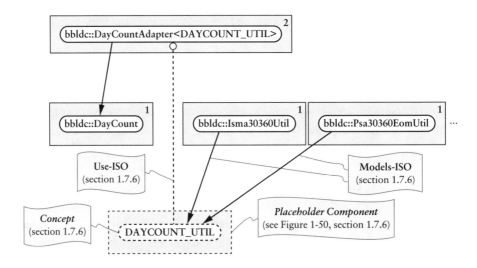

Figure 3-28: Adapting day-count utilities to a (unique) protocol class

Colocating components that change together is an important design goal. The enumeration and the higher-level wrapper component are tightly collaborative with the slowly growing set of leaf day-count components. Each time a new day count is added, both the enumeration and wrapper components must also be updated in order to present the new convention to clients

---

[67] But not *necessarily* less efficient — especially when optimizers have access to the source of inline virtual functions and templated clients as is typical with `bslma::Allocator` (see Volume II, section 4.10).

who necessarily require access to *all* conventions. By placing these highly collaborative components within a single package, we minimize the maintenance burden that arises when new components are added and the collaborative components must change.

Observation

Packages can be useful for explicitly grouping components that are, by design, necessarily syntactically (as well as semantically) similar (e.g., they all implement the same *protocol* or satisfy the same *concept*) provided, of course, that they naturally share essentially the same envelope of physical dependencies.

Recall (section 3.2.9) that, generally speaking, the semantics and physical dependencies of components, not their syntactic properties, should influence their relative packaging. In particular, sequestering nonprimitive, yet closely related, functionality — e.g., for a value type (see Volume II, section 4.2) — in a separate, higher-level package containing correspondingly named utility components is a bad idea because it impedes discovery of useful functionality intended to be consumed selectively by clients (section 3.2.9.1). In our day-count subsystem example, however, there is a clear subset of components that satisfy all the requirements described in the observation above that could be placed within a single separate package, having a prefix delineating a family of syntactically similar utilities, as illustrated in Figure 3-29.

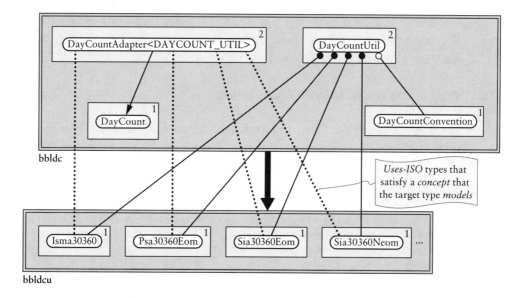

Figure 3-29: Colocating specific day-counts in their own package

The only (minor) drawback to this approach is that, whenever a new day-count component is added to the **bbldcu** package, the higher-level **bbldc** package will need to be modified as well, distributing the maintenance burden across multiple packages. Fortunately, the modifications need not occur in lockstep: A new component can be added to **bbldcu** and fully tested; then, at some later time, the highly collaborative enumeration component in **bbldc** can be extended (backward-compatibly).[68] Moreover, both packages will reside in the same UOR (i.e., the **bbl** package group) thus making the grouping of (only) the specific day-count utilities into their own separate package, **bbldcu**, a very plausible design alternative.

A compromise between the two alternative approaches would be to have just a single package, **bblx**, but provide a common prefix (e.g., **dc**) of each of the basenames (and corresponding `struct` names; section 2.4.7) of the individual day-count utilities (e.g., **bdlx_dcisma30360**, **bdlx_dcpsa30360eom**, **bdlx_dcsia30360eom**). This way, all of the day-count components naturally group together within the **bblx** package directory. What's more, day-count components satisfying subtly different concepts could be grouped accordingly in the same package (e.g., **bdlx_dc1isma30360**, **bdlx_dc2isma30360**, **bdlx_dc2psa30360eom**).[69]

3.3.8   Final Example: Single-Threaded Reference-Counted Functors

Let's now consider a classic instance of the envelope/letter pattern[70] implementing a custom suite of reference-counted functors, originally developed (c. 1998) for use in single-threaded, event-driven programming applications. We chose this example because of its many small separable logical parts, high-degree of syntactic/semantic regularity in multiple dimensions, and considerable pedagogical value.[71] After presenting an overall logical design, we'll set about rendering it optimally in components and packages.

3.3.8.1   Brief Review of Event-Driven Programming

We begin with a very brief review of single-threaded, event-driven programming. Typical functions (e.g., `sqrt`) will have no trouble using available CPU cycles to productively advance the

---

[68] Note that, as of C++11, the underlying integral type of an enumeration can be altered, thus leading to a potential ABI break. Although it now becomes possible to declare enumerations locally without their enumerators, it is precisely because the integral types may change that even these partial definitions be included using a header file associated with the defining component.

[69] Note that this final approach was the one we opted for in practice.

[70] **coplien92**, section 5.5, pp. 133–165

[71] Although this is a bona fide "real-world" example of actual production code, as of C++11, with its support for variadic templates, thread-safe reference-counted pointers (`std::shared_ptr`), and compile-time polymorphic functors (`std::function` and `std::bind`), we can now achieve essentially the same functionality more flexibly (and almost as efficiently), directly from the C++ Standard Library. Nonetheless, the architectural concepts still apply.

state of the computation toward completion. When a function is unable to proceed because some needed piece of information or resource is not yet available (e.g., a server trying to read the next request from a client), that function may block, potentially[72] allowing some other process (or thread) to take advantage of what might otherwise be an idle CPU during its operating-system-allocated time slice, as illustrated in Figure 3-30a. If, however, the same (single-threaded) process in which that function is executing is also responsible for making that information or resource available, the entire process would hang.

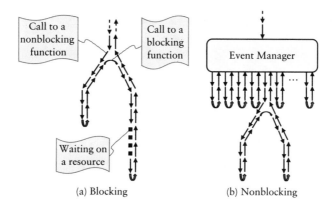

Figure 3-30: Two different programming paradigms

For a single thread of control to simulate multiple simultaneous ones, we use a classical programming paradigm known as *time multiplexing*. In this very different programming model, a global event manager (also known as an *event loop*) polls (e.g., in some sort of round-robin manner) all possible sources of events to discover which, if any, have occurred. The event loop then invokes the callback "function" associated with that event as illustrated in Figure 3-30b. For this approach to work, however, each time a function would block, it must instead explicitly *yield* its use of the CPU (i.e., `return`), but not before registering a new callback with the event manager to be invoked after the needed information or resource becomes available.

Historically (in C), a function that was called in response to an event would be passed the address of an opaque block of memory supplied by the user when the callback was registered with the event manager. As illustrated in Figure 3-31, this "user data" provides whatever *context* is needed to process the event. Notice that this C-like style of programming is neither type safe nor encapsulating and unadvisedly commingles explicit resource management with domain functionality.

---

[72] A function that burns CPU idly (e.g., through active polling) but cannot advance the state of the computation beyond a certain point until a needed resource becomes available would also be considered *blocking* (albeit less economical with hardware resources).

```
struct MyEvent {
    enum Enum {
        // ...
        e_BELOW_FREEZING,  // i.e., below 32 degrees Fahrenheit
        // ...
    };

    // ...
};

class MyEventManager {
    // ...
  public:
    void registerInterest(MyEvent::Enum  type,
                          void            (*callback)(int, void *),
                          void            *userData);
        // Associate the specified 'callback' function with the specified
        // event 'type'.  When an event of the associated 'type' occurs, invoke
        // 'callback' passing status as its first argument, and the specified
        // 'userData' address as its second.  The behavior is undefined unless
        // ...

    int run();
        // Start this event manager.  ...

    // ...
};

class MyHeatController {
    // ...
  public:
    void turnUpTheHeat(double percentCapacity);
        // Increase the power by the specified 'percentCapacity' -- i.e., as a
        // percentage of the maximum.  The behavior is undefined unless ...

    // ...
};

struct MyTurnUpTheHeatUserData {
    MyHeatController *d_controller_p;  // address of heat controller
    double           d_amount;        // percentage of capacity of heater
};

static void myTurnUpTheHeatCallback(int status, void *turnUpTheHeatUserData)
    // If the specified 'status' is good, increase the rate of heating of the
    // 'd_controller_p' by the 'd_amount' indicated, respectively, in the
    // specified 'turnUpTheHeatUserData'.  Note that, typically, this callback
    // will be invoked when an event with which it is associated occurs.
```

(continues)

(continued)

```
{
    if (0 == status) {
        MyTurnUpTheHeatUserData *p =
                reinterpret_cast<TurnUpTheHeatUserData *>(turnUpTheHeatUserData);
        (*p->d_controller_p).turnUpTheHeat(p->d_amount);
    }

    // Perhaps reregister this same callback for next time.
}

int main()
{
    MyEventManager     eventManager;

    MyHeatController heatController;
    double             percentageIncrease = 10.0;

    TurnUpTheHeatUserData data = { &heatController, percentageIncrease };

    eventManager.registerInterest(MyEvent::e_BELOW_FREEZING,
                                  &myTurnUpTheHeatCallback,
                                  &data);

    return eventManager.run();  // loop "forever"
}
```

Figure 3-31: Classical approach to event-driven programming

A more modern and sensible approach to writing event-driven programs is to register (as a callback with the event manager) not just a stateless *function* but instead a stateful *functor* ("function object") in which the registering agent has embedded *within the callback object itself* the particular context needed to respond to the event. A sketch of a prototypical reference-counted functor class template requiring exactly *N* arguments in order to be invoked is provided in Figure 3-32.

```
template <class T1, /*...*/ class TN>
class FunctorN {
    // This class template defines a functor class that requires exactly N
    // arguments to be supplied in order to be invoked.

    BaseRepresentationN<T1, /*...*/ TN> *d_letter_p;

  public:
    // CREATORS
    explicit FunctorN(BaseRepresentationN<T1, /*...*/ TN> *rep);
        // Hold on to the provided representation and increment
        // its reference count.

    FunctorN(const FunctorN<T1, /*...*/ TN>& other);
        // Hold on to the representation of the other functor
        // and increment its reference count.

    ~FunctorN();
        // Decrement the reference count of the base representation
        // provided at construction.  If that value is now zero,
        // destroy and deallocate the representation.

    // MANIPULATORS
    FunctorN<T1, /*...*/ TN>& operator=(const FunctorN<T1, /*...*/ TN>& rhs);
        // Increment the reference count in the 'rhs' functor
        // representation and then decrement the reference count in
        // this functor's representation.  If the latter value is now
        // zero, destroy and deallocate this functor's representation.
        // Hold onto the representation of the 'rhs' functor.

    // ACCESSORS
    void operator()(const T1& arg1, /*...*/ const TN& argN) const;
        // Invoke the execute method of the underlying base
        // representation, passing the specified N required arguments.
        // The user-supplied callback function will then be invoked
        // with these leading arguments followed by any additional
        // trailing arguments needed to perform its task.  Note that
        // the underlying (shared) representation may be modified.
};

// FREE OPERATORS
template <class T1, class T2, /*...*/ class TN>
bool operator==(const FunctorN<T1, /*...*/ TN>& lhs,
                const FunctorN<T1, /*...*/ TN>& rhs);
    // Return 'true' if the addresses of the underlying representations of
    // the specified 'lhs' and 'rhs' functors are the same, and 'false'
    // otherwise.

// ...
```

Figure 3-32: Sketch of generic *N*-parameter functor (envelope) interface

Absent variadic templates,[73] we were forced to create a suite of separate functor classes to accommodate varying numbers of required arguments.[74] Each `FunctorN` acts as a mapping from a caller (server) providing N arguments to a callee (callback function) expecting $N + M$ arguments. The functor holds the additional M arguments, bound in by the client creating the functor, and presents them (as trailing arguments) to its (user-supplied) callback function when the functor is invoked. A scenario, similar to the one depicted in Figure 3-31, demonstrating the flexibility of a library of properly designed, reference-counted functors — used to encapsulate arbitrary numbers of additional type-safe, user-specified arguments (e.g., `controller` and `amount`) supplied at registration — is shown in Figure 3-33.

---

[73] Variadic templates were not available in the C++ language until C++11.

[74] Note that the advice in this chapter applies generally to all languages having separate translation units, not just the latest incarnation of C++.

```
struct MyEvent { enum Enum { /* See Figure 3-31. */ }; /*...*/ };

class MyEventManager {
    // ...

  public:
    void registerInterest(MyEvent::Enum          type,
                          const Envelope1<int>& callback);
        // Associate the specified 'callback' functor with the specified
        // event 'type'.  When an event of the associated 'type' occurs, invoke
        // 'callback', passing status as its only argument.

    int run();
        // Start this event manager.  ...

    // ...
};

class MyHeatController { /* See Figure 3-31. */ };

static void myTurnUpTheHeatCallback(int              status,
                                    MyHeatController *controller,
                                    double           amount)
    // If the specified 'status' is good, increase the rate of heating of the
    // specified 'controller' by the specified 'amount'.  Note that, typically,
    // this callback will be invoked when an event with which it is associated
    // occurs.
{
    if (0 == status) {
        controller->turnUpTheHeat(amount);
    }

    // Perhaps reregister this same callback for next time.
}

int main()
{
    MyEventManager    eventManager;

    MyHeatController heatController;
    double          percentageIncrease = 10.0;

    Envelope1<int> functor;
    Function1plus2Util::makeF(&functor,
                              myTurnUpTheHeatCallback,
                              &heatController,
                              percentageIncrease);

    eventManager.registerInterest(MyEvent::e_BELOW_FREEZING, functor);

    return eventManager.run();  // loop "forever"
}
```

See Figure 3-34.

Function object to be invoked by eventManager with an int status value as its only unbound argument (see Figure 3-34)

makeF binds these two arguments into functor.

Figure 3-33: (Somewhat) more modern approach to event-driven programming

The details of implementing these reference-counted functors are many. The topic at hand, however, is physical design and how best to package this particular functor library for optimal utility. Figure 3-34 illustrates the basic pattern of every member in the functor family. The functor itself is a kind of *envelope* that holds a pointer to its *letter*, which in this case is polymorphic, depending on the number of *additional* user-supplied arguments.

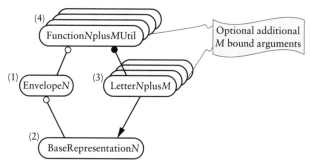

N = number of required arguments
M = number of additional, user-supplied arguments

(1) The "envelope" representing the functor itself, characterized by N and holding a pointer to an abstract base representation of its contained letter.

(2) The abstract base representation for a letter having N required arguments (corresponding to its parent envelope).

(3) The suite of N derived letter classes, each supporting a different combination of M and different kinds of callback functions (i.e., free, `const` member, and non-`const` member).

(4) A suite of utility "factory" functions used to populate a functor envelope with the appropriate letter, depending on M *trailing* arguments in the user-supplied callback function or method.

Figure 3-34: Prototypical functor taking N required arguments

Let's assume that we want to create a library that supports a combined number of up to, say, 9 (required and user-supplied) arguments. In that case, we will need (1) 10 *Envelope* classes to represent the various concrete *interface* (i.e., *vocabulary*) *types* (see Volume II, section 4.4), (2) 10 corresponding *Abstract Letters* to enable polymorphic representation of the user-supplied letters, (3) 10 + 9 + ... + 1 = 55 *Concrete Letters* (each derived from the abstract one having the same number of required arguments) in order to support all possible combinations of up to 9 required and user-supplied arguments, and (4) 55 corresponding *Factory* (utility) functions — one for each corresponding concrete letter — which clients would then typically use to populate the envelopes.

When we consider that we will also want to support both `const` and non-`const` member-function callbacks (along with the free functions contemplated above), the number of concrete *Letter* class templates, as well as the corresponding templated factory functions, swells to 165 each! If we were to place each of these logical entities in its own separate component, we would be looking at some 350 physically distinct entities, ample to robustly populate an entire package group (section 2.9). Our instincts, however, should tell us that the functionality being provided is hardly deserving of all of that physical real estate. Appropriate colocation, permitted under clause (3) — *Single Solution* — of our colocation design guideline (presented at the start of this section) will simplify things considerably.[75]

| **Observation** |

> **Package and component names can sometimes be used productively to represent orthogonal dimensions of design, but only within dead-regular frameworks.**

Choosing to keep the definition of each *Envelope* template in its own separate component makes perfect sense for a couple of reasons. First, each *Envelope* component is intended to yield a *vocabulary type* — i.e., one that is used widely in the interface of publicly accessible functions (see Volume II, section 4.4). Second, the signature (and return type) of the invocable callback defined in the interface of an event-driven library is unlikely to change from one release of the software to the next. By contrast, application clients partaking in this interface are at full liberty to adjust the functors they supply including the corresponding number of user-supplied arguments, which are, after all, essentially an implementation detail. Making clients change the headers they include whenever they change the number of optional arguments they provide would be both annoying and misguided.

Let's now consider that each concrete letter (and similarly for its corresponding factory function) is just a tiny template solving only a part of the problem it addresses directly and has absolutely no dependency on its peer solutions. Moreover, because both concrete letters and factory functions are templates, there is (at least under typical production/deployment scenarios) no issue of excessive coupling due to colocation: Each invoked (*dual-bindage*) factory function and method of the corresponding derived concrete letter class will be generated individually

---

[75] As of C++11, we have variadic templates, which (for C++ at least) obviate much of what would otherwise amount to colocation under the rubric of *single solution*.

and incorporated independently as needed (section 1.3.4). It is precisely this kind of scenario in which colocation under the *Single-Solution* criteria (see Figure 3-22a, section 3.3.1.3) is most indicated.

So how should we package our concrete letters? At least three plausible strategies for partitioning these 165 lightweight derived concrete letter class templates come to mind. Referring to Figure 3-35, we could group these concrete letters based on (1) the number of required arguments, (2) the number of additional, user-supplied arguments, or (3) the total (i.e., combined) number of required plus optional arguments.[76] All three of these suggested groupings might at first seem to produce essentially the same unbalanced result. Notice, however, that the combined choice (3) has the distinct advantage of enabling us to extend the total number of arguments to 10, 11, 12, etc., without touching existing code, simply by adding new components (but see the discussion regarding factory utility functions below).

(1) The number of required arguments			
(2) The number of additional, user-supplied arguments			
(3) The combined number of required and additional arguments			

component	(1) required	(2) additional	(3) combined
letter0	30	30	3
letter1	27	27	6
letter2	24	24	9
letter3	21	21	12
letter4	18	18	15
letter5	15	15	18
letter6	12	12	21
letter7	9	9	24
letter8	6	6	27
letter9	3	3	30
total:	165	165	165

Figure 3-35: Grouping concrete letter template classes into components

---

[76] For example, assuming we are allowing for up to a combined total of nine (required and user-supplied) argument representations for each of the three kinds of functions (i.e., free, `const` member, and non-`const` member), we can enumerate the combinations based on the total number of arguments (referred to as the *depth*; see Volume III, section 8.7) as follows. There will be three classes that take no arguments at all. There will be six classes that take one argument: Three will take a required argument and the other three will take a user-defined argument. There will be nine classes that take two arguments: Three will take two required arguments, another three will take one required and one user-defined argument, and the last three will take two user-defined arguments, and so on.

Let's now consider the corresponding utility functions and see if they shed some light on what might be the optimal grouping. Here there is a strong preference: We want to group the factory functions around the corresponding interface type, FunctorN. That is, we want to group these "populating" functions based on the number of *required* arguments. To see why, consider that any given service accepting a registration invokes its callback functor with a fixed number (and sequence of types) of *required* arguments as defined in its *interface*, which should not change (section 0.5). Any client contemplating the use of such a service will need to populate a functor of exactly that number (and those types) of required arguments, which fully implies which factory/utility component header to include.

Given that the number of any *additional* arguments is an implementation detail and much more readily subject to change, it would be silly to group the utility functions around that unstable characteristic, as changing the number of user-supplied arguments would then require the user to also change the #include directives! Minimizing the physical dependency of the utility components also leads us to reconsider our previous inclination to group the concrete letters based on the combined number of arguments, and instead group them according to the number of required arguments as well. With this packaging, each factory-function utility component need depend on only its *one* corresponding concrete letter component. Grouping based on required arguments is illustrated as choice (1) in Figure 3-35.

3.3.8.2   Aggregating Components into Packages

The classes (and functions) in each of the *letter* (and *factory*) components consisted of a regular collection of tiny peers, no one of which was independently useful, yet together formed a complete solution to a single problem: the implementation and factory for populating an envelope with a concrete letter having a specific number of required arguments. Our criteria for colocation improved usability, reduced physical complexity, and preserved optimal spatial and runtime efficiency. What we have yet to consider is whether these components belong in a single package, multiple packages, or even multiple groups (see Figure 2-72, section 2.9.3), and specifically where within the enterprise-wide structure they belong. Let's do that now.

Independent of the absolute location of these components, we must ask ourselves whether the physical dependencies vary radically from one component to the next. The answer is obviously no, and so we conclude that all of these components can properly reside within a single package group (section 2.9). Next, we consider what other components this collective facility depends on. The answer is that, apart from the low-level memory allocator protocol `bslma::Allocator` (see Volume II, section 4.10), not much. Given we believe that use of this subsystem could potentially extend to almost any domain, we might reasonably elect to place it at a fairly low level in our enterprise-wide physical hierarchy.

The next task is to determine what value, if any, there might be to distributing these components across two or more packages. Having all forty components in a single package is an outside possibility, but should this functor subsystem be extended — e.g., to introduce callbacks that return a value as opposed to only those that return `void` or, of course, to increase the maximum supported number of required arguments — the sheer number of components within the one package could become disproportionately large and cumbersome.

Conceivably one might opt to group each cluster of four components defined by the number of functor arguments within its own package. With our current maximum of nine total arguments, that grouping would result in ten packages, each having exactly four components. Such a modularization is not out of the question, but it fails to capture anything more than that these ten subsystems are independent. Moreover, having one package that will never have more than four components fails the long-term physical-fanout test (section 3.1.7).

Looking at this partitioning problem from an interface perspective, we see that the functor envelopes and utilities are entities familiar to outside clients, whereas the base representation and concrete letters are essentially implementation details. The concrete letters will be touched only by their corresponding utility functions. Along those lines, we might decide to divide these components into two packages, based on whether the components are used directly by outside clients or not. Since each required-argument slice in the family of functor component dependencies forms a diamond shape (see Figure 3-34, section 3.3.8.1), such a grouping seems quite plausible.

If we do decide that functors naturally span two packages as shown in Figure 3-36a — one representing the *interface* containing envelopes and utilities, and the other representing the implementation containing base representations and concrete letters — what would be the nomenclature? We might decide our two package prefixes will be **odef** and **odefi** (the additional **i** meaning implementation). What then will we name our components? In any two-package approach, the package is not sufficient to fully characterize the kind of component, so we will need to do that in the component name itself. For example, to describe components implementing functor envelopes taking two required arguments and returning `void`, we might settle on **odef_vfunc2** and **odef_vfunc2util**, respectively. By the same token, we might describe the corresponding base representation and concrete letter as **odefi_base2** and **odefi_letter2**, respectively. No dependency rules are violated, but how do we determine if this partitioning is optimal?

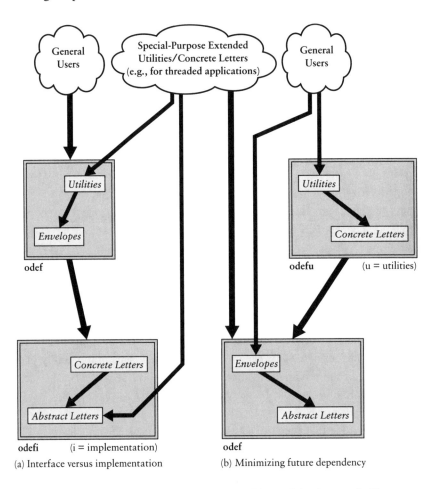

Figure 3-36: Alternative two-package partitions of the functor facility

Now suppose we consider the alternate packaging suggested in Figure 3-36b, with an eye toward extensibility and minimizing future dependencies. The envelopes are vocabulary types (see Volume II, section 4.4) whose contracts will almost certainly not change, nor will those of the abstract letters on which they depend. From a stability perspective (section 0.5), these components belong at a very low level. On the other hand, the concrete letters and utilities used to populate the envelopes with them are entirely extensible. In fact, there is no requirement that we use them at all.

While this functor facility is already fairly general, we might choose to implement (at a much higher level) a parallel set of concrete letters that explicitly support other features, say, an extensible locking mechanism for threaded applications. In that case, there would be no need for the utilities of Figure 3-36a; hence, this alternative dual-package-based partition enables such clients to avoid even coincidental dependence on such superfluous components.

Although having twenty components per package is probably close to ideal, we must also appreciate the powerful descriptive value (when appropriate) of the homogeneity of component types within a package. By distributing the four types of components into their own distinct packages, we markedly increase our ability to communicate: Our package-level vocabulary alone now suffices to fully characterize the components. What's more, we don't have to commit up front between the two modularizations in Figure 3-36.[77]

3.3.8.3   The Final Result

Given significant up-front thought, based solely on engineering reason, we have managed to arrive at the sound physical structure illustrated in Figure 3-37, in which 350 potentially separable logical entities are now consolidated into just forty components: ten *envelopes* (**odef**), ten *abstract letters* (**odefr**), ten *concrete letters* (**odefri**), and ten *factories* (**odefu**) distributed across four distinct packages. The apportionment of code was far from uniform. Functors with

---

[77] Again, this example is presented here for pedagogical purposes to illustrate optimal factoring of logical content across components and packages.

Relying on protocols (section 1.7.5) and virtual tables to provide runtime interoperability (see Volume II, section 4.6) would, in this case, likely prove prohibitively costly at run time, whereas use of a template ("policy") parameter (see Volume II, section 4.5) to achieve compile-time polymorphism and thereby generally enable inlining would necessarily invade the C++ type of the (not entirely abstract) "letters," which in turn would propagate up (and do likewise) to the concrete (*vocabulary type*) "envelopes" (see Volume II, section 4.4).

In practice, in order to achieve maximum performance for multithreaded use, we would implement thread-safe reference counting using atomic increment and decrement instructions on a counter embedded directly within the otherwise pure *abstract-letter* base class (see Volume II, section 4.7), unfortunately (but necessarily) adversely impacting performance in situations where such synchronization (e.g., single-threaded, even-driven programs) is not needed.

more required arguments necessarily require fewer factory methods and concrete letter classes. Still, this grouping was arguably a right choice given the competing design goals.

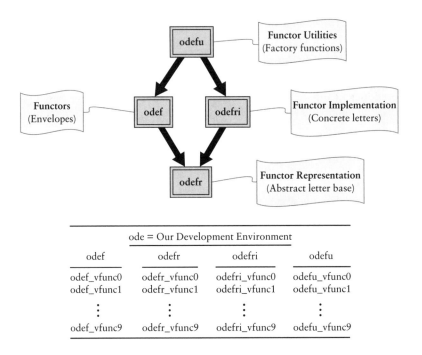

ode = Our Development Environment			
odef	odefr	odefri	odefu
odef_vfunc0	odefr_vfunc0	odefri_vfunc0	odefu_vfunc0
odef_vfunc1	odefr_vfunc1	odefri_vfunc1	odefu_vfunc1
⋮	⋮	⋮	⋮
odef_vfunc9	odefr_vfunc9	odefri_vfunc9	odefu_vfunc9

Figure 3-37: Package-level functor architecture

An important upshot of having all four package categories, in addition to flexible control over dependencies, is that the base name of every component in this extensible functor facility can be simply **vfuncN** where **N** is the number of required arguments (**v** indicates a void return type, leaving **rfuncN** available for non-void return values if needed). Notice also how the positional use of the character **f** in the package name achieves the tight logical association among a cluster of closely related packages within a larger package group, without having to resort to extra levels of explicit aggregation. Thoughtful grouping of classes and functions into components and packages makes our logical designs easier to comprehend and use.

To recap: This final example considered a specific instance of the envelope-letter pattern motivated by classical event-driven programming. We partitioned the 350 individual logical constructs of a general-purpose (reusable) family of reference-counted function objects (functors) into just forty components, based on logical cohesion and completeness. We then grouped these forty components into four packages that reinforced both vocabulary and characteristic dependencies. This rather long functor example typifies what we strive to achieve through fine-grained logical factoring and well-reasoned placement of logical content within physical modules.

3.3.9   Section Summary

To summarize this section, we presented four separate criteria that would justify colocating multiple public classes within a single component:

1. **Friendship** — I.e., so that logical encapsulation does not extend beyond the physical boundaries of a single component.

2. **Cyclic Dependencies** — I.e., so that logically interdependent constructs do not result in cyclically physical dependencies among distinct components (however, redesign is probably warranted).

3. **Single Solution** — I.e., to avoid useless physical complexity when individual logical constructs are independent peers, yet none of which is individually useful.

4. **Flea on an Elephant** — I.e., to allow for a tiny logical construct that depends on, and is typically used with, a much larger object, e.g., so that they can be documented together within a single usage example (see Volume II, section 6.16).

Auxiliary helper classes that, of necessity (i.e., not just due to laziness), have highly collaborative interfaces — especially when such interfaces are subject to change — are typically best kept private within the same component, e.g., using the extra-underscore convention (section 2.7.3), to ensure the stability of the overall component to external clients.

A "subordinate" component that is effectively an unstable implementation detail of another "client" component can often be profitably managed by placing it in the same package and using our double-underscore[78] naming convention (section 2.7.3) to ensure that it is usable only by that one local "client" component (section 2.7.5).

---

[78] Not to be confused with names containing two-consecutive underscores, which are reserved by the C++ language for use by implementers of the Standard itself.

Highly collaborative components that must be externally accessible and are also subject to change over time are far more maintainable when confined to a single UOR and ideally the same package.

Unlike utilities that provide arbitrary nonprimitive functionality on value-semantic types (see Volume II, section 4.3), components that are, by design, consumed syntactically (as well as semantically) in a highly uniform and regular way (e.g., generically) can sometimes benefit by being isolated within a package dedicated for that purpose, provided the anticipated physical dependencies of any one component do not exceed what has been specified as appropriate for the package as a whole. Common component-name prefixes within a single package can also be used to delineate such syntactic/semantic similarities.

Finally, it can be productive to exploit distinct package prefixes to identify categories of components in one dimension, while using components having corresponding base names (section 2.4.7) across all participating packages to identify another. Proper use of this approach to modularization requires that these syntactic aspects be essential (section 3.1.5) to the semantics of the architecture and that the resulting framework of packages and components is dead regular.

3.4   Avoiding Cyclic Link-Time Dependencies

Most likely you've been in a situation where you were looking at a software system for the first time and you could not seem to find a reasonable starting point or a piece of the system that made sense on its own. Not being able to understand or use any part of a system independently is a symptom of a *cyclically dependent* "design."

Consider the subsystem shown in Figure 3-38. A complex network can be modeled as a collection of subnetworks, devices, and cables. Consequently, a `Network` knows about the definitions of both `Device` and `Cable`. A device knows the network to which it belongs and can tell whether or not it is connected to a specified cable. Hence, a `Device` also knows about both `Network` and `Cable` types. Finally, a cable can be connected to a terminal of either a device or a network. Therefore, to do its job, a `Cable` must have access to the definitions of both `Device` and `Network`.

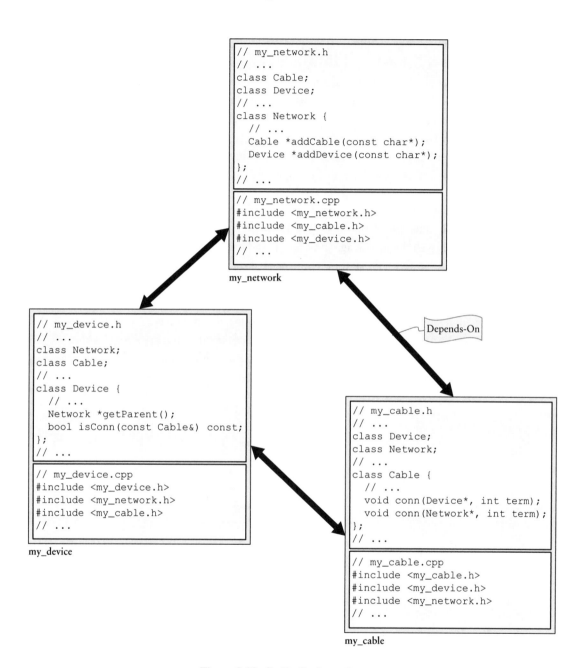

Figure 3-38: Cyclically dependent components

The definitions for each of these types reside in a separate component, ostensibly to improve modularity. Moreover, each of the other two classes is *locally declared*, avoiding cyclic includes within the preprocessor, but that doesn't make things right. Even though the implementations of these individual types are fully encapsulated by their public, programmatically accessible interfaces, the .cpp file for each component is nonetheless forced to include the header files of the other two. The physical dependency graph for these three components is *cyclic*, i.e., no one component can be used or even tested without the other two. For this and other practical reasons, our design rules proscribe (section 2.6) cyclic physical dependencies among components.

C++ objects have a phenomenal tendency to entangle themselves; designed naively, they will become tightly intertwined and fiercely resist decomposition. Consider the grossly simplified, and admittedly poor logical design provided for didactic purposes in Figure 3-39a. A *company* may have several accounts at various financial institutions. A (brokerage) *account* may, in turn, have several positions, each comprising a particular financial instrument (e.g., a *security*) and a quantity, e.g., of type double (but preferably a decimal floating-point type; **bde14**, subdirectory /groups/bdl/bdldfp/), indicating the number of units (e.g., shares) of that instrument. For accounting purposes, we might want to include the *date* on which the *position* was opened and the *price* that was paid. Each (Equity) security in our simplified model refers to exactly one underlying company, and thus the UML diagram is created.

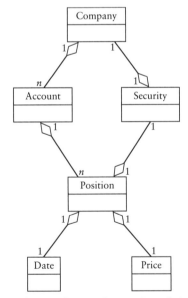

(a) Logical (UML) diagram showing class relationships

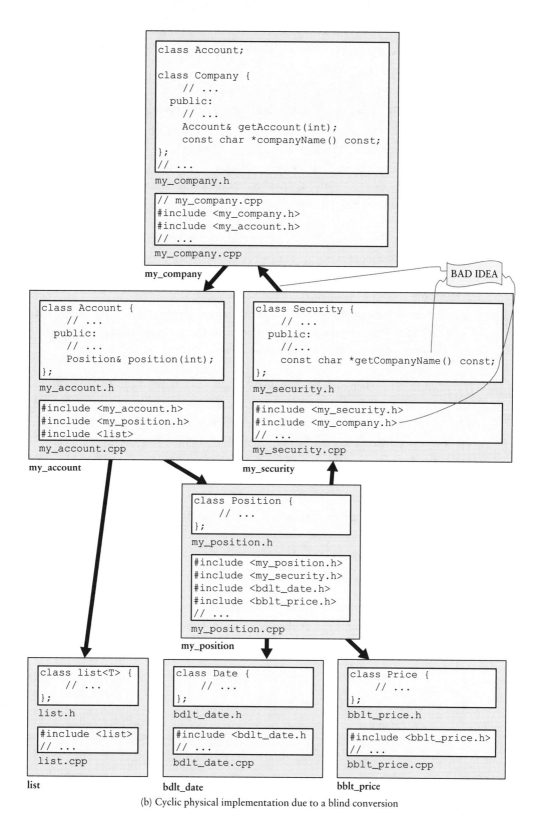

(b) Cyclic physical implementation due to a blind conversion

Figure 3-39: Cyclic physical realization of a naive entity/relation model

Figure 3-39b illustrates how a fairly straightforward translation to software could quite easily yield a cyclic physical dependency. In this admittedly (somewhat) contrived example, the class-level design shows that class `my::Company` *uses* the `my::Account` type, which, in turn, *aggregates* (via an `std::list`) instances of class `my::Position`. Examining the `#include` directives corroborates that the physical component labeled **my_company** depends on component **my_account**, which, in turn, depends on components **list** and **my_position**.

The `#include` directives further indicate that, in addition to depending on **bdlt_date** and **bblt_price**, component **my_position** depends on **my_security**. The crucial flaw, however, occurs when we allow class `my::Security` to *know* the definition of class `my::Company`, presumably in order to facilitate the implementation of the `my::Security::getCompanyName` accessor as a forward to `my::Company::companyName`. This final implied dependency (section 1.9) leaves components **my_company**, **my_account**, **my_position**, and **my_security** (physically) *cyclically dependent*!

There was a time when high-level logical designs often implied cycles. In the years following the publication of my first book,[79] it has become more and more widely recognized[80] that physical cycles implied at the logical level are bad (section 2.6), and many software designers are now actively avoiding them. Nonetheless, as high-level designs are fleshed out with more detailed specifications, the addition of organizational mechanisms and glue logic during development can sew together what would otherwise be a perfectly reasonable architecture. That is, even with a sound initial design, cycles tend to appear (1) as the details grow beyond what can reasonably be comprehended in a single diagram, (2) during the implementation phase, or (3) over time as the result of routine maintenance. Due diligence in the form of (efficiently) extracting actual dependencies (section 1.11) can help guard against such inadvertent mishaps.

Today, initial designs are often carefully planned and deliberately acyclic. In time, the unanticipated needs of clients can evoke less well-thought-out, tactical enhancements that introduce unwanted cyclic dependencies. For example, let us consider a firm-wide infrastructure

---

[79] **lakos96**

[80] **sutter05**, Chapter "Coding Style," Item 22, pp. 40–41, particularly p. 40:

> ...modules that are interdependent are not really individual modules, but super-glued together into what's really a larger module, a larger unit of release. Thus, cyclic dependencies work against modularity and are the bane of large projects. Avoid them.

containing the three separate, but widely used subsystems, **logger**, **transport**, and **mail**, illustrated in Figure 3-40. Sadly, these three subsystems are cyclically dependent, but they didn't start out that way. What's worse, with a proper understanding of *levelization techniques* (see section 3.5), no cycles would have been necessary. That said, let's take a look at how this inadvertent, not uncommon, and very unfortunate physical embroilment might have occurred.

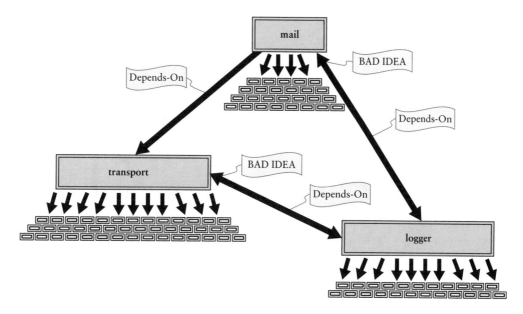

Figure 3-40: Cyclically interdependent subsystems (BAD IDEA)

Reliable transport, as we well know, is not easily achieved. Machines go down, connections are dropped, packets are lost, etc. When a problem occurs, we're going to want to know about it, when and where it happened, and so on. At the time we created the first version of our proprietary **transport** facility we did not, as yet, have a **logger** subsystem (Figure 3-41a).

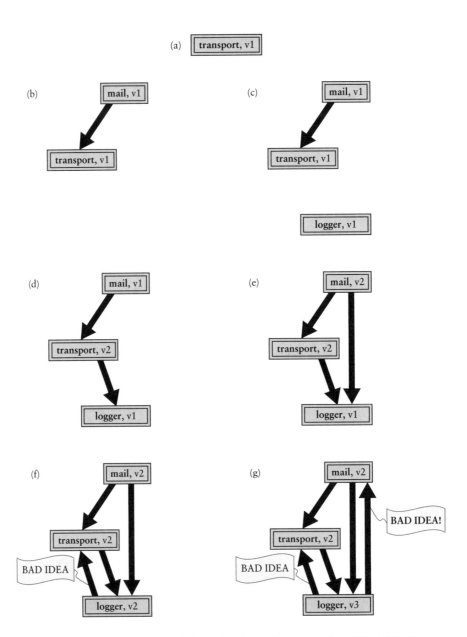

Figure 3-41: Cyclic physical dependencies evolving over time (BAD IDEA)

When something unexpected occurred, we just printed an error message to a local file (identified by an environment variable). Eventually it became clear that such a primitive solution was not adequate for our increasingly large development organization, and so a project to create a firm-wide **logger** facility was commissioned. Meanwhile, a separate project to provide an efficient firm-wide **mail** subsystem was completed and released (Figure 3-41b).

Given our glorious **transport** facility, no one even considered that there might someday be other, perhaps even significantly better ways in which email might be transmitted; hence, the **mail** subsystem was *layered* (see section 3.7.2) on top of the existing transport subsystem. Eventually the first version of the new **logger** subsystem is completed and released (Figure 3-41c).

This **logger** facility is intended to be used by applications and high-level library subsystems to extract and record information concerning the operation of a running program. An adjustable "debug" level per category (or *realm*) enables us to vary the amount and detail of information emanating from a particular subsystem. We can control these settings using environment variables, configuration files, or command-line arguments, but each of these approaches implies restarting the process. Later we might realize that we'll also need to be able to alter these settings while a given program is running (see below). Having now completed this powerful new **logger** facility,[81] the **transport** subsystem is upgraded to use it and a second version of **transport** is released (Figure 3-41d). Soon after, the **mail** subsystem is similarly upgraded (Figure 3-41e).

The nature of logging is such that efficient (inline) access to the underlying logging mechanism is an essential requirement. In particular, we will need to be able to determine instantly[82] whether a given logging statement will need to do anything at all and quickly skip over it if not. Hence, layering both the **transport** and **mail** subsystems directly on the **logger** facility is an appropriate design choice. Fortunately, there are still no cycles; the link line for a typical application built using the **mail** subsystem is straightforward:

```
$ ld main.o app.a ... mail.a tran.a log.a ...
```

---

[81] An open-source version of the **ball** (BDE Application Library Logger) package having a comparatively generous open-source license (suitable for most typical forms of commercial use) may be found in the **ball** package of the **bal** package group of Bloomberg's open-source distribution of BDE (see **bde14**, subdirectory /groups/bal/ball/).

[82] Accessing logging attributes is an ideal application for the effective use of lock-free data structures in multithreaded applications. For example, see **kliatchko07**.

Through use, it becomes apparent that having to bring down a running program in order to alter its logging attributes is not acceptable. It is proposed that the **logger** subsystem be upgraded to accept IPC connections and interpret received control messages in order to update the **logger**-configuration state on the fly. Given that there is currently only one subsystem that implements the needed IPC functionality, a quick decision is made to use **transport** to control the **logger**; however, these developers pay no attention to the physical consequences of allowing **logger** to use the **transport** subsystem directly. A second version of the **logger** facility is released. Unfortunately, we have now introduced a physical cycle between the **logger** and **transport** subsystems (Figure 3-41f).

Hence, there is no longer a guaranteed order in which the separate **transport** and **logger** libraries can be linked:

```
$ ld main.o app.a ... mail.a tran.a log.a ... tran.a log.a ...
```

Despite its physical encumbrance, the logger continues to be used. Over time, several development managers find that having to search for critical information in a log file is just too inconvenient. It is "suggested " (by senior management) that the **logger** subsystem be upgraded again — this time to allow it to send mail messages whenever a serious error occurs. Again, without considering the physical consequences, the existing **mail** subsystem is used — this time directly by **logger**. A third generation of the **logger** subsystem is released, but now there is a cyclic physical dependency involving all three major subsystems (Figure 3-41g).

The required library link order may vary from application to application, and even from one version of an application to the next:

```
$ ld main.o app.a ... mail.a tran.a log.a ... mail.a tran.a log.a ...
```

Link-time dependencies play a central role in establishing the overall *physical design quality*[83] of software. More conventional aspects of quality, such as understandability, maintainability, testability, and reusability, are all closely tied to the quality of the physical design. If not carefully prevented, cyclic physical dependencies will rob a system of this quality, leaving it inflexible and difficult to manage. In particular, a high degree of coupling associated with lower-level subsystems not only increases costs for those subsystems but can also dramatically increase the cost of developing and maintaining clients and subsystems at higher levels.[84]

---

[83] **lakos96**, section 4.13, pp. 193–201

[84] For quantitative examples of the costs associated with cycles, see **lakos96**, section 5.2, Figure 5-18, pp. 225–228.

Eliminating the cyclic dependencies among the **logger**, **transport**, and **mail** subsystems of Figure 3-40 is (perhaps) best achieved through use of the *callback* levelization technique (see section 3.5.7) using two abstract interfaces (see Figure 3-79, section 2.5.7.4.2): one for the (transport) `Channel` used to control the **logger** and one for the `Observer` used to publish logged messages. For each of these interfaces, a corresponding *adapter* (see section 3.7.5) is then supplied to the logger via a higher-level entity (e.g., `main`). From each *protocol* (section 1.7.5), we derive a concrete class that adapts the respective mechanism (i.e., the **transport** or **mail** subsystem) to that protocol. Such use of abstract interfaces and adapters will result in what we will call a *lateral* architecture (see section 3.7.5).

A word of caution (echoing warnings in **lakos96**) regarding the use of callbacks to break cycles[85]:

> Within my own team, we've seen what can be succinctly called "technically acyclic, but nonetheless cyclic designs." This happens when someone mechanically uses callbacks to break cyclic dependencies without addressing the underlying enmeshment between components. These systems are frequently even harder to understand than the cyclic ones they replaced! This is because the extra indirection of the callback makes it that much more difficult to follow the code flow.
>
> — David Sankel, Bloomberg LP (c. 2018)

In other words, there are potentially severe consequences for using callbacks to break cyclic dependencies without addressing the underlying design issues.

To summarize: cyclic physical dependencies, even if not present initially, can — over time — emerge and become a significant problem with respect to human understanding and future maintenance. In the following (atypically lengthy) section, we present a comprehensive treatment of a proven suite of *levelization* techniques that, over the years, has been used successfully to help engineer acyclic physical designs. Explicitly avoiding cyclic dependencies is an essential first step to building physically sound systems, but alone is not sufficient to mitigate the costs and risks associated with software development on an industrial scale. We must also deliberately and proactively avoid excessive (see section 3.6) or otherwise inappropriate *noncyclic* link-time dependencies (see section 3.8). The techniques that follow will prove useful for those purposes as well.

---

[85] From David Sankel's review of the manuscript for this volume

3.5   Levelization Techniques

Achieving software designs that avoid cyclic physical dependencies among cohesive physical modules, such as components, packages, and package groups, is arguably the single most important aspect of successful large-scale software design.[86] Classical development practices — particularly when applied to object-oriented software — tend to result in designs that are highly physically interdependent.

3.5.1   Classic Levelization

Nine general categories of techniques have been identified[87] as being useful for detangling physical interdependencies. These established *levelization techniques* are summarized in Figure 3-42.[88] Using such techniques to create *levelizable* designs tends to reduce the large, sometimes overwhelming, logical design space, and helps to guide developers in the direction of more maintainable architectures. It turns out that there is a "serendipitous synergy" between good *logical* design and good *physical* design; in time, and with experience, one finds that these two important design goals will come to reinforce one another.

---

[86] Note that we said design, not development. When we widen the scope to incorporate development, we must also consider having well-trained individuals, taking the long view, actually documenting and testing our code, etc. All of the techniques presented here are design techniques and have been around since I published my first book, *Large-Scale C++ Software Design*, in 1996. When I started to write **lakos96**, it was originally expected that it would be called *Large-Scale C++ Software **Development***. I explained at the time, however, that, while I believed I had deep understanding of how to design software, especially in C++, I did not yet feel ready to embark on a book that addressed more general aspects of development. Finally, some 20-odd years later, I did.

[87] **lakos96**, Chapter 5, pp. 203–325

[88] Borrowed from **lakos96**, section 5.11, pp. 524–525, specifically the unnumbered list on p. 525.

Escalation	Moving mutually dependent functionality higher in the physical hierarchy
Demotion	Moving common functionality lower in the physical hierarchy
Opaque Pointers	Having an object use another in name only
Dumb Data	Using data that indicates a dependency on a peer object, but only in the context of a separate, higher-level object
Redundancy	Deliberately avoiding reuse by repeating small amounts of code or data to avoid coupling
Callbacks	Client-supplied functions that enable (typically lower-level) subsystems to perform specific tasks in a more global context
Manager Class	Establishing a class that owns and coordinates lower-level objects
Factoring	Moving independently testable sub-behavior out of the implementations of complex components involved in excessive physical coupling
Escalating Encapsulation	Moving the point at which implementation details are hidden from clients to a higher level in the physical hierarchy

Figure 3-42: Summary of standard levelization techniques. (Lakos, John, *Large-Scale C++ Software Design,* © 1996. Reprinted and electronically reproduced by permission of Pearson Education, Inc., New York, NY.)

In the years since these levelization techniques were first published, they have been used repeatedly to achieve sound physical architectures. To this author's surprise, no profoundly new levelization techniques have emerged. Given the advances in distributed computing and even the language itself (e.g., member templates), the relative importance (and application) of some of these techniques has, however, shifted. For example, the use of (generalized) callbacks is becoming a far more common and necessary design practice. In what follows, we will present what we consider the important aspects of these techniques today. Readers interested in additional examples presented at somewhat greater length are directed to the seminal work on this subject.

3.5.2   Escalation

Moving mutually dependent functionality higher in the physical hierarchy.

The first, and still one of the most commonly used, *levelization techniques* is called *escalation*. The basic idea is that, when two components want to refer to each other, there might be some aspect of one or both of the components that can be moved to a higher level in the physical hierarchy. By *escalating* such aspects, we transform an awkward *mutual* dependency into a welcome *downward* one.

A classic example of the need for escalation can be found in two separate classes `Rectangle` and `Box`, illustrated abstractly in Figure 3-43a. Both of these classes are intended to represent the same *value* (see Volume II, section 4.1), but each concrete class has a distinct internal representation (Figure 3-43b), leading to different performance characteristics.

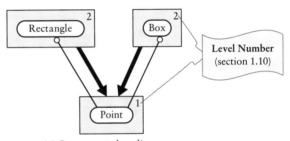

(a) Component-class diagram

```
// rectangle.h
// ...
#include <point.h>
// ...
class Rectangle {
    Point d_origin;
    int   d_width;
    int   d_length;
  public:
    Rectangle();
    Rectangle(const Point& origin,
              int          width,
              int          length);
    // ...
};
// ...
```

```
// box.h
// ...
#include <point.h>
// ...
class Box {
    Point d_lowerLeft;
    Point d_upperRight;
  public:
    Box();
    Box(const Point& lowerLeft,
        const Point& upperRight);
    // ...
};
// ...
```

(b) Elided component interfaces

Figure 3-43: Two different ways to represent a rectangular shape

Initially, these two classes may have been physically independent; over time, however, the need to convert from one to the other will inevitably become apparent (see Volume II, section 4.4). Introducing (implicit) mutual constructors, each referencing the other type, as shown in Figure 3-44b, immediately produces a cyclic interdependency between their respective components (Figure 3-44a).

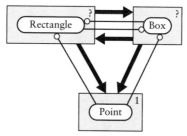

(a) Component-class diagram

```
// rectangle.h
// ...
#include <box.h>
// ...
class Rectangle {
    // ...
    Rectangle(const Box& value);
    // ...
};
// ...
```

```
// box.h
// ...
#include <rectangle.h>
// ...
class Box {
    // ...
    Box(const Rectangle& value);
    // ...
};
// ...
```

(b) Elided component interfaces

Figure 3-44: (Unacceptable) cyclic physical dependency

Having a cyclic physical dependency is unacceptable (sections 1.8, 1.9, and 2.6). Instead, we might have chosen to implement one of the classes in terms of the other, thereby eliminating any cyclic dependency. For example, we could have decided that Rectangle was the more primitive of the two classes and pushed all of the conversion functionality into Box, as illustrated in Figure 3-45. Note that, in this rendering, box.h includes rectangle.h to enable inline conversions of Rectangle to and from Box; as a result, making any change to rectangle.h will force all clients of Box to recompile. Also note that, even though rectangle.h happens to also include point.h (today), we deliberately include point.h directly in box.h to avoid a *transitive include* (section 2.6) lest that implementation detail subsequently change, thereby causing our **box** component not to compile.

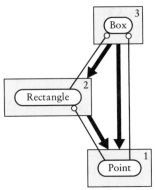

(a) Component-class diagram

```
// rectangle.h
// ...
#include <point.h>
// ...
class Rectangle {
    // ...
  public:
    Rectangle();
    Rectangle(const Point& origin,
              int        width,
              int        length);
    // ...
};
// ...
```

```
// box.h
// ...
#include <point.h>
#include <rectangle.h>
// ...
class Box {
    // ...
  public:
    Box();
    Box(const Point& lowerLeft,
        const Point& upperRight);
    Box(const Rectangle& value);
    // ...
    operator Rectangle() const;
    // ...
};
// ...
```

(b) Elided component interfaces

Figure 3-45: `Box` (and its clients) depends on `Rectangle`, but not vice versa.

Another possibility, shown in Figure 3-46, is that we decide that Box is the more fundamental and widely used class, and — while we are at it — we also decide to *insulate* (see sections 3.10 and 3.11) clients of Rectangle from changes to Box, provided, of course, that they don't also choose to use Box directly. That is, for clients that do not use **box** directly, changes to box.h will not force them to recompile.

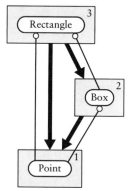

(a) Component-class diagram

```
// rectangle.h                          // box.h
// ...                                  // ...
#include <point.h>                      #include <point.h>
// ...                                  // ...
class Box;                              class Box {
// ...                                      // ...
class Rectangle {                         public:
    // ...                                    Box();
  public:                                     Box(const Point& lowerLeft,
    Rectangle();                                  const Point& upperRight);
    Rectangle(const Point& origin,          // ...
              int        width,        };
              int        length);
    Rectangle(const Box& value);
    // ...
    operator Box() const;
    // ...
};
// ...
```

(b) Elided component interfaces

Figure 3-46: `Rectangle` (and its clients) depends on `Box`, but not vice versa.

Although either of the two previous solutions are viable, a typically better, more fine-grained and decoupled solution is to *escalate* all of the mutually interdependent functionality to a higher-level component in the physical hierarchy — e.g., to a new **convertutil**, as shown in Figure 3-47.

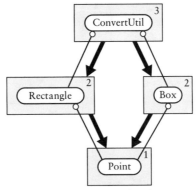

(a) Component-class diagram

```
// convertutil.h
// ...
#include <rectangle>
#include <box.h>
#include <point.h>
struct ConvertUtil {
    static Box boxFromRectangle(const Rectangle& value);
    static Rectangle rectangleFromBox(const Box& value);
    // ...
};
```

```
// rectangle.h                        // box.h
// ...                                // ...
#include <point.h>                    #include <point.h>
// ...                                // ...
class Rectangle {                     class Box {
    // ...                                // ...
  public:                              public:
    Rectangle();                        Box();
    Rectangle(const Point& origin,      Box(const Point& lowerLeft,
            int       width,                const Point& upperRight);
            int       length);          // ...
    // ...                             };
};                                     // ...
// ...
```

(b) Elided component interfaces

Figure 3-47: `Rectangle` and `Box` are mutually independent types.

Note that, in the rendering shown in Figure 3-47b, we have chosen to have `convertutil.h`
`#include` (rather than locally declare) the definitions of both `Rectangle` and `Box`,
in anticipation of implementing the two conversion routines, `boxFromRectangle` and
`rectangleFromBox`, as `inline` functions. Also note that, because class `Point` would

be used directly in the implementation (bodies) of those inlined routines, we are required to include `point.h` (defining class `Point`) directly in `convertutil.h` as well, rather than relying on either `rectangle.h` or `box.h` (illicit *transitive inclusion*) to do so. Hence — irrespective of whether or not either of `rectangle.h` or `box.h` chooses to include `point.h` — `convertutil.h` is assured of self-sufficiency with respect to compilation (section 1.6.1) as required (section 2.6).

Another common use of the *escalation* levelization technique has been to extract the creation of concrete nodes from the abstract base class from which they are derived and place them in a higher-level *factory* component. Consider a subsystem consisting of (1) an abstract base class, `Widget`, (2) a collection of derived classes `WidgetN`, and (3) a suite of `static` factory methods used to create and configure these specific widgets, returned via a (managed) pointer to their common abstract base type. Choosing to place those `static` factory methods within the abstract `Widget` base class would cause cyclic dependencies, not only between the base class and each derived class, as illustrated in Figure 3-48a, but, consequently, via transitivity (section 1.8) also among all of the derived widget classes!

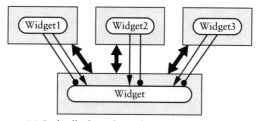

(a) Cyclically dependent subsystem (BAD IDEA)

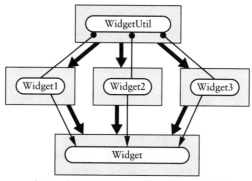

(b) Acyclic physical rendering (GOOD IDEA)

Figure 3-48: Escalating creation above use

One of the essential benefits of the object-oriented programming paradigm is that not every client of a derived object needs to know its concrete type, let alone be able to create one. Colocating the functionality to create derived types within the same component that allows clients to use them eliminates virtually all of the practical advantages *pure* interface inheritance affords (see Volume II, section 4.7) over merely switching on type. By simply escalating the `static` factory methods to a higher-level component, say **widgetutil** as illustrated in Figure 3-48b, we eliminate all physical cycles, allow each client to depend on only what is needed, and do so without sacrificing any logical functionality whatsoever!

Yet another effective use of the *escalation* levelization technique is to isolate nonprimitive (section 3.2.7) heavyweight dependencies (section 1.9) along with other kinds of problematic physical dependencies. As a simplified illustration, suppose we have a dead simple `Date` class comprising nothing more than `year`, `month`, and `day` attributes that may or may not represent a valid date value. Given such an *unconstrained attribute class* (see Volume II, section 4.2), any functionality other than to set or access the values of its attributes, obtain its memory allocator (were one needed), or compare two objects of class `Date` for equality (section 3.3.1.4) would be considered nonprimitive and properly reside in a higher-level component.

Now suppose that we want to implement an `isValidYearMonthDay` function for our naive `Date` class. All the `Date` class knows about is that it has three attributes: `year`, `month`, and `day`; it doesn't know the calendar to which they might pertain (e.g., Gregorian, proleptic Gregorian).[89] Placing that functionality with the `Date` class would restrict the class's ability to participate in other calendar contexts. What's more, there is no performance advantage to adulterating this simple, pristine attribute class with functionality that might just as well be implemented externally.

Assuming that we have settled on the proleptic Gregorian calendar for our utility functions, we can move the `isValidYearMonthDay` function and all other functionality that is based solely on the date's three attributes and expressible with no additional types to a higher-level

---

[89] Unlike the (classic) Gregorian calendar, which has eleven missing days in 1752 starting with September 3rd, and prior to that date treats every century year (e.g., 1700) as a leap year, the proleptic Gregorian calendar treats every block of 400 years the same, where years divisible by 4 are leap years unless they are also divisible by 100 (in which case they're not) unless they're also divisible by 400 (in which case they are). For all dates in the modern era, there is no difference; the difference shows up, however, when trying to express the number of days difference between a reference date and the current one whenever the reference date predates that gap in September, 1752: The number of days difference is two greater for the Gregorian calendar than it is for the proleptic Gregorian one (see **iso04**, clause 4.3.2.1).

component, **dateutil** — residing in the same package — as illustrated in Figure 3-49; see (a). Similarly, functionality such as finding the last day of the month for a supplied date according to that same calendar would also reside in DateUtil. In this way, we decouple functionality that need not have intimate access to the implementation for performance and/or is not an intrinsic part of the functionality being supplied and documented.

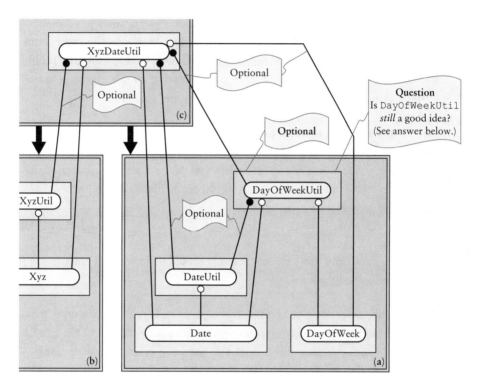

Figure 3-49: Escalating wider-scope and/or heavyweight functionality

Going a step further, we can imagine a DayOfWeek enumeration that is used to represent the day of the week corresponding to a given date. The component implementing DayOfWeek (e.g., see Figure 2-40, section 2.6) is clearly independent of both Date and the particular calendar being employed. If we want to provide functionality to determine the day of the week for a specified date, we could place that functionality in DateUtil, but that would introduce a logical, and therefore a physical, dependency of DateUtil on DayOfWeek. Given that DateUtil depends on no other types, we might instead elect to place that functionality in a new, higher-level component implementing, say, `DayOfWeekUtil`, which would be free to depend on both `Date` and `DayOfWeek`, and perhaps even `DateUtil` (if needed). Other functionality found in `DayOfWeekUtil` might include finding the *n*th day of the week in the month and year of a given `Date`.

Whether or not to partition functionality at this level of granularity is a matter of engineering judgment. Breaking code apart to this degree, while appropriate in theory, can make it more difficult for prospective "real-world" clients to know where to look for specific functionality, which in turn could make such finely factored library code more difficult to use. According to Jeffrey Olkin (in his review of the manuscript for this volume):

> If I am trying to find a function to determine the day of week, I will most likely look in `DateUtil` if I have used it before for other functions. I might not even know that `DayOfWeekUtil` exists, and though I might be surprised that such a function isn't in `DateUtil`, it would not automatically follow that I would look for another, related component.
>
> —Jeffrey Olkin (c. 2017)

Hence, the granularity to which functionality should be factored in practice can involve a measure of "art" as well as science.[90]

In this specific case, however, creating two separate utility `struct`s in order to factor nonprimitive functionality based solely on whether a specific utility function on a `Date` does or doesn't use `DayOfWeek::Enum` in its interface is not only practically undesirable — for reasons of discoverability, delineated by Jeffrey Olkin (above) — but unwarranted from a physical perspective as well!

First, the perceived intimate relationship between `Date` and `DayOfWeek` alone (ignoring its potential performance advantage for serial-date-based implementations) has already been deemed sufficient to justify that the `Date` class itself be allowed to incorporate `DayOfWeek::Enum` in its own interface (e.g., see Figure 3-102, section 3.6.1, and Figure 3-152, section 3.12.3), thereby eliminating virtually all physical advantages of virtually all subsequent factoring in higher-level utilities.

---

[90] To be fair, David Sankel points out (in his review of the manuscript for this volume) that, "While what Jeffrey has said is true, users of software written like this should immediately go to package-level and then group-level documentation [see Volume II, section 6.15] if they can't find what they are looking for."

Second, not only is `DayOfWeek::Enum` far more entwined semantically with `Date` than would a, say, `MonthOfYear::Enum` (see Figure 3-164, section 3.12.9.1), in typical usage, it will turn out that, unlike a, say, `DayOfMonth::Enum`, use of `DayOfWeek::Enum` by `Date` is inherently primitive (section 3.2.7). For example, given a serial-date implementation (see Figure 3-169b, section 3.12.11.2), the cost of returning the correct day of a week, instead of having to perform a comparatively complex arithmetic calculation can potentially reduce to just a single modulus operation:

```
DayOfWeek::Enum dayOfWeek() const
{
    return static_cast<DayOfWeek::Enum>(d_serialDate % 7);⁹¹
}
```

Such ultra-high runtime performance would simply not be possible when implemented externally to the component defining `Date`. For these reasons, the initial temptation to fully factor our utility `struct`s based on interface dependencies that are already shared by the flagship value type should ultimately be suppressed, and common nonprimitive functionality that uses only the types already used in the interface of `Date`, such as `DayOfWeek::Enum`, should reside side-by-side in the utility `struct DateUtil`⁹² (e.g., see Figure 3-165, section 3.12.10).

None of the functionality so far adds significant physical dependency, but such is certainly possible and occurs all too frequently in practice. Recall from Figure 2-74, section 2.9.3, that logical cohesion alone is not necessarily sufficient justification to colocate functionality within a single unit of release. Suppose we have a component **xyz** that has significant physical dependencies unrelated to **date**. We naturally expect that such a component would reside in a separate physical package (if not package group) as illustrated in Figure 3-49; see (b). Nonprimitive functionality pertaining to just **xyz**, however, would naturally reside along with it in the same package, but in a separate component implementing `XyzUtil`. To avoid implying that either **xyz** or **date** are required in order to use the other, we would choose to *escalate*

---

⁹¹ This implementation works provided that we have carefully established that a `d_serialDate` of 0 aligns with the 0th enumerator in `DayOfWeek`, which would warrant a rather emphatic IMPLEMENTATION NOTE so that no developer maintaining the component later inadvertently breaks this requirement. Note that the code here would necessarily be more complex for a nonproleptic implementation.

⁹² Note that providing this extra level of guidance here regarding when to (and when not to) factor utility `struct` functionality based on interface dependencies is entirely due to the thorough review process that every section in this volume has undergone by my brilliant *structural editor* (and dear friend), Jeffrey Olkin.

the (nonprimitive) functionality that depends on both **xyz** and **date** to a higher-level package defining **xyzdateutil** as suggested in Figure 3-49; see (c). In this way, we can more precisely choose to incorporate, at compile and link time, only what we truly need.

In short: *escalation* is often a great way of turning problematic mutual dependencies into welcome downward ones. When we see what appears to be an upward dependency between two components, we can often factor the lower-level one and introduce an even higher-level third component in which all of the dependencies are downward (and acyclic). The act of *escalating* nonprimitive functionality to a higher-level *utility* in the same package is, or should be, standard practice. If we see that we are introducing additional types (even from the same package) into the interface of a utility, we might want to consider *escalating* that functionality to a separate, higher-level utility component (perhaps in the same package) to support that more expansive interface. Finally, if we are considering placing functionality within an existing utility that would cause excessive coupling across UORs, we should seriously consider *escalating* that heavyweight functionality to yet another utility component located in a higher-level UOR.

3.5.3   Demotion

Moving common functionality lower in the physical hierarchy.

Demotion is the levelization technique in which functionality is refactored and placed lower in the physical hierarchy, most usually to enable wider use (reuse). For example, subsystem **xyz** in Figure 3-50a implements a piece of low-level functionality, F, that it uses internally, but is also needed by subsystem **rst** upon which subsystem **xyz** depends. Other clients of F are forced to depend on all of **xyz** and, therefore, indirectly on **rst** as well. By demoting F to a lower-level package, **abc**, as shown in Figure 3-50b, components in both **xyz** and **rst** can depend on F in **abc** without any package cycles. Moreover, other clients of F no longer need depend on **xyz** or **rst**.

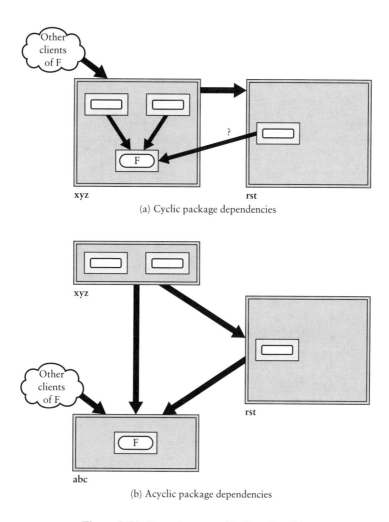

(a) Cyclic package dependencies

(b) Acyclic package dependencies

Figure 3-50: Demoting reusable functionality

A similar kind of cyclic dependency can occur at the object level. Consider a parent object, EventQueue, that manages many subordinate objects of an Event type, which is defined in a separate component. Information specific to an event is stored directly in each event's corresponding object, while information that is common to all events managed by the event queue are stored once, directly within the EventQueue object. When an event is passed to a function for processing, all of the information associated with the event, including the common information stored in the EventQueue object itself, must be available through the public interface of Event.

Figure 3-51 illustrates a straightforward way of implementing these components that satisfied the functional requirements, but results in a cyclic physical dependency between the respective components implementing EventQueue and Event. The problem arises because the Event type holds a pointer to the entire `EventQueue` object that manages it. All that is actually needed by an `Event` object, however, is to hold a pointer to the subportion of the `EventQueue` containing the common information.

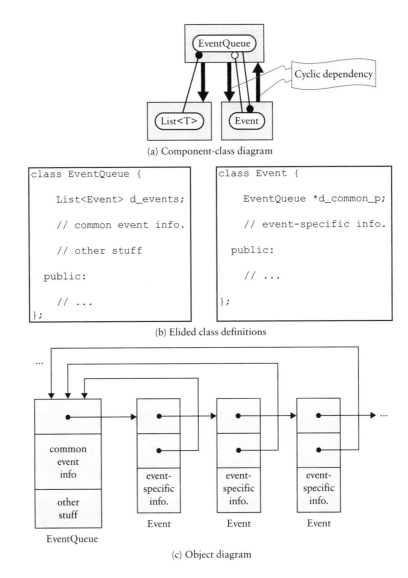

(a) Component-class diagram

```
class EventQueue {

    List<Event> d_events;

    // common event info.

    // other stuff

  public:

    // ...
};
```

```
class Event {

    EventQueue *d_common_p;

    // event-specific info.

  public:

    // ...
};
```

(b) Elided class definitions

(c) Object diagram

Figure 3-51: Cyclic `EventQueue`/`Event` implementation (BAD IDEA)

An acyclic solution is surprisingly simple. By factoring the common event information into a separate `CommonEventInfo` class, and demoting it to a physically separate component, as shown in Figure 3-52, we achieve our functional goal of allowing clients of `Event` to access all of the needed information, while avoiding a *design* cycle between EventQueue and Event. An alternative, *physically* acyclic solution employing *opaque pointers* is presented in section 3.5.4.2.

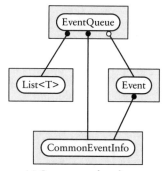

(a) Component-class diagram

```
class EventQueue {

    List<Event>      d_events;

    CommonEventInfo d_info;

    // other stuff

  public:

    // ...

};
```

```
class Event {

    CommonEventInfo *d_common_p;

    // event-specific info.

  public:

    // ...

};
```

```
class CommonEventInfo {

    // common event info.

  public:

    // ...

};
```

(b) Elided class definitions

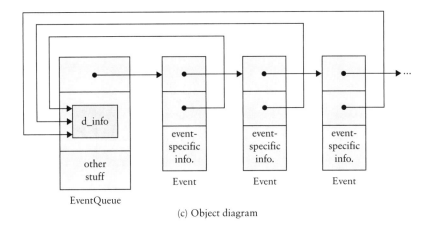

(c) Object diagram

Figure 3-52: Levelized `EventQueue` implementation (FINE)

3.5.4   Opaque Pointers

Having an object use another in name only.

The idea behind the *opaque-pointers* levelization technique is that we will declare the type of an object locally, but in no way will we depend on its definition in order to compile, link, or test the (local) component. Hence, this anomalous use of (opaque) pointers gives rise to the special symbol

used to describe an interface dependency that is *in-name-only* (section 1.7.5).

3.5.4.1   Manager/Employee Example

Recall, from Figure 3-3, section 3.1.8, the example of two cyclically dependent components respectively defining classes `Employee` and `Manager`. Here we simply reprise the explanation of the use of the *opaque-pointer levelization* technique discussed there, albeit more laconic in its commentary, and illustrated from a different, more architectural perspective.

Imagine a situation in which we have a `Manager` class that is responsible for the lifetimes of `Employee` objects. Suppose that both of these types reside in their own respective components. Also assume the requirement that an external client be able to learn the number of employees who report to a given employee's manager from any one of its employees alone — e.g., the `Employee` object is passed (by reference to `const` — a.k.a. by "`const` reference"; see Volume II, section 5.8) as the only argument to a one-parameter function.

Having a direct method on `Employee` such as `numStaff`, as depicted in Figure 3-53b, implies not only that each `Employee` be imbued with the address of its manager (at construction) but also that the component defining the `Employee` class `#include` the header defining the `Manager` class, thereby inducing a cyclic physical dependency between the respective components defining `Manager` and `Employee`, as illustrated in Figure 3-53a.

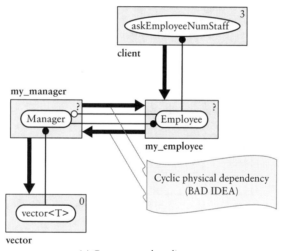

(a) Component-class diagram

```
// my_manager.h
#include <my_employee.h>
#include <vector>
// ...
class Manager {
    std::vector<Employee> d_staff;
  public:
    // ...
    int addEmployee(/*...*/);
    const Employee& employee(int id) const;
    int numStaff() const;
    // ...
};
```

```
// my_employee.h
#include <my_manager.h> ──  Problem
// ...
class Employee {
    Manager *d_boss_p;
  public:
    Employee(Manager *boss /* , ...*/);
    // ...
    int numStaff() const; ──  Problem
};
```

```
// client.h
#include <my_employee.h>
// ...
inline
int askEmployeeNumStaff(const Employee& employee)
{
    return employee.numStaff();
}
```

(b) Elided component header files

Figure 3-53: Cyclic rendering of manager/employee functionality (BAD IDEA)

Being an inherently lower-level entity, the employee simply cannot tell the (higher-level) manager what to do directly but is perfectly able to identify the manager via its opaque address (i.e., without having to #include the my_manager.h header). This new design requires a higher-level client function, e.g., askEmployeeNumStaff (Figure 3-54b), to rephrase the question to first ask the Employee object for its Manager object's address and then use that address (now in the context of the definition of the Manager class's definition) to ask that Manager object directly for the number of Employee objects it manages. The resulting levelized component-class diagram is shown in Figure 3-54a.[93]

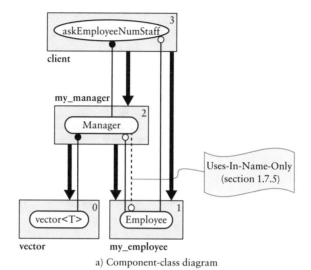

a) Component-class diagram

[93] As ever, care must be taken to ensure that an opaque pointer (which clearly doesn't manage its resource), just like any other raw pointer, not continue to be used substantively (e.g., by anyone else) beyond the lifetime of the object to which it refers.

```
// my_manager.h
#include <my_employee.h>
#include <vector>
// ...
class Manager {
    std::vector<Employee> d_staff;
  public:
    // ...
    int addEmployee(/*...*/);
    const Employee& employee(int id) const;
    int numStaff() const;           Public
    // ...                          accessor
};
```

```
// my_employee.h
// ...                              Local declaration
class Manager;
class Employee {                    Opaque
    Manager *d_boss_p;              pointer
  public:
    Employee(Manager *boss /* , ...*/);
    // ...
    const Manager *manager() const { return d_boss_p; }[94]
};
```

```
// client.h
#include <my_employee.h>
#include <my_manager.h>
// ...
inline
int askEmployeeNumStaff(const Employee& employee)
{
    return employee.manager()->numStaff();
}
```

(b) Elided component header files

Figure 3-54: Acyclic rendering of manager/employee functionality

---

[94] Note that we deliberately return a `const Manager` pointer from this `const` (*accessor*) method in order to preserve `const` correctness (see Volume II, section 5.8); by requiring a non-`const` pointer at construction (and storing it as such internally), we preserve the option to add a non-`const` (manipulator) overload returning a non-`const Manager` later (see Volume II, section 5.5).

3.5.4.2   Event/EventQueue Example

As a second example of effective use of in-name-only dependencies, consider the `Event` object from the *Demotion* solution above (see Figure 3-52, section 2.5.3), which needed full definitional knowledge, but to only a part of the parent `EventQueue` object. Suppose instead that the contained `Event` object is required to provide access to the entire `EventQueue` object but itself does not require knowing any of its parent's definition. In that case, the subordinate `Event` object can hold just an opaque pointer to its parent in order to provide clients of both with full-blown access, as shown in Figure 3-55a.

Entirely analogous to the `numStaff()` method in the `Manager` class above (Figure 3-54b, section 3.5.4.1), assume that an `EventQueue` implements a public `int numEvents() const` method. Providing such a method on an `Event` itself would require `Event` to have definitional knowledge of its parent `EventQueue`, causing the components defining these two types to be cyclically dependent. If, however, an `Event` object instead holds only the opaque address of its parent — i.e., without having a `#include` of the `EventQueue` definition anywhere in the component that defines `Event` — then `Event` can provide this opaque address to the higher-level client, which *does* `#include` the parent definition and so can now use that `EventQueue` address to invoke the `numEvents` method on the `EventQueue` object directly.

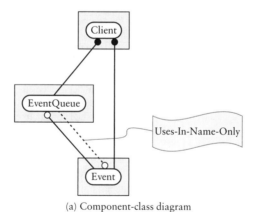

(a) Component-class diagram

```
// ...

class EventQueue;

class Event {

    EventQueue *d_parent_p;

    // ...

  public:

    Event(EventQueue *parent /* , ...*/);⁹⁵

    // ...

    EventQueue *parent();

    // ...

    const EventQueue *parent() const;⁹⁶

    // ...
};

// ...
```

(b) Elided component defining class Event

Figure 3-55: Holding an opaque "back" pointer

---

[95] Depending on the `const`-ness of the "view" of the `Event` object the `EventQueue` object happens (or is able) to provide, a returned `Event` reference may or may not afford non-`const` access that could, in turn, enable a client of that `Event` to mutate the `EventQueue`. In anticipation that mutating as well as non-mutating views of `Event` objects are possible, the (compile-time) type of the "back" pointer passed into the `Event` object at construction is non-`const` — much like how a private data member that is only sometimes modifiable is maintained internally as non-`const`.

[96] Note that the `Event` class deliberately provides two parallel methods for obtaining the parent pointer in order to preserve an important property known as *const correctness* (see Volume II, section 5.8). An object of a type, X, having this property ensures that a function taking just a single `const` reference to X is not able — without explicit casting or global access — to obtain a non-`const` reference to that same object (or portion thereof) from within the function body. Although the queue itself — `const` or not — always constructs the `Event` object with a non-`const` back pointer, it will return the `Event` as non-`const` only if it itself is non-`const`, otherwise it will return that very same address `const`-qualified, thereby ensuring overall `const` correctness.

Notice that, had the `Event` been implemented with just a single method

```
EventQueue *parent() const;
```

we could then easily (even inadvertently) construct a function, call it `stripConst`, that takes an `EventQueue` object by `const` reference and returns (or uses locally) the same object by non-`const` reference without the need for either explicit casts or global access (provided, of course, that the event queue is not currently empty):

```
EventQueue& stripConst(const EventQueue& q)                    (BAD IDEA)
{
    return *q.firstEvent()->parent();  // 'const'-correctness violation
}
```

For the original, detailed definition and exposition of the term *const correctness*, see **lakos96**, section 9.1.6, pp. 605–612.

3.5.4.3 Graph/Node/Edge Example

A similar approach can be used to create a graph consisting of collaborative, yet physically independent, nodes and edges, as illustrated in 3-56a. For example, a `Node` (Figure 3-56b) is implemented as just a collection of opaque `Edge` pointers indicating adjacent edges. An `Edge` (Figure 3-56c) consists of "edge data" plus exactly two opaque `Node` pointers: `head` and `tail`. We can implement — and even thoroughly test — `Node` without ever having seen the definition of `Edge` and vice versa.[97] It is up to the higher-level `Graph` (*manager*, see section 3.5.8) object (Figure 3-56d) to ensure that the `Node` and `Edge` objects that represent a given graph object's *value* (see Volume II, section 4.1) remain in a consistent state.[98]

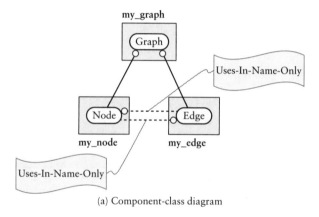

(a) Component-class diagram

---

[97] While this particular levelization technique might not be our first choice when designing from scratch, it is a valuable technique — especially when evolving a previously cyclic design, or one in which the external specifications dictate unfortunate Uses-In-The-Interface relationships among the various types. In particular, it preserves many of the existing logical properties (e.g., the ability of a client to invoke `const` methods on `Node` or `Edge` objects within a graph, given just a single reference), while also enabling independent, thorough testing of each of these piece parts. Note that this design does not attempt to mock friendship, as each of the subcomponents are stable and could be used in other similar data structures if such were appropriate. In short, this example serves as more of an illustration of what can be done, rather than a full-throated recommendation to do so.

[98] Note that we were able to achieve this goal and even return a non-`const` `Edge` pointer (primarily for illustration purposes) by setting the connectivity of an `Edge` *only* at construction and never returning a modifiable `Node` in the interface of `Graph`, which makes this sort of solution of limited utility in practice. This approach can, however, be easily generalized by providing all appropriate non-`const` `Node` and `Edge` functionality in `Graph` itself, using `const` pointers as iterators. For another, even more general solution to this specific problem, see Figure 3-94, section 3.5.10.2.

```
// my_node.h

// ...

#include <vector>

class Edge;

class Node {
    std::vector<Edge *> d_edges;

  public:
    Node();

    // ...

    void appendEdge(Edge *edge);

    Edge *edge(int edgeIndex);

    // ...

    int numEdges() const;

    const Edge *edge(int edgeIndex) const;
};

// ...
```

Note that this method cannot be applied to a Node maintained by a Graph directly but can instead be invoked (indirectly) via the appendEdge method of Graph; see (d), below.

(b) Node class holding opaque Edge pointers

```
// my_edge.h

// ...

class Node;

class Edge {
    double d_weight;  // edge data

    Node *d_head_p;
    Node *d_tail_p;

  public:
    Edge(Node *head, Node *tail);

    // ...

    void setWeight(double);

    // ...

    double weight() const;

    const Node *head() const;
    const Node *tail() const;
};

// ...
```

Notice that Node connectivity is established only upon the construction of an Edge. (This otherwise arbitrary constraint serves to simplify the example but also makes it somewhat less general.) Also note that this constructor cannot be invoked on an existing Node object within a Graph externally (as Graph exposes only const Node references), yet can be invoked internally via the appendEdge method of Graph; see (d), below.

(c) Edge class holding opaque Node pointers

```
// my_graph.h

// ...

#include <my_node.h>
#include <my_edge.h>
#include <list>

// ...

class Graph {
    std::list<Node> d_nodes;
    std::list<Edge> d_edges;

  public:[99]
    Graph();

    // ...

    const Node *appendNode();

    // ...




    Edge *appendEdge(const Node *tail,
                     const Node *head,
                     double      weight = 0.0);

    void setWeight(const Edge *edge, double weight);

    // ...

    int numNodes() const;
    int numEdges() const;
};
// ...
```

> We are using `std::list` instead of `std::vector` here (usually a bad idea) because we never want the address of any of these objects to change when a new one is appended.

> There is, by design, no way to obtain modifiable access to a Node in this graph. Hence, there is no way to invoke a non-`const` method, such as addEdge, on such a Node object directly; however, a (higher-level) appendEdge method resides in Graph, which takes two (const Node *) pointers as iterators, and invokes the (lower-level) addEdge accordingly.

> We need this method because, when traversing a graph, we will have only `const` access to its nodes and edges. Using a `const` edge pointer as an iterator enables us to set an existing edge object to an arbitrary weight value.

(d) Graph class managing sets of Node and Edge objects

Figure 3-56: Nodes and edges holding *opaque* "lateral" pointers

---

[99] An alternative design, especially given C++11 or later, might be something like an `std::vector` of `std::unique_ptr<Node>`.

Note that a coherent `Graph` object would never return a *null* `Node` or `Edge` object; hence, we might instead decide that all such objects returned from a `Graph` are done so by reference (as opposed to by address), which makes testing in isolation a tad more tricky, but not insurmountably so.[100] When it comes to representing nontransient data, however, consistently using pointers instead of references has other benefits. For example, what if we wanted to represent a vector of (un-owned) "out-of-place" elements in order to ensure that their respective addresses remained stable when other elements were added or removed:

```
std::vector<const Element *> elements;
```

We clearly cannot use a reference in this case. Other than to serve as either a `const` or *modifiable* "view" (especially with respect to a particular function call), references — due to their inherent limitations and complex semantics — are rarely preferable to pointers for representing data.

3.5.5   Dumb Data

Using data that indicates a dependency on a peer object, but only in the context of a separate, higher-level object.

The *dumb-data* levelization technique is an alternative to *opaque pointers* that, while substantially less type-safe, has the important property of being **fully** *value semantic* (see Volume II, section 4.1). For example, let's consider again how we might implement the `Graph` subsystem of Figure 3-56, section 3.5.4.3, but this time without the use of opaque pointers, such that the nodes and edges each separately represent a value that is independent of the currently running process. The idea is that conventional values such as integers and strings, though deliberately meaningless to the objects that hold them, can be understood by a client, in a higher-level context, to refer to other objects of types whose definitions are not known by the subordinate objects.

---

[100] As long as we don't do anything other than take the address of an object returned by reference, we are not (at least in practice) invoking (language) undefined behavior even if that address — e.g., `0x0` or `0xDeadBeef` (due to alignment) — could never have been that of a valid object. The same applies when an invalid address is passed by reference through the interface of a function so long as that reference is not used other than to recover the supplied address. Note that this is a gray area of the C++ Standard, but a non-issue when used for testing purposes. The purist's alternative (one that is *guaranteed* to be portable) is to create a dummy (or "mock") `Node` (or `Edge`) class in the test driver of the other component and then use the addresses of objects of that dummy type for testing purposes.

Figure 3-57a represents the new component-class diagram based on a dumb-data implementation. A `Node` class (Figure 3-57b) is now represented as an array of integer indices into some (unknown) sequence of `Edge` objects. Similarly, an `Edge` class (Figure 3-57c) is now represented as a "weight" plus a pair of integer indices identifying (albeit in a higher-level context) the adjacent `Node` objects corresponding to the respective head and tail of this edge. If we want, we could even map a negative index value onto an unconnected `head` or `tail`; the interpretation of this data is entirely in the hands of the parent (*manager*) `Graph` class.

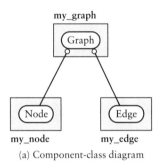

(a) Component-class diagram

```
// my_node.h

// ...

#include <vector>                    ┌─ Note that we no longer
                                     │  declare Edge locally.

class Node {
    std::vector<int> d_edgeIds;      ┌── Notice that a node in this graph
                                     │   no longer relies on fixed
  public:                            │   addresses for any adjacent edges.
    Node();

    // ...

    void appendEdge(int edgeId);     ┌── Note that we no
                                     │   longer have both
    // ...                           │   non-const and
                                     │   const versions
    int numEdges() const;            │   of member functions
                                     │   identifying edges
    int edgeId(int edgeIndex) const; │   adjacent to this node.
};

// ...
```

(b) `Node` class holding *dumb* edge "pointers"

```
// my_edge.h

// ...
            Note that we no longer
            declare Node locally.
class Edge {
    double d_weight;  // edge data

    int d_headId;
            Notice that an edge in the
            graph no longer relies on
            fixed addresses for its
    int d_tailId;
            adjacent nodes.

  public:
    Edge(int headId, int tailId);

    // ...

    void setWeight(double);

    // ...

    double weight() const;

    int headId() const;

    int tailId() const;
};

// ...
```

(c) Edge class holding "dumb" Node IDs

```
// my_graph.h

// ...

#include <my_node.h>
#include <my_edge.h>
#include <vector>

// ...

class Graph {
    std::vector<Node> d_nodes;
    std::vector<Edge> d_edges;

  public:
    Graph();

    // ...

    int appendNode();

    int appendEdge(int tailId, int headId, double weight = 0.0);



    Edge *edge(int edgeId);

    // ...

    int numNodes() const;
    int numEdges() const;

    const Node *node(int nodeId) const;

    const Edge *edge(int edgeId) const;
};

// ...
```

Note that we are no longer concerned about resizing our collections of nodes and edges, but now we are depending on O[1] access to the node or edge corresponding to its associated index.

Notice that we have provided two methods to return edge addresses given edge IDs, but only one such method for nodes. Also note that all corresponding pointers are invalidated whenever a node or edge is appended.

(d) Graph class managing *sequences* of Node and Edge objects

Figure 3-57: Holding dumb data instead of opaque "lateral" pointers

Notice that, unlike with the opaque-pointer levelization technique, there isn't even a (collaborative) local declaration of the other (Node or Edge) class type. Instead, the Graph object (Figure 3-57d) holds indexable sequences of both Node and Edge objects, which it maintains in a consistent state. When a method of Graph needs to find the node to which a given edge refers, it simply extracts the headId from the edge and uses that integer as an index into the sequence of Node objects maintained by the parent graph. This same basic technique is used to look up the adjacent edges of a given Node object.

For example, suppose we want to write a function to get the weight of the first edge adjacent to a (connected) node in a graph. With opaque pointers, all the client function needs is to be in the context of the definition of Node and Edge as illustrated in Figure 3-58a. Note that, with the *opaque-pointer* levelization technique, no knowledge of the parent graph's definition is required. When the *dumb-data* levelization technique is used, however, the client will need to know the context in which that data is to be interpreted. Although there is absolutely no knowledge whatsoever shared between the components implementing Node and Edge, objects of these types are able to collaborate, albeit indirectly, via their parent Graph object to achieve the desired results. Hence, the Graph object will have to be part of the client function's signature, as illustrated in Figure 3-58b.

```
// client.cpp

#include <my_node.h>
#include <my_edge.h>

double firstEdgeWeight(const Node *node)
{
    return node->edge(0).weight();                              // Opaque Pointers
}
```

> Desired weight information is accessible directly from the supplied Node independently of the Graph type.

(a) Implementation based on the *opaque-pointer* levelization technique

```
// client.cpp

#include <my_node.h>
#include <my_edge.h>
#include <my_graph.h>

double firstEdgeWeight(const Graph& graph, const Node *node)
{
    return graph.edge(node->edgeId(0))->weight();              // Dumb Data
}
```

> Must now also include my_graph.h; however, my_edge.h and my_node.h are still required.

> Parent Graph object must be supplied along with a Node.

(b) Implementation based on the *dumb-data* levelization technique

Figure 3-58: Contrasting client use of opaque pointers versus dumb data

Note that, in addition to including my_graph.h in Figure 3-58b, we are still required to include both my_node.h and my_edge.h directly, so as to satisfy the design rule (section 2.6) that states that clients must include directly what they use substantively (see Figure 2-45, section 2.6).

3.5.6   Redundancy

Deliberately avoiding reuse by repeating small amounts of code or data to avoid coupling.

Intentional *redundancy* is not so much a levelization technique as it is just basic common sense. Not all code is reusable, and even where it is, it might not be worth reusing from its current location. If using a particular piece of code in place would cause excessive, let alone cyclic, physical dependencies, we are far better off demoting (duplicating if necessary) that code to a lower level in the physical hierarchy. This kind of *continuous refactoring* often leads, at least temporarily, to two similar modules: the one in which the functionality was conceived and first introduced and the other one, properly located within the firm-wide repository of Software Capital (section 0.9). Accepting that there may — at least for some period of time — need to be a redundant implementation of the same functionality enables us to avoid the much more distasteful alternative of repeating some incarnation of the high-level implementation across an unbounded number of applications.

On the other hand, the mere existence of this technique does not give license to quotidian copy-paste as an expedient alternative to due diligence. If another technique, such as demotion, is practicable, it should almost always be employed. If the functionality being duplicated must necessarily remain in lockstep with the original functionality, any use of this technique is highly suspect. It is only when all other avenues have been explored, and a collective determination is made to apply this technique should it be deemed safe to do so.

For example, suppose we have, say, 20 clients using a relatively heavyweight subsystem, Subsystem A (Figure 3-59a), and, say, 200 clients using a relatively lightweight subsystem, Subsystem B (Figure 3-59b). Let's now consider two scenarios involving direct reuse versus redundancy. First let's assume that Subsystem A is being upgraded and that some reusable component in Subsystem B is appropriate — as is — for use in Subsystem A. If, for whatever reason, the reusable functionality cannot be demoted, should Subsystem A be allowed to depend on Subsystem B (A → B) or should the reusable code be duplicated? The answer to this question is that it is *probably* OK for Subsystem A to depend on Subsystem B; however, the final determination should take into account the specifics of all of the functionality involved.

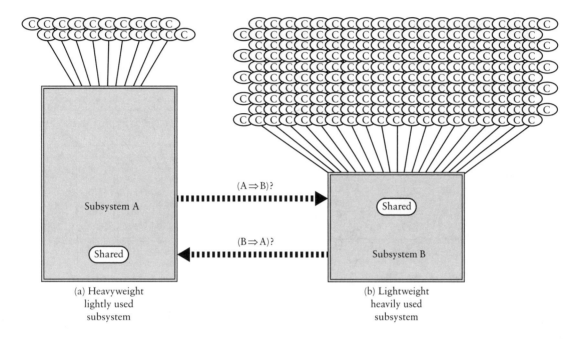

Figure 3-59: Using redundancy to avoid dependency

Now let's reverse the question and ask if, given that we find functionality in Subsystem A useful, should Subsystem B be allowed to depend on Subsystem A (B → A), or should that functionality be duplicated? The answer to this question will most likely depend on whether the component in question implements a *vocabulary type* — one used widely in the interface of functions (see Volume II, section 4.4). Without a compelling reason to do otherwise, we should be much less happy about allowing Subsystem B to depend on Subsystem A than vice versa. That is, if something other than a *vocabulary type* in Subsystem A cannot be *demoted* (i.e., moved to a mutually lower-level subsystem) immediately, we would almost certainly be better off duplicating, at least temporarily, that functionality in Subsystem B, rather than allowing Subsystem B and all of its many clients to inherit such a heavyweight dependency on Subsystem A. Again, the long-term best solution in either case, where practicable, is to demote the common (i.e., redundant) functionality to a lower level in the physical hierarchy (Figure 3-50, section 3.3), as illustrated in Figure 3-60.

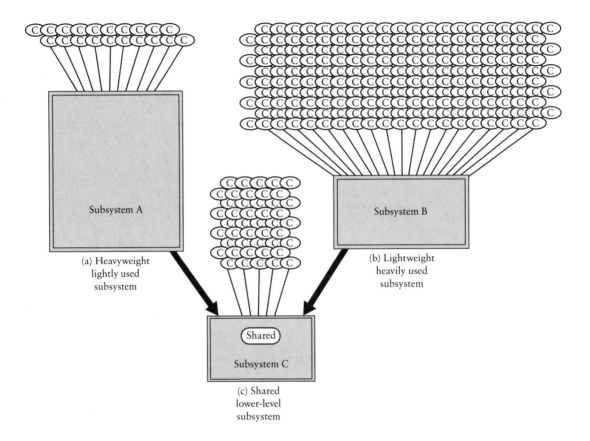

Figure 3-60: Preferring demotion over redundancy for avoiding dependency

As a second example, consider the scenario of Figure 3-61 in which we show two separate subsystems where one, Subsystem B, clearly and naturally depends on the other, Subsystem A. Now suppose that there is a tiny subset of functionality implemented, albeit more perfectly, completely, and naturally, in the higher-level Subsystem B that is later realized to be needed by the inherently lower-level Subsystem A — e.g., in order to be self-sufficient and thus reusable independently by other subsystems.

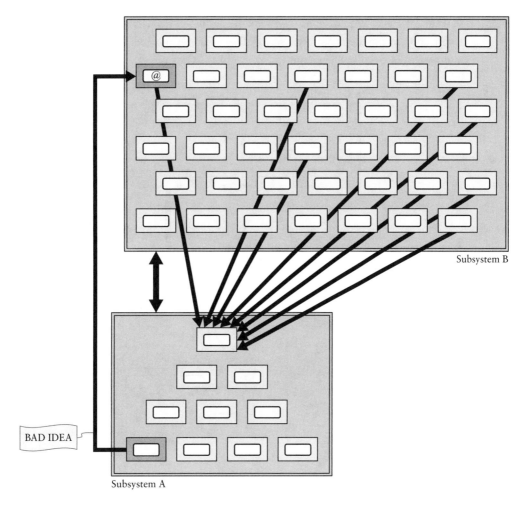

Figure 3-61: Blind reuse where it is counter-indicated (BAD IDEA)

Rather than naively opting for the short-term expedient of reusing the full-fledged functionality supplied by Subsystem B in place, and thereby tying all clients of Subsystem A to a physical dependency on Subsystem B, it is virtually always far better to extract, from the implementation of an inherently higher-level subsystem, the tiniest bit of functionality needed by the lower-level one, and without necessarily feeling obliged to eventually reuse it from the higher-level subsystem. In this way, we allow, as Figure 3-62 depicts, additional independent clients (e.g., Subsystem C) of the lower-level subsystem (Subsystem A) yet do not preclude future clients (e.g., Subsystems D, E, and F) from opting for the enhanced, more robust functionality afforded by the higher-level one (Subsystem B) if needed, and without our being fanatically obsessed with reusing every conceivable line of code regardless of the resulting collateral damage.[101] Regardless of your own experience, judicious use of a touch of redundancy as a levelization technique is not necessarily always bad design and is occasionally the only viable alternative, especially when augmenting established designs.

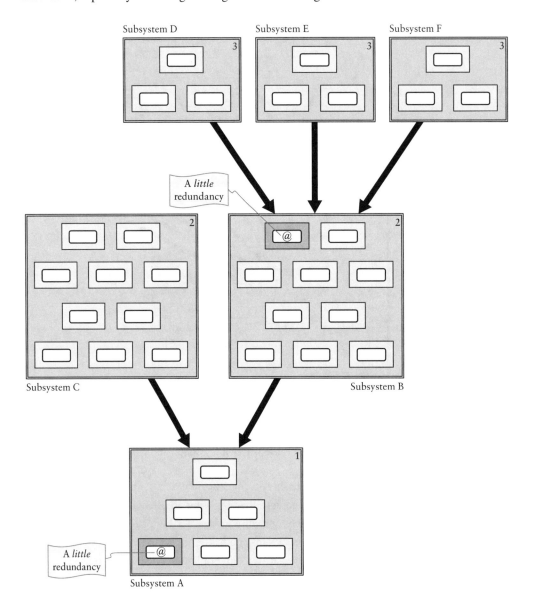

Figure 3-62: Using a *little* redundancy to avoid a *big* upward dependency

---

[101] There are those who have worked on a large codebases at both ends of the reuse spectrum: (1) places where reuse of every conceivable line of code is more or less a "fanatical obsession" and (2) places where duplication of code

3.5.7   Callbacks

Client-supplied functions that enable (typically lower-level) subsystems to perform specific tasks in a more global context.

In the years since we first published these nine levelization techniques, the use of *callbacks* in both single- and multithreaded applications has grown from a method of last resort to a first-class design strategy. The original motivation of a callback as a levelization technique was to allow a function, provided by a client, to be executed at a higher level — e.g., in the context of that client. At first, such use (misuse) of callbacks was to superficially reverse the direction of dependency of a misplaced member function. Since those early days, however, the scope and utility of callbacks has changed and they are now widely understood to include both functions and function objects[102] (i.e., "functors"; section 3.3.8), which can be bound not only at run time (e.g., via an abstract base class) but also at compile time (e.g., via a method template).[103] In what follows, we will explore five different flavors of callbacks used for levelization purposes as summarized in Figure 3-63.

1. **Data**	Passing the address of a modifiable object
2. **Function**	Passing the address of a (stateless) function
3. **Functor**	Supplying a (possibly stateful) *invocable* ("function") object
4. **Protocol**	Passing the address of a (typically) stateful concrete object accessed via the interface of a pure abstract base class
5. **Concept**	Supplying a (typically) stateful concrete object satisfying both structural and semantic requirements

Figure 3-63: Different flavors of "callbacks" used for levelization purposes

---

is standard procedure. Invariably, those who are "reuse obsessed" will tell you with absolute certainty that the drawbacks of sometimes taking reuse a bit too far pale in comparison to "duplication acceptance," where code is routinely forked and diverges. We do not disagree, but the advice here is much more nuanced than that. Again, if once in a great while, a tiny bit of redundancy is the only way to avoid a major design cycle, then do that! But if there is another way (e.g., say a practicable demotion), it's almost certainly a better alternative and one should always prefer doing that instead — even if it takes significantly more effort.

[102] Function objects and function pointers are *callables*. All callables and member function pointers are *invocable*.

[103] C++11 introduces a popular new syntax, known as *lambdas,* for concisely expressing the behavior of functors as inline code.

3.5.7.1   Data Callbacks

Perhaps the most trivial of "callbacks" is to pass the address of some storage, maintained at a higher level, down into a function that manipulates it.[104] We do this sort of thing routinely when, as illustrated in Figure 3-64, we provide an output object (particularly one that involves memory allocation; see Volume II, section 4.10) as the first argument to a function (e.g., returning status; see Volume II, sections 6.11–6.12) to decouple the supplier from the consumer.

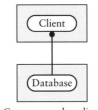

(a) Component-class diagram

```
void Client::doSomething()                              Higher-level object
{
    std::vector<std::string> answer;
    const char               criteria = "...";
    Database                 database;

    // Initialize/configure 'database'.

    int status = database.query(&answer, criteria);
    // ...
}
```

(b) Client function

```
class Database {
    // This concrete class provides a high-level interface for the ...

    // ...        Address of higher-level object

  public:
    // ...

    int query(std::vector<std::string> *result, const char *filter);
        // Load, into the specified 'result', the data collected by ...
};
```

(c) Database class

Figure 3-64: Decoupling suppliers from consumers via result-object addresses

---

[104] We readily acknowledge that referring to this subtechnique of levelization as a "data callback" is nonstandard and perhaps confusing — especially given that data is not *callable* in the conventional sense. We decided to put it here anyway. As Bjarne Stroustrup himself oft says (e.g., **stroustrup14**, p. 264), "You have been warned."

An approach similar to the one discussed above might have been used to untangle the cycle between Manager and Employee, as previously presented and solved using opaque pointers (section 3.5.4.1), but this time without having to fundamentally change the way clients interact directly with an Employee object. Suppose that, instead of passing in the address of the entire Manager object during the construction of each Employee object (Figure 3-54, section 3.5.4.1), we pass a reference to only the (private) integer data member of Manager responsible for keeping track of the current number of employees, as illustrated in Figure 3-65.[105]

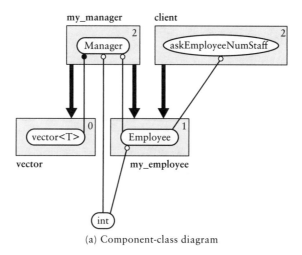

(a) Component-class diagram

---

[105] Note that the size attribute of the std::vector used to manage the Employee objects might hold this same information (redundantly), but we are unable to pass a reference to that attribute of std::vector directly given its current (standard) interface. As it turns out, however, returning the address of the internally stored size of a vector could lead to a trap if objects of the Manager class itself were to reside in a container, such as an std::vector, that, if resized, could change the location of the vector's size data member in memory. To ensure that this approach is safe under all such circumstances, it is essential that the "shadow" size "data member" (managed by the Manager class, to which the supplied back pointer refers) is *not* part of the Manager object's footprint, but instead is itself allocated dynamically, thus preserving its address if the Manager object itself moves.

```
// my_manager.h
#include <my_employee.h>
#include <vector>
class Manager {
    std::vector<Employee> d_staff;
    int d_numStaff = 0;                  New (possibly redundant) data member
  public:
    // ...
    int addEmployee(/*...*/);            Must update d_numStaff!
    const Employee& employee(int id) const;
    // ...
};
```

```
// my_employee.h
class Employee {
    const int *d_addrNumStaff_p;         Initialized at construction
  public:
    Employee(const int *addrNumStaff /* , ...*/);
    // ...                                        Data
    int numStaff() const { return *d_addrNumStaff_p; }   callback
};
```

```
// client.h
#include <my_employee.h>
inline
int askEmployeeNumStaff(const Employee& employee)
{
    return employee.numStaff();
}
```

(b) Elided component header files

Figure 3-65: Acyclic rendering of manager/employee functionality

Notice that, in this new design, there is no reference to the Manager class in the **my_employee** component — not even In-Name-Only! Instead of having a pointer to its parent class, Employee now has a pointer (providing nonmodifiable access) to just the parent's d_numStaff data member (of fundamental type int). With this address in hand, we are now free to implement the numStaff accessor directly — entirely within the Employee class (as originally desired) — but now without incurring a design cycle between Employee and Manager.

Note that the net effect of this data callback technique, as Figure 3-65a suggests, is similar to *demotion* (e.g., see Figure 3-52, section 3.5.3) in that a lower-level type (in this case the fundamental type `int`) was separated out and referred to by both `Manager` and `Employee`. Note also that this data callback was possible because it involves variation in only value, not behavior[106]:

> Use data members for variation in value; reserve virtual functions for variation
> in behavior.
>
> — Tom Cargill (c. 1992)

When the callback represents variation in behavior, however, some form of functional callback will be required.

3.5.7.2 Function Callbacks

Function callbacks are a classic yet powerful technique for decoupling libraries and frameworks from the clients they serve. For example, the traditional `qsort` library function from C requires that (the address of) a user-supplied comparison ("callback") function be provided (at run time) by clients in order to determine the relative order of two "elements" (i.e., like-sized regions of memory). This callback function is a true function, having all of the overhead associated with creating an activation record on the program stack and invoking a function via an arbitrary pointer.

By contrast, the `std::sort` function takes, as a (compile-time) template parameter, the type of an (invocable) entity (i.e., function pointer or function object) that will be used to determine the relative order of two elements (objects).[107] Making the source code of the comparison operation of a supplied "functor" (as opposed to function pointer) visible to a client's compiler when the `sort` function is instantiated makes it feasible on virtually all tool chains to eliminate the substantial invocation overhead of a conventional callback function. That is, enabling the client's compiler to `inline` the implementation of this very frequently invoked callback operation into the `sort` algorithm often results in significant performance gains when compared to a conventional C-style function callback.

---

[106] **cargill92**, section "Value versus Behavior," pp. 16–19, specifically p. 17 (see also p. 83 and p. 182)

[107] It is worth mentioning that `std::sort` also takes a runtime object of the comparator parameter's type, thus allowing for the possibility of a stateful callback (not recommended; see Volume II, section 4.5).

Conventional *function* callbacks are nonetheless useful, particularly when it comes to designing large systems. First, C-style callbacks can be used to achieve late binding. That is, the particular function being executed as a callback can be determined at run time. Second, such callback functions can be used to satisfy the open-closed principle (section 0.5). That is, a function of the appropriate structure (i.e., signature and return type) can be used to extend the functionality of preexisting library software without having to modify it in any way. Third, these runtime callbacks are inherently more scalable because their use does not imply (re)compilation of potentially vast amounts of software, but instead only (re)linking it. Even more than the first, it is this final property that turns out to be most significant in practice at distinguishing a *function* callback from its more localized, *functor* counterpart.

3.5.7.2.1   The Callback Lives with `main()`

For example, suppose we start out with a robust reusable library. We then create an application that uses this library. At the highest level, we have a single file, `main.cpp`, to bring it all together. Over time, it is observed that sometimes things go wrong: we run out of available memory, a function is called out of contract (see sections 5.2 and 5.3, and Volume II, section 6.8), or — for whatever reason — the software simply cannot proceed. A (poor) decision is made to introduce an "up call" from the library to the application (e.g., the file `main.cpp` defining `main()`, the entry point to the program), which is required to define a specific (named) function declared as

```
void saveAndExit();
```

to handle such cases. This very unfortunate state of affairs is illustrated in Figure 3-66.

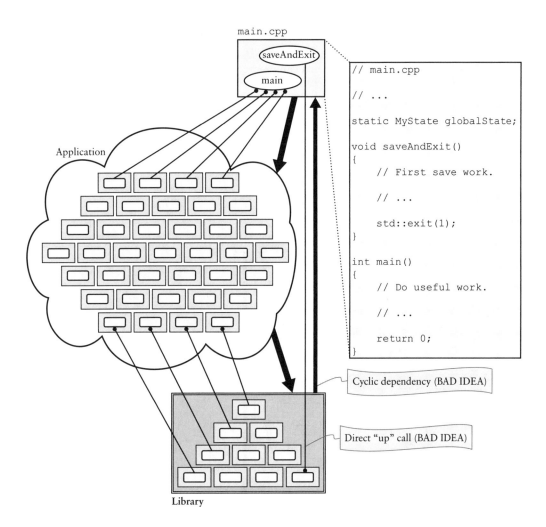

Figure 3-66: Cyclic dependency resulting from a direct "up call" (BAD IDEA)

Introducing an upward call from a library is a highly misguided expedient that should essentially always be dismissed out of hand. Instead, the library should be enhanced to accept a user-specified callback function (e.g., via a `set_lib_handler`[108] function) as illustrated in Figure 3-67. This client-specified callback will necessarily be established by `main` or at least by

---

[108] It has been suggested that a less innocent-sounding name, such as `set_fatal_exit_handler`, should be used in order to draw attention to such abject chicanery.

the owner of `main`, in order to ensure ubiquitous interoperability (see section 3.9). The name of the callback now becomes moot; only the structure remains relevant. What's more, the callback no longer requires global linkage and can be declared `static` within the file defining `main`.

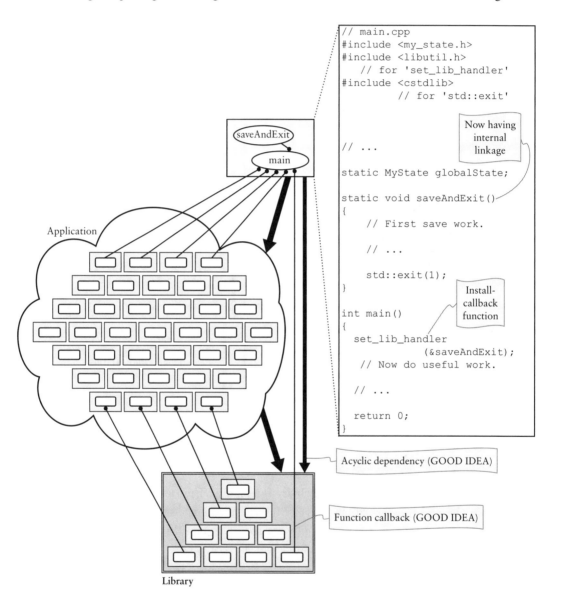

Figure 3-67: Effective (acyclic) use of function callbacks in `main`

Function callbacks have also been used historically to facilitate concurrency. As we saw in section 3.3.8.1, runtime functions (see Figure 3-31) and functors (see Figure 3-33) are supplied by clients of an event manager (see Figure 3-30b) to allow for processing in response to a specific event to occur in an arbitrary context at any level in the physical hierarchy. While this initial example use of callbacks assumed an event loop within a single thread of control, function (and functor) callbacks (see below) are also useful in a multithreaded context.[109]

3.5.7.2.2 **Event Depends Cyclically on `EventMgr`**

Figure 3-68 depicts a (naive) rendering of an event-management subsystem consisting of two separate classes, `EventMgr` and `Event` — each defined in its own separate component. In this inherently cyclic design, an event object is created and scheduled with a manager object by passing its address to the manager's `schedule` function. When the time comes for the manager to invoke the next event, it simply forwards that call to the event object's own `invoke` function resulting in a cyclic physical dependency (BAD IDEA).

---

[109] Unlike the single-threaded (time-multiplexed) example, care must be taken to ensure that all reference counting is done in a way that avoids race conditions (see Volume II, section 6.1), which today is typically accomplished using atomic instructions to increment and decrement the use count at minimal (but not negligible) runtime overhead.

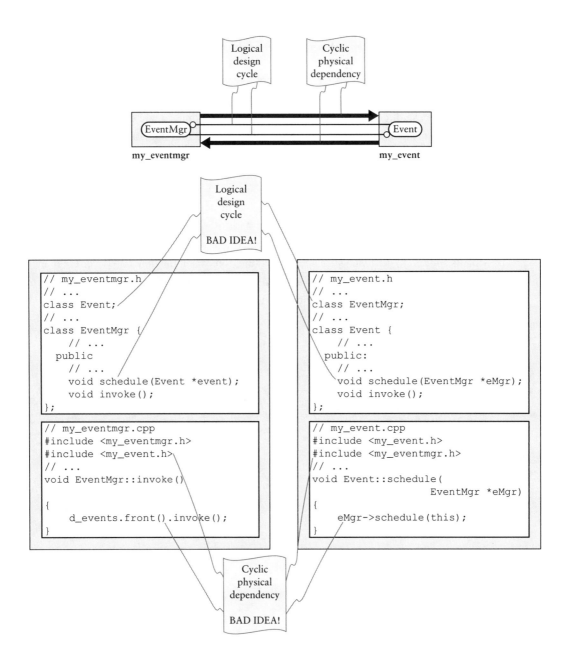

Figure 3-68: Cyclic rendering of Event/EventMgr subsystem (BAD IDEA)

3.5.7.2.3   Using Function Callbacks to Eliminate Upward Framework Dependencies

Function callbacks have long been used to eliminate any dependencies of frameworks on the user-supplied entities they are asked to manage. As an illustration, consider the simple event manager and arbitrary client suggested in Figure 3-69. The event manager class, `EventMgr`, resides at the lowest level and is unaware of any potential clients. This component publishes a specific (pure) functional interface structure, by way of a public `typedef`, e.g., `EventCb` (as shown). Would-be clients are able to schedule an object of arbitrary type (e.g., `AnyDarnThing`) by defining a (typically private) C-style function satisfying the requisite

```
void (*) (void *)
```

interface structure, such as the (file-scope `static`) `invoke` function sequestered within the `anydarnthing.cpp` file at the lower-right corner of Figure 3-69.

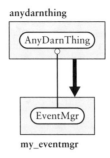

```
// anydarnthing.h                    // anydarnthing.cpp
// ...                               #include <anydarnthing.h>
class EventMgr;                      #include <my_eventmgr.h>
class AnyDarnThing {                 // ...
    // ...                           static void invoke(void *a)
  public                             {
    // ...                               AnyDarnThing *p =
    void schedule(EventMgr *eMgr);         static_cast<AnyDarnThing *>(a);
};                                       // Invoke the object using 'p'...
                                     }
                                     // ...
                                     void AnyDarnThing::schedule(
                                                         EventMgr *eMgr)
                                     {
                                         eMgr->schedule(invoke, this);
                                     }
```

```
// my_eventmgr.h                     // my_eventmgr.cpp
#include <vector>                    #include <my_eventmgr.h>
// ...                               // ...
class EventMgr {
    // ...                           void EventMgr::schedule(
  public:                                               EventCb  callback,
    typedef void (*EventCb)(void *);                    void     *data)
  private:                           {
    std::vector<EventCb> d_events;       d_events.push_back(callback);
    std::vector<void *>  d_data;         d_data.push_back(data);
    // ...                           }
  public:
    // ...                           void EventMgr::invoke()
    void schedule(EventCb  callback, {
                  void     *data);       d_events.front()(d_data.front());
    void invoke();                       // ...
                                     }
};
```

Figure 3-69: Use of function callbacks to eliminate framework dependencies

During initial scheduling, the address of this callback is supplied to the event manager along with the address of the event object itself. The type of the event object is, unfortunately, lost during scheduling; once the `invoke` function is called, however, it immediately recovers the (known) type of the object (via a `static_cast`) before proceeding to perform the desired behavior. Moreover, it is the responsibility of a client scheduling an event to ensure that the opaque data, supplied along with the function, remains valid until the function is eventually invoked on that data. When the order in which multiple events referring to the same data will be processed is not known a priori, the task of ensuring correct operation becomes even more complicated and error prone.

Although the function-callback technique has worked for years, it is decidedly ugly, manifestly nonmodular, and unequivocally plays fast and loose with the C++ type system. What's more, any sort of management for shared data must be implemented entirely from scratch. This basic callback technique, originally implemented using C-style *functions*, is now often much more effectively implemented using modern, modular, and type-safe *functors*.

3.5.7.3   Functor Callbacks

Using a (conventional) function as a callback, although often a satisfactory approach, inherently has two distinct disadvantages: A function callback (1) is itself incapable of encapsulating data specific to the supplied callback, and (2) does not[110] facilitate eliminating the runtime overhead of the callback, which — in many important cases, such as `std::sort` — can be substantial. Let us now revisit the *function*-callback solution of Figure 3-33, section 3.5.7.2.3, but this time, instead, with an eye toward using *functor* callbacks.

3.5.7.3.1   What Is a *Functor*?

Unlike a conventional C-style function, a *functor* is an object and, as such, naturally can have state. What makes a *functor* type special is that it supports one or more overloads of `operator()` and, therefore, is said to be *invocable*. By employing a *functor* (i.e., an *invocable function object*), rather than a (pure) function (i.e., one requiring externally supplied data), we make it possible to "wrap up" (i.e., encapsulate), within the callback itself, the essential user-supplied data on which the callback will eventually need to operate.

---

[110] On typical commercial platforms (absent whole-program optimization), the functor object may have its `operator()` implemented inline, thus making its body visible, whereas such is typically not the case for a function pointer.

3.5.7.3.2   Untangling Arbitrary Events from `EventMgr` Using Functor Callbacks

Figure 3-70 illustrates a revised and arguably improved functor-based solution to the cyclic conundrum depicted in Figure 3-68, section 3.5.7.2.2. The first thing to notice is that the event handler accepts a function object, implemented in terms of an `std::function` template that is parameterized by a (in this case) *member* function that both takes and returns nothing. During scheduling, the client creates the function object, passing the private `invoke` method along with the object itself.[111] When the time comes to kick off the next event, the leading callback object, along with its encapsulated user data, is invoked simply by using `()` (i.e., "function-call") syntax. In this way, we can avoid most of the unnecessary complexity and type-safety issues associated with conventional function callbacks.

---

[111] In C++03 we use `bind` as shown in Figure 3-70:

```
void anyDarnThing::schedule(EventMgr *eMgr)
{
    eMgr->schedule(std::bind(&AnyDarnThing::invoke, this));
}
```

In C++11 and later, we can instead make use of lambda expressions:

```
void anyDarnThing::schedule(EventMgr *eMgr)
{
    eMgr->schedule( [this] { invoke(); } );
}
```

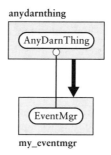

```
// anydarnthing.h
// ...
class EventMgr;
class AnyDarnThing {
    void invoke();
  public
    // ...
    void schedule(EventMgr *eMgr);
};
```

```
// anydarnthing.cpp
#include <anydarnthing.h>
#include <my_eventmgr.h>
// ...
void AnyDarnThing::invoke()
{
    // No cast needed!
    // ...
}
// ...
void AnyDarnThing::schedule(
                    EventMgr *eMgr)
{
    eMgr->schedule(std::bind(
        &AnyDarnThing::invoke, this));
}
```

```
// my_eventmgr.h
// ...
#include <functional>
#include <vector>
class EventMgr {
  // ...
  public:
    typedef
      std::function<void()> EventCb;
  private:
    std::vector<EventCb> d_events;
    // ...
  public:
    // ...
    void schedule(EventCb callback);
    void invoke();
};
```

```
// my_eventmgr.cpp
#include <my_eventmgr.h>

// ...

void EventMgr::schedule(
                    EventCb callback)
{
    d_events.push_back(callback);
}

void EventMgr::invoke()
{
    d_events.front()();
    // ...
}
```

Figure 3-70: Preferring functor callbacks to eliminate framework dependencies

Although functors greatly facilitate effective implementation, they themselves do not address all of the complexity. When the relative lifetimes of functors are not necessarily deterministic and the data they encapsulate includes references to the same noncopyable resources, it is often appropriate to employ some form of reference counting. Figure 3-71 illustrates how reference-counted functors similar to those of Figure 3-34[112], section 3.3.8.1, can be used effectively to enqueue encapsulated units of work to be processed by a thread-enabled object (see Volume II, section 6.1). Rather than make the entire functor reference counted, another approach is to reference count only the portion of the encapsulated data that is actually shared. Note that, whenever encapsulated data can be copied, and thus the coupling associated with reference counting can be avoided entirely, that approach is almost always to be preferred.

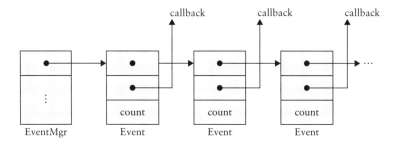

Figure 3-71: Use of reference-counted functors in multithreaded applications

3.5.7.3.3   Use of a Stateless *Functor*

Unlike stateful functors that encapsulate client-supplied data to be used by the callback once invoked, stateless functor callbacks have been used widely to customize the *logical* behavior of class templates. This kind of inherently invasive customization technique is frequently referred to as *policy-based design*.[113] Standard template containers, such as `std::map`, rely on such (stateless) functors to provide template *interface policies* (see Volume II, section 4.5) to customize the order for the elements in the instantiated container. In so doing, however, this *logical* policy also affects the C++ type of the resulting container class. Having template parameters that affect the type when the essential behavior itself is also affected is not in and of itself a problem. Template parameters that control implementation details — such as memory

---

[112] Which, as of C++11, would naturally be implemented in terms of a `std::shared_ptr` to `std::function`.
[113] **alexandrescu01**, Chapter 1, pp. 3–21

allocation, hashing algorithms, load factor — having nothing to do with intended *logical* behavior are an entirely different matter.[114,115]

Finally, note that this sort of object-based callback, like a function-based one, albeit more tightly compile-time coupled, can similarly enable access to higher-level constructs without implying `static` cyclic physical dependencies (see section 3.5.7.6).

3.5.7.4 Protocol Callbacks

Yet another form of the *callback* levelization technique involves the use of an abstract interface, a.k.a. *protocol* (section 1.7.5). Suppose we have a situation in which a "client" type c depends on some "server" type s, but the implementation of s, for whatever reason, needs to depend on c as illustrated in Figure 3-72a. By transforming the concrete class s into an abstract interface s' and a concrete derived class s'', we can always convert the cyclic component dependency (Figure 3-72a) into an acyclic one as shown in Figure 3-72b.

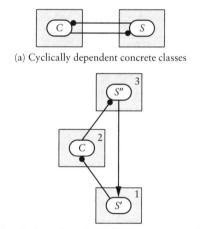

(a) Cyclically dependent concrete classes

(b) Acyclic dependency involving an abstract interface

Figure 3-72: Escalating the implementation via an abstract interface

---

[114] See Volume II, section 4.5, for a detailed discussion of the implications of such template *implementation policies* for *vocabulary types,* i.e., those used widely in the interface (see Volume II, section 4.4).

[115] Note that stateless functor callbacks are properly used to configure function templates — including via *implementation policies* — because functions are inherently structural (i.e., characterized entirely by their signature and return type, irrespective of name), and therefore do not suffer the same interoperability issues as do named types.

When employing this technique, we can create (and test) the abstract interface s' in isolation (see Volume III, Chapter 10). Next, we can use a *dummy* implementation of s' (see Volume II, section 4.9) to test c. Finally, we can use s' and c to test s''. In this way, we can avoid cyclic physical dependencies (section 2.6) and also satisfy the hierarchical testability requirement (section 2.14.3).

As a more concrete example, let's consider modeling the game of *Blackjack*, a.k.a. *21*, as illustrated in Figure 3-73.[116] Before a player can reasonably play Blackjack in a casino, he or she needs to know about a deck of cards.[117,118] The player also needs to learn the rules, which are quite involved and can vary widely among casinos.[119] Finally, a player will need to be able to "voice" each (viable) action to the dealer — such as STICK, HIT, SPLIT, DOUBLE_DOWN, INSURE[120] — perhaps represented as an enum.

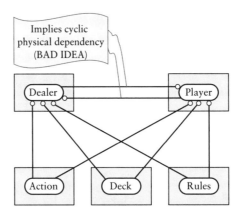

Figure 3-73: Naive (cyclic) modeling of the game of blackjack (BAD IDEA)

---

[116] Modeling Blackjack is something the author has done repeatedly (as computers have improved over time) since the mid-1970s and subsequently applied (profitably) for fun in practice — long before Jeffrey Ma pulled off his spectacular casino "scam" that was first popularized by the book *Bringing Down the House* (**mezrich02**), and followed by the hit movie *21* (2008).

[117] Each deck contains 52 distinct cards arranged in four suits (not relevant) and 13 ranks: A, 2, 3, 4, 5, 6, 7, 8, 9, T, J, Q, and K. The ranks T, J, Q, and K form an equivalence class, each member having a value of 10. The rank of A has a contextual value: either 1 or 11. For all other ranks (2 through 9) the rank represents the value.

[118] If you don't count cards (BAD IDEA), you can omit the player's dependency on the deck itself and rely on the current values of only your own cards, and, of course, those of the dealer.

[119] Fortunately, a dealer will always help a player with the specifics of the house rules, and typically (just ask) also give a player accurate advice with respect to the optimal *static* (i.e., stateless) strategy.

[120] Note that both INSURE (which pays 2-1) and DOUBLE_DOWN can be for any amount up to half or all, respectively, of the original bet.

By the same token, a dealer (representing the casino) will also need to know the rules (well), manipulate the deck[121] of cards, and listen to the specific actions the players want to take. The dealer may also need to initiate communication with a player.[122] Note that the value types (see Volume II, section 4.1) used in the interface for communication between `Dealer` and `Player` — a.k.a. *vocabulary types* (see Volume II, section 4.4) — have already been factored out into separate standalone components. Unfortunately, as Figure 3-74 delineates, a direct cyclic interaction in the interface between `Player` and `Dealer` remains.

```
// my_dealer.h
class Deck;
class Rules;
class Player;
class Dealer {
    // ...
  public:
    // ...
    void addPlayer(
            const Player *p,
            int          cash);
    void dealCards();
    void shuffleCards();
    // ...
    const Deck& deck() const;
    const Rules& rules() const;
};
```

```
// my_dealer.cpp
#include <my_dealer.h>
#include <my_player.h>
// ...
```

```
// my_player.h
class Action;
class Dealer;

class Player {
    // ...
  public:
    Player(const char *name);
    // ...
    int bet(const Dealer&
                    game) const;
    Action choice(const
            Dealer& game) const;
    const char *name() const;
};
```

```
// my_player.cpp
#include <my_player.cpp>
#include <my_dealer.h>
// ...
```

Figure 3-74: Cyclically dependent headers for `Dealer` and `Player` (BAD IDEA)

There are several ways to address this problem, including a complete refactoring of the respective components to make one of them (e.g., **my_dealer**) reside at a higher level than the other, but — for illustration purposes — we will choose to extract a protocol and split the `Player` into two parts: an abstract interface and a derived implementation. This new design is depicted in Figure 3-75.

---

[121] Often, multiple decks (typically six or eight) are used, which are placed in what is called a *shoe*.

[122] E.g., to remind him or her that it is that player's turn, ask to please take a drink off of the table, or admonish the player to stop commenting on others' play.

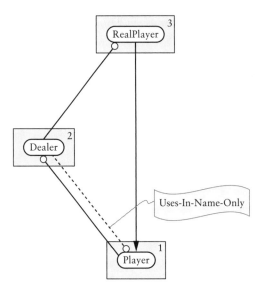

Figure 3-75: `Player` split into interface and implementation

In this new design, the **my_dealer** component remains essentially unchanged, but the `Player` class now becomes a pure abstract interface, as depicted in Figure 3-76. Although the dependencies of the **my_dealer** component on the various subcomponents do not change, those of **my_player** are now just a single (upward) Uses-In-Name-Only dependency on `Dealer`. Both `Dealer` and the class implementing `Player` (shown here as `RealPlayer`) continue to make direct substantive use of `Action`, `Deck`, and `Rules`. In this way, it is possible to test, in levelized order, the `Player` (base class), the `Dealer` (framework), and then the `RealPlayer` (derived class).

```
// my_player.h
// ...
class Action;
class Dealer;
class Player {
    // ...
  public:
    virtual ~Player();
    virtual int bet(const Dealer& game) const = 0;
    virtual Action choice(const Dealer& game) const = 0;
    virtual const char *name() const = 0;
};
// ...
```

Figure 3-76: `Player` — now an extracted protocol

This new design has the additional benefit of being extensible. We can easily accommodate radically different kinds of players without having to make changes to the `Dealer` framework. We might, for example, consider making a class, `NetworkPlayer`, derived from `Player`, that is actually a proxy for someone communicating over a network. Although perhaps initially appealing, having such a network-oriented derived class is arguably a poor candidate here because a network connection would likely (for the first time) introduce the possibility of a failure, which could significantly alter the needed signatures in the abstract interface, which is likely something we might not be prepared to entertain (see Volume II, Chapter 5). On the other hand, in a game where we have multiple players, some of which are simulated by the computer, we might reasonably choose to use inheritance to model substantially different ("avatar") game-playing strategies, such as `ConservativePlayer` versus `AggressivePlayer`.

As Figure 3-77 demonstrates, it is now also natural to create a `TestPlayer`[123] that can be used (e.g., during unit testing) to help verify the correctness of the `Dealer` class along with any other that might someday want to make use of the `Player` protocol. While this solution has advantages, it comes with the drawback that virtual functions are often not as runtime efficient as nonvirtual (especially `inline`) ones.[124]

Be aware that the introduction of an abstract interface for the sole purpose of testing — say, by *mocking* a lower-level component with a custom "test" implementation — is generally to be avoided so as not to obscure a client's perception of intended use (see Volume II). For inherently layered, as opposed to naturally lateral, designs (see section 3.7), there are typically better, less disruptive, and overall more effective ways to achieve optimal results without "messing" with the design (see Volume III).

---

[123] For designs that are naturally lateral in nature, it is good practice to always supply a well-thought-out user-configurable "test" implementation of each conjoining protocol to facilitate flexible and independent unit testing of client components making use of the protocol in the interface.

[124] Note that measurements of relatively recent enhancements (c. 2016) in optimizations for popular tool chains (e.g., GCC) have demonstrated that virtual function calls can be "devirtualized" (and therefore inlined) when the source code for both the client of the interface and the functions of the class derived from that interface are both visible to the compiler (such that the runtime type of the derived object can be deduced at compile time).

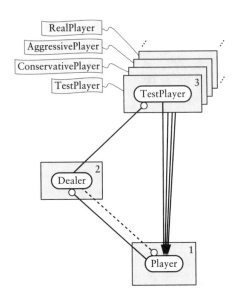

Figure 3-77: "Player" split into interface and multiple implementations

3.5.7.4.1   Injecting (Potentially Substantial) Functionality at a (Very) Low Level

A protocol can be used effectively to allow a low-level component to gain access to a (much) higher-level component or library without causing a cyclic physical dependency. Recall, from section 3.5.6, the situation where a low-level component required just a tiny amount of functionality already implemented at a higher level (see Figure 3-61, section 3.5.6). Now suppose that the required functionality is not tiny, but substantial, making the (now massive) duplication of source code ill advised.

Rather than duplicating the functionality in the low-level component, we can instead convert the concrete class in that component to an abstract one, and then escalate its implementation well above the originally higher-level component on which the new derived concrete (implementation) class needs to depend. In this modified design, however, there must be another, yet-higher-level entity (e.g., `main`) that will somehow supply the derived implementation object (via the address of its base-class type) to where it will ultimately be used. This revised, protocol-based design, as compared to the one employing (a little) redundancy (Figure 3-62, section 3.5.6), is illustrated in Figure 3-78.

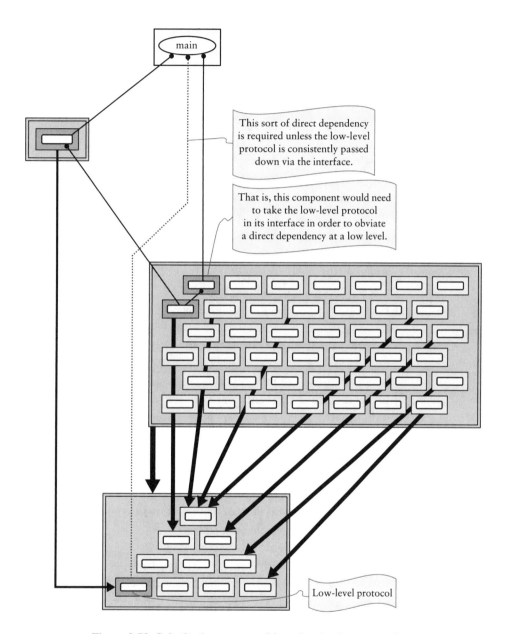

Figure 3-78: Substituting a *protocol* for a low-level concrete class

It is important to understand that applying this new protocol-based technique will require a shift in how a subsystem is used within an application. Either the highest-level entity, i.e., the `main` function, will need to install the address of this high-level implementation object (in terms of its base type) into a low-level `static` utility (i.e., at the start of program execution, after which it presumably will never change), or else each type that might need to use (directly or indirectly) this higher-level implementation must propagate the low-level protocol in its interface.

The former "singleton" approach makes sense when the implementation is intended to be program-wide and never change, such as a contract-assertion handler (see Volume II, section 6.8) or logging facility (see section 3.5.7.4.2, below). Employing this first approach also minimizes the changes needed throughout an existing subsystem. The latter "parameter" approach is indicated when immediate clients will want to supply different implementations to a given subsystem, as would be the case for memory allocators for standard container types (see Volume II, section 4.10). The downside of this alternate approach, however, is the substantial extra development effort required to implement *and test* (see Volume II, section 4.9) an extra abstract-interface parameter in every relevant component.[125]

3.5.7.4.2   Repairing the Logger-Transport-Mail Subsystems

As our final, concrete example of protocol callbacks, consider again the physically interdependent logger-transport-email configuration introduced in section 3.4. Recall that the two mutual dependencies (Figure 3-40, section 3.4) were not planned in advance but instead evolved over time. Initially, the **transport** subsystem depended acyclically on the **logger**. Then, due to a need for runtime control of the logger subsystem, **logger** was — as an expedient — allowed to depend back physically on **transport**. Similarly, **mail** was initially designed to have an acyclic dependency on **transport** and **logger**, but — due to management fiat — **logger** was then made to depend back physically on **mail**. Physical design degradation like this happens routinely in practice, and yet none of it is desirable or necessary.

Instead of allowing the **logger** subsystem to depend on **transport** directly, we can adapt our **transport** subsystem via a derived concrete implementation class (e.g., `ControlChannel`) to implement an abstract (protocol) class (e.g., `Channel`) common to all relevant transports as illustrated in Figure 3-79. The **logger** subsystem is then explicitly imbued (e.g., by `main`) with an object of type `ControlChannel` at startup.

---

[125] As of this writing, research is currently underway to determine how locally supplied memory-allocator propagation might be facilitated (and maintenance costs reduced) if incorporated into C++ as a language feature; see **meredith19**.

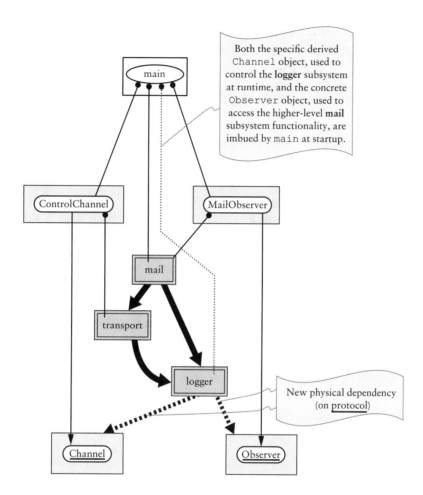

Both the specific derived
Channel object, used to
control the **logger** subsystem
at runtime, and the concrete
Observer object, used to
access the higher-level **mail**
subsystem functionality, are
imbued by main at startup.

New physical dependency
(on protocol)

Figure 3-79: Using abstract interfaces to levelize our infrastructure

Similarly, rather than allowing **logger** to depend physically on the **mail** subsystem, we can instead define an abstract interface, Observer, for all clients that want to be notified of logging events. We can then derive a concrete MailObserver class to adapt the **mail** subsystem functionality to the Observer protocol. The main program installs, at startup, an object of type MailObserver. Whenever a logging event occurs, the logger invokes the virtual publish method for each registered Observer object, thereby notifying the installed MailObserver adapter, which, in turn, invokes the needed **mail** subsystem functionality (also illustrated in Figure 3-79).

Note that this protocol-callback levelization technique is *not* always appropriate — e.g., when inlining for performance is truly essential (see section 3.5.7.5, below). For example, creating a pure abstract interface for a logging facility itself is not viable and is one of the few remaining valid uses of the C++ preprocessor.[126] First, we will need to extract the line number (__ LINE__) and filename (__FILE__) at the call site of the logging statement.[127] Second, we will need to determine — as cheaply as possible — whether the runtime logging level is sufficient to warrant invoking the publishing mechanism for *each* individual logging message — e.g., a negatively hinted if, but certainly not any kind of (noninlined) function call. Finally, and most importantly, we will need to make sure that none of the expressions that might potentially be logged are evaluated *unless* the logging statement that will ultimately transmit them is enabled at the current runtime logging level. For all of these reasons, it is not practical to reduce a concrete logging facility to just an unadorned pure abstract interface.

3.5.7.5   Concept Callbacks

Perhaps the most significant *callback* levelization technique to emerge since the publication of my previous book[128] is that of using a method template to bind (statically) to a concrete class having a syntactically consistent interface and (ideally) a contractually suitable implementation. The union of requirements on a type for it to be viable for use in such a context has come to be known as a *concept* (section 1.7.6).[129]

---

[126] Other valid uses of macros in C++03, 11, 14, 17, and even 20 include `<cassert>` and our own **bsls_assert** facility (see Volume II, section 6.8). Note that a proposal for what is essentially a superset of our (library-based) contract-checking facility (CCF) implemented as a language feature was formally adopted (June, 2018) into the C++ working paper, with the expectation of landing in C++20, but was withdrawn a year later for further consideration and (as of this writing) was actively being targeted for C++23. See also our **bsls_assert** and **bsls_asserttest** components in Bloomberg's open-source distribution of BDE (**bde14**, subdirectory `/groups/bsl/bsls/`).

[127] As of C++20, `std::source_location` provides a language-based alternative for the use of the preprocessor __FILE__ and __LINE__ macros.

[128] See **lakos96**, section 5.7, pp. 275–288.

[129] Language-level support for concepts was introduced as part of C++20. This feature (at least initially) will help programmers to detect only structural (syntactic) inconsistencies, not semantic ones. Note that this (in)ability is akin to enforcing (at compile time) that the signatures of derived-class virtual functions match the signatures of their base-class counterparts, while relying on developers to ensure that the semantics correspond as well (see Volume II, section 4.6).

As a concrete example, let us consider the notion of *serializing* the *value* of a *value-type* object such as a Date, Time, or Duration (see Volume II, section 4.1) into a byte stream, which can then be *externalized* (i.e., transmitted out of process) via some communication channel (e.g., socket, shared memory) to another process or, perhaps, a database. How would we architect such a thing in a way that scales well, and still provides maximal utility generally?

3.5.7.5.1   Plan A: Standardize on a Single Concrete **ByteStream** Class

One might, at first, consider choosing to standardize on a single concrete streaming class, ByteStream, as illustrated in Figure 3-80a. An object of this ByteStream class accumulates values, at various physical sizes, for each of the fundamental value types, such as integers, floating-point numbers, and character strings, as well as arrays of each of these fundamental objects. Figure 3-80b shows a snippet of a ByteStream interface that can be used to serialize (i.e., *write*) object data; for simplicity, however, we have omitted the de-serialize (i.e., *read*) aspect entirely. We have postulated a (toy) Date class that stores its three *salient*[130] attributes, year, month, and day, separately (see Volume II, section 4.1). The elided component implementing this Date class, depicted in Figure 3-80c, shows how each of these three date fields are sent to the ByteStream object, whose address is supplied to the Date class's streamOut method as an argument.

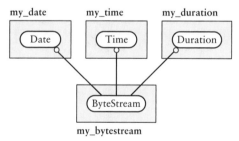

(a) Value types using ByteStream in their respective interfaces

---

[130] A salient attribute of a value-semantic type is one of its (typically observable) attributes that contributes to the overall value of the object itself. For example, year, month, and day are all salient attributes of any generally useful date class. In the case of an std::vector<int>, both the size (number of integer elements) and each individual element (in the sequence of that size) would be considered salient. Examples of nonsalient attributes would be the capacity of the vector (see Volume II, section 4.1) and the address of the mechanism (see Volume II, section 4.2) used to allocate memory (see Volume II, section 4.10).

```
// my_bytestream.h
// ...
#include <my_charbuf.h>
// ...
class ByteStream {
    CharBuf d_streamData;
    // ...
  public:
    // ...
    void putInt8(int value);
    void putInt16(int value);
    // ...
    void putFloat32(double value);
    void putFloat64(double value);
    // ...
};
```

(b) Heavily elided (and simplified) ByteStream interface

```
// my_date.h                          // my_date.cpp
// ...                                // ...
class ByteStream;                     #include <my_date.h>
// ...                                #include <my_bytestream.h>
class Date {                          // ...
    short d_year;                     void Date::streamOut(ByteStream *s)
    char  d_month;                    {
    char  d_day;                          s->putInt16(d_year);
  public:                                 s->putInt8(d_month);
    // ...                                s->putInt8(d_day);
    int day() const;                  }
    int month() const;
    int year() const;
    // ...
    void streamOut(ByteStream *s);
    // ...
};
// ...
```

(c) Elided (toy) **my_date** component using a ByteStream

Figure 3-80: Standardizing on a single concrete ByteStream class (BAD IDEA)

The fundamental problem with this approach is that how we want to stream an object can differ depending on the context in which it is streamed. For example, the streamer object might, for whatever reason, itself need to somehow encrypt as it streams. More commonly, however, we know we will want to be able to supply a TestByteStream (during development) that inserts additional sentinels and other data into the stream to ensure that, for example, an array of two integers, written to a `ByteStream`, is not (somehow) rehydrated as two separate integers or, worse, a `double`!

There is, however, another, more subtle problem. `ByteStream` and `CharBuf` reside in separate components. `ByteStream` uses `CharBuf` in its implementation to store the serialized data (Figure 3-80b). On the other hand, `CharBuf` is, itself, a value-semantic type that supports streaming natively (i.e., primitively); hence, `CharBuf` uses `ByteStream` in its interface (Figure 3-80c). As a result, there is a cyclic physical dependency between **my_bytestream** and **my_charbuf** as illustrated in Figure 3-81a.

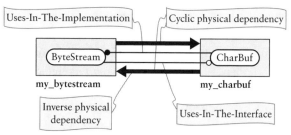

(a) Mutual dependency between `ByteStream` and `CharBuf` (BAD IDEA)

```
// my_charbuf.h
// ...
#include <cstddef> // for 'std::size_t'
class ByteStream;
// ...
class CharBuf {
    char *d_buffer_p;
    // ...
  public:
    // ...
    void appendChar(char c);
    std::size_t length() const;
    char operator[](std::size_t i) const;    Implies inverse
    // ...                                     physical
    void streamOut(ByteStream *s) const;      dependency
    // ...
};
// ...
```

(b) Elided `my_charbuf.h` file

Figure 3-81: Standardizing on a single concrete `ByteStream` class (BAD IDEA)

3.5.7.5.2   Plan B: Brute-Force Solutions Based on *Redundancy*

One brute-force solution to just the cyclic-dependency problem would be to use the *redundancy* levelization technique to create, for internal use by ByteStream, a lower-level minimal CharBuf that explicitly does *not* provide support for streaming. In that case, the component defining ByteStream becomes the lower level of the two original components and the dependency problem is resolved. Another brute-force (but not recommended) solution exploiting a (decidedly ugly) form of "redundancy" would be to create locally — in the test driver for CharBuf — a minimal mocked version of ByteStream itself for use in the initial validation of CharBuf. This second solution would require involving the build system to exclude what would otherwise be a valid dependency and is counter to the spirit of build independence (section 2.15) and unfettered interoperability advocated in our methodology (see section 3.9). What's more, neither of these solutions affords any flexibility in configuring the streaming behavior. In short, Plan B fails to address all our requirements adequately.

3.5.7.5.3   Plan C: Standardize on an Abstract `ByteStream` Interface Class

Next, we might consider employing the previously discussed *protocol*-callback levelization technique (section 3.5.7.4), separating the initial concrete streaming class into two parts: a pure abstract interface (a.k.a. *protocol*) class, ByteStream, and (at least) one implementation class (e.g., ConcreteByteStream) as shown in Figure 3-82. Logically, this design will work just fine, but — given the state of current industry-standard compilers/tool-chains — the runtime cost of invoking a virtual function on each individual streaming operation is likely to be prohibitive.[131]

---

[131] It is worth noting, however, that in certain important circumstances (see Volume II, section 4.10) — specifically when both the implementation of the derived class (e.g., ConcreteByteClass) and the class using it (e.g., CharBuf) via its base class (e.g., ByteStream) are all visible to the client's compiler (e.g., by dint of being either templates or inline functions) — even traditional compiler/tool-chain technologies (e.g., GCC) are able to "devirtualize" the function call, achieving performance comparable to the previous, cyclically dependent design. See **lakos16**.

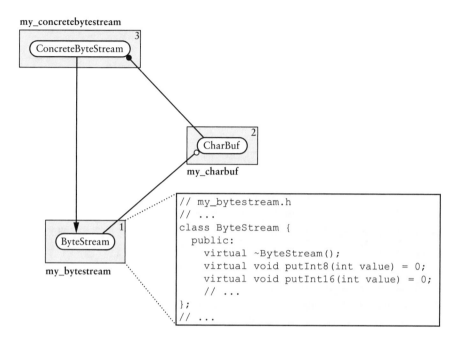

Figure 3-82: Standardizing on a protocol `ByteStream` class (BAD IDEA)

3.5.7.5.4   Plan D: Standardize on a Byte-Stream *Concept*

There is a fourth alternative, however, that — in this specific instance — turns out to be the best of both worlds. Given that we want to be able to have (compile-time) interchangeable byte-stream implementations for value types like `CharBuf` but cannot afford the potential runtime overhead of the *insulation* afforded by a virtual function call (see section 3.11.5.3), we can replace each member function in the value type (e.g., `CharBuf`) that uses an object of the `ByteStream` base-class type (e.g., `streamOut`) with an equivalent *method template*. This templated member of the value type takes, as a type parameter, any concrete class satisfying the *ByteStream* concept, as illustrated in Figure 3-83.[132] In this way, we achieve essentially *all* of the practical *logical* benefits of runtime polymorphism.[133] Moreover, because only the stream methods, and not the value type itself, are part of a template, changing the stream type does not affect the overall C++ type of the object using the stream, thereby allowing us to pass these value types as function arguments in nontemplated contexts (see Volume II, section 4.4).

---

[132] For a further description of ISO (In-Structure-Only) symbols, see Figure 1-50, section 1.7.6.

[133] Note that, along with the tight (physical) compile-time coupling, we also give up the (logical) ability to select the particular byte-stream implementation at run time. As it turns out, however, this runtime polymorphic property isn't typically useful for streaming in practice.

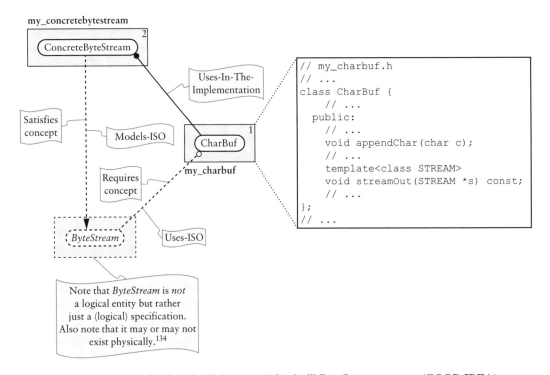

Figure 3-83: Standardizing on a "physical" ByteStream *concept* (GOOD IDEA)

Finally, the transformation from base class to concept, suggested above, has profound consequences with respect to software engineering in general and sound physical design in particular.
Relying on a *concept* rather than on an abstract base class immediately gives up any necessary
physical location where (1) the concept's *contract* (see Volume II, section 5.2) can be documented (let alone enforced), and (2) both clients and implementers must depend physically, as
suggested in Figure 3-84.

---

[134] If this component were, for any reason, to exist physically, the border of the component itself (but not the
capsule representing the ByteStream concept) would be represented as a solid line (as opposed to a dashed one).
Such a physical manifestation might be used to hold (a) documentation describing the concept and/or (b) code usable
by clients to enforce it. In either case, if the intent is for the author of the class modeling ByteStream (i.e.,
ConcreteByteStream) to #include the (now physical) component characterizing ByteStream (e.g., to make the
extent of the collaboration explicit), the arrow from the solid capsule (for ConcreteByteStream) to the dashed one
(for ByteStream) would instead be solid as well. Similarly, if the intent is to have the author of the client class
(i.e., CharBuf) include the ByteStream component's header — particularly if there were compile-time type predicates (implemented as metafunctions) available for clients to use to enforce the ByteStream concept on their own
type parameters — it too would be rendered with a solid, as opposed to a dashed, line. But even if there is nothing
whatsoever in the component but documentation — even if just an example of the required interface — there is value
in tying physically both model and client to this common contract (see Volume II, section 5.2).

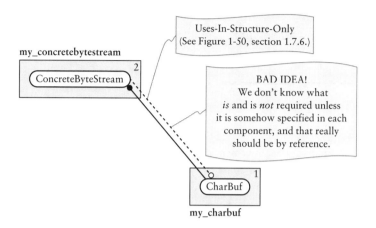

Figure 3-84: Having no unique physical node describing a *concept* (BAD IDEA)

Even before language support for concepts in C++ becomes widely available, we might consider that there be a designated component (with no source code required) that fully documents the *concept*, and on which each implementer (e.g., ConcreteByteStream, TestByteStream) and client (e.g., CharBuf, Date, Time) is expected to depend (#include) physically — just as if it were implementing a *protocol* (section 1.7.5). Doing so would go a long way toward demystifying this kind of inherently subtle architecture in a large code base.

3.5.8   Manager Class

Establishing a class that owns and coordinates lower-level objects.

The levelization technique of having a higher-level *manager class* being responsible for creating, destroying, and coordinating the instances of lower-level subordinate classes under its control is essentially just a practical design strategy. The classical example is that of a singly linked list. Is a single C++ class, as suggested in Figure 3-85, sufficient to implement a list? In particular, is it reasonable for the destructor of a Link object to destroy another object of the same type? We assert that the answer is a resounding "No!" Instead, we claim that ensuring hierarchical ownership be governed by the type system, rather than just the runtime configuration of object instances of a given type (or types), is an important design characteristic we should actively seek to achieve.[135]

---

[135] Some "clever" developers have even chosen to make the destructor of a Link object recursively destroy the next Link:

```
Link::~Link() { delete d_next_p; }
```

This "elegant" technique, apart from being absurdly slow, will sooner or later inevitably overflow the program stack on a sufficiently long list.

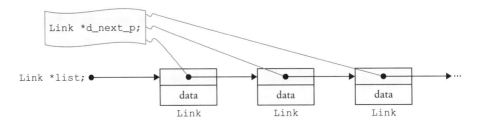

Figure 3-85: Implementing a linked list using a single C++ type (BAD IDEA)

Figure 3-86 illustrates (a) the class diagram (not including components) and (b) the runtime object layout for a typical instance of a linked list abstraction parameterized by type T. Each Link<T> is potentially nothing more than a struct containing a pointer to the next Link<T> and a data field of type T. A Link<T> manages its own instance of type T but is never responsible for affecting the lifetime of any other instance of type Link<T>. Instead, the List<T> *manager* object is solely responsible for allocating, creating, destroying, and deallocating objects of type Link<T>, and also for ensuring that each Link<T> object is configured properly — i.e., has the appropriate Link<T> address and T value.[136]

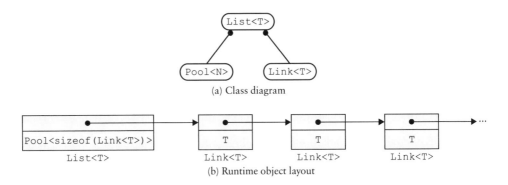

Figure 3-86: A List class manages a collection of Link objects.

Notice also that it is the manager class, List<T>, that has the additional logical dependency on the memory pool class template, Pool<N>, which it uses for allocating the individual Link objects efficiently (see Volume II, section 6.7). The definition of this pool template would most

---

[136] It has been suggested that we could have instead implemented Link<T> in a separate subordinate component, but due to its tiny size and the relative ease with which it can be tested indirectly through the straightforward testing of the principle class, the extra physical "moving parts" would be superfluous.

certainly reside in a separate component. Although there is no physical-dependency reason that would stop `Link<T>` and `List<T>` from residing in separate components, in order to allow the interaction between the list and the (trivial) link entities to remain *malleable* (section 0.5) and given that the added coupling would almost certainly outweigh any prospects for reuse (see section 3.5.6), we would likely implement the link class template as being component-private (section 2.7.1) — e.g., `List_Link<T>` in the same component that defines `List<T>`.

As a second example, consider trying to create a graph abstraction similar to the one shown in Figure 3-56a, section 3.5.4.3, but consisting of only two distinct C++ types: `Node` and `Edge`. What would such an implementation look like? Initially, we might argue that we can create a `Node` with no `Edges`, but not vice versa; hence, type `Node` is naturally at a lower level than type `Edge` (Figure 3-87a). For a client to traverse a graph, however, we will, of course, need to implement `Node` with (at least) opaque `Edge` pointers.

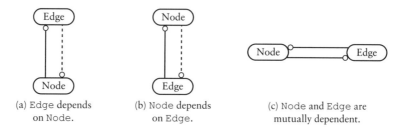

(a) Edge depends on Node.   (b) Node depends on Edge.   (c) Node and Edge are mutually dependent.

Figure 3-87: Graph implemented as just `Node` and `Edge` (BAD IDEA)

Let us now consider implementing some fundamental operations on a graph. For example, where should we place `addNode(...)`? Clearly this operation is not a method on either `Node` or `Edge`. If we were to make `addNode(...)` a free function (or, in our methodology, a `static` member of a utility `struct`), what object should keep track of this new node? That is, how can we iterate over the nodes in the graph? More to the point, what specific object represents the graph as a whole?

Similarly, suppose we want to remove a `Node`. Where should `removeNode(...)` go? Since `Node` does not know substantively about `Edge`, and yet edges hold pointers to nodes, `removeNode(...)` cannot be a member of `Node`, lest connected edges be left with dangling `Node` pointers. We might consider trying to treat `Edge` as if it were also a "Graph" and make `removeNode` a member of `Edge`, but that would be just like having `Link<T>` and `List<T>` be the same type: An `Edge` object would then be responsible for managing the lifetimes of other objects of type `Edge` (BAD IDEA).

Alternatively, having class `Node` depend unilaterally on class `Edge`, but with `Edge` having an opaque back pointer on `Node` (Figure 3-87b) is similarly problematic. If `Node` is in charge (and doing "double duty" as a "Graph"), then `removeEdge` must be an operation on `Node`, as `Edge` does not know substantively about `Node` yet holds opaque `Node` pointers. Even if `Node` and `Edge` are cyclically dependent (Figure 3-87c) — and therefore necessarily defined in the same component (sections 2.6 and 3.3.1.2) — there is no one single object that represents the "Graph" overall as a concrete value-semantic type (see Volume II, section 4.3).

Representing a graph abstraction using three distinct C++ types (including a `Graph` *manager* class (e.g., see Figures 3-56 and 3-57, sections 3.5.4.3 and 3.5.5, respectively) allows for a coherent, levelized implementation of each of the three classes in separate components and enables a single object — one whose *type* distinguishes it — to be responsible for managing the lifetimes of all of its subordinate objects. This sort of type-based hierarchical object management is, in our view, fundamental to sound physical design.

3.5.9   Factoring

Moving independently testable sub-behavior out of the implementations of complex components involved in excessive physical coupling.

Achieving an acyclic, fine-grained, component-based architecture requires assiduous attention to decomposition:

> When dependencies are analyzed, the dependencies of the interface and the implementation must be considered separately. In both cases, the ideal is for the dependency graphs of a system to be directed acyclic graphs to ease understanding and testing of the system. However, this ideal is far more critical and far more often achievable for interfaces than for implementations.[137]
>
> — Bjarne Stroustrup

Given careful up-front design, history has shown that cycles in both interface and implementation across component boundaries can *always* be productively avoided. This *factoring* levelization technique, however, addresses the reality that not all aspects of the software we

---

[137] **stroustrup00**, section 24.4.2, pp. 758–760, specifically p. 760

create are necessarily under our control. Although cycles in the interfaces of standardized (or otherwise externally specified) components are often immutable, their implementation might be amenable to a decomposition leading to separately testable, if not reusable, components.

Figure 3-88a represents abstractly a system of three logical entities A, B, and C, whose interfaces are either inherently or, more typically, *contractually* cyclically dependent. Suppose further that the functionality supported by these three types is deemed to be too large to implement and test effectively if they are all colocated in a single component. Even when we are not able to change these logical interfaces, we might still be able to factor out sufficient independently testable implementation functionality (Figure 3-88b) such that the remaining cyclically interdependent classes can reasonably reside within a single component. The better the job we do at factoring our implementations (see Volume II, section 6.4), the more testable our software becomes (see Volume III) — even when it does not turn out to be hierarchically reusable (section 0.4).

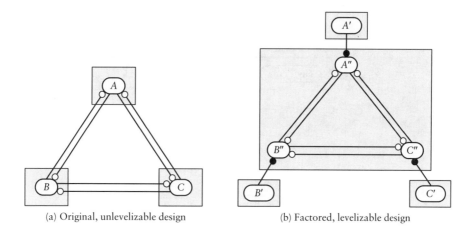

(a) Original, unlevelizable design   (b) Factored, levelizable design

Figure 3-88: Factoring out independently testable implementation details

In particular, imagine that we want to implement a Graph subsystem whose interface dependencies are explicitly constrained to be cyclic. We could imagine factoring out aspects of the implementation not contributing to the interface cycle, including the value-only portions of Node and Edge (see Volume II, section 4.1) along with implementation details of the graph itself (Figure 3-89a). In the event that we also have some latitude to change the syntax of the interface, but not the logical relationships, we might be able to reduce dependency and perhaps even make the graph more reusable by converting it to a template parameterized by value-semantic NODE and EDGE types satisfying their respective concepts (Figure 3-89b). Note that we can reduce both compile time and code size by factoring out of a templated implementation (e.g., GraphImp) as much nontemplated functionality as is reasonably possible (see Volume II, section 4.5).

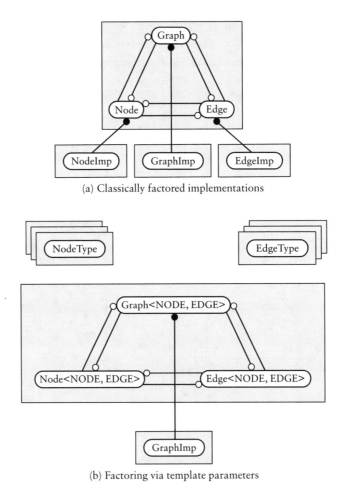

(a) Classically factored implementations

(b) Factoring via template parameters

Figure 3-89: Example of factoring for constrained Graph subsystem interface

Finally, this escalation technique is devoted to factoring given a fixed (or semi-fixed) interface. Even when the interface is entirely under our control, there will be opportunities to do factoring behind the scenes (see Volume II, section 6.4) to both (1) promote *hierarchical* reuse (section 0.4), and (2) improve testability (see Volume III); e.g., see also section 3.12.11.

3.5.10 Escalating Encapsulation

Moving the point at which implementation details are hidden from clients to a higher level in the physical hierarchy.

Sometimes the problems associated with creating a levelizable collection of fine-grained components derive not from avoiding cycles but from avoiding long-distance friendships (section 3.1.9). As component-based developers, we have become accustomed to encapsulating low-level design choices within a single component and therefore might sometimes be reluctant to allow detailed aspects of a larger implementation to "leak out" of the public interface of any component — even if nothing in that component is programmatically accessible from a higher-level, client-facing *wrapper* class. The desire to hide component-sized implementation details from the general public creates the dilemma of whether to violate the prohibition on inter-component friendship (BAD IDEA) or to make a single component excessively (perhaps even unboundedly) large (BAD IDEA).

The definition of what is and is not an *implementation component* depends on the level of abstraction we are trying to achieve. At the lowest levels of abstraction, we may have very primitive constructs such as atomic instructions, memory pools,[138] caches, and so on. Clearly, these entities with their very low levels of abstraction should not be exposed in the interface of a high-level, widely used subsystem such as a parser or logger. Still, the implementations of other, high-level subsystems should be free to depend on these important, well-thought-out, and *stable* low-level details — the very premise of *hierarchical reuse* (section 0.4). What's more, it should be possible for client-facing subsystems to alter their implementations to depend on an alternative low-level detail without forcing clients of the higher-level subsystem to rework their code (e.g., see Figure 3-171, section 3.12.11.2).

As a purely pedagogical, first example elucidating the potential benefits of *escalating* the level at which *the use of*[139] component-sized implementation details are encapsulated, consider the (vertically) *layered architecture* (see section 3.7.2) consisting of a Car, an Engine, and a SparkPlug illustrated in Figure 3-90. In this design, a Car uses its Engine in the interface. Intuitively, this logical relationship means that any client of an object of type Car (e.g., a mechanic) can open its

---

[138] Memory pools are typically pure implementation details, whereas memory allocators frequently appear as part of an object's interface (see Volume II, section 4.10).

[139] In our methodology, components do not "encapsulate" other components (see section 3.11.1), but do support the notion of *subordinate* components (section 2.7.5).

hood and access its `Engine`. In software, however, Uses-In-The-Interface (section 1.7.3) means that there exists at least some *programmatic* way of interacting with methods of a `Car` in terms of an `Engine` type. Hence, *the use of* `Engine` is *not* an encapsulated implementation detail of `Car`. That is, if we wanted to reimplement `Car` to use, say, `MyEngine` instead of `Engine`, existing clients would be forced to rework their code.

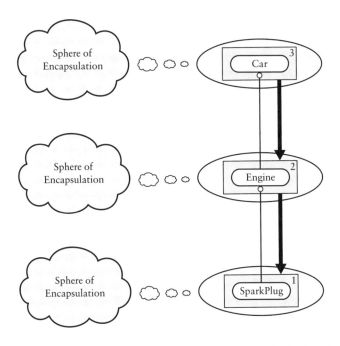

Figure 3-90: `Car` using `Engine` using `SparkPlug` — all in the interface

In this design (Figure 3-90), an `Engine`, in turn, uses type `SparkPlug` in the interface. Intuitively, if we can get to the engine of a given car, then we can also get to the spark plugs in that engine. In software terms, the consequence is that we cannot change even the type of spark plug used in the engine without potentially forcing clients of `Car` to rework their source code! Though a mechanic may need to be able to replace spark plugs for a *given* engine, it might well be the case that an owner of a `Car` does not need (or even want) to have direct access to its `Engine`. Even so, the mechanic (or component-level test driver) for `Engine` would most certainly want to be able to make effective use of `SparkPlug` objects in the interface while testing the `Engine`.

In the design of Figure 3-35, the *spheres of encapsulation* are on a per-component basis. That is, no component acts as an *encapsulating wrapper*[140] for any other component. Suppose we were to adjust our design of Car so that it no longer exposes the Engine in the interface, but Engine still continues to use SparkPlug in its public interface, as illustrated in Figure 3-91. With this new design, clients of type Car have no programmatic access to the Engine type used in the implementation. That Engine continues to use type SparkPlug in the interface is of no consequence to Car clients as there is now no programmatic access to either from the public interface of Car.[141]

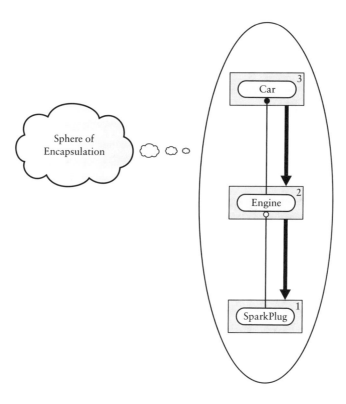

Figure 3-91: Car using Engine (along w/SparkPlug) in the implementation

---

[140] **lakos96**, section 5.10, pp. 312–324

[141] The practice of partitioning (or "telescoping") the implementation of a single complex component into two or even three separate ones — e.g., *Class* (public), *ClassImp* (encapsulated), and *ClassImpUtil* (insulated) — is discussed in Volume II, section 6.4.

By this point, the astute reader will know that we are willing to stretch an analogy (e.g., section 0.8) when doing so serves some practically useful purpose. Consider now our modified pedagogical design, as shown in Figure 3-92, in which we have substituted the functionality provided by `SparkPlug` with that of type `Fuel`. A client of `Car` cannot avoid filling up with gas, and so the interface of `Car` necessarily must allow for using `Fuel` in its interface. While it is still true that `Engine` (which is *used in the implementation* of `Car`) also depends on `Fuel`, that aspect is not relevant (logically) to clients of `Car`. Hence, a client of `Car` knows, programmatically, about `Fuel`, but not `Engine`. The takeaway here is that, were we to change the type `Engine` for another that also uses the same type (of) `Fuel` in its interface, there would be no need to rework the source code of any client of type `Car`.

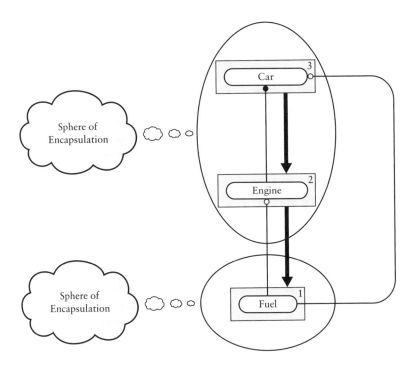

Figure 3-92: `Car` using only `Fuel`, not `Engine`, in the interface

3.5.10.1   A More General Solution to Our `Graph` Subsystem

Let us now reconsider the implementation of the simple graph subsystem of Figure 3-56a, illustrated again here in Figure 3-93, but this time along with its implementation dependencies on `std::vector`. This `Graph` class manages a collection of lower-level `Node` and `Edge` objects — each defined in separate components. In addition, `Node` maintains a sequence of (unmanaged) *opaque* `Edge` pointers. Both `Graph` and `Node` rely on `std::vector` in their respective implementations, yet `Node`, `Edge`, and `Graph` each enjoys its own individual sphere of encapsulation.

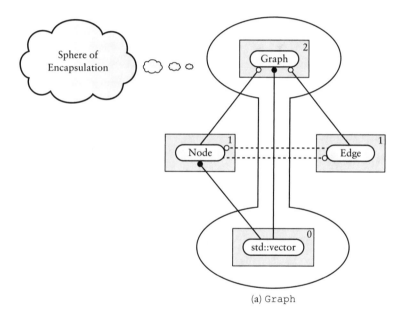

(a) `Graph`

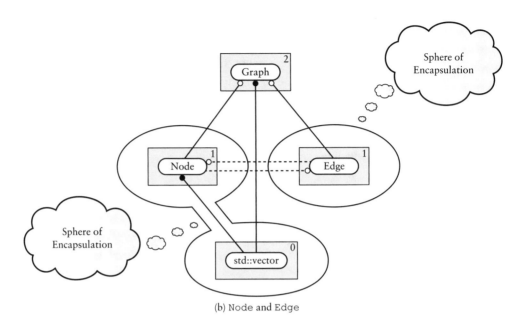

(b) `Node` and `Edge`

Figure 3-93: Individual spheres of encapsulation for `Graph`, `Node`, and `Edge`

For a `Graph` object to coordinate `Node` and `Edge` objects in this design, any ability to modify node and edge connectivity is necessarily public. That is, clients of `Graph` will have the same access to participating objects of types `Node` and `Edge` as does `Graph` itself. Although it is perfectly acceptable for arbitrary clients to create and then manipulate their own `Node` or `Edge` objects in any way they see fit, the same cannot necessarily be said for these objects when they are participating in (and therefore being managed by) a `Graph` object.

Ensuring that the invariants of `Graph` objects (see Volume II, section 5.2) are preserved — e.g., that all `Node`/`Edge` connectivity is maintained consistently across all such objects managed by each `Graph` object — forces us to severely restrict what *any* client could do with a preexisting `Node` or `Edge` object (e.g., see Figure 3-57b–c, section 3.5.5), making the previous solution fall far short of being a general one.

3.5.10.2   Encapsulating the *Use* of Implementation Components

The main idea behind this much more general levelization technique of escalating encapsulation is that the implementation of a concrete subsystem can itself be a region of encapsulation that allows open collaboration among components at a lower level of abstraction without necessarily having to hide those components from public scrutiny (see section 3.9.7) or in any way restrict their independent direct use by clients other than `Graph`.

As long as lower-level components do not contribute to the programmatically accessible interface of the client-facing subsystem, they are — for all intents and purposes — encapsulated themselves yet are still available for reuse in other subsystems. Again, by escalating encapsulation we hide the *use* of these lower-level, stable implementation components, rather than hiding them from potential new clients that might benefit from them through *hierarchical reuse* (section 0.4).

Figure 3-94 illustrates the technique of creating a larger *sphere of encapsulation* whereby only certain (in this case, *value*) types (i.e., `NodeData` and `EdgeData`) are allowed to pass through the public interface of a "wrapper" class (i.e., `Graph`). Any low-level information that must be exposed (e.g., for efficiency) across component boundaries resides in implementation-only components (i.e., those defining `Node`, `Edge`, and `std::vector`). As long as this implementation functionality is stable, there is no need to hide it from public view or grant `Graph` private access to it. Were we to change the implementation of `Graph`, we might well stop using any or all of these implementation components — replacing them with new or different ones, yet clients of this `Graph` subsystem would have no programmatic way of knowing that we did. Hence, there would be no need for clients of `Graph` to rework their source code.[142]

---

[142] For another concrete example of the benefits of proper discrete packaging of implementation details, as suggested in sections 3.1 and 3.2, see Figures 3-170–3-172, section 3.12.11.2.

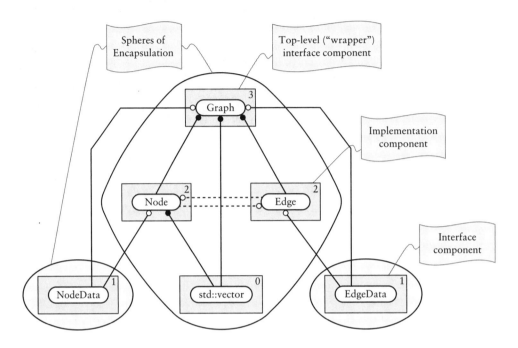

Figure 3-94: Separating interface and implementation types

Notice that, in this design neither `Node` nor `Edge` is visible in the interface of `Graph`. Hence, the *use* of these types — rather than the types themselves — remains an implementation detail of class `Graph`. Instead, only the subordinated `NodeData` and `EdgeData`, which are relevant to clients of `Graph`, are exposed (programmatically) through the interface of `Graph`. In this way, we hide the "encapsulated" implementation and expose to the client only what is needed.

It is worth emphasizing that the problems with exposing `Node` or `Edge` in the interface of `Graph` are twofold: (1) we severely limit our ability to alter the implementation — say, to convert our opaque pointers to dumb data (see Figure 3-57, section 3.5.5); (2) we are forced to constrain the functionality we are able to provide clients of `Graph`. By limiting public clients' access to objects of only the *interface* types (`NodeData` and `EdgeData`), we allow much more flexibility in what functionality we can provide in the *implementation types* (`Node`, `Edge`, and `std::vector`) and how they interact at the lower levels of the subsystem headed by `Graph`.

3.5.10.3   Single-Component Wrapper

Sometimes we don't want (or cannot afford) to rework our design entirely. Where possible, we might instead choose to create a single-component wrapper (e.g., see Figures 3-5 and 3-6b, sections 3.1.10 and 3.1.10.6, respectively) that encapsulates the use of *all* of the subsystem's components and provides indirect access to their underlying functionality. This encapsulating wrapper, sometimes called a *facade*,[143] can make public consumption easier and safer by consolidating, in a single component, only what clients truly need to use from the underlying subsystem. What's more, having a physically separate, carefully curated programmatic *view* on the low-level functionality provides an extra degree of stability, affording the flexibility to much more broadly rework and enhance the underlying implementation, without adversely impacting its public clients.

Figure 3-95 illustrates how a single-component wrapper, **xyza_pubgraph**, can serve to encapsulate the use of all of the components in a subsystem headed by a Graph manager class, which — by itself — cannot do much *syntactically* (i.e., at compile time) to help ensure that its invariants are preserved.[144] In this wrapper-based implementation, Graph is a private data member of class PubGraph, but none of the implementation of Graph — apart from common lower-level *vocabulary* types (see Volume II, section 4.4), such as std::string and bdlt::Date — is used in the interface of the wrapper component that implements PubGraph. That is, we are now able to make essentially *any* arbitrary changes to the structure of the underlying subsystem managed by Graph without reneging on promises made by the interface and contract of the (higher-level) wrapper component, **xyza_pubgraph**.

---

[143] **gamma95**, Chapter 4, section "Facade," pp. 185–193

[144] For alternatives to a purely syntactic defense against client misuse, see Volume II, sections 5.2, 5.3, and 6.8.

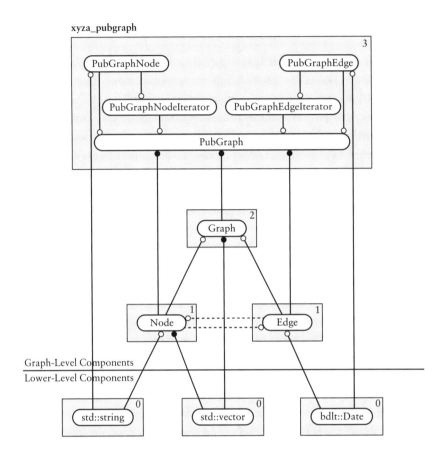

xyza_pubgraph

Figure 3-95: Creating an encapsulating `Graph`-wrapper component

Note that the example above was crafted to *explain* how this design might come into being, but not necessarily how it *should* be rendered when designed this way from the start. If given the chance, we might opt to rename `Graph` to something like `GraphImp` (or move it to a lower-level package), and then remove the "**pub**" prefix from the wrapper component name along with those of all of its contained classes, leaving the unsuspecting client oblivious to our underlying wrapper-based design. In any given situation, this renaming decision will depend on the extent to which the underlying system can be safely and more productively used directly by (at least some) public clients, along with any (measured) runtime performance improvement for doing so.

3.5.10.4   Overhead Due to Wrapping

The use of single-component wrappers is often not appropriate. In addition to not scaling to subsystems of arbitrary size (see Figure 3-6c, section 3.1.10.6), using a subsystem via a fully encapsulating wrapper (depending on the implementation and platform) might well result in additional runtime overhead compared to accessing the unwrapped system directly.[145] If it is intended that some degree of compile-time coupling is to be alleviated as well (see section 3.10.1), the resulting runtime overhead, e.g., of an *insulating wrapper* component (see section 3.11.6.1), can be dramatically higher.[146] Hence, a single-component wrapper — if employed — might well need to be situated at a sufficiently high level in the physical hierarchy so as not to impose an unacceptable degradation of runtime performance.

3.5.10.5   Realizing Multicomponent Wrappers

There are times when we might reasonably want to provide new clients of a (potentially massive) burgeoning subsystem — having a large number of "touch points" — with a more stable interface than would be possible if those clients were forced to access that subsystem directly. As we know, single-component wrappers do not scale to arbitrarily large numbers of cooperating wrapper classes, and multicomponent wrappers that conform to our component-based design rules (section 2.6) are not generally realizable by conventional means (sections 3.1.10.6–3.1.10.9). Fortunately, an important new incarnation of escalating encapsulation has emerged since its debut[147] that can be applied much more generally to create an appropriately restricted view, for select clients, of an arbitrary collection of components interacting in unstable, intimate, subtle, or error-prone ways at a lower level in the physical hierarchy.

This highly specialized — edgy yet portable — variant of the escalating-encapsulation levelization technique allows us to finally realize many of the benefits of wrapping, without *any* of the overhead often associated with a single-component wrapper. This novel solution involves

---

[145] **lakos96**, section 6.6.4, Figure 6-89, p. 466 (Systems I & II)
[146] **lakos96**, section 6.6.4, Figure 6-89, p. 466 (Systems III & IV)
[147] **lakos96**, section 5.10, pp. 312–324

the use of *shadow classes*, each implemented in its own separate component, and (typically) sequestered together in a higher-level *wrapper package*.[148]

3.5.10.6   Applying This New, "Heretical" Technique to Our Graph Example

For continuity, let us start by again considering the graph-subsystem design of Figure 3-56, section 3.5.4.3, in which we were unable to provide arbitrary `Node` or `Edge` functionality, as doing so would have exposed inappropriate functionality to public clients of `Graph`. Suppose for the moment, that `Graph`, `Node`, and `Edge` serve as a metaphor for a much larger collection of much more sophisticated classes having dozens, perhaps even hundreds, of methods each: The original motivation that led to this new twist on escalating encapsulation is captured for posterity in Figure 3-96.

HISTORICAL SIDEBAR

The use case that precipitated this new approach to escalating encapsulation was a highly efficient, arbitrarily complex self-describing data structure consisting of a couple of dozen scalar and corresponding vector types, as well as a heterogeneous list and table. The `List` class contained an object of type `Row`, which, in turn, could contain a sequence of any of the above types. Similarly, the `Table` class contained zero or more `Row` objects. In order to append a `Table` element to a `List` object, `List` would clearly have to know about class `Table`. Similarly, appending a `Row` to a table having a `List` as one of its column types would presumably force a dependency of both `Row` and `Table` on `List`. This heterogeneous data structure would be reused heavily for a wide variety of applications, so we needed to squeeze out every bit of space while maximizing runtime performance. Separately, being a deliberately closed system, we also wanted to avoid conventional solutions using a naive implementation of the composite pattern,[149] which (historically) has involved openly inheriting from an abstract interface.

---

[148] As of this writing, there is no logical or physical architectural construct in modern C++ beyond that of a translation unit to support any form of package-wide friendship (not recommended) the way there is in, say, the Java programming language. The notion of a *module* in C++ had been contemplated since the mid-2000s with an eye toward supporting the next level of software architecture directly in the language. For some time, however, its primary motivation and focus seemed, for many, to have drifted to merely improving compile-time performance.

Our novel rendering of the *escalating-encapsulation* levelization technique, presented here, seems to address (albeit clumsily) many of the relevant architectural issues about as well as can be done given the current and foreseeable limitations of C++. Know that the author — a long-time active voting member of the C++ Standards Committee representing Bloomberg LP — has been working tirelessly to bring about an architecturally sound modules feature that, in addition to being a better implementation for a *component*, will also serve to provide abridged yet *interoperable* (*encapsulating*, but not *insulating*) views on subsystems much the same way that a well-designed C-compatible procedural interface (PI) exposes (opaquely) the very same types that are used in the underlying subsystems (see section 3.11.7.12).

[149] **gamma95**, Chapter 4, section "Composite," pp. 163–173

> Placing the entire client-facing interface of this recursive data structure in a single component would have made testing and, even more importantly, client use of this substantial subsystem extremely cumbersome. By factoring out and *demoting* (described above) a suite of low-level "descriptors," invoked via *callbacks* (see above), we were able to characterize the essential *properties* of each concrete element type without having to depend on the definition of the type itself. Although we were able to eliminate all cyclic physical dependencies among the implementations of `Row`, `List`, and `Table` needed to achieve an overall levelizable design, they were at far too low a level of abstraction to be used safely by public clients directly. Still, we were determined to house the client-facing `Row`, `List`, and `Table` in their own separate components without cycles or the use of long-distance friendship. Hence, this relatively new approach to *escalating encapsulation*[150] was born.

Figure 3-96: Genesis of escalating encapsulation using multicomponent wrappers

Despite the aforementioned (historical) technical difficulties (section 3.1.10.6), what we would like to do is to somehow create a multicomponent *facade* that wraps each of these types individually in separate components and then provide only the subset of their respective functionalities that are desirable to present to public clients. The proposed solution to this perplexing problem relies on a small amount of collaborative knowledge about the physical structure of the other components participating in the cooperating wrapper subsystem and yet is a far cry from granting private access *en masse* to all the individual implementation details of each of the underlying subsystems components.

The process of translating our unwrapped `Graph` subsystem to one having a multicomponent wrapper is straightforward. The first step is to copy (a.k.a. "dupe") each of the three components implementing the respective client-facing types, `Node`, `Edge`, and `Graph`, and then rename each of the originals to reflect their respective new roles as implementation types (say, `NodeImp`, `EdgeImp`, and `GraphImp`) as illustrated in Figure 3-97a. The next step is to replace all of the data members in these new client-facing types with just a single embedded data member of its corresponding wrapped (now implementation) type as shown in Figure 3-97b. Finally, each method that we choose to expose to public clients needs to be implemented as a (typically `inline`) "magic" forwarding function that can gain access to the underlying implementation type of each object used in the interface — a few choice examples of which are shown in Figure 3-103c.

---

[150] Credit to Pablo Halpern, Vladimir Kliatchko, and Jeff Mendelsohn of Bloomberg LP (c. 2004) for their pioneering work.

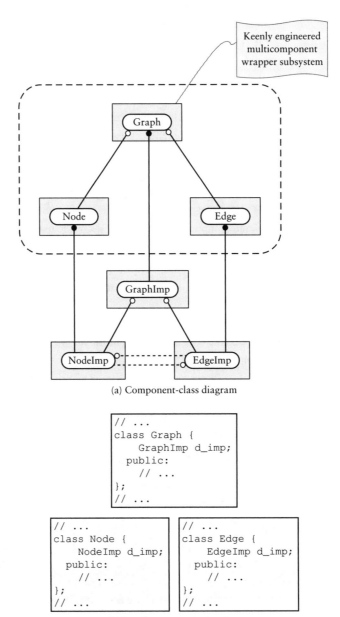

(a) Component-class diagram

```
// ...
class Graph {
    GraphImp d_imp;
  public:
    // ...
};
// ...
```

```
// ...
class Node {
    NodeImp d_imp;
  public:
    // ...
};
// ...
```

```
// ...
class Edge {
    EdgeImp d_imp;
  public:
    // ...
};
// ...
```

(b) Interface-type member data

```
inline int Graph::removeNode(const Node *node)
{
    const NodeImp *nodeImp = reinterpret_cast<const NodeImp*>(node);    // MAGIC
    return d_imp.removeNode(nodeImp);
}

inline Node *Graph::addNode(double data)
{
    NodeImp *retImp = d_imp.addNode(data);
    return reinterpret_cast<Node *>(retImp);                       // INVERSE MAGIC
}

inline Edge *Graph::addEdge(double data, const Node *head, const Node *tail)
{
    const NodeImp *headImp = reinterpret_cast<const NodeImp *>(head);   // MAGIC
    const NodeImp *tailImp = reinterpret_cast<const NodeImp *>(tail);   // MAGIC
    EdgeImp       *retImp  = d_imp.addEdge(data, headImp, tailImp);
    return reinterpret_cast<Edge *>(retImp);                       // INVERSE MAGIC
}

inline const Node *Edge::head(const Edge *edge) const
{
    const EdgeImp *edgeImp = reinterpret_cast<const EdgeImp *>(edge);   // MAGIC
    const NodeImp *retImp  = d_imp.head(edgeImp);
    return reinterpret_cast<const Node *>(retImp);                 // INVERSE MAGIC
}
```

(c) Example of "magic" forwarding functions

Figure 3-97: Collaboratively simulating a multicomponent wrapper

At first, it might not appear as if we have done anything useful here, but we have. Had we tried to use long-distance friendship with the original components, we would have openly exposed the entirety of each underlying types' implementation to the objects accessing it — a stark violation of sound engineering practice and our component-based design rules (section 2.6). On the other hand, knowing just the one "dirty little secret" (i.e., Figure 3-97b) common to each of the types participating in the wrapper subsystem allows other fellow components in that wrapper subsystem to (portably) reach in and grab access (as explained further below) to *just* the *public* functionality of the single wrapped (implementation) data member of wrapped argument objects — nothing more! That is, unlike with long-distance friendships, we continue to be free to improve (compatibly, of course) the implementations of any of the components in our underlying subsystem independently of *all* others, adding suitable wrapper components and forwarding functions only after the architecture and functionality of the implementation components have been determined to be sufficiently stable.

3.5.10.7   Why Use This "Magic" `reinterpret_cast` Technique?

This approach, admittedly not the simplest possible, provides important advantages (discussed below), especially when compared to breaking our long-distance friendship rule — even when such illicit friendships are limited to just the wrapper components. To the uninitiated, it might seem as if what we are proposing here is *undefined behavior* (see Volume II, section 5.2) or, at the very least, not fully specified in the C++ Standard and, therefore, not guaranteed to be portable across all platforms. As it turns out, not only has this specific implementation technique always worked on all real-world platforms, the C++ Standard itself requires that it be so.[151,152]

In our proposed multicomponent-wrapper design pattern, upon which we will elaborate below, the wrapper types themselves do not participate (at least not syntactically) in any inheritance relationships, nor do they have any virtual functions. Because an object of the wrapped type is the only (and therefore the first) data member of the wrapper type, their respective sizes and alignments (see Volume II, section 6.7) will naturally be the same on all platforms. Moreover, the wrapper and nested wrapped object in both C and C++ reside at the same address in memory.[153]

---

[151] In fact, as of C++17, casting such related pointers between one another, via `reinterpret_cast`, is explicitly guaranteed by the C++ Standard to work as intended on all conforming platforms (**cpp17**, section 6.9.2, paragraph 4, p. 82; styling is my own):

> Two objects a and b are pointer-interconvertible if . . . one is a standard-layout class object and the other is the first non-static data member of that object . . . If two objects are pointer-interconvertible, then they have the same address, and it is possible to obtain a pointer to one from a pointer to the other via a `reinterpret_cast`. . . .

[152] Some might argue that we can achieve the same effect more conveniently, if not more portably, by using private inheritance. We respectfully disagree. We generally discourage private inheritance (section 2.4.12) as (1) it encourages the use of `using` declarations, which would invite public clients to examine supposedly private implementation details, and (2) even if (inline) forwarding functions were provided explicitly (along with their public-facing documentation), the syntax required to create private inheritance would nonetheless necessarily appear as part of the "public" definition of the wrapper class — something we feel is entirely unacceptable in general, and especially so in the case of wrappers.

[153] The C++17 Standard defines `standard-layout types` as "Scalar types, standard-layout class types (Clause 12), arrays of such types and cv-qualified versions of these types are collectively called standard-layout types" (**cpp17**, section 6.9, paragraph 9, p. 78). `standard-layout class types` are defined in a 12-item bulleted list (**cpp17**, section 12, paragraph 7, p. 238). Finally, the layout guarantees are given (**cpp17**, section 12.2, pp. 241–251); in particular, "If a standard-layout class object has any non-static data members, its address is the same as the address of its first non-static data member" (**cpp17**, section 12.2, paragraph 24, p. 244).

When using this package-wide multicomponent-wrapper design pattern, the higher-level wrapper component is capable of unilaterally accessing the public interface of the contained wrapped component without having to modify the wrapper component defining the type of the object being accessed, say, by having to add a corresponding `friend` declaration granting long-distance access to the calling object type. Employing this implementation approach also serendipitously makes a program "ill-formed"[154] if any wrapper class used in that program has any additional data members before the wrapped object, which goes to reinforce the purity[155] of our wrapper design. This purity serves to ensure that the maintenance of the wrapper remains a straightforward mechanical process and that all of the "creativity" is relegated to the underlying implementation layer where we assert it rightfully belongs.[156] Finally, that it is "OK" to cast an interface type to its corresponding implementation type is sufficiently arcane and nonintuitive — not to mention that doing so relies on unpublished implementation details — that no reasonable public client would ever think to do such a thing themselves.[157,158]

3.5.10.8   Wrapping a Package-Sized System

Let's now consider wrapping an entire package of components, which we will call **subs**, representing an arbitrary subsystem involving various inter-component logical relationships — Is-A, Uses-In-The-Interface, and Uses-In-The-Implementation — as described in section 1.7. Let us assume that this **subs** package is under active development, and, therefore, not all of that which has been implemented so far is necessarily yet ready for widespread, public consumption. Figure 3-98 provides a high-level schematic representation of the **subs** package, which (by design) embeds several common physical design patterns that we will now exploit for didactic purposes.

---

[154] OK, hypertechnically the program is *not* ill-formed because there is no ODR violation (each wrapper is a distinct C++ type from the one it wraps), and the behavior will be undefined only if an actual attempt is made to *use* the result of a `reinterpret_cast` on a wrapper type having incompatibly-aligned member data. A program that is truly *ill-formed* cannot (by definition) be run in any way without resulting in undefined behavior. Such is not necessarily the case here.

[155] There are to be absolutely no additional data members nor non-forwarding functions (apart from inheritance-related conversions) in any wrapper class.

[156] This same sort of *purity* applies to procedural interface (PI) "wrapper" functions (see section 3.11.7.7).

[157] If you still think this approach is somehow equivalent to breaking encapsulation via providing a member function such as

```
EdgeImp& internal_details_not_for_client_use_()
```

in the wrapper, think again. Such a function amounts to an attractive nuisance, cluttering the API of the wrapper; in this approach, the client is served a clean interface containing exactly what's needed, nothing more.

[158] Ideally, the proposed new C++ modules feature will *eventually* (post C++20) address this issue far better than even we were able to do here using premodern C++ (see **lakos17a**, section 3, item I, paragraphs c and d, p. 2).

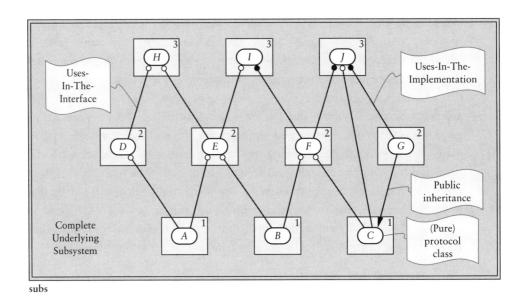

Figure 3-98: Schematic representation of a large subsystem (`subs`)

Just as we did with the `Graph` subsystem above (Figure 3-97), we will need to "dupe" the entire **subs** package — including all of its components — into a new package, which we will call **wrap**. Each class that remains in the wrapper layer — apart from those representing abstract base classes (see below) — will necessarily have a single data member that is of the corresponding type in the original **subs** package. This new, higher-level **wrap** package will now represent the public clients (stable) view of our low-level **subs** package.

The first step in the process of pruning dependencies in the wrapper package, **wrap**, is to realize that none of the Uses-In-The-Implementation dependencies that pertained in the lower-level **subs** subsystem is relevant in **wrap**. In particular, the Uses-In-The-Implementation relationship in **subs** from class I to class F, and from class J to classes F and G, simply do not exist in the **wrap** package. We have identified this property using the label (1) in the combined **subs** and **wrap** packages illustrated in (the admittedly dense) Figure 3-99, which we will endeavor to unpack over the next several paragraphs.

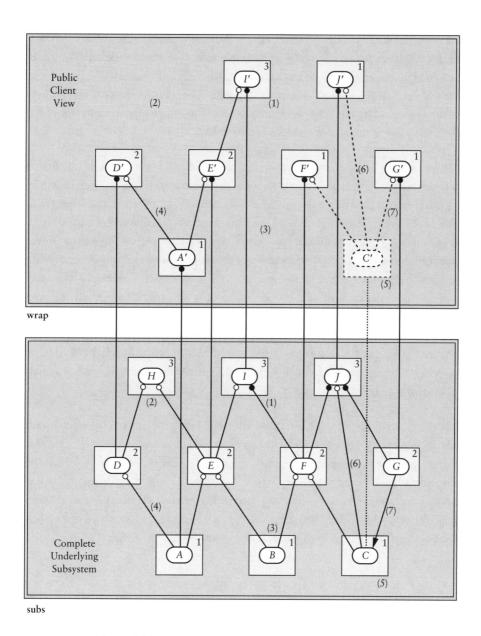

Figure 3-99: Schematic illustration of wrapped subsystem

The next step is to consider which, if any, of the components in the **subs** (subsystem) package are, for whatever reason, currently undesirable to expose more widely in the **wrap** (wrapper) package. For example, it might be that class H, label (2) in Figure 3-99, is brand new and therefore not yet "baked" enough to expose to public clients at the wrapper level. The component defining such a class could be summarily deleted from the wrapper package without having to modify any of the remaining wrapper components.

Recall that our final *levelization technique* (described in this section) is all about escalating the level at which encapsulation occurs. Suppose that there is some class B, label (3) in Figure 3-99, that is used in the interface of two other classes, E and F, all of which resided at the lower levels of the **subs** package. It might be that the communication facilitated by B exposes implementation details or is otherwise simply too dangerous to allow public clients to use directly. Failing to publish the header for class B in **subs** as a means of preventing public clients from exploiting the Uses-In-The-Interface relationship in E or F would convolve development with deployment (section 2.15) and prevent side-by-side reuse of B in programs that also incorporate **subs** (e.g., see Figure 3-129, section 3.9.7). We can, however, omit from **wrap** the component that defines B entirely and, at the same time, remove all functionality from the respective components defining E and F in **wrap** that use B in their respective interfaces. In this way, we can surgically eliminate problem functionality, while preserving that which we genuinely want our public clients to consume.

In section 3.1.10.6 (see Figure 3-6a), we articulated the problem we had when it came to wrapping an element, `bdlt::Date`, and its container, `odet::DateSequence`, using separate components, **my_date** and **my_timeseries**, respectively. Let's now zoom in on that specific issue here: label (4) in Figure 3-99. Figure 3-100a illustrates the prospect of wrapping, in separate components, an element `subs::Date` and a container of such elements `subs::DateSequence`. By virtue of knowing that each class defined in **wrap** has, as its only data member, an object of the corresponding type from **subs**, it is straightforward for `wrap::DataSequence` to reach into `wrap::Date` and grab access (as a reference[159,160]) to its (unique) `subs::Date` data member to supply to its own (unique) `subs::DateSequence` data member as illustrated in Figure 3-100b.

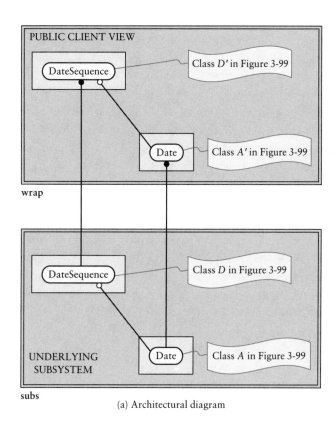

(a) Architectural diagram

---

[159] The C++17 Standard states, "[*Note*: That is, for lvalues, a reference cast `reinterpret_cast<T&>(x)` has the same effect as the conversion `*reinterpret_cast<T*>(&x)` with the built-in `&` and `*` operators (and similarly for `reinterpret_cast<T&&>(x)`). — *end note*]" (**cpp17**, section 8.2.10, paragraph 11, p. 118).

[160] Although still true in C++20, the paragraph was reworded, and the C++17 note (apparently deemed superfluous) was removed.

```
// ...
#include <iosfwd>  // for 'std::ostream'
// ...
namespace subs {

class Date {
    // ...
  public:
    Date(int year, int month, int day);
    std::ostream& print(std::ostream& stream) const;
};

class DateSequence {
    // ...
  public:
    DateSequence();
    void append(const Date& date);
};

}  // close package namespace

namespace wrap {

class Date {
    subs::Date d_imp;
  public:
    Date(int year, int month, int day) : d_imp(year, month, day) { }
};

class DateSequence {
    subs::DateSequence d_imp;

  public:
    DateSequence() : d_imp() { }

    void append(const Date& date)
    {
        const subs::Date& dateImp = reinterpret_cast<const subs::Date&>(date);
        d_imp.append(dateImp);
    }
};

}  // close package namespace
// ...
```

This is how we extract a reference to the type providing the underlying subs functionality from the wrap argument type that contains it.

(b) Illustrative source code

Figure 3-100: Addressing specific date/container example (from Figure 3-6a)

Wrapping public-inheritance relationships is inherently problematic, and we might well have chosen to ignore logical inheritance in the wrapper package entirely. That said, there is still some ability, albeit limited, to address semantic inheritance relationships in the wrapper layer, which we have chosen to present here. Although it will not be possible for clients of the wrapper layer to extend an interface through derivation, it will be possible for those clients to select from among existing derived classes to plug into types accepting the address of an in-name-only wrapper "base" class.

Referring to Figure 3-99, class c — identified in both packages by label (5) — is abstract. In **subs**, C is a pure abstract (*protocol*) base class; in **wrap**, C is an in-name-only class having no definition at all anywhere. Nonetheless, a pointer to `wrap::C` necessarily represents the same address as a pointer to its **subs** counterpart. Figure 3-101 shows, in more detail, what is transpiring among the respective components of the **wrap** and **subs** packages. Note that the argument passed via the `std::size_t numBytes` parameter of the `consume` method of class `Client` is naturally forwarded directly to the `allocate` method of the held (but not owned) `d_mechanism_p` pointer data member of abstract class `Base`, whereas the `char dummy` parameter of the constructor of concrete class `Derived` serves merely as a placeholder.

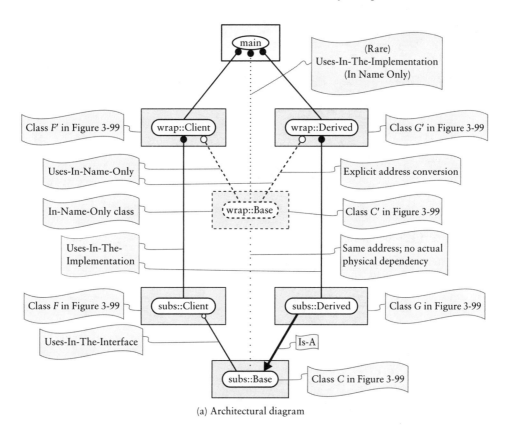

(a) Architectural diagram

```
#include <cstddef>  // for 'std::size_t'
#include <iostream>

namespace subs {                          Pure abstract interface (a.k.a. protocol)

class Base {
  public:
    virtual ~Base() { }
    virtual void *allocate(std::size_t numBytes) = 0;
    virtual void deallocate(void *address) = 0;
};
                                          Concrete client using protocol
class Client {
    Base *d_mechanism_p;
  public:
    Client(Base *mechanism);
    void consume(std::size_t numBytes);
};

class Derived : public Base {  // Concrete Derived Implementation of Protocol
    char d_dummy;  // place holder
  public:
    Derived(char dummy);
    void *allocate(std::size_t numBytes);
    void deallocate(void *address);        Definitions "Inlined"
};                                         for illustration only
                                           (See Volume II, section 6.14.)
}  // close package namespace

namespace wrap {      In-Name-Only class

class Base;
                      Concrete client using
class Client {        In-Name-Only class
    subs::Client d_imp;
  public:
    Client(Base *mechanism)
    : d_imp(reinterpret_cast<subs::Base *>(mechanism)) { }

    void consume(std::size_t numBytes) { d_imp.consume(numBytes); }
};                   Concrete "derived" implementation
                     of In-Name-Only class
class Derived {                                         Explicit pointer conversion
    subs::Derived d_imp;
  public:
    static Base *toBase(Derived *p) { return reinterpret_cast<Base *>(p); }
    static const Base *toBase(const Derived *p) { return
                                       reinterpret_cast<const Base *>(p); }
    Derived(char dummy) : d_imp(dummy) { }
```

(continues)

(continued)

```
    void *allocate(std::size_t numBytes) { return d_imp.allocate(numBytes); }

    void deallocate(void *address) { d_imp.deallocate(address); }
};

}  // close package namespace

int main()
{
    std::cout << "Using the 'subs' level directly:" << std::endl;

    subs::Derived sd('S');
    subs::Client  sc(&sd);
    sc.consume(100);

    std::cout << "Using the 'wrap' level instead:" << std::endl;

    wrap::Derived wd('W');
    wrap::Client  wc(wrap::Derived::toBase(&wd));
    wc.consume(200);

    return 0;
}
```

(b) Illustrative source code

Figure 3-101: Limited ability to wrap classes related by public inheritance

For this multicomponent-wrapper technique to work, there can be no syntactic inheritance in the wrapper layer. We can, however, still allow a client to accept a variety of derived implementations by way of an in-name-only class, label (6) in Figure 3-99. That is, to mimic the syntax of inheritance, we will need to replace the automatic standard conversion of a properly derived class in **subs** with an explicit manual one in **wrap**, label (7) in Figure 3-99. Although we are not necessarily advocating this approach to wrapping inherited relationships, we feel duty bound to present what we know is possible (see also section 3.11.7.15).

3.5.10.9   Benefits of This Multicomponent-Wrapper Technique

Using this perhaps overly artful escalating-encapsulation technique, it is now practicable to filter out problematic low-level functionality to form a new, stable, client-facing, multicomponent-wrapper interface without impacting the performance of a dynamically changing underlying subsystem. Each of the surviving components and methods in a thoughtfully abridged, much more stable, wrapper forwards directly to the corresponding method of the lower-level embedded data member, thereby eliminating all of the overhead resulting from indirect access often associated with *insulating* wrappers (see section 3.11.6). Each of these (*encapsulating*-only) wrapper types will, of course, need to know (physically) about all the other (lower-level) wrapper types that are used in the interface, along with those of corresponding wrapped types that are used in the implementation. Note that, unlike insulating wrappers, these wrapper components expose clients to the same compile-time coupling that they would experience had they included the underlying components directly[161]; a variant of this technique that uses a sufficiently large and aligned opaque byte buffer and noninline functions to achieve substantial insulation is also possible (see Volume II, section 6.6).

3.5.10.10   Misuse of This Escalating-Encapsulation Technique

What appliers of this technique should *not* do is make any attempt to augment, in any wrapper class itself, either the member data or the functionality of its underlying implementation type, with the sole exception of explicit `static` conversion functions from "derived" to (in-name-only) base-class wrapper pointers (see also sections 3.11.7.6 and 3.11.7.15). That is, apart from knowing how to access the implementation type from its corresponding interface type and to convert back again (e.g., as a return type), there should be *no* additional data or functionality defined in the wrapper class. In this way, the wrapper subsystem remains thin, providing just an appropriately narrow view of the underlying subsystem, which alone properly defines all domain-related functionality.

3.5.10.11   Simulating a Highly Restricted Form of Package-Wide Friendship

The advantages of this most recently discovered approach to escalating encapsulation are many. Since interface and implementation objects are — by design — necessarily the same size, no additional space is required. And, because the type conversion and inline forwarding are performed at compile time, there should not be *any* additional runtime overhead on modern platforms. That is, this relatively new *multicomponent-wrapper*-based escalating-encapsulation levelization technique results in increased stability for clients, greater flexibility for implementers, and (in theory) absolutely no additional runtime or spatial overhead. Note, however, that this collaborative knowledge is intentionally localized to the subsystem or package that implements the wrapper layer and falls short of an ideal modeling of inheritance relationships. Hence, this highly specialized technique is not an entirely general solution to the multicomponent wrapper problem posed in section 3.1.10.

---

[161] The modules language feature introduced in C++20 is remarkably similar *physically* (and potentially someday architecturally as well) to the wrapper components of the *encapsulating-wrapper-package* escalating-encapsulation technique discussed here. In particular, C++ modules provide additional means of *encapsulation* and might eventually also support interoperable *views* on lower-level subsystems. With respect to *insulation* (see section 3.11.1), however, C++ modules necessarily do nothing more to avoid compile-time coupling of clients on (encapsulated) implementation details than what is already supported by conventional header files.

Still, this shiny new twist on the escalating-encapsulation levelization technique is — to date — the most effective tool we have for implementing efficient general-purpose multicomponent wrappers. Until there is additional language support[162] for an architectural entity at a higher level of abstraction than a translation unit, this admittedly arcane approach is most likely the best we can do.

3.5.11   Section Summary

To recap: This section — by far the largest and arguably the most important in this volume — describes in detail nine levelization techniques that were first introduced to the world back in 1996 (repeated here from Figure 3-42, section 3.5.1).

Escalation	Moving mutually dependent functionality higher in the physical hierarchy
Demotion	Moving common functionality lower in the physical hierarchy
Opaque Pointers	Having an object use another in name only
Dumb Data	Using data that indicates a dependency on a peer object, but only in the context of a separate, higher-level object
Redundancy	Deliberately avoiding reuse by repeating small amounts of code or data to avoid coupling
Callbacks	Client-supplied functions that enable (typically lower-level) subsystems to perform specific tasks in a more global context
Manager Class	Establishing a class that owns and coordinates lower-level objects
Factoring	Moving independently testable sub-behavior out of the implementations of complex components involved in excessive physical coupling
Escalating Encapsulation	Moving the point at which implementation details are hidden from clients to a higher level in the physical hierarchy

---

[162] The nascent modules language feature, introduced as part of C++20, does *not* provide the essential (e.g., fine-grained) architectural support required to obviate this baroque *escalating-encapsulation* technique; see **lakos17a**, section 3, item I, paragraph c, p. 2.

The C++ language, along with the distributed-computing landscape, have evolved, over the years, but the basic ideas of preserving an acyclic physical hierarchy remain the same.[163] Since they were first introduced, however, two of these nine seminal levelization techniques have undergone significant expansion. Most significantly, the callback levelization technique — originally considered a refuge of last resort — has blossomed into a first-class approach, comprising five variants:

1. Data: Hold the address of higher-level data.

2. Function: Hold the address of a higher-level stateless function.

3. Functor: Incorporate an invocable object, bound at compile time.

4. Protocol: Use of runtime polymorphism to access a higher level.

5. Concept: Use of compile-time polymorphism to access a higher level.

Finally, the original *escalating-encapsulation* technique has been extended to allow for restricted use of multicomponent wrappers whereby shared knowledge within the wrapper-component community allows one wrapper object to `reinterpret_cast` another to its uniquely wrapped data member. In this way, one wrapper can unilaterally gain access to *only* the *public* interface of its wrapped subobject and then deliver (a reference to) that subobject to its own uniquely wrapped subobject.

3.6   Avoiding Excessive Link-Time Dependencies

If you have ever attempted to reuse a small amount of functionality in a library and found that your time to link and the resulting size of your program have increased disproportionately to the benefit you are deriving, then you might be incorporating excessive code due to poor physical factoring.

In object-oriented systems, it is alarmingly easy to add "missing" functionality to objects whenever a need presents itself. This seductive feature of the paradigm has tempted many conscientious developers to turn lean, well-factored software into what we call "Winnebago classes" that embody or otherwise depend on tremendous amounts of code, most of which is unused by

---

[163] For additional discussion of these nine fundamental levelization techniques, see **lakos96**, Chapter 5, pp. 203–325.

most clients. Not only are such classes difficult to navigate and generally less stable, they are also a common cause of excessive link-time dependencies and code bloat.

3.6.1   An Initially Well-Factored Date Class That Degrades Over Time

For example, consider the (well-intentioned) `Date` class shown in Figure 3-102. Like most reasonably well-designed, user-defined types, this one is complete, minimal, and primitive (section 3.2.7). A *date*, like an integer or a character string, is a part of the basic *vocabulary* in many domains, particularly those relating to finance. Like an integer or a character string, the *value* of a date is independent of its representation (see Volume II, section 4.1). Moreover, it will turn out to be desirable to have just a single type within a system, code base, or, ideally, language that is the preferred way to express that kind of value (e.g., `int`, `double`, `const char *`, `std::string`,[164] `core::Date`), particularly across interface boundaries. In order to ensure that such *vocabulary* types (see Volume II, section 4.4) can be used widely at a low level in the physical hierarchy (see section 3.7.3), it is crucial that they retain their lightweight, focused purpose — i.e., that of stably and efficiently representing a value, nothing more.

---

[164] As of C++17, `std::string_view` provides an alternative interface type useful for uniting arguments of types `const char *` and `const std::string&`.

```
// core_date.h                                                    -*-C++-*-
// ...

#include <core_dayofweek.h>
#include <iosfwd>

namespace core {

class Date {
    // This class defines a value-semantic type representing a (valid) date
    // value that falls within the range '[1/1/1 .. 9999/12/31]' in the
    // *Proleptic* *Gregorian* calendar.

    // ...

  public:
    // CLASS METHODS
    static bool isValidYearMonthDay(int year, int month, int day);
        // Return 'true' if the specified 'year', 'month', and 'day' represent
        // a valid date value, and 'false' otherwise.  A date value is valid if
        // it corresponds to a date in the *Proleptic* *Gregorian* calendar in
        // the range [1/1/1 .. 9999/12/31].

    // CREATORS
    Date();
        // Create a 'Date' object whose value corresponds to today's date.

    Date(int year, int month, int day);
        // Create an object to represent the date value corresponding to the
        // specified 'year', 'month', and 'day'.  The behavior is undefined
        // unless 'year', 'month', and 'day' correspond to a valid date value
        // within the range '[1/1/1 .. 9999/12/31]'.  See
        // 'isValidYearMonthDay'.

    Date(const Date& original);
        // Create a 'Date' object having the same value as the specified
        // 'original' date.

    ~Date();
        // Destroy this object.

    // MANIPULATORS
    Date& operator=(const Date& rhs);
        // Assign to this object the value of the specified 'rhs' object, and
        // return a reference providing modifiable access to this object.

    Date& operator+=(int days);
        // Assign to this object the value that is later by the specified
        // (signed) number of 'days' from its current value, and return a
        // reference providing modifiable access to this object.  The behavior
        // is undefined unless the resulting value would fall within the
```

See Volume II, section 4.3.

BAD IDEA!
See section 3.8.1.

(continues)

(continued)

```
        // (valid) range '[1/1/1 .. 9999/12/31]'.  Note that 'days' may be
        // negative.

    Date& operator-=(int days);
        // Assign to this object the value that is earlier by the specified
        // (signed) number of 'days' from its current value, and return a
        // reference providing modifiable access to this object.  The behavior
        // is undefined unless the resulting value would fall within the
        // (valid) range '[1/1/1 .. 9999/12/31]'.  Note that 'days' may be
        // negative.
```
See Volume II, section 6.13.
```
    Date& operator++();
        // Set this object to have the date value that is one day later than
        // its current value, and return a reference providing modifiable
        // access to this object.  The behavior is undefined unless the
        // resulting value would fall within the (valid) range
        // '[1/1/1 .. 9999/12/31]'.

    Date& operator--();
        // Set this object to have the date value that is one day earlier than
        // its current value, and return a reference providing modifiable
        // access to this object.  The behavior is undefined unless the
        // resulting value would fall within the (valid) range
        // '[1/1/1 .. 9999/12/31]'.
```
See Volume II, section 5.2
```
    void setYearMonthDay(int year, int month, int day);
        // Set this object to have the date value corresponding to the
        // specified 'year', 'month', and 'day'.  The behavior is undefined
        // unless 'year', 'month', and 'day' correspond to a valid date value
        // within the range '[1/1/1 .. 9999/12/31]'.  See
        // 'isValidYearMonthDay'.
```
See Volume II, section 6.11
```
    int setYearMonthDayIfValid(int year, int month, int day);
        // Set this object to have the (valid) date value corresponding to the
        // specified 'year', 'month', and 'day' within the range
        // '[1/1/1 .. 9999/12/31]'; return 0 on success, and a non-zero value
        // (with no effect) otherwise.  See 'isValidYearMonthDay'.

    // ACCESSORS
    int year() const;
        // Return the year, '[1 .. 9999]', corresponding to this date value.

    int month() const;
        // Return the month, '[1 .. 12]', corresponding to this date value.

    int day() const;
        // Return the day, '[1 .. 31]', corresponding to this date value.

    void getYearMonthDay(int *year, int *month, int *day) const;
        // Load, into the specified 'year', 'month', and 'day', the attributes
        // corresponding to this object's value.
```

(continues)

(continued)

```
    DayOfWeek::Enum dayOfWeek() const;
        // Return the enumerated day of the week, '[e_SUNDAY .. e_SATURDAY]',
        // corresponding to this object's value.
};


// FREE OPERATORS
bool operator==(const Date& lhs, const Date& rhs);
    // Return 'true' if the specified 'lhs' and 'rhs' objects have the same
    // value, and 'false' otherwise.  Two 'Date' objects have the same value
    // if the corresponding 'year', 'month', and 'day' attributes,
    // respectively, have the same value.

bool operator!=(const Date& lhs, const Date& rhs);
    // Return 'true' if the specified 'lhs' and 'rhs' objects do not have the
    // same value, and 'false' otherwise.  Two 'Date' objects do not have the
    // same value if any of the corresponding 'year', 'month', and 'day'
    // attributes, respectively, do not have the same value.

bool operator>(const Date& lhs, const Date& rhs);
    // Return 'true' if the specified 'lhs' value comes chronologically after
    // the specified 'rhs' value, and 'false' otherwise.

bool operator>=(const Date& lhs, const Date& rhs);
    // Return 'true' if the specified 'lhs' value is the same as or comes
    // chronologically after the specified 'rhs' value, and 'false' otherwise.

bool operator<(const Date& lhs, const Date& rhs);
    // Return 'true' if the specified 'lhs' value comes chronologically before
    // the specified 'rhs' value, and 'false' otherwise.

bool operator<=(const Date& lhs, const Date& rhs);
    // Return 'true' if the specified 'lhs' value is the same as or comes
    // chronologically before the specified 'rhs' value, and 'false' otherwise.

Date operator++(Date& object, int);        ⟨ See Volume II, section 6.13. ⟩
    // Set the specified 'object' to have the value that is one day later than
    // its current value, and return, by value, an object representing the
    // original value.  The behavior is undefined unless the resulting value of
    // 'object' would fall within the (valid) range '[1/1/1 .. 9999/12/31]'.

Date operator--(Date& object, int);
    // Set the specified 'object' to have the value that is one day earlier
    // than its current value, and return, by value, an object representing the
    // original value.  The behavior is undefined unless the resulting value of
    // 'object' would fall within the (valid) range '[1/1/1 .. 9999/12/31]'.

Date operator+(const Date& object, int days);
Date operator+(int days, const Date& object);
    // Return, by value, an object representing the date value that is,
    // chronologically, the specified (signed) number of 'days' after that of
    // the specified 'object'.  The behavior is undefined unless the resulting
```

(continues)

(continued)

```
    // value would fall within the (valid) range '[1/1/1 .. 9999/12/31]'.  Note
    // that 'days' can be negative.

Date operator-(const Date& object, int days);
    // Return, by value, an object representing the date value that is,
    // chronologically, the specified (signed) number of 'days' before that of
    // the specified 'object'.  The behavior is undefined unless the resulting
    // value would fall within the (valid) range '[1/1/1 .. 9999/12/31]'.  Note
    // that 'days' can be negative.

int operator-(const Date& date1,  const Date& date2);
    // Return the number of days that the specified 'date2' is chronologically
    // after the specified 'date1'.  Note that if 'date1 > date2', the value
    // returned will be negative.

std::ostream& operator<<(std::ostream& stream, const Date& object);
    // Write, to the specified 'stream', a human-readable representation of
    // the value of the specified 'object', and return a reference to 'stream'.

}  // close package namespace

// ...
```

Figure 3-102: Initially lean, reusable "vocabulary" type: `core::Date`

Initially, the `core::Date` class represented a date value with fairly little extra baggage. Over time, however, substantial *nonprimitive* functionality was added (Figure 3-103a)... and added (Figure 3-103b)... and added (Figure 3-103c)! Although each of the functions indicated in Figure 3-103, taken individually, might contribute relatively little weight, collectively the overhead — both in terms of code bulk and interface complexity — can become substantial.

```cpp
// core_date.h                                                   -*-C++-*-

// ...

namespace core {

class Date {

    // ...

    // ACCESSORS
    int daysDiffIsma30360(const Date& value) const;
        // Return the number of days difference, as defined by the ISMA 30/360
        // day-count convention, between the specified 'value' and the value of
        // this object.  The result will be non-negative if 'value' comes
        // chronologically at or after this object's value.  Exchanging 'value'
        // and this object negates the result.  Note that adding the result to
        // this object does not necessarily achieve the same value as 'value'.

    int daysDiffPsa30360eom(Date& value) const;
        // ...

    int daysDiffSia30360eom(Date& value) const;
        // ...

    int daysDiffSia30360neom(Date& value) const;
        // ...

};

// ...

}  // close package namespace

// ...
```

(a) Day-count conventions (see Figure 3-26, section 3.3.7)

```
// core_date.h                                                  -*-C++-*-
// ...
#include <xyza_format.h>
// ...
#include <string>
// ...
namespace core {
// ...
class Date {
    // ...
    // MANIPULATORS

    // ...

    int fromString(const char *dateSpec);
    int fromString(const char *dateSpec, xyza::Format::Type format);
        // Parse the date value from the specified 'dateSpec' and, if
        // successful, assign the unambiguous value to this object.
        // Optionally specify a 'format' (see 'xyza_format.h') to be used when
        // parsing.  If 'format' is not specified, all known formats will be
        // considered.  Return 0 on success, and non-zero (with no effect)
        // otherwise.

    // ...
```

(continues)

(continued)

```
    // ACCESSORS

    // ...

    void toString(std::string *result, xyza::Format::Type format) const;
        // Write the value of this date to the specified 'result' buffer
        // according to the specified 'format'.  The (ever-growing) enumeration
        // of known 'format' values can be found in 'xyza_format.h'.

    int toString(std::string *result, const char *format) const;
        // Write the value of this date to the specified 'result' buffer as
        // defined by the specified 'format' string comprising zero or more of
        // the supported date-field specifiers:
        //..                                            ⌐Annotation: toggle line-fill⌐
        // +======+==========================================================+
        // | Spec |                    Description                           |
        // +------+----------------------------------------------------------+
        // | %a   |   Abbreviated weekday name [Sun..Sat].                   |
        // | %A   |   Full weekday name [Sunday..Saturday].                  |
        // | %b   |   Abbreviated month name [Jan..Dec].                     |
        // | %B   |   Full month name [January..December].                   |
        // | %d   |   Day of the month as a decimal number [1..31].          |
        // | %j   |   Day of the year as a decimal number [1..366].          |
        // | %m   |   Month as a decimal number [1..12].                     |
        // | %w   |   Weekday as a decimal number [0(Sunday)..6(Saturday)].  |
        // | %x   |   Appropriate date representation [e.g., 12/03/1997].     |
        // | %y   |   Year without century as a decimal number [0..99].      |
        // | %Y   |   Year with century as a decimal number[1..9999].        |
        // | %%   |   %                    (i.e., escaped percent character)  |
        // +------+----------------------------------------------------------+
        //..
        // Return 0 on success, and a non-zero value otherwise. ...

    // ...

};
// ....
}  // close package namespace
// ...
```

(b) Parsing/formatting (see Figure 3-162, section 3.12.6)

```
// core_date.h                                                            -*-C++-*-
// ...
#include <xyza_format.h>
// ...
#include <string>
// ...
namespace core {
// ...
class Date {
    // ...
    // ACCESSORS

    // ...

    int numMonthsInRange(int month, const Date& otherDate);
        // ...

    Date nextMonth() const;
        // ...

    Date ceilMonth(int month) const;
        // ...

    Date previousMonth(int month) const;
        // ...

    Date floorMonth(int month) const;
        // ...

    Date ceilOrPreviousMonthInYear(int month) const;
        // Return the chronologically first date at or after this date that
        // falls in the specified 'month' in the same year, if such a date
        // exists, or else the chronologically last date in 'month' before
        // this date.  The behavior is undefined unless '1 <= month <= 12'.
        // Note that this function is logically equivalent to
        //..
        //  Date d = this->ceilMonth(month);
        //  return d.year() == this->year();
        //         ? d
        //         : this->previousMonth(month);
        //..
        // Also note that such dual operation with respect to business days in
        // the context of a calendar over a single month is sometimes referred
        // to in finance as *Modified* *Following*.
                                                        See Figure 3-166b,
                                                        section 3.12.10.
    Date floorOrNextMonthInYear(int month) const;
        // ...

    Date adjustMonth(int month, int count) const;
        // ...

    Date ceilAdjustMonth(int month, int count) const;
        // ...
```

(continues)

(continued)

```
    Date ceilAdjustMonth2(int month, int count) const;
        // ...

    Date floorAdjustMonth(int month, int count) const;
        // ...

    Date floorAdjustMonth2(int month, int count) const;
        // ...

    // ...
};
// ...
} // close package namespace
// ...
```

(c) Date math (see Figure 3-164, section 3.12.9.1)

Figure 3-103: Voluminous nonprimitive functionality

Figure 3-104 illustrates what can happen when the functionality provided directly within a simple date class is allowed to grow freely to satisfy the wants of all clients. Each time a new feature is added for one client, it potentially costs all of the rest of the clients in terms of increased instance size, code size, run time, physical dependencies, and overall complexity of maintenance and use, not to mention decreased stability, jeopardizing working client code. If the effort needed to incorporate `core::Date` (along with all of its implementation dependencies) continues to increase relative to the benefit a typical client derives, it becomes increasingly less likely that one would bother to use (reuse) the class, which runs counter to our general goal of reuse, especially for a *vocabulary* type — something `core::Date` should aspire to be.

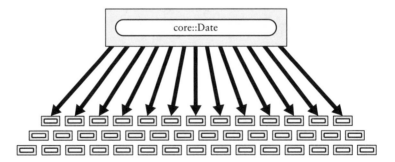

Figure 3-104: Oversized, heavyweight, nonreusable `core::Date` class

3.6.2   Adding Business-Day Functionality to a Date Class (BAD IDEA)

Let's consider a specific example. Suppose we need to know if a particular day is a holiday. Since the proposed function logically returns an attribute on dates, it might seem plausible that such a method belongs as part of the `Date` class. Upon further examination, however, this choice will turn out to be profoundly misguided. Unlike the day of the week, whether or not a particular day is a holiday (or nonbusiness day) is contextual. That is, it will depend on what kind of holiday we are talking about: Is it a *legal* holiday, a *bank* holiday, an *exchange* holiday, or a *school* holiday? These properties will also depend on the *locale* (e.g., London, New York, Tokyo). Asking the question will require the client to provide detailed parameters. It is also likely that future needs will cause the number and scope of these parameters to grow over time.

Realizing that we cannot hope to encapsulate the required information within the core date component itself, we decide to create a calendar service[165] that associates each known holiday context with its own unique string. Given a string (e.g., "NYB" for "New York Bank") and a date (e.g., January 1, 2021), this service is able to look up whether the date is a holiday. We can now use this service to implement the desired member function on our `core::Date` class:

```
bool isHoliday(const char *context) const;  // BAD IDEA
```

Doing so, however, makes `core::Date` depend on the calendar service, as illustrated in Figure 3-105, which — in addition to being a substantial body of operating-system-dependent code — requires access to a database, which must be continually updated. A better solution would be to create, at a much higher level, a utility function

```
static bool isHoliday(const core::Date&  date,
                      const char         *context);
```

in a `struct` that depends on both `core::Date` and the new `CalendarService`, as illustrated in Figure 3-106. For a better factored, more complete, and much more runtime-efficient solution to this particular problem, see section 3.12.5.

---

[165] A service-oriented architecture (SOA) is similar in spirit to a procedural interface layer in that it provides an *insulating* interface between the implementation and clients of that interface (see section 3.11.9).

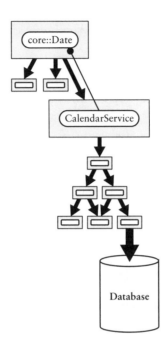

Figure 3-105: `core::Date` class with heavyweight dependency (BAD IDEA)

The sole purpose of `core::Date` should be to hold the *value* of a date, which, conceptually, is a valid year, month, and day. Depending on its internal representation — e.g., serial offset (from some epoch date), year/day-of-year, or year/month/day — certain *primitive* operations (such as advance to the next valid date, return the day of the week, return the number of actual days between two given dates, etc.) will be facilitated. Any additional *nonprimitive* operations (i.e., those not legitimately depending directly on the particular internal representation) should instead be escalated.

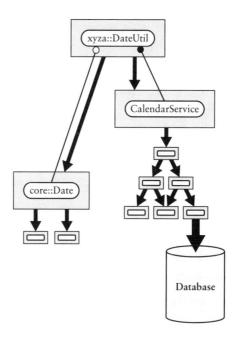

Figure 3-106: `core::Date` class without heavyweight dependency

In section 3.2.7, we discussed the importance of escalating obviously nonprimitive function-ality, such as all of the above, to higher-level components, but what if some aspect of our proposed component functionality that we have tentatively identified as primitive would nec-essarily result in a substantial increase in physical dependency? It is precisely these kinds of situations in which physical considerations provide the essential (often nonintuitive) *feedback* into our modularization choice, forcing that aspect of our design to be reworked.

3.6.3   Providing a Physically Monolithic Platform Adapter (BAD IDEA)

As a second example of the logical design implications of poor physical dependencies, suppose that we have been asked to help with the development of a trading system that requires, among other things, that information regarding individual accounts be read from, and written to, per-sistent storage. The initial design for the proposed `Account` class (Figure 3-107) provides for a constructor that takes, as its argument, a logical `accountNumber` (uniquely identifying the persistent account) and populates the account object accordingly. On destruction, the account object is persisted back to the database.

```
class Account {
    // ...
  public:
    Account(int accountNumber);
        // Create an 'Account' object containing the information in persistent
        // storage corresponding to the specified 'accountNumber'.  ...

    // ...                                              VERY BAD IDEA

    ~Account();
        // Save the value of this object associated with its unique account
        // number in persistent storage.  ...

    // ...                                        VERY, VERY BAD IDEA

    int load(int accountNumber);
        // Load the persistent information corresponding to the specified
        // 'accountNumber' into this object.  Return 0 on success, and a
        // non-zero value otherwise.  ...

    // ...                                         BAD IDEA

    int store();
        // Store the value of this object associated with its unique
        // account number to persistent storage.  Return 0 on success,
        // and a non-zero value otherwise.  ...

    // ...                                         BAD IDEA
};

bool operator==(const Account& lhs, const Account& rhs);
    // Return 'true' if both 'lhs' and 'rhs' objects have the same value, and
    // 'false' otherwise.  Two account objects have the same value if ...

// ...                                           (See Volume II, section 4.1.)
```

Figure 3-107: Elided `Account` class with database dependency (BAD IDEA)

We observe that this design is flawed in several fundamental ways. We will begin by addressing some purely logical design issues. First, looking up an account by ID might fail under ordinary conditions. Attempting to populate the account object at construction will force a design where `Account` will throw (or propagate) an exception on failure[166] — a style of C++ programming we generally do not endorse, especially at the lower levels of our hierarchically reusable

---

[166] We understand that this subject is a point of contention among software developers. We are not saying that exceptions have no place in this world, but simply that, as hierarchically reusable software developers, we choose not to *impose* them on our potential clients, thereby extending the applicability of our software in general (see Volume II, section 5.7), and also to a wider audience — e.g., embedded systems — where exceptions may not even be enabled. So, while we don't `try`, `catch`, or `throw` in our own code, all of our libraries are written to be *naturally* exception safe; we refer to this aspect of our style as being *exception agnostic* (see Volume II, section 6.1).

software where efficient, fine-grained control over all failure modes might be critically important to direct clients (see Volume II, section 5.2).

Second, attempting to persist the object to a database at destruction may cause the destructor to block (section 3.3.8.1) or, worse, fail. Throwing exceptions from destructors is more than just bad practice; if the destructor was itself invoked as the result of an exception, the second exception will kill the process (BAD IDEA). For logical reasons alone, this design will have to be reworked.

Suppose we abandon the idea that account information is hydrated/persisted at construction/ destruction but keep the explicit load and store functions. We still have the problem that these lightweight value-semantic `Account` objects embed, as part of their in-process value, their unique account number. What does it mean for two accounts to have the same value? What if two accounts have the same account number, but other attributes differ? Is that an error? What if two account numbers differ, but all other information is the same? Are their values still the same (e.g., as defined by `operator==`)?

Making `Account` a proper value type requires removing the unique ID from the account class itself (see Volume II, section 4.1). In that case, we will need a separate container type (not illustrated here) to map the in-process account IDs to their associated values. What remains now is a value-semantic type `Account` that also (somehow) provides `load` and `store` member functions, each taking (as an argument) the associated unique account number, which is still problematic. But we are not done yet.

Having addressed many purely logical design flaws, we now consider a particularly unfortunate physical implication of our design. Linking this otherwise lightweight value-semantic type to a particular persistent store constitutes a heavyweight dependency. Moreover, any client that makes use of `Account` will experience the same heavyweight dependency. For primarily physical reasons, what is needed is to escalate the very *notion* of persistence *above* the lightweight (value-semantic) type (see Volume II, section 4.3). We will revisit this topic in more detail in section 3.7.

On a larger scale, encapsulation has been used with varying degrees of success to *logically* decouple clients from the specifics of the platform on which they operate.[167] Figure 3-108 illustrates a naive rendering of such a platform. From a purely logical perspective, this approach seems to make perfect sense: applications built on top of **abc_platform** are automatically portable to every platform on which **abc_platform** has been ported. From a physical perspective,

---

[167] One such commonly used platform has been ACE, created by Douglas C. Schmidt. (See **huston03**.)

however, every application that adopts this portable framework — due to its nongranular nature (see Figure 0-17, section 0.4) — might be forced to link against a broad spectrum of platform libraries, many of which might be unnecessary for the particular application.

```cpp
// abc_platform.h
// ...

#include <cstddef> // for 'std::size_t'

namespace abc {

struct Platform {
    // ...

    static int timeOfDay();
        // Return the number of microseconds since 12:00:00.000AM UTC.

    static const char *hostName();
        // Return a network name for this (host) machine, and 0 if
        // none exists.

    static void copy(char *dst, const char *src, std::size_t numBytes);
        // Copy the specified 'numBytes' from the specified 'src'
        // address to the specified 'dst' address.  The behavior
        // is undefined if the 'src' and 'dst' ranges overlap.

    static int match(const char *src, const char *regExp);
        // Return the non-negative index in the specified 'src'
        // string matching the specified 'regExp' pattern.  ...

    static double root(double (*f)(double), double a, double b);
        // Return a solution to the expression '0 = f(x)' over the
        // interval 'a <= x <= b' if one exists, and NaN otherwise.

    // ...
};

// ...

}  // close package namespace
```

(continues)

(continued)

```
// abc_platform.cpp
#include <abc_platform.h>

// ...

namespace abc {

int Platform::timeOfDay()
{
#if defined(SUN)
    // ...
#elif defined(HP)
    // ...
#elif defined(SGI)
    // ...
#elif defined(AIX)
    // ...
#elif defined(LINUX)
    // ...
#elif defined(WINDOWS)
    // ...
#endif
}

// ...

// ...

// ...

}   // close package namespace

// ...
```

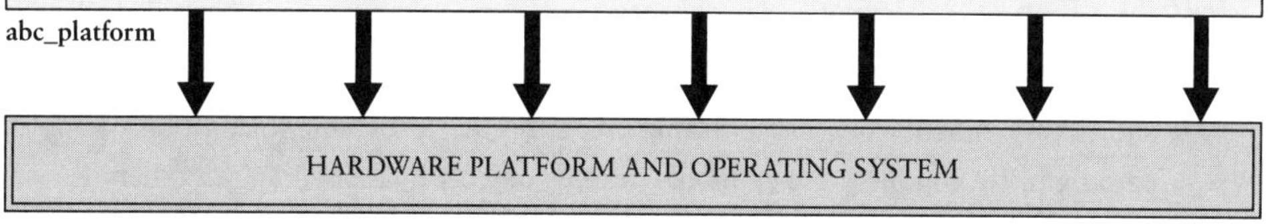

abc_platform

HARDWARE PLATFORM AND OPERATING SYSTEM

Figure 3-108: Physically monolithic platform wrapper module (BAD IDEA)

Small applications will feel the weight most acutely, as the monolithic `abc_platform` "wrapper" module[168] will completely dominate their physical characteristics. For large applications, it might not, at first, seem like this approach would present a problem since much more of the platform functionality is likely to be used at some point or another in the final program, and — in any event — the sheer girth of the application will serve to camouflage even substantial amounts of unused code. In practice, however, very large, physically sound programs are developed and tested hierarchically, with the vast majority of development and testing occurring on physically tiny subsystems (see Volume III, section 7.5). Hence, the prohibitive cost of making the adaptive platform module physically monolithic will, nonetheless, manifest.

3.6.4   Section Summary

In summary, encapsulation and layering can be an effective tool in practice, but only when applied on a granular (section 0.4) rather than on a wholesale basis. By partitioning the adaptive layer into many thoughtfully factored, individual *physical* components (section 0.7), we can, in many cases, realize the logical benefits without necessarily incurring such a high physical cost. In other cases, however, logical encapsulation and physical layering is *not* sufficient and, in fact, sometimes even entirely inappropriate. In the following section, we will examine an alternative to encapsulation and layering known as *lateral design*.

3.7   Lateral vs. Layered Architectures

Large systems often have excessive, sometimes even inappropriate, physical dependencies among the modules they comprise. Part of the reason why excessive physical dependencies creep into our large-scale designs derives from our natural desire to build on top of what we already have. In procedural programming, for example, we are used to calling lower-level subroutines and library functions in order to implement higher-level functionality. In the object-oriented paradigm, we routinely create more complex objects by embedding or otherwise substantively using simpler, more primitive ones. This basic style of programming is commonly referred to as *composition* or *layering*.[169]

---

[168] We use the term *module* here to distinguish it from the size and scope of what we would normally ascribe to a single atomic unit of logical and physical design that we normally think of when we talk about a component (section 0.7). As of this writing, the notion of a C++ module (beyond its initial, C++20 capabilities) as an *architectural* unit of both logical and physical design potentially *larger* than a component is under active development, some incarnation of which is anticipated in the next and subsequent versions of the C++ Standard; see **lakos17a**, section 3, item I, paragraphs c and d, p. 2.

[169] We sometimes prefer the term *layered* to capture private or structural inheritance (see Volume II, section 4.6) along with the concrete Uses form of composition (see Figure 1-49, section 1.7.4).

One restricted form of layered design involves isolating different levels of logical abstraction into physical bands or *layers*. Depending on the intent of the designer, components in each layer may[170] or may not[171] be permitted to interact directly with components in layers other than the one immediately beneath it (e.g., see Figure 2-70, section 2.9.1). Either way, physical (particularly link-time) dependencies of the lower levels are inherited by the higher ones. This disciplined and rigid kind of structured design is often referred to as a *layered architecture*.

Layered architectures have two significant problems: (1) they tend to standardize on a particular implementation choice, and (2) the dependencies become heavier and heavier as we proceed to higher and higher levels of abstraction. Hence, traditional layered architectures do not scale well to very large systems. In this section, we will take a closer look at layered architecture and present an alternative that addresses both of the aforementioned problems simultaneously.

3.7.1   Yet Another Analogy to the Construction Industry

Before we begin, consider the following question: Why is it that skyscrapers in major cities are never more than about 100 stories tall? One might assume the reason to be of a physical nature: The cost to build the bottom floors strong enough to support the weight of significantly taller structures would be prohibitive (but doable). This physical argument, though plausible, is — perhaps surprisingly — not the dominant one.

The true limiting factor in building height is not *physical*, but *logical*: The taller the building, the more persons per unit of lateral area (e.g., square foot) in its footprint. More people per square foot means more elevators per square foot will be needed (keeping elevator technology fixed) in order to move these people with a given average latency vertically within the building. At some height (not much higher than 100 stories, today) the proportion of usable lateral space versus required elevator-shaft space drops below economic viability. Moreover, it's not just diminishing returns: With each floor costing no more than the top one, there comes a point where adding another floor actually *reduces* the total amount of usable space per square foot for the entire building! Hence, major cities have many tall buildings, but not extremely tall ones.

3.7.2   (Classical) Layered Architectures

Let us now consider the classically *layered* architecture shown in Figure 3-109. In this design paradigm, all of the fundamental "plumbing," such as real-time data feeds and database storage, form the concrete foundation layer. The next layer consists of business ("entity") objects

---

[170] E.g., ubiquitous use of low-level libraries such as **bsl**, **bdl**, etc (see **bde14**).

[171] E.g., the layers of an operating system. See **deitel04**, section 1.13.2, pp. 35–36.

such as `Account` and `Security`, which are expected to depend directly on this (sometimes monolithic) base layer (section 3.6.3). At a higher level, we find business services such as `getAccountBalance` and `findSettlementDate` that operate directly on the business objects. At a still higher level is the presentation layer in which we find different APIs such as `TradingInterface` and `AccountingInterface`, which depend physically on all the preceding layers.

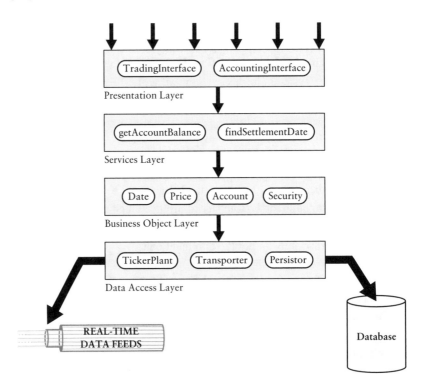

Figure 3-109: Classically layered architecture (BAD IDEA)

In this design, each business object is physically tied (directly) to the database layer. Any functionality we provide to operate on these business objects in the service layer is also similarly (directly or indirectly) encumbered. As Figure 3-110a illustrates, services such as `getAccountBalance` that necessarily depend on `Account` also — due to transitivity (section 1.8) — necessarily depend on the database. The end result (Figure 3-110b) is that virtually *everything* depends physically on the database!

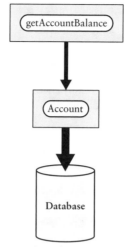

(a) Inappropriate dependencies through transitivity

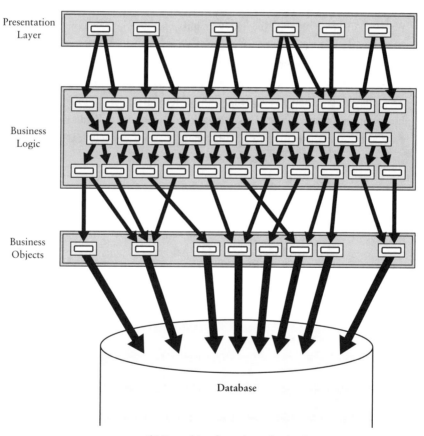

(b) Everything depends on the database!

Figure 3-110: Vertical compositional architecture (BAD IDEA)

In this strictly layered incarnation of a compositional architecture, independent understanding, testing, and reuse at the leaf level of the various higher-level subsystems is severely compromised. We cannot, for example, simply load a few business objects onto our laptop and experiment with creating new services (business logic) on our own. Any new development must be in the context of the concrete facilities provided in the lower layers. Moreover, these facilities, being concrete, are likely to have logical interfaces that are perhaps not so subtly influenced by their current implementation (see Volume II, section 5.7), making upgrading to other technologies over time both expensive and risky.

3.7.3   Improving Purely Compositional Designs

Even within purely compositional designs, there are substantial opportunities for reducing excessive physical dependencies. For example, if we refactor the classically layered design of Figure 3-110 by escalating the heavyweight dependencies (e.g., on the database) out of the low-level business objects (and closer to `main`) as suggested in Figure 3-111, we enable use (and reuse) of these important (vocabulary) objects (see Volume II, section 4.4) at will! Since these low-level "entities" are no longer encumbered, neither necessarily are the services that operate on them. We can therefore develop and deploy new business logic without having to link to a heavyweight infrastructure. This property alone reduces risk and increases productivity. It will now also be possible to reuse this business logic in new contexts, independently of how the lower-level "entity" objects come to be populated.

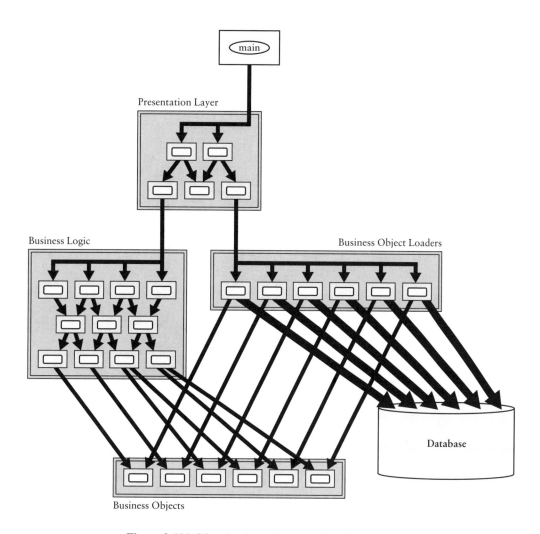

Figure 3-111: More horizontal compositional architecture

3.7.4   Minimizing Cumulative Component Dependency (CCD)

Minimizing link-time dependencies among components generally means avoiding deeply layered software. The details of how one subsystem is layered on another can directly affect this depth. For example, Figure 3-112 coarsely characterizes layering as one of three common kinds. In Figure 3-112a, subsystem S depends on subsystem R, but only from their respective highest-level component. All of the other components of S remain entirely independent of R. If S consists of multiple units of release (UORs), then only the highest-level UOR is architecturally dependent on R.

Even if s is packaged as a single UOR (e.g., as a package group) and therefore — as an architecturally cohesive whole — has an architectural dependency on *R* (section 2.2.6), depending on how subsystem *S* is *deployed* (section 2.15.9), reuse of the lower levels of *S might* have no actual physical dependence on *R* (e.g., see Figure 2-89, section 2.15.10). This *light* form of layering can be especially valuable when *R* represents some heavyweight dependency and the remainder of *S* is lightweight and independently useful.

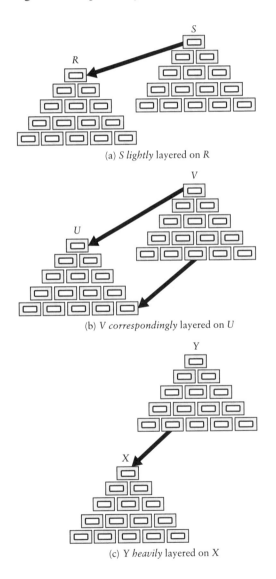

(a) *S lightly* layered on *R*

(b) *V correspondingly* layered on *U*

(c) *Y heavily* layered on *X*

Figure 3-112: Categorizing layered design patterns

Figure 3-112b illustrates a form of subsystem layering in which the components at the leaf level of subsystem *U* are used throughout subsystem *V*, but only the highest level of *V* depends (heavily) on *U*. In this layering scenario, again assuming that both *U* and *V* are released separately (each as a single UOR), reuse of any part of *V* will necessarily imply architectural dependence on all of *U*. And again, depending on how both *U* and *V* are deployed (e.g., again see Figure 2-89, section 2.15.10), reuse of the lower levels of *V* may or may not result in actual physical dependency on the whole of *U*. This kind of *correspondingly layered* architecture might occur, for example, if we wanted to build on the capabilities of a given subsystem *U* implementing, e.g., `pg1u::EquationAnalyzer`, by adding a new higher-level subsystem *V* implementing, say, `pg2v::DualEquationAnalyzer` in terms of `pg1u::EquationAnalyzer`, yet uses just a (low-level) interface type that *U* provides, say, `pg1u::Equation`, throughout the lower levels of *V*.[172]

Figure 3-112c illustrates the heaviest form of subsystem layering in which the lowest levels of subsystem *Y* depend on the highest levels of *X*. With this kind of *heavy* layering, virtually any use of *Y* will result in a physical dependency on all of *X* regardless of how *X* and *Y* are deployed. Such heavyweight dependency *might* be acceptable for relatively small or narrowly used subsystems. In almost all other cases, however, this kind of heavyweight layering is best avoided. Note, however, that ubiquitous use is appropriate for "horizontal" (see section 3.7.4.1, below) low-level reusable libraries such as **bsl** and **bdl**.[173]

3.7.4.1 Cumulative Component Dependency (CCD) Defined

Excessive link-time dependencies among individual components within even a single subsystem or UOR can directly affect the overall effort required to build and test them. Cumulative component dependency (CCD) is a physical design metric that correlates with the total link-time cost associated with creating a unique standalone test driver for each individual component within a subsystem or package.[174] NCCD (or normalized CCD) has also been used as an *objective* measure of physical design quality.[175] The original definition of CCD is provided for reference in Figure 3-113a.[176]

---

[172] Assuming the *vocabulary type* (see Volume II, section 4.4) `pg1u::Equation` is a *value type*, see Volume II, sections 4.1 and 4.3; if it is instead a protocol (section 1.7.5), see Volume II, section 4.7.

[173] These and other hierarchically reusable package groups can be found in Bloomberg's open-source distribution of BDE (see **bde14**).

[174] **lakos96**, section 4.12, pp. 187–193

[175] **lakos96**, section 4.13, pp. 193–201

[176] Two clarifying commas are added within the figure, reflecting the evolving grammatical inclinations of its author. For a comparison with other industry-standard metrics, see **lakos97b**, section 6.7, 221–226.

DEFINITION: *Cumulative component dependency* (*CCD*) is the sum, over all components C_i in a subsystem, of the number of components needed in order to test each C_i incrementally.

(a) Definition

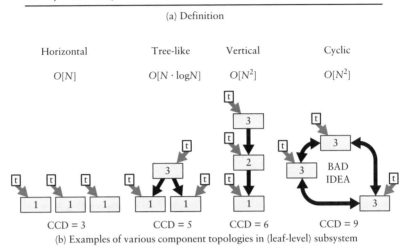

(b) Examples of various component topologies in (leaf-level) subsystem

Figure 3-113: Cumulative component dependency

Our use of CCD as a measure of link-time cost implicitly assumes that the time to link components to a test-driver program is roughly linear in the number of components linked. For example, each of the components in the *horizontal* subsystem of Figure 3-113b[177] can be tested independently. Hence, only a single component need be linked to its test driver. The cumulative link-time cost of building all of these three standalone test drivers is therefore 1 + 1 + 1 = 3. In the tree-like subsystem to the right, the cost to build the two leaf-component test drivers is again one each, but, to test the component at level 2, three components must be linked; hence, the CCD for this tree-like system is 1 + 1 + 3 = 5. For the vertical subsystem, the cost to link a (unique) standalone component test driver (see Volume III, section 7.5) increases linearly with each level. The CCD for that system is therefore 1 + 2 + 3 = 6. Finally, when we consider the (design-rule violating) cyclic subsystem (section 2.6), each component test driver requires us to link in all three components, so the CCD for that ill-conceived subsystem is 3 + 3 + 3 = 9.

3.7.4.2   Cumulative Component Dependency: A Concrete Example

Cumulative component dependency provides a fine-grain, objective (automatable) way of quantifying the benefit of avoiding deeply layered component architectures. Let us now revisit the various forms of layering discussed in Figure 3-112, applying the CCD metric.

---

[177] Borrowed from **lakos96**, Figures 4-25 and 4-26, section 4.13, pp. 194 and 195.

For illustration purposes, let us assume each system contains 15 components; hence, depending on all of the lower-level subsystem contributes a weight of 15 units toward building a test driver for that (dependent) component. For example, the CCD for subsystem S lightly layered on R (Figure 3-114a) comes in at 85 — 70 for the subsystem itself, with an extra 15 for testing the top of S linked with all of R.

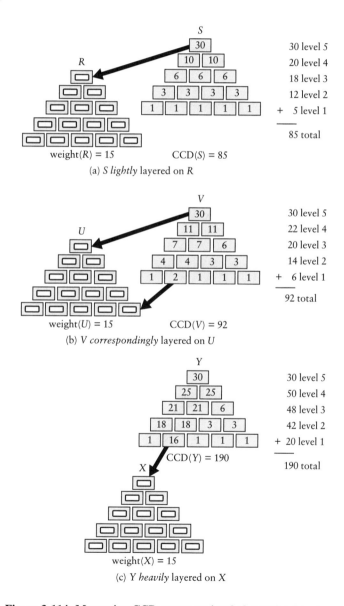

Figure 3-114: Measuring CCD across variously layered subsystems

The corresponding dependency of subsystem V on subsystem U qualitatively increases the logical coupling of these systems but increases the CCD by only 7 to 92 (just over 8%). Finally, subsystem X heavily layered on Y has more than double the CCD at 190. Even ignoring flexibility and reuse, the link-time cost to create standalone component-level test drivers should be sufficient in and of itself to demonstrate that heavily layered subsystems are inherently more expensive and less scalable than lightly layered ones. Just as in the introductory elevators-in-skyscraper analogy, both the logical and physical motivations independently lead to the same conclusion: Layering doesn't scale arbitrarily.

As we have just seen, one way of reducing link-time dependencies in a purely compositional design is by careful (re)factoring so as to minimize the proportion of layered software that relies on heavyweight dependencies. As a consequence, we typically wind up placing more independent functionality in parallel — i.e., at the same level in the physical hierarchy. The resulting design, though still entirely composition-based, is generally shallower and wider than a classically *layered* architecture.

3.7.5   Inheritance-Based Lateral Architectures

Not all designs should be purely compositional. The C++ language supports entirely different mechanisms that can and should be used for decoupling large systems into truly independent parallel subsystems. The basic idea involves replacing components having heavyweight dependencies occurring at the lower levels of a subsystem with dependencies on pure abstract interfaces (protocols). This very general approach to physical decoupling has, over decades, proven to lead to more flexible designs and yet is highly effective at minimizing CCD on a large scale.[178]

Although the same *logical* effect can sometimes be accomplished through the use of templates constrained by concepts (section 1.7.6), such *physically* motivated, architectural-level separation is invariably better suited to protocols, especially when bandwidth across the targeted interface is not an issue.[179] Keep in mind that an important benefit of lateral architectures is

---

[178] See **lakos96**, section 5.7, Figure 5-67, p. 285.

[179] On the other hand, (logically motivated) member functions used for externalizing and rehydrating the *value* of an object (see Volume II, section 4.1) — originally implemented in terms of protocols (section 3.5.7.5.3) — were quickly supplanted with member function templates constrained by concepts (section 3.5.7.5.4) purely for performance reasons. The justification is (1) that it is the client code and the library software that incurs the compile-time coupling, not the subsystems themselves, and (2) the amount of affected code is minute.

to allow clients of deployed software subsystems to mix and match capabilities at a high level without having to rework *or even recompile* the source of the subsystems they are composing.

A collateral benefit of lateral architectures is that they naturally enable a customized "dummy" implementation, derived from the (low-level, bilateral) *protocol* used in the interface of a component (section 1.7.3), to be supplied (a.k.a. "injected")[180] to simulate the often heavyweight dependencies of production software. This very popular technique, more generally referred to as *mocking*, affords component authors full control over all values (including atypical ones, such as error codes) returned back to the component via the protocol. Note, however, that the ability to mock, in and of itself, is almost never sufficient justification for introducing a protocol (see below).

As a concrete example of a physically motivated use of protocols, let us again revisit the (modi-fied) compositional architecture of Figure 3-114. In that system, each business-entity object was populated by a higher-level utility that depended physically on both that entity and a par-ticular database implementation. Escalating just the notion of persistence from the entity object was a correct decision, but suppose that we now want to decouple the Business Object Loaders from depending on a specific database implementation. What should we do now?

We can eliminate this undesirable physical dependency of even the loaders on the database by defining a suitable protocol (pure abstract interface) class (section 1.7.5) characterizing the functionality that will be needed from any database implementation suitable for use by this particular *Business-Object-Loaders* subsystem. Instead of having the loaders depend on the proprietary database directly, they depend on a custom-made protocol class (see Volume II, section 4.7), `Persistor`, as shown in Figure 3-115. At a higher level, a concrete *adapter* class, `ProprietaryPersistor`, *implements* the functionality delineated in `Persistor` using the "home-grown" database implementation, `Proprietary Database`. It then becomes the responsibility of higher levels of the application to ensure that the concrete persistor adapter is supplied (via its abstract interface) to each business object loader either at construction or as needed (e.g., per function invocation).

---

[180] The ability to supply an alternate implementation via an abstract interface is sometimes referred to as *dependency injection*.

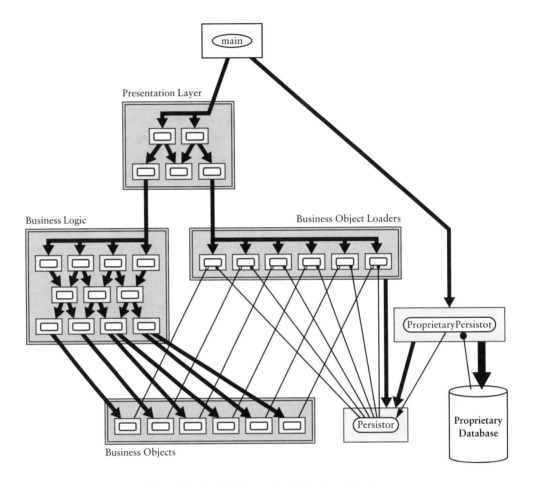

Figure 3-115: (Collaborative) *lateral* **architecture**

This use of pure abstract interface classes to decouple large systems yields what we refer to as a *lateral architecture*. Figure 3-116 illustrates four variant uses of protocols for eliminating physical dependencies. Figure 3-116a illustrates a collaborative subsystem designed expressly to implement a custom protocol in what would otherwise have been a higher-level subsystem.[181] This first approach was used in the detailed example of a collaborative database subsystem shown in Figure 3-115.

---

[181] If the protocol is packaged with the lower-level subsystem instead of the higher-level one, the topology (and resulting CCD) more closely resembles *corresponding* layering (Figure 3-114b).

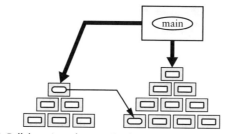

(a) Collaborative subsystem implementing a custom interface

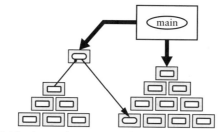

(b) Adapting a subsystem to implement a custom interface

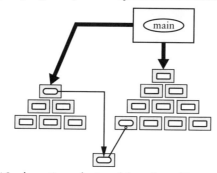

(c) Implementing and using a bilateral reusable protocol

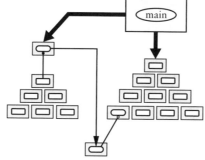

(d) Adapting and using a bilateral reusable protocol

Figure 3-116: Categorizing lateral design patterns

A more general approach, however, is to *adapt* an existing subsystem to implement the needed abstract functionality (Figure 3-116b). In this approach, the *adapter* class implementing the custom protocol typically resides in its own small UOR separate from either the implementation or the interface. An example of this kind of lateral design would be the database application similar to that of Figure 3-115, but refitted to, say, an `Oracle` database implementation via an `OraclePersistor` *adapter*, as shown in Figure 3-117. Note that the only source-code change to the application is the name of the concrete persistor type in `main` and that nothing other than `main` need be recompiled.

Figure 3-116c illustrates a subsystem that directly implements a well-known, low-level, reusable protocol that has come to be accepted as part of the vocabulary throughout the enterprise (see Volume II, section 4.4). Figure 3-116d correspondingly shows a noncollaborating technology adapted to this widely used protocol. Persistence, serialization, IPC, and memory allocation are but a few of the candidates for such standardized protocols. In our code base, for example, the abstract interface type for managing *all* memory resources has become ubiquitous (see Volume II, section 4.10).

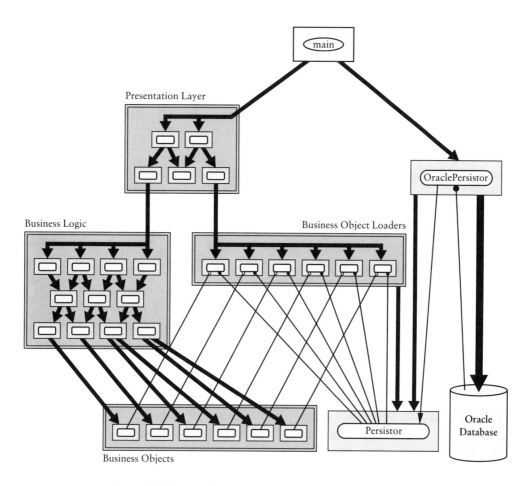

Figure 3-117: Adapting a custom protocol to a new technology

Given the database example of Figures 3-115 (see also Figure 3-111, section 3.7.3; Figures 3-105 and 3-106, section 3.6.2; and Figure 2-74, section 2.9.3), it is not hard to imagine demoting (section 3.5.3) and standardizing (see Volume II, section 4.4) the abstract `Persistor` interface (section 1.7.5) for use by multiple applications (and implementations) as indicated by Figure 3-116 parts (c) and (d).[182] We can also profitably make use of a *protocol hierarchy* (see Volume II, section 4.7) to expand the bilateral reusability (see Volume II, section 5.7) of various levels of service in distinct flavors of database implementations. In section 3.8.2, we'll discuss

---

[182] In practice, however, we would probably need separate interfaces to the functionality provided by substantially different kinds of databases (e.g., relational, embedded) in order to avoid creating what's known as a *fat interface* (see Volume II, Chapter 5).

in more detail how the use of abstract interfaces enable us to "exploit" (adapt) a new technology without having to "bet" (depend) on it.

3.7.6   Testing Lateral vs. Layered Architectures

Our classical approach to testing assumes a layered architecture. Level by level (section 1.10), each component is thoroughly tested in place in terms of the other components on which it depends, which have presumably already been tested thoroughly (section 2.14). Lateral designs admit a different sort of testing, whereby test apparatus, satisfying the syntactic requirements of the lateral "connection" (i.e., protocol for inheritance, or concept for a template), is created for the express purpose of manipulating the responses observed by a client as part of the overall plan for testing that client. This increasingly popular approach, commonly referred to as *mocking*, is effective at testing what might otherwise be hard-to-elicit failure conditions, especially when the subsystem design naturally lends itself to a lateral architecture (see Volume II, section 4.7). In other cases, however, artificial or contrived use of lateral architecture for the sole purpose of testing can, in the words of Jonathan Wakely (c. 2018, in a personal conversation), "... make a mockery of your design" by making it more complicated, less efficient, or both!

3.7.7   Section Summary

Pure logical composition or *layering* is, for many, the most natural way to design software and is the "go-to" architecture for small, well-honed, highly performant subsystems. At scale, however, such *layered* architectures become problematic for two reasons: (1) an inability to inject new technologies without reworking code, and (2) increased per-component development costs due to increasing *cumulative component dependency* (CCD).

For small, tightly woven segments of code that deliver functionality based on a single algorithm or external resource, the layered approach is ideal. Such purely compositional subsystems are easy to comprehend and also facilitate `inline`-ing and cross-function-boundary optimizations. As the size and scope of subsystems increase, however, this same tight compile-time coupling limits the ability of clients to "mix and match" lower-level (e.g., single-technology) resources at link time, causing the larger, overall system to be inflexible, if not brittle.

Physical dependencies even *within* a subsystem necessarily cause build times to increase superlinearly with component count. That is, while the lower levels of a subsystem are relatively inexpensive to build and (unit) test, the average per-component link-time costs grow rapidly with increasing distance from the leaves. This insidious cost is particularly onerous for developers who practice incremental testing approaches such as test-driven development (TDD).

Leaf components depending on other heavyweight subsystems are especially problematic as they typically incur both aforementioned drawbacks — i.e., inflexibility and high incremental development costs. Composability and developer productivity will be served by converting a purely compositional, vertical design to a more horizontal one, without sacrificing performance.

Questioning at what cost all this indirection might be realized is natural, and partitioning systems accordingly here is part and parcel of good design. Assuming that the bandwidth across subsystem boundaries is not a limiting factor, we can even replace a heavyweight low-level (e.g., leaf) dependency with a protocol. We can then create a higher-level adapter type, derived from the protocol, implemented in terms of the heavyweight subsystem and supplied to the original subsystem as needed from higher levels in the physical hierarchy.

This pattern of systematically replacing each heavyweight leaf dependency with a protocol yields what we refer to as a *lateral architecture*. By introducing protocols, we both reduce the depth of physical dependencies in the subsystems and enable other implementations and technologies to fulfill the responsibilities of the original ones without having to modify (or even recompile) the subsystem. Moreover, these protocols can be used to facilitate testing (a.k.a. "mocking") of what might otherwise be hard-to-elicit failure conditions from the adapted heavyweight module (see Volume II, section 4.7) but, when introduced solely for testing purposes, have a tendency to warp otherwise sound layered designs.

3.8   Avoiding Inappropriate Link-Time Dependencies

It is common to think of encapsulation and information hiding as sufficient to isolate any design decisions. This comforting belief is, however, inconsistent with the *physical* realities of software. The details of designing physically sound software can be subtle, and what might seem like innocent logical decisions can have a significant impact on physical dependency, stability, and even security.

3.8.1   Inappropriate Physical Dependencies

To better understand what we mean by an *inappropriate* dependency, let us again consider the interface of the core::Date class (see Figure 3-102, section 3.6.1) whose default constructor creates an instance containing today's date:

```
class Date {
    // ...
    // CREATORS
    Date();
        // Create a date initialized to today's date.   (BAD IDEA)
    // ...
};
```

This arguably useful default behavior might seem reasonable until we consider the physical implications of such a logical design decision. By documenting that a date is constructed having *today's* date by default, we impose a dependency of this lightweight core Date class on a real-time clock, presumably supported by the underlying operating system, as illustrated in Figure 3-118a, and maintained correctly (we hope) by external (untrusted) operators (see Volume II, Chapter 5). This *inappropriate* heavyweight dependency — most likely inserted for the "convenience" of clients — not only makes our core Date less portable and profoundly more difficult to test, it also opens up a potential security hole in that default date values can be "adjusted" simply by playing with the global system clock.[183]

---

[183] While it might be the case that clients will separately need to depend on some form of real-time clock anyway, building a dependency on the system clock directly into a pervasive vocabulary type (see Volume II, section 4.4) such as Date (as reiterated below) leaves *all* clients — including the reluctant ones — with no option other than to depend on it.

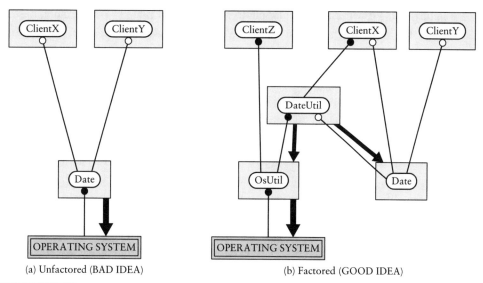

(a) Unfactored (BAD IDEA)   (b) Factored (GOOD IDEA)

```
// ...

struct DateUtil {

    // ...
                                                        (See Volume II, Chapter 5.)
    static core::Date today();
        // Return a date object having the value of today's date (UTC).

    static int loadToday(core::Date *result);
        // Load today's date (UTC) into the specified 'result'.  Return 0
        // on success, and a non-zero value (with no effect) otherwise.
                                                (See Volume II, sections 6.11 and 6.12.)
    // ...
};

// ...
```

(c) Escalated functionality operating on `Date` using `OsUtil`

Figure 3-118: Factoring out `today()` from a date component

Adding any functionality that increases the physical dependencies of `Date` would be undesirable in and of itself.[184] In this case, however, the additional dependency is more than just excessive; it qualitatively changes the physical nature of the component in that it becomes more

---

[184] In the same vein as *lightly layered designs* (see Figure 3-112a, section 3.7.4), less coupling results when the low-level types in a library or application depend on only the lowest levels supported by the platform.

tightly coupled with the particular platform on which it runs.[185] What's more, this component is, or should be, designed to be used widely in the interfaces of functions. We assert that interface types — especially those intended merely to represent a value[186] — should be kept dead simple and independent of any complicating (e.g., network or file-system) platform functionality that might not be available on every platform where such types might be needed.

Irrespective of whether such qualitatively different functionality is needed, clients of this ubiquitous *vocabulary* type (see Volume II, section 4.4) will nonetheless be forced to depend physically on it in order to remain interoperable with the rest of the system interacting with that type. Hence, such extra physical dependency on platform intrinsics, and therefore the logical functionality that implies, are both *inappropriate* here.

How a particular value for a date (including today) is obtained is clearly *not* part of the essential primitive behavior (section 3.2.7) of a (value-semantic) date type (see Volume II, sections 4.1 and 4.3). When we consider having to choose whether today's date value is determined by *universal* or *local* time and that variations in local time may affect results from one platform to the next, it becomes clear that this default logical behavior is also a form of *policy*, which — for entirely separate reasons — should be escalated (see Volume II, section 5.9) to a higher position in the physical hierarchy.

Instead, let us suppose that we factor the default constructor functionality into three separate components, as shown in Figure 3-118b. One component defines a class, `Date`, that simply holds the value of a date.[187] A second component defines a low-level utility, `OsUtil`, that encapsulates what is needed to get today's date value in some primitive form from the platform's operating system. A third component defines a higher-level utility, `DateUtil`, that

---

[185] Not all platforms are equivalent when it comes to what capabilities they support; this is particularly true of certain kinds of embedded systems, where even some "required" features of the language, such as a file system, exceptions, or even dynamic memory allocation, may simply be unavailable for client use.

[186] In practice, the types that are most likely to be needed in stripped-down (e.g., embedded) systems are the low-level types intended solely to represent process-independent (externalizable) values (see Volume II, section 4.1).

[187] Since `core::Date` objects, like other vocabulary types (see Volume II, section 4.1), are used widely by application and library developers alike, we will (as a result of practical experience) opt to have the default constructor, as is typical of value types, initialize our `Date` objects to some thoughtfully chosen, but fixed, valid default value (e.g., 1/1/1), as doing so plugs a potential security hole, preserves the invariant that a date object is always valid, and suppresses (benign) uninitialized-memory-read warnings from very valuable analysis tools such as Purify.

knows how to populate a given `Date` object from the primitive representation of a date value obtained from `OsUtil`.[188]

Users of the flagship `Date` class, such as `ClientX`, that also need the additional functionality of knowing what today's date is can elect to use that functionality explicitly via `DateUtil`. Figure 3-118c illustrates how a `DateUtil` utility `struct` (see Figure 2-23, section 2.4.9) might render the escalated, heavyweight behavior. Much more importantly, however, users of `Date`, such as `ClientY`, that need only its primitive value-representing functionality, can avoid the inappropriate dependency on the operating system and still remain interoperable with other subsystems like `ClientX`. Finally, users such as `ClientZ`, who have no need for `Date`, can still benefit from a portable platform that wraps the low-level functionality supplied by the operating system.

Let's consider again what makes a dependency inappropriate. Generally speaking, a dependency is *inappropriate* if it would profoundly (and unjustifiably) affect the inherent physical character of a component, package, or package group. Figure 3-119 enumerates some potentially inappropriate dependencies, but the list is by no means exhaustive. For example, incorporating any third-party software where we do not have access to all of the source code runs the risk that a bug or other form of incompatibility will take the ability to meet our deadlines out of our hands. For core functionality, the standard of care must be especially high. Encumbering the lightweight core `Date` type, for example, was made all the more inappropriate because clients, in order to interoperate, are virtually forced to use it.[189] The more widely used a component might become, the more essential it is to ensure its maintainability, portability, and timely deployment, as new platforms, versions, patches, etc., become available.

---

[188] In some high-performance multiprocessing environments (e.g., at Bloomberg LP), we can imagine that the values of date and time are maintained in a lock-free cache — say, in shared memory — in order to avoid the overhead of a system call.

[189] Since, in our methodology, a UOR is treated atomically at design time, care should be taken to avoid inappropriate dependencies from anywhere in the UOR. As long as the questionable dependency is in a separate component, however, we might at least have the remedy of a partitioned deployment of the UOR if needed (section 2.15.10).

Inappropriate Physical Dependencies
• Standardizing on any one technology or product (e.g., Oracle for databases, MQSeries for transport)
• Using arbitrary open-source software without either an appropriate service-level agreement (SLA) or substantial in-house familiarity with the source code
• Incorporating third-party software that imposes specific versions of other (e.g., open-source) software (e.g., in its interface)[190]
• Synchronizing with a third-party product whose versions are tied to specific versions of the compiler and/or operating system on a given platform
• Relying on a non-standard or platform-specific feature (e.g., MFC on Windows) where the essential functionality cannot be emulated efficiently on all supported platforms
• Depending on software that requires special hardware support (e.g., true concurrency with some hard minimum number of processors)

Figure 3-119: Some examples of potentially inappropriate physical dependencies

The `Date` example above demonstrates that mere encapsulation and information hiding is not sufficient to shield our core infrastructure from inappropriate physical link-time dependencies. Even with thoughtful refactoring, composition *per se* will not enable the seamless introduction of new technologies at the lower levels of the physical hierarchy. Moreover, encapsulation and layering alone provide no language-level[191] customization points for supplying a separate, instrumented "dummy" implementation of a lower-level subsystem expressly for the purpose of debugging or testing a specific instance of a higher-level client (see Volume II, section 4.9). Such flexibility is much better achieved through the use of lateral architectures (section 3.7.5).

---

[190] See **sutter05**, Chapter "Namespaces and Modules," Item 63, pp. 116–117.

[191] Providing explicit source-level customization points via abstract interfaces, callbacks, or even method templates leads to superior flexibility and interoperability over, say, having to provide "stub" implementations (e.g., by swapping `.o` files) at the binary level (see section 3.9.3). The use of template parameters to customize implementation-only aspects of class templates — often referred to as *policy-based design* — is profoundly less desirable as it can adversely impact both interoperability (see Volume II, section 4.4) and testability (see Volume III, section 7.3).

3.8.2   "Betting" on a Single Technology (BAD IDEA)

Perhaps the most common drawback of well-intentioned encapsulation and layering is that it forces one to make (and continue to live with) certain decisions long after other, more viable alternatives become available. Consider the simple TCP/IP server architecture of Figure 3-120a. In this *layered* implementation, the component **xyza_channel** encapsulates the mode of transport and contains both Channel and ChannelFactory, which are colocated due to friendship (section 3.3.1.1). The interface of ChannelFactory provides the functionality needed to set up the communication channel while the Channel interface provides only the fundamental operations (e.g., read and write) required to communicate. Although the concrete channel factory will almost certainly have features that are specific to sockets, the Channel interface itself will (ideally) hide completely any inkling of a particular implementation choice.

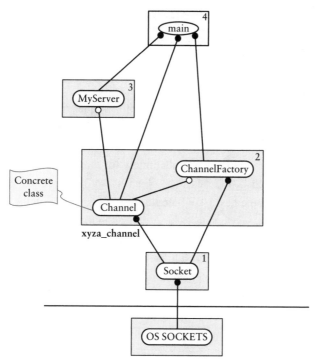

(a) Encapulation and layering: standardizing on one technology (BAD IDEA)

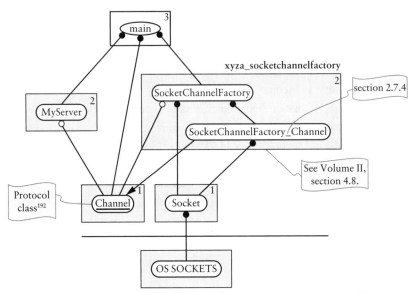

(b) Abstract interfaces and adapters: enabling new technology (GOOD IDEA)

Figure 3-120: Contrasting layered versus lateral transport architectures

Figure 3-121 shows an implementation of a simple request/response server class. In this trivial illustration, the server records (the address of) a modifiable `xyza::Channel` (Figure 3-121a) object supplied at construction. Once started, the server (Figure 3-121b) proceeds to use the held `Channel` to respond to queries indefinitely (or until an error or interrupt occurs). During each iteration of the loop, the `Channel` object's `read` method is invoked, which blocks the thread of control until the next (fixed-length) request comes in on the channel. The server then processes this request via the `generateResponse` function (definition not shown), which places the (fixed-length) result into the output buffer. Finally, the held channel's `write` method is invoked to send the calculated result back to the client — all of which is *logically* independent of both the concrete implementation of the channel and also any details on how the client connection was established.

---

[192] We sometimes use an underscore in a component/class diagram (as shown here) to indicate that a class is *abstract*.

```
// xyza_channel.h                                                   -*-C++-*-
// ...

namespace xyza {

// ...

class Channel {
    // PRIVATE DATA
    // ...

    friend class ChannelFactory;  // local friendship

    // CREATORS
    // ...

  public:
    // MANIPULATORS
    int read(char *buffer, int numBytes);
        // Read, into the specified 'buffer', the specified 'numBytes'.
        // Return 'numBytes' on success, a non-negative integer less than
        // 'numBytes' (indicating the number of bytes read) if asynchronously
        // interrupted, and a negative value on error.  The behavior is
        // undefined unless '1 <= numBytes'.

    int write(const char *buffer, int numBytes);
        // Write, from the specified 'buffer', the specified 'numBytes'.
        // Return 'numBytes' on success, a non-negative integer less than
        // 'numBytes' (indicating the number of bytes written) if
        // asynchronously interrupted, and a negative value on error.  The
        // behavior is undefined unless '1 <= numBytes'.
};

class ChannelFactory {
    //
  public:
    // CREATORS
    // ...

    // MANIPULATORS
    // ...

    Channel *allocate( /*...*/ );
        // ...

    void deallocate(Channel *channel);
        // ...

    // ...
};

}  // close package namespace

// ...
```

(a) Simple concrete `Channel` and `ChannelFactory`

```
// myserver.h
// ...

#include <xyza_channel.h>

// ...

class MyServer {
    xyza::Channel *d_client_p;  // connection to client
    // ...
    enum { k_INPUT_SIZE = 1024, k_OUTPUT_SIZE = 2048 };

    void generateResponse(char  input[ k_INPUT_SIZE],
                          char output[k_OUTPUT_SIZE]);

  public:
    // CREATORS
    explicit
    MyServer(xyza::Channel *client) : d_client_p(client) { /*...*/ }
    // ...
    // MANIPULATORS
    void run();
};

// MANIPULATORS

inline
void MyServer::run()
{
    // ...
    char  input[ k_INPUT_SIZE];  // request  buffer
    char output[k_OUTPUT_SIZE];  // response buffer

    while (1) {
        int status = d_client_p->read(input, k_INPUT_SIZE);

        if (k_INPUT_SIZE != status) break;

        generateResponse(output, input);  // Place response in output.

        status = d_client_p->write(output, k_OUTPUT_SIZE);

        if (k_OUTPUT_SIZE != status) break;
    }

    // ...
}

// ...
```

Functions defined inline here
for exposition purposes only

(b) Illustrative MyServer implementation

Figure 3-121: Simple server taking a connected `xyza::Channel` at construction

From a pure *logical*-usability standpoint, this layered implementation is effective. Figure 3-122 illustrates what is needed in order to use the server.[193] First, we create an instance of the concrete `ChannelFactory`. Then, we configure the factory to generate the appropriate connection. Next, we obtain a connection and check status. Then, if no error is encountered, we pass the valid address of that connection to the constructor of the server. Now, the server is started and proceeds to process requests on that channel until it receives an *interrupt* or *shut-down* request (from the client), at which point the server yields control back to its caller (i.e., `main`). Finally, instead of destroying the channel, we properly deallocate it back to the factory from which it was allocated (see Volume II, section 4.8), and the process terminates.

```
// main.cpp

#include <myapp_myserver.h>
#include <xyza_channel.h>                      We would generally prefer main
                                               to make a single call into the
using namespace MyLongCompanyName;             application package namespace.
using namespace myapp;

int main(int argc, const char *argv[])
{
    // Create a channel factory.              Reusable library code

    xyza::ChannelFactory factory;

    // Use socket-specific methods to configure the factory.

    factory.setPort(/*...*/);
    factory.setSocketOptions(/*...*/);

    // Allocate a channel.

    xyza::Channel *channel = factory.allocate();

    if (!channel) { /* error */ }

    xyza::ChannelScopedGuard sg(channel, &factory);
                                                       (See Volume II, section 6.1.)
    MyServer server(channel);

    return 0;                  Local to this application
}
```

Figure 3-122: Instantiating `MyServer` using a concrete socket factory

---

[193] Note that the remainder of this paragraph is written in a style reminiscent of one we often use for component-level usage examples (see Volume II, section 6.16).

Although the layered design of Figure 3-120a is modular and fully encapsulates appropriate implementation details, its logical and physical factoring leaves much to be desired. From a logical perspective, the `MyServer` class takes, as its argument, (the address of) an object of the concrete socket-based `Channel` type and hence `MyServer` is tied to that transport technology. Changing technologies (e.g., to shared memory or some third-party product) would require changing either (1) the library component **xyza_channel** (a very bad idea), or (2) the `MyServer` application class (not good either). If the server itself had been part of some reusable library, we would have had an even bigger problem. From a physical perspective, class `MyServer` depends statically on the heavyweight operating-system-level transport technology. Such logical and physical coupling is inappropriate and also unnecessary.

There are a couple of ways to address this particular problem. Given recent trends toward generic programming in general, and policy-based design in particular, it might seem prudent to parameterize the (templated) server on a transport policy. That is, instead of linking the server to any one transport, the server would be parameterized by the type of the channel passed in at construction. Thus, the server would be configured (in `main`) with the appropriate transport technology (at compile time). Depending on the complexity of the server, the allowable runtime overhead on the channel's `read` and `write` methods, the level of compiler technology, and whether the server itself will be used widely as an interface type (see Volume II, section 4.4), parameterizing the entire concrete server class *might* be a viable option (see Volume II, sections 6.3 and 6.4). More likely, however, the extra complexity, increased development effort, reduced interoperability, and very tight compile-time coupling associated with a template-policy-based solution would not be rewarded here (see Volume II, section 4.5). Relying on the preprocessor to perform conditional compilation in order to provide alternate forms of transport would be an even worse idea (see section 3.9.2).

Generally speaking, template-oriented solutions work best in the small. For larger subsystems, such as a real-world application server, we will almost always prefer the explicit structure and looser (typically link-time) coupling afforded by interface inheritance. Figure 3-120b shows this alternative, more *lateral* design in which the explicitly named `SocketChannelFactory` produces its own component-private (section 2.7.1) concrete channel type derived from the now (pure abstract) *protocol* `Channel` base class. The concrete channel factory's public interface now produces and accepts instances of only this *protocol* `Channel` type. The `MyServer` class would now take at construction an argument whose type is derived from the new abstract `Channel` protocol. Because the original concrete channel's interface (Figure 3-121a) fully encapsulated and hid the details of its implementation, an abstract version of `xyza::Channel`, as illustrated in Figure 3-123, can have virtually the same logical interface (pun intended). In fact, the only change to the usage model of Figure 3-122 is that we have replaced the use of the technology-specific concrete `Channel` class in `MyServer` with that of the more general, technology-independent `Channel` protocol.

```
// xyza_channel.h
// ...

namespace xyza {                    ⟨Note rare use of protected⟩

// ...
                                    ⟨Defined out of line and empty in the .cpp file
class Channel {                        (section 1.7.5)⟩

  protected:                                          (See Volume II, section 4.7.)
    // CREATORS
    virtual ~Channel();
        // Only the creator of a 'Channel' should destroy it.
                                                      (See Volume II, section 4.8.)
  public:
    // MANIPULATORS
    virtual int read(char *buffer, int numBytes) = 0;
        // ...

    virtual int write(const char *buffer, int numBytes) = 0;
        // ...
};

}  // close package namespace

// ...
```

Figure 3-123: Equivalent abstract `xyza::Channel` interface to Figure 3-121a

With the lateral design of Figure 3-120b, the component defining `MyServer` no longer depends physically on any aspect of the implementation of a communication channel, but only on the explicitly stated contract embedded in the bilaterally reusable abstract `xyza::Channel` *protocol* class (section 1.7.5); see also Volume II, sections 4.7, 5.7, and 6.17.

It would now be feasible to demote the server from an application package (section 2.13) to a library package where it too could be reused. Figure 3-124 illustrates how the same `Server` class can be used in three separate applications: one configured for sockets, another configured for shared memory, and a third configured to use a third-party product (e.g., MQSeries), this time via just a simple application-level *adapter* class, which might later be made into a reusable factory. In a time-multiplexed or multithreaded environment, we could easily have more than one instance of a `Server` operating with different transport technologies in the same process (see section 3.9.2).

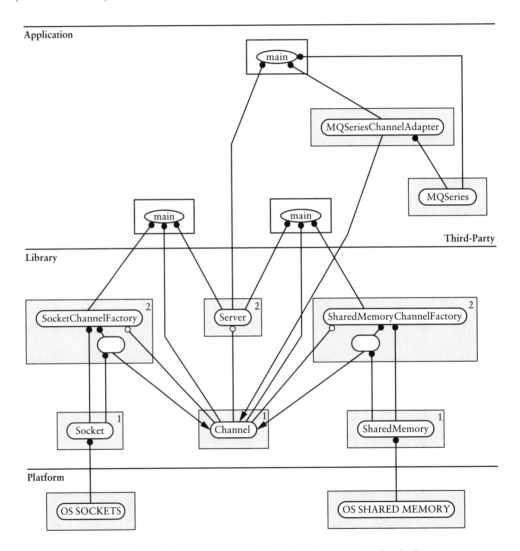

Figure 3-124: Reusing `Server` with various transport technologies

In other words, with this lateral architecture, any application can readily exploit any version of a product from a third-party vendor without having to modify the server or otherwise affect any other application. We'll elaborate on the use of lateral architectures with respect to abstract factories for modular resource management in Volume II, section 4.8.

3.8.3   Section Summary

To summarize this section, hard-coding heavyweight, operating system (OS) dependencies into otherwise lightweight (e.g., value) types is almost always inappropriate, as is "betting" (i.e., statically depending) on particular implementation choices for a much larger, layered system when other alternative technologies might well turn out to be preferable. By striving for more lateral library architectures, clients are able to compose library software more flexibly and thereby more readily achieve their design goals.

3.9   Ensuring Physical Interoperability

We now turn briefly to more mechanical concerns with respect to developing sound physical architectures. Avoiding cyclic dependencies among physical entities is such an essential "strategy" that we have elevated it to a *design imperative* (section 2.6). Preventing logical units of encapsulation from spanning physical boundaries enables the *physical* substitutability of components (see Volume II, section 5.5) as well as effective hierarchical testing (section 2.14.3; see also Volume III), and therefore it too rises to imperative status (section 2.6). In this section, we will look at other essential strategies that help to preserve interoperability (and stability) among subsystems as individual programs get larger and rely on more widespread reuse.

3.9.1   Impeding Hierarchical Reuse Is a BAD IDEA

Our perennial goal when developing software should always be to promote effective hierarchical reuse by maximizing the physical interoperability of every component's functionality.

Guideline

Minimize situations in which the use of a component, within a given program, might restrict or preclude either (1) its *own* reuse, or (2) the use of some *other* component, within that same program.

The first part of this guideline is aimed at the use (misuse) of conditional compilation or selective linking to customize a component's source code or dependencies for a particular logical domain or specific client. Such abuse implies that otherwise readily usable software (configured for one purpose) cannot necessarily be reused in the same program (configured for another). Capricious use of the singleton pattern[194] and global or static variables are other common means of inadvertently defeating component reuse within a single process.

The second part of this guideline is to call out physical modules having "selfish" or "egocentric" tendencies whose use is likely to be incompatible with others of its ilk. Such selfishness is precipitated by components that alter global properties, subsystems that require hiding header files in order to achieve logical encapsulation, and UORs that are (or depend on other UORs that are) nonportable. In what follows, we'll elaborate on each of these issues and also the use of subordinate components (section 2.7.5) as a means of addressing portability and malleability, as opposed to conventional logical encapsulation and conditional compilation.

3.9.2   Domain-Specific Use of Conditional Compilation Is a BAD IDEA

Guideline

Avoid domain-specific conditional compilation for components.

We must avoid any form of conditional compilation based on individual clients' needs if we are to ensure interoperability of independent subsystems within a single process. To understand how someone could be tempted to do otherwise, consider the program-trading system illustrated in Figure 3-125. This system establishes high-performance connectivity with different financial securities exchanges around the world. Within this system, there are a number of fairly significant, but similar subsystems, called *exchange adapters*. These subsystems are used to convert the messaging protocol defined for a particular exchange to that of a generic protocol understood and used by the trading engine itself.

---

[194] **gamma95**, Chapter 3, section "Singleton," pp. 127–136

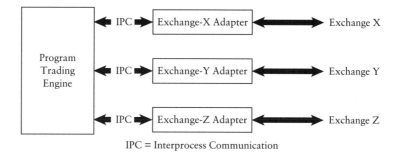

IPC = Interprocess Communication

Figure 3-125: Multiprocess-only program-trading system

As originally conceived, these exchange adapters run in independent processes within a larger system and are connected via interprocess communication links. In this configuration, the code implementing the "Exchange-X Adapter" subsystem is never part of the same executable as that implementing, say, the "Exchange-Y Adapter." Moreover, these systems are very similar yet subtly different in many tiny ways that are pervasive throughout the code base. In such circumstances, one *might* be tempted to "factor" the problem by creating a single block of code defining a "generic" adapter and then use compile-time switches to "adjust" the behavior to conform to a specific exchange, as illustrated in Figure 3-126 (BAD IDEA).

```
// ...

int beginTransaction(/*...*/)
{
    // ...

    #if NYSE_EXCHANGE
        // ...
    #elif NASDAQ_EXCHANGE          BAD IDEA
        // ...
    #elif LIFFE_EXCHANGE
        // ...
    #elif EURONEXT_EXCHANGE
       ⋮
    #endif

    // ...
}
// ...
```

Figure 3-126: Domain-specific use of conditional compilation (BAD IDEA)

Before we get to the central problem with this approach, notice that we have taken the behavior out of the language domain and pushed it up to the build scripts. We can no longer describe our testing strategy from within a single *linear* test driver and, instead, must collaborate with the build system to create many different versions that will change from one application to the next. Much of the benefit of preserving a consistent, *domain-independent* physical form (section 0.7) is lost. Moreover, this use of conditional compilation also runs contrary to the open-closed principle (section 0.5) in that the only way to extend this system to new exchanges is to modify production source code.[195]

The real problem with a design like the one in Figure 3-126, however, comes from the inherent incompatibility of two logical entities in the same process having the same name yet somehow built differently. For example, suppose it is determined that we can get a significant performance boost if we rearchitect the top level of the system to use threads instead of processes to drive the trading engine and its satellite adapters. To accomplish this task, we would need to link all of the different adapters into a single process, which is, of course, not possible with this implementation strategy. We would now need to go in and "unfactor" each of the exchange adapters, potentially leading to rampant code duplication, which is what we were trying to avoid in the first place.

The use of templated implementation policies here might, at first blush, appear to be a plausible alternative, as now the names of each adapter, though hopelessly unpronounceable, would at least be unique. As it turns out, however, the number of policies required, and the ongoing need to add new ones with each new exchange, would almost certainly make any naive application of that design pattern unworkable. What's more, we know from having implemented standard containers that the cost of thoroughly testing such policy-based design grows combinatorially with each new one added. Attempting any such template-based framework approach here would truly be utterly intractable and a recipe for disaster.

The one sure-fire long-term practical solution (Figure 3-127) is to refactor the collective implementation of "exchange adapters" into a fine-grained component hierarchy, and, with each new exchange, create a single type that addressees it (and none other). Just as with the different concrete output devices (see Figure 0-29, section 0.5), the implementation of each concrete

---

[195] Although conditional *runtime* statements tied to a specific client (e.g., controlled via a configuration file) do not necessarily preclude side-by-side reuse of the component within a single program the way client-specific conditional compilation does, they do adversely affect stability, are generally very expensive to maintain, and, therefore, are appropriate only at the application level.

exchange adapter will derive from a common interface. Moreover, as Figure 3-127 suggests, each concrete adapter will invariably be layered on and share common hierarchically reusable (section 0.4) subimplementations with other adapters as appropriate.

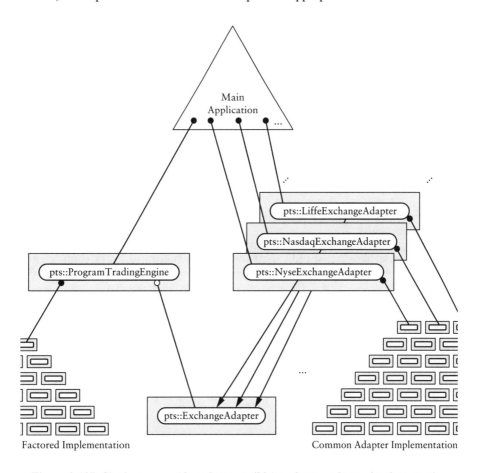

Figure 3-127: Single-process (thread-compatible) exchange-adapter implementation

Notice that, with our more *lateral* design (section 3.7.5), the addition of new exchange adapters need have no effect on existing ones! Moreover, since exchange adapters *must* be kept current with the exchanges they service, these components fall under the category of *malleable software* (section 0.5). With this factoring of the design, however, we can maintain compatibility with one exchange without touching source that would affect any other. What's more, the malleable code is maintained at a very high level in the physical hierarchy. Hence, this physically factored architecture is not only more flexible but also *more stable*, making it both easier *and less risky* to maintain.

Conditional compilation in and of itself is not the villain here. When the underlying platforms differ substantially (such as Windows versus Unix sockets, threads, etc.) to the extent that syntax on one platform will not compile on the other, conditional compilation might well be our only option. Note, however, that this use of conditional compilation is not based on "policy" imposed by a client but rather on a "trait" imposed by the underlying compiler, operating system, or hardware. Since these platform-wide traits are necessarily true of all entities that could conceivably participate in a given process, there is no potential for incoherence.[196]

3.9.3   Application-Specific Dependencies in Library Components Is a BAD IDEA

Guideline

Avoid application-specific dependencies for reusable library components.

The architectural dependencies of a UOR (section 2.2.4) in our methodology are absolute. That is, the UORs upon which a given UOR is allowed to depend is a property of the UOR itself and is independent of its clients (sections 2.8.1 and 2.9.1). Organizationally, however, the actual object code that winds up in an executable will depend on the granularity of its deployment artifacts as well as the specific technology involved (section 2.15). Allowing build dependencies to be used to customize library functionality for a particular client would again push the complexity of our logical architecture onto the build system where they do not belong. Moreover, doing so could easily prevent reuse of a component within a single process.

For example, consider a subsystem such as a pricing engine that performs its function based on a pricing model embedded in a modular "cartridge," say, a . o file. This cartridge has a well-defined binary interface, but the implementation of the cartridge will vary depending on the specific

---

[196] We, of course, prefer to isolate such platform-dependent issues, such as the preferred socket or thread handle, endianness, or the appropriate type to indicate a 64-bit integer (see Figure 3-108, section 3.6.3), in a fine-grained way (section 0.4) at as low a level in the physical hierarchy as possible.

pricing model.[197] Figure 3-128a illustrates the approach whereby the logical name of each pricing module is the same, and the appropriate implementation is determined by the build system. This approach ensures that only one `PricingModel` can be used by class `PricingEngine` within any one program (BAD IDEA). If instead we make the `PricingModel` an abstract interface (Figure 3-128b), each client is free to provide its own *uniquely named* model, irrespective of any other `PricingEngine` clients in the process.[198]

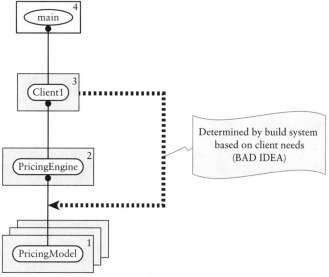

(a) Client-specific library build dependencies (BAD IDEA)

---

[197] Keep in mind that the essential work done by a typical call to a pricing-engine function is substantial, which is what allowed us to rely on the link-time binding to a `.o` file in the first place. Had that not been the case, another possibility would have been to represent each model as an object of a concrete type, constrained by a "Pricing Model" concept (section 1.7.6), supplied via a method template of `PricingEngine`.

[198] Although we may choose a deployment strategy that enables an application to load only those modules that are needed for a given invocation, we will nonetheless attempt to ensure that an architecture (1) does not require special consideration by the build system, and (2) does not preclude side-by-side use of any of the modules involved.

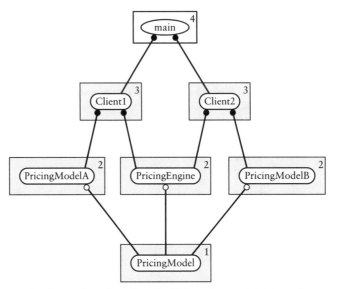

(b) Client-independent library build dependencies (GOOD IDEA)

Figure 3-128: Configuring library subsystems for specific clients

3.9.4   Constraining Side-by-Side Reuse Is a BAD IDEA

Guideline

Avoid logical constructs or patterns that artificially constrain reuse.

Clearly this strategy of avoiding patterns that artificially constrain reuse is softer and more subjective than the previous two. The intent here is to avoid any design strategy that unnecessarily
restricts use by multiple clients in a single process. For illustration purposes, consider a component that implements an IPC registry whose purpose is to track open connections between
the current process and other processes. Instead of making this registry an object of a class, it is
designed initially as a single component implementing a noninstantiable ("utility") class having
only `static` methods and `static` data. If later we decide that having one registry per thread
is a good idea, this component will be of no use for that purpose.

Very often when we think that we will need only one of something, it soon turns out that having two or three of them would be very useful.[199] Hence, another approach to implementing this singleton would be to design the registry itself as a normal, instantiable class, and then implement the singleton pattern, in a separate component, to provide an object of this registry as the designated, process-wide, globally accessible resource. The registry type itself is now perfectly reusable in new contexts. What's more, if we later decide that more than one singleton exposing a registry object for different application needs is useful — e.g., different kinds of process registries — neither the registry nor the original singleton component needs to change.[200]

3.9.5   Guarding Against Deliberate Misuse Is Not a Goal

Guideline

Design software to avoid accidental misuse, not fraud.

The only disadvantage to the "reusable"-singleton strategy — that a bogus registry could be created by a wayward client and then subsequently misused — is not significant: Such behavior would be deliberate (i.e., intentional fraud, and not merely an innocent mistake). The goal of good interface design in C++ must be to guard against accident, not fraud: Attempting to achieve the latter obfuscates the design, limits reuse, and ultimately cannot be fully successful.[201]

The advice about not wasting development cycles defending against deliberate misuse within the confines of the trusted region of a single process is important and should not be taken lightly. At the same time, this sound advice should not be confused with (optionally) defending against *accidental* misuse by trusted clients within a process (see Volume II, section 6.8) or *always* having to validate untrusted input — e.g., emanating from outside of the process (see Volume II, Chapter 5). In any event, correctly managing the lifetime of interdependent singletons (without leaking resources) is a nontrivial matter requiring explicit, process-wide coordination (see Volume II, section 6.2).[202]

---

[199] This important observation, alerting us to the benefits of upfront, fine-grained implementation factoring (see Volume II, section 6.4) with respect to the singleton pattern, is attributed to Steve Downey of Bloomberg LP while developing the initial version (c. 2007) of what has become the **ball** logger, which is in the **bal** package group of Bloomberg's open-source BDE libraries (**bde14**, subdirectory /groups/bal/ball/).

[200] For example, we have two singleton memory allocators — one for default object-memory allocations and another for default global-memory allocations — each performing essentially the same function but offering the address of a (distinct) object of the same (protocol) base class (see Volume II, section 4.10).

[201] See, for example, **lakos96**, section 3.6.2, pp. 144–146 (especially the end of p. 145).

[202] For an especially elaborate *(and entertaining)* singleton design, see **alexandrescu01**, Chapter 6, pp. 129–156.

3.9.6   Usurping Global Resources from a Library Component Is a BAD IDEA

Guideline

Avoid defining global entities outside the file that defines `main`.

There must be only one definition of any global construct within a program. When a file contains `main`, for example, it is necessarily unique throughout the program; hence, certain global *optimizations* such as redefining global operators `new` and `delete` there, especially in test drivers, *might* be acceptable (but see Volume II, section 4.10 before doing so). If two components that attempt to redefine the same global entity are pulled into the same executable, the result will be either a compile- or link-time error or, worse, an ill-formed program. By requiring that any such global redefinitions occur exclusively in the translation unit that defines `main`, we ensure a unique, program-wide point of arbitration.

Installing a global callback function (e.g., the `new` handler) from a library component means that another component doing the same cannot be used reliably in the same program without potential conflicts. By the same token, making changes to the default settings of `std::cout`, for example, could also have conflicting side effects if more than one component relying on these global features is involved. As a specific example, consider a `Date` type that overloads `operator<<` to print out its three *salient attributes*, year, month, and day (see Volume II, section 4.1). Suppose an object wanting to left-justify this output in a column sets the stream flag (a form of global variable) to do so. Now, unless the date is "smart" enough to format its three fields to a temporary buffer first, before printing it out to the output stream, only the first field will be left justified. (We have made this mistake, and we assume others have too.)

Finally, we generally want to avoid modifying the values of any global variables from within library components. Following this practice also helps ensure thread safety (see Volume II, section 6.1) in that any changes to global values can be made (from `main`) *before* any additional threads are launched.

3.9.7   Hiding Header Files to Achieve Logical Encapsulation Is a BAD IDEA

Guideline

Avoid hiding header files for the purpose of *logical* encapsulation.

Recall, from section 3.1.10.6, that creating a viable wrapper for a subsystem that spans multiple components is not easy. At times, there might be a temptation to simply hide the definitions of lower-level components in order to achieve some notion of logical encapsulation wider than a component. For example, recall the pair of classes `my::Date` and `my::TimeSeries` (see Figure 3-6, section 3.1.10.6), each of which wraps one of a pair of interacting lower-level classes `bdlt::Date` and `odet::DateSequence`, respectively. Placing the two wrapper classes in the same component (see Figure 3-6b) would allow the `my::Date` class to grant `my::TimeSeries` direct (private) access to its internal data via friendship but would violate logical/physical name cohesion (section 2.4).

Suppose instead we decide to place the two wrapper classes in separate components after all, as in Figure 3-129a, but expose the underlying `bdlt::Date` data member from `my::Date` as shown in Figure 3-129b. Then, in order to ensure that external clients of `my::Date` do not exploit this knowledge, we deliberately choose not to export the lower-level `bdlt_date.h` header file to external clients of `my::TimeSeries`.

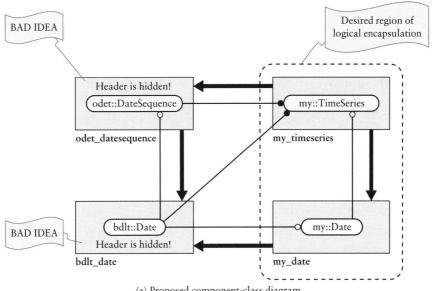

(a) Proposed component-class diagram

```
// my_date.h

// ...

namespace my {

// ...

class Date {
    bdlt::Date d_date;

  public:
    // ...

    // ACCESSORS
    bdlt::Date& privateData() const { return d_date; }
        // Do not try to use this method from outside of
        // this package; the definition of 'bdlt::Date'
        // is physically hidden from external clients.

    // ...

// ...
```

BAD IDEA

(b) Interface of class my::Date exposing private bdlt::Date data member

Figure 3-129: Hiding header files to achieve encapsulation (BAD IDEA)

Attempting to selectively hide header files for the purpose of extending the logical unit of encapsulation beyond a single component could potentially restrict side-by-side reuse of peer subsystems.[203] For example, suppose someone else creates a subsystem your::OtherSubsystem that is a peer of the UOR defining my::Date. Suppose further that this other subsystem legitimately uses bdlt::Date in its interface. Now suppose that a client, SomeClient, of my::TimeSeries decided it also wants to use your::OtherSubsystem, as illustrated in Figure 3-130. If bdlt::Date is not available, then this client of my::TimeSeries would be prevented from using your::OtherSubsystem. On the other hand, if bdlt::Date were made available to SomeClient, it would create a hole in the (unacceptably) constraining, deployment-based attempt at logical encapsulation imposed by hiding the header of the reusable bdlt::Date data member exposed in the ill-conceived interface of my::Date.

---

[203] See **lakos96**, section 5.10, pp. 312–324, especially Figure 5-96, p. 317.

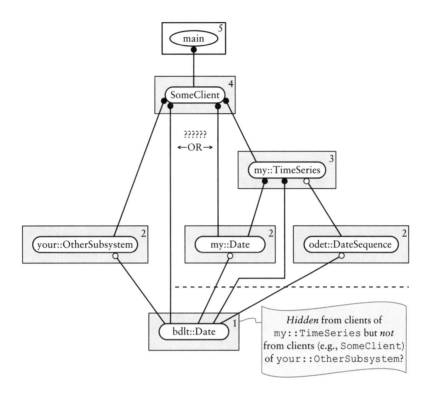

Figure 3-130: Incompatibility of peer subsystems due to hiding headers

There are other reasons why attempting to hide header files is not practical. Without providing the headers of the wrapped types, the wrapper components will not be able to use such types substantively in their own headers (e.g., as embedded data members or in the bodies of inline functions). Imposing the austere internal constraints needed to achieve *insulation* (see section 3.11.6.1) when only encapsulation is required (section 3.5.10) may be entirely inappropriate. What's more, without access to all of the source code, external clients (not to mention static analysis tools) will find debugging more difficult as well.

Separately, convolving the deployment strategy with the logical architecture of a subsystem unjustifiably complicates and constrains the build process. Keeping design and development separate from (and orthogonal to) deployment and release (section 2.15) is in itself one of the great benefits of the overall packaging structure of our methodology (Chapter 2). Note that thoughtfully choosing not to export headers of select components *purely as a build optimization for a particular deployment* is permitted so long as there is nothing in the architecture that precludes their simultaneous export in some other/future deployment. See also section 3.5.10.11.

3.9.8   Depending on Nonportable Software in Reusable Libraries Is a BAD IDEA

Guideline

Minimize and isolate the creation and use of nonportable software.

Maximizing portability is central to successful reuse. The platforms upon which any UOR of library software can be certified to run is necessarily the intersection of its own *capabilities* and those of all of the software upon which it (directly or indirectly) depends. For example, if one UOR has been certified to operate on all Sun and IBM platforms, while another UOR is capable of running on only Windows platforms, then any application or library that attempts to depend upon both will not be guaranteed to run on anything! That is, due to a lack of portability, the use of one library has precluded use of another in the same process.

For any given application, the software available for reuse will be governed by the platforms on which that application must be able to execute. If an application is expected to run on all supported platforms, then allowing it to depend on only software that has been certified to run on all currently supported platforms is necessary, but not quite sufficient. The application must also ensure that it does not use any software that cannot (might not) be easily ported (in a timely fashion) to any new platform that might suddenly need to be supported in the future. The notion of supported platforms is part of our metadata known as capabilities, or `.cap` files (section 2.16.2.2).

Portability is a dimension of quality that we find is often underappreciated. Our ability to respond quickly to new compilers and hardware is a significant part of the benefit of creating our own proprietary infrastructure. Apart from supporting clients who may be running on multiple platforms, there are several reasons why a given organization might want to have a platform-neutral infrastructure even for back-end services where the platforms being used are completely under our control:

- Use multiple compilers to better ensure compliance with the language standard.
- Avoid being held hostage by any one platform vendor.
- Facilitate migration to better compilers/hardware in the future.
- Enable the provision of hardware fault tolerance at run time.

Even when the decision is made to run on only a single platform (for now), ensuring that the code is portable generally improves its quality[204] while keeping our options open. We generally

---

[204] **kernighan99**, Chapter 8, pp. 189–213, specifically p. 189

try to avoid optimizing code for just one particular platform except, of course, in those very few places where such specialization produces measurable and needed improvement. And, when we do create platform-specific customizations (e.g., see Figure 3-108, section 3.6.3), we try to isolate the code in a *granular* (section 0.4) lower-level platform-compatibility layer or else at least mark them clearly (in place).

In all other cases, we aim for the implementations and optimizations that naturally run best in aggregate. Figure 3-131a illustrates how we can side-step nonportability[205] simply by staying within the language definition. If, for some reason, we need to get the value of the address of the most significant byte of an int on the current platform, we would prefer to factor out the platform-dependent (compile-time) notion of "endianness" once, rather than throughout the infrastructure in every place where it might be relevant (Figure 3-131b).

Nonportable   Portable

```
int i = 0, a[10];                      int i = 0, a[10];
while (i < sizeof a) {                  while (i < sizeof a) {
#if SOME_PLATFORM || ...                    a[i] = i;
    a[i] = i++;   // UB                      ++i;
#else                                   }
    a[i++] = i;    // UB
#endif
}
```

(a) Avoiding special-casing by staying within the language

Nonportable   Portable

```
char *msb(int *address) {              char *msb(int *address) {
#if SPARC || ...                        #if BSLS_PLATFORM_IS_BIG_ENDIAN
    return (char *)address;                 return (char *)address;
#else                                   #else
    return (char *)address                  return (char *)address
        + sizeof(int) - 1;                      + sizeof(int) - 1;
#endif                                  #endif
}                                       }
```

(b) Avoiding special-casing by factoring platform-specific properties

Figure 3-131: Ensuring code-level portability

---

[205] Note that both

 a[i] = i++;

and

 a[i++] = i;

are not just not portable but in fact have *language* (or *hard*) undefined behavior (UB), which means technically that almost anything could happen; see Volume II, section 5.2. In particular, there is no guarantee that the order of effects for either statement will be consistent — even within the same program on a given platform.

At a higher level, it is compelling to bring together common capabilities on diverse platforms by providing a uniform syntax at as low a level as possible. For example, the "portable" threading model on Unix platforms has, for many years, been pthreads (Figure 3-132a). Similar functionality has been available natively on Windows platforms, but with an entirely different syntax (Figure 3-132b). With care, it has been possible to create lightweight wrappers that provide sufficient common functionality, yet having a single syntax that works efficiently (i.e., with little or no overhead) on virtually all platforms (Figure 3-132c).[206,207]

Producer

```
pthread_mutex_lock(&mutex);
queue.push(request);
pthread_mutex_unlock(&mutex);
pthread_cond_signal(&cond);
```

Consumer

```
pthread_mutex_lock(&mutex);
while (queue.isEmpty()) {
    pthread_cond_wait(&cond, &mutex);
}
r = queue.top();
queue.pop();
pthread_mutex_unlock(&mutex);
```

(a) Nonportable pthreads code

Producer

```
EnterCriticalSection(&crit);
queue.push(request);
LeaveCriticalSection(&crit);
SetEvent(event);
```

Consumer

```
WaitForSingleObject(event, INFINITE);
EnterCriticalSection(&crit);
r = queue.top();
queue.pop();
if (!queue.isEmpty()) {
    SetEvent(event);
}
LeaveCriticalSection(&crit);
```

(b) Nonportable Windows code

Producer

```
mutex.lock();
queue.push(request);
mutex.unlock();
condition.signal();
```

Consumer

```
mutex.lock();
while (queue.isEmpty()) {
    condition.wait(&mutex);
}
r = queue.top();
queue.pop();
mutex.unlock();
```

(c) Portable proprietary infrastructure code

Figure 3-132: Enabling concrete solution-level portability

---

[206] In the early 2000s, there was an open-source project to create a portable pthreads implementation for Windows platforms. Though basic support for threads has been part of the Standard since C++11, the C++ Standards Committee continues to slowly flesh out unified support for more advanced concurrency constructs within C++ itself.

[207] Note that the choice of having the producer signal after unlocking was deliberate; see Volume II, section 6.1.

Once the solution domain reaches a level of abstraction where performance across its interface boundaries no longer demands tight compile-time coupling, we regain the opportunity to employ more lateral architectures (section 3.7.5). Using abstract interfaces, application developers now have the option of swapping in highly tuned, platform-specific implementations of a complex interface at that much higher level of logical abstraction. This platform-specific code is deliberately kept physically isolated from the core reusable libraries (see section 3.11.5.3). As Figure 3-133 illustrates, a large reusable library subsystem (indicated here simply as `TheServer`) can be customized to run optimally under either Windows or Unix platforms without affecting a single line of library code.

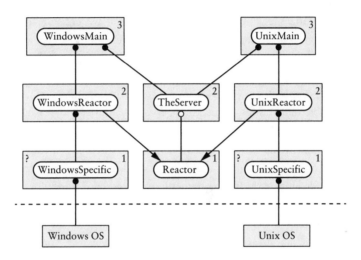

Figure 3-133: Enabling abstract solution-level portability

3.9.9   Hiding Potentially Reusable Software Is a BAD IDEA

Guideline

Minimize the need for package-local (private) components.

Recall, from section 2.7.5, our double-underscore convention for component file names. The purpose of that convention was to allow us to indicate subordinate components containing logical constructs that are not intended to be used directly from other components outside the package in which they are declared. That notation, however, goes a step further by insisting that only one "public" component within a package be allowed to refer to any particular such *package-local* component. This perhaps seemingly arbitrary, additional restriction is deliberate, and with good reason.

An important, primary use of subordinate components is for factoring template specializations of substantial classes into separate, parallel `.h`/`.cpp` pairs. In that usage model, there is just one "public" component containing the general template along with an arbitrary number of subcomponents containing the specializations. Only the component containing the general template is intended for direct use, and only that component is allowed to `#include` the other, subordinate-component header files directly. When we consider partial template specializations, it becomes useful to allow for a tree of package-local dependencies, but still rooted in just a single public component. Hence, for all *intended* purposes, the convention provides just what is needed, nothing more.

Other possible motivations for making a component private to a package are to allow its interface to be less encapsulating and/or its behavior to be more malleable. We are less sympathetic to this use of the notation. Our general approach is to promote reuse through proper factoring into stable, cohesive, atomic units of logical and physical design roughly the size of a single component. Routinely hiding non-client-facing components within a package would mean that no one outside the project will know about these "internal" components. In other words, everyone outside our project who needs similar functionality would be forced to rewrite it, write it from scratch, and invariably write it differently. Systemic, widespread use of package-local components merely to restrict unanticipated use would, in effect, limit reuse.[208] If package-local components at the lower levels of our software infrastructure became the norm, much of the productive gains from *hierarchical reuse* (section 0.4) would evaporate.

Allowing components to be only locally accessible encourages making the package and not the component the unit of design and testing.[209] The ability to hide components means that less up-front effort will be spent designing them to be generally useful. The limited nature of their use will reduce the perceived need to encapsulate and document their intended behavior. The desire to change local components will make thorough retesting of such components

---

[208] Use of `final` (in C++11 and later) is almost never appropriate and for precisely this same reason of indiscriminately limiting hierarchal reuse (section 0.4); see **lakos21**, Chapter 3, "'Unsafe' Features."

[209] The notion of package-level "access" to provide an additional level of logical encapsulation is not new. The default access in Java, for example, is package scope. Following our methodology, a package in Java would be defined similarly to our notion of a package in C++ as being a single directory of Java components, each Java component consisting of just a single `.java` file along with a *deliberately* separate, associated `_t.java` test driver file.

prohibitively expensive, which, in turn, will affect both the stability and correctness of the package as a whole. We believe that a component represents a practical level at which coherent functionality can and should be designed, validated, and preserved via regression testing by a single test driver file (see Volume III, section 7.5). Achieving a similar level of success from even a package-level boundary is dubious (see Volume III, section 7.3).

We recognize that there will, of course, be times when the interface between a "public" class defined in a component and one or more of its subordinate classes may legitimately need to evolve over time. The *extra-underscore* convention for *class* (as opposed to *component*) names (section 2.7.3) is there precisely to address this malleability issue by restricting the use of a class having an extra underscore to the component that defines it (section 2.7.1). Even so, there is a perverse temptation to make what should be stable public classes private so as to reduce the effort needed to design, document, and test them completely. Barring a bona fide stability concern, making classes private to a component is invariably short sighted, and any desire to do so should be suppressed. Hence, there is an implicit (some might argue unrealistic) expectation that each component be designed properly from the start:

> Even in the most thought-out and factored system, public components and functions will still need to be broken apart given new information. Developers should be prepared for performing these kinds of refactors.
>
> — David Sankel (c. 2018)[210]

Given that we are somehow willing to allow package-local components, limiting their use to just a single "public" component of the package mitigates much of their perceived risk. The component is private, presumably because it is an implementation detail and/or intended to be malleable. Recall from section 0.5 that *malleable* software is not reusable. Allowing two publicly reusable components to depend on the same malleable software would mean that changes on behalf of one component might adversely affect the other. Hence, malleable code is generally not appropriate to share — even by two components within the same package.

There is, however, at least one known use case for the ability to have some arbitrary subset of the logical constructs of a package designated as being local to a given package. Consider the example of Figure 3-99, section 3.5.10.8, in which a stable "view" of a subsystem under active development is being presented for use by clients. In this approach, we have used an extreme form of the escalating-encapsulation levelization technique to simulate the effects of a

---

[210] In a personal email discussion

multicomponent wrapper (see Figure 3-6, section 3.1.10.6). This approach works if our goal is to entirely encapsulate and hide *all* of the underlying implementation from the client.

Suppose now that we are actively developing a subsystem, parts of which we want our clients to start using early, but some of the types we export are *vocabulary* types (see Volume II, section 4.4), which must not be wrapped. That is, we want to provide whatever subset of types are exposed in the wrapper as the same (identical) C++ types as in the underlying subsystem. In that case, short of a single monolithic wrapper component, the only viable means of providing such a fine-grained view of the existing system would be to use a C-style procedural interface, consisting of a collection of C-style (free) functions that together enable even a C program to operate on a C++ subsystem (see section 3.11.7.12). The use of a procedural interface also has the advantage of allowing selective masking of individual members of a type, thereby yielding much finer-grained control over what is and is not exposed.[211]

Requiring fine-grained encapsulation is admittedly an additional design constraint, but one that will more than adequately repay us for the extra effort needed to achieve it. The short-to-medium-term benefits of endorsing more general use of package-local components runs directly counter to our goal of maximum productivity in the long-term steady state achieved only through hierarchical reuse. At the same time, most of the benefits of larger units of encapsulation can be realized without the loss of economies of scale, simply by thoughtfully restricting the dependencies among (the entireties of) packages and package groups. Imposing this high-level policy will indeed require firm-wide software project management, which we feel is, in itself, a genuinely good idea.

3.9.10   Section Summary

To summarize: The main objective of this section is to encourage us to maximize physical interoperability by ensuring that the design of every component does not restrict the additional use (or reuse) of that — or any other — component within a single program. Achieving this

---

[211] At its July 2017 meeting, the C++ Standards Committee voted to formally recognize *modules* as a technical specification (TS) for possible eventual inclusion into the C++ language itself. Among the goals of modules, which were initially motivated by the promise of dramatically improved compile times, now — at our behest (**lakos17a**) — also include substantial architectural properties, such as additive (non-invasive) support for fine-grained "views" on existing subsystems, while both preserving the sameness of the underlying (including imported) types (as is the case with procedural interfaces today) and eliminating the brittleness resulting from transitive includes (section 2.6). Now that modules are adopted into the language proper, we continue to be concerned that sound design beneath the module interface might be given short shrift as poorly designed, and therefore frequently updated, abstractions need not be exposed to clients, leading to the same sorts of loss in hierarchical reuse as might result by having package-private components, or component-private classes.

objective is more than just a good strategy. Like insisting on small finely graduated, granular atomic units of physical design (section 0.7), enabling physical interoperability is essential to achieving effective hierarchical reuse (section 0.4) and to our overall approach to stable library-based application development (sections 0.8–0.12). If physical interoperability is just a strategy, then it is a very important one. For more on interoperability from a purely logical perspective, see Volume II, section 4.4.

3.10   Avoiding Unnecessary Compile-Time Dependencies

Physical dependencies can manifest at compile time, link time, or both. When designing from a purely logical perspective, it is easy to ignore such issues as there are no *logical* implications of when such physical coupling occurs. From a practical engineering perspective, however, knowing the difference is important: Excessive compile-time coupling can profoundly impede our ability to maintain software.

3.10.1   Encapsulation Does Not Preclude Compile-Time Coupling

Programmatically inaccessible "encapsulated" implementation details that reside in the physical interface (e.g., the `.h` file) of a component cannot, in general, be modified without forcing all clients of that component to recompile. For even moderately large software projects, the cost[212] of having to recompile the entire system will inhibit modification of the physical interface of low-level (or otherwise widely used) components, limiting our ability to make even minor changes to the details of their implementations.

---

[212] Historically, this cost has been felt in terms of wall time, but for larger systems might perhaps be better expressed in terms of power consumption.

As an introductory example, consider the header file shown in Figure 3-134a for the **my_dstack** component. The logical interface of the `Dstack` class fully *encapsulates* its implementation. That is, there is no programmatic way for a client of `Dstack` to access any part of its array-based implementation, as doing so would preclude substitution of a list-based one (Figure 3-134b) having the identical interface.[213]

---

[213] Even with full encapsulation, not all "compliant" `Dstack` implementations are fully substitutable for each other (see Volume II, section 5.5). There are at least a few programmatic ways we could try to measure potential differences in *observable behavior*, e.g.:

1. Use the `sizeof` operator to infer that the footprint of the `Dstack` implementation on the left (Figure 3-134a) is greater than that of the one on the right (Figure 3-134b).

2. Redefine global operator `new` (in the component defining `main` per section 3.8) to help us monitor the sequence of memory requests in response to specific manipulations of a `Dstack` object. (For more on interfaces that support object-specific custom memory allocation, see Volume II, section 4.10.)

3. Keep pushing values onto a `Dstack` until all available memory is exhausted (it is highly unlikely that the two stack implementations would have the same maximum final capacity on any one particular platform, as the list-based implementation will typically use two or three times the space per element).

4. Create a performance "stress test" to see which one performed with lower (e.g., asymptotic) run time. Note that in virtually any (realistic) test scenario, on any modern computer platform, the array-based implementation will (significantly) outperform the linked-list-based one (see Volume II, section 6.7).

Programmatically observable behavioral differences at this level, however, typically manifest only through the use of white-box, component-level test drivers (see Volume III, section 8.2), and such would *not* be considered violations of *encapsulation* (see section 3.11.1) unless the contract (see Volume II, section 5.2) specifically establishes such behavior as *essential*.

```
// my_dstack.h
#ifndef INCLUDED_MY_DSTACK
#define INCLUDED_MY_DSTACK

// ...
#include <cstddef>  // 'std::size_t'

namespace my {

// ...

class Dstack {
    double     *d_stack_p;
    std::size_t d_capacity;
    std::size_t d_sp;  // first free

  public:
    Dstack();
    Dstack(const Dstack &s);
    ~Dstack();
    Dstack& operator=(const Dstack &s);
    void push(double value);
    void pop();
    double top() const;
    bool isEmpty() const;
};

// ...

}  // close package namespace

#endif
```

(a) Array-based implementation

```
// my_dstack.h
#ifndef INCLUDED_MY_DSTACK
#define INCLUDED_MY_DSTACK

// ...

namespace my {

// ...

class Dstack_Link;

class Dstack {
    Dstack_Link *d_stack_p;

  public:
    Dstack();
    Dstack(const Dstack &s);
    ~Dstack();
    Dstack& operator=(const Dstack &s);
    void push(double value);
    void pop();
    double top() const;
    bool isEmpty() const;
};

// ...

}  // close package namespace

#endif
```

(b) Linked-list-based implementation

Figure 3-134: Fully encapsulating `Dstack` interface

Even though the interface of `Dstack` fully encapsulates both implementations, any experienced C++ programmer looking at these header files can plainly see the distinct implementation strategies of the two components. These headers illustrate the inherent difficulty in concealing proprietary implementations even with encapsulating interfaces. Note that templates (see Volume II, section 6.3) and `inline` functions (see Volume II, section 6.6) can exacerbate this "security hole" by exposing clients to algorithmic details as well.[214]

---

[214] Note that the C++ feature set was not designed with "security by obscurity" as a design requirement, so we won't belabor this point further.

The desire to keep component implementations proprietary is typically *not* the dominant problem for large projects. A client has a right to expect that the logical interface of a component will not change and ideally that any changes made to the logical implementation of a component will not affect clients. In reality, however, the C++ compiler is allowed to depend on all of the logical information in a header file, including private data. If a human being can determine the implementation strategy of a component by inspecting just the source code (excluding comments) in its header, then it is likely that the programmatic clients of the component would be forced to recompile if the implementation strategy of that component changes.

All things being equal, forcing clients to recompile when only the implementation (and not the interface or behavior) changes is not a desirable physical property of a component. The more clients a component has, the more undesirable making changes to the implementation of a component with such tight, compile-time coupling can become. Failing to fully *insulate* clients from evolving implementations of widely used components can have a dramatic impact on the cost of developing large projects. A formal and thorough treatment of *insulation* (of private details) — with its properties discussed in stark contrast to those of mere *encapsulation* (of private details) — is reintroduced in section 3.11.1.

3.10.2   Shared Enumerations and Compile-Time Coupling

Low-level, widely used enumerations that change slowly over time have, historically, been an insidious source of undesirable compile-time coupling. Though ill advised, it is not uncommon to enumerate all error status codes for an entire application, system, or enterprise in a single file (at the bottom of the physical hierarchy) as illustrated in Figure 3-135. At the early stages of development, making a change that forces ubiquitous recompilation might present no significant burden. Enter the "boiling frog" metaphor.[215]

---

[215] **hunt00**, Chapter 1, section 3, pp. 7–9, specifically, the bottom of p. 8

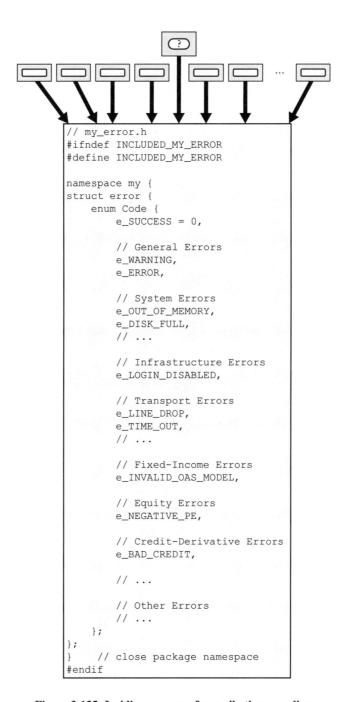

Figure 3-135: Insidious source of compile-time coupling

3.10.3   Compile-Time Coupling in C++ Is Far More Pervasive Than in C

As the system grows beyond nascence, however, the idea of making a change to a low-level header slowly but surely becomes increasingly distasteful. Sooner or later, when adding a new component, we will be tempted to "reuse" existing error codes whose names and/or documented descriptions are, perhaps, only *roughly* appropriate rather than pay the now overwhelming cost of recompiling the world. Once we have reached this point, the system has become unmaintainable.[216]

Compile-time coupling in C++ has always been a far bigger issue than it ever was in C. Typical C headers are proportionally far smaller, exposing none of the implementation details commonly seen in their C++ counterparts. The finer granularity of modular design supported by C++ (section 1.4) has led to a much more balanced distribution of source code implemented across `.h` and `.cpp` files. The more substantive headers of C++ make necessary a more complex, structured build process (sections 2.15–2.16) with well-defined UORs (section 2.2.3).[217]

Due to this extended compile-time coupling, the deployment of individual UORs cannot occur spontaneously or in arbitrary order but instead must in general be staged, proceeding through each physical level (from lowest to highest). This tighter physical coupling and more formal *build* structure necessarily reduces our ability to respond rapidly when *uninsulated* aspects of the implementation (i.e., those residing in header files) at the lower levels of our system must change. Proactive assessment of the trade-offs between compile-time coupling and runtime performance will follow us throughout our C++ development careers.

3.10.4   Avoiding Unnecessary Compile-Time Coupling

Assuming that we have decided that it is appropriate for some particular part of our system to depend on another, the precise nature of the dependency can sometimes prove pivotal to success. To illustrate why and how we should and can avoid unnecessary compile-time coupling, consider the `allocate` method of the aggressively simplified (for now) `my::Pool` class shown in Figure 3-136. Most of the time, this method simply detaches a preallocated block of the configured number of bytes and returns it much more quickly than would a more general-purpose allocation strategy (see Volume II, section 4.10). Hence, the `allocate` method is justifiably declared `inline` and defined in the header file to enable significantly improved runtime performance (and, for similar reasons, so is `deallocate`). But what about the rest of the methods? Should they too be declared `inline`?

---

[216] Separately, the very idea that specific error codes should somehow be coupled beyond a single function, let alone an entire class, never mind a hierarchy of components, is sorely misguided (see Volume II, section 5.2).

[217] Note that the modern C++ modules feature in no way addresses issues related to compile-time coupling, as private implementation details, though no longer directly usable by clients, still need to be accessible by each client's compiler. Hence, any changes to details so exposed will nonetheless force clients to have to recompile.

```
// my_pool.h                                                        -*-C++-*-
#ifndef INCLUDED_MY_POOL
#define INCLUDED_MY_POOL
// ...

namespace my {
// ...

class Pool {
    std::size_t d_size;       // number of bytes per (requested) block
    int         d_chunkSize;  // number of blocks per (allocated) chunk
    struct Link {
        Link *d_next_p;
    } *d_freeList_p;          // linked list of available memory blocks

  private:
    void replenish();
        // Make the free list non-empty.

  private: // NOT IMPLEMENTED[218]
    Pool(const Pool&);
    Pool& operator=(const Pool&);

  public:
    // CREATORS
    explicit
    Pool(std::size_t size);
        // Create a pool of memory blocks, each having the specified 'size'
        // (in bytes).

    ~Pool();
        // Destroy this object (releasing any associated memory blocks).

    // MANIPULATORS
    void *allocate();
        // Return the address (and grant ownership) of a modifiable block of
        // memory sufficiently aligned for the block size specified at
        // construction.

    void deallocate(void *block);
        // Give ownership of the specified memory 'block' back to this pool.
        // The behavior is undefined unless 'block' was previously allocated
        // from this object and has not since been deallocated.

    // ACCESSORS
    std::size_t size() const;[219]

        // Return the number of bytes per block specified at construction.
};
```

The int *here is intentional.* (See Volume II, section 4.4.)

This class has state, but no *value*; hence, generation of these operations is suppressed. (See Volume II, sections 4.1 and 4.3.)

Should this function be declared inline?

Missing optional allocator parameter (BAD IDEA) (See Volume II, section 4.10.)

Should this function be declared inline?

Should this function be declared inline?

Note that this function is not expected to be called frequently (and could even be omitted entirely).

(continues)

---

[218] Of course, in C++11 and later, we would instead write these as:
```
Pool(const Pool&) = delete;
Pool& operator=(const Pool&) = delete;
```

[219] Note that, for the purposes of thorough testing, there needs to be some way, no matter how slow or convoluted, of ascertaining (e.g., via *basic* accessors) *all* of the current state that is relevant for thorough testing to occur (see Volume III, Chapter 10).

(continued)

```
//----------------------------------------------------------------------
//                        INLINE FUNCTION DEFINITIONS
//----------------------------------------------------------------------

inline
void *Pool::allocate()            Should be inline!
{
    if (!d_freeList_p) {
        replenish();              The definition of replenish should
    }                             not reside in the header file!
    Link *tmp      = d_freeList_p;
    d_freeList_p = tmp->d_next_p;
    return tmp;
}

inline                            Should be inline!
void Pool::deallocate(void *block)
{
    reinterpret_cast<Link *>(block)->d_next_p = d_freeList_p;
    d_freeList_p = reinterpret_cast<Link *>(block);
}

inline
std::size_t Pool::size() const
{                                 Does this function really need to be declared
    return d_size;                inline and reside in the header?
}

}  // close package namespace

// ...

#endif
```

Figure 3-136: Physical interface of `my_pool` component

When performance is at stake, some people routinely `inline` everything in sight. Others, somewhat more rationally, use the size of the function body as the sole criteria for choosing whether to declare the function `inline`. For small projects, declaring functions `inline` and defining them in the header presents no problem: The machine has plenty of resources to accommodate the ensuing "code bloat," and the entire program can typically be recompiled in short order if need be. For software on an enterprise scale, however, we *do* have to consider code bloat, but even that pales in comparison to the real problem we face if the implementations of methods we might want to tune are "baked" into every client that uses them.

Let's start by considering the infrequently called accessor function, `size()`, whose definition is shown at the bottom of Figure 3-136. The body of this method is just a single statement returning the value of the `d_size` data member. Clearly the spatial overhead of making a function call here is larger than a simple memory (or register) access. Hence, the final executable size will be smaller if this function is declared `inline`. Just as clearly, a program calling `size()` will run faster if it does not have to endure the burden of creating a stack frame in order to access this data. Also consider that the client compiler, having visibility into the implementation, can typically perform more aggressive optimizations across the boundaries of an `inline` function's body defined in the header, than it can for a conventional one defined in the `.cpp` file.

This `Pool` class, however, is at a very low level in the physical hierarchy, and its header could potentially be included widely throughout the entire code base. The `size()` function — if it is called at all — is not called in any performance critical path that might warrant the "brittleness" (i.e., difficulty in making even small changes to it) of implementing it `inline`.[220] Hence, even though a program calling `size()` will be smaller and run faster if the function is declared `inline`, it is not at all clear that inlining in this case is a good idea, especially since there is reasonable chance that the underlying implementation might change — e.g., such that the requested size is no longer the same as the actual block size (which may be slightly larger).[221]

Let's now consider the constructor:

```
my::Pool::Pool(std::size_t size)
: d_size(size)
, d_chunkSize(DEFAULT_CHUNK_SIZE)
, d_freeList_p(0) 222
```

---

[220] In fact, there is no good reason, other than perhaps testing, to have a `size()` method at all! The client who created the pool object knows full well what the requested size is, as it is typically determined by the `sizeof` nodes in the parent object (e.g., container) in which it is embedded. There is simply no anticipated real-world use case where another client (i.e., in some distant scope) should ever need to rediscover the block-size attribute.

[221] Generally speaking, avoiding compile-time coupling is most valuable early in the software development lifecycle, when encapsulated adjustments to the implementation are most likely to occur. If a legitimate performance need arises, we can always choose to `inline` a function during the next scheduled release.

[222] As of C++11, we may say `d_freeList_p(nullptr)` instead.

Should this constructor definition be declared `inline` and defined in the header? There is one parameter to this constructor,[223] and it needs to make three (single-word) assignments.[224] If all we are considering is run time and code size, then the obvious choice to optimize both at once would be to declare this constructor `inline` and gain the benefits discussed earlier regarding the `size` accessor. On the other hand, by placing the definition of this constructor in the physical interface, we severely limit our ability to make urgent changes to the allocation strategy of `Pool` without also forcing all of our clients to recompile. Note also that the cost of construction is amortized over the lifetime of this object, often making this cost, along with that of destruction, entirely negligible in practice. Hence, for reasons similar to those for `size` discussed above, any constructors for this class should (at least initially) *not* be declared `inline` and *should* be defined entirely in the `.cpp` file.

Sometimes only part of a method should be defined in the header. We refer to hiding only some of the compile-time aspects from a client's compiler as *partial insulation* (see Volume II, section 6.6). For example, consider the implementation of the public `allocate` method of `my::Pool` shown in Figure 3-136. We have deliberately made the private `replenish` method noninline for a number of separate but related reasons:

1. The amount of work needed in order to replenish the pool is substantial compared with that of the overhead of a conventional function call, which alone is sufficient justification (see Volume II, section 6.7).

2. Most of the time, `d_freeList_p` will not be null, and so the cost of calling `replenish` is amortized over several calls to `allocate`.

3. Additional headers — e.g., `new` (in this case) or `bslma_allocator.h` and `bslma_default.h` (see below, and also Volume II, section 4.10) — must be included in order for the body of `replenish` to acquire the additional memory; declaring the `replenish` method `inline` would lead to additional compile-time coupling (as well as unnecessary compile-time overhead) for clients of **my_pool** by forcing such headers to be included in `my_pool.h` instead of directly in `my_pool.cpp`.

---

[223] The number of bytes per block could have been made a template parameter, but doing so would cause each uniquely sized pool to be of a distinct C++ type (see Volume II, section 4.4), causing undue code bloat (see Volume II, section 4.5) and making it incompatible with certain important use cases, such as a multipool allocator (see Volume II, section 4.10).

[224] In the less simplified, real-world, `odema::Pool` implementation discussed below, there will be two constructors (having two and three parameters, respectively) each making four assignments, but the idea remains the same.

4. Most importantly, the strategy of reallocation itself is the part of the `allocate` method that is most likely to change over time!

Declaring the private `replenish()` method `inline` would force any client of `my::Pool` to have seen not only the declaration of `replenish()` but also its definition, along with any additional headers it needs in order to compile. The logical behavior of `replenish()` is — by definition — the same whether or not `replenish` is declared `inline`. What is affected by the decision to `inline`, however, is the degree and character of the *physical coupling* between the implementation of `Pool` and its clients, and hence, so is the cost of maintaining any program using `Pool`. Our ability to tune the pooling strategy in large systems — say, to change the default chunk size or move between *fixed-size* and *adaptive* allocation strategies — in any reasonable time frame will be governed by the *physical* design decision to *not* declare strategically critical functions, such as the constructors and the (private) `replenish()` method, `inline`.

3.10.5   Real-World Example of Benefits of Avoiding Compile-Time Coupling

As a real-world example[225] of how eliminating unnecessary compile-time coupling can critically affect our ability to respond quickly to business needs, let us now suppose our department is responsible for the low-level infrastructure including reusable libraries that, among other things, help to manage memory allocation. As Figure 3-137 illustrates, the `odema::Pool` (**o**ur **d**evelopment **e**nvironment **m**emory **a**llocator `Pool`) class, formerly `my::Pool` (Figure 3-136, section 3.10.4), is used by many other departments' **d**evelopment-**e**nvironment package groups, including **e**quities (**ede**), **f**ixed income (**fde**), and **c**redit derivatives (**cde**), to amortize the cost of allocating and deallocating certain fixed-size structures for their own separate, proprietary **c**ollections packages — **edec**, **fdec**, and **cdec**, respectively. Several high-level applications depend on these collections. In fact, some of these applications (e.g., **app3**) even depend on collections that are maintained by more than one department; consequently, these collections reside in separate UORs.

---

[225] This actually happened when I was working as a financial infrastructure library developer in the F.A.S.T. Group at Bear Stearns & Co. in NYC (circa 1998).

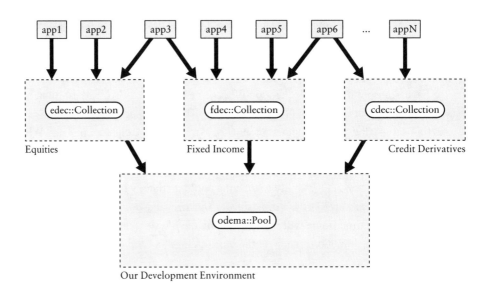

Figure 3-137: Illustrating adverse consequences of compile-time dependencies

As it turns out, **app3** is a very successful joint venture involving aspects of both equities and fixed income. One of **app3**'s principal data structures involves creating very large arrays of (node-based) `fdec::Collection` objects, which relies on `odema::Pool` to help manage its nodes, but where each collection in the array is typically very sparse (i.e., just one or two elements). The volume of **app3**'s business has been expanding so rapidly that memory consumption is beginning to bump up against the limits of the platform. Throwing more hardware at the problem is a brute-force approach providing, at best, a medium-term "Band-Aid" solution; there remains an emergent need to address the essential "ineffective" (suboptimal) pooling-strategy issue in order to avoid missed business opportunities (a.k.a. in financial parlance as "leaving money on the table"). Our department head wants to know what we can do, today!

The initial replenish strategy for `odema::Pool` was to always allocate the same fixed number of blocks at once. In this design, however, a second constructor was supplied having an additional

    int chunkSize

parameter,[226] enabling the client to specify the (positive) fixed number of memory blocks per chunk, rather than having to accept an implementation-defined default.

As Figure 3-138 shows,[227,228,229] `DEFAULT_CHUNK_SIZE`, the default value for the (fixed) number of blocks per chunk, was initially 100, but we were later able to reduce it to 32 with no appreciable loss in performance. Due to sound coding practices facilitating internal malleability (section 0.5), changing this default value in the `.cpp` file was trivial. More importantly, however, because the first constructor was not declared `inline`, changing that value from 100 to 32 did not require clients to recompile in order to pick up the new `DEFAULT_CHUNK_SIZE` value.

---

[226] We deliberately use the (unfortunately but necessarily `unsigned`) `std::size_t` to represent values, such as `blockSize`, whose maximum value is directly tied to the size of the available address space of the underlying (e.g., 32- or 64-bit) platform. In the case of `chunkSize`, however, there is no such practical dependence; hence, we generally prefer to use the more general-purpose *vocabulary type* `int` instead (see Volume II, section 4.4).

[227] This time with proper support for an optional polymorphic memory allocator in the constructors (see Volume II, section 4.10).

[228] A readily usable open-source implementation of `bslma::Allocator` and `bslma::Default` can be found in the **bslma** package of the **bsl** package group of Bloomberg's open-source distribution of the BDE libraries (see **bde14**, subdirectory `/groups/bsl/bslma/`).

[229] As of C++17, we can use the standard facilities of `std::pmr` (Polymorphic Memory Resource) to accomplish these same goals (**cpp17**, section 23.12); see also **lakos17b**, **lakos17c**, and **meredith19**.

```cpp
// odema_pool.cpp                                      -*-C++-*-
#include <odema_pool.h>
#include <bslma_allocator.h>                  (See Volume II, section 4.10.)
#include <bslma_default.h>                    (See Volume II, section 4.10.)
#include <cassert>                             (See Volume II, section 6.8.)
#include <cstddef>  // for 'std::size_t'

// ...

enum { k_DEFAULT_CHUNK_SIZE = 32 };  // was originally 100


class Link;
static const std::size_t PTR_SIZE = sizeof(Link *);  // convenient alias
```

> Note that, in this implementation, d_size is the requested size rounded up to an integral multiple of the size of a (LINK *) address on this platform.

```cpp
namespace odema {

Pool::Pool(std::size_t size, bslma::Allocator *basicAllocator)
: d_size((size + PTR_SIZE - 1) / PTR_SIZE * PTR_SIZE)
, d_chunkSize(k_DEFAULT_CHUNK_SIZE)
, d_freeList_p(0)
, d_allocator_p(bslma::Default::allocator(basicAllocator))  (See Volume II, section 4.10.)
{
    assert(size > 0);  // Assert that 'size' is greater than 0; otherwise,
}                      // 'd_size' becomes zero, and 'replenish' crashes.
                                                      (See Volume II, section 6.8.)
Pool::Pool(std::size_t size, int chunkSize, bslma::Allocator *basicAllocator)
: d_size((size + PTR_SIZE - 1) / PTR_SIZE * PTR_SIZE)
, d_chunkSize(chunkSize)
, d_freeList_p(0)
, d_allocator_p(bslma::Default::allocator(basicAllocator))  (See Volume II, section 4.10.)
{
    assert(size      > 0);
    assert(chunkSize > 0);
}
```

> Again, also assert that size > 0 (See Volume II, section 6.8.)

```cpp
void Pool::replenish()
{
    d_freeList_p = reinterpret_cast<Link *>(
                              d_allocator_p->allocate(d_size * d_chunkSize));
    Link *p = d_freeList_p;
    for (int i = 1; i < d_chunkSize; ++i) {
        Link *q = reinterpret_cast<Link *>(reinterpret_cast<char *>(p) +
                                                                    d_size);
        p->d_next_p = q;
        p = q;
    }
    p->d_next_p = 0;
}

}  // close package namespace
```

Figure 3-138: (Initial) fixed-chunk-size replenishment strategy

It is crucial to realize that compile-time coupling alone was never the issue here. Recompiling all the code, albeit (needlessly) time consuming, *could* have been done. The problem was that, in order for **app3** to take advantage of any change that involved a substantive modification to `odema_pool.h`, all of the intervening software, including **edec** and **fdec**, depending physically on the **ode** package group, would not only have had to be recompiled but also *redeployed* (section 2.15). Getting either of the responsible development organizations to rebuild and redeploy all of their libraries to production outside their normal release cycle in any reasonable timeframe would have been difficult, to say the least; getting them both to do so on very short notice was insurmountable.

Yet there was still a path forward. Because modifying the DEFAULT_CHUNK_SIZE, installed by the first `odema::Pool` constructor, did not require the intermediate libraries to be recompiled, it was possible to *patch* **app3** simply by supplying the new `odema_pool.o` file directly on the link line in front of the (statically linked) libraries for **fdec**, **edec**, and **ode** (see section 1.2.4), solving the problem until the next regularly scheduled release occurred.

Unfortunately, upon further analysis of the sparse-array usage pattern that is characteristic of **app3**, it soon became clear that no fixed-size pool replenishment strategy was workable. Although this sort of fixed strategy scaled *up* well, it failed to scale *down*, as reducing this fixed DEFAULT_CHUNK_SIZE value below 32 would have caused a noticeable reduction in performance for other applications.[230] An entirely new replenishment strategy was needed.

Changing `replenish` from a fixed chunk-size strategy to an adaptive one that allocates geometrically, e.g., starting with 1, 2, 4, 8, 16, and finally saturating at 32, would improve the spatial performance for the dominant data structure used in **app3** by an order of magnitude without inflicting significant performance degradation on any other applications. This change would obviate having to purchase and install more hardware. The only question remaining was, "Would such a change force clients of `odema::Pool` to recompile?"

This critical physical design question reduces to, "Is the first constructor[231] or the private `replenish` method for `odema::Pool` declared `inline`?" If these *infrequently used* yet *highly volatile* methods are, for some reason, currently implemented in the header, we would need to

---

[230] **lakos96**, section 10.4.3.1, pp. 702–705 (especially Figure 10-27, p. 705)

[231] Note that the constructors could still have been declared `inline` had we *partially insulated* its default chunk-size value by accessing it via a `static` class data member initialized in the `.cpp` file (see Volume II, section 6.6).

rebuild and rerelease our entire infrastructure, starting with the **ode** package group. Once that's done, we would need to get both the Equities and the Fixed Income departments to quickly rebuild, retest, and rerelease their libraries (good luck with that). Only then could **app3** be safely rebuilt.

On the other hand, if the private `replenish` method is not declared `inline`, the amortized runtime cost of calling this heavyweight method might be imperceptibly greater, but none of the strategic details of its implementation is exposed to clients. As long as the changes we make are consistent with the contract for `replenish` — i.e., "Make the free-list nonempty." — we can pretty much do as we please in the `odema_pool.cpp` file (see Volume II, section 5.5), and nothing other than that one solitary source file has to recompile.[232]

The runtime cost of construction without inlining will also likely increase, but, again, that one-time cost is amortized over the entire lifetime of the embedded pool. Provided that all of the strategic implementation[233] changes are hidden from clients' compilers, sequestered entirely in the `.cpp` file as shown in Figure 3-139, we can hand the developer of **app3** a special `odema_pool.o` *patch* file to be placed directly on the link-line ahead of the (statically linked) libraries and the emergency is resolved. Today!

---

[232] Note that having the additional constructor that allowed clients to specify the positive chunk size was a complicating factor, requiring us to preserve that capability, while supporting new functionality that would allow clients to specify, via a negative value, an arbitrary *adaptive* initial value.

[233] Thanks to a suggestion by Pablo Halpern years later, the current state-of-the-art implementation of our adaptive pool, which has always used an adaptive strategy exclusively, now — instead of first sewing together the links within each newly allocated chunk — maintains a pair of iterators into the most recent of the geometrically increasing series of chunks, thereby eliminating gratuitous (e.g., L1) cache usage, improving performance, and obviating any fixed maximum chunk size. See the **bdlma_pool** component consisting of the files `bdlma_pool.h`, `bdlma_pool.cpp`, and `bdlma_pool.t.cpp` in the **bdlma** package of the **bdl** package group of the BDE libraries (**bde14**, subdirectory `groups/bdl/bdlma/`).

```
// odema_pool.cpp                                              -*-C++-*-
#include <odema_pool.h>
#include <bslma_allocator.h>                    (See Volume II, section 4.10.)
#include <bslma_default.h>
#include <cassert>                              (See Volume II, section 6.8.)

enum { DEFAULT_CHUNK_SIZE = -1 };  // Negative implies pool is still adapting.
enum {     MAX_CHUNK_SIZE = 32 };  // The value at which chunk size saturates.

static const std::size_t PTR_SIZE = sizeof(Link *);  // convenient alias

// ...
// ...              No change to constructor definitions from Figure 3-138 with
// ...              the exception of assert(chunkSize != 0) instead of
                    assert(chunkSize > 0) in the body of the second constructor.
void Pool::replenish()
{
    int chunkSize;                              // Will hold current chunk size.

    if (d_chunkSize < 0) {                      // if chunk size is still adapting
        chunkSize = -d_chunkSize;
        if (chunkSize >= MAX_CHUNK_SIZE) {      // if chunk size has just saturated
            d_chunkSize = MAX_CHUNK_SIZE;
        }
        else {                                  // Use current chunk size.
            d_chunkSize *= 2;                   // Increase for next time.
        }
    }
    else {                                      // Chunk size already saturated.
        chunkSize = d_chunkSize;
    }
                    There is only one change from Figure 3-138 below this line:
                         d_chunkSize becomes chunkSize.

    d_freeList_p = reinterpret_cast<Link *>(
                           d_allocator_p->allocate(d_size * chunkSize) );
    Link *p = d_freeList_p;
    for (int i = 1; i < chunkSize; ++i) {
        Link *q = reinterpret_cast<Link *>(reinterpret_cast<char *>(p) +
                                                                   d_size);
        p->d_next_p = q;
        p = q;
    }
    p->d_next_p = 0;
}
```

Figure 3-139: (Replacement) adaptive-chunk-size replenishment strategy

3.10.6   Section Summary

To summarize: Changing an *encapsulated* implementation detail of a class — such as a *private data member*, the *body* of an *inline function*, or even the *signature* or *return type* of a *private* or *protected method* — will nonetheless force development tools to recompile their clients. Compile-time dependencies across UORs can be a critical design consideration for applications of even moderate size. In the next section, we discuss wholesale architectural-level approaches for *insulating* clients from any changes to *logically encapsulated* implementation details. We will revisit the topics of both *partial* and *total insulation* from an implementation-only perspective in Volume II, section 6.6.

3.11   Architectural Insulation Techniques

Compile-time coupling, introduced in the previous section, is an important consideration for larger systems, affecting both logical and physical design. In this section, we first formalize our understanding of (logical) *encapsulation* and then reintroduce the term *insulation* to mean its physical analog. Next, we present a brief discussion of the various categories of techniques used to insulate implementation details from prospective clients. Finally, we present three distinct *total* insulation techniques that necessarily affect the logical interface by which clients interact with a *fully insulated* subsystem.

3.11.1   Formal Definitions of *Encapsulation* vs. *Insulation*

> **DEFINITION**: An implementation detail of a component (type, data, or function) that can be altered, added, or removed without forcing clients to rework their code is said to be *encapsulated*.

Encapsulated implementation details, as defined here, are not programmatically accessible by clients directly.[234] As we saw at the beginning of section 3.10, hiding every aspect of observable

---

[234] Although the term *encapsulation* originally meant just bringing together (as if into a "capsule") the data manipulated by the member functions of a class, in this book we routinely use this term in its now colloquially accepted form, which, in addition to colocation of data and member functions, implies that details of the implementation — in particular, the data — are logically "hidden" (i.e., are not programmatically accessible by other than the colocated functions). Historically, however, a `struct` could have been considered to "encapsulate" its public data — even though it did not "hide" it.

behavioral differences resulting from distinct implementations in C++ is not necessarily always achievable in practice. Our goal with encapsulation, therefore, is to allow for changes to implementation details such that, for all *practical* purposes, clients will not be forced to rework their code.

DEFINITION: An implementation detail of a component (type, data, or function) that can be altered, added, or removed without forcing clients to recompile is said to be *insulated*.

Insulation is the physical analog to the logical property of encapsulation. The goal of insulation is that, in addition to clients not having to *rework* their code, they do not have to even *recompile* it. Any changes to isolated implementation details are picked up by clients at link time. Much more so than with encapsulation, insulating every aspect of a component's implementation is not necessarily the goal, and can seriously degrade performance. Hence, the form and degree of insulation that is appropriate will depend on (1) the purpose of the functionality whose implementation is being insulated, as well as (2) its relative location in the physical architecture of the code base.

3.11.2   Illustrating Encapsulation vs. Insulation in Terms of Components

To better understand the physical differences between *encapsulation* and *insulation*, consider the detailed (file-level) component-dependency graph depicted in Figure 3-140. This diagram consists of four components, denoted as **a** through **d**. Let us assume that **d** represents a client component, and that **c** represents a (reusable) library component. The client software, **d**, makes direct, substantive use of the functionality afforded by library component **c**, and so **d** — according to our design rules (section 2.6) — necessarily includes c.h *directly*. The library component **c**, in turn uses two C++ classes, A and B, each defined in their own, separate components, **a** and **b**, respectively.

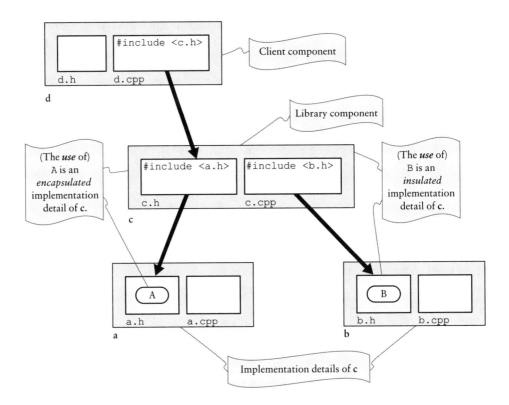

Figure 3-140: Encapsulation versus insulation of (the use of) components

In this example, **c** uses both A and B in (only) its implementation. That is, neither of these two types is part of any externally accessible *programmatic* interface defined by **c** (in c.h). It is convenient to say that both A and B are *encapsulated* by **c**, but — strictly speaking — this would not be correct. Being publicly available classes of nonsubordinate components (section 2.7.5), it is entirely possible for **c** (or any other software) to access either A or B simply by first including the corresponding header file (directly) and then proceeding to create and use objects of the desired type at will.

What we mean by the term *encapsulated* here is that, while it is possible to make new objects of these types, there is no way to make use of them in the context of **c**. That is, there is simply no programmatic orifice exposed by **c** whereby objects of such types might be inserted or extracted. To describe our intended meaning more precisely, rather than saying that

c *encapsulates* A, which it clearly does not, we could instead say that **c** encapsulates the *use* of A.[235] By dint of this notion of *encapsulation*, we could replace A with some entirely different class E, able to perform the equivalent functionality, and no proper client of **c** should have to rework their code.[236]

In this example, (the *use* of) both A and B are encapsulated by **c**. Making any substantive change to the logical interface of either A or B will force **c** to recompile, and perhaps even its source code to be reworked, but neither will force **d**'s source to change, so long as **c**'s programmatic interface and essential behavior (see Volume II, section 5.2) remain the same. Still, with respect to **c**, we can make an even stronger statement about B. While a.h is included in c.h (which, in turn, is included in c.cpp), b.h is not, and instead is included in c.cpp directly. Hence, unlike a.h, changes to b.h are *not* automatically propagated through the physical interface of **c** to **d**, and so changes to b.h do *not* necessarily require **d** to recompile! In other words, **c** *encapsulates* the use of A, whereas it (also) *insulates* the use of B.[237,238]

3.11.3   *Total* vs. *Partial* Insulation

Insulation can be classified as being either *total* or *partial*. By *total insulation*, we mean that there is essentially no aspect of the encapsulated implementation that, if changed, would force the client to recompile. *Partial insulation*, on the other hand, implies that some (ideally stable) aspects of the implementation are exposed to clients' compilers,[239] while other, more strategic

---

[235] We saw an example of this sort of "encapsulation of use" in section 3.5.10.2 (see Figure 3-94) where class Graph encapsulates the use of (implementation) classes Node and Edge, along with that of the (reusable) class template std::vector. For another, physical example of the importance of encapsulating the use of (physically distinct) implementation components, see Figure 3-172, section 3.12.11.2.

[236] Note that if a current client of **c**, e.g., **d**, happens to also use A directly, but failed to also include a.h directly, then, by swapping out A for another type, E, and removing the nested include of a.h in c.h, such a client might suddenly fail to compile. Reliance on such indirect or *transitive* includes is, however, an explicit design-rule violation (section 2.6).

[237] Note that the term *insulation* invariably implies *encapsulation* in practice. We might imagine a change to implementation detail that, while not physically requiring a client to recompile, logically forces a client to rework their code, which would, in turn, *have* to be recompiled.

[238] C++ modules, when they become widely available, will not afford much (if anything) in the way of (physical) *insulation* beyond what header files do today, as doing so would necessarily imply an unacceptably large amount of additional runtime overhead. This C++20 language feature does, however, provide a new form of *physical* encapsulation: Types used only in the implementation, e.g., for embedded (private) data members of exported (public) types, though still available for use by client compilers, will not be made available for direct use by clients of the encapsulating type, thereby actively preventing the brittle practice (and design-rule violation; section 2.6) of inadvertently relying on *transitive includes*.

[239] Usually to improve runtime performance, but sometimes to enable interoperability (see Volume II, section 4.4).

and malleable aspects are kept hidden away in the `.cpp` file. Partial insulation (as compared to no insulation) is itself an implementation detail of a single component and is discussed from that perspective in Volume II, section 6.6.[240] If total insulation is appropriate, however, then the physical architecture of the subsystem as well as the nature of the logical interface to that subsystem will most likely be affected. It is these *architecturally significant* (section 2.2.6) total-insulation techniques that we address here.

3.11.4   Architecturally Significant Total-Insulation Techniques

Historically, there have been essentially three basic architecturally significant techniques[241] for achieving total insulation of a subsystem in C++, which are summarized in Figure 3-141. Each of these techniques comes with certain advantages and disadvantages. Appropriateness of any of these techniques will depend on the specifics of the situation at hand. For example, the use of protocol classes to achieve total insulation immediately comes to mind when inheritance would otherwise be involved anyway. In such cases, the architecture already anticipates that the creator of the concrete derived type will most likely be different from the majority of clients who use it via its abstract base class. There is also the added benefit of eliminating even a link-time dependency of a protocol's clients on its (derived) implementations.

---

[240] Providing a local class declaration, say `class A;`, in a header file, say `b.h`, as opposed to including `a.h` (the header in which class `A` is defined), is typically done to insulate clients of `b.h` from changes in `a.h` where the declaration, but not the definition, of `A` is needed in `b.h` in order for it to compile in isolation as required by Component Property 1 (section 1.6.1). Such local (internal-bindage) declarations (section 1.3.4), though permitted by our component design rules (section 2.6), limit what sort of changes can be made to the client-facing interface presented in `a.h` without forcing the source code of `b.h` to be reworked. Strategies for mitigating this impediment — consistent with the basic design and packaging rules and nomenclature delineated throughout Chapter 2 — can be realized in the form of "forward"-declaring components such as **iosfwd** (see Volume II, section 5.5).

[241] **lakos96**, sections 6.4–6.5, pp. 385–445

I. The Pure Abstract Interface ("Protocol") Class
   Deriving from (or adapting to) a pure interface, where each
   concrete implementation is instantiated separately from
   typical clients that use it

II. The Fully Insulating Concrete Wrapper Component
   Creating one or more classes within a single component that
   each have exactly one data member, which is an opaque pointer
   to an instance of a unique *component-local* class defined in
   the implementation (.cpp) file and managed entirely by its
   corresponding public "wrapper" class

III. The Procedural Interface
   Providing a collection of free functions that allocate, operate
   on, and deallocate opaque objects via strongly typed pointers

---

Figure 3-141: Three basic techniques for achieving total insulation

For subsystems that must be created and managed by the same client, inheritance is not appropriate, but a fully insulating concrete wrapper component might well be. If the system is already managed by an encapsulating wrapper component — e.g., **xyza_pubgraph** (see Figure 3-95, section 3.5.10.3) — transition to a full-insulating wrapper component is straightforward (see Volume II, section 6.6). Otherwise, given that multicomponent wrappers are generally known to be notoriously difficult to realize (section 3.1.10.6), this strategy will be viable only if the number of individual wrapper classes required by the new wrapper is fixed (or very slowly growing) and will continue to remain small enough to fit within a single component — this to avoid violating the design-rule proscribing long-distance friendship (section 2.6).

Finally, for situations in which a large preexisting subsystem makes a single-component wrapper impracticable, we may be forced to resort to a procedural interface. In that approach, clients allocate, manipulate, and deallocate instances of opaque types solely via free functions. The main drawback here is that we now, in some sense, "hide" the definitions of the interface types from clients in order to gain the insulation (which is *not* the same sort of pseudological encapsulation hiding described in sections 3.9.7 and 3.9.10); hence, procedural interfaces are typically designed to also allow use by C-language clients, who wouldn't otherwise be able to use the C++ types directly anyway.[242] Let us now examine each of the three basic architecturally significant approaches to total insulation introduced above in more detail.

---

[242] As an example, see the C-style callback function, myTurnUpTheHeatCallback, invoking the turnUpTheHeat method of the MyHeatController object shown in Figure 3-31, section 3.3.8.1.

3.11.5   The Pure Abstract Interface ("Protocol") Class

Whenever we are already predisposed to using inheritance, using a protocol (section 1.7.5) to totally insulate public clients of the interface from any changes to the "reused" part of the implementation is virtually[243] always the right decision. As a contrived and (arguably) poorly designed, yet simple and pedagogically useful concrete example of the advantages of using a protocol to insulate all aspects of shared implementation in an inheritance hierarchy, consider the collection of components illustrated in Figure 3-142. This small subsystem consists of a base class, Shape, a couple of specific concrete classes, Circle and Rectangle, that derive their respective interfaces and common implementations from Shape, and several client classes, Client1, Client2, and Client3, that consume only the public interface of the Shape base class.

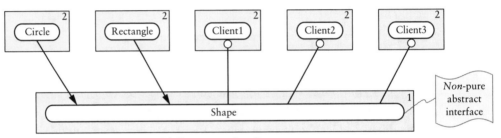

(a) Component-class diagram

```
// my_shape.h
// ...
class Shape {
    short int d_x;  // may (some day) cease being large enough
    short int d_y;  // may (some day) cease being large enough
  protected:
    Shape(int xOrigin, int yOrigin);
  public:
    virtual ~Shape();  // Defined empty in the .cpp file.
    // ...
    virtual double area() = 0;
    int xOrigin() const { return d_x; }
    int yOrigin() const { return d_y; }
    // ...
};
// ...
```

(continues)

---

[243] Pun intended.

(continued)

```
// my_circle.h
// ...
#include <my_shape.h>
// ...
class Circle : public Shape {
    short int d_radius;
  public:
    Circle(int xOrigin, int yOrigin, int radius);
    virtual ~Circle();
    virtual double area() const { return PI * d_radius * d_radius; }244
    // ...
};
// ...
```

```
// your_client3.cpp
// ...
#include <your_client3.h>
// ...
#include <my_shape.h>
// ...
static double totalArea(const std::vector<Shape *>& shapePointers)
{
    double sum = 0.0;

    for (int i = 0, n = shapePointers.size(); i < n; ++i) {245
        sum += shapePointers[i]->area();
    }
    return sum;
}
// ...
```

(b) Elided source code from selected component files

Figure 3-142: Compile-time coupling due to structural inheritance

---

244 As of C++11, we can, and probably should, annotate the `area` as being an `override` of a virtual function declared in the base class in order to help (e.g., the compiler) to ensure that its signature matches the pure virtual one that it implements:

```
virtual double area() const override;   // 'virtual' here is optional
```

245 As of C++11, we can take advantage of the range-based `for` syntax to more succinctly, but otherwise equivalently, access (in forward-iteration order) each element in the sequence of `Shape` pointers (we have deliberately elected to splurge on the extra letter in favor of readability using `Shape`, over writability using `auto`):

```
for (Shape *p : shapePointers) {
    sum += p->area();
}
```

For a thorough treatment of the effective use of these and other modern C++ language features *safely* in a large-scale industrial setting, see **lakos21**.

Originally, the author of `Shape` (who was working exclusively on 32-bit platforms at the time) knew that the useful range of coordinate values for all clients was just [−1000 .. +1000] and so, in order to minimize object size, decided to represent the coordinate values internally as `short int` data members, with the understanding that, some day, this valid range might need to increase. The specific size of the private data members used to store the coordinates is clearly an implementation detail of the `Shape` class, provided, of course, that they are capable of representing the valid range of values indicated by the contract (see Volume II, section 5.2). Subsequently replacing `short int` with `int` would not change the logical interface, which would continue to accept and return integers of type `int` as usual (see Volume II, section 6.12) albeit in a superset of the range specified in the original contract. In fact, this implementation detail is entirely encapsulated by the interface of `Shape`. Yet there is a problem.

Suppose that one fine day we learn that some of our clients are in urgent need of a larger range for coordinates than a `short int` can accommodate, and so we decide to change the type of the private coordinate data members (for everyone) from `short int` to `int`. Which of the components in Figure 3-142 would be forced to recompile? Unfortunately, the correct answer is "All of them!" including those clients that don't require this enhancement and, therefore, have no pressing need to recompile and redeploy yet must do so in order to be compatible with other clients that do.

Both `Circle` and `Rectangle` inherit from `Shape` and depend intimately on the internal physical layout of `Shape`. When any data members of `Shape` change, the internal layout of `Circle` and `Rectangle` must change accordingly and in lock step. Clients of `Shape` are no better off. In addition to incompatibilities involving the data members themselves, the position of the virtual table pointer in the physical layout of the `Shape` object will, on many platforms, be affected by the change from `short int` to `int`. Unless the dependent code is recompiled, it simply will not work.

3.11.5.1   Extracting a Protocol

Whenever any part of the implementation resides in the header file of a component, the component fails to *insulate* clients from that part of its logical implementation. Using the same base class for both interface and implementation inheritance exposes public clients to recompilation should the encapsulated details of the common partial implementation change. A pure abstract (i.e., "protocol") class, however, acts as an almost perfect insulator (see section 3.11.5.3). If we extract, from the base class, a pure abstract interface, then clients are entirely insulated from changes to that aspect of the implementation.

Figure 3-143 illustrates the modified architecture in which the original Shape class is renamed to ShapePartialImp, which now derives from the new (pure abstract) Shape protocol class. Because Shape was already an abstract class, extracting a protocol is the natural way to improve insulation without altering the usage model.[246] Runtime performance for all but the origin-related functions will be left entirely unaffected. Clients will continue to use Shape as before, but need not recompile in response to changes in the shared implementation (now residing in ShapePartialImp). Note also that a new concrete implementation of Shape, such as Box, is now able to derive from the protocol directly and, hence, is no longer forced to incur the spatial overhead associated with ShapePartialImp in the event that an alternative implementation for it is preferable.

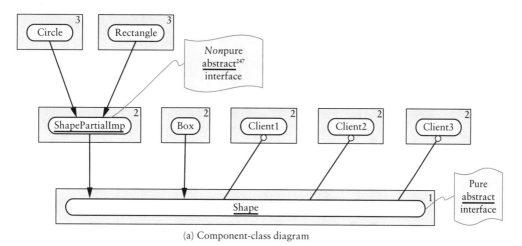

(a) Component-class diagram

---

[246] **lakos96**, section 6.6.3, pp. 653–654

[247] Note that we sometimes underscore the class name to indicate that it is an abstract interface even when it is not pure.

```
// my_shape.h
// ...
class Shape {
  public:
    virtual ~Shape();  // Defined empty in '.cpp' file.
    virtual double area() const = 0;
    virtual int xOrigin() const = 0;        Now pure virtual
    virtual int yOrigin() const = 0;
    // ...
};
// ...
```

```
// my_shapepartialimp.h
// ...
#include <my_shape.h>
// ...
class ShapePartialImp : public Shape {
    int d_x;           Now insulated from public clients
    int d_y;
  protected:
    ShapePartialImp(int xOrigin, int yOrigin);
  public:
    virtual double area() const = 0;        Still pure virtual
    virtual int xOrigin() const { return d_x; };     Implemented here
    virtual int yOrigin() const { return d_y; };
    // ...
};
// ...
```

```
// my_circle.h
// ...                                          Having a literal initializer
#include <my_shapepartialimp.h>                 for PI beyond 16 decimal
// ...                                          digits will not affect the
class Circle : public ShapePartialImp {         internal value of a typical
    static const double PI = 3.141592653589793;  (eight-byte) double.
    int d_radius;
  public:
    Circle(int xOrigin, int yOrigin, int radius)
            : ShapePartialImp(xOrigin, yOrigin), d_radius(radius) { }
    virtual double area() const { return PI * d_radius * d_radius; }
    // ...
};
// ...
```

(b) Elided source code from selected component files

Figure 3-143: Avoiding compile-time coupling via a protocol class

3.11.5.2   Equivalent "Bridge" Pattern

Interface inheritance is the only kind of inheritance that truly adds value.[248] Any use of implementation inheritance is dubious, especially for library components (see Volume II, section 4.6). Even when implementation inheritance is used, the need for separating interface from implementation inheritance goes far beyond physical insulation (see Volume II, section 4.7). Note, however, that we can always achieve precisely the same result without implementation inheritance — albeit at the cost of some additional effort on the part of derived-class authors.

An alternative to implementation inheritance would be to replace ShapePartialImp with one or more separate concrete classes, such as IntPoint and ShortPoint — sometimes identified as the *bridge pattern*[249] — as illustrated in Figure 3-144. In this design, each concrete node is independently responsible for providing its own (factored) implementation to implement the Shape protocol. If a new concrete derived shape, such as Box, wants to implement the coordinate data members itself, so be it! Note that, unless the derived-class author is also the intended client of a subsystem, it is this architectural form for library software that we typically find most effective for interface inheritance in practice.

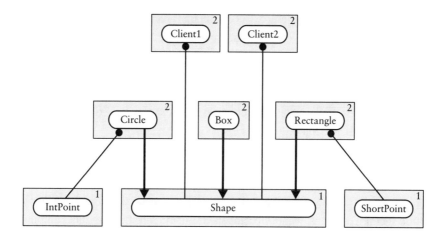

Figure 3-144: Replacing implementation inheritance with layering

---

[248] **liskov87**

[249] **gamma95**, Chapter 4, section "Bridge," pp. 151–161

3.11.5.3   Effectiveness of Protocols as Insulators

We generally find protocols, where applicable, to be the most effective of these basic architecturally significant total-insulation techniques. Protocols, being free of any clutter not specific to the interface itself, eliminate virtually all aspects of compile-time coupling associated with implementation. No data members or private member functions are exposed to clients of a pure interface. Moreover, protected functionality (intended solely for derived-class authors) is also easily escalated to partial implementations (or, alternatively, re-created in separate implementation, e.g., *utility* components) explicitly purposed for derived classes and, consequently, need never be seen by public clients' compilers either. A profoundly effective use of a protocol as a *vocabulary type* (see Volume II, section 4.4) is that of injecting local memory allocators (see Volume II, section 4.10).

3.11.5.4   Implementation-Specific Interfaces

Even the interfaces for special functions such as constructors, used by separate, higher-level clients to create and configure objects of derived (implementation) types of a protocol, are simply not visible through the abstract interface. Also eliminated, with respect to public clients, is any compile-time coupling associated with implementation-specific (nonvirtual) methods — e.g., those used to configure or access unique features of objects of derived type after they have been constructed. Note also that types used in the interface of a protocol are generally not defined via `#include` directives in the base-class component but instead are merely declared locally, thereby insulating public clients from them whenever not explicitly needed. By providing a pure interface, we effectively side-step all of the machinations normally required to *partially* insulate clients of concrete classes from individual details of their implementations (see Volume II, section 6.6).

3.11.5.5   Static Link-Time Dependencies

Even more remarkable is that, of the three architecturally significant approaches to insulation identified in this section, protocols are unique in that they also eliminate all static link-time dependencies of public clients on specific implementations. Since protocols contain no implementation, they contribute no link-time dependencies either. By depending on a protocol instead of a concrete class, we turn traditional (brittle) *layered* architectures into (more flexible) *lateral* ones (section 3.7.5).

Using interface inheritance properly (see Volume II, sections 4.6 and 4.7) to break all physical dependencies and thereby physically decouple fully what would otherwise be static dependencies on subfunctionality naturally leads to more stable (e.g., platform-independent), testable, and scalable subsystems. When `inline`-ing for runtime performance is not indicated, protocols can often be used by system-level agents (e.g., `main`) to inject (high-level) platform-specific functionality[250] as needed, rather than forcing a portable library to depend statically on multiple platform-specific ones, gated by conditional compilation.

3.11.5.6   Runtime Overhead for Total Insulation

As with any approach, using a protocol to achieve total insulation, where there was none before, comes at potentially significant additional runtime overhead. For subsystems where inheritance was not initially part of the design, it will be necessary to adapt that subsystem to the new protocol. A higher-level agent will then need to become responsible for creating and configuring the subsystem via its new *adapter*[251] object. Each of the (previously statically bound, possibly inline) accessor and manipulator function calls made by its public clients will now go through a (typically dynamically bound) virtual function. Although the relative overhead of a virtual function compared to an ordinary one is usually within a factor of two, the overhead compared with an `inline` function can be dramatically more.[252]

---

[250] An example at Bloomberg (c. 2018) would be the "transport" for a service-specific BAS (Bloomberg Application Services) client:

```
class BasTransport {
  public:
    virtual void sendMessage(RequestMessage,
                             bsl::function<void(int, ResponseMessage)>) = 0;
};

class MyService {
  public:
    MyService(std::unique_ptr<BasTransport>& transport);
    int serviceSpecificFunction();
};

int main()
{
    std::unique_ptr<BasTransport> transport (new BasTcpTransport);
    MyService                     service(transport);
    service.serviceSpecificFunction();
}
```

> Could also be
> BasHttpTransport,
> BasTestTransport, etc.

[251] **gamma95**, Chapter 4, section "Adapter," pp. 139–150

[252] **lakos96**, section 6.6.1, pp. 445–448

For subsystems that already employ inheritance, the design costs as well as the ensuing runtime overhead is likely far more modest. Extracting a protocol is mechanical, and the usage pattern remains the same.[253] Since the runtime cost of calling a pure virtual function is no greater than that of a (dynamically bound) nonpure one, the only (typical) additional runtime cost is the loss of inline access to shared implementation details residing in the (nonprotocol) base class.

If creating a protocol is to avoid both *compile-time* and *link-time* dependency for a large, heavy-weight subsystem where substantial work is performed when a typical method is invoked, there might well be no perceptible degradation in run time. If, however, the component or components being insulated make effective use of public inline functions, then the often substantial relative cost of always invoking a virtual function might be significant and, perhaps, even prohibitive. The only way to avoid ubiquitous recompilation due to changes in the implementation of high-performance, widely used types or type templates having many tiny inline functions — e.g., `bget::Point` below (see Figure 3-148, section 3.11.7.9) or `std::complex`, respectively — is to "get them right" from the start.[254]

3.11.6   The Fully Insulating Concrete Wrapper Component

The usage model for a fully insulating concrete wrapper component, unlike that for a protocol, allows for the same client that creates the wrapper to use the subsystem it insulates. In this approach to total insulation, the wrapper component provides a complete "facade"[255] for a concrete subsystem, while isolating, in the `.cpp` file, all of the various private details, such that the implementation of each class defined in the physical interface looks the same as would every other conceivable implementation when viewed from the header file alone. Where insulation via a single wrapper component is viable, this objective is often best achieved by first creating an encapsulating wrapper component, e.g., `PubGraph` (see Figure 3-95, section 3.5), and subsequently making each class within that component a fully insulating concrete class (see Volume II, section 6.6).

What makes the fully insulating wrapper component an architectural decision is not (at least not directly) the insulation, per se, but rather that all aspects of creating and using the subsystem will occur via the classes defined in the wrapper. It is typical for the types used in the interface of an insulating wrapper component *not* to be wrapped and instead are often much more widely

---

[253] **lakos96**, section 6.4.1, pp. 386–398 (especially pp. 392–393)

[254] **lakos96**, section 6.6.2, pp. 448–453

[255] **gamma95**, Chapter 4, section "Facade," pp. 185–193

used *vocabulary* types (see Volume II, section 4.4) residing at a substantially lower level in the physical hierarchy.

When the types that pass in or out of the wrapper interface are themselves wrapped, both the complexity of design and runtime overhead typically increase substantially. For example, if some public class B defined in the insulating wrapper component uses, in its interface, another such class A, then it may be necessary for the insulated implementation of B to access directly the private insulated implementation of A, making it necessary for A to declare B a friend (section 3.1.9) in the exposed physical interface of the wrapper component itself.

To enable arbitrary insulated changes, we may choose preemptively to grant friendship for B from every public type defined in the wrapper used in the interface of B (regardless of whether or not the current implementation happens to requires private access). Figure 3-145 illustrates these basic ideas applied to the encapsulating wrapper component of Figure 3-95, now implemented in an entirely separate **pub** package. Notice that we have used component-private types (sections 2.7.1 and 2.7.2) — indicated by an _i suffix — rather than forward-declaring private nested types, thereby simulating *internal bindage* (section 1.3.4), yet making those types directly accessible from anywhere in the .cpp file — e.g., a file-scope static method, a type declared in the unnamed namespace, or some other implementation (_i) type.

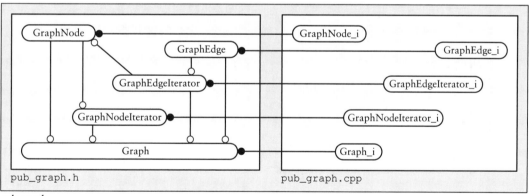

(a) Component/class diagram of fully insulating pub_graph wrapper

```
// pub_graph.h                                  // pub_graph.cpp
#ifndef INCLUDED_PUB_GRAPH                       #include <pub_graph.h>
#define INCLUDED_PUB_GRAPH                       // ...
// ...
namespace MyLongCompanyName {                    namespace MyLongCompanyName {
// ...                                           // ...
namespace pub {                                  namespace pub {
// ...                                           // ...

class GraphNode_i;                               class GraphNode_i {
class GraphNode {                                  public:
    GraphNode_i *d_this_p;                            // ...
    friend class GraphNodeIterator;                   // (creators and data only)
    friend class Graph;                               // ...
  public:                                        };
    // ...                                       // ...
    // (Public Interface)                        // (all 'GraphNode' implementation)
    // ...                                       // ...
};

class GraphEdge_i;                               class GraphEdge_i {
class GraphEdge {                                  public:
    GraphEdge_i *d_this_p;                            // ...
    friend class GraphEdgeIterator;                   // (creators and data only)
    friend class Graph;                               // ...
  public:                                        };
    // ...                                       // ...
    // (Public Interface)                        // (all 'GraphEdge' implementation)
    // ...                                       // ...
};

class GraphNodeIterator_i;                       class GraphNodeIterator_i {
class GraphNodeIterator {                          public:
    GraphNodeIterator_i *d_this_p;                    // ...
    friend class Graph;                               // (creators and data only)
  public:                                            // ...
    // ...                                       };
    // (Public Interface)                        // ...
    // ...                                       // (all 'GraphNodeIterator' impl.)
};                                               // ...

class GraphEdgeIterator_i;                       class GraphEdgeIterator_i {
class GraphEdgeIterator {                          public:
    GraphEdgeIterator_i *d_this_p;                    // ...
    friend class Graph;                               // (creators and data only)
    friend class GraphNode;                           // ...
  public:                                        };
    // ...                                       // ...
    // (Public Interface)                        // (all 'GraphEdgeIterator' impl.)
    // ...                                       // ...
};
                                                 class Graph_i {
                                                   public:
                                                     // ...
```

(continues)

(continued)

```
class Graph_i;                              // (creators and data only)
class Graph {                               // ...
    Graph_i *d_this_p;                  };
  public:                               // ...
    // ...                              // (all 'Graph' implementation)
    // (Public Interface)              // ...
    // ...
};                                      }   // close package namespace

}   // close package namespace         // ...
}   // close enterprise namespace
#endif                                  }   // close enterprise namespace
```

pub_graph

(b) Elided source files for pub_graph.h and pub_graph.cpp

Figure 3-145: Fully insulating concrete wrapper component (see Figure 3-95)

Creating a fully insulating concrete wrapper component for a low-level subsystem such as a Graph — especially when some of the fully insulating classes defined in the component return others by value — can have a devastating (order of magnitude) impact on performance.[256,257] By instead settling for less than perfect insulation, e.g., by relying on stable, but uninsulated, low-level vocabulary types in the wrapper interface, or (partially) insulating (see Volume II, section 6.6) only the strategically advantageous aspects of the wrapper classes, we can usually achieve most of the practical benefit of insulation at a fraction of the additional overhead.

3.11.6.1   Poor Candidates for Insulating Wrappers

Not all types can or should be wrapped for the purpose of achieving insulation. For example, providing an insulating wrapper class for a type that doesn't otherwise allocate memory is generally ill advised, due to the substantial overhead imposed by even a single dynamic memory

---

[256] **lakos96**, section 6.6.4, Figure 6-89, p. 466

[257] With the advent of *move semantics* in C++11, it becomes possible to define safely a *fully insulating concrete class* (see Volume II, section 6.6) employing a variant of the *PIMPL* (Pointer-to-IMPLementation idiom) in an implementation-agnostic way such that a newly constructed wrapped object returned by value could avoid the extra allocation and deallocation overhead that would normally result from having to be copied back to the caller, provided that the wrapped type itself has a semantically sensible default value. To preserve class invariants while ensuring that *move construction* is always noexcept (no-throw), a default-constructed wrapper will hold a *null* address value, and each noncreator wrapper method would have to first check whether the object was currently in the "moved from" (default-constructed) state and, if so, treat that case specially. Note that the *return-value optimization* (RVO), permitted since C++03 and required since C++17, constructs the returned object in the context of the caller, so it is likely that copying will not occur even without move semantics, making this a "just in case" scenario. All of this said, high-performance objects that allocate memory internally will continue to be ill suited for *return-by-value* even in postmodern C++ (see Volume II, section 4.10).

allocation, where before there was none. For reusable types, which if allocating we will want to also make *allocator-aware* (see Volume II, section 4.10), the act of insulating an otherwise nonallocating type will itself necessitate the addition of an optional trailing allocator-pointer parameter in each constructor of the wrapper type. Moreover, returning allocator-aware objects by value cannot be performed reliably,[258] never mind efficiently.[259] Hence, for *all reusable*[260] software, we choose *not* to return allocating objects by value, but rather via address, supplied as a leading (output) parameter (see Volume II, sections 6.11 and 6.12).

Fully insulating concrete wrappers are also generally not well suited for systems that are extensible via inheritance and virtual functions. For example, consider trying to wrap the `Shape` subsystem of Figure 3-142. We might, for example, try to create an insulating wrapper implementing a facade, say `MyShape`, through which the same client would be able to create and use shapes of polymorphic type as illustrated in Figure 3-146. In this ill-fated example, however, the constructor of `MyShape` takes the coordinates of the origin of the new shape as well as an enumerated type, `ShapeType`, that identifies the kind of shape to be constructed, thereby defeating the insulated addition of new shapes for general use. Using a character string instead of an enumeration would allow new types to be added without forcing existing clients to recompile. Such an interface would, however, recklessly circumvent compile-time type checking and is therefore not the kind of compile-time coupling that insulation seeks to eliminate.

---

[258] In both C++98 and C++03, there was no hard requirement to fully support stateful allocators. The named return-value optimization (NRVO) often, but not always, enabled the object, along with the allocator used to create it, to be constructed in place. Where that optimization failed, a copy would be performed and the currently installed default allocator is imbued in that copy. With C++11, it is possible, using move semantics, to guarantee that the behavior is as if the returned object were constructed in place. As of C++17, there are guarantees about when NRVO can be relied upon.

[259] Even with C++11 move semantics, returning an object by value requires constructing it each time the function is invoked. For functions that are called repeatedly (e.g., in a loop) or even where multiple distinct functions having the same return type are called in succession from a given scope, the necessity of constructing and destructing the returned object on each function invocation — even if it is just twice — results in needless runtime overhead, whether or not the allocating type is itself *allocator-aware (AA)*.

[260] Not all of our potential clients are performance sensitive, and therefore may choose to ignore the issue of memory allocation entirely. Though fewer in number, there are many where performance is a significant factor and will choose to make use of custom allocators if that option is available. Still fewer in number will find the qualitative and/ or quantitative advantages of having types that accept individual memory allocators on a per-object basis indispensable, and would be forced to create their own version of any type that was not so equipped. In order not to preclude *any* clients from taking full advantage of our hierarchically reusable software, it is a pillar of our design methodology to always make all types that allocate dynamic memory that can persist beyond the scope of a single method *allocator-aware* (see Volume II, section 4.10).

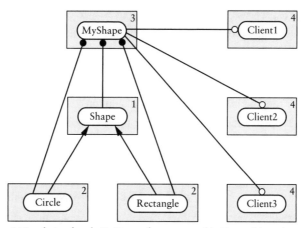

(a) Insulating facade `MyShape` for an extensible `Shape` hierarchy

```
// myshape.h
#ifndef INCLUDED_MYSHAPE
#define INCLUDED_MYSHAPE
class Shape;
class MyShape {
    Shape *d_this_p;                        What about BOX?
  public:
    enum ShapeType { CIRCLE, RECTANGLE };
    MyShape(int xOrigin, int yOrigin, ShapeType type);
    MyShape(const MyShape& shape);
    ~MyShape();
    MyShape& operator=(const MyShape& shape);
    double area() const;
    int xOrigin() const;
    int yOrigin() const;
    // ...
);
#endif
```

(b) Definition of class `MyShape` that must change if extended

Figure 3-146: Insulating wrappers for extensible abstract interface (BAD IDEA)

Even if we could add functionality that allows clients to create new shapes without having to recompile, existing clients using `MyShape` would not know how to configure instances of new concrete shapes (e.g., the size of a `Box`). This inability for existing clients to take advantage of new polymorphic types is a symptom that an insulating wrapper is not the right approach. If open-ended extensibility is a design goal, then exposing a protocol to allow higher-level agents to configure the system with specific concrete "nodes" is preferable. If we must encapsulate the creation aspect, we would do that separately — e.g., using the *Factory* design pattern,[261] at a higher level in the physical hierarchy (see Volume II, section 4.8).[262]

3.11.7   The Procedural Interface

Even when wrapping is desirable for total insulation (or even just encapsulation), it is not always feasible. Wrapper types typically require private access to other wrapper types (section 3.1) via friendship, which in turn implies colocating all such types within a single component in order to avoid long-distance friendships (section 2.6). For large, preexisting systems, especially those having many horizontal, client-facing components, wrapping is simply not a viable option. In such cases, we may need to fall back on what is commonly known as a *procedural interface*.

3.11.7.1   *What Is a Procedural Interface?*

In this more general alternative to wrapping, some or all of the underlying types of the subsystem are exposed through the interface of (nonmember) functions that may span an arbitrary number of physical entities. It is always possible to create a procedural interface and to do so without modifying the subsystem's source. The drawback to this approach, however, is that clients using the procedural interface for insulation purposes must refrain from incorporating the definitions of exposed types lest encapsulated changes to those types make the object layouts across the interface incompatible and client programs ill-formed when relinked.

---

[261] **gamma95**, Chapter 3, section "Factory Method," pp. 107–116

[262] *Type erasure* is a term commonly used to describe a technique that is a hybrid between a wrapper and a protocol. For example, consider `std::shared_ptr` (formalized in C++11), which provides reference-counted, shared access to a given object. When a `shared_ptr<T>` is constructed, it is passed an (optional) *deleter* that is to be used to clean up when the shared representation becomes orphaned. Instead of making the deleter a class-template parameter, as was done with memory allocators for standard containers in C++98 (BAD IDEA), `std::shared_ptr` employs a templated constructor as a factory method to create, in the body of the constructor, an object of an ephemerally visible templated type to hold the user-supplied deleter.

This short-lived templated type, typically *derived* from a private nested abstract base class, overrides the "destroy" method, but is itself effectively "erased" once the constructor of the shared-pointer object completes, thereby leaving the user-supplied deleter inaccessible. While this so-called *type erasure* achieves its primary mission of keeping the deleter from infecting the C++ type of the shared-pointer object, it is not generally applicable but works in this specific case because the deleter, supplied via a template argument at construction, is never needed again until it is invoked (via a private pointer to the private base class) when the reference count reaches zero.

Although type erasure was initially proposed to replace template parameters for use with memory allocators, the need to access the underlying allocator throughout the lifetime of the object made type erasure for this purpose unworkable. In C++17, the more general approach, polymorphic memory resources (PMR), of passing, into the constructor, the address of a user-supplied concrete allocator via its pure abstract (protocol) base class — was finally adopted. Note that this modern approach to memory allocation is based almost entirely on our own, original design (c. 1997), which just goes to show *old* doesn't necessarily mean *bad*.

It is worth noting that this form of insulation does not preclude side-by-side reuse of the underlying types as the types are explicitly *not* hidden for encapsulation purposes (sections 3.9.7 and 3.9.9). Hence, a client who deliberately incorporates underlying headers directly, voluntarily foregoes only the *insulation*, not the *encapsulation*, aspect of any implementation details.

3.11.7.2 When Is a Procedural Interface Indicated?

There are several important cases in which providing a procedural interface to a given subsystem might be the right decision:

I. **Legacy Subsystem** — The subsystem involves a large and mature (legacy) corpus of code. Such older software might not fully subscribe to sound principles of physical (or even logical) design and, hence, the types defined within might not be suitable for general reuse anyway. Precluding direct access to these types will likely degrade overall runtime performance to some degree, but often with an overall "net benefit" resulting from improved maintainability and usability for its clients.

II. **Active (Horizontal) Library Development** — The subsystem, though modern, is also currently under active development. If the subsystem also exposes a broad interface spanning many disparate (horizontal) components, it might not be practical, or even desirable, to wrap all of them from within a single physical component. At any given time, some aspects of the underlying subsystem will likely be changing faster than others. Forcing every client using the subsystem directly to recompile whenever *any* new functionality is added to *any* part of it is probably a poor design choice. Providing a procedural interface, on the other hand, enables granular modifications at the individual member-function level without necessarily forcing all clients of the wrapped subsystem to recompile.[263]

III. **C Language Adapter** — The subsystem, though itself written in C++, is also useful for (e.g., legacy) systems where portions are currently written in some other language, usually C. In this usage scenario, the physical interface must be compilable in the language of the client; hence, there is no possibility of direct use of member or inline functions,

---

[263] C++ modules, if and when they become widely available, could be made to support fine-grained "views" on the user-defined types in existing subsystems without having to modify the existing source code (at all), much like a procedural interface would today. The advantage of modules, however, is that a (perhaps proper) subset of (possibly templated or inline) functionality along with the types themselves would be exposed, making their direct use with no runtime overhead and (perhaps significantly) improved compile times a reality. Note, however, that the use of modules themselves will have little or no effect on the nature and extent of compile-time coupling — that is, modules are *not* useful for *insulation* (see section 3.11.1) purposes. See **lakos17a**, section 3, item I, paragraphs c and d, p. 2.

inheritance, templates, etc. As a result, there is no loss of reuse (and comparatively little in performance) resulting from insulation. A procedural interface, in this case, acts as both an insulation and a translation layer — e.g., from C++ to C linkage. As long as effective use is not overly impeded, the same procedural interface designed to support translation can also be used just for insulating higher-level C++ clients from changes to the underlying subsystem.[264]

Providing a translation layer from C++ to C is arguably the most common and general of the cases in which a procedural interface would be an appropriate *architectural* insulation technique and is the one we will focus on in the remainder of this section.[265]

3.11.7.3   Essential Properties and Architecture of a Procedural Interface

The insulating, translating procedural interface we envision will necessarily satisfy several essential properties. Use of a classically layered architecture (section 3.7.2) for creating a procedural interface will turn out also to be an intrinsic part of its overall design. Figure 3-147 illustrates the general topology of such an insulating translation layer atop the (object-oriented) C++ subsystem to which it provides access. In this example, a wrapper class, ClassW, encapsulates *the use of* implementation classes ClassX, ClassY, and ClassZ, but exposes vocabulary types ClassA and ClassB (see Volume II, section 4.4) in its interface (e.g., see PubGraph in Figure 3-95, section 3.5.10.3). C++ users of this subsystem would normally depend directly on the components defining ClassA, ClassB, and ClassW, so in order to enable full access to C-language clients, we will need to provide corresponding components for each of them in the insulating translation layer.

---

[264] Note that, on most common platforms, it will be necessary to compile the translation unit defining main using a C++ compiler (even if it contains a C-compliant subset of C++) before linking it with the remainder of a system compiled from the source code of heterogeneous languages (e.g., to initiate runtime initialization of file-scope static variables).

[265] For more on procedural interfaces including their use in other scenarios, see **lakos96**, section 6.5, pp. 425–445.

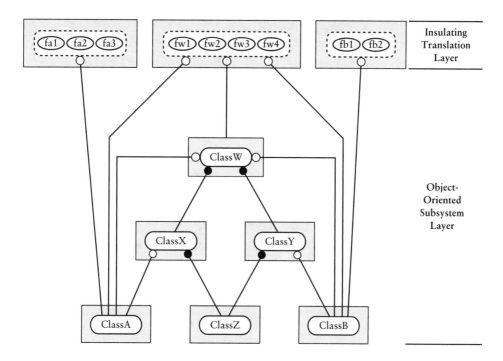

Figure 3-147: Topology of a procedural interface

On the other hand, clients of ClassW need not necessarily interact directly with the implementation classes ClassX, ClassY, and ClassZ. Since the purpose of a procedural interface here is to *insulate* and *translate*, but explicitly *not* to *encapsulate*, no sound design practice (section 3.9) is violated by deferring the implementation of their procedural counterparts in the insulating translation layer. If such "implementation" types should ever become separately useful to C clients, their defining component's counterparts can always be easily added to the procedural-interface (PI) layer on an as-needed basis without affecting any existing clients (see Volume II, section 5.5).

3.11.7.4   Physical Separation of PI Functions from Underlying C++ Components

More generally, the universe of all C-language clients (along with those C++ clients accessing the underlying subsystem exclusively through the procedural interface) is disjoint from C++ clients that access the underlying (object-oriented) C++ code directly. Arbitrary enhancements to even the physical interface of the underlying software leaves the fully insulated users of the interface unaffected. Such enhancements, however, need not be propagated immediately. Once new lower-level functionality has been proven, additional procedural-interface functions and components can be exposed to PI clients without in any way affecting the C++ clients interacting exclusively with the underlying subsystem. Moreover, clients that have no use for such a procedural interface should not be forced to even know about it, let alone depend on it. To achieve this degree of decoupling, however, it is essential that all of the (translating) PI functions remain physically separate from the C++ components they would insulate.

3.11.7.5   Mutual Independence of PI Functions

The granularity at which we will want to be able to choose to expose the functionality of the underlying C++ subsystem through the PI layer is at the individual-function level. Coupling PI functions within the same layer would impede our ability to independently select the appropriate subset of low-level functionality we might choose to expose over time. To ensure full flexibility in promoting individual lower-level functions, we will want to require that every PI function within a given PI layer be entirely independent of every other such function in that layer.

3.11.7.6   Absence of Physical Dependencies Within the PI Layer

None of the components that embody the PI functions should be permitted to `#include` (or have any collaborative knowledge of) any other such components in the PI layer. Recall, from section 3.1, the inherent difficulty in successfully creating a multicomponent wrapper. The purpose of our PI layer, on the other hand, is not to wrap it but rather to provide thoughtfully curated access to it. Allowing physical hierarchy to invade the PI layer would cloud its purpose and complicate its use. Hence, every component in the PI layer resides at the same (local) level as every other component in that layer — i.e., at level 1.

3.11.7.7   Absence of Supplemental Functionality in the PI Layer

A procedural *interface* should not provide any additional *implementation* or *functionality* beyond what exists in the underlying (object-oriented) C++ subsystem. As long as a procedural interface merely translates and insulates but does not add to existing domain-related functionality, it can be created almost mechanically. Because its use for any purpose other than insulation or translation is absent by design, we avoid any additional physical dependencies and also the temptation for the procedural layer to be pressed into service inappropriately (e.g., itself contributing to a design cycle).

3.11.7.8   1-1 Mapping from PI Components to Lower-Level Components (Using the z_ Prefix)

The next step is to adopt a strategy for systematically relating the components in the PI layer with their physically separate counterparts in the underlying (object-oriented) C++ subsystem. The approach we will take errs on the side of objectively verifiable criteria such as fine-grained factoring and regularity (as opposed to personal aesthetics). The general idea is to create a distinct, parallel "namespace" for package prefixes that will reside within the procedural interface layer. For each package, say, **abcx** that implements (object-oriented) C++ code, we will allow for an optional "sister" package **z_abcx** in the procedural interface layer whose sole purpose is to provide the procedural interface functions to access the appropriate *subset* of the functionality defined in **abcx**.[266]

Each component in package **z_abcx** will expose only the desired subset of functionality implemented in the corresponding component of package **abcx**. For example, a separate component would be created for each of the components in Figure 3-147 implementing the respective classes ClassA, ClassB, and ClassW. Ensuring this correlated, fine-grained modularity in the procedural layer helps to keep the link-time dependencies closely aligned with what they would have been if the underlying components had been used by clients directly.

For implementation-only components in package **abcx**, such as those in Figure 3-147 implementing classes ClassX, ClassY, and ClassZ, there would be no corresponding procedural interface components in package **z_abcx**.[267] Finally, the unit of release for a procedural interface — i.e., package or package group (sections 2.8 and 2.9, respectively) — would mirror that of the underlying implementation. Hence, if package group **abc** implements functionality that needs a procedural interface, then the package group **z_abc** will hold the subset of packages (e.g., **z_abcx**) that, in turn, hold the subset of components that implement the subset of functionality to be exposed to the clients of the procedural layer.

---

[266] The **z_** prefix was chosen because of its conventional use as complex impedance (i.e., resistance or insulation) in electrical engineering (and because we'd like to think we have at least some sense of humor), but is otherwise entirely arbitrary; any other prefix (**c_**, for example, to represent a C-language translation layer) would work just as well.

[267] Thus, the mapping from PI-layer components to corresponding (object-oriented) C++ components, while *1-1*, need not necessarily be *onto*.

3.11.7.9   Example: Simple (Concrete) *Value* Type

Let us now consider a simple interface type (see Volume II, section 4.4), such as might correspond to `ClassA` in the abstract diagram of Figure 3-147. As a concrete example, we will choose the lightweight `bget::Point` *value type*[268] as shown in Figure 3-148.

```C++
// bget_point.h                                                   -*-C++-*-
// ...                    Component-level documentation    (See Volume II, section 6.15.)

#ifndef INCLUDED_BGET_POINT
#define INCLUDED_BGET_POINT
                                      Forwarding header
                                        for iostream
#include <iosfwd>
// ...                                                     (See Volume II, section 4.5.)
                                     Includes for type traits
namespace MyLongCompanyName {
namespace bget {

class Point {
    // ...            Class-level documentation             (See Volume II, section 6.15.)

    int d_x;  // x coordinate
    int d_y;  // y coordinate

  public:
    // CREATORS
    Point();
        // ...                                              (See Volume II, section 6.17.)
    Point(int x, int y);
    Point(const Point& original);       Note that all function-level
    ~Point();                            documentation is elided.

    // MANIPULATORS
    Point& operator=(const Point& rhs);
    void setX(int x);
    void setY(int y);

    // ACCESSORS
    int x() const;
    int y() const;
};

// FREE OPERATORS
bool operator==(const Point& lhs, const Point& rhs);
bool operator!=(const Point& lhs, const Point& rhs);
std::ostream& operator<<(std::ostream& stream, const Point& point);
```

(continues)

---

[268] The **t** following the package-group name **bge** to form the package name **bget** had historically been used to suggest value types (see Volume II, section 4.1). This practice has long since been abandoned as basing package names on syntactic (see Volume II, section 4.2), rather than semantic, properties is almost always a bad idea (section 3.2.9).

(continued)

```
// ============================================================================
//                          INLINE FUNCTION DEFINITIONS
// ============================================================================

// CREATORS
inline
Point::Point()
: d_x(0), d_y(0)
{
}

inline
Point::Point(int x, int y)
: d_x(x), d_y(y)
{
}

inline
Point::Point(const Point& original) 269
: d_x(original.d_x), d_y(original.d_y)
{
}

inline
Point::~Point() 269
{
}

// MANIPULATORS
inline
Point& Point::operator=(const Point& rhs) 269
{
    d_x = rhs.d_x;
    d_y = rhs.d_y;
    return *this;
}

inline
void Point::setX(int x)
{
    d_x = x;
}

inline
void Point::setY(int y)
{
    d_y = y;
}
```

(continues)

---

[269] In C++11 (and later), we would instead use the =default syntax in the interface.

(continued)

```
// ACCESSORS
inline
int Point::x() const
{
    return d_x;
}

inline
int Point::y() const
{
    return d_y;
}

}  // close package namespace

// FREE OPERATORS
inline
bool bget::operator==(const Point& lhs, const Point& rhs)
{
    return lhs.x() == rhs.x()  && lhs.y() == rhs.y();
}

inline
bool bget::operator!=(const Point& lhs, const Point& rhs)
{
    return lhs.x() != rhs.x()  || lhs.y() != rhs.y();
}
                         Specializations for type traits
// ...                                                            (See Volume II, section 4.5.)

}  // close enterprise namespace
#endif
```

(a) Header file `bget_point.h`

```
// bget_point.cpp                                                    -*-C++-*-

#include <bget_point.h>
#include <ostream>

namespace MyLongCompanyName {

namespace bget {  // empty

}  // close package namespace

// FREE OPERATORS
std::ostream& bget::operator<<(std::ostream& stream, const Point& point)
{
    return stream << '(' << point.x() << ','
                          << point.y() << ')' << std::flush;
}

}  // close enterprise namespace
```

(b) Implementation file `bget_point.cpp`

Figure 3-148: Component implementing lightweight class `bget::Point`

Notice that almost the entire implementation of this class is exposed in its header file (Figure 3-148a) — the only exception being that of the stream-out operator, `operator<<`, which is implemented in the `.cpp` file (Figure 3-148b). Insulating the implementation of this class from our internal C++ users could easily have a devastating impact on overall performance. Instead, we will wisely choose to provide a physically separate, procedural interface for use by our external C clients, but which is also interoperable with C++ clients — just in case such might prove advantageous (as discussed later in this section).

3.11.7.10   Regularity/Predictability of PI Names

We now turn to the detailed task of promoting the desired subset of (object-oriented) C++ functionality to the PI layer. The components and functions that make up the procedural interface should have names that are regular and predictable, exhibiting logical and physical name cohesion. Ideally, the physical location and packaging for every PI function will be implied by its underlying C++ operation, method, or function, along with its component, package, and package group name. Keep in mind that, in our methodology, the names of the underlying (logical) classes are *UpperCamelCase* (section 1.7.1), while the names of physical entities, such as component files (section 2.6), packages (section 2.8), and package groups (section 2.9), are *all_lowercase* (section 2.10). Figure 3-149 illustrates how we might implement the insulating, translating PI component, **z_bget_point**, corresponding to the **bget_point** component of Figure 3-148, section 3.11.7.9.

```cpp
// z_bget_point.h                                                   -*-C++-*-

#ifndef INCLUDED_Z_BGET_POINT
#define INCLUDED_Z_BGET_POINT

#ifdef __cplusplus
extern "C" {
    namespace MyLongCompanyName {
    namespace bget {
        class Point;
    }  // close package namespace
    }  // close enterprise namespace
    typedef MyLongCompanyName::bget::Point z_bget_Point;
#else
    typedef struct z_bget_Point z_bget_Point;
#endif

// CREATORS
z_bget_Point *z_bget_Point_fCreate();
z_bget_Point *z_bget_Point_fCreateInit(int x, int y);
z_bget_Point *z_bget_Point_fCreateCopy(z_bget_Point *original);
void z_bget_Point_fDestroy(z_bget_Point *object);

// MANIPULATORS
void z_bget_Point_fAssign(z_bget_Point *object, z_bget_Point *other);
void z_bget_Point_fSetX(z_bget_Point *object, int x);
void z_bget_Point_fSetY(z_bget_Point *object, int y);

// ACCESSORS
int z_bget_Point_fX(const z_bget_Point *object);
int z_bget_Point_fY(const z_bget_Point *object);
int z_bget_Point_fAreEqual(const z_bget_Point *object,
                           const z_bget_Point *other);
int z_bget_Point_fAreNotEqual(const z_bget_Point *object,
                              const z_bget_Point *other);

#ifdef __cplusplus
}  // close extern "C" linkage
#endif

#endif  // internal include guard
```

(a) Header file z_bget_point.h

```
// z_bget_point.cpp                                              -*-C++-*-

#include <z_bget_point.h>
#include <bget_point.h>
#include <cassert> ─────────┐ Defensive precondition checks    (See Volume II, section 6.8.)

// CREATORS
z_bget_Point *z_bget_Point_fCreate()
{
    return new z_bget_Point;
}

z_bget_Point *z_bget_Point_fCreateInit(int x, int y)
{
    return new z_bget_Point(x, y);
}

z_bget_Point *z_bget_Point_fCreateCopy(z_bget_Point *original)
{
    return new z_bget_Point(original->x(), original->y());
}

void z_bget_Point_fDestroy(z_bget_Point *object)
{
    delete object;
}

// MANIPULATORS
void z_bget_Point_fAssign(z_bget_Point *object, z_bget_Point *other)
{
    assert(object);                                    (See Volume II, section 6.8.)
    assert(other); ──────┐ Defensive precondition checks
    *object = *other;
}
```

(continues)

(continued)

```
void z_bget_Point_fSetX(z_bget_Point *object, int x)
{
    assert(object);                                                    (See Volume II, section 6.8.)
    object->setX(x);
}
```
Defensive precondition check

```
void z_bget_Point_fSetY(z_bget_Point *object, int y)
{
    assert(object);                                                    (See Volume II, section 6.8.)
    object->setY(y);
}
```
Defensive precondition check

```
// ACCESSORS
int z_bget_Point_fX(const z_bget_Point *object)
{
    assert(object);                                                    (See Volume II, section 6.8.)
    return object->x();
}
```
Defensive precondition check

```
int z_bget_Point_fY(const z_bget_Point *object)
{
    assert(object);                                                    (See Volume II, section 6.8.)
    return object->y();
}
```
Defensive precondition check

```
int z_bget_Point_fAreEqual(const z_bget_Point *object,
                           const z_bget_Point *other)
{
    assert(object);                                                    (See Volume II, section 6.8.)
    assert(other);
    return *object == *other;
}
```
Defensive precondition checks

```
int z_bget_Point_fAreNotEqual(const z_bget_Point *object,
                              const z_bget_Point *other)
{
    assert(object);                                                    (See Volume II, section 6.8.)
    assert(other);
    return *object != *other;
}
```
Defensive precondition checks

(b) Implementation file `z_bget_point.cpp`

Figure 3-149: Insulating (translating) procedural interface (see Figure 3-148, section 3.11.7.9)

Due to the translation aspect, the logical interface of the PI layer is forced to conform to the limitations of the C language. In particular, no function or operator overloading is available. To allow for components defining more than one public type, we must encode the *type* (and not merely the *component*) name into each free function. Hence, the name of each function associated with type `bget::Point` begins with `z_bget_Point_` and not `z_bget_point_` (section 1.7.1);

logical and physical name cohesion (e.g., see Figure 2-22c, section 2.4.9) ensures that we will be able to find the component from the function name easily. For member functions that are overloaded on type, such as is required for constructors, we are forced to synthesize unique function names such as `z_bget_Point_fCreate`, `z_bget_Point_fCreateInit`, and `z_bget_Point_fCreateCopy`.[270] We will also want to ensure that such artificial names are consistent throughout (at least) the entire PI layer.

Notice that, in Figure 3-149, we have not (yet) elected to export the functionality allowing us to format a `bget::Point` to an `std::ostream`. This functionality is, however, something we may choose to expose in the future, but that would require providing a procedural interface for `std::ostream` in a (physically) *separate* UOR corresponding to (at least that aspect of) the C++ Standard Library. Also notice that, in this rendering style, we have deliberately chosen to make the symbol representing the opaque type alias for `bget::Point` carry the `z_` prefix as well (i.e., `z_bget_Point`). Having the function prefix match the name of the type exactly is consistent with nominal cohesion (section 2.4) and seems to make the intent clearer: The `z_` in the type clearly indicates that it is an alias that is itself always opaque.[271]

3.11.7.11 PI Functions Callable from C++ as Well as C

It is a requirement of our PI design that the translating functions in the insulating PI layer are also callable from translation units compiled using a C++ compiler.[272] In return for enabling C++ clients to use our translating PI, we can now have a multicomponent insulating "view" on a subsystem that is too voluminous for a single fully insulating wrapper component (section 3.11.6) to be practical. Notice that we have made use of conditional compilation at the top of the `z_bget_point.h` file (Figure 3-149a) in order to make a PI header compile in both C and C++.

If the client component is being compiled for C, the compiler will do nothing with `__cplusplus`, which will remain undefined. For C-language clients, we will employ the classic C idiom of

---

[270] This style of making the function part of the name start with a lowercase f followed by an `UpperCamelCase` descriptive function name, for many, improves maintainability — i.e., clarity (e.g., that it is part of a PI layer) and searchability (e.g., `z_*_f[A-Z]*`) — in source code, but is otherwise entirely arbitrary.

[271] The extra `z_` prefix also allows older code bases that formerly used logical package prefixes to have a separate symbol to represent the opaque version of the type. Although the visual cue can be exceedingly helpful, the `z_` prefix for the type alias is not strictly necessary; replacing the type `z_bget_Point` with just `bget_Point`, for example, can also work, despite a somewhat increased risk of collision with C and (legacy) C++ code in the global namespace.

[272] Note that clients written in other languages can typically adapt more easily by leveraging the C-language PI layer.

declaring a `struct` and, in the same statement, aliasing it to a C type whose name has the same spelling as that of its tag. From a C client's perspective, what is being returned is an address having a unique opaque pointer type. In reality, however, no definition corresponding to that type's declaration exists.

If, on the other hand, the client component is being compiled in C++, the compiler will define the `__cplusplus` preprocessor symbol. The class `Point` will be declared in the `bget` namespace, nested within the `MyLongCompanyName` namespace. Then, for the remainder of the translation unit, the `typedef` name `z_bget_Point` will be an alias for `MyLongCompanyName::bget::Point`. For all C++ clients of `z_bget_point.h` (including `z_bget_point.cpp`), `z_bget_Point` becomes a fully qualified C++ type name, which can be used anywhere within a C++ program, including from within the `MyLongCompanyName::bget` namespace:

```
// test.cpp
#include <z_bget_point.h>
#include <bget_point.h>
namespace MyLongCompanyName {
    namespace bget {
        Point        *p1;  // unqualified type declaration
        z_bget_Point *p2;  // fully qualified type declaration
    }
}
```

Note that `p1` and `p2` (above) are *by design* of the (identically) same C++ type.

3.11.7.12 Actual Underlying C++ Types Exposed Opaquely for C++ Clients

As mentioned earlier in this section, trying to achieve total insulation through a fully insulating concrete wrapper can lead to untenable run times. One way we can mitigate excessive performance loss is to publish a stable subset of the underlying, low-level *vocabulary* types (see Volume II, section 4.4), such as `bget::Point`, for consumption by C++ clients of the PI layer. In doing so, we enable such clients to gain direct access to the underlying C++ type definitions, which — in turn — enables those specific types to be manipulated and accessed using their native inline and overloaded C++ functions. At the same time, by not publishing all of the low-level headers, we preserve insulation for other, less stable aspects of the underlying subsystem, such as, say, the wrapper class, `ClassW`, shown above (see Figure 3-147, section 3.11.7.3).

In order for C++ clients of the PI layer to be able to successfully exploit direct access to the underlying types used in the still-insulated part of the interface (e.g., `ClassW`), however, it is imperative that each such interface type declared (opaquely) in a PI component refer to *precisely the same type* as the one defined in the corresponding C++ component. This important "sameness" property of procedural interfaces is consistent with that of physical interoperability discussed in section 3.9.[273]

3.11.7.13   Summary of Essential Properties of the PI Layer

It is worth reiterating that each component implementing a procedural interface *must* be both physically and architecturally separate from the underlying C++ components it insulates; that is, clients that require neither insulation nor translation must not be forced to depend on any UOR containing PI code. All components and functions within the PI layer should be mutually independent, and supply no additional functionality other than what is needed for insulation or translation purposes. We will want to make it easy to find the component that defines a given C++ function to which a given PI function provides access, and vice versa (given that such a PI function exists). We will want all of the functions within a PI layer to have mnemonic, consistent, and predictable names to (1) promote ease of use, and (2) avoid the possibility of collisions as new functionality is promoted to the PI layer over time.

In order to keep all of our options open, we will not want to preclude use of this insulating PI layer from direct use by C++ components. Finally, to achieve maximum flexibility, we will want C++ clients of the PI that are also granted direct access to (any subset of) the underlying C++ headers to be able to use them *interoperably* with the opaque types exported by the PI components themselves — i.e., those C types need to be (opaque) aliases to the actual underlying C++ types. In this way, addresses returned by the PI layer in the presence of appropriate C++ headers enable C++ clients having an otherwise opaque object pointer to interact with that object directly — e.g., via inline functions, overloaded operators, inheritance, templates, etc. These essential properties of the (insulating and translating) PI functions reprised above are again summarized for reference in Figure 3-150.

---

[273] Note that this desirable property of types exposed through different *library*-delivery mechanisms, such as via C++ classes directly versus through a translating PI layer, is also critically important for different C++ *language*-delivery mechanisms, such as conventional header files versus the highly anticipated C++ module facility, as the latter becomes more widely available; see **lakos17a** and **lakos18**.

Each insulating and translating PI function in a given PI layer will have all of these important physical (and logical) properties:

1. Be physically separate from the C++ component it accesses

2. Be entirely independent of every other PI function

3. Reside in components having no physical interdependencies

4. Be devoid of *any* supplemental domain functionality

5. Reside in a component having a 1-1 mapping to an underlying component

6. Be named in a natural, regular, and predictable way

7. Be callable from both C and C++

8. Expose (opaquely) the actual underlying C++ types

Figure 3-150: Properties of a translating insulating procedural interface

3.11.7.14   Procedural Interfaces and Return-by-Value

Apart from creative, yet consistent, naming of overloaded methods and operators, there are other considerations that complicate the fully mechanical creation of procedural interfaces. To begin with, we cannot efficiently return any opaque object by value.[274] Naively allocating a new instance of each object in such cases would not only be grossly inefficient, it would violate important resource-allocation guidelines (see Volume II, section 4.8). For example, consider wrapping the method of `bget::Polygon` — which is similar to, but much simpler than, `our::Polygon` (see Figure 3-18, section 3.2.8.15) — that returns the `i`th vertex by value:

```
namespace bget {
    // ...
    class Polygon {
        // ...
        // ACCESSORS
        Point operator[](int vertex) const;
        // ...
    };
    // ...
}
```

---

[274] Note that returning an appropriately `const`-qualified pointer in C where a reference would have been appropriate in C++ is perfectly fine.

Instead of having the procedural interface function dynamically allocate a new `bget::Point` (Figure 3-151a), we will require the PI client to pass in the instance of `bget::Point` to be populated (Figure 3-151b). In this way, the amount of dynamic memory allocation is minimized, and the process of allocation and deallocation of objects can be confined to a single lexical scope, where "peephole" source-code analysis tools can verify correspondence between local allocations and deallocations, thereby crudely approximating the safety afforded by automatic variables and destructors in C++.

```
#include <z_bget_polygon.h>
#include <z_bget_point.h>
#include <bget_point.h>
#include <bget_polygon.h>

#include <cassert>

z_bget_Point *
z_bget_Polygon_fVertex(const z_bget_Polygon *polygon, int index)
{
    assert(polygon);
    assert(0      <= index);
    assert(index <  polygon->length());

    using namespace MyLongCompanyName;
    bget::Point *p = new bget::Point();

    *p = (*polygon)[index];
    return p;
}
```

(a) Allocating returned object dynamically (BAD IDEA)

```
void
z_bget_Polygon_fVertex(z_bget_Point          *result,
                       const z_bget_Polygon *polygon,
                       int                   index)
{
    assert(result);
    assert(polygon);
    assert(0      <= index);
    assert(index <  polygon->length());

    *result = (*polygon)[index];
}
```

(b) Returning result through argument list (GOOD IDEA)

Figure 3-151: Accommodating lightweight objects returned by value

3.11.7.15   Procedural Interfaces and Inheritance

Writing procedural interfaces for C++ objects is further complicated in the presence of inheritance. For C and C++ clients accessing (object-oriented) C++ functionality exclusively via the PI layer, there is no access to the low-level base classes and therefore no way to derive new concrete types. Hence, inheritance hierarchies become closed systems that cannot be extended. By ensuring compatibility of our opaque C types with the underlying C++ type definitions, however, we retain the option to expose just the base class headers, thereby reopening the possibility of derivation by C++ clients.

Standard conversions among pointers in an underlying inheritance hierarchy must be implemented explicitly. We will want to choose a consistent and predictable nomenclature for these explicit conversion functions in order to improve programmer productivity. We will need to identify both types (including their unique package names) coupled with a consistent initial function name (e.g., `fConvert`). To ensure consistent modular packaging, we will choose to associate conversion routines with the class at the physically higher level (i.e., the one being converted from)[275,276]:

```
ToType *
FromType_fConvert2ToType(FromType *from);
```

For example, an implicit standard conversion from a derived `Circle` type to its base type, `Shape`, might look as follows:

```
z_abcx_Shape *
z_xyza_Circle_fConvert2abcx_Shape(z_xyza_Circle *from);
```

It will be also necessary to supply an explicit `const` version of each conversion function (see Volume II, section 5.8):

```
const z_abcx_Shape *
z_xyza_Circle_fConvertConst2abcx_Shape(const z_xyza_Circle *from);
```

---

[275] Note that the component design rule prohibiting physical cycles (section 2.6) ensures that even for user-defined conversions among classes defined in separate components, the implementation of the underlying C++ conversion operation will reside in either the higher-level component if one depends on the other (see Figure 2-47, section 2.6) or in a separate "utility" component if the two types are physically independent (see Figure 2-48, section 2.6).

[276] In keeping with our C++ function-level design methodology, argument order is consistent: outputs, inputs, parameters (see Volume II, section 6.11).

In deep or multiple inheritance hierarchies (not recommended), we will need to implement a pair of explicit conversion functions to each *exposed* base type. Note that, since no additional inheritance is possible, designs that follow our guidelines need not expose partial implementations such as `ShapePartialImp` in Figure 3-143, section 3.11.5.1.[277]

3.11.7.16   Procedural Interfaces and Templates

Template notation is another casualty of the C-compatible translating procedural interface. For example, how should we represent C++ types such as

```
std::vector<int>
```

or

```
xyza::HashTable<std::string, double>
```

in a procedural interface? In theory, we can call the C aliases for either of these types anything we like as long as the naming convention is consistent and there are no conflicts:

```
z_IntVector z_xyza_StrDoubleHashTable        (BAD IDEA)
```

Although careful use of mixed case capitalization and abbreviation here seems to improve both readability and ease of use, this approach, unfortunately, does not scale.

Notice that, just as with template specialization (section 1.3.15), there is a many-to-one relationship between components implementing the procedural interface for different instances of a given underlying C++ class template. The template type arguments used to create these unique instantiations may come from different packages (e.g., `matlab::Int`, `pod::string`), and the number of useful distinct instantiations may continue to grow over time. We want to make sure that our naming convention scales predictably, without collisions and without the need for developers to consult a global registry each time there is a need to wrap a new template instantiation (e.g., `std::vector<xyza::Int>`).[278]

---

[277] For further discussion on deep and multiple inheritance hierarchies, see **lakos96**, section 6.5.5, pp. 441–445.

[278] Recall that the purpose of unique package prefixes (section 2.4.5) and part of the motivation for cohesive naming of the logical entities within them (sections 2.4.8–2.4.9) is to decentralize and eliminate "race conditions" in naming for everything below the unit of release (section 2.9.4).

Given this many-to-one relationship and the express need for predictability and uniqueness, we might be well advised to choose to have the physical naming of these separate instantiations of a template borrow from the conventional use of additional underscore(s) (section 2.9.3) for C++ component names (section 2.9.5) — minus the restrictions on nonlocal access for extra-underscore names beginning with **z_**:

```
z_std_vector_int.h     z_xyza_hashtable_std_string_bdlt_date.h
```

Notice that the component header names above are guaranteed to be distinct from others (see below) arising from instantiations of types having similar names (e.g., `int`/`Int`, `string`/`String`, `Date`), but residing in different packages (e.g., none, **std**, **matlab**, **bdlt**, **odet**):

```
z_std_vector_matlab_int.h      z_xyza_hashtable_pod_string_odet_date.h
```

And, because only fundamental type names (e.g., `int`, `double`) are not package-prefixed, they cannot (syntactically) represent a package name; hence, this naming convention scales predictably and is independent of other parallel development efforts.

3.11.7.17   Mitigating Procedural-Interface Costs

Given this approach to physical naming, we might reconsider the logical names in order to achieve logical and physical name cohesion (section 2.4) within our procedural interface modules[279]:

```
z_std_Vector_int                z_xyza_HashTable_std_String_double
z_std_Vector_matlab_Int         z_xyza_HashTable_fxln_String_double
```

This kind of verbose notation is admittedly painful, but it is necessary in order to achieve consistency, predictability, and interoperability of our procedural interface layer over the long term.

Sometimes, however, providing a complete procedural interface to a C++ subsystem with a rich or elaborate interface might not be the right answer: (1) The long, ugly procedural names might make the C procedural interface unduly painful for developer use, and (2) calling a

---

[279] The decision to capitalize `Vector` and `String` in the type alias shown here favors the C user rather than the C++ implementer and is consistent with encouraging library developers' retracting and hiding complexity rather than propagating it to their application clients (section 0.10). Keeping the lexical conventions independent of the specific underlying type names achieves a more consistent and intuitive procedural interface layer, especially for C developers not familiar with the C++ Standard Library.

C function for every low-level get/set operation might induce unacceptable overhead at run time. Instead, we might opt to create a *facade* or *dashboard* at the C++ level (perhaps even customized for a particular client), but in a separate (higher-level) UOR, that translates and consolidates the needed functionality into a much smaller and narrower C++-wrapper interface. By providing an insulating C procedural interface for just this new C++ wrapper (along with essential operations for any required interface types), we minimize both library and application development effort while potentially improving runtime performance. Note that, even if the full procedural interface for the underlying subsystem were already available, we might still choose to create a new customized facade in C++, and then promote its interface to the PI layer if only to reduce the volume of painful C code new PI clients would need to write.

3.11.7.18   Procedural Interfaces and Exceptions

Lastly, exceptions pose their own interesting challenges to PI authors and users alike. Over the years, compilers have used various and very different strategies for implementing exceptions. One approach has been to pass additional information on the program stack. Doing so changes the standard calling sequence, which means that C++ translation units that were compiled with exceptions enabled, and translation units (C++ or otherwise) that were not, may be inherently incompatible. Moreover, this approach often caused significant additional runtime overhead — even when exceptions were not used. On these kinds of platforms in particular, it is absolutely imperative that exceptions not "leak out" of the subsystem of components that were compiled with exceptions enabled.[280]

Some compilers, instead of passing exception information on the program stack, maintain a separate exception stack. In this model, the C++ compiler manages exceptions via the C++ run time — the same run time that orchestrates the construction of file- or name-space scope objects before `main` is entered (see Volume II, section 6.2). For exceptions to work on these platforms, it is mandatory that `main` be compiled using the C++ compiler, and that the program

---

[280] **sutter05**, Chapter "Namespaces and Modules," Item 62, pp. 114–115

be appropriately postprocessed by the C++ linker.[281] As long as both of these two conditions are simultaneously met, C++ exceptions can exist in a mostly C client.

The issue now becomes how to prevent exceptions from leaking out across the procedural layer. One way to address the issue — brute force — is to put a `try`/`catch` block around the body of every function, e.g.:

```
z_bget_Polygon *z_bget_Polygon_fCreate()
try282 {
    // ...
    // normal function body
    // ...
} catch (...) {
    // ...
    // What now?
    // ...
}
```

The trouble here is that, if an exception is thrown, there is not much we can do besides log it. If the underlying use of exceptions follows our guidance for library interface design (see Volume II, Chapter 5), there will be no such use mentioned as part of the essential behavior (see Volume II, section 5.2) in any function-level documentation (see Volume II, section 6.17); hence, the wrapped software was unexpectedly unable to satisfy the terms of the contract (e.g., because the system is out of virtual memory). We could try to convert the "breach of contract" to a failure status (e.g., by returning 0), but there will be little the caller can do either, beyond exiting gracefully. A more robust and *defensive* (see Volume II, Chapter 5) way to address an out-of-memory exception is via the `new_handler` (which itself must be wrapped). By *replacing* the *out-of-memory* exception mechanism with a callback, the client application can control

---

[281] For the underlying C++ code to work properly, the translation unit implementing `main` must be compiled using a C++ compiler and linked using a C++ linker; hence, there will typically be a *library* component of the form

```
#include <cmain.h>  // extern "C" int cmain(char *, char *[]);

int main(char *argc, char *argv[])
{
    return cmain(argc, argv);
}
```

that will be pulled in by the linker (section 1.2), and — in turn — call the client's `cmain` program, compiled using a standard C compiler (resulting in `extern "C"` linkage).

[282] N.B.: This is not a syntax error.

(at the highest level) what is to happen when a truly exceptional condition occurs without adding all of the bulky status checking that exceptions were meant to avoid. In our view, the use of a catchall exception is for the purpose of debugging; hence, the proper action for the body of a catch within a procedural interface function is most likely to print a nice message such as

```
assert(!"An uncaught exception has been detected.");
```

and terminate (see Volume II, section 6.8).

3.11.8   Insulation and DLLs

One final testament to the value of total insulation is the ability to replace dynamically loaded libraries transparently. Once you have a fully insulated library implementation, you can then provide (binary-compatible) performance enhancements and bug fixes (see Volume II, section 5.5) without impacting your clients at all! Clients, in order to use a new update, are not forced to recompile or even relink. As long as we can ensure consistent versioning throughout their program, all they need to do is reconfigure their environment to point to the new dynamically loaded libraries, restart their program, and off they go!

3.11.9   Service-Oriented Architectures

As a brief aside, a service-oriented architecture (SOA) is architecturally similar to a procedural interface in that it resides at a high physical level and fully insulates its clients from the underlying implementation. The main difference between a procedural interface and an SOA is that, in an SOA, the subsystem typically runs in a separate process from the client, often on a remote machine, and message passing replaces function calls. The significantly increased runtime latency, due to message passing, means that the work done by services generally have to be more substantial in order to sustain the increased invocation overhead. Note that, just as with PI functions, the SOA interface layer resides above the underlying C++ implementation; unlike a PI, however, clients of an SOA-based subsystem have no *link-time* dependency on the implementation of that subsystem. Our fine-grained reusable components naturally form an ideal substrate for implementing services in an SOA as well as the SOA framework itself.[283]

---

[283] For example, BAS (Bloomberg Application Services) is Bloomberg's core microservice architecture and has enabled scaling of software beyond what resides on a typical machine in a single executable. It essentially combines software reuse, as described here, with reuse of the hardware that executes it.

3.11.10 Section Summary

To summarize: In this section, we have formalized what it means for a component to (1) *encapsulate*, and (2) *insulate the use of* an implementation detail from its clients. A component **c** *encapsulates the use of* a class, A, if replacing A by an equivalent class (defined in a separate component) does not necessitate the code of any client of **c** to be reworked. On the other hand, a component **c** *insulates the use of* a class B if replacing B does not force any client of **c** even to recompile.

Three separate architecturally significant total-insulation techniques (see Figure 3-141, section 3.11.4) were presented: (I) the pure abstract interface ("protocol") class (section 3.11.5), (II) the fully insulating concrete wrapper component (section 3.11.6), and (III) the procedural interface (section 3.11.7). Each of these approaches has certain advantages and disadvantages. Protocols are indicated when (1) the design is already formulated in terms of an inheritance hierarchy, (2) the client of the interface is distinct from the one creating instances of concrete objects of derived type, and (3) they would not incur any additional runtime overhead (e.g., by possibly losing inline access to shared data). Moreover, this form of total insulation is unique in that it also eliminates even link-time dependencies of public clients on derived-class implementations.

When the client creating the subsystem is the same as the one using it, having an insulating wrapper component can be the right answer, provided the number of distinct fully insulating concrete classes can reasonably fit within a single component. Given that we already have an encapsulating wrapper, the process of achieving total insulation by modifying the classes within the wrapper to be fully insulating (see Volume II, section 6.6) is straightforward. Otherwise, an entirely new wrapper component will have to be engineered. Either way, such total insulation will increase run time, sometimes unacceptably. Relaxing total insulation for stable interface types is one way to mitigate this overhead.

Finally, if neither of the previous two approaches is suitable, as might be the case for a large, legacy corpus of code, we might be forced to resort to a procedural interface, consisting entirely of free functions trafficking in pointers to opaque user-defined C-style types. Such a procedure-only interface will necessarily incur the concomitant runtime overhead associated with noninline function calls, pointer indirection, and dynamic memory allocation. Written properly, however, such interfaces typically also serve as a natural bridge to client subsystems written entirely in C.

Of the three architecturally significant, total-insulation techniques presented in this section, we generally find protocols, where practicable, to be the most effective. Irrespective of the method used, however, achieving total insulation, where before there was none, invariably comes at a price in the form of a significant increase in runtime overhead. As an alternative, consider using *partial insulation techniques* (see Volume II, section 6.6) as was done for the adaptive `Pool` example discussed in the latter half of section 3.10.

3.12   Designing with Components

So far in this chapter, we have explored several important facets of sound physical design and factoring. Most of the examples have been small and focused, illustrating a specific idea, approach, or technique. In this final new-content section before the chapter summary, we will use a real-world example to demonstrate how we develop *hierarchically reusable software* (section 0.4) in our day-to-day jobs as software infrastructure (SI) engineers. The vehicle for our demonstration will be in satisfying an actual request to extend our, then nascent, repository of Software Capital (section 0.9) to incorporate substantial new functionality involving dates and calendars at the behest of an application-level business client in the form of an overly specific enhancement request having characteristically sketchy and incomplete requirements. This section is dedicated to walking through that process, "soup to nuts."

3.12.1   The "Requirements" as Originally Stated

Let us suppose that our client is tasked with developing a new financial service, let's call it *Stock Studio*,[284] that requires evaluating a portfolio of financial instruments over some specified set of time horizons against some other specified set of market scenarios. To do that, it will be necessary to determine valid business dates on which payments can be made (known as *settlement dates*) and, to do that, we will need to know what calendar days are business days. We'll also need to be able to determine today's date (i.e., have access to a real-time clock) so that it can provide current valuations of a portfolio. Instead of identifying each of these needs individually, the original "specification" came as a single (almost comically) conflated request:

> Write me a date class that tells me whether today is a business day.[285]

---

[284] *Bond Studio* was an actual product developed at Bear Stearns in the late 1990s and early 2000s by two (now fellow Bloomberg) software engineers, Sumit Kumar and Wayne Barlow, which made extensive use of the component-based methodology espoused throughout this book.

[285] **lakos12**

The first thing to realize in software infrastructure is that the customer is usually right when it comes to the spirit of the request, but less often so with respect to design advice that typically accompanies it — e.g., that there ought to be such a thing as a `Date` class that can tell whether today is a business day! We know of the critical importance of having a firm-wide "date" class as a pervasive *vocabulary type* (see Volume II, section 4.4), and we have already seen (section 3.6.2) that what constitutes a holiday is context-sensitive and is clearly not an intrinsic property of a date; hence, a `Date` object should not itself know if the date it holds is a holiday. We also have seen (section 3.8.1) that creating a date class that itself can directly obtain today's date forces an otherwise lightweight `Date` class to have an inappropriate, heavyweight dependency on a real-time clock; moreover, supporting this feature within the type itself would open up a Pandora's box of logical issues related to time zones. Based on these caveats alone, we can conclude that the requirements must be disentangled from the design suggestions, and the latter discounted in their entirety.

More generally, it is often the case that a substantial enhancement request that properly requires the addition of one component will also lead to the creation of other components, even when the functionality that they provide was not explicitly requested. It is common for less seasoned developers to try to cram a complete solution into one component so as not to have to be bothered with separately developing and testing multiple components. Doing so, however, is a rookie mistake[286] for at least two distinct and important reasons:

1. It is dramatically easier to understand, test, and maintain several smaller components, each having a single, focused purpose (e.g., see Volume III, Chapter 10).

2. Our ability to use, reuse, and ultimately *hierarchically reuse* software depends critically on this sort of fine-grained, focused logical (see Volume II, section 4.2) and physical (sections 0.4 and 0.7) packaging — well beyond what is necessary to address the current business need.

In what follows we will go out of our way to prevent our zeal to address the immediate objective quickly from interfering with our long-term-greedy goal of properly capturing hierarchically reusable Software Capital in the process (section 0.9), and — to some extent — vice versa.

---

[286] For example, the need for having multiple separate *domain-specific* sections — as opposed to non-domain-specific ones, such as CREATORS, MANIPULATORS, and ACCESSORS (see Volume II, section 6.14) — in the *interface* of an *instantiable* class (as opposed to a utility `struct`) is an indication that the class might lack sufficient focus, and is a candidate for further logical and physical factoring.

3.12.2   The Actual (Extrapolated) Requirements

The first step for SI engineers will be to extrapolate this "work order" — as stated — into a well-reasoned series of requirements:

1. **Represent a date value in terms of a C++ class.** Based on what was stated in the initial request, it is fair to conclude that the requester envisions passing date values around as C++ objects. So, at a minimum, we will want to have a C++ type that performs that function satisfactorily. What "satisfactorily" entails (see Volume II, section 4.3) might not be immediately obvious to the uninitiated, but — at the highest level of design — some such type suitable for representing date values will be needed.

2. **Determine what** *date value* **"today" is.** The original request leaves little question that whatever we come up with will somehow have to be able to ascertain the current date — presumably from the underlying operating system. While we might think to require that the current date be supplied as input, that most likely isn't what the author of the enhancement request had in mind; otherwise, they would have said, "... that tells me whether a *given* date is a business day."

3. **Determine if a given date value is a** *business day.* Once we have today's date value, we will want to know if it represents a valid business day, presumably by loading that value into an object of our new `Date` class and then supplying that object to some facility that is able to determine, given a `Date` object (necessarily representing a valid [*date*] value), whether it also represents a *business day.* Keep in mind that what constitutes a business day will necessarily be sensitive to the application context and potentially subject to constant updates. Hence, any attempt to hard code the data into the software component itself would be a fool's errand.[287]

4. **Render the solution as hierarchically reusable components.** As always, being SI library developers (as opposed to application developers), we are attempting to solve not just this specific problem quickly but rather to solve thoroughly the subdomain of problems that implementing the implied collection of well-factored components naturally addresses, thereby allowing future projects to progress more quickly. Moreover, we will want to identify any closely related functionality that, while not explicitly requested, is likely to be needed in the foreseeable future. It will be up to the SI

---

[287] Separately, note that just having a large number of data members is often indicative of insufficient factoring of the implementation.

developer to determine (or anticipate) whether such functionality is (or should be) part of the initial set of deliverables, or can be deferred, just as will determining whether such functionality properly resides with the set of components to be delivered initially or, perhaps, at a higher level in the physical hierarchy where it can be added incrementally (at some future date) without having to perturb already delivered (and therefore desirably stable) production software.

After some rethinking (and diplomatic negotiation), we finally agree with our client (application business sponsor) on the following modified request:

> Create for me (and others) a well-factored suite of finely graduated, granular, stable (hierarchically reusable) components — properly distributed throughout the firm-wide physical hierarchy of UORs that make up our Software Capital infrastructure — such that (among other things) we will be able to determine, both easily and efficiently, whether (or not) today is a business day in the context of our client's application domain.

There is, of course, a lot of independent functionality that must be assembled and refined to achieve a robust, well-factored, *hierarchically reusable* solution satisfying these revised requirements along with many other, more subtle ones that we will no doubt discover along the way. Without a reasonably mature repository of Software Capital (section 0.9) already in place, however, the cost of "doing it right" could seem prohibitively expensive in terms of up-front development time. Yet, because we are convinced that the compounding benefits of creating a fine-grained, hierarchically reusable library infrastructure are absolutely and incontrovertibly worth the additional up-front cost over the long haul (section 0.8), we will assume that much of the low-level groundwork has already been done, and that any new components that we might add will invariably contribute to significantly reduced time-to-market for future projects.

3.12.3   Representing a Date Value in Terms of a C++ Type

Without much analysis, it seems pretty clear that — absent a standard or otherwise ubiquitously used Date class in our enterprise-wide repository — providing a Date vocabulary type (see Volume II, section 4.4) would be a good place to start.[288] The date class we envision will natu-

---

[288] For a real-world discussion of how one might go about designing an effective *standard* date class, see **pacifico12**.

rally serve two purposes: The first is to hold a date value; the second is to provide primitive and/or universally useful operations on that value such as dayOfWeek and isLeapYear. It will turn out that each of these features will properly result in the creation of a new component.

In the first instance, returning the day-of-week (in a compile-time checked, type-safe manner) will lead to the creation of a DayOfWeek enumeration. As Figure 2-38 of section 2.6 suggests, we will want each such reusable enumeration to be defined as its own separate component, thereby (1) facilitating its routine manufacture (see Volume III, Chapter 10), and (2) increasing its potential for independent reuse (section 0.4).[289] In the second instance, isLeapYear and other such useful functions provide a separate opportunity for factoring, but from the perspective of reuse in entirely different situations (with distinct clients), rather than based on the immediate needs of the current client. We will return to the idea of factoring from an implementation perspective once we have laid out the initial design in terms of just the client-facing components for the current client.

Because this Date type is intended to represent a value that makes sense outside of the current process (see Volume II, section 4.1), it can be externalized. There exist two distinct ways in which values can be externalized: (1) *from above*, i.e., via the public API, and (2) *from below*, i.e., directly from the implementation. If we are to rely on the first method, then we do not need to address it now, as it is completely *additive*.[290] On the other hand, because a date type is a very stable, very low-level vocabulary type (see Volume II, section 4.4), the overhead of externalizing via the public API might be too much to bear.

Originally (c. 1998), we provided primitive streaming functions to externalize and rehydrate values out of, and back into, an object in a given process via a pair of *aspect*[291] (section 2.4.8) member functions, streamOut and streamIn, using (pure abstract) *protocol* classes (section 1.7.5)

---

[289] A similar method for returning an enumerated month, e.g., monthOfYear, might be considered as a future addition, but we would still want to accept a value delineated by a sequence of three integers to represent the year, month, and day, respectively.

[290] By "additive" we mean that we can unilaterally add to the existing code base to extend it without having to modify it — i.e., any of its current source files — in any way.

[291] An *aspect* is a common cross-cutting feature that, by design, is named the same way, and serves the same purpose for every type to which it pertains (in every component in which it appears). For example, begin and end are aspect methods of a container, just as print (and its corresponding output operator, operator<<), bdexStreamIn, and bdexStreamOut are aspect functions for a value-semantic type.

bdex_OutStream and bdex_InStream,[292] respectively. We soon observed, however, that the state of optimization technology — being comparatively primitive at that time — made the use of virtual functions prohibitively expensive in this context, while adding no practical business value for the added runtime flexibility. For such critical, low-level, performance-sensitive types, we soon developed a pair of enterprise-wide externalization[293] concepts (c. 2003) that we now refer to as *BDEX* streaming. To continue to avoid adding dependencies on specific stream implementations, we changed our aspect methods to a pair of template member functions, bdexStreamOut and bdexStreamIn, which write to and read from anything that models the concepts *BdexOutStream* and *BdexInStream*, respectively. Models for both *BdexOutStream* and *BdexInStream* (for both testing and production) can be found in the low-level **bslx** package of the **bsl** package group of our open-source BDE distribution.[294,295]

For the purposes of this discussion, let us assume that BDEX streaming is a library-author–imposed subrequirement of this value-semantic (see Volume II, section 4.3) Date class and that the client either has access to the **bslx** package, or otherwise can manage to model the two streams locally (if needed). A proposed interface for our fully value-semantic Date class itself is shown in Figure 3-152.[296]

---

[292] Note that this use of the older style of having logical package prefixes (c. 1998) predates the widespread availability/use of C++ namespaces.

[293] The process of extracting the *value* of an object and representing it in a process-independent way so that it may be transmitted externally is often referred to as *serialization*.

[294] **bde14**, subdirectory /tree/master/groups/bsl/bslx/

[295] BDE originally stood for (either) "Bloomberg" or "Basic" Development Environment, depending on the context in which it was being used. For historical consistency, BDE has now become a recursive acronym that stands for BDE Development Environment.

[296] Note that this class design, rendered in the hypothetical grouped (*grp*) package namespace (grppk), is similar to that found for core::Date in Figure 3-102, section 3.6.1, except that it now wisely sidesteps certain suboptimalities, such as depending directly on the system time (e.g., for the default constructor), adding support for BDEX-style streaming, and providing somewhat more standard, potentially better wording for its function-level documentation (see Volume II, section 6.17). Despite the redundancy, we feel that there is affirmative value in seeing essentially the same type rendered twice, using essentially the same general methodology — i.e., both the similarities and differences are instructive.

```
// grppk_date.h                                                 -*-C++-*-
// ...                                              (See Volume II, section 6.15.)
namespace MyLongCompanyName {
// ...
namespace grppk {

class Date {
    // This class implements a complex-constrained, value-semantic type for
    // representing dates according to the Unix 'cal' calendar function.  Each
    // object of this class *always* represents a *valid* date value in the
    // range '[0001JAN01 .. 9999DEC31]' inclusive.  ...

    // ...    (all encapsulated implementation details omitted for now)

  public:
    // CLASS METHODS[297]
    static bool isValidYearMonthDay(int year, int month, int day);
        // Return 'true' if the specified 'year', 'month', and 'day' represent
        // a valid value for a 'Date' object, and 'false' otherwise.  'year',
        // 'month', and 'day' represent a valid 'Date' value if they correspond
        // to a valid date as defined by the Unix (POSIX) calendar confined to
        // the year range '[1 .. 9999]' inclusive.  See {Valid Date Values and
        // Their Representations} for details.  ...

                            // Aspects[298]

    static int maxSupportedBdexVersion(int versionSelector);
        // Return the maximum valid BDEX format version, as indicated by the
        // specified 'versionSelector', to be passed to the 'bdexStreamOut'
        // method.  Note that it is highly recommended that 'versionSelector'
        // be formatted as "YYYYMMDD", a date representation.  Also note that
        // 'versionSelector' should be a *compile*-time-chosen value that
        // selects a format version supported by both externalizer and
        // unexternalizer.  See the 'bslx' package-level documentation for more
        // information on BDEX streaming of value-semantic types and
        // containers.
```

(continues)

---

[297] In our methodology, class functionality is grouped according to well-established major categories (e.g., CLASS METHODS, CREATORS, MANIPULATORS, ACCESSORS) and rendered in alphabetical order (see Volume II, section 6.14). There are, however, occasions where it makes sense to subdivide a major category into arbitrary subcategories, which also serve to segment alphabetization (see below).

[298] The subcategory Aspects happens to be special in that an *aspect* (section 2.4.8) here is a class entity — typically a member function, such as begin or end — whose name and semantics are deliberately kept common across a wide range of disparate classes.

(continued)

```
// CREATORS
Date();
    // Create a 'Date' object having the earliest supported date value,
    // i.e., having a year/month/day representation of '0001/01/01'.299

Date(int year, int month, int day);
    // Create a 'Date' object having the value represented by the specified
    // 'year', 'month', and 'day'.  The behavior is undefined unless
    // 'year', 'month', and 'day' represent a valid 'Date' value (see
    // 'isValidYearMonthDay').

Date(const Date& original);
    // Create a 'Date' object having the value of the specified 'original'
    // date.

~Date();
    // Destroy this object.300

// MANIPULATORS
Date& operator=(const Date& rhs);
    // Assign to this object the value of the specified 'rhs' date, and
    // return a reference providing modifiable access to this object.
```

(continues)

---

[299] An alternative approach — one we have opted historically not to take — is to create a valid date object having an indeterminate value such that any attempt to access that value would be considered undefined behavior (see Volume II, section 5.2). Although theoretically viable, academically satisfying, and in some cases potentially more efficient, the benefit of making the "value" of an uninitialized date object defined, known, and conspicuous facilitates practical debugging when, for example, someone wants to inspect (e.g., print) the value of a suspicious date object created (perhaps uninitialized) remotely. As we would never be tempted (or even able) to change the default value, there is comparatively little benefit to not making that information part of the contract for Date.

[300] Many would argue that there is no need to document the behavior of a destructor unless it does something other than release in-process (only) memory and end the logical lifetime of the object. In our methodology, we have chosen to document every function and to make this exception would take more effort (in terms of training and education) than not. What's more, it removes the potential concern that needed documentation was deferred, and then simply overlooked. In much the same manner as one is asked to "tick" a box to acknowledge acceptance of a contract on the internet, we require some form of acknowledgment that a contract has been supplied here.

It has also been suggested that instead of "Destroy this object." that we, perhaps, should just leave the text portion blank

```
~Date();
    //
```

or indicate our desire to leave it blank

```
~Date();
    // This comment intentionally left blank.
```

or somehow otherwise indicate that we don't need to comment

```
~Date();
    // <SSIA>
```

which, in this context, stands for "Signature Says It All." (We say "Destroy this object." Enough said.)

(continued)

```
Date& operator+=(int numDays);
    // Assign to this object the value that is later by the specified
    // (signed) 'numDays' from its current value, and return a reference
    // providing modifiable access to this object.  The behavior is
    // undefined unless the resulting value falls within the range of dates
    // supported by this class (see 'isValidYearMonthDay').  Note that
    // 'numDays' may be negative.

Date& operator-=(int numDays);
    // Assign to this object the value that is earlier by the specified
    // (signed) 'numDays' from its current value, and return a reference
    // providing modifiable access to this object.  The behavior is
    // undefined unless the resulting value falls within the range of dates
    // supported by this class (see 'isValidYearMonthDay').  Note that
    // 'numDays' may be negative.

Date& operator++();
    // Set this object to have the value that is one day later than its
    // current value, and return a reference providing modifiable access to
    // this object.  The behavior is undefined if the year/month/day
    // representation of the current value is '9999/12/31'.[301]

Date& operator--();
    // Set this object to have the value that is one day earlier than its
    // current value, and return a reference providing modifiable access to
    // this object.  The behavior is undefined if the year/month/day
    // representation of the current value is '0001/01/01'.
```

(continues)

---

[301] Rather than supplying a manifest constant in the documentation, it has been suggested that we define the highest and lowest legal values for instances of the class — e.g., k_MaximumDate and k_MinimumDate, respectively — and then refer to those named constants in the documentation instead. We choose not to do so for several reasons:

i. The specific literal values inform whether they impose any concern for overflow (these typically impose none).

ii. Such constants are rarely, if ever, needed in code as the valid range of use in our intended application is virtually always (substantially) smaller, and sequestered well within this supported range.

iii. If rendered in code, widening the range would no longer be considered a truly *backward-compatible* change (see Volume II, section 5.5), the way it would be if implemented as shown here — e.g., valid client code such as

```
assert(bdlt::Date::k_MaximumDate == bdlt::Date(9999, 12, 31));
```
might fail.

iv. Clients are free to define these constants locally (for their own use), which would be guaranteed to remain valid in all future releases of the library (as the range might grow, but would never shrink).

v. If rendered as code, partial insulation (see Volume II, section 6.6) would be required to avoid having to immediately recompile all clients in the case of a patch (e.g., see Figure 3-139, section 3.10.5).

```
int addDaysIfValid(int numDays);302
        // Set this object to have the value that is later by the specified
        // (signed) 'numDays' from its current value, if the resulting value
        // falls within the range of dates supported by this class (see
        // 'isValidYearMonthDay').  Return 0 on success, and a non-zero value
        // (with no effect) otherwise.  Note that 'numDays' may be negative.

    void setYearMonthDay(int year, int month, int day);
        // Set this object to have the value represented by the specified
        // 'year', 'month', and 'day'.  The behavior is undefined unless
        // 'year', 'month', and 'day' represent a valid 'Date' value (see
        // 'isValidYearMonthDay').

    int setYearMonthDayIfValid(int year, int month, int day);
        // Set this object to have the value represented by the specified
        // 'year', 'month', and 'day' if they comprise a valid 'Date' value
        // (see 'isValidYearMonthDay').  Return 0 on success, and a non-zero
        // value (with no effect) otherwise.303

                            // Aspects

    template <class STREAM>
    STREAM& bdexStreamIn(STREAM& stream, int version);
        // Assign to this object the value read from the specified input
        // 'stream' using the specified 'version' format, and return a
        // reference to 'stream'.  If 'stream' is initially invalid, this
```

(continues)

---

[302] To be fair, the true motivation for this function is not at all obvious. An important invariant of this Date type is that it holds a valid date value. It is highly improbable that someone is going to add some reasonable number of days to a date in the valid range, i.e., January 1, 0001 to December 31, 9999, and have it overflow (or underflow) in practice — at least not in the financial context for which, it so happens, it was initially designed. The reality, however, is that, in large development organizations, the folks who write the code to get a date value from a user are not necessarily the same folks who process the date, and sometimes the date obtained isn't valid, yet no one has bothered to check it before creating the date object.

One could argue that those UI folks should be trained to do a better job, and we would not disagree. One could also argue that our Date object must *always* check the inputs and "throw something" if they are invalid, to which we would disagree (see Volume II, Chapter 5) — especially in the context of reusable library software. Still, there remains a pressing need to be able to ask the "taboo" question, "does this date object really hold a valid date?" knowing full well that, even if it does, it doesn't necessarily mean that the valid date value is correct!

Our almost too-clever-by-half solution to this vexing interface-design conundrum was to provide this function, which (1) has a plausible and valid use case, and — much more importantly — (2) has the "accidental" behavior that adding 0 days to a valid date object will *always* return 0 (for success) reliably, but if you happen to have a date object whose internal representation currently does not represent a valid value, it *might* (and, in practice, always will) return a non-zero value (indicating something other than success), in which case you know that you have entered into the world of *undefined behavior* (see Volume II, section 5.2). In other words, this function subtly enables yet another (redundant) check that can be used to defend against client misuse, but — please — only in an appropriate *assertion-level build* mode (see Volume II, section 6.8).

[303] Notice that the return type for this setYearMonthDayIfValid "MANIPULATOR" method, as well as that of addDaysIfValid, is int, whereas the return type for the (static) "CLASS METHOD" isValidYearMonthDay is bool. (N.B., we exploit common method prefixes, e.g., isValid, and suffixes, e.g., IfValid, in a pseudo aspect-like way; see Volume II, section 6.11.) In our methodology (see Volume II, section 6.14), we strive to segregate functions that answer a question (typically without changing state) from those that attempt to "do something" (which necessarily implies a state change). Questions having yes-or-no answers are phrased in that form — e.g., isValid, hasProtocol, areParallel — and always return a bool where true means "yes" and false means "no." By contrast, manipulator methods either "succeed" or "fail." As there is just one way to succeed, but potentially many ways to fail, we follow the Unix tradition of returning 0 on success, and a non-zero value otherwise (see Volume II, section 6.12).

(continued)

```
              // operation has no effect.  If 'version' is not supported, this object
              // is unaltered and 'stream' is invalidated, but otherwise unmodified.
              // If 'version' is supported but 'stream' becomes invalid during this
              // operation, this object has an unspecified, but valid, state.  Note
              // that no version is read from 'stream'.  See the 'bslx' package-level
              // documentation for more information on BDEX streaming of
              // value-semantic types and containers.

    // ACCESSORS
    int day() const;
              // Return the day of the month in the range '[1 .. 31]' of this date.

    DayOfWeek::Enum dayOfWeek() const;
              // Return the day of the week in the range
              // '[DayOfWeek::e_SUNDAY .. DayOfWeek::e_SATURDAY]' of this date.

    void getYearMonthDay(int *year, int *month, int *day) const;
              // Load, into the specified 'year', 'month', and 'day', the respective
              // 'year', 'month', and 'day' attribute values of this date.

    int month() const;
              // Return the month of the year in the range '[1 .. 12]' of this date.

    int year() const;
              // Return the year in the range '[1 .. 9999]' of this date.

                            // Aspects[304]
    template <class STREAM>
    STREAM& bdexStreamOut(STREAM& stream, int version) const;
              // Write the value of this object, using the specified 'version'
              // format, to the specified output 'stream', and return a reference to
              // 'stream'.  If 'stream' is initially invalid, this operation has no
              // effect.  If 'version' is not supported, 'stream' is invalidated, but
              // otherwise unmodified.  Note that 'version' is not written to
              // 'stream'.  See the 'bslx' package-level documentation for more
              // information on BDEX streaming of value-semantic types and
              // containers.

    bsl::ostream& print(bsl::ostream& stream,
                        int           level = 0,
                        int           spacesPerLevel = 4) const;
              // Write the value of this object to the specified output 'stream' in a
              // human-readable format, and return a reference to 'stream'.
              // Optionally specify an initial indentation 'level', whose absolute
              // value is incremented recursively for nested objects.  If 'level' is
              // specified, optionally specify 'spacesPerLevel', whose absolute value
```

> Note that this is now a primitive operation of this class (see below).

(continues)

---

[304] As previously stated, it is our practice to alphabetize functions within each major section. When we feel that some other ordering is needed, our convention is to insert a centered title to break the flow and restart the alphabetization. Any arbitrary title accomplishes this break; as it happens, however, the title `Aspects`, to which this footnote is attached, is reserved ubiquitously to indicate a region of interface where respective functions are uniform in both name and semantics across all of our types and, ironically, is therefore itself an *aspect* (section 2.4.8); see also Volume II, section 6.14. Note that, had we felt the need, we could have inserted an arbitrary centered title — either before day or after year, to separate the getYearMonthDay method so that the individual field accessors grouped together.

(continued)

```
        // indicates the number of spaces per indentation level for this and
        // all of its nested objects.  If 'level' is negative, suppress
        // indentation of the first line.  If 'spacesPerLevel' is negative,
        // format the entire output on one line, suppressing all but the
        // initial indentation (as governed by 'level').  If 'stream' is not
        // valid on entry, this operation has no effect.  Note that this
        // human-readable format is not fully specified, and can change without
        // notice.
};

// FREE OPERATORS
bool operator==(const Date& lhs, const Date& rhs);
    // Return 'true' if the specified 'lhs' and 'rhs' objects have the same
    // value, and 'false' otherwise.  Two 'Date' objects have the same value if
    // each of their 'year', 'month', and 'day' attributes (respectively) have
    // the same value.[305]

bool operator!=(const Date& lhs, const Date& rhs);
    // Return 'true' if the specified 'lhs' and 'rhs' objects do not have the
    // same value, and 'false' otherwise.  Two 'Date' objects do not have the
    // same value if any of their 'year', 'month', and 'day' attributes
    // (respectively) do not have the same value.

bsl::ostream& operator<<(bsl::ostream& stream, const Date& date);
    // Write the value of the specified 'date' object to the specified output
    // 'stream' in a single-line format, and return a reference to 'stream'.
    // If 'stream' is not valid on entry, this operation has no effect.  Note
    // that this human-readable format is not fully specified, can change
    // without notice, and is logically equivalent to:
    //.. ─────────────────────────────
    //   date.print(stream, 0, -1);        Annotation: toggle line-fill
    //.. ─────────────────────────────

bool operator<(const Date& lhs, const Date& rhs);
    // Return 'true' if the specified 'lhs' date value is earlier than the
    // specified 'rhs' one, and 'false' otherwise.[306]

bool operator<=(const Date& lhs, const Date& rhs);
    // Return 'true' if the specified 'lhs' date value is earlier than or the
    // same as the specified 'rhs' one, and 'false' otherwise.

bool operator>(const Date& lhs, const Date& rhs);
    // Return 'true' if the specified 'lhs' date value is later than the
    // specified 'rhs' one, and 'false' otherwise.
```

(continues)

---

[305] To understand what we mean by *value*, see Volume II, section 4.1. To understand what it means for a type to have *value semantics*, see Volume II, section 4.3.

[306] This and the other three relational operators that follow are above and beyond what is addressed by value semantics, which is limited in scope to properly representing the *same* value (or not). That is, not all value-semantic types have (or should have) relational operators.

(continued)

```
bool operator>=(const Date& lhs, const Date& rhs);
    // Return 'true' if the specified 'lhs' date value is later than or the
    // same as the specified 'rhs' one, and 'false' otherwise.

Date operator++(Date& date, int);307
    // Set the specified 'date' object to have the value that is one day later
    // than its current value, and return the value of 'date' on entry.  The
    // behavior is undefined if the value of 'date' on entry is '9999/12/31'.

Date operator--(Date& date, int);
    // Set the specified 'date' object to have the value that is one day
    // earlier than its current value, and return the value of 'date' on entry.
    // The behavior is undefined if the value of 'date' on entry is
    // '0001/01/01'.

Date operator+(const Date& date,    int          numDays);
Date operator+(int         numDays, const Date& date);
    // Return the date value that is later by the specified (signed) 'numDays'
    // from the specified 'date'.  The behavior is undefined unless the
    // resulting value falls within the range of dates supported by this class
    // (see 'isValidYearMonthDay').  Note that 'numDays' may be negative.

Date operator-(const Date& date, int numDays);
    // Return the date value that is earlier by the specified (signed)
    // 'numDays' from the specified 'date'.  The behavior is undefined unless
    // the resulting value falls within the range of dates supported by this
    // class (see 'isValidYearMonthDay').  Note that 'numDays' may be negative.

int operator-(const Date& lhs, const Date& rhs);
    // Return the (signed) number of days between the specified 'lhs' and 'rhs'
    // dates.  Note that if 'lhs < rhs' the result will be negative.

// FREE FUNCTIONS
template <class HASHALG>
void hashAppend(HASHALG& hashAlg, const Date& object);
    // Pass the specified 'object' to the specified 'hashAlg'.  This function
    // integrates with the 'bslh' modular hashing system and effectively
    // provides a 'bsl::hash' specialization for 'Date'.

}  // close package namespace
// ...
}  // close enterprise namespace
// ...
```

Figure 3-152: Proposed interface for value-semantic `Date` class

---

[307] Unlike the prefix increment and decrement operators, the corresponding postfix operators return objects *by value* and are therefore properly implemented as free (i.e., non-member) functions, in part to inhibit the operator from modifying an unnamed temporary, which is almost certainly a bug, and not just because it can be implemented efficiently in terms of its prefix counterpart, thus avoiding the need for friend access (see Volume II, section 6.13).

Note that, for more general consumption, it might later turn out to be worthwhile for our `Date` class to support date values in the form year/day-of-year (as well as year/month/day). Also note that we had originally chosen to employ the (nonproleptic) Gregorian calendar, which is consistent with the Unix (POSIX) standard, because that was what was prevalent at the time `Date` was originally conceived (c. 1997). Since then, the world has seemed to standardize on the proleptic Gregorian calendar, which necessitated our making a very difficult change indeed.[308] We will discuss physical design considerations that anticipate making such fundamental changes to this crucial vocabulary type (see Volume II, section 4.4) later in this section.

A sketch addressing the `Date`-class portion of our initial design, including only the essential client-facing components needed to satisfy all aspects of the first of our four synthesized requirements, is provided for reference in Figure 3-153. Notice that both the `Date` class itself and its subsidiary `DayOfWeek` enumeration — each residing in its own separate component — are both (fully) value-semantic types (see Volume II, section 4.3) and, as such, represent values that make sense outside (as well as inside) the current running process. In order for both of these new types to be able to participate in (efficient) externalization of their values using BDEX streaming, each will require method templates relying (implicitly) on the related BDEX concepts.

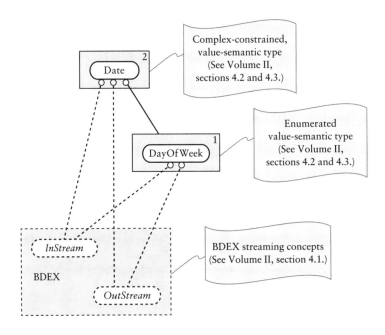

Figure 3-153: `Date` class along with its subsidiary client-facing components

---

[308] For reasons having to do with business risk, we ultimately chose to defer the adoption of this change internally.

Notice that, for now, we have omitted any notion (section 2.4) of the packages in which the final components will reside. Although absolute physical location (section 3.1.4) will ultimately be of critical importance to successful reuse, we are still in the early stages of the macroscopic design. Once the initial design is complete and the implementation components have been identified and more fully articulated, we can then begin to think about assigning each of the new components to their proper respective positions in the enterprise-wide repository comprising our Software Capital, while preserving their relative physical dependencies, of course (e.g., see Figure 0-56, section 0.9).

3.12.4   Determining What Date Value *Today* Is

Our next objective is to satisfy our second requirement of making it possible, and ideally convenient, for clients to ask our library for the value of the current date. While this task might seem like a relatively simple one, there are many complicating factors, such as distinguishing between local time and UTC.[309] No doubt our library will need to supply both kinds of time values, and so we will want corresponding zero-argument functions, e.g., `local()` and `utc()` — each returning a `Datetime` object by value (see below) — appropriately nested as `static` methods within a utility `struct` (see Figure 2-23, section 2.4.9). In keeping with our nomenclature, we will want to append the suffix `Util` to whatever descriptive name we choose for this, and other similar `struct` types (section 3.2.9.2).

How we choose to name this utility will turn out to be important. Because the utility we propose carries with it a substantial physical dependency (i.e., on the underlying OS), we would not, for example, want to call it simply `DatetimeUtil`. Moreover, we might well (and, in fact, we already know we will) want it to return values of time-related types other than `Datetime`. Hence, for both of these reasons, we will deliberately choose *not* to name our needed utility `struct DatetimeUtil`. Instead, we have chosen a more specific and descriptive name, `CurrentTimeUtil`, the detailed reason for which will be made clearer shortly (just below Figure 3-155). Meanwhile, a sketch of the initial interface (along with elided function-level documentation) for this utility component is provided in Figure 3-154.[310]

---

[309] Note that UTC stands for Coordinated Universal Time, formerly GMT (Greenwich Mean Time). Although the two are often interchanged or confused, GMT is a time *zone*, while UTC is a time *standard*.

[310] As ever, this original design will continue to evolve and grow over time to accommodate other features that were not motivated by the initial use case. For example, other types, such as `DatetimeTz` (which carries with it a time-zone offset), should also be made available to return the current time via a `static` method, such as `asDatetimeTz`. Moreover, in some multiprocessing contexts, it can be more efficient to access the current time from a location in shared memory that is repeatedly being updated by its own dedicated process (employing another processor) than by making a system call (employing the same processor). Hence, a more mature implementation of this utility would most likely support that capability (via a user-supplied callback and supporting static methods) as well. Finally, we will want to be sure to delineate all of the pair-wise thread-safety guarantees properly (see Volume II, section 6.1) in component-level documentation (see Volume II, section 6.15).

```
// grppk_currenttimeutil.h
// ...

namespace bsls { class TimeInterval; }

namespace grppk {

class Datetime;

struct CurrentTimeUtil {
    // This 'struct' provides a namespace for current-time-retrieval
    // procedures.  ...

  public:
    // CLASS METHODS
    static Datetime local();
        // Return the 'Datetime' value representing the current date/time in
        // the local time zone.  ...

    static bsls::TimeInterval now();311

        // Return the 'TimeInterval' value between 'EpochUtil::epoch()' and
        // the current date/time.  ...

    static Datetime utc();
        // Return the 'Datetime' value representing the current date/time in
        // Coordinated Universal Time (UTC).

    // ...
};312


// ...

}  // close package namespace
// ...
```

> Note that this function returns a
> higher-resolution value than the others.

Figure 3-154: Initial sketch of interface for struct CurrentTimeUtil

Notice that we have anticipated one additional function, now(), that returns an object of the preexisting, low-level bsls::TimeInterval class, which will ultimately be needed in order to address our overall design's third implied requirement — i.e., that of determining whether a given Date object represents a business day — as described below.

---

[311] That this function returns a time interval rather than an absolute time is, in part, due to historical reasons related to time functions in Unix employing this epoch-based convention.

[312] As shown, the functionality provided here is *unmockable*, which many would consider a bad design as clients of this utility would find it difficult to fully exercise (and test) the aspects of their implementation that depended on this functionality. What is not shown here, however, is that there is a way to install a callback allowing users to intercept the call to the OS (1) for testing, but also (2) for cases where the current time can be kept in, say, shared memory and accessed by multiple processes far more efficiently than having to make costly system calls.

This `CurrentTimeUtil struct` traffics in objects of type `Datetime`, as opposed to just `Date`, because getting the time of day along with the date is a more general operation than getting the date alone. A `Datetime` comprises two independent values of types `Date` and `Time`, respectively; the latter provides the time of day and originally had a maximum resolution of milliseconds.[313]

For those without at least some domain-specific background, it might come as a surprise that the units of a time *duration* are not the same as those of a time *point* (e.g., `Datetime`). While the difference of two unitless integers is itself an integer, the difference of two time points is a duration (e.g., `DatetimeInterval`). What's more, the notion of a duration turns out to be logically *prior* to that of a time point. That is, all of the operations on a duration that do not involve another type result in a duration. The same cannot be said for a time point. For example, the sum or difference of two durations is again a duration:

```
DatetimeInterval operator+(const DatetimeInterval& lhs,
                           const DatetimeInterval& rhs);
DatetimeInterval operator-(const DatetimeInterval& lhs,
                           const DatetimeInterval& rhs);
```

The difference of two time points, on the other hand, is not a time point, but a duration (and there is no meaningful notion of adding two time points):

```
DatetimeInterval operator-(const Datetime& lhs,
                           const Datetime& rhs);
```

Hence, a component defining a duration type naturally resides at a lower level in the physical hierarchy than a compatible time-point one. In other words, the logical functionality in the component that defines our `Datetime` class is allowed to know about (and make use of) the component that defines our `DatetimeInterval` class, but not vice versa. The complete design so far — incorporating our solution to our first synthesized requirement of representing a date value in isolation — is provided for reference in Figure 3-155.

---

[313] Due to the MiFID regulatory requirements for the financial industry (c. 2015), the `Time` and, hence, `Datetime` types would later need to be modified to represent microsecond resolution — ideally without impacting existing clients (see Volume II, section 5.5).

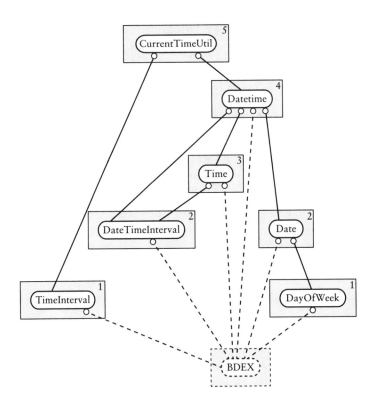

Figure 3-155: `CurrentTimeUtil` and its subsidiary client-facing components

As we saw previously, we have chosen to incorporate, in `CurrentTimeUtil`, a method, `now()`, that returns the current date and time value as an offset (duration) from a known "epoch" time point. The preexisting type used to represent this particular duration value is `TimeInterval`. Given that both `TimeInterval` and `DatetimeInterval` are durations, it would seem like we should have chosen one or the other (see Volume II, section 4.4). As it turns out, however, these two durations have different properties (e.g., object size, precision) and serve almost entirely disjoint client bases.

To begin with, a `TimeInterval` is intended to be used in conjunction with system-level operations, such as timeouts, which (historically) have required higher levels of precision (e.g., nanoseconds) than time points geared toward an application domain such as finance. In finance, millisecond time-point resolution has (historically) been sufficient, and only relatively recently have regulatory requirements pushed us to incorporate additional precision (e.g., microseconds) in the likes of `Time` and `Datetime`. Note that even with microsecond resolution, an eight-byte object footprint is sufficient to identify every time point within a 10,000-year range, which is all that our `Datetime` type promises to support.

What's more, the range of values required of a high-precision system-level time offset (duration) is always much smaller in practice than is typically needed for a time point. As limiting the representation of such values to what will fit within a typical machine word is generally preferred (e.g., for performance and/or concurrency reasons), it is possible to achieve the higher resolution and still keep it to an eight-byte footprint by significantly shortening the representable range of values for this duration type.[314] Finally, since we already know that we will need to get the current time in terms of this specific type later anyway (to be used as a timeout), we have elected to incorporate this eminently reusable functionality, `now()`, now.

3.12.5   Determining If a Date Value Is a *Business Day*

Having addressed the synthesized requirements of representing a date as well as loading the value of today into a `Date` object, we now turn to the more complex task of designing the components that will enable clients of our library to determine whether a given date is a business day. From section 3.6.2 we know that functionality such as `isHoliday` or — more to the point — `isNonBusinessDay` cannot possibly be methods on `Date`. One (at least physically sound) design (illustrated in Figure 3-106, section 3.6.2) suggested that there be some `CalendarService` facility that, when supplied a date object, would return its business/holiday properties. While this approach can work for some applications, it is entirely unsatisfactory for others. As promised back in section 3.6.2, we will now explore a more modular, flexible, and runtime-efficient solution in terms of a value-semantic type (see Volume II, section 4.3).

---

[314] Note that, at microsecond resolution, an eight-byte time point is capable of addressing a span of roughly $2^{64} / (10^6 \cdot 60 \cdot 60 \cdot 24 \cdot 365.25)$ or just over 584,542 years (plenty for our `Datetime` type). At nanosecond resolution, however, the maximum span of a valid range drops to under 585 years, but — even with a signed value — 292 years is still plenty large for any practical system-time offset (e.g., timeout) that one might need in practice.

3.12.5.1   Calendar Requirements

We will begin by identifying several of the actual requirements — including performance requirements — and then explore how they will shape our design and govern our component implementations. The general requirement states that we need to efficiently determine whether a given date is a business day. What is not stated explicitly, however, is that, for many important applications (including the one at hand), this specific question might be asked and answered repeatedly, over and over again — potentially trillions of times — in a single run.

Hence, the amortized cost of determining whether a given date in a given context is a business day *must* be dead minimal. Any solution that requires going out of process on each such determination is a nonstarter. What's needed instead is a way of organizing the information *up front* such that the incremental runtime cost of determining, in a series of contiguous dates, whether the next date is a business day is vanishingly small.

This extremely high runtime-performance requirement, however, is not the only constraint. For financial systems, it is common to have dozens, if not hundreds (or even thousands) of distinct contexts in which a date might be queried. For example, nonbusiness days (e.g., weekends and holidays) in one jurisdiction or *locale* (e.g., New York City) might well not be the same as for another (e.g., London). In fact, what constitutes a business day will depend on what, precisely, we are talking about. For example, there are days on which the stock market might be closed, and yet banks are open. Special dates for bonds, known as settlement dates, might be different than days on which a financial instrument may be traded.[315] As one might expect, there are no

---

[315] Thus, within a given locale it is possible that what is considered a valid "business day" to perform a transaction for one kind of financial instrument (e.g., equities) might not be considered a business day for another (e.g., mortgage-backed securities, commercial paper). Moreover, whether a given day of the week is a recurring non-business day (i.e., a weekend day) cannot be hard coded either. For example, in some geographic regions of the world, it is common for *Friday* and *Saturday* to be weekend days, whereas, in other regions, there might be a six-day work week with just one weekend day.

natural laws that govern such data. Moreover, this information is subject to change on short notice, and hence it must frequently be retrieved (expeditiously) anew from an external data source (e.g., in the form of a C++ object). So, in addition to being able to access the data to answer business-day information quickly, we must also be able to store this data compactly for efficient transmission across process boundaries.

A *calendar*, in our lexicon, is a kind of C++ type whose *value* represents a set of *business days* over some contiguous range of dates. How this information is obtained is of no more relevance to our calendar-class design than it would be if we were implementing an std::vector. Hence, a sufficient (and complete[316]) set of manipulator methods must be provided for adding (individual) holidays and (recurring) "weekend" days.[317] A heavily elided interface for our proposed Calendar type is provided for reference in Figure 3-156.[318]

---

[316] **booch94**, section 3.6, pp. 136–143 (especially pp. 136–137 and the summary on p. 143). "Sufficient" means enough for the first use. "Complete" means enough for all similar uses.

[317] Although it was not originally contemplated, recurring weekend days, like time zones, sometimes change over time, and so an additional, more elaborate interface for specifying recurring non-business days — i.e., other than just setting the set of weekend days for the entire calendar — eventually became necessary.

[318] In addition to knowing whether a given date is a business day, it is also sometimes useful to know which holiday (if any) resulted in a given date being a non-business day. Although not as ubiquitous as a *date*, a Calendar type can nonetheless be fairly widely used in public interfaces (see Volume II, section 4.4). Hence, we would ideally want to have only one C++ class to represent it in (most) public interfaces. On the other hand, keeping the in-memory size of calendar data small is also an essential design goal, as there are potentially thousands of locales that may need to be imported into, and be co-resident within, a single process. We must also make sure not to burden our users with any development overhead associated with storing elaborate holiday information in each instance, and any physical dependency on a holiday repository is simply out of the question. Moreover, there must be no speed or space overhead for users that do not care why a day is not a business day. Given these constraints, our solution will be to allow interested clients to associate holiday information within a Calendar via dumb data (section 3.5.5) in the form of a small integer index called a *holiday code*. It will then be up to the client to use these indices to look up the needed information regarding a particular holiday in an appropriate, but separately managed, table (e.g., of type std::vector<string>).

```
// grppk_calendar
// ...

#include <dayofweek.h>

#include <iosfwd>

namespace MyLongCompanyName {

namespace bslma { class Allocator; }

namespace grppk {

class PackedCalendar;
class Date;
class BusinessDayConstIterator;
class DayOfWeekSet;
class HolidayConstIterator;
class WeekendDaysTransitionConstIterator;

class Calendar {
    // This class implements a runtime-efficient, value-semantic repository of
    // weekend and holiday information over a *valid* *range* of dates.  ...

  public:
    // TYPES

    // ...    ('typedef's for [e.g., business-day, holiday] iterators omitted)

    // CLASS METHODS
                                    // Aspects

    static int maxSupportedBdexVersion(int versionSelector);

    // CREATORS
    explicit Calendar(bslma::Allocator *basicAllocator = 0);
    Calendar(const Date&        firstDate,
             const Date&        lastDate,
             bslma::Allocator *basicAllocator = 0);
    explicit Calendar(const PackedCalendar&  packedCalendar,
                      bslma::Allocator       *basicAllocator = 0);
    Calendar(const Calendar& original, bslma::Allocator *basicAllocator = 0);
    ~Calendar();

    // MANIPULATORS
    Calendar& operator=(const Calendar& rhs);
    void addDay(const Date& date);
    void addHoliday(const Date& date);
    void addWeekendDay(DayOfWeek::Enum weekendDay);
    void addWeekendDays(const DayOfWeekSet& weekendDays);
    void intersectBusinessDays(const Calendar& other);
```

> Creates a speed-efficient calendar from a space-efficient one (discussed below)

> Multiple locales

(continues)

(continued)

```
      void intersectNonBusinessDays(const Calendar& other);
      void removeAll();
      void removeHoliday(const Date& date);
      void setValidRange(const Date& firstDate, const Date& lastDate);

                                // Aspects
      template <class STREAM>
      STREAM& bdexStreamIn(STREAM& stream, int version);
      void swap(Calendar& other);

      // ACCESSORS
      BusinessDayConstIterator beginBusinessDays() const;
      BusinessDayConstIterator beginBusinessDays(const Date& date) const;
      HolidayConstIterator beginHolidays() const;
      HolidayConstIterator beginHolidays(const Date& date) const;
      WeekendDaysTransitionConstIterator beginWeekendDaysTransitions() const;
      BusinessDayConstIterator endBusinessDays() const;
      BusinessDayConstIterator endBusinessDays(const Date& date) const;
      HolidayConstIterator endHolidays() const;
      HolidayConstIterator endHolidays(const Date& date) const;
      const Date& firstDate() const;
      int getNextBusinessDay(Date *nextBusinessDay, const Date& date) const;
      int getNextBusinessDay(Date          *nextBusinessDay,
                             const Date&   date,
                             int           nth) const;
      Date holiday(int index) const;
      bool isBusinessDay(const Date& date) const;
      bool isHoliday(const Date& date) const;
      bool isInRange(const Date& date) const;
      bool isNonBusinessDay(const Date& date) const;
      bool isWeekendDay(const Date& date) const;
      bool isWeekendDay(DayOfWeek::Enum dayOfWeek) const;
      const Date& lastDate() const;
      int length() const;
      int numBusinessDays() const;
      int numBusinessDays(const Date& beginDate, const Date& endDate) const;
      int numHolidays() const;
      int numNonBusinessDays() const;
      int numWeekendDaysInRange() const;
      const PackedCalendar& packedCalendar() const;
```

> Provides read-only access to underlying space-efficient *calendar* type, discussed below

```
      // ...                 (various reverse-iterator accessors omitted)

                                // Aspects

      bslma::Allocator *allocator() const;
      template <class STREAM>
      STREAM& bdexStreamOut(STREAM& stream, int version) const;
```

(continues)

(continued)

```
    std::ostream& print(std::ostream& stream,
                        int           level = 0,
                        int           spacesPerLevel = 4) const;
};

// FREE OPERATORS
bool operator==(const Calendar& lhs, const Calendar& rhs);
bool operator!=(const Calendar& lhs, const Calendar& rhs);
std::ostream& operator<<(std::ostream& stream, const Calendar& calendar);

// FREE FUNCTIONS
template <class HASHALG>
void hashAppend(HASHALG& hashAlg, const Calendar& object);
void swap(Calendar& a, Calendar& b);

// ...                    (various iterator-class definitions omitted)

}   // close package namespace

// ...
```

Figure 3-156: Initial (elided) sketch of interface for `Calendar` class

3.12.5.2   Multiple Locale Lookups

Financial software often requires adjusting a given date based on whether a particular day is a *business day* in more than one locale. For example, determining a date on which a particular trade can settle may require repeated attempts to ascertain whether a given date is a business day in two distinct regions — e.g., that of both the buyer and of the seller — simultaneously.[319] One way of addressing this issue is to create two calendars, ask the question twice, and intersect the results. This approach, however, has two drawbacks.

The first problem with requiring multiple calendar objects is that common algorithms, such as *modified following* (see section 3.12.10), implemented as a function taking just a single calendar and a date, could not be reused — at least not nearly as easily as if there were just a single calendar parameter. The second problem is that such subroutines are often applied (e.g., over a cross product of many portfolios, time horizons, and scenarios) an inordinate number of times. Performing two or more lookups — one for each locale — and then intersecting them each time we need to know if a given date is a valid settlement day in multiple locales would, in many important cases, be unacceptably inefficient.

---

[319] For complex "multilegged" transactions, the number of regions could be three, four, or more.

Fortunately, because a `Calendar` can be thought of as a set of business days over a range, we can define semantics for basic set operations such as `and`, `or`, `xor`, and `sub`. For example, the logical `and` of two calendars represents the intersection of the ranges and of the business days of these two calendars.[320] Operations resembling `or`, `xor`, and `sub` for calendars can also be defined if needed; however, intersection (i.e., `and`) is by far the most useful of the set-like operations on a calendar, and the only one needed here.[321] By quickly precalculating a composite calendar as the intersection of the business days of original calendars for the respective regions, we simultaneously achieve superior interoperability, reuse, and runtime performance!

Given all of these requirements for calendar information on top of the fine-grained physical rendering implicit in hierarchically reusable software, we are going to have to create a number of complex, high-performance *client-facing*[322] components before we can even begin to provide the complete interface for this `Calendar` type. The first step will be to capture the raw information in a space-efficient form in a class that we will call a `PackedCalendar`.

A `PackedCalendar` object holds the same sort of *value* (see Volume II, section 4.1) as a `Calendar`, and therefore must contain all of the information needed to represent a `Calendar`, but in an ultra-space-efficient manner incapable of delivering sufficiently high runtime performance (see below). Each instance of a `PackedCalendar` must represent the valid range of dates, which days within that range are holidays, and which days of the week are considered weekend days.[323]

---

[320] A *holiday code* for a given holiday, for example, could remain in the result value only if it is present in *both* initial calendars for a given date in the valid range of the result. An alternative, perhaps more useful, behavior might be to retain the holiday code if it is in *either* of the initial calendars for a given date within the valid range of the result. Providing either or both behaviors is acceptable so long as the precise behavior (see Volume II, section 5.2) is fully specified for the calendar method that performs the operation (see Volume II, section 6.17).

[321] The meanings of operations resembling `or`, `xor`, and `sub` are less obvious and can lead to calendar ranges that are not contiguous; hence, the contract (see Volume II, section 5.2) of the calendar might have to be extended, and the additional behavior defined carefully so as not to invalidate its invariants (see Volume II, section 5.5). Alternatively, these operations can be omitted entirely until some business need presents itself (see Volume II, section 5.6).

[322] By client-facing, we mean components that are intended to be used directly by clients of this subsystem as opposed to those additional, lower-level, "implementation" components (not programmatically accessible through the client-facing ones), which are provided only to achieve a fully factored (see Volume II, section 6.4), hierarchically reusable (section 0.4) subsystem.

[323] Just as with `Calendar`, a `PackedCalendar` object may have associated with each non-recurring non-business date, one or more unique, small non-negative integer holiday codes. For `PackedCalendar` objects having no associated holiday codes — just as for classes having no virtual functions (see Volume II, section 4.6) — there must be (essentially) zero runtime overhead (see Volume II, section 6.7) imposed for retaining this supplemental functionality.

We can represent the business days in a `PackedCalendar` type internally in terms of a starting date, an ending date, a byte-sized[324] `DayOfWeekSet` class containing the set of weekend days, and a (space-efficient) array of unsigned integer offsets (see below) from the starting date, with each offset indicating a holiday. All empty calendar ranges are equivalent and represented *canonically* (see Volume II, section 4.4) by having the start and end dates hold the maximum and minimum values, respectively (a.k.a. known as an "imploded range").[325]

Until `PackedCalendar`, none of the types we have discussed implementing have needed to allocate memory dynamically. Given that there will be embedded data structures in a `PackedCalendar` — e.g., the one representing the sequence of holidays — that require variable (if not unbounded) amounts of memory, and that a `Calendar` object has, as one of its data members, a `PackedCalendar`, objects of both types of calendar class will potentially need to allocate memory throughout their lifetimes. Whenever a reusable type potentially incorporates dynamically allocated memory as a managed resource of its objects,[326] we will want to be able to specify precisely from where that memory is coming. For various reasons (e.g., runtime performance, whole-object placement, and per-object metrics), which we will explore further in Volume II, section 4.10, we want to be able to control the dynamic memory source on a per-object basis, and do so without affecting the C++ type of the object. Our solution will be to allow clients to supply, at construction, the address of a particular concrete allocator that implements the (pure abstract) `bslma::Allocator` protocol; if no allocator is supplied, an appropriate *default allocator* (typically `bslma::NewDeleteAllocator`) is used instead (see Volume II, section 4.10). A high-level diagram of the client-facing components needed to supply an initial interface for our `Calendar` class, properly integrated into our previous component-based design, is provided for reference in Figure 3-157.

---

[324] Given that we can denote the presence of each of the seven days of the week with a single bit, a class implementing the power set of these seven days will fit within a single byte (with one bit to spare); hence, there is no need for dynamic memory allocation here.

[325] Note that, if there are no associated holiday codes for any holiday, the entire data structure representing such codes is never created (analogously to typical implementations of `std::vector` or `std::string`).

[326] I.e., the dynamic allocation/deallocation sequence is not limited to the scope of a single public member function of the object (see Volume II, section 4.10).

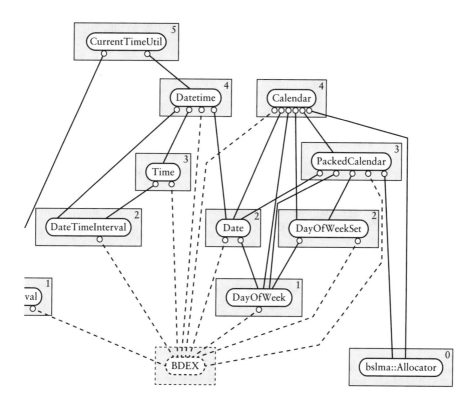

Figure 3-157: Calendar along with its subsidiary client-facing components

3.12.5.3   Calendar Cache

At this point, the client-facing infrastructure portion of this design would appear complete. Given a Calendar populated with the appropriate business-day information, we can now use it to determine if a given date is a business day. Are we done? No. In order for application developers to use this infrastructure, we will need to supply some sort of general apparatus for the system to get specific information into a calendar, and to find that calendar from disparate parts of the program. That is, we will need a place within the running process to store Calendar data associated with some locally unique (e.g., character string) identifier. We will refer to such a facility as a *calendar cache*.

In our design, class `CalendarCache` is a *mechanism* (see Volume II, section 4.2) that provides a mapping of unique character-string names to calendar data. This class, however, is more than just a simple `std::map<std::string, Calendar>`. How the calendar data is represented internally could be in terms of `Calendar`, `PackedCalendar`, or something else. Moreover, there are other aspects of a `CalendarCache` — such as what to do on a cache miss, and when lingering data is considered stale — that are essential to its intended purpose, and that a raw `std::map` simply couldn't accommodate.[327]

To make a `CalendarCache` sufficiently flexible to permit general reuse, we will need to provide an extensible mechanism by which higher-level clients (e.g., `main`) can program an instance of a `CalendarCache` to load the associated calendar data on demand. The architectural approach we take here (Figure 3-158a) is again *lateral* in nature (section 3.7.5). We will define an abstract interface type `CalendarLoader`. Each instance of `CalendarCache` will, at construction, be provided the address of an appropriate concrete class derived from this (pure abstract) `CalendarLoader` protocol (Figure 3-158b). When a calendar is requested (by name) for which no such calendar entry exists, the virtual `load` method of the held `CalendarLoader` object is invoked by the `CalendarCache` (Figure 3-158c) to populate an object of type `PackedCalendar` supplied by reference (address) as the first argument. If the call is successful, the associated `Calendar` data is made available to the original client of `CalendarCache`; otherwise, a bad status (e.g., a null pointer) is returned instead (Figure 3-158d).[328]

---

[327] Even if the current implementation of a `CalendarCache` were no more than a string-to-calendar mapping, future enhancements could make preserving the stability of such an unencapsulated implementation problematic (see Volume II, section 5.6); hence, we would choose to encapsulate even that particular implementation in a named class (i.e., not a `typedef`) as was done here.

[328] Note that returning a `Calendar` by pointer makes it difficult to invalidate the cache for a given process; on the other hand, if calendar data changes, a calendar date returned by value will not be up to date. In typical financial applications, if calendar data needs to change intraday, it is not uncommon to simply "bounce" (restart) the process in order to reset the cache. There are, however, better, more robust ways, such as returning a proxy object (e.g., a shared pointer) to achieve such goals.

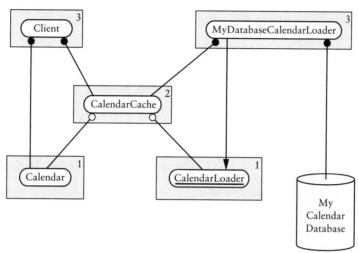

(a) Architectural component/class diagram

```
// grppk_calendarcache.h                                              -*-C++-*-
// ...
namespace grppk {

class CalendarCache {

    // ...

  private:
    // NOT IMPLEMENTED
    CalendarCache(const CalendarCache&);
    CalendarCache& operator=(const CalendarCache&);

  public:
    // CREATORS
    explicit
    CalendarCache(CalendarLoader   *loader,
                  bslma::Allocator *basicAllocator = 0);
        // Create an empty calendar cache that uses the specified 'loader' to
        // load calendars on demand and has no timeout.  Optionally specify a
        // 'basicAllocator' used to supply memory.  If 'basicAllocator' is 0,
        // the currently installed default allocator is used.  Calendars loaded
        // into this cache remain valid for retrieval until they have been
        // explicitly invalidated (via either the 'invalidate' or
        // 'invalidateAll' methods), or until this object is destroyed.   The
        // behavior is undefined unless 'loader' remains valid throughout the
        // lifetime of this cache.

    CalendarCache(CalendarLoader          *loader,
                  const bsls::TimeInterval&  timeout,
                  bslma::Allocator         *basicAllocator = 0);329
        // Create an empty calendar cache that uses the specified 'loader' to
        // load calendars on demand and has the specified 'timeout' interval
        // indicating the length of time that calendars remain valid for
        // subsequent retrieval from the cache after they have been loaded.
        // Optionally specify a 'basicAllocator' used to supply memory.  If
        // 'basicAllocator' is 0, the currently installed default allocator is
        // used.  The behavior is undefined unless
        // 'bsls::TimeInterval() <= timeout <= bsls::TimeInterval(INT_MAX, 0)',
        // and 'loader' remains valid throughout the lifetime of this cache.
        // Note that a 'timeout' value of 0 indicates that a calendar will be
        // loaded into the cache by *each* (successful) call to the
        // 'getCalendar' method.
```

(continues)

---

329 This particular strategy for caching — i.e., temporally (rather than physically) constrained — was motivated by users who felt they required some mechanism to ensure that the callers were not *too* out-of-date (e.g., as a backup to a frequently failing database trigger). A fixed-memory-based constraint (e.g., LRU) would be a more typical algorithm, and it has been suggested that both the default caching algorithm and the factoring of functionality here is suboptimal. (*Nolo contendere.*)

(continued)

```
    ~CalendarCache();
        // Destroy this object.

    // ...
};
// ...
}  // close package namespace
// ...
```

(b) `CalendarCache` takes the address of a `CalendarLoader` at construction

```
// grppk_calendarloader.h                                    -*-C++-*-
// ...
namespace grppk {

class PackedCalendar;

class CalendarLoader {
    // This class defines a protocol used to load calendars from a specific
    // source.  Each repository of calendar information can be supported by a
    // distinct implementation of this protocol.

  public:
    // CREATORS
    virtual ~CalendarLoader();
        // Destroy this object.

    // MANIPULATORS
    virtual int load(PackedCalendar *result, const char *calendarName) = 0;
        // Load, into the specified 'result', the calendar identified by the
        // specified 'calendarName'.  Return 0 on success, and a non-zero value
        // otherwise.  If the calendar corresponding to 'calendarName' is not
        // found, 1 is returned with no effect on '*result'.  If a non-zero
        // value other than 1 is returned (indicating a different error),
        // '*result' is valid, but its value is undefined.
};

}  // close package namespace
// ...
```

(c) `CalendarLoader` is invoked by `CalendarCache` on a miss

```
// grppk_calendarcache.h                                            -*-C++-*-
// ...
namespace grppk {

class Calendar;

class CalendarCache {

    // ...

    const Calendar *lookup(const char *locale) const;330
        // Return the address of a calendar loaded with the information
        // corresponding to the specified 'locale' key, or 0 if no such
        // key can be found.  The address of each calendar object
        // returned will remain valid until the 'CalendarCache' object is
        // destroyed.

    // ...

};
// ...
}  // close package namespace
// ...
```

(d) CalendarCache is where clients get Calendars by name

Figure 3-158: Interaction between CalendarCache and CalendarLoader

What we have discussed here is only the high-level component architecture. We will leave subtle issues, such as whether the cache can be invalidated (flushed) explicitly, to the developer charged with the detailed interface and contract design (see Volume II, Chapter 5) of the component implementing CalendarCache. What is important at this stage of design, however, is that the loader, when invoked, be supplied writable access to a PackedCalendar designated by the CalendarCache object from which that loader is being invoked. Hence, while the CalendarCache interface itself must be sufficient to add new name/calendar pairs, it must also be possible to associate new or updated calendar values from raw data returned (via a reference to a PackedCalendar object in the argument list) from a call to the client loader (supplied at construction). The result of incorporating both CalendarCache and CalendarLoader into the component-class diagram of Figure 3-157, section 3.12.5.2 — including the previously anticipated (see Figure 3-155, section 3.12.4) use of TimeInterval (for timeout purposes) in the interface of CalendarCache — is provided for reference in Figure 3-159.

---

[330] Note that we might also have returned the calendar object by value or via the argument list as was done in load above. In practice, however, we will instead opt to return the calendar via a shared-pointer-based proxy object (providing only non-modifiable access to a Calendar) in order to facilitate thread-safe updates of the in-process calendar data. E.g.,

```
bsl::shared_ptr<const Calendar> getCalendar(const char *calendarName);
```

See the bdlt_calendarcache.h header file of the **bdlt_calendarcache** component (**bde14**, subdirectory /groups/bdl/bdlt/).

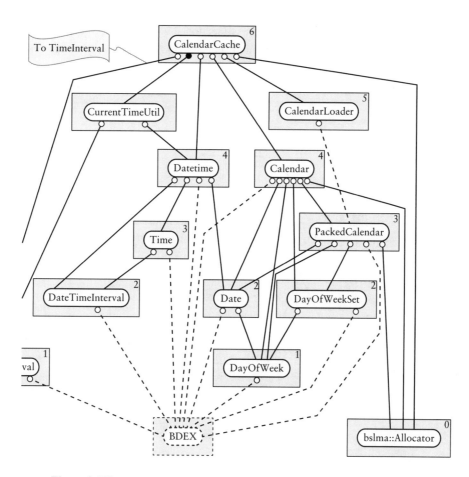

Figure 3-159: `CalendarCache` **and its subsidiary client-facing components**

3.12.5.4   Application-Level Use of Calendar Library

Getting back to the original problem, we want to provide the needed infrastructure to allow an application developer to determine whether today is a business day in their context. To that end, we are almost done. We might now be tempted to assert that the calendar cache is a process-wide resource and to design it as a singleton. Doing so, however, would be a mistake. It is entirely reasonable that some clients will have a cache of bank holidays, while others will need a cache of retail-store holidays. It is suboptimal to make such clients mutually exclusive in a single process (section 3.9.4). Instead, we might create an abstract interface for the client-side functionality of a `CalendarCache`. We might call this interface a `CalendarFactory` and adapt the appropriate subfunctionality of `CalendarCache` using the adapter `CacheCalendarFactory`,[331] as shown in Figure 3-160a.

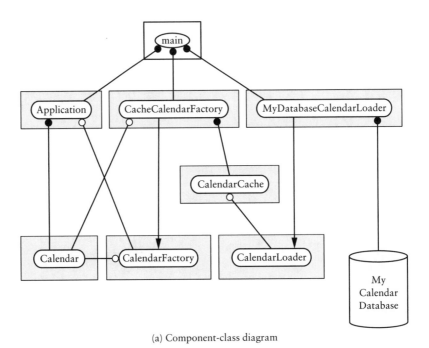

(a) Component-class diagram

---

[331] Note that identifying a concrete implementation of an abstract interface by prefixing the protocol name with an implementation-descriptive phrase is one of our standard naming idioms (see Volume II, section 6.10).

```
// main.cpp
// ...

#include <xyza_mydatabasecalendarloader.h>
#include <abcz_cachecalendarfactory.h>
#include <jsl_application.h>

int main(int argc, const char *argv[])
{
    // Create an appropriate concrete calendar loader.

    xyza::MyDatabaseCalendarLoader loader("my-date-info");

    // Create an appropriate concrete calendar factory node.

    abcz::CacheCalendarFactory calendarFactory(&loader);

    // Create an instance of my application that needs calendars.

    jsl::Application app(&calendarFactory);

    return app.run();
}
```

(b) Configuring the application in `main`

```
// jsl_application.cpp
// ...

#include <jsl_application.h>

#include <calendar.h>
#include <calendarfactory.h>
#include <currenttimeutil.h>
#include <date.h>
#include <datetime.h>

namespace jsl {

bool Application::isTodayBusinessDay() const
{
    // Get the appropriate Calendar for this region (e.g., New York Bank).

    Calendar nybcal;
    int status = d_calendarFactory_p->lookup(&nybcal, "NYB");
    if (0 != status) { /* Houston, we have a problem */ }

    // Get today's date.

    Date today = CurrentTimeUtil::local().date();

    // Return whether today is a business day for banks in New York.

    return nybcal.isBusinessDay(today);
}

}   // close package namespace
```

(c) Using the infrastructure within the application

Figure 3-160: Application-level use of date/calendar infrastructure

In the preface of his book, *The C++ Programming Language*, 4th Ed., Bjarne Stroustrup quotes David J. Wheeler: "All problems in computer science can be solved by another layer of indirection, except for the problem of too many layers of indirection,"[332] and that is exactly what we are about to observe is going on here. Configuring such a seemingly elaborate infrastructure is nonetheless surprisingly straightforward and easy, as is illustrated in Figure 3-160b. First, we create a concrete object, such as `MyDatabaseCalendarLoader`, derived from `Calendar-Loader`. Then, we create an instance of a concrete type, such as `CacheCalendarFactory`, derived from `CalendarFactory`, and (at its construction) pass it the address of the concrete

---

[332] **stroustrup00**, "Preface," p. v

calendar loader defined directly above it in the source code. Now, we create an instance of an entire subsystem or application, represented here by the type `jsl::Application`. Finally, we proceed to run the application and return its boolean result.

Using the infrastructure from within the application, as illustrated in Figure 3-160c, is also easy and efficient. First, we get a calendar for the proper domain and locale (e.g., days banks are open in New York). Then, we get today's date. Next, we look up that date in the calendar. Finally, we return the result of determining whether the current day is a business day. By introducing a calendar factory, we have provided a well-factored, physically sound, highly flexible infrastructure that application and infrastructure clients will be able to use and extend.

Although often a useful design strategy, any additional flexibility afforded by having an abstract `CalendarFactory` interface is probably overkill for what we are likely to need for financial (e.g., "settlement day") purposes. We typically create protocols when we expect we will need variation in behavior, as opposed to variation in value.[333] Since we already have a concrete type to represent the value of a calendar, and a sufficiently flexible way of configuring how we get a valid calendar that we don't already have (i.e., via the `CalendarLoader` protocol), this extra level of indirection serves no useful purpose. Hence, we may reasonably choose to forgo this superfluous customization point and simply create one or more, possibly globally accessible (e.g., singleton), objects of type `CalendarCache` to be used throughout the application, which is what we have successfully elected to do in practice. A detailed architectural diagram illustrating this more minimalist approach is provided for reference in Figure 3-161.

---

[333] **cargill92**, section "Value versus Behavior," pp. 16–19, specifically p. 17 (see also p. 83 and p. 182)

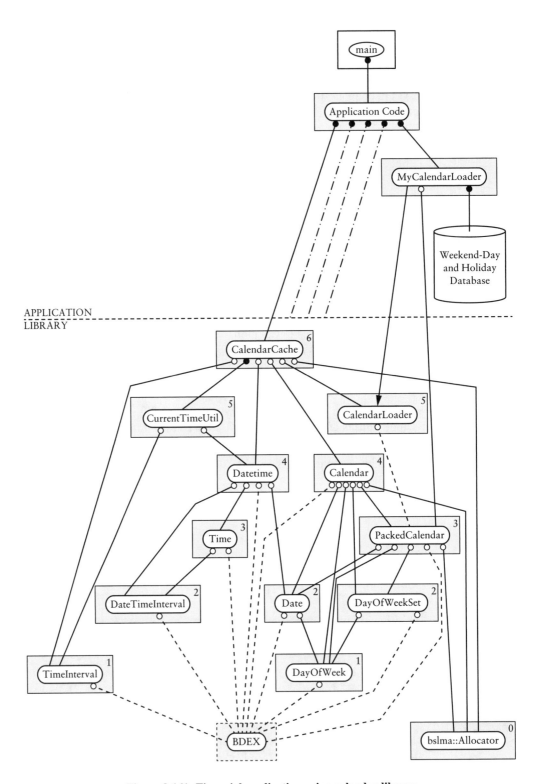

Figure 3-161: Financial application using calendar library

3.12.6   Parsing and Formatting Functionality

In addition to the basic requirements clearly implied by our initial client request, there is an enormous amount of generally useful functionality related to dates to be identified and productized. For example, properly addressing all of the formats in which a `Date` value can be written — let alone read — would result in a substantial body of software in and of itself, which is likely to grow and evolve over time. For this reason, it is generally a mistake to incorporate functionality to parse or even format (in any domain-specific customizable way) a textual representation of a value-semantic type within the same component that defines it. Note that containers in the standard library provide no such output routines whatsoever.

Let us, for a moment, consider incorporating the `istream` (input) operator on a `Date` as a free operator in the same component:

```
std::istream& operator>>(std::istream& stream, Date& date);
```

Figure 3-162 illustrates just some of the many considerations that can arise and will continue to arise over time. The substantial added complexity, dependency, and unavoidable instability of even rendering a value on an output stream is why our standard co-resident value-semantic operators are limited to only writing the value of an object (to an `std::ostream`), and in just one nonspecific, human-readable format (for debugging only), but not necessarily in any particular well-defined (or even parsable) format (e.g., that would be suitable for reading from an `std::istream`).[334]

---

[334] It has been suggested that it would be nice if the standard containers provided a similar facility for the same reason.

What constitutes a valid format?	
`yyyy/mm/dd`	`; slash-delimited four-digit year, month, day`
Do we accept a two-digit year?	
`yy/mm/dd`	`; two-digit year`

Supplying just two digits for year
implies that the resulting date is some
not especially obvious (or unique)
function of the current year.

`41/12/07 in 1998`	`; probably 1941`
`41/12/07 in 2008`	`; 1941 or 2041?`
`41/12/07 in 2018`	`; probably 2041`

Do we accept other styles (that might
depend on location)?

`dd/mm/yyyy`	`; European Style`
`mm/dd/yyyy`	`; American Style`

These two styles can result in different
dates for the same text:

`01/02/2003`	`; January 2nd or February 1st?`
Are internal spaces permitted?	
`yyyy / mm / dd`	`; 2000 / 12 / 31`

What about tabs? newlines?
other white-space?

`yyyy / mm / dd`	`; 2000\n/12\n/31`
Can we drop leading zeros?	
`yyyy/m/d`	`; 2001/1/1`
Can we use alphabetic months?	
`yyyy/mon/dd`	`; 2001/jan/01`
Is the month case-sensitive?	
`yyyy/Mon/dd`	`; 2001/Jan/01`
Do we accept the full month name?	
`yyyy/Month/dd`	`; 2001/September/30`
Do we accept any other abbreviations?	
`yyyy/Mont/dd`	`; 2001/Sept/30`
Do we permit any other separators?	
`yyyy-mm-dd`	`; 2001-09-30`
`yyyy:mm:dd`	`; 2001:09:30`
`yyyy\mm\dd`	`; 2001\09\30`

(continues)

(continued)

Can we omit the printable separators?	
yyyy mm dd	; 2001 09 30
Can we omit separators altogether?	
yyyymmdd	; 20010930
What if we attempt to parse an	
invalid date?	
2001/02/29	
JAN/FEB/MAR	
Chocolate	
Is a trailing digit or character	
considered an error?	
2001/01/02a	; 2001/Jan/02 or error?
2001/01/025	; 2001/Jan/02 or 2001/Jan/25?
2001/01/125	; 2001/Jan/12 or error

Figure 3-162: Complexity and instability in parsing a simple date value

Instead of forcing an unwieldy parser into the source code of a highly reusable `Date` type (Figure 3-163a), we deliberately factor out the parsing (along with the corresponding domain-specific custom formatting) into a separate logical entity, such as the utility `struct DateParserUtil`, defined in its own separate component:

```
struct DateParserUtil {

    // ...

    static
    int parseDate(bdlt::Date *result, const char *input, ...);
    static
    int parseDate(bdlt::Date *result, std::istream& input, ...);
        // Load, into the specified 'result', the date value read
        // from the specified 'input'.  Return 0 on success and a
        // non-zero value (without affecting '*result') otherwise.

    // ...
};
```

This logical functionality uses class `Date` in its interface and hence, as shown in Figure 3-163b, the physically separate component defining the date-parsing utility would depend directly on the one defining `Date`.

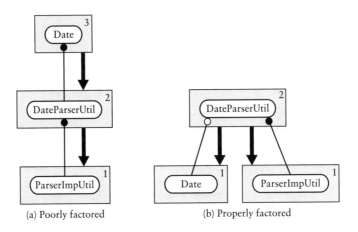

(a) Poorly factored   (b) Properly factored

Figure 3-163: Factoring out "parsing" from a date component

In addition to depending on the component defining `Date`, `DateParserUtil` itself will most likely be layered on more general parser functionality collected in a separate, substantially-lower-level component,[335] such as `ParserImpUtil`, which we may reasonably assume already exists. By relegating the definition of any reliable format to a component at a higher level than the `Date` type, new formatter-parser components can be added without affecting existing ones or ever having to modify the underlying component defining `Date`. Moreover, since such a date-parser component can be developed separately — entirely on top of our immediately needed ones — we can defer its creation to a later project with no risk to the stability of the currently requested subsystem.

3.12.7   Transmitting and Persisting Values

In almost any real-world business application today, the ability to transmit, save, and restore information across process boundaries will be essential. From section 3.6, we know that layering otherwise lightweight value-semantic types on heavier-weight functionality, especially a specific persistence scheme or mechanism, leads to severe physical coupling and is almost always to be avoided (see Figures 3-105 and 3-106, section 3.6.2). Then, in section 3.7, we talked about how various forms of lateral architectures can be used to eliminate such dependencies

---

[335] Or perhaps multiple components.

(see Figures 3-112 and 3-116, sections 3.7.4.1 and 3.7.5, respectively). Since any transport or persistence mechanism will properly be layered on top of (or else reside laterally relative to) our lightweight `Date` class, and because neither is needed for the current project, we are free to defer their design and implementation with no risk of having to rework later the code that is being developed now.

3.12.8   Day-Count Conventions

Some industrial financial applications, as we first learned about in section 3.3, depend on baroque day-count conventions (see Figure 3-26, section 3.3.7). As discussed in section 3.6, we would not even think of adulterating our fairly lean, value-semantic (see Volume II, section 4.3) `Date` class with such nonprimitive functionality (see Figure 3-103a, section 3.6.1). Rather than placing this highly specialized functionality within a separate component locally (i.e., within the same package, or even the same package group), we would instead relegate it to a separate package, such as **bbldc**, in the higher-level package group **bbl** (see Figure 3-27, section 3.3.7). Note that in no way is this sort of functionality relevant to the design of our `Date` class's interface or that of any of the rest of the immediately needed client-facing components. Nonetheless, this arcane functionality might well influence the implementation of `Date`, should such functionality be deemed part of a primary use case of preferred clients.

3.12.9   Date Math

Additional opportunities for providing rich, highly reusable, yet nonprimitive (section 3.2.7), functionality that operates on our soon-to-be ubiquitous `Date` type abound. One fairly broad category of functionality involves operations that adjust or determine a date value based on calendar information that is independent of any external weekend or holiday database. We sometime refer to such self-contained, independently implementable library-suitable function-ality as *date math* (e.g., see Figure 3-103c, section 3.6.1).

For example, given two dates, an "accessor" function of a utility `struct` (see Figure 2-23, section 2.4.9) such as

```
static int numMonthsInRange(const Date& a, const Date& b);
```

might (ignoring the day fields) return the signed number of months spanned by the two supplied `Date` arguments. E.g.,

```
numMonthsInRange(2020-01-31, 2020-02-01)   ➔   2
```

Similarly, a "manipulator" function (of a utility `struct`) such as

```
static int advanceMonth(Date *target, int numMonths);
```

might be used to advance, by the specified (signed) integer `numMonths`, the month field in the `Date` object identified by the specified `target` address, adjusting the year up or down when appropriate and adjusting down (if needed) the day-of-month field (so as to ensure a valid date value), and returning zero on success, and a nonzero value (with no effect) otherwise.

3.12.9.1   Auxiliary Date-Math Types

Such date-math functionality might sometimes benefit from other auxiliary types as well. We may, for example, eventually want to support efficient operations involving months. Enumerating the months sometimes affords certain advantages with respect to reducing coding errors,[336] so we may decide to create a component defining a class `MonthOfYear` that holds a nested enumerated type, `Enum`, along with all of the typically needed auxiliary functionality that normally accompanies one of our enumeration classes (see Figure 2-40, section 2.6).

Programmers in the financial industry can often make use of solutions to questions posed in terms of a date and a month of the year, or perhaps even a set of months of the year. For example, a "manipulator" function (of a utility `struct`) such as

```
static int advanceMonth(Date *target, MonthOfYear::Enum month);
```

might advance the month field in the `Date` object (identified by the specified `target` address) to the next month of year represented by the specified `month` argument, adjusting the year up or down when appropriate and adjusting down (if needed) the day-of-month field (so as to ensure a valid date value), and returning zero on success, and a nonzero value (with no effect) otherwise.

A `MonthOfYearSet`, not to be confused with the much less space- and runtime-efficient `std::set<MonthOfYear::Enum>`, is a nontemplated type employing no dynamic memory allocation and having only a tiny (2-byte) footprint (of which just 12 bits are used). For example, a "manipulator" function (of a utility `struct`) such as

```
static int advanceMonth(Date *target, MonthOfYearSet months);
```

---

[336] See Volume II, section 6.8 for a thorough treatment of defending against failure to satisfy the preconditions of an invoked function's contract (see Volume II, section 5.2).

might advance the month field in the `Date` object (identified by the specified `target` address) to the next valid month-of-year (represented in the specified `months` parameter), adjusting the year up or down as appropriate and adjusting down (if needed) the day-of-month field (so as to ensure a valid date value), and returning zero on success, and a nonzero value (with no effect) otherwise.

There are, of course, numerous variations on these functions, such as having an additional (signed) integer argument to indicate the number of months that are to be skipped over[337]:

```
static
int advanceMonth(Date                   *target,
                 MonthOfYear::Enum   month,
                 int                     numMonths);

static
int advanceMonth(Date                       *target,
                 const MonthOfYearSet&   months,
                 int                         numMonths);
```

And, of course, there are countless other conceivably useful operations involving months (and sets of months) as well:

```
static
int numMonthsInRange(const Date&       first,
                     const Date&       last,
                     MonthOfYear::Enum month);

static
int numMemberMonthsInRange(const Date&          first,
                           const Date&          last,
                           const MonthOfYearSet& months);

static
int numNonMemberMonthsInRange(const Date&           first,
                              const Date&           last,
                              const MonthOfYearSet& months);

        .       .            .              .              .
        .       .            .              .              .
        .       .            .              .              .
```

---

[337] Note that these like-named `static` functions act as (and in fact are) *overloads* only if they reside in the same (named) utility `struct`.

Though not nearly as complex as parsing a date value, rendering this sort of date-math function-ality can be painstaking and time consuming, but — assuming that we have implemented our Date interface appropriately (as was done for Polygon; see Figure 3-18, section 3.2.8.15) — often need not be primitive. Instead of making the day-of-month-related functions above mem-bers of Date (Figure 3-164a), we might instead wisely choose — as we thought to do (albeit less wisely) with DayOfWeek (see Figure 3-49, section 3.5.2) — to distribute this functionality across two separate utilities based solely on interface dependency (Figure 3-164b). Those nonprimitive date-math functions that use MonthOfYearSet would be placed in the MonthOfYearSetUtil utility struct, and the nonprimitive date-math operations associated with just MonthOfYear placed in MonthOfYearUtil, with each utility struct residing in its own separate compo-nent. Note that, much like Date naturally depends semantically on DayOfWeek, some methods of MonthOfYearSet naturally use MonthOfYear::Enum in the interface as well.

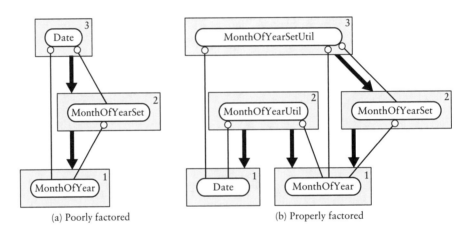

(a) Poorly factored   (b) Properly factored

Figure 3-164: Factoring out "month calculations" from the date component

This dependency-oriented approach to partitioning has some distinct advantages over other, more conventional, "logically cohesive" criteria. The first is objectivity: It is clear (section 1.9) that use in the interface implies physical dependency. The second is useful physical modularity: Clients who are interested in performing date-math with respect to individual months, but not sets of months, are not necessarily forced to compile or link with the month-set component. The third is stability: Changes or additions to MonthOfYearSet or MonthOfYearSetUtil have no effect on clients who use just Date, MonthOfYear::Enum, and MonthOfYearUtil. The fourth is incremental extension: We can add MonthOfYear and then MonthOfYearUtil to our repository of reusable components without necessarily having to add MonthOfYearSet or MonthOfYearSetUtil immediately. By the same token, we can defer *all* of the month-related components to a later project, without incurring additional costs due to refactoring in the future.

The bottom line here is that these sorts of extensions to nonprimitive functionality are purely *additive*, and that any additions or modifications of any kind to month-related functionality in higher-level components have absolutely no impact on clients who make exclusive use of the ubiquitous value-semantic (see Volume II, section 4.3) `Date` vocabulary type (see Volume II, section 4.4).

3.12.10 Date and Calendar Utilities

Given the nature of the initial request, we would be remiss if, as proactive SI developers, we failed to anticipate the most likely intended use cases for our new flagship value-semantic types, `Date` and `Calendar`. For example, there are many nonprimitive operations that require nothing more than what is already represented in the interface of the component that defines `Date`. We assert that such common nonprimitive operations on `Date` objects properly belong in a utility `struct`, `DateUtil`, defined in a separate (higher-level) component that depends directly on the components defining `Date` and `DayOfWeek`, respectively, as illustrated in Figure 3-165a. An example of the interface and contract for a typical function, `nthDayOfWeekInMonth`, that one might reasonably find in such a utility `struct` is provided for reference in Figure 3-165b.

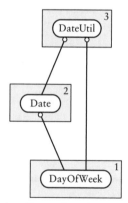

(a) Component-class diagram featuring a separate `DateUtil`

```
// grppk_dateutil.h                                                 -*-C++-*-
// ...

namespace grppk {

struct DateUtil {

    // ...

    static Date nthDayOfWeekInMonth(int               year,
                                    int               month,
                                    DayOfWeek::Enum   dayOfWeek,
                                    int               n);
        // Return the date in the specified 'month' of the specified 'year'
        // corresponding to the specified 'n'th occurrence of the specified
        // 'dayOfWeek'.  If 'n < 0', return the date corresponding to the
        // '-n'th occurrence of the 'dayOfWeek' counting from the end of the
        // 'month' towards the first of the 'month'.  If '5 == n'338 and a
        // result cannot be found in 'month', then return the date of the first
        // 'dayOfWeek' in the following month.  If '-5 == n' and a result
        // cannot be found in 'month', then return the date of the last
        // 'dayOfWeek' in the previous month.  The behavior is undefined unless
        // '1 <= year <= 9999', '1 <= month <= 12', 'n != 0', '-5 <= n <= 5',
        // and the resulting date is neither earlier than 0001/01/01 nor later
        // than 9999/12/31.
        //
        // For example:
        //..
        //  nthDayOfWeekInMonth(2004, 11, DayOfWeek::e_THURSDAY, 4);
        //..
        // returns November 25, 2004, the fourth Thursday in November, 2004.

    // ...
};
// ...
}  // close package namespace
// ...
```

(b) Typical date-math algorithm involving `Date` and `DayOfWeek`

Figure 3-165: Nonprimitive operations involving just the `date` component

---

338 Note that, for the specific case of == (only), we have historically tried always to put the literal (or otherwise non-modifiable) value on the left of the operator to guard against accidentally typing a single =; we deliberately make no such effort for any of the other five relational operators: !=, <, <=, >, and >=.

While nonprimitive functionality that involves only `Date` and perhaps also `DayOfWeek` properly belongs in the component having only those physical dependencies, there are also operations that require information that would naturally be supplied by a `Calendar` object. Such functionality also has a greater envelope of dependencies — e.g., on the component that defines `Calendar` — and, as such, cannot belong in `DateUtil`. Again, from section 3.2.7, we know that such nonprimitive functionality does not properly reside in the same component as the `Calendar` type either. We assert that such common nonprimitive operations on `Date` and `Calendar` objects properly belong in a separate utility `struct`, `CalendarUtil`, defined in its own (higher-level) component[339] that depends directly on the components defining, among other things, `Date` and `Calendar`, respectively, as illustrated in Figure 3-166a. An example of the interface and contract for a widely used financial function, `shiftModifiedFollowingIfValid`, having the requisite interface dependencies, is provided for reference in Figure 3-166b.

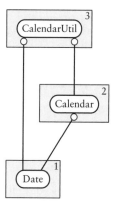

(a) Component-class diagram featuring a separate `CalendarUtil`

---

[339] In practice, there might be several different calendar utilities depending on the particular domain.

```cpp
// grppk_calendarutil.h                                                -*-C++-*-
// ...

namespace grppk {

class Date;
class Calendar;

struct CalendarUtil {
    // This 'struct' provides a namespace for utility functions that operate on
    // dates in the context of supplied calendars.

    // ...

    static int shiftModifiedFollowingIfValid(Date           *result,
                                             const Date&     original,
                                             const Calendar& calendar);
        // Load, into the specified 'result', the date of the chronologically
        // earliest business day that is on or after the specified 'original'
        // date, unless a date cannot be found in the same month, in which case
        // load the chronologically latest business day before the 'original'
        // date based on the specified 'calendar'.  Return 0 on success, and a
        // non-zero value, without modifying '*result', if the 'original' date
        // is not within the valid range of 'calendar' or a valid business date
        // cannot be found according to the above algorithm within the valid
        // range of 'calendar'.

    // ...
};
// ...
} // close package namespace
// ...
```

(b) Classical "Modified Following" (financial) settlement-day algorithm

Figure 3-166: Nonprimitive operations involving both `Date` and `Calendar`

The result of putting it all together and inserting these utilities back into the design of Figure 3-161, Figure 3-167 depicts a component-class diagram showing the actual Uses-In-The-Interface relationships between the client-facing logical entities rooted in the two components defining `DateUtil` and `CalendarUtil`, respectively. In theory, any component defining a type (e.g., `PackedCalendar`) used in the interface of a type (e.g., `Calendar`) after which a utility is named (e.g., `CalendarUtil`) would be suitable for use in the interface of that utility. In practice, however, there is no useful functionality in a packed calendar that would be appropriate for general clients of `Calendar` objects so that direct Uses-In-The-Interface relationship (between `Calendar` and `PackedCalendar`) is shown (in Figure 3-167) in light gray; see also sections 3.12.11.3 and 3.12.11.4.

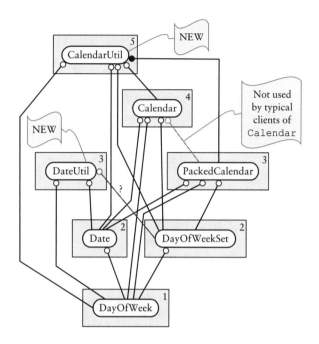

Figure 3-167: Anticipated (imminently useful) utility components

On the other hand, DayOfWeekSet is entirely independent of Date and, hence, would not naturally be considered for use in the interface of DateUtil. Yet, due to its lightweight nature and close semantic relationship to the DayOfWeek::Enum type, we might choose to allow that dependency (tagged in Figure 3-167 with a '?') rather than creating a separate DayOfWeekSet utility. As ever, "there is no substitute for wisdom, judgment, and good taste."[340] Such fine-grained, subjective, client-facing design decisions — in any particular instance — are left to the reader.

Ensuring optimal performance is addressed by providing a highly efficient implementation of a value-semantic Calendar type and also a collaboratively efficient implementation of Date — e.g., in terms of a serial date (discussed below) — suitable for optimizing performance-critical operations such as date difference (see Volume II, section 6.7):

```
int operator-(const Date& lhs, const Date& rhs);
```

It bears repeating that this fine-grained, factored approach allows potentially useful functionality, such as in CalendarUtil, to be deferred in a way that does not require revisiting existing components when the time comes to implement it.

---

[340] Bjarne Stroustrup (c. 1990, personal conversation)

3.12.11   Fleshing Out a Fully Factored Implementation

At this point, we are prepared to declare our initial client-facing design complete. Having given due consideration to current — as well as future — client-focused functionality, we now turn from the client's perspective to consider what sorts of reusable components are needed in order to realize a hierarchically reusable foundation for the implementation of our new date/calendar library subsystem (see Volume II, section 6.4).

3.12.11.1   Implementing a Hierarchically Reusable Date Class

Recall from section 3.2.5 that an important motivation for factoring occurs when distinct clients require different levels of functionality. Some operations on dates make sense on date values even without a Date class. For example, determining whether a given year is a leap year in the traditional Gregorian calendar[341] can be implemented as a small, straightforward function of the year (suitable for inlining), as illustrated in Figure 3-168. This function can be used in the implementation of our Date class, but also separately by clients having just the year (represented as an integer).

```
// grppk_primitivedateutil.h                                          -*-C++-*-
// ...

namespace grppk {
// ...

inline  // static
bool PrimitiveDateUtil::isLeapYear(int year)
{
    assert(0 <= year); assert(year <= 9999);[342]        (See Volume II, sections 5.2 and 6.8.)

    return 0 == year % 4
        && (   year <= 1752
            || year >  1752 && (0 != year % 100 || 0 == year % 400));[343]
}
// ...
}  // close package namespace
// ...
```

Figure 3-168: Determining whether a given (integral) year is a leap year

---

[341] Note that since the design of our original Date class, the industry has moved away from the ANSI-standard Gregorian calendar, having all of its irregular complexities, to the POSIX-standard proleptic Gregorian calendar, which treats all blocks of 400 years the same as those from 2000/01/01 .. 2399/12/31. Converting from Gregorian to proleptic Gregorian has almost no effect on dates in the modern era, except that the number of days since 0001/01/01 goes down by two, which can lead to inconsistencies in programs that explicitly take this difference, e.g., using the (free) operator- for Date objects that attempt to represent values in the premodern era (i.e., prior to September 14, 1752).

Other widely used functionality — such as determining whether a given year/month/day combination represents a valid date in this same calendar system — can also be factored out, tested, and used directly without necessarily pulling in the definition and concomitant dependencies of a value-semantic date type. That is, the component that implements the `Date` class can make use of (section 1.9), and (therefore) depend on (section 1.8), this lower-level basic functionality, but clients that need this low-level functionality, yet have no need for our value-semantic `Date` class, are not forced to depend on it.[344]

3.12.11.2   Representing Value in the `Date` Class

Precisely how our `Date` class represents its value internally, while having no effect on semantics (see Volume II, section 5.2), will affect various aspects of its performance, as well as the kinds of functionality we will need in order to implement it. Our `Date` class supports the year/month/day format in its interface, and could naturally be implemented internally using three

---

[342] This function returns `true` if the specified year is a leap year according to the Gregorian calendar (as implemented by the `cal` command on most traditional Unix systems). The behavior is undefined unless the year falls within the range [1 ... 9999]. The asserts are there to defend (if so desired) against client misuse (see Volume II, sections 5.2 and 6.8). Note that splitting two asserts to form a range check is one of the very few cases where, in our opinion, placing two statements on a single line is both appropriate and beneficial as together they represent a range.

[343] As is our habit, we would rewrite the above to a more optimal form:

```
return 0 == year % 4
    && (year <= 1752 || 0 != year % 100 || 0 == year % 400)
```

Note that

```
!A || A && B
```

and

```
!A || B
```

represent the same boolean-valued function of A and B. We are inclined toward such tight code — even if a compiler would typically be able to achieve the same result in an unoptimized mode — partly because we are perfectionists, but also because of the exceptionally thorough component-level test drivers that are omnipresent in our component-based development methodology (see Volume III).

[344] Generally speaking, given a *value type* named `Foo`, a *utility* `struct` that uses `Foo` in its interface would be named `FooUtil` while a utility used in the implementation of `Foo` would be named `FooImpUtil`, with the name `FooImp` reserved for an intermediate instantiable implementation class (see Volume II, section 6.4).

separate integral fields, as shown in Figure 3-169a.[345] Yet, in order to optimize certain kinds of primitive operations, including those performed by (members)

```
Date& operator++();
DayOfWeek::Enum dayOfWeek() const;
```

and (free)

```
int operator-(const Date&, const Date&);
```

(i.e., returning the [signed] number of *actual* days between two given dates), a serial-date representation can be employed internally, as shown in Figure 3-169b.

```
class Date {
    short  int  d_year;
    signed char d_month;
    signed char d_day;

  public:

    // ...

};
```

```
class Date {
    int d_serialDate;

  public:

    // ...

};
```

(a) Separate-fields implementation   (b) Serial-date implementation

Figure 3-169: Alternative implementation strategies for class `Date`

If we decide to go the serial-date route, we will need efficient routines to convert to and from the serial representation. If, on the other hand, we were to choose to represent our date internally using three separate fields, no serial conversion routines would be needed; however, other primitive date functionality, such as efficiently adjusting a valid year/month/day representation to the next or previous one, or calculating the day-of-week, given separate year, month, and day integral values, would be needed instead.

When developing a fully factored solution to a given business need there will be both essential functionality that must be implemented now and also related functionality that can be deferred to a later project. Deferring unnecessary development mitigates some of the high initial cost of creating fully factored software. Assuming we choose a *serial*-date implementation, we can defer creating primitive functionality that operates directly on a year/month/day representation; we will then, however, require the conversion routines immediately.

---

[345] Note that the data members are sized to hold the independently maximum values of year, month, and day, 0001/01/01 ≤ date ≤ 9999/12/31, as delineated by the invariants of the contract for `Date` above (see Figure 3-152, section 3.12.3).

Consistent with our overall methodology, we want our publicly available conversion routines to admit: (1) *hierarchical* reuse (section 0.4), and also (2) direct (component-level) testing (see Volume III, section 7.3). One expedient, yet inferior, way to expose this conversion functionality would be as public `static` methods of `Date` itself. Sound logical design principles, however, are sufficient to discourage us from taking this shortcut. For starters, the level of abstraction of these serial date conversion routines is significantly lower than for a value-semantic `Date` class. Clients of `Date` will rarely require these conversions, and their presence in that interface would add unnecessary clutter, making `Date` harder to understand and use for its intended audience. Placing this functionality, instead, in a separate utility (Figure 3-170) forms a natural intermediate interface — a logical firewall — behind which we can isolate and test independent low-level design decisions (section 0.7).

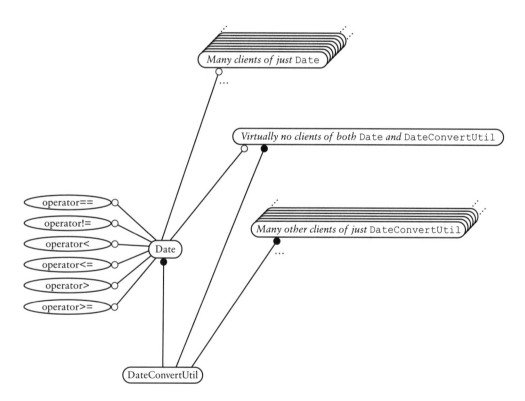

Figure 3-170: Logical design and usage of `Date` and `DateConvertUtil`

Our preferred, albeit less straightforward, implementation choice for `Date` — i.e., that of employing a serial-date representation to optimize key operations — is the inspiration for `DateConvertUtil`. The `DateConvertUtil struct` provides a suite of `static` methods that convert between the three most common date formats — serial date, year/month/day, and year/day-of-year — when represented in terms of separate integral fields.[346] Its functionality is well-defined, stable, and generally applicable even to clients who might not need a `Date` object.

Given that the appropriate logical design consists of two separate classes (a `class` and a utility `struct`) and a handful of free operators on class `Date`, the question now becomes how best to collect these logical constructs into their respective physical containers (i.e., components). Figure 3-171 shows the only two plausible componentization alternatives: (a) the definitions for both logical types reside in the same component, or (b) each of these C++ types is defined in its own separate component.

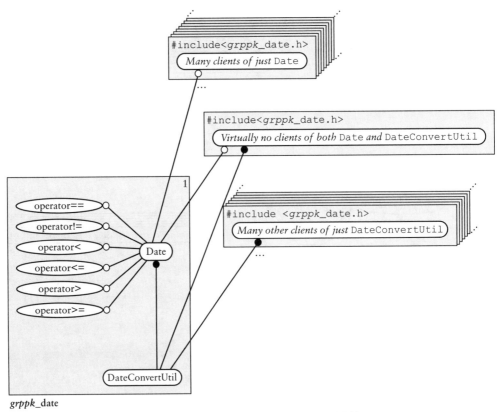

(a) Both classes in the same component (BAD IDEA)

---

[346] Incorporating year/day-of-year conversions requires relatively little extra work as it is already an intermediate form in the implementation; in this kind of situation, the marginal effort to craft and implement a complete interface right from the start, in such cases, is almost always the best decision in the long run, provided that at least some potential clients are likely to benefit eventually.

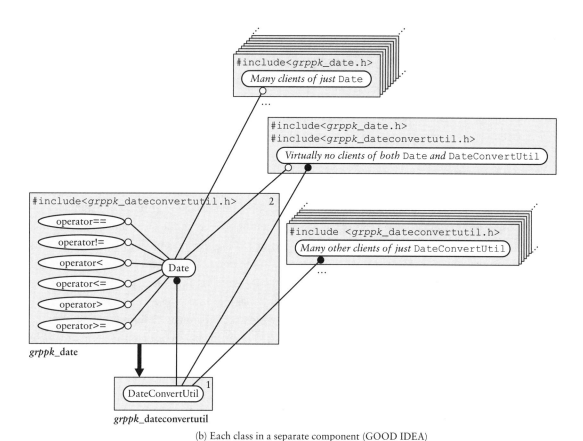

(b) Each class in a separate component (GOOD IDEA)

Figure 3-171: Two modularizations for `Date` and `DateConvertUtil`

Again, recall (section 3.5.6) that segregating functionality having distinct clients and/or participation levels was recommended as a useful criterion for modularization. Whether we place these classes in one component or two will have no effect on logical behavior. The amount of functionality in either class is not overwhelming and, given that all of this functionality is very closely related (at least from an implementation perspective), it might seem quite reasonable to put it all in a single component (Figure 3-171a). Yet doing so would make the system less flexible by eliminating potentially valuable future design alternatives. As we are about to understand in detail, preferring (up front) the finer physical granularity resulting from separate components (Figure 3-171b) in these sorts of situations is generally the superior choice.

Semantic cohesion alone rarely justifies the physical coupling that results from colocating classes in the same component (section 3.3.1.3). In the case of Figure 3-171a, however, there is no semantic cohesion: The physical colocation is at best an implementation expedient — nothing more. With just a single component, clients of only `DateConvertUtil` would be forced to drag in extra code pertaining to `Date`. Any changes pertaining to just the `Date` type in the component header would nonetheless force clients of `DateConvertUtil` to recompile. Clients of either `Date` or `DateConvertUtil` would still be forced to skip over substantial documentation delineating functionality that they probably do not care about (in much the same vein as what we wanted to avoid by not placing the static conversion methods within class `Date` itself).

Let's now consider the potential stability of our subsystem in the long run. For example, suppose it turns out that incrementing the date and getting the day of the week are not as common and time-sensitive as they used to be, and that extracting the year-month-day information is the critical, high-performance moneymaker! At some point, a decision is made to change the fully encapsulated, internal representation of `Date` from its (original) serial-date format to a (new) discrete year-month-day format, thereby making `Date`'s use of `DateConvertUtil` obsolete.[347] The utility class, `DateYmdUtil` (which we previously deferred), would now be needed to perform the needed operations efficiently on dates represented in terms of three distinct integer fields. Figure 3-172 shows how minor deficiencies resulting from a suboptimal initial implementation choice are compounded by having the (publicly accessible) implementation `struct` reside (physically) in the same component as `Date`, leading to poor physical modularity as otherwise encapsulated, entirely private logical details change over time.

---

[347] See Volume II, section 6.7, for another implementation approach (using table lookup) that achieves exceptionally high performance (over a relatively small but heavily trafficked subrange) for both kinds of usage patterns simultaneously.

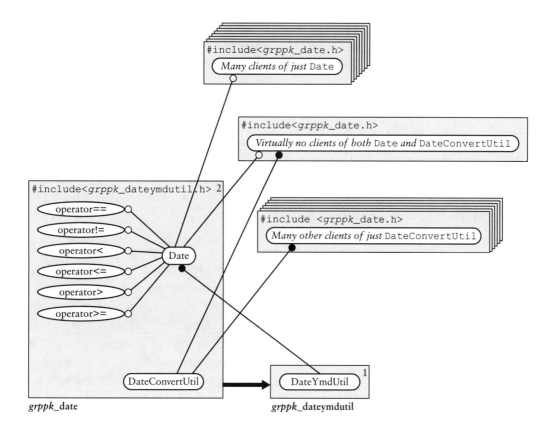

Figure 3-172: Poor modularity resulting from a poor initial design choice

Assuming both logical entities are colocated in the ***grppk*_date** component, the `DateConvertUtil` `struct` cannot simply be removed from the component implementing `Date` because of the many clients that access `DateConvertUtil` via direct inclusion of the component implementing `Date`:

```
#include <grppk_date.h>
```

Clients of `Date` continue to pay (e.g., in link time and executable size) for supporting both utility `struct` implementations. Moreover, clients of `DateConvertUtil` — in addition to paying for `Date` — now also pay for `DateYmdUtil`! On the other hand, isolating `Date` and `DateConvertUtil` within their own, separate components *from the start* avoids all of the problems described here. By giving `DateConvertUtil` its own separate header, we have in effect encapsulated its use (see Figure 3-140, section 3.11.2), thereby escalating its "encapsulation" (section 3.5.10) to that of the component defining `Date`. Finally, colocating the operators that operate on `Date` in the same component that defines `Date` is not only consistent with the fourth guideline for proper colocation (section 3.3.1.4), it is also explicitly required by our component design rules (section 2.6). In short, the logical/physical packaging of Figure 3-171b is the proper choice here.

Stepping back, we observe that there are aspects of the implementation of our value-semantic date type, such as `isLeapYear`, that will be needed irrespective of our data-member representation. We might well choose to place such basic implementation functionality in its own separate lower-level component, e.g., `PrimitiveDateUtil`. Hence, we have identified two (immediately needed) "implementation" utilities (`PrimitiveDateUtil` and `DateConvertUtil`), an enumeration `struct` (`DayOfWeek`), and an important *vocabulary* (see Volume II, section 4.4) class (`Date`). Given that our `Date` class and `DayOfWeek::Enum` enumeration are both value-semantic types (see Volume II, section 4.3), certain basic facilities such as one that enables streaming will be needed. Again, we have assumed that the concept of BDEX streaming, i.e., providing the needed externalization functionality, already exists and is available (see Volume II, section 4.1). The component-class diagram depicting our burgeoning hierarchically reusable implementation components is illustrated in Figure 3-173.

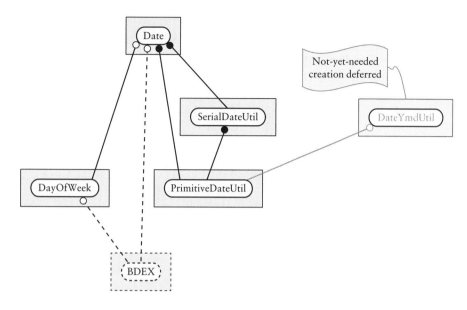

Figure 3-173: Value-semantic `Date` class with `DayOfWeek` `enum` subsystem

Note that direct clients of `Date`, such as `DateParserUtil`, will use the static `isValidYearMonthDay` method of the `Date` class (which would be `inline` forwarded to call the corresponding functions in `PrimitiveDateUtil`) in order to validate a date value *before* population occurs. This validation functionality — being intimately tied to the invariants of the `Date` class itself — serves all populators (including direct clients of `Date`) and therefore is properly "republished" as a `static` method of the `Date` class (within the component defining `Date`).[348]

3.12.11.3   Implementing a Hierarchically Reusable `Calendar` Class

Recall that our objective in creating `Calendar` is to create a type that is suitable for general efficient use. Although a `PackedCalendar`, by design, represents the same *value* as a `Calendar`,[349] a `PackedCalendar` cannot deliver the performance required for high-volume settlement-day calculations involving algorithms such as *Modified Following* (see Figure 3-166b, section 3.12.10). For these operations, we will require functions such as

---

[348] Note that `std::chrono` — available as of C++11 — is intended to solve many of the same problems as `bdlt::Time`, and in similar ways, but follows a different interface design philosophy compared to **bdlt**. Note that, as of C++20, `std::chrono` supports dates as well as times, complete with time-zone support. Prior to C++20, however, we had only time support (and clocks) at varying granularities.

[349] I.e., we can convert between the two with no loss of *salient* information (see Volume II, section 4.1).

isBusinessDay[350] to be as fast as possible. Experience shows that compact, table-based solutions are often the most efficient (see Volume II, section 6.7), and so we employ that approach here in the form of a value-semantic `BitArray` that caches the business days in a compact (i.e., 8 days per byte) tabular form yet suitable for ultra-efficient lookup.[351,352] With this implementation, determining whether a given (serial) date *is* a business day involves only three `inline` methods. The first method simply inverts the logical sense of the question before forwarding to the second:

```
inline
bool Calendar::isBusinessDay(const bdlt::Date& date) const
{
    return !isNonBusinessDay(date);
}
```

The second method, the one more likely to be called from within a tight loop, determines the date offset from the start of the calendar before forwarding that to its (private) nested `BitArray` object.

```
inline
bool Calendar::isNonBusinessDay(const bdlt::Date& date) const
{
    return d_bitArray[date - d_startDate];  // Stored in terms of
}                                           // "negative logic".
```

The third method, part of `BitArray` itself, calculates and returns the boolean value at the supplied *offset* index:

```
inline
bool BitArray::operator[](std::size_t index) const
{
    const std::size_t WORD_SIZE = sizeof *d_words_p;  // 'constexpr'
    return d_words_p[index / WORD_SIZE] & (1 << index % WORD_SIZE);
}
```

---

[350] It turns out that the operation that requires the maximum optimization in practice is `isNonBusinessDay`.

[351] The implementation-defined nature of the performance characteristics of `std::vector<bool>` immediately disqualifies it from being an option here. What's more, critical operations, such as AND-ing and OR-ing entire arrays, cannot be implemented efficiently, given its public interface.

[352] `std::bitset` is, of course, also available, but fails to provide the dynamic (runtime) resizing needed.

That is, determining that a given date is *not* a business day can be accomplished by one division operation, one array dereference, one mod operation,[353] one shift operation, one bitwise integer `and` operation, and one implicit integer-to-boolean conversion, or roughly as many assembly instructions and, on modern architectures, considerably fewer clock cycles due to aggressive parallelism (e.g., pipelining and concurrent execution of these instructions). This heightened runtime efficiency comes at a cost in terms of object size: A `BitArray` sufficient for representing each day in, say, a 30-year calendar alone would consume roughly $30 \cdot 365.25 / 8 = 1370$ bytes — almost twice as much as what will be needed for just the equivalent compact `PackedCalendar` representation (see section 3.12.11.4).

The effort needed to implement an efficient, general-purpose `BitArray` is surprisingly larger than many might first expect. In order to implement efficient set operations (e.g., AND, OR, XOR, and SUB), we will want to perform these operations by explicitly exploiting maximal parallelism in the underlying hardware. That is, we will want to use (for the purposes of data transfer) an integer — or perhaps an even larger, user-defined data type (see Volume II, section 6.7) — whose size is at least that of the data path in the underlying hardware (e.g., 256 bits).

When we consider that we might reasonably want to apply subranges of one `BitArray` to arbitrary offsets in another, achieving optimal performance will require different algorithms depending on whether the physical alignment of the bits in corresponding words in the source operand are (1) below, (2) the same as, or (3) above those in the destination operand. Moreover, the case where the starting and ending bits are in the same word (for both the source and the destination) will probably need to be treated as a special case of the general algorithm where the starting and ending bits are in separate words (separated by zero or more whole words). The point here is that writing an efficient `BitArray` — though very valuable — is non-trivial, which is precisely why we should do it and do it right, once and for all.

In order to implement efficient subset operations for `BitArray`, we will also need to perform efficient mask operations on individual words. Such functionality is itself eminently reusable and worthy of a separate utility, `BitUtil`, residing in its own component. Through the use of static tables,[354] we can synthesize masks that cover an arbitrary contiguous subsequence of bits in a machine word by AND-ing the result of two look-ups in *insulated* static arrays

---

[353] Note that the (integer) *division* and *mod* operations have constant divisors that are powers of 2, so they will get *strength-reduced* to trivial *bit-shifting* and *masking* operations, respectively.

[354] On some architectures, generating such masks "on the fly" with a small number of bitwise operations might prove more efficient even than referencing static arrays that might not be resident in cache; isolating this logic in `BitUtil` allows for easy microbenchmarking of different implementation strategies.

(see Volume II, section 6.6). `BitUtil` would also provide many other low-level operations —
e.g., counting the number of 1-bits in a word. By factoring out as much functionality as possible
(see Volume II, section 6.4), we improve our ability to test, if not to reuse. As it turns out, the
`BitUtil` facility might well prove useful (not shown here) in implementing the functionality of
the `DayOfWeekSet` as well.

Often the need for further factoring presents itself only after initial attempts at implementation are well underway. Such might arguably be the case here with the intermediate utility
`struct BitStringUtil`. A `BitArray` is a value-semantic type that both represents a value
(i.e., a sequence of boolean values of arbitrary length) and also provides several useful operations on objects of that type. `BitUtil`, on the other hand, is a very low-level utility `struct`
that performs complex bitwise operations, such as `numBitsSet`[355] (a.k.a. *population count*) that
returns the number of 1-bits in a single machine word.

Between those two levels of logical abstraction, however, exists an enormous chasm of intricate
functionality involving operations on contiguous strings of binary words that is both worthy
of direct testing and also eminently reusable in other data structures and value-semantic types.
By further factoring the mechanisms used to define the operations provided so cleanly for retail
use by `BitArray`, we improve both the quality of our implementation and the opportunities
for hierarchical reuse.

Given the fundamental importance and ubiquitous use of a memory allocation protocol and a
designated default allocator mechanism (see Volume II, section 4.10), we have assumed that
they already exist in a package called **bslma** (BDE Standard Library Memory Allocators). All
generally reusable objects that make use of dynamic memory that persists between primitive
operations on the object will depend on this package. Note that all of these reusable value types
(see Volume II, section 4.1) also "depend" (at least conceptually) on **bslx** for externalization.
Those types, such as `Calendar`, `PackedCalendar`, and `BitArray`, that represent a value
and require dynamic memory allocation naturally depend[356] on both facilities. The component-class diagram depicting `Calendar`, along with its interface dependencies and any new
non-*client-facing* components (darker gray) that will be needed for this implementation only
(but not for long) are illustrated in Figure 3-174.

---

[355] See Volume III, sections 8.3 and 8.4, for a thorough discussion on how to test various implementations of this and
other similar functions.

[356] Understand that, because of the concept-based nature of the BDEX facility, the dependency on it (as depicted
here) is only collaborative, not physical.

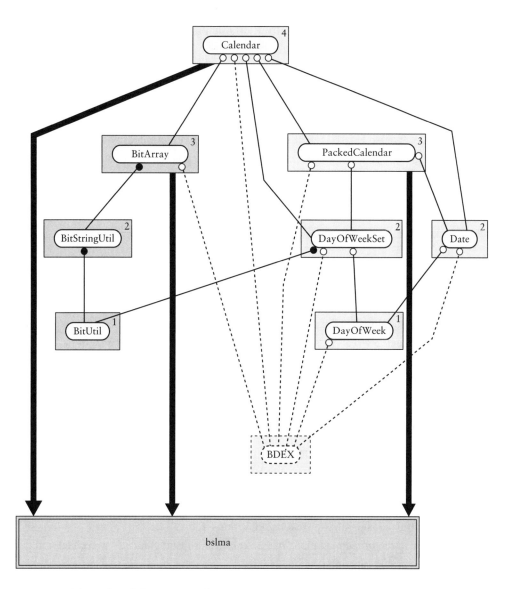

Figure 3-174: Implementation dependencies of the `calendar` component

3.12.11.4   Implementing a Hierarchically Reusable `PackedCalendar` Class

The purpose of a `PackedCalendar` is to represent all of the needed calendar data as compactly as practicable and, ideally, still provide all of the same services as an object of class `Calendar`, albeit much more slowly, in many important cases. In practice, we know that a typical calendar — e.g., one for valuing thirty-year bonds — will span a sequence of contiguous days whose length is well within what can be represented by a two-byte unsigned integer (65,535 days or about 179.3 years). Given that we can realize substantial savings for representing holidays when the range of a calendar in days can be indexed (from its start date) by an unsigned `char` or `short` integer, rather than a full `int`, it makes sense to create a potentially reusable `PackedIntArray`, that, for example, adapts its internal element size based on the magnitude of the maximum unsigned integer value it contains.[357]

A packed 30-year calendar (spanning just under eleven thousand days) having about one holiday per month can be represented with a couple of integers (identifying the range), a (one-byte) `DayOfWeekSet`, and an array of about $30 \cdot 12 = 360$ short (2-byte) integers, for a total of roughly 0.75K bytes on most platforms. Hence, we can expect the storage requirements of a typical 30-year (high-speed) `Calendar` object, which contains a `PackedCalendar` (~750 bytes) and also a `BitArray` (~1400 bytes), to be on the order of 2150 bytes (or just over 2K bytes) total. Note that, unless we take care to limit the amount of allocated memory explicitly, the number of bytes allocated for both a `PackedCalendar` and a `Calendar` could be as much as nearly twice the number of bytes actually needed (used).

As is typically the case for space-efficient (but otherwise general-purpose) data types, such as `BitArray` (section 3.12.11.3), that cannot provide direct C++ references to their individual elements, `PackedIntArray` inherently does not conform to the requirements of an STL-style standard container, and therefore does not play well with standard algorithms. After more thoughtful consideration, custom algorithms for `PackedIntArray` — initially embedded directly in the implementations of `PackedCalendar` methods — were factored out into separately reusable functions.

---

[357] Just as this section was being reviewed for submission (October 2017), the need for another kind of space-efficient vector-like data structure — this one optimized for representing sequences of highly repetitive values — was identified for use in a proposed new "time table" component that maps `Datetime` values to "transition codes" (state-transition IDs), e.g., to store trading schedules for financial exchanges. The proposed implementation for this new component was to employ the Flyweight pattern (see **gamma94**, Chapter 4, section "Flyweight," pp. 195–206) using two vectors: the first to hold the set of unique exemplars, and the second to represent the sequence of non-negative integers referencing those exemplars via unsigned offsets into the first vector. Given the nature of the vector of offsets, however, the `PackedIntArray` is never less space efficient than `std::vector<std::size_t>` and superior in the expected case — e.g., when the number of exemplars does not exceed 2^8 (or even 2^{16}) — and especially when the length of the sequence would dominate the overall storage requirements.

As a result, we decided to introduce a new utility `struct`, `PackedIntArrayUtil`, providing generally useful integer-array operations, such as `isSorted`, `lowerBound`, and `upperBound`, implemented in terms of the (intimately associated) `PackedIntArrayConstIterator` type (not shown). Due to its inherent need for friendship, this iterator type is necessarily defined in the same component as its "befriender," `PackedIntArray` (section 3.3.1.1). It is precisely these kinds of carefully crafted, high-performance data types that require the scrupulous test-data–selection methods proposed in the third volume of this book (e.g., see Volume III, Chapter 8).

The immediately essential subsystem resulting from the design of just `PackedCalendar` — including its dependencies on implementation-only components (darker gray) — is illustrated in Figure 3-175.

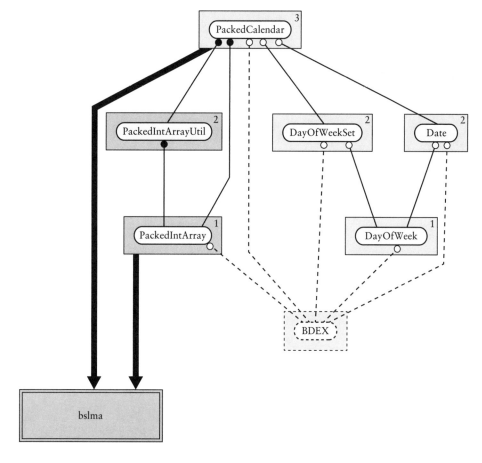

Figure 3-175: Components/packages needed just to create a `PackedCalendar`

3.12.11.5   Distribution Across Existing Aggregates

Now that we understand the principal classes that make up the system, we will need to make sure that we aggregate our components appropriately (sections 2.2, 2.9, 2.10, and 3.1.4). Some of the very low-level types and facilities discussed here, such as `bslma::Allocator` and the BDEX concept, are widely used, and presumed to exist in the lowest-level package group, **bsl**. Much of the newly designed infrastructure (e.g., `Date` and `Calendar`) is basic, reusable, and could easily belong to a single package (e.g., **bdlt**) in a slightly higher-level package group, **bdl**, which depends directly on **bsl**. Other components, such as those implementing more application-specific functionality (e.g., our `MyDatabaseCalendarLoader`) clearly do not belong in the same UOR as the more generally useful components, and in fact properly reside at a much higher level — nearer to (or along with) the applications that use them. A summary diagram emphasizing all the relevant aspects of what was discussed in this section is provided in Figure 3-176.[358]

---

[358] For a comprehensive overview of the material leading up to the design depicted in his figure, see **lakos13**; a discussion of this specific problem begins at 1:33:18.

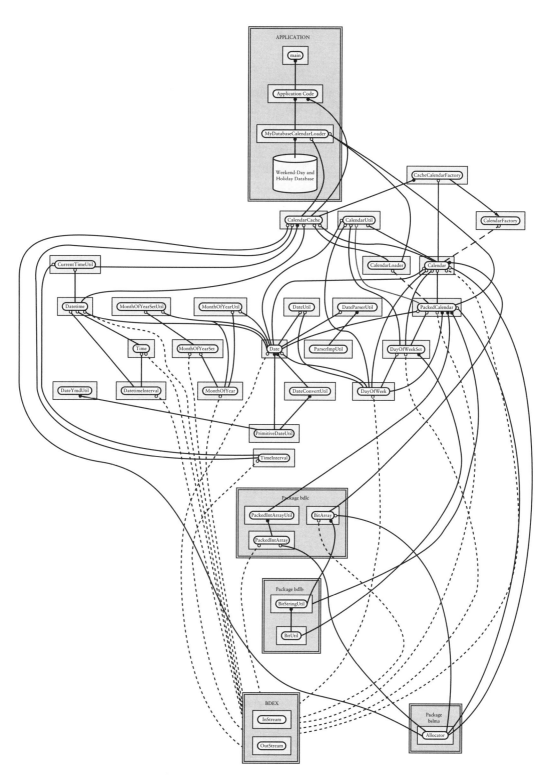

Figure 3-176: Elided view emphasizing just our date/calendar subsystem

When showing complex component diagrams involving more than just a handful of components, it is common (in order to reduce clutter resulting from overlapping dependency arrows) to elide actual direct dependencies that, if removed, would not affect the levelization of the graph depicting the overall design. Such elision is more generally known as *transitive reduction* (see Figure 1-59, section 1.8). For example, consider the subsystem (Figure 3-177a) headed by a Date class that uses DayOfWeek in its interface, and both DateConvertUtil and Assert in its implementation. The Assert "class,"[359] shown here at level 1 (section 1.10), is also used directly by both DayOfWeek and DateConvertUtil; hence, each of these structs is at level 2, and class Date is at level 3. Although there happens to be a Uses-In-The-Implementation relation (section 1.7.2) between Date and Assert, which implies (section 1.9) an actual direct physical dependency (section 1.8) between their respective components, that dependency is also implied (transitively) by both

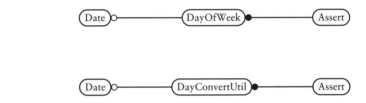

and

So by removing the explicit direct dependency implied by

as in Figure 3-177b, we reduce the number of edges, yet do not affect the level numbers of the nodes in the overall graph.

---

[359] We are using "class" Assert here to represent our widely used **bsls_assert** component (**bde14**, subdirectory /groups/bdl/bdlt/), which provides a general (macro-based) facility for implementing compile-time-configurable defensive checks (see Volume II, section 6.8) — as in *Defensive Programming for narrow contracts* (see Volume II, Chapter 5) — to ensure at run time that arguments, supplied by the client, are at least consistent with the preconditions (see Volume II, section 5.2) of each library function for which such checks are enabled.

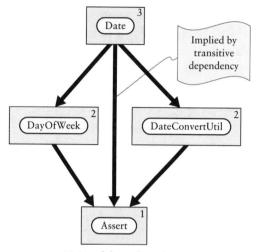

(a) Actual direct dependencies

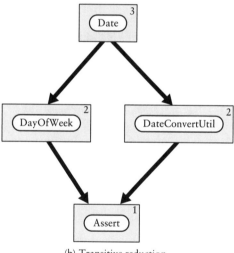

(b) Transitive reduction

Figure 3-177: Eliding direct dependencies implied by transitivity

The transitive reduction of the complete dependency graph used to implement `bdlt::CalendarCache` — resulting from many years of application of our, now proven, component-based methodology — is provided for reference in Figure 3-178.[360] If we had been asked to do all of this work from scratch for this project, it likely wouldn't have been possible. Fortunately, we did not have to, and, the next time we approach a new development task, we won't need to re-create the well-honed parts of this hierarchically reusable subsystem. By carefully aggregating only widely reusable components that have no undue or heavyweight dependencies, and implementing more domain-specific functionality (e.g., the **bbldc** package) in (physically) separate UORs, we incrementally begin to achieve what will soon become our hierarchically reusable infrastructure — i.e., our Software Capital (section 0.9).

---

[360] This design was extracted from the actual BDE open-source library distribution (**bde14**) and rendered in March 2019, by Steven Breitstein and Clay Wilson of the BDE team at Bloomberg LP.

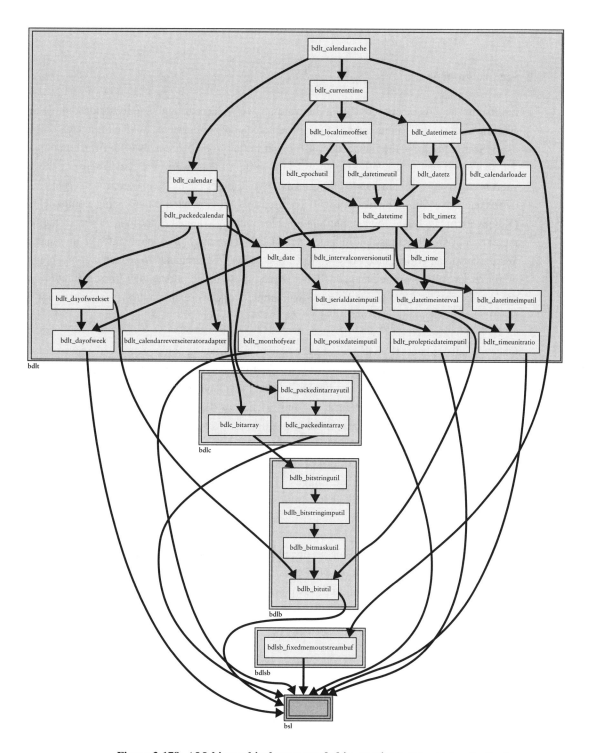

Figure 3-178: *ALL* hierarchical reuse needed in creating `bdlt::CalendarCache`

3.12.12 Section Summary

In this final section of new content in this volume, we walked through a real-world example of creating a substantial, hierarchically reusable date/calendar subsystem suitable for a wide range of applications, e.g., in the financial industry. Our initial "specification" was far from complete, and so we first set out to synthesize what the true requirements were, and also to separate those valid needs from any ham-handed design advice that might have come along for the ride. We then sketched a fine-grained (physical) hierarchy of our intended client-facing components (along with most of their logical interrelationships) that satisfied all of the client's stated (legitimate) needs as well as those additional urgent ones that we might reasonably infer or anticipate. We also made an effort to look beyond the initial project requirements to see what components might reasonably be needed and added, but wisely chose not to pursue their implementation in the initial effort, as there would be more than ample work in creating a proper implementation for just what was immediately needed.

Once we satisfied ourselves that all of the essential client-facing components were represented, we turned our attention to considering what sort of missing hierarchically reusable implementation infrastructure was needed, what was already available, and — most critically — what was not! We then proceeded to flesh out and extend our design to include a full hierarchy of well-factored, highly performant "implementation-only" subcomponents that are designed with an eye toward maximizing their own potential future reuse (see Volume II, section 5.7), but without regard for their absolute placement within our growing repository of Software Capital (section 0.9). Finally, we suggested how we might distribute these components across the packages and UORs that comprise our ever-growing, enterprise-wide software infrastructure.

As is typical, the final rendering we produced looked nothing like the one the client suggested initially; instead, it was much more well-considered, robust, testable, usable, and — of course — *hierarchically reusable* in future development efforts.

3.13   Summary

Developing software on a large scale requires knowledge of both logical and physical design. In order to achieve our goal of fine-grained factoring, however, our knowledge of each of these two dimensions of design must be applied simultaneously and synergistically. In this chapter, we have focused on physical design strategies that result in fundamentally superior software structure, as well as specific *levelization* and *insulation* techniques to facilitate its creation.

With this essential information in hand, we are now prepared to address the unbounded logical design issues that we will face throughout our software-development careers (see Volume II).

3.1 Thinking Physically

Classical software design has, historically, been *logical* design. In our component-based methodology, however, physical design provides a dimension of structure and of direction — both vertical and lateral — that gives meaning to the notion of the relative position of components. Thoughtful use of physical design techniques, such as transposing the relative physical positions of interface and implementation, for example, can lead to more flexible and stable (e.g., *lateral*) designs.

Determining precisely what our needed logical functionality must do remains essential. However, determining how that functionality should be distributed across our enterprise-wide libraries is also critically important if we are to be able even to find it, let alone maximize its usefulness. Effective high-level design strategies, phrased in terms of packages and package groups (Chapter 2), help us avoid many of the organizational problems that commonly plague ongoing large-scale development efforts.

Both semantic cohesion and physical dependencies will play important roles when determining optimal physical location. Such optimality does not happen by chance, and far too rarely by design. Hence, every library developer must be accountable, not just for the exciting new functionality he or she implements, but also for how it is successfully incorporated into the packages and package groups that make up our repository of Software Capital (section 0.9). Ubiquitous use of package prefixes and corresponding (coherent) namespaces serve as constant reminders that, ultimately, the absolute location of library functionality simply cannot be ignored.

Our physical design rules (section 2.6) impose constraints that govern the kinds of logical designs that are possible. The strategies we use to render our software, subject to these rules, derive from substantive and enduring architectural and semantic properties, rather than superficial and syntactic ones. Among the most important of rules is the imperative proscribing any sort of cyclic physical dependency across physical boundaries. Cyclic physical designs must always be reworked to yield an acyclic physical dependency graph. Anything less quickly leads to chaos and madness.

How logical content requiring private access is best aggregated is also strongly influenced by the design imperative proscribing long-distance friendship. In particular, the scope of encapsulated low-level design decisions is strictly limited to a single component. Given that a component's size is bounded by our ability to test it, there are fairly hard limits on how much logical content a single component can contain (see Volume III, section 7.5). Multicomponent wrappers are generally not feasible. Attempting to share private implementation details across an unbounded number of classes is precluded by our methodology: Such designs must be reworked to be more modular — both logically and physically.

3.2 Avoiding Poor Physical Modularity

It has been said that the road to hell is paved with good intentions. Yet, failing — for whatever reason — to apply appropriate modularization criteria to our components can easily lead to horribly suboptimal designs that are unnecessarily difficult to understand, use, and maintain. It is therefore essential that we employ substantial and meaningful criteria for modularization, such as semantics and physical dependencies, rather than superficial ones (e.g., based on language syntax).

Early on, for example, we sometimes naively used a `t` suffix (e.g., **bdet**) to indicate a package consisting entirely of value-semantic types and a `tu` suffix (e.g., **bdetu**) to indicate a package consisting exclusively of *utility* components (i.e., containing nonprimitive functionality implemented as `static` methods of a `struct` that operated on the value types defined in correspondingly named components in the **bdet** package). That turned out to be a bad idea because it (1) made useful functionality hard to discover by clients and (2) prevented other value-semantic types in **bdet** from depending on the nonprimitive functionality in **bdetu** (lest we violate package levelization).

Given that C++ is not just an object-oriented language but rather a *multiparadigm* one, it generally does not make sense to artificially restrict the kinds of logical constructs that can go into a component for a particular package. Instead, we should use whichever logical constructs are the most appropriate to productively render coherent semantic content in each component of every package, colocated based on other, more substantial logical and physical criteria.

The purpose of every component should have a narrow focus. Within that focus, the component should be *sufficient* to address the needs of most any client with respect to its intended purpose. Designed properly, according to the *open-closed principal* (section 0.5), a truly *complete* component will allow for almost arbitrary extension (i.e., via additional nonprimitive functionality) without having to modify the source code of the component itself.

Avoiding excessive functionality that is not strictly needed by the majority of clients is also an important aspect of fine-grained reusable components. In order to ensure that components are easy to understand, we generally want them to be *minimal*. That is, functions supplied within the component will ideally be uniquely useful rather than providing multiple equivalent ways of accomplishing the same task.

In order to ensure stability and scalability, we want the functionality implemented within a component that defines an instantiable type to be primitive. By *primitive*, we mean functionality that cannot be implemented efficiently without private access to the implementation (internal representation) of the type upon which it operates. Functionality that can be implemented efficiently outside of the component — i.e., in terms of other primitive functions — is not considered primitive. Refactoring a component to contain only *primitive* functionality reduces clutter and improves stability. Providing a complete (but minimal) set of primitive functions enables additional functions to be written efficiently without perturbing the component *a la* the open-closed principal. Except for free operators and operator-like *aspect* functions, such as `swap`, essentially all nonprimitive functionality should be escalated to a "utility" `struct` in a separate component — sometimes in a separate package (or UOR). Hence, when writing reusable components, we strive to create interfaces that are at once complete, minimal, and primitive.

Modularity is an essential aspect of good design. Poor physical modularity can take many forms. At an architectural level, poor modularity reflects the absence of a global, long-term strategy. Absent a centralized repository, carefully curated and maintained by an autonomous core team (section 0.10), application developers will be hard-pressed to avoid embedding highly reusable functionality within their own application source. This *absence* of architectural modularity inevitably leads to ill-conceived (unstable) inter-application dependencies, rampant cut-and-paste, and repeated reinvention.

Even within a single UOR, there are many forms of poor physical factoring. Putting all of the enumerations in one package and all of the classes in another is an extreme example of poor physical modularization. Another example — almost as bad — is to colocate lightweight reusable classes (e.g., `Stapler`) in the same physical module (i.e., component) as a much more heavyweight object (e.g., `Table`). The use of physical dependency as a criterion for logical factoring to achieve sound physical modularity and effective reuse is therefore a staple of sound modular design.

When new, appropriate functionality is needed that cannot be implemented in terms of existing primitive functionality, rather than writing a new member function addressing only that one specific need, an effort should be made to implement the *essence* of what would have been needed in order to implement that new functionality without having had to modify the underlying object's source code, thereby enabling additional new similar functionality to be added thusly in the future. By consistently designing (and refining) sufficient, complete, and minimal interfaces, and escalating any nonessential functionality to higher levels within our fine-grained, physical hierarchy, we minimize complexity, enhance stability, and generally promote effective reuse.

3.3 Grouping Things Physically That Belong Together Logically

By default, our desire for fine-grained factoring will encourage us to place each publicly accessible class or `struct` within its own separate component. Sometimes, however, it is necessary to place more than one such top-level logical entity within the same physical module. There are four situations in which colocation is indicated (see Figure 3-20, section 3.3.1): (1) friendship is required, (2) cyclic dependencies would result, (3) "peer" entities (each typically small) that only together comprise a useful *whole*, or (4) a tiny class (e.g., a `ScopedGuard`) or function (e.g., `operator==`) that (a) adds no additional dependencies, (b) depends on a heavyweight class (e.g., a logger) in the same component, and (c) is an essential part of common usage for that component. These four criteria for colocation of public classes are delineated in greater detail in Figure 3-179.

---

(1)   FRIENDSHIP: The goal of modularity must be to isolate each individual low-level design choice within a single module (i.e., component). The design rule (section 2.6) forbidding private access to span component boundaries helps to reinforce this fine-grained approach to modularity. As long as we do not violate its contract, a change to the implementation of one component should never require a corresponding change to another, but see the package-wide "hack" — described at the end of section 3.5.10 — used when *escalating encapsulation* for an entire package in order to simulate a multi-component wrapper. A container and its iterator(s), or a (derived) concrete factory and its widget(s), are common examples of the need for colocation due to friendship. Ensuring that logical encapsulation does not span component boundaries is by far the most common valid reason for colocation of classes.

(2)   IMPLIED CYCLIC PHYSICAL DEPENDENCY: Far less common is the legitimate need for two classes to collaborate in ways that would force a physical dependency were the two classes to be packaged separately. Note, however, that in almost all cases, the cycle is gratuitous and can easily be eliminated through thoughtful design, perhaps employing one or more of the levelization techniques presented in section 3.5. Again, the primary reason for colocation is avoiding inter-component friendships.

(3)   SINGLE SOLUTION: There are occasionally times when we require a number of peer classes to represent a cohesive whole. (Although placing these classes into separate components would not violate any design rules per se, it would needlessly increase the physical complexity of the system and is therefore counterindicated.) If the nature of these classes is such that (a) none of them depends on another, and (b) only taken together do they comprise a complete implementation of a single solution, then it can make the most sense for all of these cohesive parts to be colocated within a single component. A set of partial implementations for a small metafunction or the suite of polymorphic representations corresponding to varying numbers of optional arguments (e.g., for a functor having a given required number of arguments) are both potential candidates for colocation.[361] The legitimate need for private access via friendship, however, remains — by far — the dominant valid reason for colocation.

(4)   FLEA ON AN ELEPHANT: When we have nonprimitive functionality that is both (a) ultra-lightweight and (b) essential to typical usage, we may pragmatically elect to allow it to reside within the same component as the heavyweight class on which it depends — not only to reduce needless physical clutter, but also to facilitate the documentation of realistic usage examples (see Volume II, section 6.16). We must, however, avoid the temptation for abuse: The nonprimitive functionality must truly be only a "flea" on the back of the principle "elephant" class. Such situations occur infrequently compared to the one frequently recurring valid reason for colocation — i.e., friendship.

Figure 3-179: Detailed justification for colocating public classes

---

[361] As of C++11, we now have support for both variadic templates and variadic macros.

All other things being equal, placing in proximity code that is likely to change together tends to ease the process of maintaining, enhancing, and releasing software. This age-old fundamental axiom of modularity extends from individual classes and functions, through components and packages, all the way up to package groups and units of release. At the component level, we will sometimes create highly collaborative classes that are not intended for use outside of a single component. Such classes can be implemented entirely within the .cpp file, made private nested members of a public class (generally not recommended), or exploit the "extra under-score" convention (section 2.7.3) that designates a programmatically visible class as being local to the component (section 2.7.1), and not suitable for external use.

Colocating collaborative components at the package level is also important. For example, in the case of substantial templated entities that require template specialization, it is often desirable to implement each specialization in a separate .h/.cpp. Although these specializations could be used directly, no one of them comprises a complete solution. Moreover, if the general template changes, each of these specializations will have to change in lock-step. It is therefore appropriate to have all specializations reside within the same component (or, if not, at least the same pack-age) as the general template (and make use of the double-underscore convention [section 2.7.3] as needed to make the subordinated nature [section 2.7.5] of their defining-component relation-ships explicit).

Some library software is inherently malleable (section 0.5), e.g., a system that enumerates a slowly growing number of named entities (e.g., day-count conventions). Each time a new entity is created, the enumeration must be extended and the manager utility that is aware of all of them must change in lock-step. Placing the enumeration in a separate UOR from the top-level utility would mean that each time a new entity is added, the two UORs must be released in lock-step. Any intervening UORs would have to be released simultaneously as well; hence, the severity of this problem is unbounded. Another common example of tight intercomponent col-laboration results from separately packaged encoder and decoder classes for a given encoding. If the encoding strategy changes at all, both components would naturally be affected. Note that the decoder is routinely allowed to depend on the encoder purely for (e.g., "fuzz") testing pur-poses (see Volume III, section 8.6).

3.4 Avoiding Cyclic Link-Time Dependencies

Avoiding cyclic dependency among physical modules at any level of aggregation is a central design imperative within our methodology. Whenever a component dependency graph has a sub-set of nodes that is strongly connected, we say that those components are cyclically dependent.

Such proscribed dependencies could arise from `#include` directives residing in the `.h` or the `.cpp` files of participating components; either way, the resulting physical dependency graph will be the same.

Supporting cyclically interdependent subsystems on a large scale can be a nightmare, and effective modular testing is often impossible. Cyclic dependencies impact the development process in that larger and larger bodies of code must be enhanced, tested, and deployed as a single entity. Repetition of static libraries on the link line becomes onerous, lengthening and destabilizing the build cycle. Objective measures of physical design quality — e.g., cumulative component dependency (CCD), discussed in section 3.7.4 — suggest that low-level cycles are the most damaging. By contrast, hierarchical physical designs (having no cyclic dependencies) are relatively easy to understand, test, and reuse incrementally.

Even physically sound, high-level logical designs described cleanly (e.g., in UML) can inadvertently result in cyclic physical dependencies when implemented. If a `Company` has an `Account`, which in turn holds an object of type `Position` that refers to a `Security` that points back to the underlying `Company`, a naive implementation could lead to a cycle. Even if the high-level design is acyclic, cycles can emerge as the design is fleshed out, implemented, or maintained and enhanced over time. Hence, a development system that detects and rejects physical design cycles at check-in (and ideally throughout the development process) can be invaluable in this regard.

3.5 Levelization Techniques

The classical levelization techniques (see Figure 3-42, section 3.5.1), discussed in detail throughout section 3.5, can be used to break physical design cycles and otherwise reduce excessive physical dependencies. Surprisingly, no profoundly new levelization techniques have been discovered since they were first published in **lakos96**, but the relative importance of some have changed, primarily due to the increasing prominence of asynchronous programming. In particular, the use of *callbacks* is no longer "a technique of last resort" and is properly used often and in many disparate contexts. *Escalation* followed by *demotion*, however, continue to be the techniques we find ourselves employing most frequently in our day-to-day work. The use of *dumb data*, more so than *opaque pointer*, has proven, on a number of occasions, to be very useful in totally eliminating explicit dependency, invariably with (non-negative) integer indices — e.g., `Calendar` holiday indices discussed in section 3.12.11.3. And unlike opaque pointers, the use of dumb data also lends itself to externalization of values via (e.g., BDEX-style) serialization (see Figure 3-153, section 3.12.3).

The technique of *redundancy* (an alternative to demotion) amounts to a judgment call that we find ourselves employing less of, but still consider a valid alternative to excessive coupling. Preserving a compile-time-observable ownership hierarchy via a *manager class* remains an integral part of our design strategy, and *factoring* out independently testable (if not reusable) subcomponents continues to be indicated when the interface (1) is provided for us, (2) is immutable, and (3) dictates a Uses-In-The-Interface (logical) design cycle. Finally, *escalating encapsulation* — e.g., via a wrapper class — is an essential part of achieving hierarchical reuse. In this approach to levelization, we understand that the components that make up the low-level implementation need not themselves be encapsulated and kept private — it is only their *use* that must remain hidden from clients of the higher-level classes. Since this technique was first proposed, we have extended it to allow a wrapper package to simulate a weak form of package-level friendship using some admittedly sketchy (but legal) casting techniques.[362]

3.6 Avoiding Excessive Link-Time Dependencies

While cyclic physical dependencies are explicitly disallowed by our methodology, excessive — yet legal — link-time dependencies can also interfere with the effectiveness of otherwise lightweight, highly reusable software by dragging in significant amounts of code that will never be used by most clients. A Date class, for example, should be able to represent a date value (in some unpublished internal format) and efficiently manipulate that value using commonly needed operations (e.g., operator- for the number of *actual* days between two dates). Additional dependencies required by functionality such as "day-count" conventions (which are specific to the financial industry), formatting functions (which are unstable and likely to change), and date-math functions, such as finding the nth weekday in a particular month and year (which, although they do not require access to a database, are nonetheless far from primitive), impose a needless burden (e.g., at design and/or link time) on clients of an otherwise lightweight, easy-to-understand, easy-to-use, value-semantic, vocabulary Date type. Depending on poorly factored functionality (e.g., a monolithic wrapper) is yet another source of excessive link-time dependency.

---

[362] Ideally, a C++-modules facility will someday prove vastly superior at accomplishing what such inelegant syntactic "hackery" clumsily tries in vain to achieve.

Our natural tendency is to build on top of what we already have. This mindset can lead to the use of composition (or layering) to an extent beyond where it is appropriate. For small systems that require high performance across component interface boundaries, composition achieved via explicit physical dependency is efficient, easy to understand, and often the right approach. For much larger systems, however, an architecture based solely on composition is flawed in two important ways: (1) it is inflexible, effectively standardizing on a single de facto implementation, and (2) the dependencies grow with each increasing level of abstraction, making development — especially component-level (a.k.a. "unit") testing — onerous. For these reasons, classically "layered" architectures do not scale.

The most proximate alternative to a deeply layered architecture is a more *lateral* one. There are at least two basic ways to achieve a lateral design. One way involves refactoring value-semantic types (see Volume II, sections 4.1–4.3) so that the functionality that populates these types (e.g., from a database) and the functionality that uses these types (e.g., business logic) reside as independent peers — each depending on the lower-level value type. This more *lateral*, yet still compositional design is also more stable, flexible, and testable than a classical *layered* architecture because the people developing the business logic are unaffected by additions or modifications involving the populators (and vice versa).

The other common approach to achieving more lateral architectures is to define a pure abstract interface that defines the services expected by a client. We can then create our own implementations or exploit others, including third-party or open-source solutions, via the use of an *adapter* — i.e., a class that inherits from an abstract interface, or *protocol*, and uses a concrete type in its implementation. Several variations on this theme are possible (see Figure 3-116, section 3.7.5). Concrete implementations of such abstract interface types are provided by a higher-level agent (e.g., `main`) to client objects — either at construction or supplied along with each invocation of a particular method.

For reasons pertaining to runtime performance, we may choose instead to make the particular method, normally taking an adapter base class (by pointer or reference), a method *template*, which can often be more readily bound at compile time on conventional platforms than virtual functions, though those too can be "devirtualized" under certain important circumstances (see Volume II, section 4.10). Through the use of member function templates, we can achieve a physically independent, flexible, and runtime-efficient (albeit highly collaborative and tightly compile-time-coupled) lateral design.

Although we typically characterize (e.g., in metadata) component dependencies across packages and package groups coarsely (section 2.16), we are still well advised to be aware of the individual component dependencies in order to achieve minimal physical coupling in practice — e.g., after deployment (see Figure 2-89, section 2.15.10). In particular, we can mitigate the inherent cost of layered systems by choosing a *lightly layered* approach as opposed to a *heavily layered* one (see Figure 3-112, section 3.7.4). These costs can be quantified using the *cumulative component dependency* (CCD) physical-design-quality metric (see Figure 3-114, section 3.7.4.2).

The trade-offs between lateral and layered architectures are an essential aspect of large-scale software design. On a moderate scale, there are economies in creating compositional architectures in which components explicitly depend on lower-level ones. The cost of lateral architectures, whether at run time (via virtual functions) or compile time (via member function templates) is more generally, and perhaps more appropriately, measured in terms of complexity (human cognition). In this way, a layered subsystem is analogous to a single multistory skyscraper (section 3.7.1). Past a certain point, however, costs associated with inflexibility, along with the link-time costs required to perform thorough component-level testing, become prohibitive. Hence, large-scale software — like most major cities — will scale better laterally than vertically.

3.8 Avoiding Inappropriate Link-Time Dependencies

Lateral architectures are particularly effective at avoiding heavyweight, unpredictable, or otherwise undesirable software, especially at the lower levels of a system. Some dependencies, however, are more than just excessive; they are qualitatively inappropriate. One example of an inappropriate dependency is tying a lightweight, value-semantic type (e.g., `Date` or `Calendar`) to a platform's operating system or to a particular vendor's database. Other examples include (1) incorporating, into core libraries, open-source or third-party software for which there is not a sufficient SLA (service-level agreement) or that requires a specific version of some other piece of software not under our control, (2) relying on nonstandard features of a particular operating system that cannot be emulated efficiently on all supported platforms, or (3) depending on software that requires special hardware support.

Classical layered architectures can also be inappropriate in that they typically force us to standardize on a single implementation. Restricting ourselves to, say, a particular concrete transport mechanism (e.g., sockets) impedes our ability to communicate optimally between processes. As time goes on, new technologies may appear (e.g., shared memory, openSSL, MQSeries, ASIO), perhaps with significant benefits (e.g., performance, security, fault tolerance, productivity) that we would like to exploit — possibly even side by side along with other technologies in the same process. Relying on third-party products can be risky; however, leveraging them need not be. By adapting functionality to stable interfaces in a more lateral design, we are able to exploit a new technology without necessarily having to *bet* on it.

In a typical lateral design, an object of a concrete class derived from a protocol would be constructed as an automatic variable by a higher-level agent (e.g., `main`) and then subsequently configured. The address of this object would then be passed (via its base class) to the constructor of another concrete class, this one derived from some other pure abstract base class at the same low physical level as the first one, but at a higher level of logical abstraction. The address of this (concrete) object could, in turn, be used to create an object of yet a third concrete class, and so on.

Substituting one low-level technology for another is accomplished simply by modifying the sequence of statements (e.g., in `main`) used to create the subobjects used to instantiate that technology as well as any subsequent objects used to configure it (e.g., see Figure 3-122, section 3.8.2). Alternatively, an abstract interface, concrete mechanism, or remote service can be supplied by a client with each invocation of a method at either run time or compile time. Unlike layered designs, however, there is no practical limit to the scalability of lateral designs.

3.9 Ensuring Physical Interoperability

In order to maximize reuse, we would like to ensure certain fundamental physical interoperability properties among our components. In particular, we want to avoid situations in which the use of a component restricts its use or reuse within the same program. We also want to minimize situations in which the use of one component restricts the use of some other component within the same program. There are several specific manifestations of poor physical interoperability that we will want to avoid: domain-specific conditional compilation; application-specific dependencies for library software; logical constructs (e.g., a `static` variable) or design patterns (e.g., a *singleton*) that artificially constrain reuse; defining global entities outside the file that defines `main`; hiding header files for the purpose of logical encapsulation; and unisolated use of, and dependency on, nonportable software. Failure to ensure physical interoperability in these ways will impede our ability to compose new solutions from the parts of existing ones — i.e., it will impede hierarchical reuse (section 0.4).

Avoiding unnecessary compile-time dependencies is another important aspect of good physical design. The term *encapsulation* (with information hiding implied) means that some implementation detail is not, under normal usage, programmatically accessible. That is, changes to an encapsulated implementation detail will not require production clients to rework their code. The term *insulation*, however, connotes a stronger property than encapsulation. Changing an insulated implementation detail of a component does not require clients even to *recompile* their code. Formal definitions for these terms are provided in section 3.11.1.

Insulating implementation details makes it possible to change them without having to recompile the client, which in turn can dramatically reduce the amount of time it takes to rebuild an entire system. Moreover, insulating critical low-level implementation details makes it possible to *patch* (see below) defects quickly, rather than having to rebuild the entire system — layer by layer — using a traditional, deliberate, and time-consuming standard release process. This critical difference between *encapsulation* and *insulation* can be of enormous importance for developers of widely used Software-Infrastructure libraries.

For instance, rebuilding the entire system to fix critical bugs between releases can be prohibitively expensive (if not outright impossible due to the unavailability of critical staff). A *patch* is a local change to a previously released version of software. When critical bugs are encountered between releases, making a patch is typically less expensive and far less disruptive than re-releasing the entire system. As long as the physical interface and contract of a component is not altered, the modified implementation can often be recompiled and dropped in place without having to recompile other components.

The more insulated the implementation of a component, the more likely it is that it can be repaired locally (without forcing the recompilation of clients). Our ability to patch and rerelease a system quickly is directly related to the degree to which implementation details are insulated from clients throughout that system. Hence, insulating implementation details across major interface boundaries, where feasible, should generally be a design goal.

There are two basic kinds of insulation techniques: *total* and *partial*. Total insulation means no aspect of the implementation, if changed, would force clients to recompile. Partial insulation means that clients are immune to recompilation due to changes in some aspects of the implementation, but not others. If total insulation is the goal, then there are architectural implications;

if only partial implementation is needed, the nature and degree is entirely an implementation detail (see Volume II, section 6.6).

There are essentially three separate ways in which to achieve total insulation: (1) a pure abstract interface; (2) a fully insulating wrapper component; (3) a procedural interface. A client using a pure abstract interface is not only shielded from all compile-time dependency, but also side-steps direct link-time dependency on any one implementation — the caveat being that the agent instantiating the derived implementation of the abstract interface exists at a higher physical level than the client using it. Note that, whenever inheritance is involved, extracting a *protocol* class is a general insulation technique that should be used for factoring the interface and implementation of a non-pure-abstract base class — irrespective of the (perceived) value of the resulting insulation.

When employing a fully insulating wrapper component, the same client that instantiates a given object can use that object without being affected (i.e., having to recompile) due to changes in that component's implementation. The client will still inherit the dependencies of the wrapped implementation. Making wrapper components fully insulating can, however, result in enormous runtime overhead. Moreover, it is not in general possible to create multicomponent wrappers for preexisting systems without the use of long-distance (i.e., intercomponent) friendships (section 3.1.10.6). Hence, for an existing subsystem, a procedural interface is often the only viable total-insulation option.

A procedural interface is always achievable but not always appropriate (or the best choice) in that there is typically significant overhead and loss in fidelity (e.g., with regard to inheritance and templates). It should never be used in a context that might limit the possibility of side-by-side reuse. There are, however, two cases in which a procedural interface is often the right decision: (1) to isolate a legacy system in which the underlying types were not designed to be reusable, and (2) to provide a translation layer (e.g., from C++ to C). In either of these scenarios, there is no cost resulting from loss of reuse.

An effective procedural interface (PI) typically has eight characteristic properties (see Figure 3-150, section 3.11.17.13). Each PI function resides *physically* in a separate component (and typically UOR) from what it accesses and is *logically* independent of every other one. Each component implementing a PI function is independent of every other such component, provides no additional domain functionality beyond what is needed for mechanical translation, and maps 1-1 with the underlying C++ component it "wraps" (whose *view* it presents). Finally, each PI function is named in a predictable way, is callable from either C or C++, and traffics (albeit opaquely) in the actual underlying C++ types; hence, a PI is — by design — *not* a true *wrapper.*

Finally, when designing with components, we must consider logical and physical design simultaneously. What might, at first, appear to be primitive behavior for a class may have physical consequences that transcend its initial requirements. In order to achieve a modular, maintainable design, the proposed class might have to undergo substantial refactoring, resulting in perhaps several components. As long as the totality of software provides an effective solution, the myriad benefits of careful factoring leading to hierarchical reuse will invariably offset the (typically trivial) adjustment in client usage.

In the course of creating software infrastructure, we must consider the long-term landscape, yet defer implementation of peripheral components not germane to the current business need. All required foundation software must, of course, be implemented first, and in fully factored form. Software that can be implemented later in terms of the more urgently needed components should be considered upfront, but then must be deferred until an appropriate future project, lest the latency of delivery preclude any use of this overall component-based-development approach. During development, we must resist the temptation to place more than one class in the same component based solely on logical cohesion (section 3.3.1). Doing so can affect stability or eliminate important design alternatives down the road (e.g., see Figure 3-172, section 3.12.11.2).

The profound advantage of our design methodology derives from the hierarchical reuse that we are able to achieve by deliberately feeding back (section 0.1) well-designed, finely graduated, granular components (section 0.4) into our enterprise-wide repository of Software Capital (section 0.9), which we continue to grow over time (section 0.10). Each time we endeavor to solve a new business problem or provide a new capability in an existing system, we will need to consider carefully how that solution best maps onto our existing hierarchically reusable infrastructure. The original specification will need to be atomized and reassembled meticulously (section 0.11) into well-reasoned, focused, client-facing components conforming to well-understood categories (see Volume II, section 4.2).

Once the specification of the "interface" components is largely complete, the development mindset changes. Instead of looking at the system from the external client's perspective, we must now begin to consider the reusable hierarchy of non-client-facing components that will be needed to implement the client-facing ones. Each component, in turn, becomes a new subsystem, and the process of developing it as if it were a top-level client-facing component recurses until a component of manageable size and complexity is reached — much like what was done in our quantifying analogy (section 0.8). It is only once we reach this unusually aggressive level of decomposition that we begin to dig into the lower-level details of design, implementation, rendering (see Volume II), and testing (see Volume III).

Conclusion

Ultimately, the goal of this chapter has been to demonstrate the importance of, as well as how to achieve, a physically sound, well-factored, fine-grained software infrastructure. Reduced reliability, increased maintenance costs, increased executable size, and reduced runtime performance are among the likely consequences of a poor physical design. All other things being equal, each of the above are to be avoided. As Figure 3-180 illustrates, reduced testability, reduced usability, and reduced modifiability are three important primary causes of these undesirable consequences.

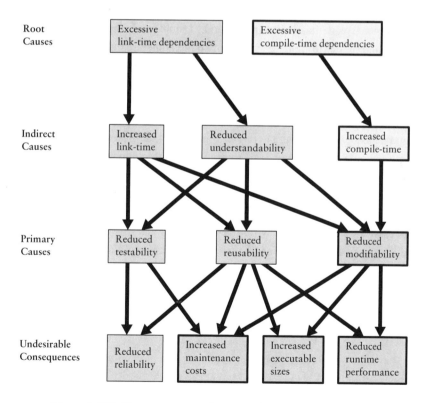

Figure 3-180: Consequences and causes of a poor physical design

If a system is harder to test, it will be tested less, be less reliable, and therefore require more maintenance. Software that should be (but is not) reusable is less used, hence less proven, and therefore typically less reliable. Less reuse means more duplication, so there is more code to maintain; hence, it costs more to maintain it. More code to do the same thing in a program means larger executable size, which — in turn, due to caching considerations — might impact runtime performance. Finally, reduced modifiability means that it will be harder (cost more) to make changes (e.g., to optimize for physical parameters like executable size and runtime performance).

Indirect causes of these undesirable consequences include increased link time, reduced under-standability, and increased compile time. If it costs more to link a test driver to its subject code, less testing will get done per testing dollar. Similarly, if link time is disproportionately increased by reusing a body of code, that code is less likely to be reused. Once code is modified, it must be tested; hence, if code is more expensive to test, it is necessarily more expensive to modify. For quite different reasons, reduced understandability correlates closely with increased link time. If code is hard to understand, it simultaneously becomes harder to test, harder to reuse, and harder to modify without breaking something else. Finally, increased compile time affects a system in that our ability to make modifications is attenuated. This malady, unlike increased link time, can be addressed incrementally and on a case-by-case basis.

The root cause of all of these problems can often be traced to excessive link-time and compile-time dependencies among the physical modules that make up a system, application, or library. Both compile-time and link-time dependencies affect physical design quality by increasing the time needed to compile and link programs. But much more importantly, excessive link-time dependencies compromise understandability, and therefore both usability and maintainability. Moreover, cyclic, excessive, or otherwise inappropriate link-time dependencies can undermine successful reuse across many unrelated applications. It is by proactively minimizing or elimi-nating physical dependencies that we achieve truly profound quality in our software designs.

Appendix

Quick Reference

The following is a summary of the Definitions, Corollaries, Design Imperatives, Design Rules, Guidelines, and Observations discussed throughout this book.

1   Definitions

Chapter 1:

- A *declaration* is a language construct that introduces a name into a scope. (p. 154)
- A *definition* is a language construct that uniquely characterizes an entity within a program and, where applicable, reserves storage for it. (p. 154)
- A C++ construct has *internal bindage* if, on typical platforms, use of a declared name of that kind of construct and its corresponding definition (or meaning) is *always* effectively bound at compile time. (p. 160)
- A C++ construct has *external bindage* if, on typical platforms, a corresponding definition must not appear in more than one translation unit of a program (e.g., in order to avoid multiply-defined-symbol errors at link time). (p. 161)
- A C++ construct has *dual bindage* if, on typical platforms, (1) a corresponding definition can safely appear in more than one translation unit of the same program, and (2) use of a declared name of that kind of construct and its corresponding definition can be bound at link time. (p. 162)
- A type is *used in the interface of a function* if that type is named as part of the function's signature or return type. (p. 220)
- A type is *used in the (public) interface of a class* if the type is used in the interface of any (public) *member* function of that class. (p. 220)
- A type is *used in the implementation of a function* if that type is referred to anywhere in the definition of the function but not named in its public (or protected) interface. (p. 221)
- A type is *used in the implementation of a class* if that type is not used in the public (or protected) interface of the class, but is (1) used in a member function of the class, (2) referred to in the declaration of a data member of the class, or (3) [rare] derived from privately (i.e., is a private base type of the class). (p. 223)

- A *protocol class* is a class that (1) has only pure virtual functions except for a non-`inline` virtual destructor (defined in the `.cpp` file), (2) has no data members, and (3) does not derive from any other class (directly or indirectly) that is not itself a protocol class. (p. 226)
- A component y Depends-On a component x if x is needed to compile or link y. (p. 238)
- A component y exhibits a *compile-time dependency* on component x if x.h is needed to compile y.cpp. (p. 239)
- A component y exhibits a *link-time dependency* on component x if the object file y.o (produced by compiling y.cpp) contains an undefined symbol for which x.o is required by the linker to resolve that symbol. (p. 240)
- Acyclic physical dependencies admit the canonical assignment of (non-negative) level numbers:
  Level 0:   A non-local component.
  Level 1:   A local component not depending physically on any other local component (a.k.a. a *leaf component*).
  Level N: A local component that depends physically on at least one local component at level $N - 1$ (for $N \geq 2$), but none at level N or higher.
  (p. 252)
- A software subsystem rendered in terms of components that can be assigned level numbers is said to be *levelizable*. (p. 252)
- A component, x, *Includes* another component, y, if the contents of y.h are ultimately incorporated into the translation unit corresponding to x.cpp at compile time (for *any* of the supported build targets). (p. 258)

Chapter 2:

- An *aggregate* is a cohesive physical unit of design comprising logical content. (p. 275)
- A *component* is the innermost level of physical aggregation. (p. 275)
- A *unit of release* (*UOR*) is the outermost level of physical aggregation. (p. 277)
- An aggregate y Depends-On another aggregate x if any file in x is required in order to compile, link, or thoroughly test y. (p. 278)
- A logical or physical entity is *architecturally significant* if its name (or symbol) is intentionally visible from outside of the UOR in which it is defined. (p. 278)
- A *manifest* is a specification of the collection of physical entities — typically expressed in external metadata (see section 2.16) — intended to be part of the physical aggregate to which it pertains. (p. 281)
- An *allowed dependency* is a physical dependency — typically expressed in external metadata (see section 2.16) — that is permitted to exist in the physical hierarchy to which it pertains. (p. 281)
- A *package* is the smallest architecturally significant physical aggregate larger than a component. (p. 300)
- The *base name* of a component is the root name of the component's header file, excluding its package prefix and subsequent underscore. (p. 310)
- An *aspect function* is a named (member or free) function of a given signature having ubiquitously uniform semantics (e.g., `begin` or `swap`) and, if free, behaves much like an operator — e.g., with respect to argument-dependent lookup (ADL). (p. 311)

- A *transitive include* implies that a client is relying on the use of one header to include another in order to make direct use of the functionality afforded indirectly via the nested include. (p. 359)
- A *component-private* class (or `struct`) is one defined at package-namespace scope that must not be used directly by logical entities located outside of the component in which it is defined. (p. 371)
- A *subordinate component* is one that must not be `#include`d (or used) directly by any component other than the one (located within the same package) to which that component has been explicitly designated as being subordinate; a component can be subordinate to at most one nonsubordinate one. (p. 382)
- A *package* is an architecturally significant collection of components (1) organized as a physically cohesive unit, and (2) sharing a common package namespace. (p. 386)
- A *package group* is an architecturally significant collection of packages, organized as a physically cohesive unit. (p. 402)
- A package group g Depends-On another UOR u if any package in g Depends-On u. (p. 407)
- A package is *irregular* if it is not composed entirely of proper components, each adhering to our design rules, especially those pertaining to cohesive naming. (p. 431)

Chapter 3:

- Functionality that intrinsically requires private access to objects of a type on which it operates in order to be implemented efficiently is said to be a *primitive* operation of that type. (p. 528)
- An implementation detail of a component (type, data, or function) that can be altered, added, or removed without forcing clients to rework their code is said to be *encapsulated*. (p. 790)
- An implementation detail of a component (type, data, or function) that can be altered, added, or removed without forcing clients to recompile is said to be *insulated*. (p. 791)

2   Corollaries

Chapter 2:

- The name of each package must be unique throughout the enterprise. (p. 300)
- Every library component filename must be unique throughout the enterprise. (p. 303)
- The fully qualified name (or signature, if a function or operator) of each logical entity declared within an architecturally significant component header file must be unique throughout the enterprise. (p. 311)
- Allowed (explicitly stated) dependencies among packages must be acyclic. (p. 323)
- The `.h` file of each component must compile in isolation. (p. 354)
- Transitive includes are not permitted, except to access a public base class of a type whose definition is included directly. (p. 360)
- The name of each package group must be unique throughout the enterprise. (p. 402)

3   Design Imperatives

Chapter 2:

- Allowed (explicitly stated) dependencies among physical aggregates must be acyclic. (p. 293)
- Cyclic physical dependencies among components are not permitted. (p. 362)

- Access to the private details of a logical construct must not span the boundaries of the physical aggregate in which it is defined — e.g., "long-distance" (inter-component) friendship is not permitted. (p. 367)
- Cyclic physical dependencies among packages, as defined by their (explicitly stated) *allowed dependencies*, are not permitted. (p. 394)
- Allowed (explicitly stated) dependencies among UORs must be acyclic! (p. 411)
- Hierarchical Testability Requirement: Every physical entity must be *thoroughly testable* in terms only of other physical entities that themselves have already been tested thoroughly. (p. 439)

4   Design Rules

Chapter 2:

- The name of every architecturally significant entity must be unique throughout the enterprise. (p. 292)
- Component files (`.h`/`.cpp`) must have the same root name as that of the component itself (i.e., they differ only in suffix). (p. 302)
- Every component must reside within a package. (p. 303)
- The (all-lowercase) name of each component must begin with the (all-lowercase) name of the package to which it belongs, followed by an underscore (_). (p. 304)
- Each logical entity declared within a component must be nested within a namespace having the name of the package in which that entity resides. (p. 307)
- Each package namespace must be nested within a unique enterprise-wide namespace. (p. 309)
- The name of every logical construct declared at package-namespace scope — other than free *operator* and *aspect* functions (such as `operator==` and `swap`) — must have, as a prefix, the base name of the component that implements it; macro names (`ALL_UPPERCASE`), which are not scoped (lexically) by the package namespace, must incorporate, as a prefix, the entire uppercased name of the component (including the package prefix). (p. 311)
- Only classes, `structs`, and free operator functions (and operator-like *aspect* functions, e.g., `swap`) are permitted to be *declared* at package-namespace scope in a component's `.h` file. (p. 312)
- A component header is permitted to contain the declaration of a *free* (i.e., nonmember) operator or *aspect* function (at package-namespace scope) only when one or more of its parameters incorporates a type defined in the same component. (p. 317)
- Neither `using` directives nor `using` declarations are permitted to appear outside function scope within a component. (p. 331)
- A component must comprise exactly one `.h` file and (at least) one corresponding `.cpp` file having the same root name, which together satisfy the four fundamental properties (sections 1.6 and 1.11) of components. (p. 343)
- COMPONENT PROPERTY 1: A component's `.cpp` file includes its corresponding `.h` file as the first substantive line of code. (p. 343)
- COMPONENT PROPERTY 2: Each logical construct effectively having external linkage defined in a component's `.cpp` file is declared in that component's `.h` file. (p. 344)

- COMPONENT PROPERTY 3: Each logical construct effectively having external bindage declared in the .h file of a component (if defined at all) is defined within that component. (p. 344)
- COMPONENT PROPERTY 4: A component's functionality is accessed only via a #include of its header file and never by a local extern declaration. (p. 346)
- Every logical construct we write outside of a file that defines main must reside within a component. (p. 346)
- The .h file of each component must contain a unique and predictable include guard: INCLUDED_*PACKAGE_COMPONENTBASE* (e.g., INCLUDED_BDLT_DATETIME). (p. 353)
- Logical constructs having other than internal bindage (e.g., inline functions) that are exported by a component must be first declared (within the header file) and then defined separately (within the same component), with all free (e.g., operator) functions defined outside the namespace in which they were declared. (p. 354)
- Runtime initialization of file- or namespace-scope static objects is not permitted. (p. 354)
- Any *direct* substantive use of one component by another requires the corresponding #include directive to be present *directly* in the client component (in either the .h or .cpp file, but not both) unless indirect inclusion is implied by intrinsic and substantial compile-time dependency — i.e., public inheritance (nothing else). (p. 359)
- Avoid the use of an underscore character (_) purely as a separator in logical names except between two all-uppercase words or for established (lowercase) single-character prefixes and suffixes (i.e., d_, s_, e_, k_, and _p). (p. 371)
- A logical entity declared in a component header at package-namespace scope whose name contains an *extra* underscore — i.e., other than as required (1) as a valid separator (e.g., between all-uppercase words or as part of an established prefix/suffix), or (2) for nominal cohesion (e.g., in *subordinate* components) — is considered to be local to the component that defines it and must not be accessed directly from outside that component; the lowercased name up to the (first) *extra* underscore must match exactly the component's *base name*. (p. 372)
- A component, c, having an underscore in its base name is reserved to indicate that the component is *subordinate* to another component (in the same package) whose name is a prefix all the way up to (but not including) an underscore in the base name of c. (p. 382)
- Anticipated *allowed* (direct) *dependencies* of each package must be stated explicitly. (p. 389)
- Anticipated *allowed* (direct) *dependencies* of each package group must be stated explicitly. (p. 408)
- The (all-lowercase) alphanumeric name of every package group must be exactly three characters and form a valid identifier:
  <Package Group Name> ::= [a-z] [a-z0-9] [a-z0-9]
  (p. 423)
- The (all-lowercase) name of each package within a package group must begin with the name of the group, followed by one, two, or three lowercase alphanumeric characters that uniquely distinguish the package within its group.
  <Grouped Package Name> ::= <Package Group Name> [a-z0-9] ([a-z0-9] ([a-z0-9])?)?
  (p. 424)

- The (all-lowercase) name of each standalone package must begin with a lowercase alphabetic character and either (1) consist of more than six (or exactly three, which is RARE) alphanumeric characters, or (2) be followed by an underscore, a letter, and then zero or more alphanumeric characters (note that the prefix "z_" is treated specially; see Figure 2-75, section 2.10.3).

  <Ungrouped Package Name> ::= <Package Group Name> ([a-z0-9])⁴ ([a-z0-9])*

  | <Package Group Name>   *VERY RARE*

  | [a-y] _ [a-z] ([a-z0-9])*   *z_ is special.*

  (p. 425)
- The allowable names for applications (i.e., application-level "packages") must be disjoint from those of all other kinds of packages. (p. 436)
- All code within an application package must be local (private) to that package — i.e., *nothing* outside the package is permitted to depend on software defined within an application-level package. (p. 436)
- Associated with every component (and having the same root name) must be a *unique*, physically separate test driver having a consistent suffix (e.g., .t.cpp). (p. 441)
- The component test driver resides (physically) in the same directory as the component it tests. (p. 445)
- The hierarchical *direct* (physical) dependencies of a test driver must not exceed those of the component under test. (p. 445)
- The dependencies of a test driver on external data or other apparatus that is not explicitly part of our supported (portable) build environment must not exceed those of the component under test. (p. 454)
- Neither relative nor absolute path names (i.e., no directory names) are permitted to be used when #include-ing a component header file. (p. 459)
- Any additional organizational partitioning employed solely for deployment purposes must not be architecturally significant. (p. 464)

5   Guidelines

Chapter 2:

- Every physical aggregate should be treated atomically for design purposes. (p. 277)
- Architecturally cohesive logical entities should be tightly encapsulated within physical ones. (p. 294)
- The *use* of each logical entity declared at package-namespace scope should alone be sufficient to indicate the component, package, and UOR in which that entity is defined. (p. 301)
- Avoid architecturally significant use of the C++ namespace construct except for the enterprise-wide namespace and directly nested package namespaces. (p. 341)
- The .h file should contain only those #include directives (or, where appropriate, local ["forward"] class declarations) necessary to ensure that the header file compiles in isolation. (p. 355)
- Aim for one (public) class per component unless there is an engineering justification to do otherwise. (p. 369)
- Avoid *defining* a nested class within the lexical scope of its enclosing class. (p. 373)
- Avoid *declaring* nested classes altogether. (p. 375)

- Each package should, if possible, be part of an appropriate package group. (p. 419)
- Allowed package-group dependencies should be (1) minimal, and (2) seldom increased. (p. 420)
- The name of each (sharable) UOR within an enterprise should be registered (and reserved) with a central authority *before* it is used. (p. 426)
- There should be a well-defined subset of the invocation interface for each test driver that is standard across the enterprise. (p. 456)
- The "user experience" for each test driver should (ideally) be standard across the enterprise. (p. 458)

Chapter 3:

- Always try to factor and, when time allows, proactively *demote* generally useful functionality created for a specific application to its appropriate location in the physical hierarchy of our ever growing repository of *Software Capital*. (p. 518)
- Avoid colocating more than one public class in a component unless there is a compelling *engineering* reason to do so. (p. 522)
- Especially avoid colocating classes expected to have largely disjoint clients. (p. 524)
- Avoid colocating functionality expected to have largely disjoint clients. (p. 526)
- Each component we design should have a tightly focused purpose. (p. 527)
- The functionality provided by a reusable component should be *complete* yet *minimal*. (p. 528)
- Almost all of the (domain-specific) functionality implemented within a component that defines an instantiable type should be *primitive*. (p. 529)
- Most nonprimitive functionality that operates on an instantiable type should be implemented in a higher-level utility `struct`. (p. 530)
- Strive for an interface that affords maximum runtime efficiency while keeping implementation options as open and flexible as practicable. (p. 534)
- Prefer providing low-level, reusable primitive functionality rather than implementing primitive application-level functionality directly. (p. 539)
- Strive to provide sufficient primitive functionality to support the *open-closed principle* (section 0.5) by ensuring that each component's functionality is *complete*: Arbitrary application functionality should be implementable (e.g., by a client) in a separate, higher-level component. (p. 545)
- Prefer semantics and physical dependency over syntax as a modularization criteria, especially at the package level. (p. 552)
- Avoid defining more than one *public* class within a single component unless there is a compelling engineering reason to do so (see Figure 3-20, section 3.3.1). (p. 555)
- Colocate software that must change together. (p. 560)
- Limit tight mutual collaboration across public components to a single UOR. (p. 565)
- Minimize situations in which the use of a component, within a given program, might restrict or preclude either (1) its *own* reuse, or (2) the use of some *other* component, within that same program. (p. 753)
- Avoid domain-specific conditional compilation for components. (p. 754)
- Avoid application-specific dependencies for reusable library components. (p. 758)
- Avoid logical constructs or patterns that artificially constrain reuse. (p. 760)

- Design software to avoid accidental misuse, not fraud. (p. 761)
- Avoid defining global entities outside the file that defines `main`. (p. 762)
- Avoid hiding header files for the purpose of *logical* encapsulation. (p. 762)
- Minimize and isolate the creation and use of nonportable software. (p. 766)
- Minimize the need for package-local (private) components. (p. 769)

6   Observations

Chapter 1:

- A compile-time dependency often results in a link-time dependency. (p. 241)
- The Depends-On relation for components is transitive. (p. 242)
- C++ preprocessor `#include` directives alone are sufficient to deduce *all* actual physical dependencies among the components within a system, provided the system compiles. (p. 258)

Chapter 2:

- The Depends-On relation among aggregates is transitive. (p. 278)
- The definition of every physical aggregate must comprise the specification of (1) the entities it aggregates, and (2) the external entities that it is *allowed* to depend on *directly*. (p. 281)
- To maximize human cognition, peer entities within a physical aggregate should be of comparable physical complexity (e.g., have the same level of physical aggregation). (p. 284)
- More than three levels of appropriately balanced physical aggregation are virtually always unnecessary and can be problematic. (p. 287)
- Package groups support logically and physically cohesive library development. (p. 414)
- Package groups allow acyclic application libraries to evolve over time. (p. 417)
- Package groups support decentralized package creation. (p. 421)
- Choosing package names within a package group is automatically decentralized. (p. 427)
- The coarse physical granularity of UORs that must be assumed (architecturally) during development often exceeds that of deployed software. (p. 464)

Chapter 3:

- Physical implementation dependencies strongly govern modularization. (p. 521)
- Anticipated client usage significantly influences modularization. (p. 523)
- Iterators often dramatically reduce what would otherwise be considered *manifestly primitive* operations. (p. 529)
- The degree of flexibility in the implementation might affect what can be considered *primitive*. (p. 535)
- Packages can be useful for explicitly grouping components that are, by design, necessarily syntactically (as well as semantically) similar (e.g., they all implement the same *protocol* or satisfy the same *concept*) provided, of course, that they naturally share essentially the same envelope of physical dependencies. (p. 575)
- Package and component names can sometimes be used productively to represent orthogonal dimensions of design, but only within dead-regular frameworks. (p. 584)

Bibliography

[abrahams05]

David Abrahams and Aleksey Gurtovoy, *C++ Template Metaprogramming: Concepts, Tools, and Techniques from Boost and Beyond* (Boston, MA: Addison-Wesley, 2005)

[alexandrescu01]

Andrei Alexandrescu, *Modern C++ Design: Generic Programming and Design Patterns Applied* (Boston, MA: Addison-Wesley, 2001)

[alliance01]

Agile Alliance, "Manifesto for Agile Software Development," 2001
https://www.agilealliance.org/agile101/the-agile-manifesto/

[austern98]

Matthew H. Austern, *Generic Programming and the STL* (Reading: MA: Addison-Wesley, 1998)

[baetjer98]

Howard Baetjer Jr., *Software as Capital* (Los Alamitos, CA: IEEE Computer Society, 1998)

[bde14]

https://github.com/bloomberg/bde/

[beck00]

Kent Beck, *Extreme Programming Explained* (Reading, MA: Addison-Wesley, 2000)

[bellman54]

Richard Bellman, "The Theory of Dynamic Programming," *Bulletin of the American Mathematical Society*, 60 (1954) (6):503–516

[boehm04]

Barry Boehm and Richard Turner, *Balancing Agility and Discipline: A Guide to the Perplexed* (Boston, MA: Addison-Wesley, 2004)

[boehm81]

Barry Boehm, *Software Engineering Economics* (Englewood Cliffs, NJ: Prentice Hall, 1981)

[booch05]

Grady Booch, James Rumbaugh, Ivar Jacobson, *The Unified Modeling Language User Guide*, second ed. (Reading, MA: Addison-Wesley, 2005)

[booch94]

Grady Booch, *Object-Oriented Analysis and Design with Applications,* second ed.
(Reading, MA: Addison-Wesley, 1994)

[bovet13]

Daniel Pierre Bovet, "Special Sections in Linux Binaries," LWN.net, 2013
https://lwn.net/Articles/531148/

[brooks75]

Fred Brooks, Jr., *The Mythical Man-Month* (Reading, MA: Addison-Wesley, 1975)

[brooks87]

Fredrick P. Brooks, "No Silver Bullet: Essence and Accidents of Software Engineering,"
IEEE Computer 20(4):10–19

[brooks95]

Fred Brooks, Jr., *The Mythical Man-Month*, 2nd ed. (Reading, MA: Addison-Wesley, 1995)

[brown90]

Patrick J. Brown, *Formulae for Yield and Other Calculations* (Washington, DC:
Association of International Bond Dealers, 1990)

[cargill92]

Tom Cargill, *C++ Programming Style* (Reading, MA: Addison-Wesley, 1992)

[cockburn02]

Alistair Cockburn, *Agile Software Development* (Boston, MA: Addison-Wesley, 2002)

[coplien92]

James O. Coplien, *Advanced C++ Programming Styles and Idioms* (Reading, MA:
Addison-Wesley, 1992)

[cormen09]

Thomas H. Cormen et al., *Introduction to Algorithms,* third ed. (Cambridge, MA: MIT
Press, 2009)

[cpp11]

Information Technology — Programming Languages — C++, INCITS/ISO/IEC
14882-2011[2012] (New York: American National Standards Institute, 2012)

[cpp17]

Programming Languages — C++, ISO/IEC 14882:2017(E) (Geneva, Switzerland:
International Organization for Standardization/International Electrotechnical
Commission, 2017)

[deitel04]

Harvey Deitel, Paul Deitel, and David R. Choffnes, *Operating Systems*, third ed.
(Upper Saddle River, NJ: Pearson, 2004)

[deitel90]

Harvey Deitel, *Operating Systems*, second ed. (Reading, MA: Addison-Wesley, 1990)

[dewhurst05]

Stephen Dewhurst, *C++ Common Knowledge* (Boston, MA: Addison-Wesley, 2005)

[dijkstra59]

E. W. Dijkstra, "A Note on Two Problems in Connection with Graphs," *Numerische Mathematik* 1 (1959): 269–271

[dijkstra68]

Edsger W. Dijkstra, "The Structure of the 'THE'-Multiprogramming System," *Communications of the ACM* 11 (1968) (5):341–346

[driscoll]

Evan Driscoll, "A Description of the C++ typename Keyword." http://pages.cs.wisc.edu/~driscoll/typename.html

[ellis90]

Margaret Ellis and Bjarne Stroustrup, *The Annotated C++ Reference Manual* (Reading, MA: Addison-Wesley, 1990)

[faltstrom94]

P. Faltstrom, D. Crocker, and E. Fair, RFC 1741: "MIME Content Type for BinHex Encoded Files," Internet Engineering Task Force (IETF), December 1994 https://www.ietf.org/rfc/rfc1741.txt

[felber10]

Lukas Felber, *ReDHead — Refactor Dependencies of C/C++ Header Files*, Master's Thesis, HSR Hochschule für Technik, Rapperswil, Switzerland.

[fincad08]

FinancialCAD Corporation, "Day Count Conventions and Accrual Factors," 2008 http://docs.fincad.com/support/developerfunc/mathref/Daycount.htm

[foote99]

Brian Foote and Joseph Yoder, "Big Ball of Mud," *Fourth Conference on Patterns Languages of Programs,* Monticello, Illinois, June 26, 1999 http://www.laputan.org/mud/mud.html

[fowler04]

Martin Fowler, *UML Distilled*, third ed. (Reading, MA: Addison-Wesley, 2004)

[freed96]

N. Freed and N. Borenstein, RFC 2045: "Multipurpose Internet Mail Extensions (MIME) Part One: Format of Internet Message Bodies," Internet Engineering Task Force (IETF), November 1996 https://tools.ietf.org/html/rfc2045

[gamma95]

Erich Gamma, et al. *Design Patterns: Elements of Reusable Object-Oriented Software* (Reading, MA: Addison-Wesley, 1995)

[helbing02]

Juergen Helbing, "yEncode - A Quick and Dirty Encoding for Binaries,"
Version 1.2, Feb. 28, 2002
http://www.yenc.org/yenc-draft.1.3.txt

[hirsch02]

E. D. Hirsch, Joseph F. Kett, and James Trefil, *The New Dictionary of Cultural Literacy,*
third ed. (Boston, MA: Houghton Mifflin Harcourt, 2002)

[hunt00]

Andrew Hunt and David Thomas, *The Pragmatic Programmer: From Journeyman to
Master* (Boston, MA: Addison-Wesley, 2000)

[huston03]

Stephen Huston, et al., *The ACE Programmer's Guide: Practical Design Patterns for
Network and Systems Programming* (Boston, MA: Addison-Wesley, 2003)

[iso04]

*Data Elements and Interchange Formats — Information Interchange —
Representation of Dates and Times,* ISO 8601:2004 (Geneva, Switzerland:
International Organization for Standardization, 2004)
https://webstore.ansi.org/preview-pages/ISO/preview_ISO+8601-2004.pdf

[iso11]

Information Technology — Programming Languages — C++, ISO/IEC 14882:2011
(Geneva, Switzerland: International Organization for Standardization/International
Electrotechnical Commission, 2011)
https://www.iso.org/standard/50372.html

[kernighan99]

Brian Kernighan and Rob Pike, *The Practice of Programming* (Reading, MA:
Addison-Wesley, 1999)

[kliatchko07]

Vladimir Kliatchko, "Developing a Lightweight, Statically Initializable C++ Mutex:
Threadsafe Initialization of Singletons," *Dr. Dobb's Journal*, 32(6):56–62

[lakos12]

John Lakos, "Date::IsBusinessDay() Considered Harmful! (90-minutes)," *Proceedings of
the ACCU*, Oxford, UK, April 2012

[lakos13]

John Lakos, "Applied Hierarchical Reuse: Capitalizing on Bloomberg's Foundation
Libraries," C++Now, Aspen, CO, May 15, 2013
https://www.youtube.com/watch?v=ASPj9-4yHOO

[lakos16]

John Lakos, Jeffrey Mendelsohn, Alisdair Meredith, and Nathan Myers, "On Quantifying
Memory-Allocation Strategies (Revision 2)," P00891R, February 12, 2016
http://www.open-std.org/jtc1/sc22/wg21/docs/papers/2016/p0089r1.pdf

[lakos17a]

John Lakos, "Business Requirements for Modules," P0678R0, June 16, 2017
http://www.open-std.org/jtc1/sc22/wg21/docs/papers/2017/p0678r0.pdf

[lakos17b]

John Lakos, "Local ('Arena') Memory Allocators - Part I," Meeting C++ 2017
https://www.youtube.com/watch?v=ko6uyw0C8r0

[lakos17c]

John Lakos, "Local ('Arena') Memory Allocators - Part II," Meeting C++ 2017
https://www.youtube.com/watch?v=fN7nVzbRiEk

[lakos18]

John Lakos, "C++ Modules and Large-Scale Development," *Proceedings of the ACCU,*
Belfast, UK, April 20, 2018
https://www.youtube.com/watch?v=HmI1XFEu_uY

[lakos19]

John Lakos, "Value Proposition: Allocator-Aware (AA) Software," C++Now 2019
https://www.youtube.com/watch?v=dDR93TfacHc

[lakos21]

John Lakos and Vittorio Romeo, *Embracing Modern C++ Safely*, manuscript, 2021

[lakos96]

John Lakos, *Large-Scale C++ Software Design* (Reading, MA: Addison-Wesley, 1996)

[lakos97a]

John Lakos, "Technology Retargeting for IC layout," *Proceedings of the 34th Annual
Design Automation Conference (DAC)*, Anaheim, CA, June 9–13, 1997, pp. 460–465
http://dl.acm.org/citation.cfm?id=266201

[lakos97b]

John Lakos, *Dynamic Fault Modeling, Physical Software Design Concepts, and
1C Object Recognition*, Ph.D. Dissertation, Columbia University, 1997

[lindskoog99]

Nils Lindskoog, *Long-Term Greedy: The Triumph of Goldman Sachs*, second ed.
(McCrossen, 1999)

[lippincott16a]

Lisa Lippincott, "Procedural Function Interfaces," P0465R0, October 16, 2016
http://www.open-std.org/JTC1/SC22/WG21/docs/papers/2016/p0465r0.pdf

[lippincot16b]

Lisa Lippincott, "What Is the Basic Interface?" (part 1 of 2), *C++ Conference (CppCon)*,
Bellevue, WA, 2016
https://www.youtube.com/watch?v=s70b2P3A3lg

[lippincot16c]

Lisa Lippincott, "What Is the Basic Interface?" (part 2 of 2), *C++ Conference (CppCon)*, Bellevue, WA, 2016
https://www.youtube.com/watch?v=Uzu5CuGfmGA

[liskov87]

Barbara Liskov, "Data Abstraction and Hierarchy," *Addendum to the Proceedings on Object-Oriented Programming Systems, Languages, and Applications (OOPSLA)*, Orlando, FL, October 4–8, 1987, pp. 17–34

[martin03]

Robert C. Martin, *Agile Software Development, Principles, Patterns, and Practices* (Upper Saddle River, NJ: Pearson, 2003)

[martin95]

Robert C. Martin, *Designing Object-Oriented C++ Applications Using the Booch Method* (Upper Saddle River, NJ: Prentice Hall, 1995)

[mcconnell96]

Steve McConnell, *Rapid Development: Taming Wild Software Schedules* (Redmond, WA: Microsoft Press, 1996)

[meredith19]

Alisdair Meredith and Pablo Halpern, "Getting Allocators Out of Our Way," *C++ Conference (CppCon)*, Aurora, CO, September 18, 2019
https://www.youtube.com/watch?v=RLezJuqNcEQ

[meyer95]

Bertrand Meyer, *Object-Oriented Software Construction* (Upper Saddle River, NJ: Prentice Hall, 1995)

[meyer97]

Bertrand Meyer, *Object-Oriented Software Construction*, second ed. (Upper Saddle River, NJ: Prentice Hall, 1997)

[meyers05]

Scott Meyers, *Effective C++,* third ed. (Boston, MA: Addison-Wesley, 2005)

[meyers97]

Scott Meyers, *Effective C++*, second ed. (Boston, MA: Addison-Wesley, 1997)

[mezrich02]

Ben Mezrich, *Bringing Down the House* (New York: Free Press, 2002)

[modules18]

Programming Languages — Extensions to C++ for Modules, ISO/IEC TS 21544:2018 (Geneva, Switzerland: International Organization for Standardization/International Electrotechnical Commission, 2018)
https://www.iso.org/standard/71051.html

[myers78]

Glenford J. Myers, *Composite/Structured Design* (New York: Van Nostrand Reinhold, 1978)

[pacifico12]

S. Pacifico, A. Meredith, and J. Lakos, "Toward a Standard C++ Date Class," N3344=12-0034, 2012
http://www.open-std.org/jtc1/sc22/wg21/docs/papers/2012/n3344.pdf

[parnas72]

D. L. Parnas, "On the Criteria to Be Used in Decomposing Systems into Modules" *Communications of the ACM* 5 (1972) (12):1053–1058

[pemberton93]

Steven Pemberton, "enquire.c," version 5.1a, 1993
https://homepages.cwi.nl/~steven/enquire/enquire.c

[pike]

Colby Pike, "cxx-pflR1 The Pitchfork Layout (PFL): A Collection of Interesting Ideas," accessed September 16, 2019
https://raw.githubusercontent.com/vector-of-bool/pitchfork/spec/data/spec.bs

[potvin16]

Rachel Potvin and Josh Levenberg, "Why Google Stores Billions of Lines of Code in a Single Repository," *Communications of the ACM*, 59(7):78–87
http://cacm.acm.org/magazines/2016/7/204032-why-google-stores-billions-of-lines-of-code-in-a-single-repository/fulltext

[siek10]

Jeremy Siek, "The C++0x Concepts Effort," *Generic and Indexed Programming.* International Spring School (SSGIP 2010), Oxford, UK, March 22–26, 2010, pp. 175–216

[stepanov09]

Alexander A. Stepanov, *Elements of Programming Style* (Boston, MA: Addison-Wesley, 2009)

[stepanov15]

Alexander A. Stepanov, *From Mathematics to Generic Programming* (Boston, MA: Addison-Wesley, 2015)

[stroustrup00]

Bjarne Stroustrup, *The C++ Programming Language: Special Edition,* third ed. (Boston, MA: Addison-Wesley, 2000)

[stroustrup12]

B. Stroustrup and A. Sutton (Editors), "A Concept Design for the STL," N3351=12-0041, 2012
http://www.open-std.org/jtc1/sc22/wg21/docs/papers/2012/n3351.pdf

[stroustrup14]

Bjarne Stroustrup, *Programming: Principles and Practice Using C++*, 2nd ed. (Boston, MA: Addison-Wesley, 2014)

[stroustrup85]

Bjarne Stroustrup, *The C++ Programming Language* (Reading, MA: Addison-Wesley, 1985)

[stroustrup94]

Bjarne Stroustrup, *The Design and Evolution of C++* (Reading, MA: Addison-Wesley, 1994)

[subbotin15]

Oleg Subbotin, https://github.com/bloomberg/bde-tools/blob/master/bin/bde_runtest.py

[sutter05]

Herb Sutter and Andrei Alexandrescu, *C++ Coding Standards* (Boston, MA: Addison-Wesley, 2005)

[sutton13]

Andrew Sutton, Bjarne Stroustrup, and Gabriel Dos Reis, "Concepts Lite: Constraining Templates with Predicates," N3580, 2013 http://www.open-std.org/jtc1/sc22/wg21/docs/papers/2013/n3580.pdf

[tragakes11]

Ellie Tragakes, *Economics for the IB Diploma* (Cambridge, UK: Cambridge University Press, 2011)

[unisys87]

"Unisys A15," *Computers* (Delran, NJ: Datapro Research Corp., 1987) http://bitsavers.informatik.uni-stuttgart.de/pdf/burroughs/A-Series/datapro/ 70C-944YT-50_8707_Unisys_A15.pdf

[voutilainen19]

Ville Voutilainen, "Allowing Contract Predicates on Non-First Declarations," P1320R1, 2019 www.open-std.org/jtc1/sc22/wg21/docs/papers/2019/p1320r1.html

[winters18a]

Titus Winters, "Standard Library Compatibility Promises," P0922R0, 2018 http://www.open-std.org/jtc1/sc22/wg21/docs/papers/2018/p0922r0.pdf

[winters18b]

Titus Winters, "Standard Library Compatibility Guidelines (SD-8)," *C++ Conference (CppCon)*, Bellevue, WA, 2016 https://www.youtube.com/watch?v=BWvSSsKCiAw

[zarras16]

Dean Zarras, "Software Capital — Achievement and Leverage," *Hacker Noon*, January 9, 2016 https://hackernoon.com/software-capital-achievement-and-leverage-2c30f6f01ed9

Index